Fiji

a Lonely Planet travel survival kit

Robyn Jones
Leonardo Pinheiro

aghty for their work on the language section. Thanks also to Dan Levin for showing great clemency in the soft font department.

Thanks

Many thanks to the travellers who used the last edition and wrote to us with helpful hints, useful advice and interesting anecdotes:

Jon & Tali Adini, Eve Alpern, Joan Anderson, Mark Ashley, John Ayers, S P Barnard, Y Bennett, Derek Bissell, Kirsty Blackstock, Steve Booth, Jerry Bounds, A Bracken, Alan Bradley, Donna Bray, D Bray, Nick Bron, Sally & Alison Brooke, Diana Brown, Marilyn Carter, Eva Cermak, Les Charters, James Christer, Alicia Close, D Connelly, Mary Dawson, Susan Dennis, Naz Dessous, Ann Diamond, Julia Ditrich, Rev J Dominitz, Nadia Duguay, Arad Eldad, Steve Elliott, Mike Fee, Dan Fowler, Lucille Frauenstein, Jo Gibbons, Phillip Gittus, Alan Goldsmith, Ian Gordon, Jane Gresle-Farthing, Ulrich Guenther, Annie Hawkins, Carl Henderson, Escher Imhof, T & B Jakobsson, Michael Jiew, C Johnson, Ernst Junker, Mel Kay, George Keller, Prof Ruprecht Keller, Garry Kemp, G F Kortschak, Martin Kyllo, Caroline Long, Julie Louttit, Mabel MacDonald, Ricky Lee Martin, Paul Martin, Sue Mathieson, Tracey McGregor, Jim McNamara, John Messenger, Kirsty Morris, K J Morrissey, Dr Catriona Moxham, Heidi Mulcock, James Muller, Daniel Munday, Pauline Neale, Runol Ohlsson, Marcia Ouellette, Paige Passano, Ryan Paulsen, Sharon Pearton, Richard Penrose, Jo Pilkington-Down, Elizabeth Pollard, Mary-Sarah Ratumaiyale, Alaisdair Raynham, Michelle Reeves-Elliott, Penelope Reilly, Peter Reilly, Bernt Ringvold, Adrienne Robinson, Donna Roemling, Peni Rokolaga, Su Roper, Benny Rotem, C Rounds, Stephen Rush, F Salthouse, Robert Saunders, Rob Scholten, Clive Searle, Gregory Sherwood, Angela Simonett, B J Skane, Elaine Slade, Palle Sorensen, Jenny Thomson, Nick Thow, Geoffrey Tickell, M Tranter, Frank Van Kampen, Franz Vettiger, Gerry Vineberg, Jenny Visser, J & S Waggett, Baerbel Whitney, Alita Whittier, Philip Winter, Kalane Wong, Janice Woodward, Patrick Zebedee, Suellen Zima, Amir & Simone Zimmermann, Ralfs Znotins

Warning & Request

Things change – prices go up, schedules change, good places go bad and bad places go bankrupt – nothing stays the same. So, if you find things better or worse, recently opened or long since closed, please tell us and help make the next edition even more accurate and useful.

We value all of the feedback we receive from travellers. Julie Young coordinates a small team who read and acknowledge every letter, postcard and email, and ensure that every morsel of information finds its way to the appropriate authors, editors and publishers.

Everyone who writes to us will find their name in the next edition of the appropriate guide and will also receive a free subscription to our quarterly newsletter, *Planet Talk*. The very best contributions will be rewarded with a free Lonely Planet guide.

Excerpts from your correspondence may appear in updates (which we add to the end pages of reprints); new editions of this guide; in our newsletter, *Planet Talk*; or in the Postcards section of our Web site – so please let us know if you don't want your letter published or your name acknowledged.

Contents

Boxed Text

Map Legend

BOUNDARIES

.... International Boundary

.... Regional Boundary

ROUTES

.... Freeway

.... Highway

.... Major Road

.... Unsealed Road or Track

.... City Road

.... City Street

.... Railway

.... Underground Railway

.... Tram

.... Walking Track

.... Walking Tour

.... Ferry Route

.... Cable Car or Chairlift

AREA FEATURES

.... Parks

.... Built-Up Area

.... Pedestrian Mall

.... Market

.... Cemetery

.... Reef

.... Beach or Desert

.... Rocks

HYDROGRAPHIC FEATURES

.... Coastline

.... River, Creek

.... Intermittent River or Creek

.... Rapids, Waterfalls

.... Lake, Intermittent Lake

....................................Canal

.... Swamp

SYMBOLS

✪ CAPITAL	......................National Capital	
◉ Capital	......................Regional Capital	
◍ CITY	.... Major City	
● City	.... City	
● Town	.... Town	
● Village	.... Village	

■	▼	.........Place to Stay, Place to Eat		
⚓	♟	.... Cafe, Pub or Bar		
✉	☎	.... Post Office, Telephone		
❶	❾	.... Tourist Information, Bank		
◒	🅿	.... Transport, Parking		
⛬	⛨	...............Museum, Youth Hostel		
⛺	🅰	Caravan Park, Camping Ground		
⛪	➡	.... Church, Cathedral		
🕌	🕍	.... Mosque, Hindu Temple		
✛	★	Hospital, Police Station		
◒	🐾	.............Embassy, Petrol Station		

✈	✚	.... Airport, Airfield
🏊	🤿	.........Swimming Pool, Dive Site
❖	🐘	...............Shopping Centre, Zoo
🍷	⛱	...Winery or Vineyard, Picnic Site
←	A25	One Way Street, Route Number
⛫	⚱	.........Stately Home, Monument
⛩	▣	...........................Castle, Tomb
⌒	⛺	.... Cave, Hut or Chalet
▲	※	.... Mountain or Hill, Lookout
⛯	⚓	.............Lighthouse, Shipwreck
)(	◎	.... Pass, Spring
🦅	⚲	..................Beach, Surf Beach
✿	❶	.... Garden, Toilet
∴		...... Archaeological Site or Ruins
		.... Ancient or City Wall
		........Cliff or Escarpment, Tunnel
		.... Railway Station

Note: not all symbols displayed above appear in this book

Introduction

The Fiji archipelago has over 300 islands, of which only about one third are populated. The country's central position in the south-west Pacific and relatively large land area has favoured its development as one of the most important nations of the region.

When most people think of Fiji they imagine beautiful white-sand beaches, coral islets, azure waters and tropical resorts. Fiji has these and much more. The larger islands are of volcanic origin and have rugged highland interiors with striking landscapes and picturesque villages. Travellers can snorkel and dive in the clear warm waters, explore gorgeous coral reefs teeming with underwater life, trek to waterfalls and through tropical forests, see historical and archaeological sites, and visit Fijian villages.

Fiji has an interesting blend of various cultures, namely Melanesian, Polynesian, Indian, European and Chinese. This mix is reflected in Fijian food, language and architecture. Food includes Fijian *lovos* (feasts in which food is cooked in a pit oven), Indian curries, European steak & chips and Chinese stir fry. While the common language is English, the universal greeting is a warm *Bula!* Most people also speak one of the many Fijian dialects or Fiji Hindi or Urdu. Hindu temples, Islamic mosques, Christian churches and traditional Fijian houses (*bures*) contrast with modern buildings.

While Fiji once had a fearsome reputation as the 'Cannibal Isles', paradoxically it is now renowned for its easy-going and friendly people. In the 19th century, Fiji was the trade centre of the South Pacific and in 1874 the islands became a British colony. The British brought Indian indentured labourers to work on the sugar plantations and their descendants are now fourth-generation Fiji Indians. Fiji remained a British colony for almost 100 years, gaining independence in 1970.

Unlike many countries the indigenous people of Fiji have not lost their land rights, retaining ownership of 83% of the country's land. Access to land and political rights for

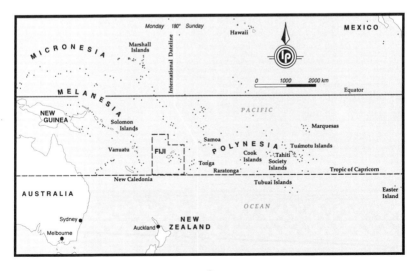

all of Fiji's ethnic groups are currently controversial topics.

Despite the influences of Western values, the indigenous Fijian culture and social structure has remained strong. Many rural people live a semisubsistence village lifestyle under the authority of a local chief. Traditional values and culture are maintained through *mekes* (dance performances telling stories and legends), kava ceremonies, bure construction, and crafts such as bark-cloth making and pottery. However, many Fijian customs such as elaborate hairdressing and body painting, as well as the old religion, disappeared during the imposition of Christianity by missionaries.

With its pleasant tropical climate, Fiji is a relatively easy country to travel in: it's malaria free, has a wide range of options for activities and accommodation, and has an extensive transportation network of buses, ferries and small planes. You can have a great time discovering Fiji's above and underwater beauty regardless of whether you are on a tight budget or indulging yourself at an exclusive island resort. You can travel solo or in a group, use local transport, hire a car, or take an organised tour or cruise. Fiji can be a stopover or a destination in itself. It is suitable for a short trip or, even better, for spending a month or two exploring some of the many islands.

Facts about the Country

HISTORY
Vitian Culture

'Fiji', the name given to the island group after European colonisation and the arrival of Christian missionaries, actually comes from the Tongan name for the islands. Before the arrival of Europeans, the inhabitants called their home Viti.

Vitian culture is a complex blend of influences. It has been shaped by Polynesian, Melanesian and some Micronesian peoples who came and went during 35 centuries of settlement. Evidence from pottery suggests that Fiji experienced various periods of significant cultural change before the arrival of Europeans.

The Lapita people first settled the Fiji islands about 1500 BC. They were mainly coastal dwellers who relied on fishing. Theories based on linguistic studies suggest that the Lapita people came from Vanuatu or the eastern Solomons. These original shore-dwellers may have lived in relative peace, but from about 2500 years ago a shift towards agriculture occurred alongside an expansion of population and an increase in feuding between tribes. Cannibalism became common and villages moved to fortified sites, returning when warring diminished.

About 1000 years ago Tongans and Samoans invaded from the east, prompting larger scale, more organised wars. More Tongans invaded in the 18th century and villagers again sought refuge in fortified sites. While there were also extended periods of peace, Viti was undergoing intense social upheaval at the time of first European settlement. By the early 19th century, local skirmishes between tribes were verging on civil wars. This led the Europeans to believe that the islands were in a constant state of war.

No community was fully self-sufficient. Certain villages produced specialised products which were traded through networks operating throughout the islands, even extending to Tonga and Samoa. Viti was, however, never politically unified and there were local variations in culture.

Vitian society centred around *mataqali* (extended family groups) which were headed by a hereditary village chief or *turaga-ni-koro* who was usually male. The chief's everyday role was to chat and solve problems while village men worked in the fields and the women fished, cooked and made crafts. Ownership was collective but the chiefs controlled the allocation of land and labour. A chief's immense power over the community was reinforced by the belief that he or she was *tabu* or sacred, their mana derived from a special relationship with an ancestral god.

Chiefs were polygamous and intermarriage led to complex interrelationships between mataqali. Villages were grouped under a paramount chief. Normally the position of chief passed through a generation of half-brothers before turning to their sons, but the appointment was often debated by village elders. Rivalry and power struggles were common, resulting in fighting and sometimes all out war between close neighbours who were invariably related. To further complicate matters, a chiefly woman's sons could claim ownership over property of her brothers from other villages. This was known as the *vasu* system.

A startling array of vicious weapons including barbed spears, javelins, bows and arrows, slinging stones, throwing clubs, skull-piercing battle hammers and innumerous varieties of clubs can be seen at the Fiji Museum in Suva.

European Explorers

During the 17th and 18th centuries, Europeans crossed the south-west Pacific searching for *terra australis incognita*, or 'unknown southern land'.

Cannibalism

Archaeological evidence from food-waste middens shows that cannibalism was practised in Viti from 2500 years ago until the mid to late-19th century, by which time it had become an ordinary, ritualised part of life. In a society founded on ancestor worship and belief in the afterlife, cannibalising an enemy was considered the ultimate revenge. A disrespectful death was a lasting insult to the enemy's family.

Bodies were either consumed on the battlefield or brought back to the village spirithouse, offered to the local war god, then butchered, baked and eaten on the god's behalf. The triumph was celebrated with music and dance. Men performed the *cibi*, or death dance, and women the *dele* or *wate*, an obscene dance in which they sexually humiliated corpses and captives. Torture included being thrown alive into ovens, bled or dismembered, forced to watch their body parts being eaten or even to eat some themselves!

Women and children joined in the eating, but were banned from the formal sacrificial rites and feasting in the spirithouse and men's house. Raw and cooked human flesh was handled like any other meat and eaten with fingers. As living representatives of the gods, however, priests and chiefs could not touch any kind of food, their hands and lips were considered tabu. They were normally fed by a female attendant who carefully avoided touching the lips, but for cannibalistic feasts they fed themselves with special long-pronged wooden forks. Considered sacred relics, these forks were named and kept in the spirithouse and were not to be touched by others.

Momentos were kept of the kill to prolong the victor's sense of vengeance. Necklaces, hairpins or ear-lobe ornaments were made from human bones, and the skull of a hated enemy was sometimes made into a *tanoa*, or *yaqona* drinking bowl. Meat was smoked for snacks, and the war clubs were inlaid with teeth or marked with tally notches. To record a triumph in war, the highlanders of Viti Levu placed the bones as trophies in branches of trees outside their spirit houses and men's houses. The coastal dwellers used leg bones to make sail needles and thatching knives, so sexual organs and foetuses were suspended in trees instead. Rows of stones were also used to tally the number of bodies eaten by the chief.

Early European visitors and settlers were obsessed with cannibalism, recording gruesome but nevertheless fascinating stories. ∎

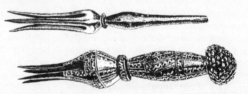

Ornate forks used for cannibalistic feasts

The first known European to visit Fijian waters was Abel Tasman, who, on his way to Indonesia on a voyage for the Dutch East India Company, sailed past the group in 1643. He negotiated the treacherous reefs north-west of Vanua Levu and Taveuni. His descriptions of the reef system kept mariners out of Fijian waters for the next 130 years.

After claiming Australia for Britain, the English navigator Captain James Cook met some Fijians in Tonga (then known as the Friendly Islands) who described the Fijians as formidable warriors and ferocious cannibals. Despite this, Cook stopped at Vatoa in the southern Lau group in 1774. The reputation Fiji gained, however, deterred sailors from visiting the islands for some time.

After the famous mutiny on the *Bounty* in 1789, Captain William Bligh and 18 others were cast adrift near Tonga. In their small open boat, with only a few provisions and navigation instruments, they sailed for Timor in the Dutch East Indies, a 6000-km trip lasting 41 days. They passed through southern Lau, across the Koro Sea and between Vanua Levu and Viti Levu (through a channel now known as Bligh Water). Almost clear of the 'Cannibal Isles' without incident, they were chased by two Fijian war canoes near the Yasawas. Bligh made rudimentary charts along the way and during another voyage in 1792 he added to these charts, sailing through the Lau group, the Koro Sea, and past Kadavu.

Traders & Beachcombers

Tongans had long been trading with the Lau group and other Fiji islands. Trade items included weapons, *masi* (printed bark cloth) and colourful kula-bird feathers, which were highly valued for their use in ceremonial dress. From the early 19th century, Europeans began to arrive. Whalers, sandalwood and bêche-de-mer (sea cucumber) traders had a significant and disruptive impact on the Fijian population, introducing arms and foreign capitalist values. Some chiefs even sold their land for guns to use in warfare.

Sandalwood Trade

Tongans traded with the Fijian chiefs of Bua Bay on Vanua Levu, obtaining sandalwood, which they in turn traded with Europeans. Oliver Slater, a survivor of the shipwrecked *Argo*, discovered the location of the supply and spread the news.

There was high demand in Asia for the fragrant timber, and Europeans began to trade directly with Fijians in 1805. It was a high-risk, high-profit business for the traders. The timber was initially bartered for items such as metal tools, tobacco, cloth, muskets and powder, and then sold for an average profit of between 400% and 600%. Chiefs, however, began to drive harder bargains, and often demanded assistance in wars against other chiefs. By 1813 the accessible supply of sandalwood was exhausted.

The timber, a source of wealth and advantage for the chiefs of Bua and Bau (south-east Viti Levu), led to jealousy and conflict with others. The introduction of firearms and the resulting increase in violent tribal warfare were a lasting consequence of the trade.

Bêche-de-Mer Trade

Asia was a lucrative market for bêche-de-mer where it was considered a delicacy. Like sandalwood, this trade was also short-lived due to over-exploitation, only lasting from 1830 to 1835 and 1844 to 1850.

Hundreds of workers were required for a bêche-de-mer station. Fijian labour was used in the intensive process which involved collection from the reefs, cleaning, boiling, and cutting wood, drying, smoking and packaging. Certain chiefs sent their villagers to work on the trade in order to increase their wealth and power, and this impacted on the lives and economies of communities. The chief of Bau received 5000 muskets and 600 kegs of powder in return for helping suppress objections to the trade.

Beachcombers

During the 17th and 18th centuries, deserting or shipwrecked sailors and escaped convicts from the British penal settlements in Australia lived with Fijian villagers. Some didn't survive for long before being eaten, while others were recruited into Fijian society and given special treatment for helping the chiefs in war. Beachcombers made themselves useful by serving as interpreters and go-betweens, carpenters, arms-owners and marksmen.

Charles Savage, a Swede, was an especially influential beachcomber. After being shipwrecked on the *Eliza* in 1808, he retrieved muskets and ammunition from the wreck. Savage helped Bau's chief to became one of the most powerful in Fiji. In return for service in war he received a privileged position and many wives, surviving about five years before being killed in battle. His skull was preserved as a kava bowl. Paddy Connel played a similar role in neighbouring Rewa.

Many of these beachcombers adopted Fijian dress, hairstyles and body painting for convenience or at the insistence of their hosts and protectors. To be a conspicuous white man in battle was not wise.

Expanding Chiefdoms

By 1829 the chiefdom of Bau controlled the coastal areas in the north and east of Viti Levu and Lomaiviti, where trade with Europeans had been most intense. For reasons of intermarriage, Bau's chiefly family exerted influence over Rewa and Cakaudrove, much of Northern Lau, Ovalau and Moturiki. Wealth, tools, weapons and influence had been accumulated from dealings with traders and beachcombers. From Bau's strategic location, enormous canoes were used to

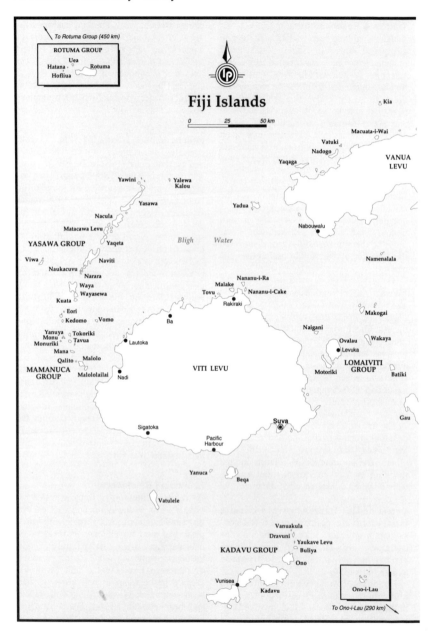

Cikobia

Vetauua

Quelevu

Drua
Tutu
Mali
• Labasa

Nukusemanu

Nukubasage
Nukubalati

Rabi   Yavu   Cobia
Yanuca

Kioa

• Savusavu

Matagi
Somosomo   Laucaia
Qamea

Nanuku Lailai
Nanuku Levu

Wailagi Lala

Somosomo Strait

TAVEUNI

*Nanuku
Passage*

Naitaba

Malima

Avea
*Kaibu Island
Resort*
Kaidu

Kanacea

Vanua Balavu
Cikobia-i-Lau
Lomaloma Resort

Koro

Yacata

Nukutolu

Namalata   Susui
Munia

Vatu Vara

Mago

Karafaga

Vekai

180°

Tuvuca

Nairai

Cicia

LAU GROUP

Yarous

*KORO
SEA*

Nayau

Lakeba

Aiwa

Vanua Vatu

Oneata

Moala

Olorau   Moce

Komo

Tavua Na Sici

Namuka-i-Lau

Vuaqava

Kabara

Navutu-i-Ra   Yagasa
Navutu-i-Loma

Totoya

Marabo

Matuku

Vatoa   *To Vatoa (140km)*

Fulaga

Ogea Levu

Ratu Seru Cakobau dressed in *masi* (bark cloth) robes

assert the chief's power by carrying out raids or intervening in disputes.

The competing chiefs of the south-eastern regions of Bau, Rewa and Verata involved their people in vicious power struggles, and war was the norm from the late 1840s to the early 1850s. Ratu Seru Cakobau, who succeeded his father Chief Tanoa, was by 1850 at the height of his influence. He was known to foreigners as Tui Viti (King of Fiji) despite having no real claim over most of Fiji. His former allies eventually turned against him because of the unreasonable demands he placed on local custom.

Tongan Influence

In the early and mid-19th century, Tonga began to have more influence on Fijian affairs. The chiefdoms of Bau, Rewa and Cakaudrove became dependent on Tongan canoe building and seafaring skills, and Bau also received Tongan military support.

In 1848 the Tongan noble Enele Ma'afu led an armada of war canoes to capture the island of Vanua Balavu in the Lau group. His ultimate goal was to conquer all of Fiji, annex it to Tonga, and convert the people to Christianity along the way. In 1853 his cousin, the King of Tonga, made him governor of all Tongans in Lau. By 1854 Ma'afu had become a serious threat to Cakobau's power, especially in the Lau group. In the late 1850s much of Fiji was taking sides either with Cakobau or Ma'afu, with the Tongan becoming the controlling force in eastern Fiji. Local chiefs, however, still presided over much of western Viti Levu and other remote areas.

Missionaries

Missionaries were drawn to Fiji to find converts for Christianity and to preach against cannibalism. They first entered the Lau group from the east, via Tahiti and Tonga. In the 1830s the London Missionary Society sent Tahitian pastors to Oneata, and the Wesleyan Methodist missionaries David Cargill and William Cross set up in Lakeba. Cross and Cargill developed and taught a language system using a single letter to represent each Fijian sound (b for mb, c for th, d for nd, g for ng and q for ngg).

The Tongan population of Lau converted fairly easily, but Fijians were not very interested in giving up their own gods. Progress was slow for the missionaries due to Fiji's lack of political unification. They realised that in order to convert the Fijian people it was necessary to convert the chiefs first, principally the powerful chiefs of eastern Viti Levu. Bau and Rewa were warring intensely at the time and it was not until 1839 that the missionaries' first real victory was achieved. The high chief of Viwa Island (three km from Bau) converted to the new religion, setting a precedent for his villagers and other chiefs under his influence.

The influential Bauan chief, Cakobau reluctantly adopted Christianity in 1854 on the threat of withdrawal of Tongan support. The Methodist Church saw his conversion as a triumph. There was a setback, however, when the Reverend Baker, attempting to spread the Gospel in the western highlands in 1867, was killed and eaten by locals who resisted the imposition of ideas associated with Bau. See the 'Reverend Baker' aside in the Viti Levu chapter.

Some chiefs endured the presence of missionaries in their village because of trade opportunities. Others converted because they were impressed by the new god's power, as demonstrated by the machines, guns and warships of its followers. Missionaries and Fijian ministers gradually displaced the priests of the old religion and assumed privileged positions. The concept of holiness was accepted for its similarity to the existing belief of tabu. The influence of missionaries and Europeans on traditional culture and everyday life was all pervasive: dress and once-elaborate body decoration and hairdressing became conservative; rituals such as initiation tattooing were discouraged; tribal warfare was suppressed; and Bauan was promoted over other dialects as the written language. Many Fijians adopted Christianity while continuing to worship their own gods and ancestor spirits.

European Settlement & Levuka

By the 1830s a small whaling and beachcomber settlement was established at Levuka, Ovalau. The foreigners married local women and Levuka became one of the main ports of call in the South Pacific for traders and warships. A US expedition, led by Commandant Charles Wilkes, arrived in Fiji in 1840 with the aim of exploring the Pacific. His team of scientists, artists and a language expert produced the first reasonably complete chart of the Fijian islands. While surveying the islands, Wilkes negotiated a port regulation treaty with powerful chief Tanoa of Bau. The chief would be paid in return for the protection of foreign ships and the supply of provisions.

In 1846 John Brown Williams was appointed as American commercial agent. The British, fearful that America or France might try to annex the group, sent WT Pritchard to Levuka in 1858 to act as their consul.

The chiefs of Bau and the early foreign settlers of Levuka had a mutually beneficial association, using one another for political advantage. Relations deteriorated when the settlement was razed by fires in 1841 and Cakobau was suspected of being behind it. During the 1849 American Independence Day celebrations, the home of Williams on Nukulau Island was accidentally destroyed by fire, and locals helped themselves to his possessions. Williams held Cakobau, as 'King of Fiji', responsible for the actions of his people and sent him a substantial damages bill. This set a precedent and claims against Cakobau for compensation for the loss of American property rose to an inflated amount of US$45,000.

Cakobau, under increasing pressure from all sides, while still claiming to have power over the whole of Fiji, proposed to Pritchard that in return for paying his debts he would cede the islands to Britain. The 1862 offer was not seriously considered at the time, but representatives were sent to investigate the attractiveness of the proposition. Rumours and speculation caused a large influx of British settlers via Australia and New Zealand. Settlers bickered between themselves and disputes erupted with Fijians over land. Levuka town had become a lawless, greedy outpost bordering on anarchy and race war.

Cakobau's debt was not cleared until 1868 when the Polynesian Company agreed to pay it in exchange for land (see the Suva section of the Viti Levu chapter). Various attempts were made to form a local Fijian government with limited success. In 1865 a council of chiefs was established but it only lasted for a couple of years, after which regional governments were formed in Bau (headed by Cakobau) and Lau (headed by Ma'afu) and in Bua. Finally in 1871 Cakobau formed a Fiji-wide government based at Levuka. It only lasted two years, however, as Cakobau's opponents accused his government of extravagance, ineptness and corruption.

Blackbirding

Other Pacific Islanders were brought to

labour on cotton, copra and sugar plantations in Fiji. The American Civil War indirectly stimulated the trade in labourers by prompting a world-wide cotton shortage which resulted in a cotton boom in Fiji.

Levuka was a centre of the trade, and planters paid the recruiters up-front to secure labour. Initially people were coaxed into agreeing to work for three years in return for minimal wages, food, clothing and return passage. Later, chiefs were bribed and men and women traded for ammunition.

Most labourers were islanders from the south-west Pacific, especially from the Solomons and New Hebrides (now Vanuatu), but Fijians were also coerced. For a short time the chiefs of Ra traded their people for guns to use in defence against raiding war parties from the hills. In 1871 Cakobau sold the Lovoni people of the interior of Ovalau into virtual slavery on the plantations (see the Lovoni aside in the Ovalau chapter).

By the 1860s and 1870s blackbirding had developed into an organised system of kidnapping. Stories of atrocities and abuses by recruiters resulted in pressure on Britain to stop the trade. In 1872 the Imperial Kidnapping Act was passed, but this had limited success in regulating the traffic because Britain had no power to enforce it.

Cession to Britain
Cakobau's attempt at government did not successfully maintain peace, and in 1873 JB Thurston, the acting British consul, again requested that Fiji be annexed by Britain. This time Britain was interested, citing blackbirding as its principal justification. Cakobau felt that Fiji was in a vulnerable position due to internal instability. Annexation by Britain was seen as preferable to annexation by other European powers such as France and Germany who were increasing their presence in the Pacific.

Fiji was pronounced a British crown colony on 10 October 1874 at Levuka. The islands of Fiji were in effect given to Queen Victoria, her heirs and successors. Signatories to the deed of cession were Cakobau (King of Fiji and warlord), Ma'afu (then

chief of Lau, Taveuni and much of Vanua Levu) and 11 other chiefs. It is significant that all but one of the high chiefs who signed the deed were from eastern Fiji: cession was not universally accepted by Fiji's chiefs.

The Colonial Period
Colonial Government Sir Hercules Robinson, the then governor of NSW, was sent to determine the terms of the cession contract and was then instated as provisional governor of the new colonial government. His replacement, Sir Arthur Gordon, arrived in the new colony in June 1875 and stayed for five years.

Along with the end of the US Civil War came a slump in the world cotton market. The local economy was depressed and unrest and epidemics followed. Cholera and the common cold took their toll and an outbreak of measles wiped out about a third of the indigenous Fijian population.

The recent Maori-Pakeha wars in New Zealand and the fact that Europeans were greatly outnumbered, prompted fears that racial war could break out in Fiji. Like the missionaries before it, the colonial government appreciated the influence of the chiefs. If they could be persuaded to collaborate then Fiji would be most easily, cheaply and peacefully governed. The last significant conflict in Fiji was the Kai Colo Uprising of 1875-76. This involved the highlanders of western Viti Levu, who had no part in the ceding of their land to Britain and were not happy with the imposition of new laws. The viability of the colonial administration was being threatened. Gordon's strategy was to pit Fijians against Fijians to quash the 'rebellion'. See the Kai Kolo Uprising aside in the Viti Levu chapter.

Christianity was an effective form of social control, helping the colonial government enforce and protect their new capitalist economic order. To reinforce the chiefs' traditional support, Gordon introduced a system of administration which incorporated the existing Fijian hierarchy. Fijian institutions were developed to provide a line of authority extending from the village chief to the governor.

Levuka's geography hindered expansion, so the administrative capital was officially moved to Suva in 1882. The early 1880s saw a considerable infusion of capital from New Zealand and Australia.

A land commission was set up to determine whether Europeans who had obtained land prior to cession had acquired it honestly and at a fair price. All tribal land was to be retained by traditional owners and the remainder of the land designated crown or government land. It was the policy of the colonial government to protect Fijian land rights by forbidding sales to foreigners. Between 1905 and 1909, however, the rules of inalienability of land, as agreed by the deed of cession, were temporarily waived to attract investors. The system was successful in retaining land rights for the indigenous owners, and 83% of the land is still owned by Fijian communities.

Fijian Labour Gordon was apparently keen to protect Fijians from being exploited, and he prohibited the employment of Fijians as labourers on the plantations. His reasons were perhaps paternalistic, but they were also aimed at maintaining good relations between the new colonial government and indigenous Fijians. Fijian labour had been exploited in the harvesting of sandalwood, in the processing of bêche-de-mer, and in cotton and copra production, and this had proved disruptive to village life. Fijians were becoming increasingly reluctant to take full-time wage work, preferring subsistence work which was less regimented and satisfied their village obligations. Fijian labour, however, did generate wealth for the colony as village agricultural produce was appropriated by the government in the form of a tax.

The colonial government was placed under increasing pressure from Britain to make the Fijian economy self-sufficient. Plantation crops such as cotton, copra and sugar cane were a solution, but demanded large pools of cheap labour. Slavery had been abolished, blackbirding was under control,

Gordon was opposed to using Fijian labour, and Fijians were unwilling to leave their communal lands to work on the plantations anyway. Having served in Mauritius and Trinidad, where he had experienced an indentured-labour system using Indian workers, Gordon set about establishing a similar system in Fiji.

Indentured Labour Negotiations with the Indian government were made in 1878 for labourers to come to Fiji. The contracts were for five years, after which the labourers, or *girmitiyas*, were free to return to India at their own expense. If they stayed for another five years the return passage was paid.

Some Indians saw the system as a way to escape poverty, conflict with family or with authorities, or as a chance to start a new life. Others were recruited by trickery and deceit. Many Indians were reluctant to go because the journey would involve loss of caste and extensive purification ceremonies upon their return. *Arkatis* (agents under commission) promised fine prospects or failed to explain the penalty clauses of the contract. Most girmitiyas were transported from the ports of Calcutta in north-east India and Madras in the south.

The Indians soon discovered the reality of life on the plantations. It was in the overseers' and foremen's interest to overload the workers, as they often received a bonus from their employers for work done quickly and cheaply. Heavy work allocations were given and food was strictly rationed; if the girmitiyas failed to compete the daily task the result was no wages and often prosecution. Corporal punishment and human rights' abuses by the overseers were rife, checks were rare and there was little or no recourse to legal aid. In this high-pressure situation, crime, suicide, sickness and disease were common.

About 80% of the labourers were Hindus, 14% were Muslim and the remainder mostly Sikhs and Christians. Caste rules governed all aspects of a Hindu's life, dictating eating habits, dress, marriage and the level of personal physical purity. Overcrowded accommodation gave little privacy, and people of different caste and religion were forced to mix. The overseers were not sympathetic to these matters and the result was a breaking down of the caste system.

The Indian government initially insisted that there be a ratio of 10 men to every four women, but this was not enforced. Women were fought over and rape and adultery were common. Girls married and became mothers at a young age, and remarriage became widespread though illegal in traditional law. The social and religious structure was crumbling; there was a lack of traditional leaders, very little knowledge of correct religious rituals, and there was no education for children other than in Christian missionary schools.

Even though they may have been through great hardship or *narak* (hell), the vast majority of Indians decided to stay in Fiji once they had served their contract and even bought their families from India. Some people of lower caste had much greater prospects if they stayed in Fiji. Those who returned were usually given the social standing of outcastes or untouchables, the lowest status in India.

By the early 1900s the Indian government was being pressured to abolished the indenture system. The missionary CF Andrews highlighted the plight of the girmitiyas, and others, including Mahatma Ghandi, denounced the civil and human rights' abuses that were occurring on the plantations. The Indian lawyer Manilal Maganlal Doctor from Mauritius, who arrived in Fiji in 1912, helped focus and give political direction to the Indian labourers. However, strikes by Indians against low wages, the 12-hour working day, rising prices and unfair taxes had little immediate effect. Recruiting stopped in 1916 and indenture ended officially in January 1919. About 2000 Indians had been transported each year from 1879 to 1916, a total of 60,537.

Power Play Interaction between Indians and Fijians was discouraged by the colonial government. Indians, restricted from buying land from the indigenous Fijians by the colo-

nial administration, instead moved into small business, trade and bureaucracy, or took out long-term leases as independent farmers. Differences in wealth began emerging between north and south Indians. The former, who arrived earlier, tended to be more prosperous.

Up until 1904 the legislative council had been all-European and nominated by the governor. The constitution was subsequently amended to include six elected Europeans and two Fijians nominated by the Great Council of Chiefs. It was not until 1916 that the governor nominated one Indian member, and 1929 that the first Indian members were elected to the government. The 1920s brought the first major struggle for better conditions for Indians.

By the mid 1930s Australian dominance in the Fijian economy had extended beyond the sugar sector into gold-mining. The working classes were becoming more assertive and many indigenous Fijians laboured in mining. Occupational and geographical concentrations of labour developed along broadly racial lines as did labour organisations. The government resisted the introduction of fairer labour laws and instead promoted further racial fragmentation of the trade union movement to 'divide and conquer'. Working Fijians viewed themselves principally as Fijians, rather than as members of a social class.

Meddling, stirring and manipulation by a section of the local European community aimed to protect that community's capital and to quell labour troubles within the Indian-dominated workforce. By taking sides with the Fijians they diverted attention from their monopoly on freehold land and their power and influence in the civil service. It was convenient to blame all problems on the Indian community and to provoke fears that the Indian population would surpass the number of indigenous Fijians.

In the 1940s Britain allocated money to development funds and Europeans involved in the planning process diverted money to infrastructure, favouring the growth of tourism.

CSR

The sugar industry was the mainstay of the colonial capitalist economy, and the Australian-owned Colonial Sugar Refining Company (CSR) gained phenomenal power in Fiji. In the early 1880s CSR established mills on the banks of the Rewa River (at present day Nausori), on the Ba River at Rarawai, and at Lautoka and Labasa in Vanua Levu. Another mill at Rakiraki, northern Viti Levu, was taken over by CSR in 1926.

The colonial government, keen to attract foreign investment, facilitated the purchase of land and arranged for cheap labour through the indenture system. CSR initially developed its own plantations, but later shifted the burden of heavy production costs to others by subcontracting the sugar-growing work. In 1894 the company began leasing land to ex-indentured Indians, a minority of whom became rich cane farmers, leading to resentment among White plantation owners. CSR profits hinged on long working hours (a 50-hour week) and a heavy task system. During the period 1914 to 1924, CSR reaped the best profits in its history. After the abolition of indenture and the resulting labour shortage, company land was divided and rented to small tenant farmers.

From 1942 to 1960 industrial trouble between mill owners, workers and growers over wages, cane prices and conditions led to the establishment of the Sugar Advisory Board & Advisory Council. CSR pulled out of Fiji in 1972 due to reduced profits, and the plant and its freehold land was nationalised. ∎

World Wars Fiji had only a minor involvement in WWI. Being distant from the conflict, the war was of little relevance, except that Britain was involved. However, about 700 of Fiji's European residents and about 100 Fijians were sent to serve in Europe.

The conflict in the Pacific during WWII was obviously closer to home. Around 8000 Fijians were recruited into the Fiji Military Force (FMF) and trained by American and New Zealand forces, and from 1942 to 1943 Fijians fought against the Japanese in the Solomon Islands. There was no armed combat in Fiji, but air-raid shelters and batteries were built in Suva and cannons placed at Momi Bay near Sigatoka and at Vuda Point near Nadi.

Understandably, after the racism and exploitation experienced in the cane fields during and since the indenture period, Indians did not rush to enlist. The Fijian and European leaders chose to see this action, together with the cane farmer's strike of 1943, as cowardly and unpatriotic.

The after effects of WWII included additional exposure to Western ways, growth in the FMF, greater links with the New Zealand government, who assisted in the administration and training of the FMF, and increased control by Fijian citizens over their own affairs. Traditional divisions and local prejudices were partially broken down as Fijian officers commanded groups of Fijians who had been thrown together from different regions.

Fijian troops, who had gained a reputation for jungle fighting in WWII, served again in the 1952 Malaya conflict against communism. Malaysia, with its indigenous Malay population and Chinese immigrants, was later to serve as a role model for some economic and political development. Since 1978 the FMF have served in the Middle

East and Zimbabwe as part of the United Nations' peacekeeping forces.

Independence

After WWII, Fijians became more conscious of the need for democratically elected government and the importance of forming organisations such as trade unions. The 1960s saw the formation of ministerial government, voting rights for women, the establishment of political parties, constitutional changes and a movement towards self-government. Increasingly, more members of the government were elected by the people rather than being nominated by the governor.

The Alliance Party, led by Ratu KT Mara, represented indigenous Fijians and other races. It was interested in keeping a link with the British Crown and in introducing a racially divided voting roll. By supposedly embracing multiracialism and making peace with sections of the Indian community they hoped to weaken support for a common electoral role. The National Federation Party, led by AD Patel, represented Indians and wanted independence from Britain and the introduction of a common electoral roll. The Alliance gained the majority in the 1966 elections and a ministerial system was created with Ratu Mara as the chief minister.

In 1963 the legislative council had consisted of 38 members, divided equally between Fijian, Indian and European groups, with each racial community voting from separate rolls. In 1966 a new constitution expanded the legislative council to 40 members, changed the racial balance of the council by reducing the proportion of seats reserved for Europeans, and incorporated a system of cross-voting in which all voters also elected members from the different racial groups.

Fiji became independent on 10 October 1970, after 96 years of colonial administration. The 1970 constitution followed the British model of two houses with a senate, comprised of Fijian chiefs, and a house of representatives, comprised of 22 Fijians, 22 Indians, and eight general electors (Europeans, part-Fijians and Chinese).

In the rush towards independence, important problems, such as land ownership and leases, how to equally protect the interests of a racially divided country, the voting system, and appropriate development, were not resolved. The long history of segregation in Fiji was continued in the division of political seats and with parties being separated along racial lines.

Postindependence Fiji

In the immediate postindependence years Fiji experienced a period of prosperous economic development. The road system and airstrips were upgraded, hydroelectricity developed, building, commerce, tourism, sugar cane and pine plantations expanded and urbanisation increased. The high growth rate lasted throughout most of the 70s, falling during the early 80s with the decline in the price of sugar, the main source of wealth generation. Along with the perceived benefits derived from foreign investment came foreign debt.

Fiji's first postindependence election was won by the Alliance Party, led by Ratu Mara. Although the Alliance promoted itself as pro-multiculturalism, the results in the polls showed a clear racial division of voting. The following year Ratu George Cakobau, the paramount chief of indigenous Fijians, became the new governor general. Ironically he was a descendent of the great chief Cakobau who had ceded Fiji to Britain almost one hundred years before!

Ethnic Tensions In the first few years after independence, Fijians were optimistic, especially in towns and urban centres, and people of different races mixed well. There were, however, underlying tensions which became more apparent as the economy worsened. In 1975 there was a rise in nationalism led by Mr Sakesai Butadroka who called a parliamentary motion to repatriate the entire Indian community, despite the fact that most of its members were fourth-generation Fijians. The motion was rejected by both the National Federation Party (NFP) and the Alliance Party, but many Fijians agreed with the idea. The following elections in 1977 saw Butadroka's Fijian Nationalist Party (FNP) divide Alliance voters, allowing the Indian NFP to win. Their victory was short lived, however, as the governor general called for a new election, and the Alliance regained its majority.

In both urban and rural areas most retail outlets and transport services were (and still are) run by Indian families. A racial stereotype developed portraying Indians as obsessed with making money. The vast majority of Indians, like the vast majority of Fijians, belonged in fact to the poorer working classes.

Meanwhile the economic aspirations of indigenous Fijians were changing: while some wanted to preserve their traditional ways, others sought to modernise their values and practices. In the subsistence economy of the villages Fijians were, and still are, relatively self-sufficient. In a cash economy, however, traditional obligations and a communal way of thinking are a definite disadvantage; instead, individualism, entrepreneurship and access to capital are required.

Prior to independence there had been an anti-Fijian bias in lending policies, and the economic boom had not directly affected most indigenous Fijians. They were mostly employed in agriculture, the unskilled workforce and in the tightly controlled gold-mining industry. Efforts were made by the government to encourage Fijians to enter business through a 'soft loan scheme' developed by the Fiji Development Bank. However, many new businesses failed because they attempted to move into already competitive areas. Competition in business, education and employment tended to be seen in purely racial terms.

The Alliance Party was perceived to be failing indigenous Fijians in their hopes for economic advancement, and Fiji Indians were tired of the fighting between the Hindu and Muslim factions within the NFP. Greater unity among the working classes led to a shifting of loyalties and the formation of the Fiji Labour Party (FLP) in 1985, led by Dr Timoci Bavadra.

In the April 1987 elections an FLP-NFP coalition defeated the Alliance Party by winning 28 of the 52 house of representative seats; 19 of the elected FLP-NFP members were Indians. Despite having a Fijian prime minister and a cabinet with an indigenous-Fijian majority, the new government was labelled 'Indian dominated'.

Military Coups

The victory of the coalition immediately raised racial tensions in the country. The extremist Taukei movement, supported by eastern chiefs and the Fijian elite, launched a deliberate destabilisation campaign. In a demonstration in Suva, 5,000 Fijians marched in protest against the new government.

Taukei leaders played on Fijian fears of losing land rights and of Indian political and economic domination. They suggested that development would result in the loss of Fijian culture, using the suppression of Maori and Australian Aboriginal cultures as examples.

In the following weeks there were violent incidents against Fiji-Indian owned businesses around the country and petrol bombs

General Rabuka, leader of the May 1987 military coup.

were thrown into the government offices in Suva. On 14 May 1987, only a month after the elections, there was a surprise invasion of parliament by armed soldiers led by Lieutenant Colonel Sitiveni Rabuka. He took over the government in a bloodless coup and arrested Dr Bavadra and his cabinet.

A state of emergency was declared by Governor General Ratu Penaia Ganilau; however, he was unable to reverse the situation. Rabuka formed a civil interim government, comprised mostly of members of the previous Alliance government, with himself as military member directing a council of ministers. His 'government' was supported by the Great Council of Chiefs. In the face of international condemnation, Rabuka attempted to legitimise his government. He negotiated a deal with Ganilau to head the council of ministers, with himself heading the security forces and home affairs.

Talks were held between the imposed new government and the opposition parties to amend the constitution and prepare for new elections. Taukei extremists, however, were radically opposed to any ideas of unification and staged a series of violent protests. In September 1987, when the government was about to announce that elections would be held, Rabuka again intervened with military force. The 1970 constitution was invalidated and Fiji declared a republic. Rabuka proclaimed himself head of state and appointed a new council of ministers which included leaders of the Taukei movement and army officers. Arrests of community leaders and academics followed, a curfew was imposed in urban centres, newspapers closed and all political activities were restricted.

In October 1987, Ratu Ganilau resigned as governor general and Fiji was dismissed from the Commonwealth. By December, Rabuka had nominated Ratu Mara as the prime minister, and Ratu Ganilau returned as the president of the new republic.

Background to the Coups Much has been written proposing different theories as to what motivated the coups. One is that the CIA were involved to protect US interests in the South Pacific nuclear-weapons testing ground. The FLP-NFP coalition were opposed to nuclear testing.

Another theory implies that the nationalistic movement within the Methodist Church was behind the coups. The majority of indigenous Fijians are Methodist and are supporters of the deposed Alliance Party. Church leaders took part in the racist Taukei movement and postcoup, Sunday observances were imposed on the whole country by the military government.

There were underlying tensions and some jealousy on the part of Fijians against the Fiji Indians, but these racial differences were deliberately exaggerated by the Fijian elite who stood to lose by the Alliance Party's defeat. The FLP-NFP coalition with its western Fijian and Indian members threatened the political power of the traditional hierarchy of the Great Council of Chiefs, which was dominated by eastern chiefs.

The coups, supposedly benefiting all Fijians, in fact caused immense hardship and benefited only a minority. When the Fiji Indian element was effectively removed, tensions within the Fijian community itself were exposed. Clear examples of this are the conflicts and contradictions among chiefs from eastern and western Fiji; between paramount chiefs and village chiefs; urban and rural divisions; and within the church and trade-union movement.

Interim Government
The economic consequences of the coups were drastic. By the end of 1987, Fiji experienced negative growth in GDP, a devalued dollar, inflation, price increases and wage cuts. The economy's two main sources of income were seriously affected: Fiji Indian sugar farmers refused to harvest their crops, and tourism declined significantly. Aid from Australia and New Zealand was temporarily suspended and large numbers of people, including thousands of Fiji Indians, skilled tradespeople and professionals, began emigrating.

Although there were a number of interruptions in sugar-cane harvesting and crushing while the interim government was in power, Fiji managed to largely recover from the economic effects of the coups. The government created a tax-free zone for export business, and loans were offered to start new businesses in tourism, timber and construction.

In 1989 the government relaxed the Sunday observance rules. In protest, the Methodist Church fundamentalist leader Manasa Lasaro organised demonstrations and roadblocks in Labasa, resulting in the arrest of 57 people, including his own. Methodist Church groups also firebombed and destroyed three Hindu temples.

Ratu Mara, the interim government's prime minister, became antagonistic towards Rabuka for his incompatibility with the old cabinet traditions and political interests, and suggested he return to the military forces. In late 1989, Rabuka resigned from his position in the cabinet and took command of the army as major-general.

New Constitution
Early in 1990, diplomatic problems between Fiji and India resulted in the closure of the Indian High Commission in Suva.

On 25 July 1990 a new constitution was proclaimed by President Ratu Ganilau. The constitution increased the political power of the Great Council of Chiefs, giving them the right to appoint the president and a majority of senators as well as authority over any legislation relating to land ownership and common rights. The Native Lands Trust Board (NLTB) was one of the public bodies excluded from the jurisdiction of the courts. The president was given the right to appoint the prime minister from indigenous Fijian members of the house of representatives. Two seats in cabinet were reserved for the army, and the military was given ultimate responsibility for the welfare of the country. The constitution also granted the military, including Rabuka, the police and the prison forces, special immunity from legal prosecution in relation to the coups-d'état of 1987.

The constitution reserved a majority of seats in the house of representatives for indigenous Fijians. An electoral gerrymander ensured an advantage for the eastern chiefly elite while discriminating against those provinces that were not as supportive of the regime. Compulsory Sunday observance was legislated, imposing Christian religious values on the whole population.

Indian political leaders immediately opposed the constitution claiming it was racist and undemocratic and that it condemned Fiji Indians to perpetual minority status. In protest a group of academics ceremonially burnt a copy of the constitution. A University of the South Pacific (USP) lecturer was kidnapped and tortured while being questioned about the protest. The soldiers involved in the Dr Sigh kidnapping were fined and set free under suspended jail sentence.

Recent Elections
As 1991 advanced and the election approached, anticipation of change grew. The Great Council of Chiefs disbanded the multicultural Alliance Party in March 1991. In its place they formed a new party, the Soqosoqo-ni-Vakavulewa-ni Taukei (Party of Policy Makers for Indigenous Fijians; SVT). The General Voters Party was formed to represent Europeans, part-Fijians and Chinese. The Fiji Indian NFP and the FLP considered boycotting the election, but in the end decided to participate. Differences between the two parties ruled out the possibility of a coalition.

Rabuka gave up his military career to pursue politics full time and in November 1991 he was elected president and party leader of the SVT. Rabuka's position as army commander was taken over by the president's son, Brigadier Ratu Epeli Ganilau.

Industrial unrest by trade unions grew after the introduction of new anti-labour legislation. Strikes occurred at the Emperor Gold Mine in Vatukola, in garment factories and in the public service.

To suit his political ambitions, Rabuka changed his hardline approach and became increasingly populist. Prior to the 1992 elections he promised to repeal labour laws affecting trade unions, to review the constitution and to extend Fiji-Indian farmers' land leases. The SVT won the first postcoup general election held in May 1992, but did not obtain a clear majority in the lower house and thus had to seek coalition partners. Amazingly, in order to gain a majority and be appointed prime minister, Rabuka secured the support of the Fiji-Indian members of the house of representatives who had belonged to the same parties that he had expelled in the 1987 coup. Soon after the election, the GVP agreed to form a coalition with the SVT, thereby strengthening the new government's position.

However, the postelection promises made to the FLP by the SVT – constitutional change, labour reform, land tenure, and the scrapping of a value added tax (VAT) – were not fulfilled.

The new government faced a faltering economy with growing unemployment, crime, and urbanisation of the population. To promote indigenous-Fijians in business, companies with more than 50% indigenous Fijian ownership were offered a 20-year tax exemption.

The concept of a government representing the interests of all groups in society was discussed in parliament, but predictably chiefs and members of the Taukei movement condemned the idea. FLP members eventually walked out of parliament in protest against the delay in revising the constitution and Rabuka's failure to keep promises.

To add to the poor economic situation Hurricane Kina hit at the start of 1993, causing widespread damage. Later in the year the government presented a budget with a large deficit. The proposed budget was defeated when seven members of the SVT-GVP coalition voted against it and formed a new political party, the Fijian Association. Parliament was dissolved and a new general election called. During the election campaign the president, Ratu Penaia Ganilau, died and the Great Council of Chiefs elected Ratu Mara in his place.

In the election, held in February 1994, the SVT won 31 of the 37 seats reserved for indigenous Fijians in the parliament, a one seat increase. The new Fijian Association won two seats in the Lau province. Fiji-Indian allegiance shifted with the FLP losing seven seats and the NFP increasing its tally from 13 to 20. Rabuka was re-appointed as prime minister and continued as leader of the SVT-GVP coalition. The previously defeated budget remained unchanged and was approved by parliament.

Recent Events

1995 began with revelations that the Public Trustee's Office had been borrowing funds for nonexistent developments, resulting in criminal charges being laid. But the main event of the year was the confirmation of the bankruptcy of the National Bank of Fiji. World Bank figures revealed debts mounting to F$150 million. As a rescue effort, the government considered bringing 28,000 paying Chinese migrants from Hong Kong to boost the economy by hundreds of millions of dollars. The idea, however, was not pursued.

On a positive note, 1995 saw the lifting of the Sunday observance decree and its ban on Sunday trading, although to a large extent this is still followed.

In 1996 France, the UK and the US signed a comprehensive test-ban treaty at the South Pacific Forum headquarters in Suva. Prime Minister Sitiveni Rabuka declared it a day of joy and celebration for the people of the South Pacific.

Constitutional Review A Constitutional Review Commission (CRC) was established in 1995. The SVT's submission to the commission called for continued political dominance by Fijians and the retention of the 1990 constitution because 'Fijians don't trust Indians politically'.

In response, a multiracial, multi-interest group called the Citizens' Constitutional Forum (CCF) submitted a report to the CRC. It proposed a move beyond ethnic issues to a national perspective, in nonracial and secular terms. It argued that the present constitution perpetuates racial differences; is undemocratic and divisive; weak on accountability; lumps all indigenous Fijian interests together; and is contributing to economic and social decline.

In September 1996 the Constitutional Review Committee presented its findings. The 800-page report called for a return to a multi-ethnic democracy and suggested that the 70 seats of the house of representatives be broken down as follows: 12 Fijian and Pacific Islanders, 10 Indians, one Rotuman, two other races, and 45 open seats (three each from 15 heterogeneous constituencies). While accepting that the position of president be reserved for an indigenous Fijian, it proposed no provision of ethnicity for the prime minister.

Public expectations of reform and a fairer electoral system are high in Fiji. There is a widespread lack of confidence in the political system and a lack of national identity. It remains to be seen whether the government will act on the CRC's recommendations. Nationalists have publicly spat on, burnt and destroyed copies of the report in acts of symbolic defiance against it.

GEOGRAPHY

The Fiji islands are located in the south-west Pacific Ocean, south of the equator and north of the tropic of Capricorn. Australia lies 3160 km to the south-west, and New Zealand lies 2120 km to the south. Other nearby Pacific islands include Tonga, 770 km to the east, and Vanuatu, 1100 km to the west.

Fiji's territorial limits cover an area of over 1.3 million sq km, but less than 1.5% of this is dry land. Fiji's total land area is about 18,300 sq km, and the Fiji islands lie between latitudes 12 degrees and 21 degrees south of the equator, and between longitudes 177 degrees east and 175 degrees west. The 180-degree meridian cuts across the group at Taveuni, but the international date line has been diverted eastward to keep all islands within the same time zone – 12 hours ahead of Greenwich Mean Time. The archipelago comprises 300 islands, or many more, depending on how you apply the definition of island. Their size varies from tiny patches

of land a few metres in diameter to Viti Levu (big Fiji), which is 10,390 sq km. The second-largest island is Vanua Levu (big land), with an area of 5538 sq km. Only about one-third of the islands are inhabited, mainly due to isolation or lack of fresh water.

Viti Levu has the highest peak in Fiji, Mt Tomanivi (Mt Victoria) 1323m, near the north end of the dividing range which separates east from west. Suva, the country's capital is situated in south-eastern Viti Levu. Nadi, home to the country's main international airport, and Lautoka, the second most important port after Suva, are on the western side. Viti Levu has the largest rivers and the most extensive transport and communication system. The Kings Road and Queens Road are the main roads around the island's perimeter.

Vanua Levu, north-east of Viti Levu, has an irregular shape and a deeply indented coast with many bays of various shapes and sizes. There is a huge bay between the Natewa Peninsula and the remainder of the island. Like Viti Levu, the island is divided by a mountain range. Vanua Levu's mountain range is significantly lower than Viti Levu's, with Nasorolevu as the highest peak at 1032m. Most roads are unsealed, but a sealed stretch links the two main towns – Savusavu in the south and Labasa in the north.

Taveuni, the third-largest island, is separated from Vanua Levu by the Somosomo Strait. It is rugged with rich volcanic soil and luxuriant vegetation, and is known as 'Fiji's garden island'. Its mountainous backbone of volcanic cones includes Uluigalau (1241m) the second-highest summit in Fiji.

Kadavu, south of Viti Levu, is of similar size to Taveuni. The Kadavu group includes Ono and a number of small islands within the Astrolabe Reef. The main island is composed of three irregularly shaped, rugged land masses linked by isthmus. Like Taveuni, Kadavu is very scenic with beautiful reef lagoons, mountains, waterfalls and dense vegetation.

The remainder of Fiji is comprised of relatively small islands classified in groups:

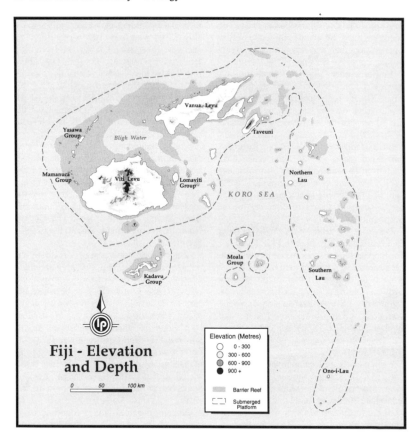

Fiji - Elevation and Depth

Elevation (Metres)
- 0 - 300
- 300 - 600
- 600 - 900
- 900 +

Barrier Reef

Submerged Platform

Lomaiviti, Lau, Moala, Yasawa, Mamanuca and Rotuma. Beqa and Vatulele are small islands off southern Viti Levu. Refer to individual chapters for the geography of specific islands.

GEOLOGY

Apart from Kadavu and the islands of the Koro Sea, all of the Fijian islands belong to one massive horse-shoe-shaped submarine platform. The largest land masses, Viti Levu and Vanua Levu, are situated on the broader and higher north-west end of the platform. The eastern arm of the platform extends

almost 500 km to the southern end of the Lau group. The whole platform is tilted to the south-east resulting in deeper waters at the narrower south-eastern end. The waters of the Koro Sea almost cut the platform in two at Nanuku Passage, the north-east shipping gateway to the Fijian islands.

About 300 million years ago Fiji was part of a large Melanesian continent which covered Eastern Australia, New Zealand, and South-East Asia; it extended as far north as the Philippines and as far east as Fiji. A complex series of geological events built and shaped the archipelago over a long period of

Types of Islands & Coral Reefs
The Fijian islands are of three different types: coral, limestone, or most commonly, volcanic.

Volcanic Islands These are generally of high relief with a series of conical hills rising to a central summit. Sharp pinnacles indicate the sites of old volcanoes, and crystallised lava flows often reach the coast as ridges to form cliffs or bluffs. Between these ridges are green valleys, and on the coast, beaches and mangrove communities. Flat land is only found in the river valleys of the larger islands. The sides of the islands facing the prevailing winds get more rain and therefore perennial forest vegetation thrives. The leeward hills are home to grasslands with only a sparse covering of trees.

There are no active volcanoes in Fiji, but there is plenty of geothermal activity in Vanua Levu, and in Savusavu some locals use the hot springs to do their cooking! Viti Levu, Taveuni and Kadavu are also volcanic islands.

Limestone Islands These are characteristically rocky land masses uplifted from the sea. They have a series of cliffs undercut by the sea, with shrubs and trees growing on the top. Generally there is a central depression forming a basin with fertile undulating hills. Volcanic materials also thrust up through the limestone mass. Vanua Balavu in the Lau group is an example of a limestone island.

Coral Islands These are small low islands without many topographic variations. Generally they are situated in areas protected by barrier reefs, and so don't get washed away by the sea. Surface levels raise only to the height at which waves and winds can deposit sand and coral fragments. These islands support simple, yet luxuriant vegetation, composed mostly of overhanging palms, broad leafed trees, shrubs, vines and grasses. The coast has bright, white-sand beaches and mangroves in the shallows of lagoons. Examples of coral islands are Beachcomber and Treasure Island in the Mamanuca group, and Leluvia and Caqelai in the Lomaviti group.

Fringing Reefs These are usually narrow stretches of reef linked to the shore and extending seaward. Sometimes they can extend up to five kilometres out from the shore. During low tide the reefs are exposed. Often the bigger fringing reefs have higher sections at the open-sea edge and drainage channels on the inside, which remain filled with water and are navigable by canoes and small boats. Rivers and streams break the reefs, the fresh water preventing coral growth. The Coral Coast on southern Viti Levu is an example of an extensive fringing reef. Most islands in Fiji have sections of fringing reefs somewhere along their coast.

Barrier Reefs These are strips of continuous reef, broken only by occasional channels some distance from the coastline and sometimes encircling islands. They often occur in combination with fringing reefs. The biggest barrier reef in Fiji is the Great Sea Reef which extends about 500 km from the coast of south-western Viti Levu to the northernmost point of Vanua Levu. A section of this barrier is unbroken for more than 150 km, and lies between 15 and 30 km off the coast of Vanua Levu. Other smaller well-known reef barriers include the one encircling Beqa Lagoon, and the Great Astrolabe Reef of Kadavu.

Atolls These are small islands, rising just above sea level, situated on a ring of coral reef enclosing a lagoon in their middle. An atoll where the land forms a complete circle is rare, and invariably small when it does occur.

Despite the idyllic idea given of atolls in tales of the South Pacific, most have inhospitable environments. The porous soil derived from dead coral, sand and drift-wood retains little water, and unless the atoll is situated within a rain belt it is subject to droughts. The vegetation is typically small and hardy with species such as pandanus and coconut palms, shrubs and coarse grasses. Fiji has only a few islands that can be classified as atolls. The most well known is Wailagi Lala island east of Nanuku Passage in the Lau group. There are, however, a number 'looping' barrier reefs that encircle islands. ■

time, with volcanic material and sediments being deposited on the ancient platform.

Viti Levu is believed to be the oldest of the Fijian islands. Its characteristic volcanic mountains were formed by upthrusts of masses of magma from below the platform.

Around 150 million years ago, four long periods of volcanic activity began and uplifts resulted in the formation of sediments and limestone deposits.

Erosion over about 35 million years formed river deltas such as the Rewa near Suva, and the sand hills of Kulukulu near Sigatoka.

CLIMATE

Fiji has a mild and mostly stable tropical maritime climate throughout the year. The main reason for this stability is the large expanse of ocean surrounding the islands. The sea surface heats and cools slowly, unlike land masses, which can change temperature in just a few hours, causing local atmospheric disturbances.

The climate in Fiji, however, has local variations, from hot and dry to warm and wet. The prevailing winds are the easterly and the south-east Trade Winds. All the large islands have mountain ranges lying across the path of these prevailing winds, resulting in frequent cloud and greater rainfall on the windward eastern sides. The leeward sides are drier, with clear sky for most of the year and more variable temperatures and wind direction. Smaller islands tend to have dry and sunny microclimates.

Most of the resorts are concentrated in areas of plentiful sunshine on the south-western side of Viti Levu and the Mamanuca group, while Suva is notorious for its cloudy, wet weather.

Fiji's 'wet season' extends from November to April, and the 'dry season' from May to October, but rainfall occurs throughout the year. Suva, which is in a typical windward locality, has an average rainfall of around 3100 mm per year. In comparison, Nadi, on the leeward side of Viti Levu, gets just under 2000 mm. The heaviest rains fall from December to mid-April, and during this period the leeward side can get wetter than the windward sides. Strong thunderstorms can occur at any time during the year, but are more frequent around March and rare in July-August.

Fiji has mild average temperatures of

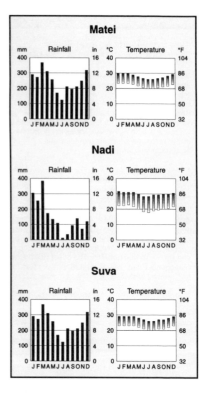

around 25˚C, but on a hot summer day it can reach 30˚C. During the coolest months, July and August, the temperature can drop to between 18˚C and 20˚C. In the mountainous interiors of the main islands it can be much cooler, especially at night. Temperatures on the smaller islands are even more stable. Fiji's warm tropical waters are great for snorkelling and diving, with average temperatures between 25˚C and 28˚C throughout the year.

Humidity is high, with averages ranging from 60% to 80% in Suva and 60% to 70% in Lautoka. Hot, windless, summer days with humidity levels of up to 90% can become oppressive. Most of the year, however, humidity is offset by pleasant sea breezes.

Tropical Cyclones

Tropical cyclones, or hurricanes, are most feared from November to April, the so-called 'hurricane season'. Cyclones originate from low-pressure centres near the equator and travel to higher latitudes, accelerating along a curving path. They often reach their full power at latitudes such as Fiji's.

Strong, destructive cyclones are, however, a fairly rare phenomenon. Fiji has been hit by an average of 10 to 12 cyclones per decade, with two or three of these being very severe. Of the 52 storms recorded between 1940 and 1980 only 12 were considered severe. On the other hand, in 1985 four cyclones hit Fiji within four months, including Eric and Nigel which caused deaths and millions of dollars worth of damage to towns, agriculture and the tourism industry. The last hurricane that caused extensive damage was Cyclone Kina early in 1993. It caused severe flooding, completely destroying the bridge over the Ba River in the north-west of Viti Levu.

ECOLOGY & ENVIRONMENT

In the past the population limited itself through warfare, disease, famine, sexual abstinence and even infanticide. About 2500 years ago the population increased and began moving inland. This was accompanied by extensive forest burning and clearing of land for agriculture, which resulted in widespread erosion. With the arrival of Europeans, concepts of individual wealth changed the traditional communal and subsistence use of land, leading to more intensive use and environmental damage.

Since the 1960s more than 100,000 hectares (between 11% and 16%) of Fiji's forests have been cleared. Most of the deforestation is concentrated in drier lowland forests and whole coastal forest ecosystems have disappeared completely. Forests in the interior of the large islands have been cut more sparingly. Logging practices are poor and have been one of the main causes of land degradation.

Unsustainable agricultural practices such as steep-land sugar cane and ginger farming have increased natural erosion. This has led to large areas of land becoming unproductive as fertile topsoil is washed away. Landowners seeking short-term gain through extensive and uncontrolled commercial agriculture, are the principal cause of deforestation. Fiji has also developed a pine plantation reforestation programme on dry and degraded lands.

Unplanned urban development resulting from increased urbanisation of the population is creating pressure on resources, infrastructure and services, and prompting racial tensions.

Fiji's plentiful freshwater resources are not well managed, even in areas where water shortages can be a problem. In urban centres water quality is good, but supply and quality in many rural areas is poor.

Marine pollution near Suva is severe and in certain areas fish consumption is a health hazard. Destructive fishing techniques such as the use of poisons and explosives are commonly employed in Fiji without much control. Despite previous 'boom and bust' exploitation of bêche-de-mer and clams, over-fishing continues around the most populated areas. The use of driftnets for fishing is officially opposed.

Waste management is a national problem. Many villages dispose of their garbage as they always did, as if it were still biodegradable. In urban areas like Suva, only 60% of sewage goes into a sewerage system and it isn't always processed before being discharged into the sea. There are a number of industries using a variety of toxic chemicals and materials without any serious data on the types and extent of pollution generated.

The government departments of environment, agriculture, tourism and forestry are working in association with the Foundation for People of the South Pacific (FSP), USP, Fiji Museum, National Archives, and National Lands Trust Board (NLTB) to revise environmental legislation. They are also working together on specific projects, such as the choice between logging and ecotourism on Ovalau.

Landowners are being encouraged to

become involved in activities based on ecotourism. The potential for low-impact tourism exists, but it also has associated problems, especially in remote areas. While benefiting from the cash infusion, villages are faced with additional pollution and rapid cultural change. When visiting remote areas, including the ocean, consider taking your rubbish away with you, especially items like batteries, disposable nappies and plastic. Avoid bumping against or walking on coral reefs and don't take coral and shells as souvenirs.

Conservation groups in Fiji include the South Pacific Action Committee for Human Ecology and Environment (SPACHEE), at the University of the South Pacific, and the World Wildlife Fund, also in Suva.

FLORA & FAUNA

Much of Fiji's indigenous flora and fauna is related to that of Indonesia and Malaysia. Plant and animal species are thought to have migrated to the islands on the prevailing winds and sea currents. Another theory for the dispersal of species in the South Pacific is that during prior ice ages one large Australasian continent linked parts of South-East Asia, Australia, New Zealand and the South Pacific.

Flora

Fiji has over 3000 identified species of plants, with one third of these being endemic. Fijians use much of the native flora for food, medicine, implements and building materials.

Rainforest Plants There are hundreds of different species of fern in Fiji, a number of which are edible and are known as *ota*. *Balabala* (tree ferns) are similar to those found in Australia and New Zealand. Tree fern trunks, traditionally used on the gable ends of *bures* (traditional houses), are now used for orchid stands and carved garden ornaments. Some *wakalou* (climbing fern) species were used to secure thatched roofing and to distinguish the chief's house and temples.

Forest giants include valuable timbers such as *dakua* (Fijian kauri) and *yaka*. These very hard, durable timbers have a beautiful grain and are used for furniture making. Due to unrestricted logging and the absence of an efficient planting programme these trees are becoming less common in Fiji.

Degeneria vitienses is a primitive flowering plant found only in Fiji. It is related to the ornamental magnolia. The leaves, known as *masiratu*, were used in the past as sand paper for wood carving.

Fiji has various species of pandanus and at least two of these are endemic. These trees are cultivated around villages and the leaves provide the raw material for thatching roofs and making baskets and mats.

Fiji's national flower is the *tagimaucia* or *Medinilla waterhousei*. This flower only grows at high altitudes on the island of Taveuni and on one mountain of Vanua Levu. Its petals are white and its branches bright red.

Orchids are abundant in Fiji's rainforests. Vanilla is a common orchid and there is a renewed commercial interest in its cultivation for use as a natural flavouring by the food industry.

Edible Plants The Fijian root crops *tavioka* and *dalo* are the country's food staples. Tavioka, also known as cassava, is a shrub with starchy tuberous roots that grows up to three metres high. The leaves are also edible but are usually only eaten by people from the Lau group. Dalo, also known as taro, has a high protein content and is more nutritious than cassava. Its leaves are often used to cook traditional Fijian dishes. Fijians distinguish 80 different varieties of dalo.

Another important staple food is obtained from the breadfruit tree that grows up to 18 metres tall. The fruit, up to 25 cm in diameter can be eaten boiled, roasted or fried, or it can be fermented underground to produce a type of edible sourdough. In the past its wood was used to make canoes. The jackfruit is another large tree. Its seeds are used by Fiji Indians in curries, and when ripe the flesh of the fruit can be eaten (if you can cope with the unpleasant smell). Bananas are common, as are pawpaw and mangoes.

Piper methysticum, or kava, a plant belonging to the pepper family, is widely cultivated in Fiji. The roots are dried, ground and then mixed with water to make *yaqona*, a beverage drunk socially and in yaqona ceremonies.

Garden Plants Many of Fiji's common garden plants were introduced by JB Thurston during the 19th century. The hibiscus, introduced from Africa, is Fiji's most common and well-known garden plant and is used for decoration, food, dye and medicine. Two common plants, both introduced from Brazil, are the bougainvillea and the allemanda, the latter producing large yellow flowers all year round. Frangipani, or *bua*, with its scented white flowers, is also an introduced species.

Coastal & River Plants The most distinctive plant communities found along coastlines are mangrove forests. They cover large areas around river deltas and are important for the protection of sea shores against damage by sea and wind. The aerial roots, sulphurous mud and saline water of mangrove forests provide breeding grounds for various fish species. Mangrove hardwood is used for firewood and for building houses, which has led to the destruction of many mangrove communities.

Casuarina, also known as ironwood or *nokonoko*, grows on sandy beaches and atolls. As its name suggests, the timber is heavy and strong and was used to make war clubs and parts of canoes.

The coconut palm has been an important part of the history of human occupation throughout the Pacific. Its nuts provide food and drink, its shells are used for making cups and charcoal, its leaves are used for baskets and mats, and its oil is used for cooking, lighting homes, and for body and hair lotion.

Other common coastal plants include the beach morning glory, with its purple or lavender flowers, wild passionfruit and the beach hibiscus or *vau*. The latter has large yellow flowers and its light wood was used in the past to build canoes.

Aquatic Plants Plants are integral to the structure and energy balance of reefs. The most common is the variety of algae that grows as a film over dead coral. Grape weed or *nama*, is an algae which looks like miniature green grapes and is often found in lagoons; Fijians consider it a delicacy. Large submerged meadows of sea grass also grow abundantly in lagoons.

Fauna
Over 3500 years ago the first settlers introduced poultry and probably dogs and pigs. This coincided with the extinction of at least three bird species (two megapodes, or mound-building birds, and a giant fruit pigeon).

Mammals Fiji has relatively few native mammals due to its distance from other land masses. Its six species of bats are the only native terrestrial mammals found on Fiji. The most common are the large fruit bats, also known as flying foxes or *beka*, which roost in large numbers in tall forest trees. Two species of insectivorous bats live in caves and are therefore seldom seen. The sheath-tailed bat, or *bekabeka*, is the smaller of the two and the other is the free-tailed bat.

All other land-dwelling mammals have been introduced to Fiji. Perhaps the most common wild animal in Viti Levu and Vanua Levu is the small Indian mongoose, and it will often be seen scurrying across roads. They were introduced in 1883 to control rats in the sugar-cane plantations, which they did, but they also ate native snakes, toads, frogs, and birds and their eggs. Although mongooses are often blamed for the depletion of banded iguanas, it is more likely that feral cats and habitat destruction are the cause. Other domestic animals turned feral include the pig, introduced by the Polynesians, and goat, which was brought by missionaries. Both cause damage to the native vegetation.

Apart from these animals, three species of

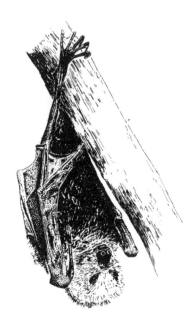

Fruit bats are a common sight in Fiji's inland forests

rat have also been introduced. In the 19th century, Europeans inadvertently brought with them the brown and black rat and the house mouse. The Polynesian rat came to Fiji much earlier, probably as a food source.

Dolphins, pilot whales and the occasional sperm whale visit Fiji's waters. Baleen whales also pass by on their annual migration to escape the Antarctic winter.

Tabua, the teeth of sperm whales, have a special ceremonial value for Fijians. They are still used as negotiating tokens symbolising esteem or atonement.

Reptiles Fiji has 20 species of land-dwelling reptiles, four species of turtle and four species of sea snake.

Fiji's crested iguana, which was only identified in 1979, is found on Yadua Taba (a small island off Bua), Vanua Levu and the Yasawas. It may reach one metre in length.

Since there are no other species of crested iguana found in South-East Asia, its ancestors are thought to have floated to Fiji on vegetation from South America! The banded iguana is found on Fiji as well as other Pacific islands, including Wallis, Futuna, and Tonga. Iguanas have been bred in captivity at the Orchid Island Cultural Centre near Suva.

There are about seven types of gecko in Fiji. The smallest grows only to a maximum length of 80 mm, while the giant forest gecko, which yaps like a dog and changes colour, can reach 30 cm. Various types of skink (slim, quick lizards) are also common, with large ones growing to 250 mm.

Two types of terrestrial snakes are found in Fiji. The Pacific boa constrictor reaches two metres in length. The burrowing snake *Ogmodon vitianus*, recognisable by a cream chevron on the top of its head, is venomous but seldom seen. Pacific boas were in the past considered sacred snakes. They were raised in rubble-filled pits or around the stone plinth of a spirithouse for consumption by chiefs and priests during religious rituals, and their vertebrae were used to make necklaces.

There are four sea snakes in Fiji, two being semiterrestrial. The *dadakulaci*, or banded sea krait, is Fiji's most common snake and you are likely to see it when snorkelling or diving. Occasionally they enter freshwater inlets, and mate and lay eggs on land. They

The banded sea krait is more venomous than the Indian cobra

Despite restrictions on their capture, turtles can still be found in Fijian markets

are placid and locals may tell you that they cannot open their jaws wide enough to bite humans, but don't risk it: the sea krait's venom is three times more potent than the venom of the Indian cobra. The yellow-bellied sea snake is found throughout the Pacific, it is able to remain submerged for up to two hours and can be aggressive. Another aquatic snake is *Hydrophis melanocephalus*.

Turtle species found in Fiji include: the hawksbill, the loggerhead (which visits but does not breed in Fiji); the green turtle (named after the colour of its fat), and the leatherback. The leatherback is the largest, growing up to two metres, and is under strict protection to prevent its extinction. Their meat as well as their eggs are considered a delicacy in Fiji as in many other parts of the world. Taking eggs is now banned in Fiji and it is illegal to catch adults with a shell length under 46 cm. This doesn't make much sense though as the turtles only reach breeding age at sizes considerably larger than this! Unfortunately turtle meat is still sold at the Suva market. The shells, especially of the endangered hawksbill turtle, are still found in shops and markets even though most countries prohibit its import.

Amphibians You are sure to come across the cane toad. It was introduced from Hawaii in 1936 to control insects in the cane plantations and has now become a pest itself, competing with the native ground frog in coastal and lowland regions. The tree frog

and ground frog have retreated deeper into the forests and are not as easy to find.

Birds Fiji has a varied and interesting bird life. There are around 100 species of bird, and about 23 of these are endemic. Fijian names imitate the bird's sounds; *kaka* for parrots, *ga* for ducks, *kikau* for honeyeaters. Despite the relatively short distance between islands, some species, such as the Kadavu parrot or the Taveuni dove, are present on one island only.

Around densely populated areas like Suva, introduced species are common. More aggressive introduced species, such as mynahs and bulbuls brought from India, have taken over and forced native birds into the forest. Taveuni and Cicia have imported the Australian magpie.

Fiji has seven species of nectar-eating parrot, three lory, eight species of pigeon and dove (including the Malay turtledove), as well as ducks and wild fowls, cuckoos and warblers. Tropical sea birds include the kingfisher, the frigate bird and the booby. The Fiji petrel, pink-billed parrot finch, red-throated

The Feather Trade

Parrot feathers obtained from the endemic kula lory and kaka, or red-breasted musk parrot, were a symbol of chiefly and priestly status in Fiji as well as Polynesia. Priests and chiefs wore headbands made of a strip of pandanus leaf to which red, and sometimes green and blue feathers were glued. A trade in parrot feathers persisted between Fiji, Tonga and Samoa until the 20th century when it was banned by the colonial government for reasons of nature conservation. Seafaring Tongans would come to Fiji to obtain the feathers and then trade them with Samoans for fine mat kilts bordered with the feathers. The demand was so high that Tongans were even willing to fight for them. Originally they were traded for a few nails, but after the sandalwood era the Fijians became more demanding. According to Thomas Williams, who lived on Taveuni in 1844, they were traded for 'European ironware, yaqona bowls, or use of their wives, sisters and daughters for a night or two'. ∎

lorikeet, and long-legged warbler are rare or endangered species. A good reference for the bird-watcher is *Birds of the Fiji Bush* by Fergus Clunie. The best areas for bird-watching in Fiji are Taveuni, eastern Vanua Levu and Kadavu.

Insects Fiji, like other islands in the Pacific, is a paradise for insects, and there are many thousands of different species. Initial isolation hindered an extensive colonisation of the islands by insects, but with human movements came a number of different insect species, some of which have eventually formed new species unique to Fiji. Most of Fiji's insects haven't yet been described and catalogued. There are plenty of mosquitoes, but fortunately no malaria.

Marine Life Fiji's richest diversity of fauna lies underwater, especially inside its reefs

and protected lagoons. There are hundreds of species of hard coral, soft coral, sea fan and sea sponge, and these are often intensely colourful and fantastically shaped.

In order to survive, coral needs sunlight and oxygen, which therefore restricts it to depths above 60m. Wave-breaks on shallow reefs are a major source of oxygen. Corals on a reef-break are generally densely packed and able to resist the force of the surf. Fewer corals grow in lagoons, where the water is quieter, but more fragile corals such as staghorn can be found in these places. Reefs near populated areas can be damaged by alluvial run off, sewage, chemicals, reef-walking, and the use of dynamite to kill fish. Infestations of the crown-of-thorns starfish also kill reefs.

There is a seemingly infinite variety of fish with exquisite colours, and of different sizes and shapes. Many have equally attrac-

---

Coral

Coral is usually stationary and often looks decidedly flowery but it's an animal, and a hungry carnivorous animal at that. Although a 3rd century AD Greek philosopher surmised that coral was really an animal it was still generally considered to be a plant until only 250 years ago.

Corals are Coelenterates, a class of animals which also includes sea anemones and jellyfish. The true reef-building corals or Scleractinia are distinguished by their lime skeletons. It is this relatively indestructible skeleton which actually forms the coral reef, as new coral continually builds on old dead coral and the reef gradually builds up.

Coral takes a vast number of forms but all are distinguished by polyps, the tiny tube-like fleshy cylinders which look very like their close relation, the anemone. The top of the cylinder is open and ringed by waving tentacles which sting and draw into the polyp's stomach (the open space within the cylinder) any passing prey. Each polyp is an individual creature but each can reproduce by splitting to form a coral colony of separate but closely related polyps. Although each polyp catches and digests its own food, the nutrition passes between the polyps to the whole colony. Most coral polyps only feed at night: during the daytime they withdraw into their hard limestone skeleton, so it is only at night that a coral reef can be seen in its full colourful glory.

Hard corals may take many forms. One of the most common and easiest to recognise is the staghorn coral, which grows by budding off new branches from the tips. Brain corals are huge and round with a surface looking very much like a human brain. They grow by adding new base levels of skeletal matter and expanding outwards. Flat or sheet corals, like plate coral, expand at their outer edges. Many corals can take different shapes depending on their environment. Staghorn coral can branch out in all directions in deeper water or form flat tables when they grow in shallow water.

Like their reef-building relatives, soft coral is made up of individual polyps, but does not form a hard limestone skeleton. Without the skeleton which protects hard coral, it would seem likely that soft coral would fall prey to fish but it seems to remain relatively immune either due to toxic substances in its tissues or due to the presence of sharp limestone needles which protect the polyps. Soft corals can move around and will sometimes engulf and kill off hard coral.

Corals catch their prey by means of stinging nematocysts (a specialised type of cell). Some corals can give humans a painful sting and the fern-like stinging hydroid should be given a wide berth.

Tony Wheeler

tive names, such as soldier fish, surgeon fish, trumpet fish, red lizard fish, goat fish, bat fish, butterfly fish and parrot fish. The ribbon or leaf-nose eel is especially interesting. During its life cycle it changes colour and sex from being a young black male to a brilliant blue male or bright yellow female. The territorial anemone fish, or clown fish, lives in a symbiotic relationship with the sea anemone, having developed an immunity to its poisonous sting. Some of the most beautiful fish and marine creatures, such as the scorpion fish and lion fish, are also highly venomous. If in doubt, don't touch!

Species such as the barracuda, jackfish, sting ray, small reef shark and large parrot fish are found cruising along channels and the edges of reefs. In open sea and deeper waters, larger fish are common, including tuna, bonito, sword fish, rays and sharks. Large sharks normally stay away from the coast. The grey reef shark is most often seen on steeper outer-reef drops. It has a reputation for being aggressive, but it feeds primarily on small fish. Large manta and devil rays feed on zooplankton and small fishes. Sting rays are most often found near swamp areas and among mangroves.

For an insight into the lives of molluscs, crustaceans, sea slugs, feather stars, starfish, christmas-tree worms, and other marine life, pick up a copy of Paddy Ryan's *The Snorkeller's Guide to the Coral Reef*.

Cruelty to Animals

According to an opinion poll held in Fiji in 1996, 57% of those polled said cruelty to animals was a big problem in Fiji. Fijians and Fiji Indians generally view animals in terms of their practical use. Working animals such as horses and bullocks are sometimes badly nourished, and are often whipped as they work. Village animals are rarely treated for worms and parasites. Cockfighting is practised for entertainment, though in secret. Travellers will notice that animals used for horse riding are not always well tended. Many resorts and tours promote game fishing as a sport.

Turtle is banned from restaurants but is sometimes found at markets. Turtle meat and eggs are considered a delicacy and are still eaten by some villagers, as are bats and giant clams.

National Parks & Protected Areas

Fiji's potential for land and sea reserves is excellent. There are a number of places with outstanding natural beauty, interesting landscapes and vegetation, and rare or unique animals and birds. Archaeological and historical sites and monuments have great potential for tourism.

Since 1971, environmental policies and national development plans have been proposed by government. Implementation, however, has been minimal and there aren't many legally protected conservation areas in Fiji. The few areas selected as 'nature reserves' by Fiji's Department of Forestry have not had their ecological attributes fully evaluated. The existing legislation is adequate, but due to a lack of resources and commitment to conservation, legal preservation of sites is not happening. Because of the increased popularity of ecotourism, a few forest parks and reserves have recently been declared. A good example is the Lavena Coastal Walk on eastern Taveuni.

Significant sites include Sovi Basin and

The lion fish is as beautiful as it is deadly

Colo-i-Suva Park in Naitasiri province near Suva; the Bouma Forest Reserve on Taveuni Island; Abaca National Park in the Mount Evans Range near Lautoka, Viti Levu; Tunuloa Silktail Reserve in the Cakaudrove district on Vanua Levu; and the Sigatoka Sand Dunes, Viti Levu. Refer to their respective chapters for more information.

GOVERNMENT & POLITICS

The Republic of Fiji is presently governed by the SVT-GVP coalition led by Prime Minister Sitiveni Rabuka. It was Rabuka who led the two military coups-d'état of 1987. The president is Ratu Sir Kamisese Mara, who has been prominent in the Fijian political scene since the 1960s. The leader of the opposition is Jai Ram Reddy, of the NFP.

The government is divided into 16 ministries. For administrative purposes the country has four political divisions: Western, Northern, Eastern and Central. Local government includes city, town and municipal councils.

Parliament & the Judiciary

The 1990 constitution provides for a parliament consisting of a president, a house of representatives and a senate.

The president has executive authority and serves for a period of five years. The position is reserved for a Fijian appointed by the Great Council of Chiefs and requires support from a majority in the house of representatives.

The senate (upper house) consists of 34 members appointed by the president. Of these, 24 are appointed on the advice of the Great Council of Chiefs, one on the advice of the Rotuman Island Council and nine on the advice of other communities. The role of the senate is to revise bills and debate issues.

The house of representatives (lower house) consists of 70 members from 52 constituencies. Of these seats, 37 are reserved

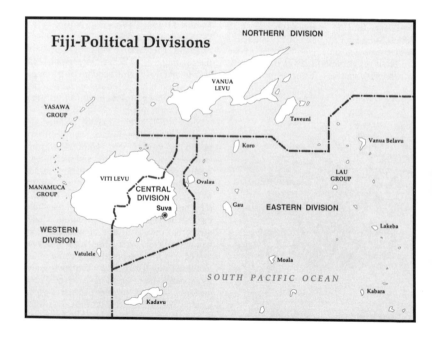

Fiji-Political Divisions

for Fijians, 27 for Indians, one for Rotumans (Polynesians) and five for general electors.

The positions of prime minister, police and civil service commissioners and army commander are also reserved for indigenous Fijians.

The judiciary is comprised of three courts: a high court, court of appeal and supreme court.

The present constitution is seen by many as racist and detrimental to the country as a whole. Constitutional review and the issue of renewal of land leases are particularly important issues facing the government. Refer to the history section for details on recent political events.

Political Parties

After a long history of segregation in Fiji, political parties remain mostly separated along racial lines. The country's political parties include:

Soqosoqo-ni-Vakavulewa-ni Taukei (SVT)
   Dubbed the chief's party, the SVT is a Fijian nationalist group sponsored by the Great Council of Chiefs and supported by the Taukei movement.
National Federation Party (NFP)
   Comprised mostly of Fiji Indians. It was part of the NFP-FLP coalition, which won the 1987 election and was then deposed in the first coup.
Fiji Labour Party (FLP)
   Comprised of Fijian and Indian trade-union members.
Fijian Association
   An ultranationalist party intent on preserving traditional chiefly power.
General Voters Party
   Comprised of European, part-Fijian, Chinese, and other Pacific Islanders.
Fijian Nationalist United Front (FNUF)
   A Fijian ultranationalist party advocating indigenous Fijian rule.

Fijian Administration & the Great Council of Chiefs

Parallel and intertwined with government administration is the traditional chiefly system. Chiefs make decisions at a local level as well as being extremely influential at a national level through the Bose Levu Vakaturaga or Great Council of Chiefs

National Symbols

Although Fiji is a republic, and since the coups no longer a Commonwealth member, the British influence is retained in the national symbols and the national anthem – *God Bless Fiji*. Queen Elizabeth II still figures on all currency.

The Fijian coat of arms features two warriors with war club and spear, a *takia* (Fijian canoe) and a shield. The shield bears a heraldic lion clasping a cocoa pod, sugar cane, a coconut palm, bananas and a dove of peace. The words Revevaka na Kalou ka doka na Tui, meaning 'fear God and honour the queen', also appeared on the flag of the Cakobau 'government' before cession.

The Fijian Flag has the British Union Jack on a light-blue background and the shield from the coat of arms. ■

The basic unit of Fijian administration is the *koro* (village) headed by a hereditary chief, the *turaga-ni-koro*, who is appointed by the village elders. Several koro are linked as a *tikina*, and several tikina form a *yasana* or province. Fiji is divided into 14 provinces, and each has a high chief.

The Great Council of Chiefs includes members of the lower house as well as nominated chiefs from the provincial councils. The council was originally created to strengthen the position of the ruling Fijian elite, and has gained great power since the military coups and the introduction of the 1990 constitution. The council appoints the president, who in turn is responsible for appointing judges, in consultation with the Judicial & Legal Services Commission. It also has authority over any legislation related to land ownership and common rights.

ECONOMY

Tourism and sugar are Fiji's main earners and together employ about 80,000 people. Fiji also exports molasses, gold, timber, fish, copra and coconut oil, and clothing. Recent diversification has occurred with the exportation of forest wood chips, sawn timber, and an expansion in manufacturing to include products such as leather and furniture.

Fiji is facing many economic problems. The population is increasing and people's expectations are rising. Poverty and inequality are growing, along with unemployment and increasing urbanisation due to a shift away from subsistence farming.

Unemployment is especially high among youth. The semisubsistence village economy is no longer able to absorb large numbers of young people. Cash is required for clothing, school fees, church levies, imported goods and community projects. Urban children lead a different life, away from the discipline and structure of village life. Theft in the cities and towns is increasing.

The traditional Fijian and modern economic systems have different and often contradictory requirements. Traditional economic systems rely on kinship and village structure to sustain them. With the global push for internationalisation of production and trade, Fiji is becoming more export orientated and open to increased competition.

Government policy includes down-sizing of the public sector, tax reform, encouragement of overseas investment and increased indigenous-Fijian participation in business. The public sector accounts for 40% of all formal employment. Both the size of the armed forces and parliament increased in 1987. Fiji has long been reliant on overseas aid from Australia and New Zealand, and more recently, Japan.

Economic growth is needed to service Fiji's massive loans. In 1994 foreign debt stood at F$190 million and internal debt at F$800 million, and in 1995 it was confirmed that the National Bank of Fiji was bankrupt. Growth is being hindered by the public's reluctance to invest and make long-term commitments due to uncertainty over land leases, racial tension and constitutional problems. Many skilled and educated workers, especially Fiji Indians, are leaving Fiji in search of security.

Tourism Fiji receives about 300,000 visitors per year and since 1989 earnings from tourism have amounted to 17% of GDP, surpassing sugar as the primary source of foreign-exchange earnings. Most visitors are from Australia and New Zealand, while increasing numbers are coming from Japan and Korea. The industry is promoted by the Fiji Visitors Bureau (FVB) and the Tourism Council of the South Pacific (TCSP).

Travellers should be aware that there is a 10% value added tax (VAT) on all goods and services. Since tourism has been going through a bit of a low, there are good deals being offered by resorts desperate for cash flow.

Agriculture Agriculture is the largest sector of the economy. Only about 16% of Fiji's land is suitable for agriculture, and this occurs mainly along the coastal plains and river valleys and deltas of the two main islands. The main cane-growing areas are western Viti Levu and western Vanua Levu, with mills at Lautoka, Ba, Rakiraki and Labasa. Dairy farming is concentrated in the Rewa Delta, near Suva. Other produce includes molasses, copra and coconut oil, cocoa, ginger, rice, vanilla, fruit and vegetables.

The sugar industry has been the mainstay of the economy for most of the 20th century. It currently provides employment for almost a third of the population. The prosperity of the industry is therefore extremely important to the economy, providing taxes to the government and rent from leased land to landowners. To counteract the problem of falling markets, there is a need to focus on greater productivity, investment in technology and long-term planning.

Due to historical and constitutional reasons the industry is compartmentalised along racial lines. Most cane is grown by Fiji-Indian farmers on land leased by indigenous landowners. Indigenous Fijians own 83% of the total land area, and, due to rules of ownership, Fiji Indians cannot own this land. Long-term land leases begin to expire in 1997 and farmers feeling vulnerable and anxious about the future are therefore discouraged from long-term planning and investment.

Other Economic Activities The fisheries industry produces canned tuna, bêche-de-mer, trochus shell and trochus-shell buttons and shark fin.

Pine plantations are common on the western sides of Viti Levu and Vanua Levu. Most forest is on communally owned native land, and has been planted by Fiji Pine Limited.

Gold is being mined at Vatukoula near Tavua in northern Viti Levu, and at Mt Kasi in Vanua Levu.

Fiji's manufacturing sector includes clothing and small-scale footwear production, and cigarette, food and beverage industries. Aluminium and plastic products, agricultural equipment, boats, cement, furniture, and handicrafts are also manufactured.

Trade Agreements In 1994 Fiji became a signatory to the General Agreement on Tariffs and Trade (GATT). The South Pacific Regional Trade and Economic Cooperation Agreement (SPARTECA) provides for duty and quota-free access to New Zealand and Australian markets, and this has benefited Fiji. However, Australia is now removing its trade protection. The Lome Convention gives Fiji preferential access to the European Union, and the Generalised System of Preferences does the same in the US and Japan. Fiji is currently pursuing trade links with the markets of South-East Asia.

POPULATION & PEOPLE

Fiji has a total population of about 772,000, according to 1993 estimates. About half of the population is under the age of 20 and about two-thirds under 30. Youths aged between 15 and 24, comprising about 20% of the total population, are facing high unemployment.

The most populated island is Viti Levu, with 75% of the overall population, followed by Vanua Levu with 18%. The remaining 7% of the population is spread over 100-odd islands. About 39% of the population are urban dwellers. The highest densities occur in the major urban centres of Suva, Nadi, Lautoka and in the sugar-cane growing areas of Rewa and Ba.

The population is the most multiracial of South Pacific countries. Some areas have a higher proportion of particular races due to historical factors such as indenture. The Fijian administration categorises people according to their racial origins and therefore there is a lack of national identity. The term 'Fijian' is used for indigenous Fijians only, even if a person's family has lived in Fiji for generations. Fiji Indians are referred to as 'Indians', and the naming system for 'Chinese' and other Pacific Islanders is similar. People of Australian, New Zealand, American or European decent are all labelled 'Europeans'. Those people with a mixed descent of European and indigenous Fijian are called 'part-Europeans'.

Fijians also use the following terms: *kaiviti* for indigenous Fijian, *kaihidi* for Fiji Indians, and *kaivelagi*, or literally 'people from far away', for Europeans. The term 'pre-mix' is occasionally used informally to describe people of mixed race. Generally though, there is relatively little marriage between racial groups.

From the late 1940s until the military coups of 1987, indigenous Fijians were outnumbered by Fiji Indians. Indigenous Fijians presently account for about 50% of the population and Fiji Indians for about 45%.

Indigenous Fijians

Indigenous Fijians are predominantly of Melanesian origin, but have a strong Polynesian influence both physically and culturally, especially in the eastern islands (Lau group) due to their proximity to Tonga. Darker Melanesian features and frizzy hair are mixed with lighter Polynesian features and straight hair.

Fiji Indians

Most Fiji Indians are descendants of indentured labourers. Initially most of the Indians sent to Fiji came from the states of Bengal (Bangladesh), Bihar and Uttar Pradesh in

Racial Issues

Race relations on an everyday level between ordinary people are generally harmonious, however, racial divisions are entrenched in Fijian history, language and politics. Underlying concerns and fears have been deliberately played upon and exploited for political gain, and religion and consequently education reinforce differences. The extremist slogan 'Fiji for Fijians' is still used, and Fiji Indian and Chinese shop owners in remote areas protect themselves behind barricades.

Ironically, government publications say that:

The country's 1990 constitution guarantees and promotes racial equality. It is unlawful to discriminate on the grounds of colour, race or ethnic origins and it is an offence to incite racial disharmony.

However, many argue that the constitution re-enforces racial inequality and that the government is showing little willingness to address the issue. The Citizens Constitutional Forum (CCF) argues that a change in government policy is needed to heal the 'suspicion and division which has been the legacy of the coups and the 1990 constitution'.

The government's racial policies are also having a negative effect on the economy. Indo-Fijian farmers are concerned that land leases which begin expiring in 1997 will not be renewed and with this insecurity there is no incentive to invest. One Indo-Fijian farmer told us, 'we cannot call our homes our own. Whatever we have here doesn't belong to us even though our parents struggled to build this for us'. It has even been suggested by some indigenous Fijians that all Indo-Fijians in the sugar-cane industry should be replaced by the year 2000.

The government's policy of 'positive discrimination' favouring indigenous Fijians in public institutions is also very controversial. Fiji Indians complain that less experienced or qualified indigenous-Fijian colleagues receive promotions, and in competition for scholarships indigenous-Fijian children are given preference even when their marks are lower.

Those who are most frustrated and disillusioned are leaving the country, including large numbers of skilled workers in professional and technical areas. The rate of Indian emigration almost doubled during the few years after the coups, and continues to maintain relatively high levels. The resulting brain drain is imposing huge costs on the economy. ■

north-eastern India. Later, large groups of southern Indians arrived. The great diversity of languages, religions, customs and subcultures has merged to a certain extent over the years.

Other Indians, mostly Punjabis and Gujeratis, voluntarily came to Fiji soon after the end of the indenture system. Both groups are now a kind of business elite in Fiji.

Other Groups

There are about 4,500 so-called 'Europeans' who were born in Fiji, and over 10,000 'part-Europeans'. Some of these families established themselves at Levuka during the early 19th century as traders and ship-builders or on the copra plantations of Vanua Levu, Lomaiviti and Lau. Europeans tend to work in agriculture, business, tourism and the public sector. Other 'Europeans' include temporary residents.

The 8600 Fijians from Rotuma are of Polynesian origin. Most of them live and work in Suva away from their remote island. Among the other 9000 Pacific Islanders in Fiji are Tongans and Samoans and 3000 Banabans – Micronesians whose own island was stripped by phosphate mining, and who were resettled on Rabi Island after WWII. There are also more than 8000 descendants of blackbirder labourers from the Solomon Islands, most living in communities near Suva and on Ovalau.

About 0.7% of the population (5000 people) are Chinese or part-Chinese, the majority of whose ancestors arrived early in the 20th century to open general stores and other small businesses. More Chinese have migrated to Fiji in the past decade. Most are living in urban centres and tend to work in restaurants and commerce. The first Chinese settlers married Fijian women, but today the

Chinese tend to form their own groups within the community.

Standard of Living

About 70% of the population has access to a piped water supply. Many rural villages and settlements in the interior and outer islands rely on diesel generators or do not have electricity. The government provides some housing assistance for low-income earners. Food is relatively plentiful and many rural people live a semisubsistence village life-style. The urban poor are less well off and support networks and extended families are less intact. About 8% of households have an annual income of less than F$3000. The 1986 census showed that 21% of women had jobs outside the home. Life expectancy is 61.4 years for men and 65.2 for women.

EDUCATION

Fiji has a reasonably good education system, and is considered the educational centre of the South Pacific. Education is not compulsory, but primary and lower secondary education are accessible almost all round the country, and the country's literacy rate is high (87% according to a 1990 estimate).

About 25% of the population is school-aged. Almost 100% of children attend primary school and most complete lower secondary education. The government provides incentives for poor rural children in the form of free tuition for primary and secondary students, and per capita grants. The government has also been trying to reduce the disparity between rural and urban schools by upgrading teacher quality and student assessments. Nearly all rural Fijian children at some stage during their education move away from their home villages to attend boarding schools or live with relatives in towns.

Education is not officially segregated, but schools are run by the major religions. Normally, Fiji-Indian children attend Hindu or Muslim schools while indigenous Fijians attend Christian schools. English is the official language taught in all educational establishments in Fiji. The government has been encouraging the learning of either Fijian or Hindi in all schools in an attempt to increase the interaction between different communities. Special provisions have been made for more scholarships and education facilities for indigenous Fijians, in an effort to increase their representation in higher education.

The University of the South Pacific is a regional university established in 1968 belonging to 12 Pacific island countries. Its main campus is based in Suva, but it also has a campus in Western Samoa and centres in the other member countries. USP has over 2600 students enrolled at the Suva campus and another 6000 students in extension programmes. The Fiji School of Medicine opened in 1985 to provide medical training in the region. The Fiji College of Agriculture, in conjunction with the USP, offers training in tropical agriculture and receives students from other South Pacific countries. The main centre for technical education is Suva's Fiji Institute of Technology (FIT). The FIT runs 10 different programmes, some in association with local industry, and also has offices at Labasa and Lautoka.

ARTS

Fijian villagers still practise traditional arts, crafts, dance and music. Some arts remain an integral part of the culture, others are practised solely to satisfy tourist demand. Other cultural groups also retain many of their traditional arts.

New movements include fashion and, though not common, painting and photography. The paintings of Debora Veli, which feature on postcards, are stylised, almost naive scenes mainly of the forest and mythology. There are local fashion designers, and a clothing and fabric industry on Viti Levu. A theatre group in Suva showcases local playwrights, and drama is taught at the university.

Dance

Visitors are often welcomed at resorts and hotels with a *meke*, a dance performance that enacts stories and legends. Every subtle movement as well as the arrangement of the group has a significance in a meke, and important guests and onlookers are given special positions of honour to avoid offence. While performances for tourists may seem staged, meke is an ongoing tradition.

In the past, Fijian mekes involved chanting by 'spiritually possessed seers' or a chorus, and were often accompanied by rhythmic clapping, the thumping and stamping of bamboo clacking sticks, the beating of slit drums, and dancing. They were held purely for entertainment, for welcoming visitors, or on important religious and social occasions – including births, deaths, marriages and property exchanges between villages. Mekes were handed down through generations and new ones were composed for special events. Traditionally, chants included laments at funerals, war incitement dirges, and animal impersonations.

Men, women and children participated in mekes. Men performed club and spear dances and women fan dances. In times of war, men performed the *cibi*, or death dance, and women the *dele*, or *wate*, a dance in which they sexually humiliated enemy corpses and captives. Paddles were used as

Fijian legends are told through dance performances called *mekes*

dance props in areas of Tongan influence. Dancing often took place by moonlight or torch light, the performers in costume, bodies oiled and faces painted, combs and flowers decorating their hair.

The Dance Theatre of Fiji performs regularly at the cultural centre at Pacific Harbour. Its performances are produced and composed by Manoa Rasigatale, who is intent on keeping alive old ceremonies through dances choreographed for modern audiences. The group has been on many international tours, including a performance at England's Wembley Stadium for the opening of a World Cup rugby match.

Traditional Chinese dancing is still practised, and Indian classical dance, including Bharat Natyam and *kathak*, is taught at Indian cultural centres.

Music

While in Fiji, try to attend at least one meke and a church service to witness fantastic choir singing. Guitar is now the most commonly used instrument. Popular local musicians include Seru Serevi, the Black Roses, Danny Costello, Michelle Rounds, the Freelancers, Karuna Gopalan, Laisa Vulakoro, Soumini Vuatalevu, and the more mellow Serau Kei Mataniselala. Reggae has been influential and is very popular, and there are jazz bands in Suva. Tapes of local bands can be found in music shops such as SPR and Morris Hedstrom.

Music from 'Bollywood' films (Indian melodramas) is popular among Fiji Indians. Local bands, such as His Masters Orchestra, do covers of Indian songs. Vocal/harmonium, tabla (percussion) and sitar lessons are given at Indian cultural centres.

Pottery

Fiji's best known potters are Diana Tugea of Nakabuta in the Sigatoka Valley, and Taraivini Wati of Naisilai on the Rewa River near Nausori. The pottery-making tradition in these villages has been handed down through the centuries. Different areas had different techniques and styles.

Tugea's clay pots are smooth with a wide

Traditional Musical Instruments

Traditional nose flutes were once quite common in the Pacific but are now almost, if not completely, extinct in Fiji. The instrument was typically a single section of bamboo about 70 cm long, closed at each end by a node, and carved with intricate patterns. The musician lay on a pandanus mat, with his or her head resting on a bamboo pillow. Small panpipes, commonly worn around the neck, were made of two to 12 hollow cane barrels.

Wind instruments were informally played by both men and women while serenading, and the flute reputedly had the power to attract the opposite sex.

Other instruments such as shell trumpets and whistles were used for communication. *Lali*, large slit drums made of resonant timbers, are audible over large distances, and they are still used to beckon people to the chief's *bure* or to church. Portable war drums were used for warning and communicating tactics on the battlefield. ■

belly, open neck and outward curving lip. They are used for cooking. The food is wrapped in banana or *rourou* (taro) leaves and the pot is sealed with coiled leaves.

Wati's pots are highly decorated and traditionally used for water storage. These pots were originally reserved for use by high chiefs. Most of her pots have a smooth outer belly with a raised pattern of triangular spikes and a narrow neck and lip with patterned incisions. The raised spikes are a traditional motif and are thought to represent a type of war fence which was used to defend ring-ditch villages in the Rewa Delta. She also makes replicas of elaborately designed drinking vessels used in the 19th century.

A series of wooden paddles of various shapes and sizes are used to beat the pots into shape, while the form is held from within using a pebble anvil. Coil and slab-building techniques are also used. Once dried they are then fired outdoors in an open blaze on

Vitian Pottery

Pottery serves as one of the main archaeological records of Vitian culture, showing that Vitian people and culture have varied greatly over time. Shards of Lapita pottery (named after the Lapita people, the early inhabitants of the islands) dating back to 1290 BC have been found in the Sigatoka area, and shards dating back to 1030 BC on nearby Yanuca Island. These pots, decorated with intricate, paddle-impressed geometric patterns, are thought to be ceremonial and suggest an involved social structure. Other impressed pottery found on Yanuca dates back to 710 BC and at Vuda and Navuta from 100 BC to 1100 AD. A later plain-pottery phase lasted from 1250 AD to European arrival.

Simple, functional pots replaced the more sophisticated Lapita pottery at the time of a population explosion and increase in agriculture 2500 years ago. People were moving inland and warring; cannibalism and the use of defensive forts also increased. About 2000 years ago there was another abrupt change in pottery which is thought to have been caused by further influxes of Melanesians. Vitian pottery of 100 BC to 1000 AD is characterised by a chequered decoration.

Cooking pots were usually perched on three hollow earthenware stands on the hearth. Drinking vessels ranged widely in shape and form. In the 19th century, drinking vessels with bizarre shapes were made for the chiefs of south-east Viti Levu and Bau. Forms ranged from an interconnected grouping of citrus fruit, shaped as tabua (whale's teeth), to turtles, canoe hulls or combinations of these.

Pot making seems to have generally been the work of women from seafaring mataqali, who traded these items for agricultural and land produce. ■

coconut husks. Pots are often sealed with resin varnish from the *dakua* tree.

Wati and her work can be seen at the Fiji Museum each Thursday and Friday, and the two potters give joint demonstrations on the first Thursday of each month. Both villages receive visitors. Refer to the Sigatoka and Rewa sections in the Viti Levu chapter.

Wood Carving

Traditional wood-carving skills are being kept alive by the tourist trade, which provides a ready market for war clubs, spears and chief's and priest's cannibal forks. Yaqona drinking bowls, or *tanoas*, are still widely used in everyday life in Fiji. In areas of Tongan influence, wooden articles are inlaid with ivory, shell and bone. Traditional designs are still made by the Lemaki people of Kabara, Southern Lau, (descendants of Tongan and Samoan wood carvers and canoe builders who settled in Viti in the 18th and 19th century).

Carvings in human and animal forms were generally restricted to religious objects such as yaqona vessels. They were traditionally made of sacred *vesi* timber. Yaqona bowls shaped like turtles are thought to have derived from turtle-shaped *ibuburau* (vessels used in indigenous Vitian yaqona rites).

The Fiji Museum is the best place to see authentic traditional wood carvings. Beware that many of the artefacts for sale at handicraft centres are not genuinely Fijian and that the quality varies greatly.

Bark Cloth & Traditional Textiles

Masi, also known as *malo* or *tapa*, is bark cloth with designs printed in black and rust. Masi played an important role in Vitian culture and its motifs had symbolic meaning. Today Fijian masi is mostly made for tourists and used for postcards, wall hangings and other decorative items. The beautiful tapa panels that hang in parliament house are perhaps a symbolic reference to the ancestor spirits. Textile designers are now incorporating traditional masi motifs in their fabrics.

Masi's status and symbolic worth was of similar importance to yaqona and tabua (whales' teeth). It has long been associated with the marking of special occasions and was worn by men in the form of snowy white male loincloths during initiation rituals, for renaming ceremonies following killings, and as an adornment in dance, festivity and war. The finest sheet tissue was worn as sashes, waistbands, trains and turbans by priests and chiefs, and was also used to wrap the cord with which a man's widows were strangled for burial with him so that they would accompany him into the afterlife. Masi was an important exchange item and was used in bonding ceremonies between related tribes. Chiefs would dance swathed in a huge puffball of masi cloth, and then give it to members of the other tribe, who then clad themselves in it. Local motifs and patterns were sometimes used to signify allegiance to a particular tribe.

While men wore masi, production was traditionally a woman's role. The cloth is made from the inner bark of the paper mulberry bush. The bark is peeled and the inner white bark is stripped, soaked in water, scraped clean and stored in rolls. The bark is beaten and widened and felted together for hours until it has a fine even texture. Large sheets of 2m by 2.2m are not uncommon. Rich, oily, brown cloth is made by soaking the material in coconut oil and smoking it over burning sugary leaves. Intricately painted designs are done by hand or using stencils. In areas of Tongan influence patterns are obtained by rubbing the cloth over a tablet made of raised leaf strips. Rusty coloured paints are traditionally made from an infusion of candlenut and mangrove bark; pinker browns from red clays; and blacks from the soot of burnt dakua resin and charred candlenuts. Modern paints and glues are now used as shortcuts.

Mat & Basket Weaving

Woven mats made of pandanus leaves are used in most Fijian homes as floor coverings, dining mats and as finer sleeping mats. They are much in demand as wedding presents, and for baptisms, funerals and presentations to chiefs.

Most village girls learn the craft; traditionally it was the hereditary role of the women of certain tribes. The pandanus leaves are cut and laid outdoors to cure, then stripped of the spiny edges, boiled and dried. The traditional method of blackening the leaves for contrasting patterns is to bury them in mud for days and then boil them with certain leaves. The dried leaves, made flexible by scraping with shells, are split into strips of about one to two cm. The borders of mats used to be decorated with parrot feathers, but now brightly coloured wools are used instead.

Literature
The indigenous-Fijian oral tradition of telling tall stories, myths and legends around the kava bowl is still strong, both as entertainment and for passing on history. English is the principal written means of expression. *Myths & Legends of Fiji & Rotuma* by AW Reed & Inez Hames is an interesting collection of these stories.

Fiji has a small but strong community of poets, playwrights and other writers. Contemporary literature includes works by Joseph Veramu, the author of the short story collection *The Black Messiah* and the novel *Moving Through the Streets*, which is about urban teenagers in Suva. Jo Nacola's work includes the play *I Native No More*. The Fiji Writers Association has published *Trapped: A Collection of Writings From Fiji*. The Fiji issue of *Mana*, a South Pacific journal of language and literature, vol. 9, no. 1 has a selection of local poetry, short stories and critiques of Fijian literature by male and female writers. Other notable authors are short-story writer Marjorie Crocombe and Rotuman playwright Vilsoni Hereniko.

Fiji Indians continue writing poetry in Hindi, but since the 1970s some, principally USP academics, began to write poetry in English. Some important writers include Subramani, Satendra Nandan, Raymond Pillai and Prem Banfal. The theme of the injustice of the indenture experience rates highly in Fiji-Indian literature, showing its importance on the psyche, and interestingly the natural environment is often portrayed as harsh and alien. As a body of work it is not necessarily representative of the contemporary or historical Fiji-Indian identity, as it often dwells on a sense of hopelessness. Prem Banfal's work is written from a female perspective.

The 'Niu Wave Writers', from the Fiji Writers Association, perform music and comedy monthly at Trapps Bar in Suva.

Architecture
Traditional The most beautiful example of a traditional village is Navala, in the highlands of Viti Levu. It is the only village remaining where every home is a bure. Bures are cheap and relatively quick to build, and young rural men still sometimes build themselves a bure if they need a home. Most villagers, however, now live in simple rectangular, pitched-roof houses built from modern materials, which require less maintenance. While a bure's structure is able to withstand cyclones, the government offers incentives to build concrete cyclone-proof houses.

Most traditional bures are rectangular with a hipped or gabled roof. However, in areas of Tongan and Samoan influence such as Lau, round-ended plans are common. With few windows, the interior space is normally quite dark. Pandanus mats cover a packed-earth floor and there is often a sleeping compartment at one end, behind a curtain. Cooking is now normally done in a separate bure. Bure building is a skilled trade passed from father to son, although the whole community helps when a bure is under construction, and most village people would know how to maintain their bure walls and roof. Skills are also kept alive for the tourist industry with its demand for authentic-looking buildings.

Colonial Levuka, the old European trader settlement and former capital of Fiji, has been officially designated an historic town. A number of buildings date from its boom period in the late 19th century and the main streetscape is surprisingly intact, giving the impression of a town that has stopped in time.

Suva's British influence is reflected in its many colonial buildings, including Government House, the Suva City Library, the Grand Pacific Hotel and government buildings.

Modern Much of Fiji's modern architecture combines traditional aesthetics, knowledge and materials with modern technology. Notable buildings include the new parliament complex, the USP campus in Suva, and the *bure bose* (meeting house) at Somosomo on Taveuni.

Many of the resorts have fairly predictable tropical-style designs. Those whose architecture stands out are the up-market Vatulele Island Resort (combining American Santa Fe style with traditional design); Namale Resort near Savusavu, Vanua Levu; and the smaller Natadola Beach Resort. Young architects, with new ideas for tropical architecture, are also making an impact on the commercial and resort scene.

SOCIETY & CONDUCT
Traditional Culture
Indigenous Fijians Many features of Viti's richly diversified past were suppressed with the old religion in the mid to late-19th century. Pre-Christian costumes, hairdressing and body decoration are far removed from today's conservative dress style. However, many aspects of the communal way of life are still strong, despite changing influences and pressures. Even through the colonial era the chiefly system and village structure remained intact, partly due to laws protecting Fijian land rights and prohibiting Fijian labour on the plantations.

Most indigenous Fijians live in villages in mataqali (or extended family groups) and acknowledge a hereditary chief who is usually male. Each mataqali owns land, and wider groups have a paramount chief. Clans gather for births, deaths, marriages, *lovo* feasts (where food is cooked in a pit oven), mekes and to exchange gifts. Yaqona drinking is still an important social ceremony. A family is allocated land for farming. Communal obligations also have to be met, including farming for the chief, preparing for special ceremonies and feasts, fishing, building and village maintenance. Village life is now only semisubsistent; cash is needed for school fees, community projects and imported goods.

Village life is based on interdependence and is therefore supportive, providing a

Traditional Fijian Face & Body Painting

Face painting reached its artistic peak in the mid-19th century. The indigenous pallet of red, yellow, black and white, was joined by the vermilion and blue introduced by traders. Vermilion became 'equal to gold' and was traded with the Europeans for baskets of bêche-de-mer.

An endless variety of creative designs were used fairly informally for everyday cosmetic decoration. Faces could be striped, zigzagged, spotted, bisected or plain black except for a red nose. There were special rules for certain festive occasions or war. Face painting was perhaps a convenient disguise in wars against close neighbours, although warriors generally wished to gain glory and notoriety. The bodies of dead or dying women were adorned with turmeric or vermilion paint. Turmeric was used to paint babies and women for the first three months of pregnancy and after the birth until the baby was weaned. During this time a woman was under sexual tabu and males were ridiculed if they were found smudged with yellow paint. Young men were also covered in turmeric for *buli yaca* (puberty) ceremonies, or renaming ceremonies celebrating the first killing. Men mostly used red and black (associated with war and death) on their faces and sometimes chests. Women favoured yellow, saffron, pink and red. Fine black circles drawn around the eyes were considered beautiful.

Before painting, skin was oiled and scented with coconut oil. Black pigment was obtained from the soot of burnt candlenut or kauri resin, or from charcoal or fungus spores, then mixed with coconut and other oils. Yellow was obtained from a type of ginger root as well as from turmeric. ■

strong group identity. It is also conservative; independent thinkers are not encouraged, and being different or too ambitious can threaten the stability of a village. There is sometimes conflict between those who want change and those who don't. Profits from any additional business are normally expected to be shared with the whole village.

Traditional Fijian Hairdressing

Prior to European contact, a Fijian's head was considered sacred, and hairdressing in Viti was an art form. Early Europeans were astonished by the variety of elaborate styles and the custom was deliberately suppressed by missionaries, who regarded it as a 'flagrant symbol of paganism' not suitable for the 'neat and industrious Christian convert'.

Before initiation, girls either wore a cascade of bleached or reddened corkscrew ringlets, or had their heads shaven except for two ringlets, which sometimes reached the hips. These *tobe* ringlets represented the prawns they were destined to fish in later life. Once married, the tobe were removed and often the entire head shorn. Women kept their crown shaven or close-cropped in uniform length, sometimes ringed by a ruff of hair dyed rusty brown or yellow. Their hairstyle had to be inferior to their husband's, with the exception of female chiefs who could wear huge regal hair-dos.

Until initiation boys were bald except for one or two upstanding tufts. A man's hair, however, was a symbol of his masculinity, vanity and social standing. Men grew flamboyant, extravagant, fantastic, often massive hair-dos. Styles ranged from the relatively conventional giant puffball (up to 30 cm tall) to shaggy or geometric shapes with variations of ringlets, tufts and ruffs. Ringlet style was more appropriate for those with more Polynesian ancestry and wavier, less frizzy hair. The hair was dyed black, grey, sky blue, rust, orange, yellow, white or multicoloured. Before the introduction of the razor and mirror by traders, beards and moustaches were also grown long.

Hairdressers were employed to prick up the hair, stiffen it with burnt lime, and have it teased and singed into a sculpted form. People slept on uncomfortable-looking raised wooden pillows to keep their coiffure from being spoilt. The head was especially dressed up for festive occasions. Accessories included hair scratchers (practical for lice), ornamental combs, scarlet feathers, wreaths of small flowers and vines, larger flowers at the ears, and grated sandalwood as a perfume.

Shaving one's head was a profound sacrifice for a man. There were special wigs for balding men or for those who had sacrificed their hair in mourning or to appease a wrathful ancestral spirit. Tobe ringlets (the long ones could take 10 years to grow) were popular war trophies.

A chief's head was considered tabu and required a special hairdresser. The work could take two days to complete. The circumference of a chief's hair could reach more than 1.5m. Huge turbans of fine bark cloth were often worn, but would be removed in the presence of a superior as a token of submission and respect. ■

Concepts such as *kerekere* and *sevusevu* are still strong, especially in remote areas. Kerekere is where someone, especially a friend or relative, asks for something – you cannot refuse (property is considered communal). This can put employees of businesses in difficult situations, as it is especially difficult to say no if the person is of higher rank! Sevusevu is the presentation of a gift such as yaqona or, more powerfully, a tabua in exchange for certain favours. The receiver is obligated to honour your request. In remote areas the role of men and women is clearly demarcated. The hill villagers still obey a strong hierarchy and adhere to customs such as the rule that a brother and sister-in-law cannot converse.

Regional cultural and social differences which were noticeable in the past are, however, disappearing quickly. Fijians are travelling more and the Bauan dialect is now being used widely for business purposes. Fiji is also becoming increasingly urbanised. Villages are no longer self-sufficient and many young people travel to the cities for education, employment or to escape the restrictions of village life. For those who have grown up in the relative security and disciplined structure of a village, adapting to urban life is not easy. Together with increased freedom comes competition for jobs and a less supportive social structure. Traditional values and the wisdom of elders are less respected in urban areas. Television, which has only just been introduced in Fiji, presents opposing values and contradictory messages.

Indigenous Fijians own about 83% of the land, some of which is leased to others for farming and tourism. In addition to agriculture, mining and the public service, many indigenous Fijians are employed in the tourist industry, so there is some pressure placed on Fijians to retain the more exotic aspects of their culture.

While most of the larger resorts are foreign-owned, there are some smaller-scale projects that bring tourist dollars directly to villages.

Fiji Indians Most Fiji Indians are descended from indentured labourers whose families have been in Fiji for four or five generations. The majority of these labourers were young, illiterate farmers from communal villages. Traditional social structures and cultural traditions have been partially broken down through the experience of indentured labour, intermarriage and mixing over the years. Fiji Indians of different religions and diverse cultural and religious backgrounds were and still are stereotyped as a single group.

Extended families often live in the same house, but the trend is towards nuclear families. Females generally have a stricter upbringing than boys. In rural areas it is common for girls to marry at a young age and marriages are often arranged. Hindu married women wear a red spot between the brows. Girls often wear decorative coloured *bindi* spots. Hindu women usually wear saris and Muslims wear traditional robes and head coverings. Dress codes are more cosmopolitan in Suva.

Fiji Indians are often involved in farming on leasehold land, commerce and transportation. Most Gujeratis (from the north of Bombay) and Punjabis (mostly Sikhs from north of Delhi) arrived as free settlers, traders and merchants, and their descendants now monopolise shops and businesses. Gujeratis and Punjabis have stronger social networks and links with India.

The Fiji-Indian community share an interest in soccer and 'Bollywood' movies – escapist melodramas with lots of romance, violence and music, which are made by India's equivalent of the Hollywood film industry. While cut off from mainstream Indian traditions for a long period, there has been a recent movement to maintain and preserve cultural values. Indian cultural centres have been established to promote Indian culture with lectures, language classes, theatre, music and dance lessons. The four centres are at Ba (☎ 676 800), Suva (☎ 676 800), Labasa (☎ 814 433) and Nadi (☎ 703 144).

The Department of Indian & Multi-Ethnic

Affairs publishes the *Fiji Indian Cultural Newsletter*.

Dos & Don'ts

Indigenous Fijians have quite complicated codes of behaviour. Travellers need to be aware of local customs in order to show appropriate respect and good manners. If you are unsure of the appropriate way to behave, just ask. If you are travelling with children, impress on them the need to be obedient, quiet indoors, and respectful to their elders. When choosing tours consider those which support local people, services and conservation, and expect to pay a fair price.

Village Visits Try not to show up to a village uninvited, or, if you do, ask the first person you meet if it is possible to visit their village. They will probably take you to see the chief. Never wander around unaccompanied. Gardens, backyards, and bures are someone's private realm. Even in remote areas the land, beaches and reefs are usually owned by a mataqali.

Fijian culture demands that visitors should be treated as honoured guests. Often villagers invite visitors into their home and offer food, even if they are very poor. It is polite to accept, and also a good chance to talk to locals. Try to reciprocate hospitality by leaving some basic groceries such as sugar, tea or tinned meat, which you can buy at the village shop. If you intend to travel outside the main tourist areas, consider taking some extra clothes to give away in return for villagers' kindness. Second-hand clothes are OK, especially for kids.

Always take a sevusevu when visiting a village. About 500g of *taga yaqona*, (pounded kava, which costs about F$14 per kg) is acceptable, or, even better, take a bundle of *waka* (kava roots). Kava is available at markets, some shops and service stations. Don't bring alcohol; it may be banned in the village. In most villages yaqona is drunk every day, but some villages do abstain from drinking it, so ask the person taking you on the visit. Request to present the yaqona to the turaga-ni-koro (chief) who will welcome you in a small ceremony on behalf of the village. This may develop into a friendly *talanoa* (gossip session) around the yaqona bowl, where you will probably have to give your life story.

When entering a bure, remove your shoes and leave them outside. Stoop when entering (doorways are often low anyway), and quietly sit down cross-legged on the pandanus mat. If you are in the presence of someone of high social rank, such as the chief and his family, it is polite to keep your head at a lower level than theirs. Fijians consider the head as private, even sacred, so never touch a person's head or hair.

Do not question the authority of a *ratu* (male chief) or *adi* (female chief) or *tui* (king). It is considered rude to speak badly of anyone or to criticise people personally and its not polite to push people to talk about contentious topics such as politics if they are hesitant.

It is unusual for villagers to use a tourist unreasonably as a source of money, but it can happen. On the other hand, tourists sometimes take advantage of Fijian hospitality. If you do stay in a village, contribute food or money (about F$10 per day to cover your costs). Don't camp outside if you have been offered a place to sleep inside a home. It may be interpreted that the bure is not good enough and embarrass the hosts. When taken somewhere by private boat always offer to pay your share to cover fuel costs. Usually Fijians will not ask you for money or let you know when you are behaving in an insensitive manner or have overstayed your welcome.

Children or even adults may ask you for your shoes, jewellery or other travelling gear. This is the custom of shared property or kerekere. If you don't want to give the item away, you can usually get out of awkward situations by saying that you can't do without it. Try not to flash around expensive items that are beyond the reach of villagers.

Many locals think that all tourists are wealthy and that the standard of living is much higher in other countries. Travellers are often asked to become a pen pal or to sponsor someone to migrate. A polite refusal should be OK.

Sunday is considered a day of rest when families spend time together and attend church. It is therefore not a good day to visit as the disruption may not be appreciated by the chief.

Yaqona Drinking Yaqona, or kava, is an infusion prepared from the mildly narcotic root of *Piper methysticum*, a type of pepper plant, dried and ground to a powder. It is extremely important in Fijian culture and in the past was used ceremonially by chiefs and priests only. Today yaqona is part of daily life, not only in villages, but across the different races and in urban areas. 'Having a

grog' is used for welcoming and bonding with visitors, for storytelling sessions or for just passing time.

Certainly soon after your arrival in Fiji you will be offered a drink of kava. When visiting a village you will usually be welcomed with a short ceremony, and it is good manners to bring a bunch of kava or powdered root with you for presentation to the chief.

There are certain protocols to be followed at a kava ceremony and in some remote villages it is still a semireligious experience. Sit cross-legged, facing the chief and the large wooden bowl or tanoa. Women usually sit behind the men and don't get offered the first drink unless they are the guest of honour. Never walk across the circle of participants, turn your back to the tanoa or step

---

The Yaqona Ritual

A daily *burau* (a ceremonial yaqona-drinking ritual) was an integral part of the old Fijian religion. In ancient times the priest knelt or lay on the floor to drink the liquid from a *tanoa* bowl, an earthenware vessel or an elegant, shallow dish made of *vesi* wood, which was considered a sacred timber. For tabu reasons priests were not meant to touch either food or drink with their hands, and to this end a straw was sometimes used.

Yaqona drinking in the past was the prerogative of chiefs, priests and important male elders, and often drunk inside spirithouses. Late in the 18th century, Tongan contact saw the introduction of a different way of drinking yaqona, and yaqona started to be served using coconut-shell cups and deep wooden tanoa bowls. Tongans also introduced the kava circle ritual, which was a less religious yaqona ceremony, and the habit of chewing the kava root. Youths of both sexes were employed to chew the root prior to preparing the infusion. By the mid-19th century, these rituals were widespread in Fiji.

Long, elaborately plaited, egg-cowry (a symbol of divine fertility) and studded cords on kava bowls are a relatively recent innovation. The cord is extended towards the principal chief present, forming a link with the spirits. It was believed that if the cord was crossed, death would result. After drinking from the bowl the participant in the formal ritual would clap and say *mana, yaqona*, thanking the god.

The traditional Fijian yaqona ceremony, being an essential part of the religion, was condemned by the missionaries. The more Tongan kava ceremonies were tolerated and remain to the present. Yaqona is still an extremely important part of the culture and is ritually served on important occasions. Remote villages still practise quasi-religious ceremonies around the kava bowl. Galvanised or plastic buckets are now often used for social drinking. ■

Gunusede

A *gunusede*, literally 'drink money' is a village fundraising activity. You may be invited to attend one, and it is considered offensive to refuse. You will need to take some money, and if you are on a tight budget, don't take more than you can afford to give away. You should spend every cent you take to a gunusede. If you participate, even to a small extent, it will be appreciated. At a gunusede, people buy drinks, usually yaqona, for themselves and others. The price is usually a token 10 cents. If someone buys a drink for you and you can't stand another drop (this happens with yaqona) you can get out of it by bidding a higher price for someone else to drink it. Otherwise you must drink what is bought for you. These fundraising parties are used to pay for things like school fees for the village children. It is an example of how the community works together, and it is usually a fun get together.

Emma Hegarty

over the cord that leads from the tanoa to a white cowry, as this represents a link with the spirits.

The drink is prepared in the tanoa. The powdered root, wrapped in a piece of cloth, is mixed with water and the resulting concoction looks (and tastes) like muddy water. You will then be offered to drink a *bilo* (half a coconut shell). Clap once, accept the bilo, and say *bula* (meaning cheers or literally 'life') before drinking it all in one go (best to get it over with quickly anyway!). Then clap three times in gratification. The drink will be shared until the tanoa is empty. You are not obligated to drink every bilo offered to you, but it is polite to drink at least the first one.

Kava is a mild narcotic and has been used as a diuretic for pharmaceutical purposes. After a few drinks you may feel a slight numbness of the lips. Long sessions, however, with stronger mixes will probably make you drowsy. Some heavy drinkers develop *kanikani*, or scaly skin, and excess use has led to complaints of impotence from wives!

Dress Precolonial Fijians wore very little. Children ran around naked. Girls from about seven to puberty used a skimpy apron and afterwards the short *liku*, the skirt of womanhood made out of grasses or strips of pandanus leafs. Men wore just the *malo*, a loincloth. The missionaries, however, imposed a puritanical dress code. Today, indigenous Fijian women generally wear

long dresses with underskirts, and men wear shirts and *sulus* (skirts to below the knees), or long pants. Similarly most Fiji-Indian women cover up in long saris. The dress code in the urban centres is not so strict, with a mix of traditional and Western styles.

Modest dress is expected everywhere except resorts. Don't swim or sunbathe naked or topless, unless at an exclusive or remote resort. When in a village, don't wear hats or caps – if you want protection from the sun, use sunblock, look for a tree for shade or use an umbrella! It's also rude to wear sunglasses, especially when meeting people. Cameras and carry bags should be carried in the hands, not over the shoulder. Shoulders should be covered and women should wear knee-length dresses or skirts rather than long trousers or shorts.

Socialising It is rare to see public displays of affection between men and women. To avoid offence you should not be openly affectionate in public.

At a dance or in a disco, if a man asks a woman to dance and she refuses, she must then refuse every other man who asks.

Fiji-Indian Temples Visitors are asked to abstain from eating meat prior to visiting a Hindu temple and to remove their shoes before entering.

Photography Fijians usually enjoy having their photo taken, but always ask permission first and perhaps ask if they would like copies sent to them. During a yaqona ceremony you normally have to wait until after the formal ritual; check first.

RELIGION

Religion is extremely influential and important in all aspects of Fijian society, affecting politics, government, education, and interaction within and between different races. Only 0.4% of the population are nonreligious. Different Christian sects together command the largest following (52.9% of the population), followed by Hindus (38.1%), Muslims (7.8%), Sikhs (0.7%), and other religions (0.1%).

Traditional Fijian Religion

The old Fijian religion, based on ancestor worship, extended to every aspect of life, including medicine and mythology. There were many gods and spirits, and the souls of outstanding ancestors were made into local deities. A hero in battle could become a war god, or an outstanding farmer could become a god of plenty. Appeasing and thanking the gods shaped all aspects of life in Viti. Spirithouses were built for each significant god.

Hereditary chiefs and priests were considered representatives of the gods, and the priests served as a medium through which a god spoke to its descendants. Relics and idols kept in the temple were also mediums. Images were carved from sacred vesi wood or whales teeth and sometimes took a human form. Offerings included food and yaqona roots or tabua for important issues.

Various mutilatory rituals, mourning sacrifices and initiation ceremonies were demanded by the gods. Belief in the afterlife was a strong incentive for actions in life. Mourning sacrifices included amputation of finger joints and self-induced burns. Shaving one's head was the ultimate religious or mourning sacrifice for a man. For a woman the equivalent was being strangled to accompany her husband to the afterlife. Women were tattooed and men circumcised in initiation rituals. It was believed that the demon guardians of the spirit path would ambush and inspect each ghost to see if it had been properly tattooed or circumcised and that its ear lobes had been plugged and little fingers lopped. Concerned friends and family would often try to trick priests and spirits by painting on designs or chopping off a dead person's fingers.

The early missionaries dreaded the worship of idols and 'heathen' deities and translated the Fijian word for gods, *tevoro*, as devil. The tevoro were not necessarily evil, but the label stuck. Many beliefs and practices were wiped out or at least suppressed, but traces and attitudes remain and some have been fused with Christianity.

Tabua

Tabua (whale's teeth) were carefully polished and shaped and believed to have a special spiritual essence because they formed the shrines of ancestor spirits. Tabua were highly valued, diplomatically essential items. Tabua were used as *sevusevu*, presents given as a token of esteem or atonement, and are still used for this purpose today. Their acceptance binds a chief morally and spiritually to the presenter and their desired outcome.

Tabua, a war club or a musket was meant to accompany a man's corpse to the grave to help defend his spirit on its hazardous journey to the afterworld. The soul of his wives, who were strangled and buried with him, would follow to care for him in the spirit world, otherwise his spirit would be left in 'lonely limbo'.

Originally tabua were rare items, obtained from washed up sperm whales or through trade with Tonga. The European traders brought an influx of whale's teeth and replicas were carved in whalebone, elephant and walrus tusks. Thousands of these negotiation tools became concentrated in the hands of a few increasingly powerful chiefdoms. ■

Initiation Ceremonies

After having proven their skill at fishing and crafts, girls underwent a prolonged and painful initiation into adulthood. This normally took place between about seven years and puberty. The *veiqia* rite involved elaborate tattooing of the pubic area and in some cases was extended as a band around the hips so that it resembled 'dark, skin-tight, intricately patterned shorts'. Girls were told that it would enhance their beauty and sex drive.

Each village had a female *duabati* (hereditary tattoo specialist) who had a special hut on the outskirts of the village or a more distant hide-out. Often a few girls were operated on at once, taking turns to hold each other down. The ritual was carried out during the day when men were out, so they wouldn't hear the screaming. It was extremely painful, taking weeks, months, even up to a year. Many could not stand the whole procedure. The blue-black (soot mixed with oil) designs were tapped into the flesh with a special spiked pick and light mallet, and lines were made with bamboo slivers or sharp shells. A celebratory feast was held on the fourth day after completion of the operation and the young woman was then entitled to wear the *liku* (skirt of womanhood) and to marry.

Designs were similar to those found on masi, woodcarving, pottery and nose flutes. The patterns represented everyday items such as net sinkers and floats, and special designs were reserved for chiefly women. To signify that a woman had undergone initiation, a pair of dots or crescents were tattooed at the corners of her mouth. In some regions, if a woman had her whole hips tattooed then her mouth was surrounded in a spotted or chequered pattern, although this was also sometimes done just to hide wrinkles.

It was believed that untattooed women would be persecuted by the ancestor spirits in the afterlife, be slashed about the pubic region or pounded to a pulp and fed to the gods. This was a dreaded fate and girls were loath to defy the custom. Even into the 20th century, fake tattoos were sometimes painted on dead girls to bluff the gods. Church authorities regarded tattooing, with its religious and sexual significance, as a symbol of paganism and were intent on its suppression. In some regions it was still practised into the 1930s, for sexual rather than religious motives. Other cosmetic tattoos were and still are common on the faces and limbs of both sexes.

Boys had to endure the less painful initiation ritual of circumcision. After having his bravado tested for four nights, a boy was entitled to use the loincloth of manhood, grow his hair and move to the men's bure. Boys trained in the use of arms and dodging missiles from infancy, and were only granted a real man's name once they had killed an enemy.

Everyone had to have their ear lobes pierced and dilated to take an ornamental plug. Ear lobe piercing and expansion to accept ornamental plugs was obligatory or the soul would suffer persecution in the afterlife. According to Fergus Clunie, former director of the Fiji Museum and author of *Yalo i Viti*, intact ear lobes 'doomed the ghost to a severe beating with clubs and a meal of snotty phlegm and possibly manure'! ■

Christianity

Most indigenous Fijians adhere to one of the Christian sects and almost every village and settlement has at least one church. In small villages which retain a hierarchical society, people generally follow the religion of the chief. Church attendance is high and spiritual leaders are very influential. Where a village has a number of religions this can sometimes lead to jealousy and conflict. Only about 2% of Fiji Indians are Christians.

Of the all the Christian sects in Fiji the Methodist Church is the most powerful and influential. Extremist factions of the church were supporters of the nationalist movement and the subsequent military coups, and played a role in the Sunday ban on business activities. Other denominations include the Catholic, Seventh Day Adventist, Anglican, and Presbyterian churches, and more recently there has been a growth in the Assembly of God, Mormons and Jehovah's Witnesses.

Even if you are not at all religious, try to attend a church service in a Fijian village. The singing is usually fantastic and visitors are welcome. Leave a small donation to help with community projects.

Indian Religions

There are many tiny, beautiful temples and green and white mosques scattered around

Fire Walking

Fijian The *vilavilairevo* (literally, 'jumping into the oven') is practised on Beqa Island. The ability to walk barefoot on white-hot stones without being burned was, according to local legend, granted to a local chief by the leader of the *veli*, a group of little gods. Now the direct descendants of the chief (*Tui Qalita*) serve as the *bete* or priests that instruct the ritual of fire walking. The little people spirits are summoned to watch the performance in their honour.

Preparations for fire walking used to involve the whole village for nearly a month. The work involved collecting firewood, selecting appropriate stones, making costumes and performing various ceremonies. Fire walkers had to abstain from sex, and not eat any coconut for up to a month before the ritual. No fire walker's wife could be pregnant, or it was believed the whole group would receive burns. Pregnant women were also not allowed near the pit preparation.

Traditionally, fire walking was only performed on special occasions in the village of Navakaisese. Nowadays it is performed for commercial purposes and has little religious meaning. Other villages on Beqa Island, as well as villages from neighbouring Yanuca Island, use fire walking as a source of income. Time and cost considerations in modern resort performances led to a reduction in the size of original fire pits, which were much larger, took longer to prepare and required a tremendous amount of firewood. Costumes can now be re-used, and tabu periods have been reduced to a few days. There are regular fire walking performances at Pacific Harbour Cultural Centre, at Suva's annual Hibiscus Festival, and at some resort hotels such as the Regent.

Hindu Hindu fire walking is part of an annual religious festival coinciding with a full moon in July or August and lasting 10 days. It takes place at many temples in Fiji, including the Mariamma Temple in Suva.

Preparations for the ceremony are overseen by a priest and take three to 10 days with the fire walking as the climax of the ritual. During this period participants isolate themselves, abstain from sex and eating meat, and meditate to worship the goddess Maha Devi. They rise early and pray until late at night without getting much food or sleep and dress in red and yellow, symbolising the cleansing of physical and spiritual impurity. Yellow turmeric is smeared on the face as a symbol of prosperity and power over diseases.

On the final day the participants at the Mariamma Temple bathe in the sea and further rites are performed by the priests who pierce the tongues, cheeks and bodies of the fire walkers with three-pronged skewers. The fire walkers then dance in an ecstatic trance for about two km back to the temple for the fire walking.

Devotees' bodies are whipped before and during the ceremony. The Tamil word for fire pit, *poo kuzhi*, is the same as for flower pit. If they are focused on the divine Mother they should not feel pain. A decorated statue of the goddess is placed facing the pit for her to watch and bless the ceremony. It only takes about five seconds to walk along the pit, which is filled with charred wood raked over glowing coals, and the walk is repeated about five times. The ceremony is accompanied by sacred chanting and drumming.

Hindu fire walking is a religious sacrament performed mostly by descendants of south Indians. It is a means by which a devotee aspires to become one with the Mother. Their body should be enslaved to the spirit, and denied all comforts. They believe life is like walking on fire: a disciplined approach, like the one required in the ceremony, helps them to achieve a balanced life, self-acceptance and to see good in everything. ■

Fiji's countryside, especially in the cane-growing areas of Viti Levu and Vanua Levu. Indentured labourers established temples in the new country to pursue their own faith and add a feeling of security. There were, however, a lack of spiritual leaders, and knowledge of the philosophy behind the religions was partly lost. After generations of separation from their homeland, Fiji Indians are generally less orthodox in terms of caste and religion, and religious differences are more tolerated than in India. Most are Hindus or Muslims, and Sikhism (combines Hindu and Islamic beliefs) is practiced by some descendants of north-west Indians. Hare Krishnas also have a small following. They have a temple in Lautoka and run good vegetarian restaurants both there and in Suva.

Islam Muslims believe in peace and submission to Allah (God), following the teachings of the Prophet Mohammed and the holy book the Koran. Religious festivals include Ramadan (30-day dawn-to-dusk fasting), the Eid festival to celebrate the end of fasting, and the Prophet Mohammed's birthday.

Hinduism Hindus believe in reincarnation and that the consequence of all past deeds will be faced, thus the importance of a good moral life. Most Hindu homes in Fiji have small shrines for family worship. High-caste Hindus who are relatively economically secure tend to be less devoted to their religious activities.

Hindus worship one supreme power, Brahman, who assumes many forms and names in order to be better understood. The characteristic Hindu form of God is the Great Mother. She is the personification of nature, which gives life, meaning and purpose to all things. The greatest goddess is Maya Devi. She is all powerful, all knowing, all pervading. All energy is believed to come from her and she is symbolised by water (the life giver) and fire (the purifier or destroyer). She shows compassion to those who surrender to her, and punishes those who disobey. Devotees see every woman as the personified

Hindu Symbolic Rites
A Hindu temple symbolises the body, in which the soul resides. Union with God is achieved through prayer and by ridding the body of impurities. Meat cannot be eaten before you enter the temple and shoes must be removed, as leather, coming from sacred cattle, is considered impure.

Fire and water are used for blessings. Water carried in a pot with flowers is symbolic of the Mother. Burning camphor symbolises the light of knowledge and understanding. When illuminated, the soul merges with the Great Soul. The trident is the protector, representing fire and three flames. It stands for purity, light and knowledge.

Singing, drumming and dancing are used to acclaim the Mother and anklets jingled in praise of her holy feet.

The breaking of a coconut represents the cracking of three forms of human weakness: egotism (the hard shell), delusion (the fibre) and material attachments (the outermost covering). The white kernel and sweet water represent the pure soul within. ■

essence of the Divine Mother. The green goddess Parvati symbolises nature, the dark blue Kali is time personified, and red Lakshmi represents wealth. Other goddess forms include Durga, Maari and Shakti.

Descendants of southern Indians perform a fire-walking ritual in July or August at many temples, including the Mariamma temple in Suva. A group of orthodox Hindus, of north-Indian origin, perform Durga Gram Puja each August at Wailekutu, near Suva. The goddess Durga is worshipped by undergoing ordeals including whipping, having the tongue and body pierced with metal instruments, the hands immersed in boiling ghee (oil), and dancing on upturned knife blades. Important Hindu festivals include Holi (festival of colours), Diwali (festival of lights) and the Birth of Lord Krishna. Refer to the Facts for the Visitor chapter for dates.

LANGUAGE

One of the reasons why many visitors from the English-speaking world find Fiji such a congenial place to visit is because they don't have to learn another language: most local people who come into contact with tourists can speak English, and all signs and official forms are also in English. At the same time, for almost all local people English is not their mother tongue: indigenous Fijians speak Fijian at home and Fiji Indians speak Fiji Hindi. So, if you really wish to have a better knowledge of the Fijian people and their culture, it is important that you know something of the Fijian languages – and, no matter how poor your first attempts, you will be greatly encouraged by the response from Fijians.

Fijian

The many regional dialects found in Fiji today all descend, at least partly, from the language spoken by the original inhabitants. They would have come from one of the island groups to the west, either the Solomons or Vanuatu, having left their South-East Asian homeland at least a 1000 years previously and spread eastwards by way of Indonesia, the Philippines and Papua New Guinea. From Fiji, groups left to settle the nearby islands of Rotuma, Tonga and Samoa, and from there they spread out to inhabit the rest of Polynesia, including Hawaii in the north, Rapanui (Easter Island) in the east, and Aotearoa (New Zealand) in the south. All the people in this vast area of settlement speak related languages belonging to the language family known as 'Austronesian'.

There are some 300 regional varieties (dialects) of Fijian, all belonging to one of two major groupings. All varieties spoken to the west of a line extending north-south, with a couple of kinks, across the centre of Viti Levu belong to the Western Fijian group, while all others are Eastern Fijian.

Fortunately for the language learner there is one variety, based on the eastern varieties of the Bau-Rewa area, which is understood by Fijians all over the islands. This standard form of Fijian is popularly known as 'Bauan' *(vosa vakabau)*, though linguists prefer to call it standard Fijian. It is used in conversation among Fijians from different areas, on

the radio and in schools, and is the variety used in this section.

In Fijian, there are two ways of saying 'you', 'your', and 'yours'. If you are speaking to someone who is your superior, or an adult stranger, you should use a longer form (the 'formal' form). This formal form is easy to remember because it always ends in *nī*. In all other situations, a shorter form (the 'informal' or familiar' form) is used.

Pronunciation Fijian pronunciation is not especially difficult for the English speaker, since most of the sounds in Fijian are similar to English sounds. The standard Fijian alphabet uses all the English letters, except 'x'. The letters 'h' and 'z' occur only rarely, in borrowed words.

Since the Fijian alphabet was devised relatively recently (in the 1830s), and by a missionary who was also a very competent linguist, it is almost perfectly phonetic. That means that each letter has only one sound, and each sound is represented by only one letter.

As with all Pacific languages, the five Fijian vowels are pronounced much as they are in languages such as Spanish, German and Italian:

a	as in 'f**a**ther'
e	as in 'b**e**t'
i	as in 'mach**i**ne'
o	as in 'm**o**re'
u	as in 'z**oo**'

Vowels can be pronounced short or long, with the long vowel having a significantly longer sound. A long vowel is marked in this book with a macron above it, eg: *mamā*. An approximate English equivalent is the difference between the final vowel sound in 'icy' and 'I see'. To get the right pronunciation and meaning of a word, it's important that the length of the vowel sound is correct. For example, *mama* means 'a ring', *mamā* means 'chew it', and *māmā* means 'light' (in weight). Note that *māmā* takes about twice as long to pronounce as does *mama*. In some long words there is also a secondary stress, that is, a less heavy accent, and this is marked in this book by a bolded letter, for example, v**a**lenivuli (classroom).

Most consonants are pronounced as they are in English, but there are differences.

b	'mb' as in 'timber'
c	'th' as in 'this' (not 'thick')
d	'nd' as in handy
g	'ng' as in 'sing' (not 'angry')
j	'ch' without following puff of breath
k	'k' without following puff of breath
p	'p' without following puff of breath
q	'ngg' as in 'angry' (not 'sing')
r	rolled
t	't' without a following puff of breath, often 'ch' before 'i'
v	with lower lip against upper lip, somewhere between a 'v' and a 'b'

Occasionally on maps and in tourist publications you'll find a variation on this spelling system which is intended to be easier for English speakers. In this system, Yanuca is spelt 'Yanutha', Beqa 'Mbengga', and so on.

Basics

Yes.	*Io.*
No.	*Sega.*
Thank you (very much).	*Vinaka (vakalevu).*
Hello.	*Bula!*
Hello. (reply)	*Io, bula/Ia, bula (more respectful)*
Good morning.	*Yadra.*
Goodbye. (if you don't expect to see them again)	*Moce.*
See you later.	*Au sā liu mada.*
Sorry. (general)	*(Nī) Vosota sara.*

Small Talk

Where are you going?	*O(nī) lai vei?*

(used as we ask 'How are you?')

Nowhere special, just wandering around.	*Sega, gādē gā.*

(As with the response to 'How are you', there's no need to be specific.)

Let's shake hands.	*Daru lūlulu mada.*
What is your name?	*O cei na yacamu(nī)?*
My name is ...	*O yau o ...*
Pleased to meet you.	*Ia, (nī) bula.*

Where are you from?	*O iko/kemunī mai vei?*
I am from ...	*O yau mai ...*
How old are you?	*O yabaki vica?*
I am ... years old.	*Au yabaki ...*
Are you married?	*O(nī) vakawati?*
How many children do you have?	*Lē vica na luvemu(nī)?*
I don't have any children.	*E sega na luvequ.*
I have a daughter/son.	*E dua na luvequ yalewa/tagane.*

Language Problems

I don't speak Fijian/English.	*Au sega ni kilā na vosa vakaviti/vakavālagi.*
Do you speak English?	*O(nī) kilā na vosa vakavālagi?*
I understand.	*Sā macala.*
I don't understand.	*E sega ni macala.*

Getting Around

I want to go to ...	*Au via lako i ...*
Where is the ...?	*I vei na ...?*
airport	*rārā ni waqavuka*
bus station (central)	*basten*
bus stop	*ikelekele ni basi*

What time does the ... leave/arrive?	*Vica na kaloko e lako/kele kina na ...?*
bus	*basi*
plane	*waqavuka*
boat	*waqa*

Directions

Where is ...?	*I vei na ...?*
How do I get to ...?	*I vei na sala i ...?*
Is it far?	*E yawa?*
Can I walk there?	*E rawa niu taubale kina?*
Can you show me (on the map)?	*Vakar**a**itaka mada (ena mape)?*

Go straight ahead.	*Vakadodonu.*
Turn left ...	*Gole i na imawī ...*
Turn right ...	*Gole i na imatau ...*

Compass bearings (north etc) are never used. Instead you'll hear:

on the sea side of ...	*mai ... i wai*
on the land side of ...	*mai ... i vanua*
the far side of ...	*mai ... i liu*
this side of ...	*mai ... i muri*

Around Town

I'm looking for ...	*Au vāqarā ...*
a church	*na valenilotu*
the ... embassy	*na ebasī/valeni-volavola ni ...*
the market	*na mākete*
the museum	*na vale ni yau māroroi*
the police	*na ovisa*
the post office	*na posi(tōvesi)*
a public toilet	*na valelailai*
tourist information office	*na valenivolavola ni saravanua*

What time does it open/close?	*E dola/sogo ina vica?*
Can I take your photograph?	*Au tabaki iko mada?*
I'll send you the photograph.	*Au na vākauta yani na itaba.*

Accommodation

Where is ...?	*I vei ...?*
a cheap hotel	*ōtela saurawarawa*
a hotel	*dua na ōtela*

A note of caution. The term 'guesthouse' and its Fijian equivalent, *dua na bure ni vulagi*, often refer to establishments offering rooms for hire by the hour.

I'm going to stay for ...	*Au na ...*
one day	*siga dua*
one week	*mācawa dua*

I'm not sure how long I'm staying.	*Sega ni macala na dedē ni noqu tiko.*
Where is the bathroom?	*I vei na valenisili?*
Where is the toilet?	*I vei na valelailai?*

Staying with a Family Should you be invited to stay with a Fijian family, prepare yourself for a novel and heart-warming experience. Fijians are masters at entertaining and go out of their way to make guests feel as comfortable as possible.

When you visit a Fijian family, bring some *yaqona* (kava) with you. This is for your *sevusevu* – a formal presentation, comparable to bringing a bottle of wine when you visit friends back home.

Some phrases you may need include the following:

Where can I buy yaqona?	*E volitaki i vei na yaqona?*
What kind of yaqona?	*Yaqona cava?*
ground yaqona	*yaqona qaqi*
pounded yaqona	*yaqona tuki*
a bundle of yaqona root	*dua na ivesu waka*
How much for one bag?	*E vica dua na taga?*
I've brought a little yaqona.	*Dua na yaqona lailai au kauta mai.*
Thank you for having me.	*Dua noqu kā ni veivuke lailai.*

(this is used when offering money or a gift for your board; literally, 'Just a little help from me')

Food

restaurant	*valenikana*
Chinese restaurant	*valenikana ni kai Jaina*
Indian restaurant	*valenikana ni kai Idia*
food vendor	*volitaki kākana*
breakfast	*katalau*
lunch	*vakasigalevu*
dinner	*vakayakavi*

Shopping

How much is it?	*E vica?*
I'm just looking.	*Sarasara gā.*
That's too expensive for me.	*Au sega ni rawata.*
bookshop	*sitoa ni vola*
clothing shop	*sitoa ni sulu*
laundry	*valenisavasava*
market	*mākete*
pharmacy	*kēmesi*

Time & Dates

What time is it?	*Sā vica na kaloko?*
today	*nikua*
tonight	*na bogi nikua*
tomorrow	*nimataka*
yesterday	*nanoa*
Monday	*Mōniti*
Tuesday	*Tūsiti*
Wednesday	*Vukelulu*
Thursday	*Lotulevu*
Friday	*Vakaraubuka*
Saturday	*Vakarauwai*
Sunday	*Sigatabu*

Numbers

0	*saiva*
1	*dua*
2	*rua*
3	*tolu*
4	*vā*
5	*lima*
6	*ono*
7	*vitu*
8	*walu*
9	*ciwa*
10	*tini*
11	*tínikadua*
12	*tínikarua*
20	*rúasagavulu*
21	*rúasagavulukadua*
30	*tólusagavulu*
100	*dua na drau*
1000	*dua na udolu*

Health

I need a doctor.	*Au via raici vuniwai.*
Where is the hospital?	*I vei na valenibula?*
I'm constipated.	*Au sega ni valelailai rawa.*
I have a stomach ache.	*E mosi na ketequ.*
I am diabetic.	*Au tauvi matenisuka.*
I am epileptic.	*Au manumanusoni.*
I'm allergic to penicillin.	*E dau lako vakacā vei au na penisilini.*
I have my own syringe.	*E tiko na noqu icula.*
I'm on the pill. (contraceptive)	*Au gunu vuanikau ni yalani.*
condoms	*rapa, kodom*
contraceptive	*wai ni yalani*
diarrhoea	*coka*
medicine	*wainimate*
nausea	*lomalomacā*
sanitary napkin	*qamuqamu*

Emergencies

Help!	*Oilei!*
Go away!	*Lako tani!*
Call a doctor!	*Qiria na vuniwai!*
Call an ambulance!	*Qiria na lori ni valenibula!*
I've been robbed!	*Butako!*
Call the police!	*Qiria na ovisa!*
I've been raped.	*Au sā kucuvi.*
I am lost.	*Au sā sese.*
Where are the toilets?	*I vei na valelailai?*

Further Reading A good introduction to the language is Lonely Planet's *Fijian phrasebook*, written by Paul Geraghty, which provides all the essential words and phrases travellers will need, along with grammar and cultural points. Those interested in further studies of Fijian will find George Milner's *Fijian Grammar* (Government Press, Suva, 1956) an excellent introduction to the language. Likewise, Albert Schütz's *Spoken Fijian* (University Press of Hawaii, Honolulu, 1979) is a good primer for more advanced studies.

Fiji Hindi

Fiji Hindi (sometimes called Fiji Hindustani) is the language of all Fiji Indians. It has features of the many regional dialects of Hindi spoken by the Indian indentured labourers who were brought to Fiji from 1879 to 1916. (Some people call Fiji Hindi Bhojpuri, but this is the name of just one of the many dialects that contributed to the language.)

Many words from English are found in Fiji Hindi (such as room, towel, book and reef). But some of these have slightly different meanings. For example, the word 'book' in Fiji Hindi includes magazines and pamphlets; and if you refer to a person of the opposite sex as a 'friend', this implies that he/she is your sexual partner.

Fiji Hindi is used in all informal settings, such as in the family and among friends. But the 'Standard Hindi' of India is considered appropriate for formal contexts, such as in public speaking, radio broadcasting and writing. The Hindu majority write in Standard Hindi using the Devanagari script with a large number of words taken from the ancient language Sanskrit. The Muslims use the Perso-Arabic script and words taken from Persian and Arabic. (This literary style is often considered a separate language, called Urdu.) Fiji Indians have to learn Standard Hindi or Urdu in school along with English, so while they all speak Fiji Hindi informally, not everyone knows the formal varieties.

Some people say that Fiji Hindi is just a 'broken' or 'corrupted' version of standard Hindi. In fact, Fiji Hindi is a legitimate dialect with its own grammatical rules and vocabulary unique to Fiji.

Pronunciation Fiji Hindi is normally written only in guides for foreigners, such as this, and transcribed using the English alphabet. Since there are at least 42 different sounds in Fiji Hindi and only 26 letters, some adjustments have to be made. The vowels are as follows:

a	as in 'about' or 'sofa'
å	as in 'father'
e	as in 'bet'
i	as in 'police'
o	as in 'obey'
u	as in 'rule'
ai	as in 'hail'
åi	as in 'aisle'
au	as in 'own'
oi	as in 'boil'

Fiji Hindi also has nasalised vowels, as in French words such as *bon* and *sans*. This is shown with a tilde (~) over the vowel or with the letter 'n' if there's a following consonant.

The consonants 'b', 'f', 'g' (as in 'go'), 'h', 'j', 'k', 'l', 'm', 'n', 'p', 's', 'v', 'y', 'w', and 'z' are similar to those of English. The symbol 'č' is used for the 'ch' sound as in 'chip' and 'š' is used for the 'sh' sound as in 'ship'.

Pronunciation of other consonants is a bit difficult. First, Fiji Hindi has two 't' sounds and two 'd' sounds – all different from English. In 't' and 'd' in English, the tip of the tongue touches the ridge above the upper teeth, but in Fiji Hindi it either touches the back of the front teeth (dental) or is curled back to touch the roof of the mouth (retroflex). The dental consonants are shown as 't̪' and 'd̪' and the retroflex ones as 'ṭ' and 'ḍ', and they're important in distinguishing meaning. For example:

āt̪ā	coming
āṭā	flour
t̪ab	then
ṭab	tub
d̪āl	dhal (lentils)
ḍāl	branch

You can susbstitute the English 't' and 'd' for the retroflex ones and still be understood. There are also two 'r' sounds different from English. In the first, written as 'r', the tongue touches the ridge above the upper teeth and is flapped quickly forward, similar to the way we say the 't' sound in 'butter' when speaking quickly. In the second, written as 'r̤', the tongue is curled back touching the roof of the mouth (as in the retroflex sounds) and then flapped forward. You can sometimes substitute English 'rd' for this sound.

Finally, there are 'aspirated' consonants. If you hold your hand in front of your mouth and say 'Peter Piper picked a peck of pickled peppers', you'll feel a puff of air each time you say the 'p' sound. This is aspiration. But when you say 'spade, spill, spit, speak', you don't feel the puff of air, because in these words the 'p' sound is not aspirated. In Fiji Hindi, aspiration is important in distinguishing meaning and is shown with an 'h' following the consonant – for example:

pul	bridge
phul	flower
kālā	black
khālā	valley
ṭāli	clapping
ṭhāli	brass plate

Other aspirated consonants are:

bh	as in 'grab him' said quickly
čh	as in 'church hat' said quickly
ḍh	as in 'mad house'
gh	as in 'slug him'
jh	as in 'bridge house'
ṭh	as in 'out house'

Note that some books use a different system of transcription. For example, 'aa' is used for 'ā' and 'T', 'D', 'R' for 'ṭ', 'ḍ' and 'ṛ'.

Basics

Yes.	*hã*
No.	*nahī*
Maybe.	*sāyiṭ*
I'm sorry (for something serious).	*māf karnā*

There are no equivalents for 'please' and 'thank you'. To be polite in making requests, people use the word *ṭhoṛā* ('a little') and a special form of the verb ending in *nā* – for example:

Please pass the salt.	*ṭhoṛā nimak denā.*

They also use the polite form of the word 'you', *āp*, instead of the familiar form, *tum*.

For 'thanks', people often just say *ačhā* ('good'). The English 'please' and 'thank you' are also commonly used. The word *ḍhanyavāḍ* is used to thank someone who has done something special for you. It means something like 'blessings be bestowed upon you'.

Greetings There are no exact equivalents for 'hello' and 'goodbye' in Fiji Hindi. The most common greeting is *kaise* ('How are you?'). The usual reply is *ṭik* ('fine'). In parting, it's common to say *fir milegā* ('We'll meet again').

More formal greetings are:

namasṭe (for Hindus)
salām alaikum (for Muslims); the reply is *alaikum salām.*

Small Talk

What's your (polite/ familiar) name?	*āpke/ṭumār nām kā hai?*
My name is ...	*hamār nām ...*
Where are you from?	*āp/ṭum kahã ke hai?*
I'm from ...	*ham ... ke hai*
Are you married?	*šāḍi ho gayā?*
How many children do you have?	*kiṭnā laṛkā hai?*
I don't have any children.	*laṛkā nahī hai*
Two boys and three girls.	*ḍui laṛkā aur ṭin laṛki*

Language Difficulties

Do you (polite/familiar) speak English?	*āp/ṭum English bolṭā?*
Does anyone speak English?	*koi English bole?*
I don't understand.	*ham nahī samajhṭā*

Getting Around

I want to go to ...	*ham ... jāe mangṭā*
Where is the ...?	*... kahã hai?*
shop	*ḍukān*
airport	*eyapoṭ*
bus station (central)	*basṭen*

market	*mākeṭ*
temple	*manḍir*
mosque	*masjiḍ*
church	*čeč*

You can also use the English words hotel, guesthouse, camping ground, toilet, post office, embassy, tourist information office, museum, cafe, restaurant, telephone.

Is it near/far?	*nagič/ḍur hai?*
Can you go by foot?	*paiḍar jāe sakṭā?*
Go straight ahead.	*sidhā jāo*
By the ...	*... ke pās*
coconut tree	*nariyal ke peṛ*
mango tree	*ām ke peṛ*
breadfruit tree	*belfuṭ ke peṛ*
sugar-cane field	*gannā kheṭ*

Please write down the address.	*ṭhoṛā eḍres likh denā*
What time does the ... leave/arrive?	*kiṭnā baje ... čale/pahunče?*
ship	*jahāj*
car	*moṭṭar*

You can also use the English words bus, plane, boat.

Numbers

1	*ek*
2	*ḍui*
3	*ṭin*
4	*čār*
5	*pānč*
6	*čhe*
7	*sāṭ*
8	*āṭh*
9	*nau*
10	*das*
100	*sau*
1000	*hazār*

Note: English numbers are generally used for 20-99.

Food & Drink

to eat, food	*khāna*
to drink	*pinā*
tea	*čā*

yaqona (kava)	*nengonā, grog*
liquor	*ḍāru*
beer	*bia*
water	*pāni*

I don't drink alcohol.	*ham ḍāru nahī piṭā*
I don't eat hot (spicy) food.	*ham ṭiṭā nahī khāṭā*
I don't eat meat.	*ham gos nahī khāṭā*
I eat vegetables.	*ham ṭarkāri khāṭā*
Just a little.	*ṭoṛā ṭhoṛā*
very good	*bahuṭačhā*
Enough!	*bas!*

Time & Dates

What time is it?	*kiṭnā baje?*
It's ... o'clock.	*... baje*
When?	*kab?*
today	*āj*
tomorrow	*bihān*
yesterday	*kal*
day	*roj*
tonight	*āj rāṭke*

English days of the week are generally used.

Health

I am constipated.	*peṭ kaṛā ho gayā*
I feel nausea.	*hame čhānṭ lage*
I have a stomach ache.	*hamār peṭ pirāwe*
I am diabetic.	*hame čini ke bimāri hai*
I am epileptic.	*hame mirgi awe*
I am asthmatic.	*hame sãs fule ke bimāri hai*
I get sick from penicillin.	*penesilin se ham bimār ho jāi*
condom	*konḍom, raba*
contraceptive	*pariwār niyojan ke dawāi*
medicine	*dawāi*
sanitary napkin	*peḍ, nepkin*
tampon	*ṭampon*

Staying with a Family Fiji Indians are very hospitable. If you're invited to someone's

HOLGER LEUE

ROBYN JONES

ROBYN JONES

ROBYN JONES

ROBYN JONES

LEONARDO PINHEIRO

ROBYN JONES

A	B
C	D
E	F

A: Hibiscus basket, Turtle Island
B: Woven bamboo wall cladding
C: Parrot fish at Suva market
D: Palm, Lautoka Botanical Gardens
E: Tropical flower, Thurston Gardens
F: Fungi, Nausori Highlands

HOLGER LEUE

HOLGER LEUE

ROBYN JONES

ROBYN JONES

ROBYN JONES

ROBYN JONES

Faces of Fiji

house, you'll certainly be offered a cup of tea and usually a delicious meal.

In rural areas, men and women socialize and eat separately. Many Indian men enjoy drinking yaqona as much as the Fijians. But it isn't the custom for guests to bring yaqona with them. If you want to bring something, sweets for the kids are usually appreciated. Some men also drink alcohol, often following yaqona (called 'washdown'). Women tourists who feel like drinking can be considered honorary men for the occasion!

Note that the custom throughout Fiji is to finish drinking yaqona and/or alcohol before the meal. This can mean some very late dinners.

Emergencies

Help me.	hame maḍaḍ karo
Go away!	jāo!
Call the doctor/police.	ḍokṭā ke/pulis ke bulāo
Where is the hospital?	āspaṭāl kahã hai?
I've been robbed.	čori ho gayā
I've been raped.	koi hame reip karis

English Words & Phrases with Different Meanings in Fiji:

Fijian English	English
grog	kava
bluff	lie, deceive
chow	food, eat
set	OK, ready
step	cut school, wag
good luck to ... !	it serves ... right!
not even!	no way!

Facts for the Visitor

PLANNING

When to Go

Fiji can be enjoyed all year round, and is a great place to escape either southern or northern hemisphere winters. Probably the best time to visit, however, is during the so-called 'Fijian winter' or 'dry season', from May to October. This time of year has lower rainfall and humidity, milder temperatures, and less risk of tropical cyclones.

The end of the year is often busy, coinciding with school holidays in Australia and New Zealand and people visiting relatives. February and March, on the other hand, are quiet months for tourism in Fiji, with accommodation discounts and vacancies more likely. See also the Climate, Activities and special events sections.

What Kind of Trip?

Fiji is one of the South Pacific's major transit hubs. If you are just passing through it would be a shame to only spend a couple of days in the country. Fiji is an excellent place for the independent traveller to explore, either solo or with friends or family. You could either try to cover as many islands as possible in a mad dash; stay in one or two spots and pursue special interests such as diving or trekking; or just vegetate on the beach for your entire stay.

There are countless accommodation options and resorts for different budgets. Alternatively, there are also many tours on offer. Whatever you do, try to include the beach and water sports, a jaunt to the mountains, and some contact with the local culture.

Maps

The best place to buy maps of the Fiji islands, and some town maps, is the Lands and Surveys Department (☎ 211 395; fax 304 037), in Suva. There are 1:50,000 scale topographical maps of most areas, useful if you are going trekking, for under F$5. Aerial

photographs are also available of some islands. Enquire at Room 10, Records and Reprographic Subsection, Government Buildings, Suva. The office is open from 9 am to 3.30 pm Monday to Thursday (3 pm on Friday), closed from 1 to 2 pm for lunch. Orders can also be made from overseas.

Bookshops, including Desai, sometimes stock town maps, and the tourist brochure *Welcome to the Fiji Islands* also has simple town maps. At the Fiji Visitors Bureau, or specialist book and map shops overseas, you may be able to purchase the 1995 Hema map of Fiji. It is a topographical map with an index for islands, towns and some resorts, plus general visitor information and town maps on the back.

Specialist marine charts are expensive in Fiji, so its best to buy them overseas. Failing this, enquire at the Suva Yacht Club.

What to Bring

Pack as little as possible – it will mean less to lug around and less to lose. Backpacks should ideally be the fold-away type – compact, comfortable, waterproof – and have double zips that can be padlocked. A chain is handy for locking gear to a fixture in shared rooms, or in a hotel's safe-deposit room. Carry cash, some travellers' cheques and important documents in a money belt. You will need a day pack, and waterproof stuff bags are handy for carrying stationary (notebook, addresses etc), photocopies (of important documents) and camera gear on boat trips.

Appropriate dress for Fiji's tropical climate is light, cotton casuals, but you will need to respect local traditions when outside the main tourist areas. As well as bathers, shorts, and T-shirts that cover the shoulders, pack or buy a *sulu* (a length of material wrapped around as a skirt). Women should include below-the-knee dresses or skirts. Only pack low-fuss, wash-and-wear items. Take a light jumper as it can get cool in the highlands and elsewhere in the winter months, especially between May and August. Include a light raincoat or compact umbrella, sunglasses, a malleable hat and a light-weight towel or chamois. Refer also to the Women Travellers section.

Make sure that shoes are worn-in before travelling; the last thing you want is blisters causing infections. You can live in a good pair of walking sandals, but you will need walking boots if you are going hiking in muddy conditions. An old pair of sneakers or reef walking shoes may be useful (walk over dead coral or sand only!). The dress code for Suva or Nadi's night spots requires neat shoes.

Pack toiletries in small containers to reduce bulk and weight. Take resealable plastic bags to avoid disastrous leaks. Pharmacies and large supermarkets in the main towns stock condoms, tampons and baby items such as disposable nappies, formula and sterilising solution. Most resorts have a shop with basic toiletries. If you are going directly to a remote island, however, it is probably best to bring your personal needs from home. It's advisable to carry an emergency supply of toilet paper when travelling. Include a good insect repellent, containing plenty of DEET, vitamins if you will be on the road for an extended period, tiger balm, prescription medicines (with a copy of scripts), spare glasses or contact lenses (disposables are handy). Refer to the Health section for a list of medical items.

Keen snorkellers should consider taking their own mask, snorkel and fins, and divers their own gear and scuba certification card. Equipment, however, can be hired at most resorts and dive shops. Lycra suits for summer or three-mm wetsuit for winter are recommended for divers.

Consider how you will be travelling when choosing photographic equipment, and bring plenty of film. (See Photography later in this chapter.) Photos make great thank-you gifts. Other equipment could include a Swiss army knife, torch, compass, travel alarm, calculator or electronic organiser (if you're addicted to technology) and spare

batteries (you should be able to get them there, but bring some to avoid the hassle of searching). A needle and thread, laundry soap and traveller's clothesline should be included.

Most accommodation provides mosquito nets or screened windows, but you may want to take a sleeping sheet for hostels. Campers and self-caterers should take a light-weight waterproof tent, possibly a camping stove (kerosene is readily available), plastic plate, cup, utensils and matches.

SUGGESTED ITINERARIES

Even if you have a few months you will only be able to visit a small proportion of the 300 Fijian islands. If you are just after swimming beaches it's best to head for one of the smaller offshore coral islands. High volcanic islands like Viti Levu, Vanua Levu and Taveuni have few good beaches. Rugged Taveuni and Kadavu should be a high priority for nature lovers. Just about all of the islands have access to good snorkelling and diving. Note that the eastern sides of the larger islands have wetter climates.

Depending on the time available, your pace and budget, the following itineraries could be considered:

Day Trips from Nadi
    Cruise or fly to the Mamanucas for swimming, snorkelling or diving.
    Go on an organised tour to the Nausori Highlands or to Abaca National Park.
    Drive or bus along the Queens Road.
    Visit the Sigatoka Sand Dunes and Tavuni Hill Fort.
    Take the Coral Coast Scenic Railway from near Sigatoka to Natadola Beach, Viti Levu.
    Go rafting on the Ba River (or Navua River from Suva).
One Week
    Take a bus, or hire a car or 4WD, and explore Viti Levu for at least four days. Include Natadola beach, Sigatoka (Tavuni Hill Fort and the Sigatoka Sand Dunes), the Coral Coast, Suva, the Kings Road and Rakiraki. If you have a 4WD head up to Navala and the Nausori Highlands, then return to Nadi. Spend a couple of days on offshore islands, such as the Mamanucas or Nananu-i-Ra for water sports.
    Alternatively, combine day trips from Nadi

with either a flight to Taveuni Island (four days minimum, see the Bouma Falls and hike the Lavena Coastal Walk), or take a cruise to the Yasawa islands.

Two Weeks

Spend one week exploring Viti Levu as above, including day trips to offshore islands and the highlands. Spend the second week in Taveuni or the Yasawas.

One Month

Travel around Viti Levu, the Nausori Highlands, offshore islands including Ovalau (visiting the historic town of Levuka, and hiking to Lovoni) for about two weeks. Fly or ferry to Taveuni Island and take a trip to the Yasawas.

Two Months & Over

Follow the one month suggestions, adding Kadavu and eastern Vanua Levu including Savusavu and the Natewa Peninsula. Western Vanua Levu is not a high priority, but if you have the funds Vanua Levu is a good island to explore by 4WD.

THE BEST & THE WORST

Top 10

1 Innumerable snorkelling and dive spots – fantastic fish, coral and warm water
2 Small plane flights – incredible views of rugged highlands and of gorgeous coral islands and reefs
3 Trekking in the Viti Levu Highlands or Taveuni's Lavena Coastal Walk and Bouma Falls
4 Village visits, especially the picturesque Navala village
5 Exploring the larger islands by 4WD
6 The Fiji Museum, Suva
7 Tavuni Hill Fort, and the Sigatoka Sand Dunes
8 Cruising or sailing in the Yasawas or Mamanucas, or kayaking in the outer islands
9 Surfing or wave jumping at Wilkes and Malolo passages in the southern Mananucas
10 Church service or *meke* for great singing

Bottom 10

1 Slaughtered turtles in the Suva market
2 After a fantastic time snorkelling, finding you can't move because of sunburn
3 Trips in a small boat in rough weather
4 Overcrowded backpacker 'resorts'
5 Low tide in some areas with fringing reefs (no swimming)
6 Tropical sores
7 Being hassled by Nadi shop vendors
8 Litter
9 The food after a few weeks – somehow everything begins to taste like cucumber!
10 Excessive kava *(yaqona)*

TOURIST OFFICES

The Fiji Visitors Bureau (FVB) is the major tourist information body in Fiji and overseas. The head office is in Suva, but your first encounter is likely to be at Nadi International Airport. If you arrive here by plane you will be greeted by an FVB representative. Their office is on the left, just past the ANZ bank as you come out of arrivals. There will be many other faces smiling at you, including travel agents or representatives of resorts and other accommodation. The FVB have a 24-hour toll-free help line for complaints or emergencies available from anywhere in Fiji (see Local Fiji Visitors Bureau Offices).

The Fiji Hotel Association, the Ministry of Information and the Tourism Council of the South Pacific all have offices in Suva (see the Information section for Suva in the Viti Levu chapter). Other useful sources of information include:

Fiji Magic – an excellent source of information essential to backpackers and anyone not staying in a resort. Has details and prices of accommodation, restaurants, activities and tours and is free and widely available (try the FVB and airline offices). Although re-issued monthly the information is not always up to date.

Fiji Islands Travel Guide – an annual magazine published by the FVB

Affordable Fiji – a brochure published by the FVB specifically for the budget traveller (costs F$5)

Welcome to the Fiji Islands and the South Pacific – a free booklet, with useful information and maps

The Other Side of Fiji – a magazine published by Air Pacific

The Yacht Help Booklet, Fiji – useful information for yachties including tide tables and clearance formalities, available from marinas

The Fiji Hotel Association – Suva

The Ministry of Information – Suva

Local Fiji Visitors Bureau Offices

Fiji has Visitors Bureau Offices in Suva and Nadi:

Suva

Thomas St, GPO Box 92 (☎ 302 433; fax 300 970; email: infodesk@fijifvb.gov.fj)

Nadi

Nadi Airport Concourse, Box 9217, Nadi Airport (☎ 722 433 or toll free 0800 721 721; fax 720 141)

Fiji Visitors Bureau Offices Abroad

Fiji also has Visitors Bureau Offices in the following countries:

Australia
Level 12, St Martins Tower, 31 Market St, Sydney 2000 (☎ 02-9264 3399 or toll free 1800 25 1715; fax 02-9264 3060)

Germany
Dircksenstrasse 40, 10178 Berlin (☎ 30-2381 7628; fax 30-2381 7641)

Japan
NOA Building, (10th floor), 3-5, 2 Chome Azabuudai, Minato-ku, Tokyo 106 (☎ 03-3587 2038; fax 03-3587 2563)

New Zealand
5th floor, 48 High St, PO Box 1179, Auckland (☎ 09-373 2133; fax 09-309 4720)

UK
375 Upper Richmond Rd, West London SW14 7NX (☎ 0181-392 1838; fax 0181-392 1318)

USA
5777 West Century Blvd, Suite 220, Los Angeles, CA 90045 (☎ 310-568 1616 or toll free 1800-932 3454; fax 310-670 2318)

VISAS & DOCUMENTS
Passport & Visas

Visitors must have an onward or return ticket, and their passport must be valid for at least six months from the intended date of departure from Fiji. Vaccinations for yellow fever and cholera may be required if you are coming directly from an infected area.

Tourist visas of four weeks are automatically granted on arrival to citizens of the following countries: most countries belonging to the Commonwealth, North America, Western Europe, Antigua, Argentina, Barbuda, Belize, Bolivia, Brazil, Chile, Colombia, Tanzania, Ecuador, Iceland, Indonesia, Israel, Japan, Mexico, Paraguay, Peru, Philippines, Taiwan, Thailand, Tunisia, Turkey, Uruguay and Venezuela. There is no charge for the initial visa or subsequent extensions.

Others will have to apply for visas through a Fijian embassy prior to arrival. Fees are F$65/110 for single/multiple entry visas. Allow at least two weeks for the processing of applications.

Those entering Fiji by boat are subject to the same visa requirements as those travelling to Fiji by plane. Yachts can only enter through Suva, Lautoka and Levuka. Moves are also underway to set up an immigration point at Savusavu. Yachts have to be cleared by immigration, health and customs, and it is prohibited to visit any outer islands before doing so. To visit the Lau group, yachts need to apply for special written authorisation (see Travel Permits).

Visitors cannot partake in political activity or study, and work permits are needed if you intend to live and work in Fiji. Foreign journalists will require a permit if they are in Fiji for more than 14 days (see the Work section).

Visa Extensions Try to have your initial visa granted for the maximum four-month stay rather than the usual four weeks. Otherwise visa extensions are given for four weeks at a time, and you must apply before the initial visa expires. You can apply for visa extensions at the Department of Immigration at Nadi airport, Lautoka or Suva. You'll need to show your passport, return ticket and, occasionally, proof of adequate funds. You can apply through police stations in Ba, Tavua, Taveuni, Savusavu, Labasa and Levuka, but allow at least a week for the paperwork. If you wish to stay longer than four months you'll have to leave and then re-enter the country. The Department of Immigration has the following offices:

Suva
Gohil Building, Toorak (☎ 312 672; fax 301 653)
Nadi
Nadi International Airport – open for all international arrivals (☎ 722 263; fax 721 720).
Lautoka
Namoli Ave (☎ 661 706; fax 668 120)
Nausori
International Airport (☎ 478 785)

Photocopies

Keep photocopies of vital documents in a separate place in your luggage, together with an emergency stash of about F$50. Include a copy of your passport's data pages, birth certificate, credit cards, airline tickets, travel insurance, the serial numbers of your travellers' cheques, driving licence, vaccination details, prescriptions, employment documents and education qualifications. Also leave a copy of all these things with someone at home.

Travel Permits
Travel to the outer islands such as the Lau group requires special permits. Yachties will need a customs cruising permit and a permit to cruise the islands from the Ministry of Foreign Affairs (☎ 211 458; fax 301 741) at 61 Carnarvon St in Suva, or from the Commissioner's office in Lautoka or Levuka. They will ask to see customs papers and details of all crew members.

Travel Insurance
A travel insurance policy to cover theft, loss and medical problems is a good idea. There is a wide variety of policies available and your travel agent will be able to make recommendations. The policies handled by STA Travel and other student travel organisations are usually good value. Some policies offer lower and higher medical-expense options but the higher ones are chiefly for countries such as the USA, which have extremely high medical costs. Check the small print:

- Some policies specifically exclude 'dangerous activities' which can include scuba diving, motorcycling, even trekking. If such activities are on your agenda you don't want that sort of policy. A locally acquired motorcycle licence may not be valid under your policy.
- You may prefer a policy which pays doctors or hospitals direct rather than you having to pay on the spot and claim later. If you have to claim later make sure you keep all documentation. Some policies ask you to call back (reverse charges) to a centre in your home country where an immediate assessment of your problem is made.
- Check that the policy covers ambulances or an emergency flight home. If you have to stretch out you will need two seats and somebody has to pay for them!

Driving Licence & Permits
If you hold a current driving licence from an English-speaking country you will be allowed to drive in Fiji. Otherwise you will need an international driving permit, which

should be obtained in your home country before travelling.

Hostel Card
There are two Hostelling International (HI) affiliated hostels in Fiji where you can get a discount as a member, one in Nadi and other in Suva. They will also issue new HI membership cards.

The Australian Nomads Dreamtime Card is also accepted by some backpacker hostels in Fiji, principally the Cathay chain, which has accommodation in Korovou and Suva on Viti Levu. It may be worth getting if you also intend travelling around Australia. To obtain a card contact Nomads Backpackers International Pty Ltd (☎ 61 8 224 0919; fax 224 0972), c/o Ayers House, 288 North Terrace, Adelaide SA 5000, Australia.

Student & Youth Cards
STA travel agents give discounts on international airfares to full-time students who have an International Student Identity Card (ISIC). Application forms are available at STA Travel offices. Have the completed form stamped at the registry office of your school or university, and return it to the STA office. Upon payment of about A$10 your card will be issued on the spot. Student discounts are occasionally given for entry fees, restaurants and accommodation in Fiji. If you get sick in Suva you can also use the student health service at the University of the South Pacific.

EMBASSIES
Fijian Embassies Abroad
Fiji has diplomatic representation in the following countries:

Australia
9 Beagle St, Red Hill, ACT 2600, Canberra, or PO Box E 159, Queen Victoria Terrace, ACT 2600 (☎ 06-239 6872; fax 06-295 3283)
Belgium
66 Avenue de Corteberg, 1000 Brussels, Boîte Postale 7, (☎ 02-736 9050; fax 02-736 1458)
Japan
10th Floor, Noa Building, 3-5, 2-Chome, Azabudai, Minato-Ku, Tokyo 106 (☎ 03-3587 2038; fax 03-3587 2563)

Malaysia
  2nd floor, Suite 203, Wisma Equity, 150 Jalan Ampang, 50450 Kuala Lumpur (☎ 03-264 8422; fax 03-262 5636)
New Zealand
  PO Box 3940, 31 Pipitea St, Thorndon, Wellington (☎ 04-473 5401; fax 04-499 1011)
Papua New Guinea
  4th floor, Defense House, Champion Parade, Port Moresby, NCD, PO Box 6117 (☎ 211 914; fax 217 220)
USA
  2233 Wisconsin Avenue, NW, Suite 240, Washington, DC 20007 (☎ 202-337 8320; fax 202-337 1966)
United Nations
  Fiji Permanent Mission, 630 Third Avenue, 7th Floor, New York, NY 10017 (☎ 212-687 4130; fax 212-687 3963)
UK
  34 Hyde Park Gate, London SW7 5BN (☎ 0171-584 3661; fax 0171-584 2838)

Foreign Embassies in Fiji
Refer to the Suva chapter for details.

CUSTOMS
If you are travelling with expensive camera or computer equipment, carry a receipt to avoid hassles when returning home.

Visitors can enter Fiji without paying duty on the following: up to F$400 per passenger of duty assessed goods; two litres of liquor or four litres of wine or four litres of beer; 500 cigarettes or 500g of cigars/tobacco, or all three under a total of 500g; and personal effects. Pottery shards and trochus shells cannot be taken out of the country.

Quarantine
Importation of vegetable matter, seeds, animals, meat or dairy produce is prohibited without licence from the Ministry of Agriculture & Fisheries. Domestic pets require a permit to enter Fiji and will be kept in quarantine in Suva for a week.

MONEY
The local currency is the Fiji dollar (F$). All prices quoted herein are in F$ unless otherwise noted.

Always ensure that you confirm whether prices of accommodation, food or transport etc are being quoted with or without VAT (value added tax) a 10% sales tax on goods and services introduced in July 1992. Prices quoted in the book include VAT. Travellers and locals alike have to pay this tax.

The commercial banks operating in Fiji include Fiji Westpac, ANZ, National Bank of Fiji (government owned), Bank of Hawaii, Bank of Baroda and Habib Bank. Bank business hours are 9.30 am to 3 pm Monday to Thursday (4 pm on Friday). The ANZ at Nadi airport provides 24-hour service. While banks in larger towns keep standard business hours, branches in smaller towns may not open every day. In a small branch you may have trouble exchanging money if it is a public holiday in the home country of your currency (a regional branch may worry if they can't get the latest exchange rate).

Costs
Travelling independently in Fiji is relatively economical for solo travellers, families or the elderly. Since the whole country is so heavily geared to tourism and resorts, it can be very easy to spend a lot of money. To give an idea of overall expenses, a local phone call by cardphone costs 20 cents, the *Fiji Times* costs 60 cents, one litre of long-life milk is F$1.20, and a glass of beer F$2. See also the Accommodation and Food sections. Following are some money-saving hints:

- If you are on a tight budget follow the locals to the cheaper restaurants and avoid trendy joints aimed at tourists. Self-catering may be a good idea; try the local market for fresh fruit and vegetables.
- Carry lots of small notes and coins, essential for bargaining or when taking taxis, which sometimes have no change.
- Be careful with transport; a bit of planning can save a lot of money. Interisland hopping and fuel for boats is fairly expensive.
- When looking for a taxi, always try for one that will bring you back. Refer to the Getting Around section.
- Hitching is also quite easy, the locals do it all the time. It is courteous to pay the equivalent of the bus fare.
- Accommodation prices vary enormously in Fiji, from backpacker beds for F$5 to F$10 and cheap hotel rooms for F$35, to luxury resorts for F$1000 per night. Some of the bottom and middle-range

places give access to the same activities and sites as the resorts, for a fraction of the price. Some resorts offer package deals. Enquire about local rates.

Carrying Money

While it is relatively uncommon for travellers to be robbed in Fiji, it does happen. Avoid becoming suddenly destitute by hiding money in inside pouches and secret stashes, and by not keeping your wallet in a back pocket.

Cash

Bank notes come in denominations of F$50, F$20, F$10, F$5 and F$2. There are coins to the value of F$1, 50, 20, 10, five, two and one cents. Even though Fiji is now a republic, notes and coins still have Britain's Queen Elizabeth on one side.

Travellers' Cheques & Credit Cards

Travellers' cheques can be changed in most banks, exchange houses, larger hotels and duty-free shops. However, it is best to change plenty of money before travelling to remote areas. It's a good idea to take travellers' cheques in a variety of small and large denominations to avoid being stuck with lots of cash when leaving.

Most restaurants, shops, middle to upper-range hotels, car rental agencies, tour and travel agents will accept all of the major credit cards. Visa, American Express, Diners Club and MasterCard are widely accepted. Beware – some resorts will charge an additional 5% for payment by credit card.

American Express has a good reputation for replacing lost or stolen cards or cheques quickly. It has a representative at 25 Victoria Pde, Suva (☎ 302 333; fax 302 048) and at the Nadi Airport Concourse (☎ 722 325). Diners Club International (☎ 300 552; fax 301 312) is on the 5th Floor of ANZ House, Victoria Parade, Suva.

ATMs

At the time of writing the only ATM was at the Bank of Hawaii in downtown Suva.

International Transfers

Cash advances are available through credit cards at most banks, but always confirm this before travelling to a remote area.

Currency

The best currencies to carry are Australian, New Zealand or US dollars.

Currency Exchange

At the time of writing the exchange rates were as follows:

Australia	A$1	=	F$1.09
Canada	C$1	=	F$1.01
France	1FF	=	F$0.27
Germany	DM1	=	F$0.92
Japan	¥100	=	F$1.26
New Zealand	NZ$1	=	F$0.96
Vanuatu	VT100	=	F$1.27
UK	UK£1	=	F$2.15
USA	US$1	=	F$1.38

Changing Money

The 24-hour ANZ bank at Nadi International Airport charges a transaction fee of F$2. Other banks and exchange bureaus don't normally charge a fee.

Black Market

There is not an obvious black market in Fiji, but you may occasionally get people on the street wanting to buy US dollars from you.

Tipping & Bargaining

Tipping is not expected or encouraged in Fiji; however, many of the resorts have a Staff Christmas Fund to which you may choose to contribute.

Indigenous Fijians generally do not like to bargain, but always expect to do so in Fiji-Indian stores, especially in Nadi. It is considered bad luck for a shop owner or taxi driver to lose their first customer of the day, so arrive first thing to drive an especially hard bargain!

POST & COMMUNICATIONS

Fiji Posts & Telecommunications Ltd provides a wide range of services throughout the islands, and since Nadi International Airport is a major flight hub, international deliveries are usually quite efficient. Post offices are open from 8 am to 4.30 pm.

Postal Rates

To mail a postcard or standard letter (under 15g) from Fiji costs 13 cents within the country, 31 cents to New Zealand, 44 cents to Australia, 63 cents to the USA and 81 cents to Europe.

Sending Mail

Sending mail is straightforward. Use surface mail if your items are too heavy and expensive to send by air mail, and if you don't mind a long delivery time. An international express mail service is also available through the main post offices.

Receiving Mail

It is possible to receive mail at all major post offices through general deliveries. Mail is held for up to two months. It is also possible to receive faxes from FINTEL (Fiji International Telecommunications) and the major post offices. See below.

Telephone

Most public telephones require a phonecard which can be purchased at post offices, some pharmacies and newsagents. It's a good idea to buy a few at the airport when you arrive (shop near departures). The plastic phonecards come in denominations of F$3, 5, 10, 20 and 50, and have interesting designs. Avoid buying the large denomination cards though as phonecards are very easy to leave behind! Phones are generally not too hard to find.

Remote areas such as Kadavu have a telephone exchange service. Calls to radio phones may have to go through the operator. Local calls on public phones cost 20 cents per call; calls from town to neighbouring towns cost around 20 cents per 45 seconds; more distant calls (eg Nadi to Suva) cost 20 cents for each 15 seconds. FINTEL, in downtown Suva, provides an international phone service.

In the major towns the telephone exchanges are automatic. Islands are linked by cable and satellite to worldwide networks.

The majority of middle and top-end hotel rooms are equipped with telephones. There are also many phonecard payphones and some coin-operated payphones, though the latter are being phased out. Coin-operated payphones accept 20 cent coins, but only those minted since 1990. Mobile phones can be rented from the local cellular service provider and some car rental agencies.

Hotels can frequently add hefty surcharges on calls so the cheapest and most convenient way to make international calls is by public cardphone. They are also a good way to limit costs. In Suva try the FINTEL office. Most post offices have public phones, although not always functioning. Collect calls are more expensive and when using operator assistance the minimum charge is three minutes. Trunk calls within Fiji between 6 pm and 6 am Monday to Friday and midnight Friday to midnight Saturday cost at least 50% less. If you want to charge calls to your home telephone, Telecom Calling Card or Telecom Credit Card, call the operator for assistance.

Some useful numbers include:

000	Emergency
010	Operator assistance and reminder calls
011	Local directory enquiries
030	Local collect calls – follow with the local number
031	International collect calls – follow with the number
012	International operator assistance, bookings
022	International directory enquiries

The international dial-in code for Fiji is 679 followed by the local number. There are no area codes.

To use IDD (International Direct Dial) dial 05 plus:

Australia, 61; New Zealand, 64; Tonga, 676 (F$1.76 per minute)

French Polynesia, 689; Vanuatu, 678 (F$1.87 per minute)

France, 33; Germany, 49; Japan, 81; USA, 598 (F$2.97 per minute)

Off-peak calls to Australia and New Zealand between 11 pm and 6 am are F$1.20.

Fax, Telegraph & Email

In Suva you have a choice of using the services of the post office or FINTEL (☎ 312 933, 301 655; fax 301 025). FINTEL deals with international services only (telephone calls, faxes and telegrams), and has booths and sells phonecards for this purpose. The FINTEL fax service is cheaper if you wish to send multiple pages. Ring to enquire if you have incoming faxes. The office is open from 8 am to 8 pm Monday to Saturday, but is closed on Sunday and public holidays.

At FINTEL fax charges are as follows:

Regional countries – F$7.70 for the first page plus F$3.30 for each additional page
Other countries – F$8.80 for the first page plus F$4.40 for each additional page
Incoming faxes cost F$1.10 per page

At post offices fax charges are as follows:

Local – F$2.20 per page plus 55 cents handling fee
Regional countries – F$5.50 per page plus F$3.30 handling fee
Other countries – F$7.70 per page plus F$3.30 handling fee
Incoming faxes cost F$1.10 per page

Post offices offering fax services include:

Suva (GPO)	(fax 306 088)
Labasa	(fax 813 666)
Lautoka	(fax 664 666)
Nadi Airport	(fax 720 467)
Savusavu	(fax 880 359)
Waiyevo, Taveuni	(fax 880 459)

HF radio and telegraph services are available Monday to Friday from 8 am to 5 pm at any post office. The minimum charge per minute is 31 cents. Dial 013 and ask the operator to book your call.

Email While email is not yet common in Fiji, it is starting to take off. The University of the South Pacific has a direct Internet connection to AARnet via Melbourne. The general public can gain Internet and CompuServe access via Fiji Telecom. If you don't wish to dial a personal service back home, then you will have to get an email account locally.

Calling home via a modem can be expensive and time consuming, and email delivery can depend on the quality of the telephone line. However, if you have your own notebook, modem and server overseas, go to the telecom office in Suva and they will allow you to hook-up and charge the regular international time fees.

If you need to print documents, all resorts and big hotels should let you use their facilities. Note that some exclusive resorts such as Vatulele discourage the use of personal computers, telephones and faxes, as they believe it interferes with your holiday!

There are several shops that sell PCs in Suva. If they don't do repairs themselves they should be able to put you in touch with others that do.

BOOKS

Refer to the Literature section in Facts about the Country for contemporary Fijian Literature. For those with a specific interest in the area, *South Pacific Literature – From Myth to Fabulation*, published by the Institute of Pacific Studies, 1992, is a survey of Pacific Islanders and there work, and has an extensive bibliography.

Most books are published in different editions by different publishers in different countries. As a result, a book might be a hard-cover rarity in one country while it's readily available in paperback in another. Fortunately, bookshops and libraries search by title or author, so your local bookshop or library is best placed to advise you on the availability of the following recommendations.

Lonely Planet

Also published by Lonely Planet are the *Fijian phrasebook* by Paul Geraghty, an excellent aid to talking with locals, and *Travel with Children* by Maureen Wheeler, which is packed with useful information for family travel and contains a section on Fiji.

History & Politics

History books that cover precolonial history include:

Yalo i Viti – A Fiji Museum Catalogue by Fergus Clunie, 1986.

Matanitu – The Struggle for Power in Early Fiji by David Routledge, 1985.

Fiji and the Fijians – Vol. 1, The Islands and Their Inhabitants by Thomas Williams, a 1982 reprint of the 1858 original.

A History of Fiji by RA Derrick, 1950, now only available in libraries, deals with the period up to 1874.

My Twenty-One Years in the Fiji Islands by Totaram Sanadhya, 1991, an interesting first-hand account of the indenture system. Written in the 1910s, a new edition is available at the Fiji Museum.

Other general history books include the following:

Fiji in the Pacific – A History and Geography of Fiji by Donnelly, Quanchi & Kerr, 1994, designed as a school textbook, but a good introduction to the country.

Fiji Times – A History of Fiji by Kim Gravelle, 1979.

Beyond the Politics of Race, An Alternative History of Fiji to 1992 by William Sutherland.

Broken Waves – A History of the Fiji Islands in the Twentieth Century by Brij V Lal, 1992.

The titles below deal specifically with the military coup and postcoup era:

Power and Prejudice – The Making of the Fiji Crisis by Brij V Lal, 1988.

More Letters From Fiji, 1990 – 1994, First years under a post-coup Constitution by Len Usher.

Fiji – The Politics of Illusion by Deryck Scarr, 1988.

Rabuka – No Other Way by Eddie Dean & Stan Ritova, 1988.

Fiji – Shattered Coups by RT Robertson & AT Amanisau, 1988.

Literature by Non-Fijian Writers

A number of novels about Fiji have been written by Westerners:

Life in Feejee, or, Five Years Among the Cannibals by A Lady (Mary Davis Wallis), 1851, reprinted 1983, is the memoirs of the wife of a Yankee trading captain. It can be purchased at the Fiji Museum shop.

Fiji by Daryl Tarte, 1988, is the ultimate trashy Fijian novel, a sprawling saga following over a century of Fijian history through the experiences of a plantation family. It's based on the Tarte family of Taveuni, whose old colonial farm is now a backpacker and dive resort (Nomui Lala). It's easy to read and covers a wide range of historical topics.

General

A range of books have been written about Fiji, some of which cover specialist topics:

Children of the Sun by Glen Craig with poetry by Bryan McDonald, 1996, has stunning photography of mostly smiling locals with perfect teeth as well as spectacular landscapes. The book is humorously and interestingly designed and has photos taken over an eight-year period on Craig's many visits to Fiji. You should be able to purchase a copy at the Fiji Visitors Bureau.

Fiji Celebration by James Siers, 1985.

Fiji's Natural Heritage by Paddy Ryan, 1988, covers Fiji's flora, fauna and environment.

The Snorkeller's Guide to the Coral Reef, also by Paddy Ryan, 1994, with photographs by the author and Peter Atkinson.

Mai Veikau – Tales of Fijian Wildlife by Dick Watling, 1986, may not be available in bookshops.

Secrets of Fijian Medicine by MA Weiner.

The Fiji Islands – A Geographical Handbook by RA Derrick, 1951, is still a good reference text, available at libraries.

Myths and Legends of Fiji and Rotuma by AW Reed & Inez Hames, 1967.

ONLINE SERVICES

Travellers may be interested in accessing the following Internet sites:

The Fiji Visitors Bureau
    http://www.fijifvb.gov.fj
    http://www.fijifvb.gov.fj/fijidb/sites.htm
Fiji Magic
    http://www.fijimagic.com
The Tourism Council of the South Pacific
    www.infocentre.com/spt

FILMS

Both the original 1948 *Blue Lagoon* film starring Jean Simmons and the 1979 remake with Brooke Shields were shot in the Yasawa islands. *Return to the Blue Lagoon* was filmed in Taveuni in 1991.

∞∞∞∞∞∞∞∞∞∞∞∞∞∞∞∞∞∞∞∞∞∞

Freedom of the Press

The concept of a free press is still in its infancy and there is no freedom-of-information legislation in Fiji. The government at one moment assumes a position of commitment to openness and at another introduces media legislation to secure confidentiality and privacy for certain citizens.

There are opposing views regarding media freedom. Journalists and academics are strong promoters of media freedom, advocating the right of every citizen to have access to information, especially government information. Others oppose the application of 'Western concepts', arguing that media freedom is disruptive to traditional institutions and endangers the harmony of Fijian customs, values and hierarchical systems of authority. This last view is supported by the government. On the one hand the government wishes to promote Fiji's development using modern forms of information and communication, yet on the other it is concerned with secrecy of government information. ■

∞∞∞∞∞∞∞∞∞∞∞∞∞∞∞∞∞∞∞∞∞∞

NEWSPAPERS & MAGAZINES

The *Fiji Times*, founded in Lavuka in 1869, is the oldest media organisation in the country. Now owned by Rupert Murdoch, it has a circulation of 38,000. Its slogan is 'the first newspaper published in the world today', due to its proximity to the dateline. The *Fiji Times* also publishes the newspapers *Nai Lalaki*, in Fijian, and *Shanti Dut*, in Hindi. The *Daily Post*, established in 1987, has a circulation of about 16,000, and also publishes *Nai Volasiga* in Fijian. Magazines include *Pacific Islands Monthly* and *Island Business* which cover regional issues, and *The Review*, which is Fiji oriented.

Australian newspapers (at least a few days old) are available at the Desai Bookshop in Suva and some newsagents for an inflated price. The *Sydney Morning Herald* costs F$8.75 and the *Australian* F$8. Alternatively, try embassy reading rooms.

Refer to the Tourist Office section for magazines with information for travellers.

RADIO & TV

The government-sponsored Fiji Broadcasting Commission has two stations in English (Radio Fiji 3 and FM 104), one in Fijian (Radio Fiji 1) and two in Hindi (Radio Fiji 2 and 98 FM).

Running since 1990, FM 104 has music programmes including the World Chart Show, Take 40 Australia, Roots Rhythm, UK Top 10, and shows featuring dance and reggae. The station is supposed to play 10% local content: listen for Seru Serevi, Danny Costello, Michelle Rounds, Karuana Gopalan, The Freelancers and The Black Roses.

The independent commercial station FM 96 began as Communications Fiji Limited in 1985. It has 24-hour broadcasting with music, sports and community information in English and Hindi.

Radio Pacific (FM 88.8), a new station managed by the University of the South Pacific Student's Association, began broadcasting in May 1996. Student volunteers run programmes with music and information from different Pacific countries as well as some academic programmes. The government licence binds them to avoid political and religious topics.

Fiji received its first TV transmission in October 1991, when Television New Zealand played a live telecast of World Cup rugby matches. The Fiji Television Company received its licence in August 1993. There is one station – Fiji One. Check the *Fiji Times* or the fortnightly *TV Guide* magazine for programming. Cable TV was to be introduced in 1996.

VIDEO SYSTEMS

The various video systems – PAL, NTSC, and SECAM – are incompatible. The system used in Fiji is PAL G, as in Australia and New Zealand. When buying video recordings ensure they are compatible with the system in your home country.

PHOTOGRAPHY & VIDEO
Film & Equipment

Film and photography equipment is readily available in Fiji, although it is probably best to buy films in bulk before leaving your country. Always check expiry dates and, if intending to take lots of shots, buy 36-exposure films which will be less bulky to carry. While for most conditions 100 ASA will be OK, also take some 400 ASA film for darker, forest conditions. There are labs with same-day processing services in Nadi, Lautoka and Suva.

For travel photography (portraits, landscapes, architecture, wildlife and macro shots) it is best to have equipment that gives you flexibility. An SLR with a combination wide angle and zoom lens is great. However, weight and simplicity of operation are also of prime importance. Make sure your equipment and flash are working well, take spare batteries and consider bringing a polariser.

Don't leave your camera gear exposed to the sun, heat, humidity or salty sea air. Fungal growth on camera lenses can be a problem. If you plan to stay in Fiji or the tropics for more than a few weeks, it may be a good idea to keep equipment in airtight containers with activated silica gel (available at pharmacies). If travelling around in small boats, store your camera and films in a waterproof bag or container.

Photography

Most importantly make sure you are familiar with the operations of your camera equipment.

Avoid flat shots of landscapes with no foreground: they may look gorgeous in real life, but boring as a photo. Experiment with a variety of subjects, taking into consideration composition (framing, balance, centre of interest and position of horizons) and modelling (direction and intensity of light on the subject). Fiji's midday sun can be bright and harsh, leading to overexposed photos, so you'll need to adjust your camera settings accordingly. The best light conditions are generally in the early morning and late afternoon. Be careful that dark-skinned people don't turn out as silhouettes on bright backgrounds. In this situation it might be best to overexpose, or use the contrast-adjustment setting on some cameras. A flash can also be used to highlight foregrounds.

Underwater Photography As an introduction to underwater photography, novelty cameras are fun. Some resorts and dive centres offer underwater cameras for hire, and some have tuition and processing facilities. Special underwater cameras are an expensive investment. Alternatively, standard cameras can be used with special waterproof housings and an underwater strobe flash, or on sunny days, with underwater slide film. As a general rule close-up shots will be more successful. Give preference to high shutter speeds to avoid camera shake and blurred fish. Water absorbs certain wavelengths, and red filters can be used to reduce the exaggerated blue. If you are bringing your own equipment make sure your lights can be charged on 240V, or bring a converter.

Video

For a good travel video, make sure you are familiar with your camera and its limitations first. Consider light conditions, avoid glare, panning too quickly and camera shudder. Give a running commentary to entertain the viewers and avoid wind, which can be noisy. As with any photography, try to take creative shots, with variety, humour and plenty of close-ups. Protect your gear from humidity, heat and sea air.

Restrictions

During a yaqona ceremony you will normally have to wait until after the formal ritual; check first. Don't wander around villages photographing and filming people's private space, unless invited. Try not to flash expensive gear around.

Photographing People

Fijians usually enjoy having their photo taken, but always ask permission first and ask if they would like copies sent to them.

Airport Security

Repetitive exposure to airport x-ray machines can damage film, especially those of high speed. Carry films in a lead-lined bag, or in a clear plastic bag and ask for them to be checked by hand.

TIME
While the 180° meridian passes through the Fiji islands the international date line is diverted for convenience so all islands lie to the west of it. Fiji is 12 hours ahead of GMT/UTC. Daylight is from about 6 am to 6 pm. Fiji does not have daylight saving (summer time). The concept of time in Fiji is fairly flexible ('Fiji time'), so don't get too stressed if people are not punctual for appointments; just go with the flow.

When it's noon in Suva corresponding times elsewhere are as follows:

noon	Auckland same day
11 am	New Caledonia & Vanuatu
10 am	Sydney same day
midnight	London previous day
7 pm	New York previous day
4 pm	San Francisco previous day
1 pm	Samoa previous day
1 pm	Tonga same day

Add one hour to these times if the other country has daylight saving.

ELECTRICITY
Voltage & Cycles
Electricity in Fiji is supplied at 240V, 50 Hz AC, as in Australia. Many remote areas and island resorts rely on solar and generator power. It is best to buy adaptors prior to leaving but they are also available in duty-free shops. Many of the resorts and hotels have universal outlets for 240V or 110V shavers and hair dryers.

Plugs & Sockets
Outlets are of the three-pin type and use flat two or three-pin plugs of the Australian type.

WEIGHTS & MEASURES
Fiji follows the metric system, hence distance is measured in km, goods bought in kg or litres, and temperature registered in degrees Celsius. Refer to the conversion chart on this book's inside back cover.

LAUNDRY
Most resorts and hotels will do your laundry for a small fee. F$5 a load is the standard. People travelling away from cities, towns, resorts should carry laundry soap and a scrubbing brush, although village stores usually stock these items. In rural areas women sit down in the creeks or rivers fully clothed to do their washing. Same-day laundry and dry-cleaning services are available in Nadi and Suva. Consult the telephone directory (Fiji *Yellow Pages*).

TOILETS
Toilets are the sit-down type. Fiji has public toilets in cities and larger towns, hotels and resorts, and sometimes near small groups of shops on country roads. Toilets in restaurants and in resort and hotel foyers are usually cleaner than those outside. Its a good idea to carry an emergency supply of toilet paper.

Most remote villages don't have toilets or any facilities for washing bodies and clothes except a creek. Ask about the local customs for bathing, don't just strip off near the village. For a toilet, make do with the bush or the beach, and bury your toilet paper.

HEALTH
Travel health depends on your predeparture preparations, your day-to-day health care while travelling and how you handle any medical problem or emergency that does develop. While the list of potential dangers can seem quite frightening, with a little luck, some basic precautions and adequate information, few travellers experience more than upset stomachs.

If you've arrived directly from a temperate climate the tropical heat and humidity may be a bit overwhelming at first. Health risks for travellers to Fiji include infected cuts and, if you are unlucky, ciguatera poisoning, or the mosquito transmitted diseases, filariasis and dengue fever.

Travel Health Guides
There are a number of books on travel health:

Staying Healthy in Asia, Africa & Latin America, Dirk Schroeder, Moon Publications, 1994. Probably the best all-round guide to carry, as it's compact but very detailed and well organised.

Travellers' Health, Dr Richard Dawood, Oxford University Press, 1995. Comprehensive, easy to read, authoritative and also highly recommended, although it's rather large to lug around.

Where There is No Doctor, David Werner, Macmillan, 1994. A very detailed guide intended for someone, like a Peace Corps worker, going to work in an underdeveloped country, rather than for the average traveller.

Travel with Children, Maureen Wheeler, Lonely Planet Publications, 1995. Includes basic advice on travel health for younger children.

Predeparture Planning

Health Insurance See Travel Insurance in the Visa & Documents section of this chapter.

Medical Kit It's wise to carry a small, straightforward medical kit. The kit should include

- Aspirin or paracetamol (acetaminophen in the US) – for pain or fever. It may, however, be preferable to use paracetamol rather than aspirin in areas where dengue fever is endemic.
- Antihistamine (such as Benadryl) – useful as a decongestant for colds and allergies, to ease the itch from insect bites or stings, and to help prevent motion sickness. There are several antihistamines on the market, all with different pros and cons (eg a tendency to cause drowsiness), so it's worth discussing your requirements with a pharmacist or doctor. Antihistamines may cause sedation and interact with alcohol so care should be taken when using them.
- Antibiotics – useful if you're travelling well off the beaten track, but they must be prescribed and you should carry the prescription with you.
- Some individuals are allergic to commonly prescribed antibiotics such as penicillin or sulpha drugs. It would be sensible to always carry this information when travelling.
- Loperamide (eg Imodium) or Lomotil for diarrhoea; prochlorperazine (eg Stemetil) or metoclopramide (eg Maxalon) for nausea and vomiting. Antidiarrhoea medication should not be given to children under the age of 12.
- Rehydration mixture – for treatment of severe diarrhoea. This is particularly important if travelling with children, but is recommended for everyone.
- Antiseptic such as povidone-iodine (eg Betadine), which comes as a solution, ointment, powder and impregnated swabs – for cuts and grazes.
- Calamine lotion or Stingose spray – to ease irritation from bites or stings.
- Bandages and Band-aids – for minor injuries.
- Scissors, tweezers and a thermometer (note that mercury thermometers are prohibited by airlines).
- Cold and flu tablets and throat lozenges.
- Insect repellent, sunscreen, suntan lotion, chap stick and water-purification tablets.
- A couple of syringes, in case you need injections in a country with medical hygiene problems. Ask your doctor for a note explaining why they have been prescribed.

Ideally antibiotics should be administered only under medical supervision and should never be taken indiscriminately. Take only the recommended dose at the prescribed intervals and continue using the antibiotic for the prescribed period, even if the illness seems to be cured earlier. Antibiotics are quite specific to the infections they can treat. Stop immediately if there are any serious reactions and don't use the antibiotic at all if you are unsure that you have the correct one. In many countries, if a medicine is available at all it will generally be available over the counter and the price will be much cheaper than in the West. However, be careful if buying drugs in developing countries, particularly where the expiry date may have passed or correct storage conditions may not have been followed. Bogus drugs are common and it's possible that drugs which are no longer recommended, or have even been banned, in the West are still being dispensed in many Third World countries.

In many countries it may be a good idea to leave unwanted medicines, syringes etc with a local clinic, rather than carry them home.

Health Preparations Make sure you're healthy before you start travelling. If you are embarking on a long trip make sure your teeth are OK; there are lots of places where a visit to the dentist would be the last thing you'd want.

If you wear glasses bring a spare pair and your prescription. Losing your glasses can be a real problem, although in many places you can get new spectacles made up quickly, cheaply and competently.

If you require a particular medication take an adequate supply, as it may not be available locally. Take the prescription or, better still, part of the packaging showing the generic rather than the brand name (which may not be locally available), as it will make getting replacements easier. It's a wise idea to have a legible prescription or a letter from your doctor with you to show that you legally use the medication – it's surprising how often over-the-counter drugs from one place are illegal without a prescription or even banned in another.

Immunisations Vaccinations provide protection against diseases you might meet along the way. For some countries no immunisations are necessary, but the further off the beaten track you go the more necessary it is to take precautions.

It is important to understand the distinction between vaccines recommended for travel in certain areas and those required by law. Essentially the number of vaccines subject to international health regulations has been dramatically reduced over the last 10 years. Currently yellow fever is the only vaccine subject to international health regulations. Vaccination as an entry requirement is usually only enforced when coming from an infected area.

Occasionally travellers face bureaucratic problems regarding cholera vaccine even though all countries have dropped it as a health requirement for travel. Under some situations it may be wise to have the vaccine despite its poor protection, eg for the trans-Africa traveller.

On the other hand a number of vaccines are recommended for travel in certain areas. These may not be required by law but are recommended for your own personal protection.

All vaccinations should be recorded on an International Health Certificate, which is available from your physician or government health department.

Plan ahead for getting your vaccinations:

some of them require an initial shot followed by a booster, while some vaccinations should not be given together. It is recommended you seek medical advice at least six weeks prior to travel.

Most travellers from Western countries will have been immunised against various diseases during childhood but your doctor may still recommend booster shots against measles or polio, diseases still prevalent in many developing countries. The period of protection offered by vaccinations differs widely and some are contraindicated if you are pregnant.

In some countries immunisations are available from airport or government health centres. Travel agents or airline offices will tell you where.

Vaccinations include:

Tetanus & Diphtheria Boosters are necessary every 10 years and protection is highly recommended.

Polio A booster of either the oral or injected vaccine is required every 10 years to maintain our immunity from childhood vaccination. Polio is a very serious, easily transmitted disease which is still prevalent in many developing countries.

Typhoid Available either as an injection or oral capsules. Protection lasts from one to five years depending on the vaccine and is useful if you are travelling for long in rural, tropical areas. You may get some side effects such as pain at the injection site, fever, headache and a general unwell feeling. A new single-dose injectable vaccine, which appears to have few side effects, is now available but is more expensive. Side effects are unusual with the oral form, but occasionally an individual will have stomach cramps.

Hepatitis A The most common travel-acquired illness which can be prevented by vaccination. Protection can be provided in two ways – either with the antibody gamma globulin or with a new vaccine called Havrix.

Havrix provides long-term immunity (possibly more than 10 years) after an initial course of two injections and a booster at one year. It may be more expensive than gamma globulin but certainly has many advantages, including length of protection and ease of administration. It is important to know that being a vaccine it will take about three weeks to provide satisfactory protection – hence the need for careful planning prior to travel.

Gamma globulin is not a vaccination but a ready-made antibody which has proven to be very successful in reducing the chances of hepatitis infection. It should be given as close as possible to departure because it is at its most effective in the first few weeks after administration and the effectiveness tapers off gradually between three and six months.

Hepatitis B Travellers at risk of contact (see Infectious Diseases section) are strongly advised to be vaccinated, especially if they are children or will have close contact with children. The vaccination course comprises three injections given over a six-month period then boosters every three to five years. The initial course of injections can be given over as short a period as 28 days then boosted after 12 months if more rapid protection is required.

Yellow Fever Yellow Fever vaccinations are only required on entering Fiji if the traveller is coming from an infected area (some parts of South America and Africa). Protection lasts 10 years. Vaccination is contraindicated during pregnancy but if you must travel to a high-risk area it is probably advisable.

Rabies Pretravel rabies vaccination involves having three injections over 21 to 28 days and should be considered by those who will spend a month or longer in a country where rabies is common, especially if they are cycling, handling animals, caving, travelling to remote areas, or children (who may not report a bite). If someone who has been vaccinated is bitten or scratched by an animal they will require two booster injections of vaccine.

Cholera Not required by law but occasionally travellers face bureaucratic problems on some border crossings. Protection is poor and it lasts only six months. It is contraindicated in pregnancy.

Basic Rules

Care in what you eat and drink is the most important health rule; stomach upsets are the most likely travel health problem (between 30% and 50% of travellers in a two-week stay experience this) but the majority of these upsets will be relatively minor. Don't become paranoid; trying the local food is part of the experience of travel, after all.

Water The water in Fiji's major towns, hotels and resorts is generally safe to drink, but the same cannot be said of all villages. If you don't know for certain, always assume the worst. The number-one rule is *don't drink the water* and that includes ice. Reputable brands of bottled water or soft drinks are generally fine, although in some places bottles refilled with tap water are not unknown. Only use water from containers with a serrated seal – not tops or corks. Take care with fruit juice, particularly if water may have been added. Milk should be treated with suspicion, as it is often unpasteurised. Boiled milk is fine if it is kept hygienically. Tea or coffee should also be OK, since the water should have been boiled.

Water Purification The simplest way of purifying water is to boil it thoroughly. Vigorous boiling for five minutes should be satisfactory; however, at high altitude water boils at a lower temperature, so germs are less likely to be killed.

Simple filtering will not remove all dangerous organisms, so if you cannot boil water it should be treated chemically. Chlorine tablets (Puritabs, Steritabs or other brand names) will kill many but not all pathogens, including giardia and amoebic cysts. Iodine is very effective in purifying water and is available in tablet form (such as Potable Aqua), but follow the directions carefully and remember that too much iodine can be harmful.

If you can't find tablets, tincture of iodine (2%) or iodine crystals can be used. Four drops of tincture of iodine per litre or quart of clear water is the recommended dosage; the treated water should be left to stand for 20 to 30 minutes before drinking. Iodine crystals can also be used to purify water but this is a more complicated process, as you have to first prepare a saturated iodine solution. Iodine loses its effectiveness if exposed to air or damp so keep it in a tightly sealed container. Flavoured powder will disguise the taste of treated water and is a good idea if you are travelling with children.

Micropur water filters are useful for long trips. They filter out parasites, bacteria and viruses, and although expensive they are more cost effective than buying water.

Food There is an old colonial adage which says: 'If you can cook it, boil it or peel it you can eat it...otherwise forget it'. Salads and fruit should be washed with purified water or peeled where possible. Ice cream is usually OK if it is a reputable brand name, but beware of Third World street vendors and of ice cream that has melted and been refrozen. Thoroughly cooked food is safest but not if it has been left to cool or if it has been reheated. Shellfish such as mussels, oysters and clams should be avoided as well as undercooked meat, particularly in the form of mince. Steaming does not make shellfish safe for eating.

If a place looks clean and well run and if the vendor also looks clean and healthy, then the food is probably safe. In general, places that are packed with travellers or locals will be fine, while empty restaurants are questionable. The food in busy restaurants is cooked and eaten quite quickly, with little standing around, and is probably not reheated.

Ciguatera The ciguatera toxin is found in some predatory fish, especially on reefs which have been upset by dredging or storms. The toxin is contained in algae, which is eaten by the smaller reef fish, which are in turn the prey of larger fish. The larger the fish the more likely it is to have higher concentrations built up over its lifetime. It is best to avoid eating big reef predators such as snapper, barracuda and groupers. Pelagic (open ocean) fish such as tuna, wahoo and Spanish mackerel are safe to eat, and small reef fish that the locals eat and recommend should be OK.

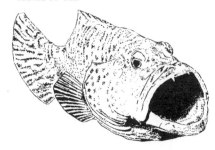

Large reef predators such as the grouper can contain the poisonous ciguatera toxin

The symptoms of ciguatera poisoning include nausea, vomiting, diarrhoea and stomach cramps, alternating fevers and chills, and tingling in the skin and mouth. A feeling of weak muscles and joints and aching pain in the fingers and feet may last weeks or even months. Hot may feel cold and vice versa. According to Peter Dunn-Rankin in *Fishing the Reefs* Mannitol, a simple intravenous medication, has been used to treat the poisoning.

Nutrition If your food is poor or limited in availability, if you're travelling hard and fast and therefore missing meals, or if you simply lose your appetite, you can soon start to lose weight and place your health at risk.

Make sure your diet is well balanced. Eggs, tofu, beans, lentils (dhal in India) and nuts are all safe ways to get protein. Fruit you can peel (bananas, oranges or mandarins for example) is usually safe and a good source of vitamins (melons can harbour bacteria in their flesh and are best avoided). Try to eat plenty of grains (including rice) and bread. Remember that although food is generally safer if it is cooked well, overcooked food loses much of its nutritional value. If your diet isn't well balanced or if your food intake is insufficient, it's a good idea to take vitamin and iron pills.

In hot climates make sure you drink enough – don't rely on feeling thirsty to indicate when you should drink. Not needing to urinate or dark-yellow urine is a danger sign. Always carry a water bottle with you on long trips. Excessive sweating can lead to loss of salt and therefore muscle cramping. Salt tablets are not a good idea as a preventative, but in places where salt is not used much adding salt to food can help.

Everyday Health Normal body temperature is 98.6°F or 37°C; more than 2°C (4°F) higher indicates a high fever. The normal adult pulse rate is 60 to 100 per minute (children 80 to 100, babies 100 to 140). You should know how to take a temperature and a pulse rate. As a general rule the pulse increases about 20 beats per minute for each °C (2°F) rise in fever.

Respiration (breathing) rate is also an indicator of illness. Count the number of breaths per minute: between 12 and 20 is normal for adults and older children (up to 30 for younger children, 40 for babies). People with a high fever or serious respiratory illness (like pneumonia) breathe more quickly than normal. More than 40 shallow breaths a minute may indicate pneumonia.

In Western countries with safe water and excellent human-waste disposal systems we often take good health for granted. In years gone by, when public health facilities were not as good as they are today, certain rules attached to eating and drinking were observed, eg washing your hands before a meal. It is important for people travelling in areas of poor sanitation to be aware of this and adjust their own personal hygiene habits.

Clean your teeth with purified water rather than straight from the tap. Avoid climatic extremes: keep out of the sun when it's hot, dress warmly when it's cold. Avoid potential diseases by dressing sensibly. You can get worm infections through walking barefoot or dangerous coral cuts by walking over coral without shoes. You can avoid insect bites by covering bare skin when insects are around, by screening windows or beds and by using insect repellents. Seek local advice: if you're told the water is unsafe due to jellyfish or sharks don't go in. In situations where there is no information, discretion is the better part of valour.

Medical Problems & Treatment

Potential medical problems can be broken down into several areas. Firstly there are the problems caused by extremes of temperature, altitude or motion. Then there are diseases and illnesses caused through poor environmental sanitation, insect bites or stings, and animal or human contact. Simple cuts, bites and scratches can also cause problems.

Self-diagnosis and treatment can be risky, so wherever possible seek qualified help. Although we do give drug dosages in this section, they are for emergency use only. Medical advice should be sought where possible before administering any drugs. Local doctors will be able to advise on preventative medicine and the sorts of health problems visitors may encounter.

An embassy or consulate can usually recommend a good place to go for such advice. So can five-star hotels, although they often recommend doctors with five-star prices. (This is when that medical insurance really comes in useful!) In some places standards of medical attention are so low that for some ailments the best advice is to get on a plane and go somewhere else.

Environmental Hazards

Sunburn In the tropics you can get sunburnt surprisingly quickly, even through cloud. Use a sunscreen and take extra care to cover areas which don't normally see sun – eg your feet. A hat provides added protection, and you should also use zinc cream or some other barrier cream for your nose and lips. Calamine lotion is good for mild sunburn.

Remember that too much sunlight, whether it's direct or reflected (glare), can damage your eyes. If your plans include being near water, sand or snow, then good sunglasses are doubly important. Good quality sunglasses are treated to filter out ultraviolet radiation. However, poor quality lenses cause pupil dilation, thereby absorbing more ultraviolet light than they would if no sunglasses were worn. Excessive ultraviolet light will damage the surface structures and lens of the eye.

Prickly Heat Prickly heat is an itchy rash caused by excessive perspiration trapped under the skin. It usually strikes people who have just arrived in a hot climate and whose pores have not yet opened sufficiently to cope with greater sweating. Keeping cool but bathing often, using a mild talcum powder or even resorting to air-conditioning may help until you acclimatise.

Heat Exhaustion Dehydration or salt deficiency can cause heat exhaustion. Take time to acclimatise to high temperatures and make sure you get sufficient liquids. Wear loose clothing and a broad-brimmed hat. Do not do anything too physically demanding.

Salt deficiency is characterised by fatigue, lethargy, headaches, giddiness and muscle cramps and in this case salt tablets may help. Vomiting or diarrhoea can deplete your liquid and salt levels. Anhydrotic heat exhaustion, caused by an inability to sweat, is quite rare. Unlike the other forms of heat exhaustion it is likely to strike people who have been in a hot climate for some time, rather than newcomers.

Heatstroke This serious and sometimes fatal condition can occur if the body's heat-regulating mechanism breaks down and the body temperature rises to dangerous levels. Long, continuous periods of exposure to high temperatures can leave you vulnerable to heat stroke. You should drink lots of water and avoid excessive alcohol or strenuous activity when you first arrive in a hot climate.

The symptoms are feeling unwell, not sweating very much or at all and a high body temperature (39°C to 41°C). Where sweating has ceased the skin becomes flushed and red. Severe, throbbing headaches and lack of coordination will also occur, and the sufferer may be confused or aggressive. Eventually the victim will become delirious or convulse. Hospitalisation is essential, but meanwhile get victims out of the sun, remove their clothing, cover them with a wet sheet or towel and then fan continually.

Fungal Infections Fungal infections, which occur with greater frequency in hot weather, are most likely to occur on the scalp, between the toes or fingers (athlete's foot), in the groin (jock itch or crotch rot) and on the body (ringworm). You get ringworm (which is a fungal infection, not a worm) from infected animals or by walking on damp areas, like shower floors.

To prevent fungal infections wear loose, comfortable clothes, avoid artificial fibres, wash frequently and dry carefully. If you do get an infection, wash the infected area daily with a disinfectant or medicated soap and water, and rinse and dry well. Apply an anti-fungal cream or powder like the widely available Tinaderm. Try to expose the infected area to air or sunlight as much as possible and wash all towels and underwear in hot water as well as changing them often.

Motion Sickness Eating lightly before and during a trip will reduce the chances of motion sickness. If you are prone to motion sickness try to find a place that minimises disturbance – near the wing on aircraft, close to midships on boats, near the centre on buses. Fresh air usually helps; reading and cigarette smoke don't. Commercial motion-sickness preparations, which can cause drowsiness, have to be taken before the trip commences; when you're feeling sick it's too late. Ginger (available in capsule form) and peppermint (including mint-flavoured sweets) are natural preventatives.

Jet Lag Jet lag is experienced when a person travels by air across more than three time zones (each time zone usually represents a one-hour time difference). It occurs because many of the functions of the human body (such as temperature, pulse rate and empty-ing of the bladder and bowels) are regulated by internal 24-hour cycles called circadian rhythms. When we travel long distances rapidly, our bodies take time to adjust to the 'new time' of our destination, and we may experience fatigue, disorientation, insomnia, anxiety, impaired concentration and loss of appetite. These effects will usually be gone within three days of arrival, but there are ways of minimising the impact of jet lag:

- Rest for a couple of days prior to departure; try to avoid late nights and last-minute dashes for travellers' cheques, passport etc.
- Try to select flight schedules that minimise sleep deprivation; arriving late in the day means you can go to sleep soon after you arrive. For very long flights, try to organise a stopover.
- Avoid excessive eating (which bloats the stomach) and alcohol (which causes dehydration) during the flight. Instead, drink plenty of noncarbonated, nonalcoholic drinks such as fruit juice or water.
- Avoid smoking, as this reduces the amount of

oxygen in the aeroplane cabin even further and causes greater fatigue.

- Make yourself comfortable by wearing loose-fitting clothes and perhaps bringing an eye mask and ear plugs to help you sleep.

Infectious Diseases

Diarrhoea A change of water, food or climate can all cause the runs; diarrhoea caused by contaminated food or water is more serious. Despite all your precautions you may still get a mild bout of travellers' diarrhoea, but a few rushed toilet trips with no other symptoms is not indicative of a serious problem. Moderate diarrhoea, involving half-a-dozen loose movements in a day, is more of a nuisance. Dehydration is the main danger with any diarrhoea, particularly for children where dehydration can occur quite quickly. Fluid replacement remains the mainstay of management. Weak black tea with a little sugar, soda water, or soft drinks allowed to go flat and diluted 50% with water are all good. With severe diarrhoea a rehydrating solution is necessary to replace minerals and salts. Commercially available ORS (oral rehydration salts) are very useful; add the contents of one sachet to a litre of boiled or bottled water. In an emergency you can make up a solution of eight teaspoons of sugar to a litre of boiled water and provide salted cracker biscuits at the same time. You should stick to a bland diet as you recover.

Lomotil or Imodium can be used to bring relief from the symptoms, although they do not actually cure the problem. Only use these drugs if absolutely necessary – eg if you *must* travel. For children under 12 years Lomotil and Imodium are not recommended. Under all circumstances fluid replacement is the most important thing to remember. Do not use these drugs if the person has a high fever or is severely dehydrated.

In certain situations the need for antibiotics may be indicated by:

- Watery diarrhoea with blood and mucous. (Gut-paralysing drugs like Imodium or Lomotil should be avoided in this situation.)
- Watery diarrhoea with fever and lethargy.

- Persistent diarrhoea not improving after 48 hours.
- Severe diarrhoea, if it is logistically difficult to stay in one place.

The recommended drugs (for adults only) would be either norfloxacin 400 mg twice daily for three days or ciprofloxacin 500 mg twice daily for three days.

The drug bismuth subsalicylate has also been used successfully. It is not available in Australia. The dosage for adults is two tablets or 30 ml and for children it is one tablet or 10 ml. This dose can be repeated every 30 minutes to one hour, with no more than eight doses in a 24-hour period.

The drug of choice in children would be co-trimoxazole (Bactrim, Septrin, Resprim) with dosage dependent on weight. A five-day course is given.

Ampicillin has been recommended in the past and may still be an alternative.

Giardiasis The parasite causing this intestinal disorder is present in contaminated water. The symptoms are stomach cramps, nausea, a bloated stomach, watery, foul-smelling diarrhoea and frequent gas. Giardiasis can appear several weeks after you have been exposed to the parasite. The symptoms may disappear for a few days and then return; this can go on for several weeks. Tinidazole, known as Fasigyn, or metronidazole (Flagyl) are the recommended drugs for treatment. Either can be used in a single treatment dose.

Dysentery This serious illness is caused by contaminated food or water and is characterised by severe diarrhoea, often with blood or mucus in the stool. There are two kinds of dysentery. Bacillary dysentery is characterised by a high fever and rapid onset; headache, vomiting and stomach pains are other symptoms. It generally does not last longer than a week, but it is highly contagious.

Amoebic dysentery is often more gradual in the onset of symptoms, with cramping abdominal pain and vomiting less likely; fever may not be present. This is not a self-limiting disease: it will persist until treated and can recur and cause long-term health problems.

A stool test is necessary to diagnose which kind of dysentery you have, so you should seek medical help urgently. In case of an emergency the drugs norfloxacin or ciprofloxacin can be used as presumptive treatment for bacillary dysentery, and metronidazole (Flagyl) for amoebic dysentery.

For bacillary dysentery, norfloxacin 400 mg twice daily for seven days or ciprofloxacin 500 mg twice daily for seven days are the recommended dosages.

If you're unable to find either of these drugs then a useful alternative is cotrimoxazole 160/800 mg (Bactrim, Septrin, Resprim) twice daily for seven days. This is a sulpha drug and must not be used by people with a known sulpha allergy.

In the case of children the drug cotrimoxazole is a reasonable first-line treatment. For amoebic dysentery, the recommended adult dosage of metronidazole (Flagyl) is one 750 mg to 800 mg capsule three times daily for five days. Children aged between eight and 12 years should have half the adult dose; the dosage for younger children is one-third the adult dose.

An alternative to Flagyl is Fasigyn, taken as a two-gram daily dose for three days. Alcohol must be avoided during treatment and for 48 hours afterwards.

Viral Gastroenteritis This is caused not by bacteria but, as the name suggests, by a virus. It is characterised by stomach cramps, diarrhoea, and sometimes by vomiting and/or a slight fever. All you can do is rest and drink lots of fluids.

Hepatitis Hepatitis is a general term for inflammation of the liver. There are many causes of this condition: drugs, alcohol and infections are but a few.

The discovery of new strains has led to a virtual alphabet soup, with hepatitis A, B, C, D, E, G and others. These letters identify specific agents that cause viral hepatitis. Viral hepatitis is an infection of the liver, which can lead to jaundice (yellow skin),

fever, lethargy and digestive problems. It can have no symptoms at all, with the infected person not knowing that they have the disease. Travellers shouldn't be too paranoid about this apparent proliferation of hepatitis strains; hep C, D, E and G are fairly rare (so far) and following the same precautions as for A and B should be all that's necessary to avoid them.

Viral hepatitis can be divided into two groups on the basis of how it is spread. The first route of transmission is via contaminated food and water (leading to hepatitis A and E) and the second is via blood and bodily fluids (resulting in hepatitis B, C and D).

Hepatitis A This is a very common disease in most countries, especially those with poor standards of sanitation. Most people in developing countries are infected as children; they often don't develop symptoms, but do develop life-long immunity. The disease poses a real threat to the traveller, as people are unlikely to have been exposed to hepatitis A in developed countries.

The symptoms are fever, chills, headache, fatigue, feelings of weakness and aches and pains, followed by loss of appetite, nausea, vomiting, abdominal pain, dark urine, light-coloured faeces, jaundiced skin and the whites of the eyes may turn yellow. In some cases you may feel unwell, tired, have no appetite, experience aches and pains and be jaundiced. You should seek medical advice, but in general there is not much you can do apart from resting, drinking lots of fluids, eating lightly and avoiding fatty foods. People who have had hepatitis must forego alcohol for six months after the illness, as hepatitis attacks the liver and it needs that amount of time to recover.

The routes of transmission are via contaminated water, shellfish contaminated by sewerage, or foodstuffs sold by food handlers with poor standards of hygiene.

Taking care with what you eat and drink can go a long way towards preventing this disease. But this is a very infectious virus, so if there is any risk of exposure, additional cover is highly recommended. This cover comes in two forms: Gammaglobulin and Havrix. Gammaglobulin is an injection where you are given the antibodies for hepatitis A, which provide immunity for a limited time. Havrix is a vaccine which allows you to develop your own antibodies and gives lasting immunity.

Hepatitis E This is a very recently discovered virus, of which little is yet known. It appears to be rather common in developing countries, generally causing mild hepatitis, although it can be very serious in pregnant women.

Care with water supplies is the only current prevention. As there are no specific vaccines for this type of hepatitis. At present it doesn't appear to be too great a risk for travellers.

The following strains are spread by contact with blood and bodily fluids:

Hepatitis B This is also a very common disease, with almost 300 million chronic carriers in the world. Hepatitis B, which used to be called serum hepatitis, is spread through contact with infected blood, blood products or bodily fluids, for example through sexual contact, unsterilised needles and blood transfusions, or via small breaks in the skin. Other risk situations include having a shave or tattoo in a local shop, or having your body pierced. The symptoms of type B are much the same as type A except that they are more severe and may lead to irreparable liver damage or even liver cancer. Although there is no treatment for hepatitis B, a cheap and effective vaccine is available; the only problem is that for long-lasting cover you need a six-month course. People who should receive a hepatitis B vaccination include those who anticipate contact with blood or other bodily secretions, either as a health-care worker or through sexual contact with the local population and particularly those who intend to stay in the country for a long period of time.

Hepatitis C This is another recently defined virus. It is a concern because it seems to lead to liver disease more rapidly than hepatitis B.

The virus is spread by contact with blood – usually via contaminated transfusions or shared needles. Avoiding these is the only means of prevention, as there is no available vaccine.

Hepatitis D Often referred to as the 'Delta' virus, this infection only occurs in chronic carriers of hepatitis B. It is transmitted by blood and bodily fluids. Again there is no vaccine for this virus, so avoidance is the best prevention. The risk to travellers is certainly limited.

Typhoid Typhoid fever is another gut infection that travels the faecal-oral route – ie contaminated water and food are responsible. Vaccination against typhoid is not totally effective and it is one of the most dangerous infections, so medical help must be sought.

In its early stages typhoid resembles many other illnesses: sufferers may feel like they have a bad cold or flu on the way, as early symptoms are a headache, a sore throat, and a fever which rises a little each day until it is around 40°C or more. The victim's pulse is often slow relative to the degree of fever present and gets slower as the fever rises – unlike a normal fever where the pulse increases. There may also be vomiting, diarrhoea or constipation.

In the second week the high fever and slow pulse continue and a few pink spots may appear on the body; trembling, delirium, weakness, weight loss and dehydration are other symptoms. If there are no further complications, the fever and other symptoms will slowly diminish during the third week. However, you must get medical help before this because pneumonia (acute infection of the lungs) or peritonitis (perforated bowel) are common complications, and because typhoid is very infectious.

The fever should be treated by keeping the victim cool and dehydration should also be watched for.

The drug of choice is ciprofloxacin at a dose of one gram daily for 14 days. It is quite expensive and may not be available. The alternative, chloramphenicol, has been the mainstay of treatment for many years. In many countries it is still the recommended antibiotic but there are fewer side affects with Ampicillin. The adult dosage is two 250-mg capsules, four times a day. Children aged between eight and 12 years should have half the adult dose; younger children should have one-third the adult dose.

People who are allergic to penicillin should not be given Ampicillin.

Worms These parasites are most common in rural, tropical areas and a stool test when you return home is not a bad idea. They can be present on unwashed vegetables or in undercooked meat and you can pick them up through your skin by walking in bare feet. Infestations may not show up for some time, and although they are generally not serious, if left untreated they can cause severe health problems. A stool test is necessary in order to pinpoint the problem, and medication is often available over the counter.

Tetanus This potentially fatal disease is found worldwide, occurring more commonly in undeveloped tropical areas. It is difficult to treat but is preventable with immunisation. Tetanus occurs when a wound becomes infected by a germ which lives in soil and in the faeces of horses and other animals, so clean all cuts, punctures or animal bites. Tetanus is also known as lockjaw, and the first symptom may be discomfort in swallowing, or stiffening of the jaw and neck; this is followed by painful convulsions of the jaw and whole body.

Tuberculosis (TB) Tuberculosis is a bacterial infection which is widespread in many developing countries. It is usually transmitted from person to person by coughing, but may be transmitted through consumption of unpasteurised milk. Milk that has been boiled is safe to drink, and the souring of milk to make yoghurt or cheese also kills the bacilli. Typically many months of contact with the infected person are required before the disease is passed on so it is not considered a serious risk to travellers. The usual site of the disease is the lungs, although other organs may be involved. Most infected people never develop symptoms. In those who do, especially infants, symptoms may arise within weeks of the infection occurring and may be severe. In most, however, the disease lies dormant for many years until, for some reason, the infected person becomes physically run-down. Symptoms include fever, weight loss, night sweats and coughing. Vaccination against tuberculosis may prevent serious disease so is recommended especially for young children who are likely to be heavily exposed to infected people.

Diphtheria Fiji has a little diphtheria, although most people are vaccinated against the disease. Diphtheria can be a skin infection or a more dangerous throat infection. It is spread by contaminated dust contacting the skin or by the inhalation of infected

cough or sneeze droplets. Frequent washing and keeping the skin dry will help prevent skin infection. The mainstay of treatment of the diphtheria throat infection is an intravenous infusion of diphtheria antitoxin. The antitoxin is produced in horses so may be associated with allergic reactions in some people. Because of this it must be administered under close medical supervision. Antibiotics such as erythromycin or penicillin are then given to eradicate the diphtheria bacteria from the patient so that it is not transmitted to others. A vaccination is available to prevent the throat infection.

Sexually Transmitted Diseases Sexual contact with an infected sexual partner spreads these diseases. While abstinence is the only 100% preventative, using condoms is also effective. Gonorrhoea, herpes and syphilis are the most common of these diseases; sores, blisters or rashes around the genitals, discharges or pain when urinating are common symptoms. Symptoms may be less marked or not observed at all in women. Syphilis symptoms eventually disappear completely but the disease continues and can cause severe problems in later years. The treatment of gonorrhoea and syphilis is with antibiotics.

There are numerous other sexually transmitted diseases, for most of which effective treatment is available. However, there is no cure for herpes and there is also currently no cure for AIDS.

Fiji, as in many Pacific island countries, has high STD rates compared to Australia and New Zealand. The human papilloma virus, an STD associated with cervical cancer, is almost epidemic in Fiji.

HIV/AIDS HIV, the Human Immunodeficiency Virus, may develop into AIDS, Acquired Immune Deficiency Syndrome. HIV is a major problem in many countries.

Any exposure to blood, blood products or bodily fluids may put the individual at risk. In many developing countries transmission is predominantly through heterosexual sexual activity. This is quite different from industrialised countries where transmission is mostly through contact between homosexual or bisexual males, or via contaminated needles shared by intravenous drug users. Apart from abstinence, the most effective preventative is always to practise safe sex using condoms. It is impossible to detect the HIV-positive status of an otherwise healthy-looking person without a blood test.

HIV/AIDS can also be spread through infected blood transfusions; some developing countries cannot afford to screen blood for transfusions. It can also be spread by dirty needles – vaccinations, acupuncture, tattooing and ear or nose piercing can be potentially as dangerous as intravenous drug use if the equipment is not clean. If you do need an injection, ask to see the syringe unwrapped in front of you, or better still, take a needle and syringe pack with you overseas – it is a cheap insurance package against infection with HIV.

Fear of HIV infection should never preclude treatment for serious medical conditions. Although there may be a risk of infection, it is very small indeed.

Insect-Borne Diseases

Fiji is malaria free, though some neighbouring countries, such as Vanuatu, have the disease. Obtain a doctor's advice about antimalarials if you also plan to visit such countries.

Dengue Fever Dengue can be dangerous for the elderly and can kill infants. The arboviral disease complex includes dengue fever, dengue haemorrhagic fever and its subsequent dengue shock syndrome. There is no prophylactic available for this mosquito-spread disease; the main preventative measure is to avoid mosquito bites, especially when epidemics are reported. A sudden onset of fever, headaches and severe joint and muscle pains are the first signs before a rash starts on the trunk of the body and spreads to the limbs and face. The rash can be unbearably itchy and children may need to be bandaged so they won't scratch

their skin raw. After a further few days, the fever will subside and recovery will begin.

The patient should rest, drink lots of water to avoid dehydration, and take codeine to ease the aches. Depression is a symptom for some and dengue sufferers are notoriously grumpy and rude to their carers. Serious complications are not common but full recovery can take up to a month or more. Visitors may catch it and not get sick until they've left the country. Doctors in other countries may not know how to deal with dengue.

Filariasis This is a mosquito-transmitted parasitic infection which is found in many parts of Africa, Asia, Central and South America and the Pacific. There is a range of possible manifestations of the infection, depending on which filarial parasite species has caused the infection. These include fever, pain and swelling of the lymph glands; inflammation of lymph drainage areas; swelling of a limb or the scrotum; skin rashes and blindness. Treatment is available to eliminate the parasites from the body, but some of the damage they cause may not be reversible. Medical advice should be obtained promptly if the infection is suspected. In Fiji the disease is prevalent in the wet south-east sides of coastal areas of the larger islands, as well as in some small island communities.

Cuts, Bites & Stings

Cuts & Scratches Skin punctures can easily become infected in hot climates and may be difficult to heal. Treat any cut with an antiseptic such as povidone-iodine and try to keep flies away. Where possible avoid bandages and Band-aids, which can keep wounds wet. If the sore is not healing and starts spreading, consult a doctor as antibiotics will probably be needed.

Coral cuts are notoriously slow to heal and if they are not adequately cleaned small pieces of coral can become embedded in the wound. Avoid coral cuts by wearing shoes when walking on reefs, and clean any cut thoroughly with sodium peroxide if available.

Bites & Stings Bee and wasp stings are usually painful rather than dangerous. Calamine lotion or Stingose spray will give relief and ice packs will reduce the pain and swelling or ask locals for traditional remedies. There are some spiders with dangerous bites but antivenenes are usually available.

Certain cone shells found in Australia and the Pacific can sting dangerously or even fatally. There are various fish and other sea creatures which can sting or bite dangerously or which are dangerous to eat (refer to Food in Basic Rules above). Again, local advice is the best advice.

Snakes Fiji's most common snake is the *dadakulaci*, or banded sea krait, and you are likely to see it when snorkelling or diving. Although placid, its venom is three times more potent than that of the Indian cobra. The yellow-bellied sea snake can be aggressive, and the burrowing snake is venomous but seldom seen. To minimise your chances of being bitten do not approach any sea snake, and wear boots, socks and long trousers when walking through undergrowth where snakes may be present. Don't put your hands into holes and crevices, and be careful when collecting firewood.

Snake bites do not cause instantaneous death, and antivenenes are usually available. Keep the victim calm and still, wrap the bitten limb tightly, as you would for a sprained ankle, and then attach a splint to immobilise it. Then seek medical help, if possible with the dead snake for identification. Don't attempt to catch the snake if there is even a remote possibility of being bitten again. Tourniquets and sucking out the poison are now comprehensively discredited.

Jellyfish Local advice is the best way of avoiding contact with these sea creatures, which have stinging tentacles. Stings from most jellyfish are rather painful. Dousing in vinegar will de-activate any stingers which

have not 'fired'. Calamine lotion, antihistamines and analgesics may reduce the reaction and relieve the pain.

Bedbugs & Lice Bedbugs live in various places, but particularly in dirty mattresses and bedding. Spots of blood on bedclothes or on the wall around the bed can be read as a suggestion to find another hotel. Bedbugs leave itchy bites in neat rows. Calamine lotion or Stingose spray may help.

All lice cause itching and discomfort. They make themselves at home in your hair (head lice), your clothing (body lice) or in your pubic hair (crabs). You catch lice through direct contact with infected people or by sharing combs, clothing and the like. Powder or shampoo treatment will kill the lice and infected clothing should then be washed in very hot water.

Leeches & Ticks Leeches may be present in damp rainforest conditions; they attach themselves to your skin to suck your blood. Trekkers often get them on their legs or in their boots. Salt or a lighted cigarette end will make them fall off. Do not pull them off, as the bite is then more likely to become infected. An insect repellent may keep them away. You should always check your body if you have been walking through a potentially tick-infested area as ticks can cause skin infections and other more serious diseases. If a tick is found attached, press down around the tick's head with tweezers, grab the head and gently pull upwards. Avoid pulling the rear of the body as this may squeeze the tick's gut contents through the attached mouth parts into the skin, increasing the risk of infection and disease. Smearing chemicals on the tick will not make it let go and is not recommended.

Women's Health
Gynaecological Problems Poor diet, lowered resistance due to the use of antibiotics for stomach upsets and even contraceptive pills can lead to vaginal infections when travelling in hot climates. Maintaining good personal hygiene, and

wearing skirts or loose-fitting trousers and cotton underwear will help to prevent infections.

Yeast infections, characterised by a rash, itch and discharge, can be treated with a vinegar or lemon-juice douche, or with yoghurt. Nystatin, miconazole or clotrimazole suppositories are the usual medical prescription.

Trichomoniasis and gardnerella are more serious infections; symptoms are a smelly discharge and sometimes a burning sensation when urinating. Male sexual partners must also be treated, and if a vinegar-water douche is not effective medical attention should be sought. Metronidazole (Flagyl) is the prescribed drug.

Pregnancy Most miscarriages occur during the first three months of pregnancy, so this is the most risky time to travel as far as your own health is concerned. Miscarriage is not uncommon, and can occasionally lead to severe bleeding. The last three months should also be spent within reasonable distance of good medical care.

A baby born as early as 24 weeks stands a chance of survival, but only in a good modern hospital. Pregnant women should avoid all unnecessary medication, but vaccinations and malarial prophylactics should still be taken where possible. Additional care should be taken to prevent illness and particular attention should be paid to diet and nutrition. Alcohol and nicotine, for example, should be avoided.

WOMEN TRAVELLERS
Attitudes to Women
Domestic violence is quite a problem in Fiji. There has been a campaign to curb this and you will see 'real men don't hit women' stickers in public areas and buses. The problem is found in both the Fiji Indian and indigenous Fijian communities.

In general, female travellers should have nothing to fear from men in Fiji, especially if you are travelling with a partner. Unfortunately, however, some men will assume you are fair game if travelling alone; several

female readers have complained of being annoyed and harassed. One found Suva 'a complete hellhole', as she couldn't walk on her own after dark without being remarked at and grabbed.

I really did find visiting Nadi and Lautoka during the day a hassle, with Indian men deliberately blocking my path, or stretching out to lightly grab my arm as I walked. Likewise, an afternoon spent alone on the beach at Pacific Harbour was full of hassles – the calls of 'Hello' and 'Where are you from' were not just innocent greetings, but led to offers of movies and visits to houses etc. It made me uncomfortable either to deal with or ignore these comments.

Y Bennet

Another wrote:

Fiji is very difficult for a single, White woman. I was harassed by men, constantly. The Fijian men wanted to talk to me, to know where I was from and what I thought of Fiji. The Indian men wanted me to marry them, go to the beach with them etc. One man told me he would meet me in my hotel room. Fortunately, by this time I had learned to lie and was very rude to him...I was never physically touched by the men...cab drivers, store clerks and even minibus drivers lied to me, always telling me I had to pay more. I realise that this is part of their culture, but it gets extremely annoying. I felt like I had to be on the defensive all the time.

A Whittier

You may even strike the opposite problem of being totally ignored, especially by Indian men. If you get a blank response when trying to get information or buy a ticket, seek help from someone who does acknowledge your existence.

If you become uncomfortable or bored in a male-dominated situation, such as an evening around the yaqona bowl, seek the company of Fijian women instead, and you will see another side of village life (see the Dos and Don'ts section in the Facts about the Country chapter).

Safety Precautions
Ask local women for practical advice if you are unsure of how to act, or if any male behaviour towards you is making you uncomfortable. Here are a few tips:

- Don't hitchhike alone.
- Avoid walking at night through dimly lit streets, especially in Nadi and Suva.
- Don't go drinking with Fijian men, however friendly they are to begin with. It's rare but the friendliness may be false and you could end up losing your wallet. Unfortunately the likelihood of a Fijian man becoming violent rises dramatically if he is drunk.
- Wearing a wedding ring may deter unwelcome comments or advances.
- Draw the curtains! There are 'window shoppers' or peeping toms in some rural areas. If a man is interested in a woman he may come to her window at night. Evidently there is no need to be distressed, but it can give a fright! Just tell him to go away.

What to Wear

The Fijian dress code is conservative, especially in the rural areas. Indian women generally wear long saris and Fijians big floral caftans down to the ankles. A woman in short skirts, brief shorts or sleeveless tops is unusual and such dress is considered inappropriate except in resorts or in Suva where attitudes are changing. To avoid hassles respect the local dress code. Refer to the Dos & Don'ts section for local attitudes to dress and behaviour.

Organisations

There are several women's organisations in Suva where you might be able to meet local women, including:

Fiji Women's Crisis Centre
88 Gordon St, Suva (☎ 313 300)
Fiji WIP Project – National Council of Women
30 Clarke St, Suva (☎ 311 880)
Fiji Women's Federation for World Peace
52 Raisara Rd, Rarawai (384 226)
Women's Action for Change
16 Goodenough St, Suva. (☎ 314 363)
Fiji Women's Rights Movement
88 Narseys Building, Renwick Rd, Suva (☎ 313 156). This prominent community organisation deals with things like domestic violence, women in trade unions and women's legal rights. It also assists rape victims.

GAY & LESBIAN TRAVELLERS

While homosexuality is outlawed in Fiji, socially it is tolerated as long as it's kept private. There are some resorts which are decidedly gay unfriendly (notably Turtle Island) and one which targets the gay and lesbian market (Man Friday on the Coral Coast). Some of the bars in Suva are also gay friendly.

There are words for male and female homosexuality in Fijian, suggesting that sexuality may not have been an issue until the missionaries came along.

Organisations

For pre-trip planning advice consult the latest *Spartacus International Gay Guide*, *Outrage* magazine, and the ALSO Foundation, or check out www.qrd.org and www.infoqueer.org on the Internet.

DISABLED TRAVELLERS

Disabled people in the Pacific are simply part of the community, looked after by family where necessary, but still expected to play some useful role. In some cities there are schools for disabled children. Access facilities such as ramps, lifts and braille are rare. Airports and some hotels and resorts are accessible. If you are intending to stay at a particular resort, check if they suit your needs. It may be best to be booked in ground-level rooms. Some of the middle and top-end resorts have better wheelchair access than others, but most are designed with multiple levels and lots of stairs.

Alicia Close, a reader who travelled to Fiji with a group of people with various disabilities, highly recommends the Hideaway Resort on the Coral Coast, Viti Levu, for catering to their special needs:

The staff at our hotel...came with us wherever we went to help carry (literally) the people in wheelchairs up stairs, over curbs, into and out of (wheelchair-inaccessible) buses, interisland ferries etc!

Organisations

For pretrip planning advice try the Internet and disabled people's associations in your home country. The Fiji Disabled People's Association (☎ 311 203), 355 Waimanu Rd, Suva, may also be able to provide advice.

SENIOR TRAVELLERS

Fiji is a good place for senior travellers who want to either stay at resorts, take tours, travel in groups or independently. Some travel agents offer group discounts and discounts for those with senior's cards. It is easy to hire vehicles and explore the larger islands, and Fiji is relatively disease-free. For pre-trip planning advice try the Internet and senior traveller's associations in your home country.

TRAVEL WITH CHILDREN

Fiji is a major family destination and is extremely child friendly. Some resorts cater specifically for children with baby-sitting and child-minding services, cots and high chairs, organised activities and children's pools. Other smaller exclusive resorts, however, ban children or relegate them to a specific time period during the year. Some resorts have sand paths which may make life a bit difficult for transporting young children in a stroller. The Fijian on Viti Levu is reportedly great for kids and the Tokatoka Resort Hotel is good if you want to stay near Nadi Airport.

Ignoring resorts and travelling around with kids should also be fairly easy compared to many places. Some car-rental companies will provide baby seats. If you intend to take public transport, a backpack for transporting young children is a good idea. Long-life milk is readily available, as is bottled spring water and fruit juice. Nappies, formula and sterilising solution are readily available in pharmacies and supermarkets in the main cities and towns, but if you are travelling to remote areas or islands it would be best to take your own supplies. Disposable nappies can be bought in any town, but, as they're not really environmentally friendly, try to use cloth nappies wherever you can.

Children are highly valued in Fiji, and child care is seen as the responsibility of the extended family and the community. Everyone will want to talk with your kids and invite them to join activities or visit homes. Fijian men play a large role in caring for children and babies, so don't be surprised if they pay the kids a lot of attention. Fijian children are expected to be obedient and happy and spend lots of time playing outdoors. Backchat and showing off is seen as disruptive to the fabric of the community. So when visiting a village try to curb your children's crying, tantrums and noisy behaviour.

Lonely Planet's *Travel With Children* has useful advice on family travel, and has a section on Fiji.

DANGERS & ANNOYANCES

Crime, theft and assault are unfortunately on the increase in Fiji. Be careful when walking around at night, even as a couple. While it is still relatively safe, assault of travellers in Nadi is becoming more common. Don't hitchhike alone. (See the Women Travellers section earlier). Use a money belt and keep your valuables in a safe place. Travellers are sometimes asked on the street if they want drugs – ignore such questions.

Sword sellers are not as common as they used to be, since the FVB have tried to curtail the practice. If anyone becomes overly friendly, wants to know your life story and begins carving your name on a piece of wood, just walk away, even if they pursue you claiming that you have to pay for the rubbishy item.

If you are unlucky enough to be caught in a natural disaster such as a cyclone or flood, ask the advice of locals. Another annoyance includes developing tropical ulcers from something as simple as a mosquito bite or scratch.

If you are travelling for an extended period you may tire of being asked 'where are you from' followed by 'where are you staying'. While this is often just innocent conversation, it is also a way of judging how much you are paying or willing to pay.

In some areas at peak season, the sheer number of tourists may be a nuisance.

Swimming

Contrary to Fiji's image overseas, many beaches, especially on the large islands, aren't that great for swimming. Coral reefs can become shallow at low tide. Be careful of currents and tidal changes when swimming and snorkelling, and avoid swimming alone. Always seek local advice on conditions. At some locations, at some times of the year, sea lice or stingers can be annoying.

Some of the most beautiful sea creatures such as the scorpion fish and lion fish are also highly venomous. Keep your hands to yourself! Sea urchins, crown-of-thorns starfish and stone fish can be poisonous or cause infections. Eels hide in coral crevices and can be dangerous, jelly fish and fire coral can cause nasty stings, cone shells often have a tiny harpoon containing venom, barracuda may bite, and sea snakes have a venomous bite.

Shark attacks on divers and snorkellers are rare in Fiji. We did hear of a shark attack on a local spear fisher carrying the day's catch around his waist! Avoid places near wastewater outlets (especially where people have been cleaning fish), the mouths of rivers or murky waters. If you are lucky enough to see a shark, move away calmly. Reef sharks don't normally attack humans for food, but they can be territorial.

LEGAL MATTERS

The only drug you are likely to come across is marijuana. Don't seek it out, and in the city don't buy any – the risk is too high. It is not uncommon for drug users in Fiji to be imprisoned in the lunatic asylum. It is illegal to drink and drive. Refer also to the Customs and Gay & Lesbian sections.

BUSINESS HOURS

Fijians are not known for their punctuality, often adhering to 'Fiji time'. However, most businesses open from 8 am to 5 pm, Monday to Friday, with some opening on Saturday from 8 am to 1 pm. Government offices are open Monday to Thursday from 8 am to 4.30 pm (4 pm on Fridays). Many places close for lunch from 1 to 2 pm. The Sunday observance's ban on trading, enforced after the coup, has now been lifted. But still practically nothing happens on Sunday and for

Fijians it is a day for church, rest and spending time with the family. Resorts are often exempt, but activities may be restricted.

PUBLIC HOLIDAYS & SPECIAL EVENTS

Fijians celebrate a great variety of holidays and festivals:

1 January
New Year's Day holiday. Celebrated all over Fiji. In villages festivities sometimes last all of the first week in villages or even the whole month of January.

February or March
Hindu Holi or Festival of Colours. People squirt coloured water at each other; it is best observed in Lautoka.

March
National Youth Day holiday

March or April
Ram Naumi (Birth of Lord Rama). A Hindu religious festival and party on the shores of Suva Bay.
Good Friday and Easter Monday holidays

May
Ratu Sir Lala Sukuna Day holiday. Commemorates the man considered Fiji's greatest statesman, soldier, high chief and scholar. Includes cultural shows and games.

June
Queen's Birthday holiday

July
Bula Festival – Nadi
Constitution Day holiday
Prophet Mohammed's Birthday holiday

August
Hibiscus Festival. Held in Suva; lots of floats and processions.
Hindu ritual fire walking performed by South Indians in many of their temples.

August or September
Birth of Lord Krishna

September
Sugar Festival – Lautoka

early October
Fiji Day (Independence Day)

October or November
Diwali Festival holidays or Festival of Lights. Hindus worship Lakshmi (goddess of wealth and prosperity), houses are decorated and business settled.

25 & 26 December
Christmas Day and Boxing Day

Refer to the Religion section in Facts about the Country for further information on Indian festivals.

ACTIVITIES

Your trip to Fiji can be as active or inactive as you like. Laze around and do very little, or alternatively pack in lots of different activities.

Cycling

Fiji is a great place for mountain-bike tours, or for the independent cyclist, and cycling is a good way to explore Viti Levu, Vanua Levu, parts of Ovalau and Taveuni. Apart from the Kings and Queens roads, most roads, especially inland, are rough, hilly and unsealed, so mountain bikes are the best option. Watch the traffic, there are lots of mad drivers! It can be hot so make sure you carry plenty of water to avoid dehydration. The best time to go would be in the 'drier' season, and note that the east side of the islands receive higher rainfall. Take waterproof gear and a repair kit to be self-sufficient as it is difficult to get bike parts in Fiji. Maps are available from the Department of Lands & Survey in Suva.

Some resorts have bikes for hire. Expect to pay about F$8 for a half day. Independent Tours, in Korovou near Sigatoka, run guided mountain-bike tours on Viti Levu, including half day/day tours for F$39/69. Three-day/two-night trips to the highlands are F$275, and an annual eight-day trip around Viti Levu costs F$385. Mountain bikes provided are 21-speed and there is a 15% discount if you bring your own. Food and drinks are carried in a support truck. Refer to the Viti Levu chapter for more details.

Trekking

It is culturally offensive for people to simply trek anywhere – they need to ask permission, be invited or go on a tour. For more details see the Society & Conduct section in the Facts about the Country chapter, or Camping under Accommodation later in this chapter. Travellers should ask local villagers or staff at their hotel to organise permission and a guide. It is best to go trekking in the dry season when it won't be so muddy. Always make sure people know where you are heading in case you get lost or have an accident. Good boots are essential and carry plenty of water, good maps, a compass, a warm jumper and a waterproof coat.

Viti Levu and Taveuni are the best islands for trekking and Kadavu is more isolated but equally beautiful. Colo-i-Suva Forest Park on Viti Levu and the Lavena Coastal Walk and Bouma Falls on Taveuni Island are two good trekking places that have marked trails and don't require guides. Other good places for trekking are Taveuni's Lake Tagimaucia, Mt Tomanivi on Viti Levu near Nadarivatu, and Abaca National Park and Mt Koroyanitu near Lautoka. For an easy but scenic walk follow the Coral Coast Scenic Railway from the Fijian Resort to the beautiful Natadola beach. If you will be in Fiji for a month or so, consider contacting the Rucksack Club in Suva. Many companies organise trekking to Viti Levu's highlands, including Rosie Tours, Peni's Inland Adventures, and German International Eco-Touring. On the Suva side of Viti Levu, Discover Fiji Tours also have one and three-day treks. The tours offer different standards of service but expect to pay about F$50 to F$60 for a day trip, and up to F$100 a day for longer trips of four to six days. Refer to the Viti Levu and Taveuni chapters.

Village Visits

Avoid visiting villages on Sunday as this is considered a day for church and rest. Most tours will include a village visit with the obligatory kava presentation. Navala, in Viti

Bure building is a skill handed down from father to son

Levu's highlands, is the most picturesque village. Refer to the Dos & Don'ts section under Society & Conduct in the Facts about the Country chapter.

Archaeological Sites

Fiji has a number of fascinating archaeological sites. The Tavuni Hill Fort near Sigatoka is the only site set up for visitors. There are also many ring-ditch sites in the Sigatoka Valley and Rewa Delta. Labasa has a ceremonial *naga* site (a stone enclosure where religious rites were carried out), and Nukubolu near Savusavu has the remains of an extensive village and pools with hot spring water. In Taveuni the old Vuda village defensive site is partly on Vatuwiri Farm Resort land.

Bird-Watching

The best places for bird-watching are Taveuni and Kadavu islands. Taveuni has a better infrastructure than Kadavu, and is cheaper and easier to travel around. Colo-i-Suva Forest Park near Suva on Viti Levu is also a good spot. *Birds of the Fiji Bush*, by Fergus Clunie & Pauline Morse, Fiji Museum, 1984, is a good reference.

Horse Riding

There are a few places in Fiji where horse riding is an organised activity. Ratuva's, near Sigatoga on Viti Levu's Coral Coast, charges F$15 to F$20 per hour. At Vatuwiri and Nomui Lala resorts in Southern Taveuni a four-hour ride through rainforest to a volcanic crater costs about F$25 per person.

Surfing

Surfing over crystal-clear reefs and warm turquoise-blue waters can make for a very special experience. It is believed that surfing has existed in Fiji for hundreds of years. Winter is the best time to go due to low pressures bringing in big surf, but if you want to stay at popular surf resorts such as Tavarua, book well in advance. Most of Fiji's coral reefs are not suitable for surfing and the majority of surf breaks are on offshore reefs, normally requiring boat trips. When choosing accommodation also consider the price of getting to the surf.

The best surf spots are in barrier-reef passages – where powerful swells from the open ocean break onto the reefs – along southern Viti Levu (Frigates Passage south of Yanuca Island near Beqa Lagoon) and along eastern Viti Levu (Malolo and Wilkes passages in the southern Mamanuca group).

Accommodation near the breaks in the southern Mamanucas is available at the Tavarua Island Resort, Namoto Island Resort, and on the mainland at Seashell Surf and Dive Resort. Riding these dangerous reef-breaks should only be attempted by experienced surfers.

There are only a few places on mainland Viti Levu where you can paddle out to the surf, including the beach-break at Club Masa, near the Sigatoka Sand Dunes, and the reef-break near Hideaway Resort on the Coral Coast. Club has budget accommodation, but Hideaway is discontinuing its dormitory rooms. Natadola Beach sometimes has small surf, good for beginners, and Waidroka Bay Resort on the Coral Coast has a couple of breaks half-an-hour's paddle away, or a half-hour boat trip away at Frigates Passage. There is another break near the Suva Lighthouse, but you need a boat to get there. You can also get to Frigates Passage from Pacific Harbour and there is a surf camp on Yanuca Island.

A less known spot is Kadavu Island's Cape Washington, which reportedly has good surf but no place to stay, and there is apparently surf on the passages near Matava, The Great Astrolabe Hideaway on north-east Kadavu. Lavena Point on Taveuni also has rideable waves, but they are reportedly inconsistent. The Little Dolphin Treehouse in Matei hires surfboards at F$15 per day and can arrange surfing trips.

You should be aware that Fijian villages usually have fishing rights to, and basically own, adjacent reefs. Some resorts pay the villages for exclusive rights leading to controversy between competing surfing or diving operations. If you would like to explore lesser known areas you will need the

T RESORT

LEONARDO PINHEIRO

HOLGER LEUE

Beaches
Top: Tokoriki Island, Mamanuca Islands
Middle: Matei, Taveuni
Bottom: Snorkelling, Blue Lagoon cruise, Yasawa Islands

HOLGER LEUE

HOLGER LEUE

HOLGER LEUE

Top Left: Yaqona ceremony, Yasawa Islands
Top Right: Market, Suva
Bottom: Coconut leaf fishing, Yasawa Islands

permission of the local villagers and to respect local traditions.

It is difficult to hire surfboards and it is fairly easy to lose or snap a board. Bring your own (ideally three, with two over two metres). Take a light wet suit or vest for the winter; surfing booties and a helmet are also a good idea.

If you are staying in Fiji for an extended period, contact Ian Muller (☎ 721 866 Nadi) or Ed Lovell (☎ 361 358, Suva) from the Surf Rider's Association. Membership is F$20 per year entitling you to enter surf contests and receive their newsletter.

Windsurfing

Many of the resorts have windsurfers for use by guests. Wave jumpers should consider the surf-break off the Namoto Island Resort, Namoto Island (Magic Island) in the Mamanucas. Refer to the Mamanuca chapter. You will have to take your own board though. One of the owners and managers is wave-jumping champ Mike Waltze.

Another option is to use your sailboard as a means of transportation! We received a letter from a couple who spent seven months travelling through Fiji by sailboard, visiting 40 different islands, camping and staying at budget accommodation along the way.

They sailed from southern Lau to Taveuni, to Vanua Levu, down to Ovalau, around northern Viti Levu to the Mamanucas and along the Yasawas. Obviously only experienced windsurfers should try something like this, and to visit the Lau group you should have a permit. Refer also to the Climate section in the Facts about the Country chapter.

Boat Chartering & Fishing

The reefs and their fishing rights are owned by villages so you cannot just drop a line anywhere; seek permission first. Many of the more expensive resorts specialise in game fishing with boat chartering and fishing tours. Matagi Island Resort, in the Taveuni island group, specialises in salt-water fly fishing. The smaller resorts will also arrange for local boats to take you fishing. Consider

the south-east Trade Winds when choosing the location to go fishing, the leeward sides of the islands are generally calmer. For boat chartering for the Mamanucas, handline fishing and night fishing in Nadi Bay, contact Bay Cruises (☎ 722 696, 720 147), South Sea Cruises (☎ 701 445, 720 095), or for Suva try the Ocean Pacific Club (☎ 304 864; fax 361 577). Also refer to the *Fiji Magic* magazine.

Peter Dunn-Rankin, author of *Fishing the Reefs*, 1994, a guide to top-water spinning in Hawaii and the South Pacific, rates Fiji as the most promising area in the South Pacific for sports fishing. He promotes the 'catch and release' motto, especially for large breeding-age fish.

Rafting

Bilibili (bamboo rafting), canoeing and white-water rafting trips can be made on the Ba River and the Navua River, Viti Levu. Contact Eco Touring Fiji for the Ba River and on the Suva side of Viti Levu, Wilderness Ethnic Adventure Fiji and Discover Fiji Tours. Day trips are F$55 to F$85 per person. A quick but expensive thrill (F$55) is the Shotover Jet through the mangroves at Denarau Island near Nadi.

Sailing

Visitors to Suva can experience old-style sailing on the Fiji Museum's double-hulled canoe *Tabu Tabu Soro*.

Yachties sometimes look for extra people to crew their boats. Approach the marinas, ask around and look on the notice boards. Fiji's marinas include the Suva Yacht Club, Neisau Marina at Lautoka, Vuda Point Marina between Nadi and Lautoka, Levuka Marina on Ovalau, Savusavu Marina on Vanua Levu, and Musket Cove Marina on Plantation Island in the Mamanucas. Designated ports of entry are Suva, Levuka and Lautoka. Refer to the Visas & Documents section earlier in the chapter.

June, July and August is the main yacht season, but there are yacht races and regattas throughout the year.

For organised cruises and charters refer to

the individual island chapters. The Moorings at the Musket Cove Marina hires yachts for sailing around the Mamanucas and Yasawas. A 12m to 15m boat suitable for six people will cost F$880 per day, discounted to F$605 in the low season (January to March when there's a greater chance of squalls and cyclones). Obviously the Fijian reefs require good charts and sailing experience.

Contact individual yacht clubs for further information, and pick up a copy of the *Yacht Help Booklet, Fiji*. A popular reference for sailors is *Landfalls of Paradise – The Guide to Pacific Islands*, by Earl R Hinz, University of Hawaii Press, 1979.

Sea & Dive Kayaking

Sea and dive kayaking is becoming increasingly popular in Fiji. It is a great way of exploring the coast at a gentle pace. Dive kayaks, which can carry lunch, snorkelling gear and scuba gear, can be double the fun. Many of the resorts have kayaks for use by guests, or for hire at about F$20/30 for a half/full day. There are also special kayaking tours available during the drier months between May and November. Some combine paddling with hiking into rainforest, snorkelling, fishing and village visits, and have support boats which carry camping gear and food. They don't necessarily require previous experience.

Independent travellers planning extended trips should check weather forecasts, watch the tides and currents, and wear a life jacket, hat and plenty of sun block. Ideally take a signalling device or even a mobile phone or radio and always let someone know of your plans.

The islands of Taveuni, Vanua Levu, Yasawa and Kadavu are great for kayaking. Some keen kayakers paddle Taveuni's rugged Ravilevu Coast, but generally the western sides of the islands are preferred as they are sheltered from the south-east Trade Winds.

On Taveuni there are ocean kayaks for hire at the Garden Island Resort, and Little Dolphin Treehouse in Matei has outrigger canoes. Ringgold Reef Kayaking at Bever-

ley Beach also rents kayaks and conducts kayaking/camping tours. Fiji by Kayak offers seven-day tours along Natewa Bay on Vanua Levu, for US$1040. Southern Sea Ventures run 10-day trips to the Yasawas for A$1395. On Kadavu, Dive Kadavu at the Matava Resort has diving kayaks for hire and professional instruction is available. It intends to run trips from the resort around Kadavu, as does Jona's Paradise Resort on Ono Island, northern Kadavu.

Refer to individual island chapters for more detail.

Snorkelling

Snorkelling in Fiji's warm waters is a definite highlight. In many areas there are beautiful reefs teeming with amazing life very close to the coast, making it a relatively inexpensive and easy pastime compared to diving. Many snorkellers get a taste for the underwater experience and use it as a stepping stone to diving, while others are content without the fuss. All you need is a mask, snorkel and fins. Ideally wear a T-shirt and waterproof sunscreen as it is easy to become absorbed by the spectacle, lose sense of time, and burn your back and legs.

If you have never snorkelled before or are not a confident swimmer, familiarise yourself with the equipment in a pool or shallow water. Learn how to clear your snorkel, so that you don't panic, tread all over fragile coral, or drown! Keep to the surface if you feel more comfortable and never dive too deep. It is best to swim with a partner, always use fins and ask locals about currents. Some operators who take snorkellers on their dive trips may just dump you overboard with a buoy, on a barrier reef, far from land. If you are not confident ask for a life jacket. It is common to see reef sharks but don't panic, they are probably more scared of you. The most beautiful creatures can be poisonous so avoid touching any creature or being washed against the reef as coral cuts can turn into nasty infections.

You are likely to see brilliant soft and hard corals, multitudes of colourful fish of various shapes and sizes, sponges, sea cucumbers,

Trumpet Shells are one of the many varieties of shell to be seen along Fijian coasts

urchins, starfish, Christmas-tree worms and molluscs. Crustaceans are more difficult to spot and many only come out at night. Night snorkelling is supposed to be a fantastic experience, if you can overcome the fear of the unknown!

Snorkelling becomes even more enjoyable if you can recognise different species. Paddy Ryan's *The Snorkeller's Guide to the Coral Reef* is recommended, and you may like to pick up a laminated Fiji fish identification card (available from dive shops).

Snorkelling Sites Most resorts offer snorkelling and/or diving and many have equipment for hire. However, always check first when going to a remote budget resort. It can be frustrating if you are in a gorgeous location without any equipment. If you are a keen snorkeller it may be worth having your own equipment for greater flexibility. Dive operations usually take snorkellers to outer reefs if there is room on the boat, although some prefer to keep the activities separate and special snorkelling trips.

Perhaps the best snorkelling sites are on the outer islands. Notable sites include: the Mamanucas and Yasawas (superb reefs with mostly hard coral); Vanua Levu's rocky coastline, especially near Mumu's Resort; Taveuni's Prince Charles Beach and Vuna Reef; Kadavu, off the Matava, The Great Astrolabe Resort and Jona's Paradise Resort on Ono Island; the Lomaviti group's Caqelai and Leluvia islands. Viti Levu's Coral Coast is not that great for snorkelling as it is usually a long way to the drop, much of the reef is dead, and in many places you can only swim at high tide. Better sites on Viti Levu are at Natadola Beach (watch the current), Nananu-i-Ra Island and Beqa Lagoon.

Diving

Fiji's warm, clear waters and abundance of reef life and its well-established dive industry make the islands a magnet for divers. Visibility regularly exceeds 30m, though this is reduced on stormy days or when there is a heavy plankton bloom. In terms of visibility the drier months of April to November are more reliable, but in different seasons the diver will see different things.

Fiji provides access to great diving regardless of whether your accommodation budget is bottom end or luxury. Your choice of accommodation will also depend on whether you want to do nothing but dive or whether you want to pursue other activities as well. Some resorts specialise in diving, and exclusive resorts often include diving in the daily tariff. Refer to individual island chapters for specific information on dive operators and resorts.

Average dive prices range from F$35 to F$60 for a single-tank dive; F$60 to F$130 for a two-tank dive; F$50 to F$80 for a night dive. Most operators rent equipment (in varying states of maintenance) if you don't want to lug around your own gear. It may be a good idea to bring your own buoyancy control jacket, regulator, mask, snorkel and fins.

Many travellers take the opportunity to

The Bends

The bends, or decompression sickness, occurs when gas bubbles form in the body due to a rapid transition from a high-pressure environment to one of lower pressure. This can occur in divers when, having descended into the water to a substantial depth, not enough time is allowed while rising to the surface to let the body's tissues expel the gases, the main one being nitrogen. If the gases are not expelled slowly, bubbles will form in the tissues. It's the forming of these bubbles in the brain, spinal cord or peripheral nerves that results in the bends, the symptoms of which include difficulties with muscle coordination, numbness, nausea, speech defects, paralysis and convulsions, as well as personality changes. Small nitrogen bubbles trapped under the skin can cause a red rash and an itching sensation known as diver's itch, but these symptoms usually pass in 10 to 20 minutes. Excessive coughing and difficulty in breathing, known as the chokes, indicate nitrogen bubbles in the respiratory system. Other symptoms include chest pain, a burning sensation while breathing, and severe shock.

Relief from the bends can usually be achieved only by recompression in a hyperbaric, or decompression, chamber in which the air pressure can be varied slowly to return people from abnormal pressure to atmospheric pressure. However, permanent tissue damage can still remain after recompression. It is important to get a diver suffering from the bends to a decompression chamber as quickly as possible.

Chris Wyness

learn scuba diving while in Fiji, and most operators offer courses for beginners as well as certification and advanced courses. Open water certification courses, either PADI (Professional Association of Diving Instructors) or less commonly NAUI (National Association of Underwater Instructors), take four to five days to complete and cost between F$275 and F$550. There are other speciality courses which cost F$200 to F$400. Equipment rental is about F$15 to F$30 per day. Make sure your instructor is qualified and that your travel insurance covers scuba diving and emergency treatment. If you need an air transfer and stint in a recompression chamber you will be glad to have insurance! Some dive operators offer courses in languages other than English. Mana Island, in the Mamanuca group, has instruction in Japanese, and Vuna Reef Divers on Taveuni Island in German. Check with the Fiji Dive Operators Association (FDOA) or Fiji Visitors Bureau.

There is a recompression chamber in Suva (☎ 850 630, 305 154, or 362 172 for 24-hour service) and a medevac system which transfers dive accident victims to the chamber. About 40 of Fiji's dive operators belong to the FDOA, which requires its members to abide by international diving standards, a code of practice and a code of ethics, as well as support the Fiji Recompression Chamber Facility. Other operators may offer cheaper diving, but perhaps less reliable instruction, equipment and safety procedures.

For further information contact the FDOA (☎ 850 620; fax 850 344; email: seafijidive @is.com.fj), PO Box 264, Savusavu. The Fiji Visitors Bureau publishes an annual glossy *Fiji Islands Dive Guide*. Also try the Internet and diving magazines.

See also the Sea & Dive Kayaking section, and the Photography & Video section for advice on underwater photography.

Dive Sites Fiji has vast unexplored regions as well as many dive sites of world renown such as the soft corals of the 'Great White Wall' of the Somosomo Strait near Taveuni. Beqa Lagoon off southern Viti Levu and the Astrolabe Reef off Kadavu are equally famous.

However, there is no such thing as the best diving site, especially in Fiji. Every dive site has something special or unique to see and dives range from safe and easy to wall dives in fast currents, and dives with reef sharks.

Mamanuca Group There is a wide range of dive sites in the Mamanucas, including the supermarket shark dive, which are easily accessed from Nadi and Lautoka. The Malolo Barrier Reef protects the group, and the currents through its passages provide nutrients, promoting soft and hard coral growth. Inside the barrier reef the waters are generally calm with many coral reefs and abundant fish life. There are exciting dive sites outside the barrier reef at the Namotu and Malolo passages, where you can see large pelagic fish, manta rays and turtles. It often gets rough here and should therefore only be attempted by experienced, adventurous divers.

Despite the large number of tourist resorts in the Mamanucas, the coral ecosystems there haven't been destroyed. Some divers underestimate the quality of diving here, but there is a world-class selection of sites. There are many dive operators, including Aqua-Trek, Subsurface and Mamanuca Diving.

Yasawa Group The Yasawas have plenty of spectacular reefs with vibrant corals, walls, underwater caves and unexplored areas. Diving activity has been fairly low with most tourists visiting the islands by tour ship. The up-market Yasawa Island Lodge and Turtle Island Resort offer diving for their guests and there is also a diving operation run by locals called Dive Trek Wayasewa, on Wayasewa Island. West Side Water Sports have begun a new dive operation on Tavewa Island, which promises to be good for backpackers. The Seafari Cruise to the Yasawa islands also includes diving.

Viti Levu As well as the Mamanucas, other dive sites off Viti Levu include the Coral Coast, Beqa Lagoon and Nananu-i-Ra.

The main advantage of diving on the Coral Coast is the proximity of sites to the coast, and the wide range of accommodation available. The inside reefs can be reached by small boat, currents are usually moderate, and you will see reasonably good coral and small reef fish. To see bigger pelagic fish and more spectacular coral you have to dive the

outer reefs and passages. Sea Sports caters for the Coral Coast resorts as most don't have their own diving operations. Waidroka Resort is carrying out exploratory dives just past Korolevu, in a section of Coral Coast reef not previously dived.

The large barrier reef surrounding Beqa and Yanuca islands forms Beqa Lagoon, considered one of the world's top diving locations. The reef and its various passages have a number of excellent dive sites, with coral heads, walls, tunnels, undercuts, abundant soft coral and large fish. Pacific Harbour dive operators take trips to the lagoon, and Marlin Bay Resort on Beqa Island has diving for its guests.

There are many dive sites and unexplored areas around Nananu-i-Ra Island, which is situated just off the northernmost point of Viti Levu. Divers can expect to see soft and hard coral, black coral, walls, caves, large fish, dolphins, turtles, and sometimes even whales cruising through Bligh Waters.

Ovalau & the Lomaviti Group This area is relatively unexplored. Ovalau Divers based in Levuka began in 1995, and the backpacker resort on Leluvia Island has diving.

Kadavu Kadavu's reputation for excellent diving was established on the Great Astrolabe and Solo reefs during the 80s, and now many more diving sites have been found. The reefs north of the island are equally beautiful and are sheltered from the southwest Trade Winds. The best dives are in the passages to the open sea and outside face of the barrier reefs. Expect to find abundant soft and hard coral, vertical walls and, of course, lots of fish.

Kadavu is a remote and rugged island away from the main-stream tourist destinations, and remains a relatively new frontier for diving in Fiji. There is lots of scope for exploratory diving, and there is a small range of resorts and diving operators to choose from for various budgets. Dive Kadavu at Matana Resort is easily accessible, has very good facilities and dorm beds as well as up-market accommodation. Other options include: Nukubalavu Adventure Resort & Dive Centre; Matava, The Great Astrolabe Hideaway; Albert's Place; and the up-market Malawai Resort.

The North: Taveuni & Vanua Levu Fiji's northern region has developed a reputation as one the best areas for diving in Fiji. The vast number of reefs offer all that the diver could wish for: lots of soft coral, huge walls, over-hangs and caves, reef and pelagic fish.

The best sites, including the Rainbow Reef and the Great White Wall, are on the outer barrier reefs in the Somosomo Strait, between the islands of Vanua Levu and Taveuni. Somosomo dive sites often have strong currents and involve drift diving.

Dive operations on Taveuni include Dive Taveuni, Garden Island Resort (Aqua-Trek), Vuna Reef Divers and Aquaventure.

Most of the diving on Vanua Levu is concentrated in the Savusavu area. Operations include the Eco Divers, L'Aventure Jean-Michel Cousteau and Dive Kontiki. Nukubati Island Resort is the only resort diving the Great Sea Reef off northern Vanua Levu.

Lau The Lau Group, due to its distance from the rest of Fiji as well as restrictions on tourism, is still relatively unexplored in terms of diving. The up-market Lomaloma Resort near Vanua Balavu and Kaimbu Island Resort both in northern Lau have their own dive operations. There is reportedly great potential for the area, with dive sites as good as or better than the best found in the rest of the country.

Live-Aboard Operators Due to the number of readily accessible dive sites in Fiji, live-aboard operators are not as popular as in some dive localities. They are, however, a good option for exploring reefs where land-based dive operations won't go. The *Matagi Princess II*, based at Matagi Island Resort east of Taveuni Island, offers diving and luxury cruising in the waters of Somosomo Strait, and around the Ringgold Isles north-

east of Taveuni and the Exploring Islands in the Lau group.

Nai'a Cruises operates out of Lami, near Suva, and cruises can be taken to Beqa, the Lomaiviti group, and Namena, and special charters can be taken to Lau. The Ocean Pacific Club of Fiji also operates out of Lami.

COURSES

If you are going to spend some time in Fiji enquire about informal courses at USP and check the *Fiji Times* diary page, which sometimes advertises classes. Other organisations which may run classes include the Western Art & Craft Society (☎ 663 595) or Language Instruction (☎ 313 802) at 16 Goodenough St, Suva. Indian cultural centres have three month programmes including classical dance *(kathak)*, vocal/harmonium, tabla, sitar, yoga and Hindi language. While classes are mostly for local children you may be able to negotiate something.

WORK

Working visas are difficult to get and need to be organised prior to travelling to Fiji. Application forms can be obtained from any Fiji embassy and must be completed and sent by the applicant to the immigration authorities in Fiji. Applications will normally only be approved if supported by a prospective employer and if your skills cannot be found locally. If you want to conduct business in Fiji, contact the Fiji Trade and Investment Board (☎ 315 988; fax 301 783), 3rd floor, Civic House Town Hall Rd, PO Box 2303, Government Buildings, Suva.

Volunteer Work

Volunteers are required to apply for a work permit.

There are two types of volunteer work available to foreigners in Fiji. One is through an overseas aid organisation such as the American Peace Corps, Australian Volunteers Abroad, or British Voluntary Service Overseas. Responsible organisations will only go where invited, pay their people local wages, and teach volunteers the local language and respect for traditional culture and customs. The other option, usually taken up by ex-pats, is to help a Fijian charitable or community organisation such as the Fiji Women's Rights Movement (refer to the Women Travellers section earlier). There have been problems in the past when volunteers with good intentions imposed their unconscious political agendas in culturally insensitive ways. The Fiji Museum in Suva is always looking for volunteers: see Suva in the Viti Levu chapter.

ACCOMMODATION

Tourism is one of Fiji's largest industries and there is no shortage of accommodation options, ranging from dorm beds with rock-bottom prices (about F$5 per night) to world-class luxury resorts charging up to F$1000 per night! Accommodation prices are subject to 10% VAT. Always check if this tax is included in the price quoted before signing in. Prices herein are VAT inclusive. Prices often vary between low season (February and March) and high season, and there are also lower 'local rates'. There are a few homestays and B&B type accommodation and many hostels, hotels and resorts.

The Nadi/Lautoka area has a large range of places to stay. While Nadi itself is nothing special, it is a good base from which to plan your trip, organise tours or cruises and seek up-to-date advice from other travellers.

Reservations

If you are after a short stay in one place, it is often best to prebook hotel or resort accommodation from home, thus avoiding higher walk-in rates. Booking well in advance is a good idea for popular resorts. During the quiet periods you may be able to take advantage of cheaper package deals.

While it is handy to have somewhere to crash on the first night, the independent traveller should adopt a flexible approach – keep your options open and avoid paying for too many nights in advance. There are many places to choose from so if you are not happy for some reason, just move on.

Some remote islands, however, such as Kadavu, have few places to stay and the main form of transportation is by boat. In this case it is best to prebook to ensure you'll be met at the airport or ferry and won't be left stranded with no vacancy within your price range.

Camping

Don't just set up camp anywhere without permission. Most of Fiji's land, even in seemingly remote areas, is owned by the indigenous population, by mataqali or villages. If you are invited to camp in villages, avoid setting up next to someone's bure, this can be misinterpreted as camping outside a house not good enough for you to stay in. There are designated camping areas on all of the main islands. Expect to pay about F$5 per person per night. For details of the location of camping areas refer to the individual island chapters.

Rental Accommodation

Most long-term rental accommodation can be found in Suva, Pacific Harbour and to a lesser extent Nadi. Renting apartments or rooms with weekly rates may save money if you are looking for a fixed base from which to take day trips. Normally apartments have cooking facilities, and if you are in a small group a joint effort to buy groceries, fresh fruit and vegetables from the local market can save a fair bit of money.

Hostels

There is a hostel affiliated with IYHF in both Suva and Nadi, and the Suva YWCA has a few beds for women. There are some other low-end hotels claiming to be youth hostels, and many hotels with dormitory accommodation.

Guesthouses

Guesthouses are normally cheap hotels. Beware, sometimes the term is used for hotels rented by the hour and used by local prostitutes. There are also government guesthouses, generally situated in remote areas. They are mostly used by government workers, but travellers are usually accepted if there is a vacancy.

Hotels

Fiji has many budget hotels, especially in the Nadi/Lautoka area, the Coral Coast and Suva on Viti Levu. Spartan rooms are available for F$20 to F$30 a double. Many budget hotels have dormitories for about F$5 to F$10 a night. These are a good option if you are travelling alone and want to meet other travellers. Some have communal cooking facilities.

Middle-range hotels are plentiful. Prices vary between F$35 and F$80 for doubles, and discounts may apply if the hotel is not busy. Amenities usually include air-con, tea and coffee-making facilities, restaurant, bar and pool.

Resorts

The term 'resort' is used very loosely in Fiji and can refer to any accommodation anywhere near the sea, ranging from backpacker style to exclusive luxury. If you are prepared to put up with rudimentary facilities and services you can find an inexpensive piece of paradise. There are some beautiful little islands where you can stay in simple thatched-roof bures in idyllic settings at low cost.

Wailoaloa Beach (Newtown Beach) near Nadi has a small concentration of 'backpacker resorts'. Although the black-sand beaches aren't that great and the distance can be a bit restricting, they are an alternative to staying in the centre while you decide where else to go or wait for your flight out. There are many backpacker resorts on the offshore islands, including the Yasawas, Mana Island in the Mamanucas, Kadavu, Nanui-i-Ra, and Leluvia and Caqelai Islands near Ovalau. Normally they ask for payment up front, so before embarking try to get information from travellers who have just been there. Some (such as Mana and Leluvia) are notorious for overcrowding. Transport is usually by small open boat, which can be risky in rough weather.

For those who are happy to spend up to a few hundred dollars per day for extra comfort, services and activities there are many popular resorts in the Mamanucas, on the Viti Levu's Coral Coast as well as on more remote islands. While mainland resorts have the advantage of more options for tours, entertainment and shopping, if you are looking for water sports and a relaxing time on the beach choose an offshore island. There is a trend towards small, exclusive resorts such as Natadola Beach Resort on Viti Levu, Nukubati Island Resort on Vanua Levu, Lomaloma Resort in the Lau group and Vatulele Island Resort off southern Viti Levu. These are best suited to couples with a large bank balance or on a honeymoon spree.

FOOD
Local Food

Being the multicultural hub of the Pacific, Fiji's food is a blend of indigenous Fijian, Polynesian, Indian, Chinese and Western eating habits. Traditional Fijian foods include cassava (*tavioka*) and taro (*dalo*) roots, boiled or baked fish and seafood in coconut cream (*lolo*). Meat (pork or beef) is fried and eaten accompanied with the same roots and taro leaves in coconut cream. *Kokoda* is another popular traditional dish made of raw fish marinated in coconut cream and lime juice. Tropical fruits include guava, pineapple, and mangoes when in season. Fiji-Indian dishes tend to be heavily spiced. A typical meal is a meat curry with rice, lentil soup and roti (a type of flat bread). Chinese dishes are mostly stir fries, fried rice or 'Chinese curries', and some restaurants have *bêche-de-mer* on the menu.

If you are lucky enough to be invited to share a meal with a Fijian or Fiji-Indian family, you are likely to be given a taste of authentic Fijian food. Fijians at home generally eat with their hands and sit on mats on the floor. In Indian homes there may be a strict protocol for eating, using a particular hand etc. Ask your hosts for advice. Normally you will be provided with plenty of food, whether they can afford it or not. Some may even wait for you to have your fill

Bêche-de-Mer

European traders flocked to Fiji in the early 19th century to obtain bêche-de-mer (sea cucumber), which could be sold for huge profits in Asia, where it is considered a delicacy. You are likely to see some of these ugly slug-like creatures while snorkelling or diving. There are various types: some are smooth and sticky, others prickly; some are black while others are a multitude of different colours. They feed on organic matter in the sand and serve an important role as cleaners in the lagoon ecosystem.

After being cut open and cleaned, they are boiled to remove the salt, then sun-dried or smoked. Many find the taste revolting, but sea cucumber is highly nutritious, consisting of 50% to 60% protein. Bêche-de-mer is still a lucrative commodity. Locals dive in deep waters for the creature, often risking their health by using faulty or dirty diving equipment. ■

before they start eating – if that is the case, leave enough for everybody. Try to reciprocate by buying some groceries.

Another interesting experience is to taste Fijian 'bush food'. While hiking in the interior your guides might catch some freshwater prawns and cook them on the spot. Cassava and then prawns are roasted on a small open fire. Banana leaves in a circle of rocks are used to hold a mixture of water, salt, lime juice and chillies. Once the cassava and prawns are baked, dip them into the banana-bowl mixture and eat.

Unfortunately, turtle meat can still be found in markets. If villagers offer you *vonu* (turtle), politely refuse. As turtles are an endangered species there are strict controls on their capture and eating. An adult female is about 20 to 50 years old before she can lay eggs and she does not do so every year.

Crabs swarm along beaches on nights with a full moon, and village children catch them for a feast. Fishing for flounder is also popular under moonlight, and involves wading into shallow water to spear or net the fish.

Avoid eating large predatory reef fish such as snapper, barracuda and gropers, as these sometimes carry the ciguatera toxin. Refer to the Health section earlier in this chapter.

Fast Food

Fijians are facing increasing problems with nutrition and diabetes as they forgo traditional foods for Western-style tinned and packaged foods. The number of fast-food outlets is quickly growing in Fiji's main towns. Pizzas are now fairly popular, as are takeaways with lots of fried greasy Indian or Chinese dishes. The first McDonald's opened in Nadi in early 1996.

Restaurants

Fiji's main towns, especially Nadi and Suva, have a good variety of restaurants ranging from cheap cafes to fine dining. Most have a combination of adapted Chinese, Indian and Western dishes. Cheap restaurants charge between F$5 and F$10 for main meals. If you are on a long trip and a tight budget, restaurant and cafe food may become boring with everything beginning to taste the same!

Boiled Bat

Beka (bat) was once a popular food, but now tends to be eaten only by older people. The smell of boiling bat is disgusting and they taste foul. Fortunately it is not considered rude to refuse an offer to eat it. ■

Many restaurants serve imported beef, as local beef can be of poor quality.

Nadi has one good Fijian restaurant but generally it is difficult to find traditional Fijian food or fresh fruit and vegetables, unless you visit someone's home or shop at the markets. Many resort restaurants, however, have Fijian buffets (or *lovo* nights),

which are often accompanied by a meke performance. Lovos are traditional Fijian banquets in which the food is slowly prepared in an underground oven. A hole is dug in the ground and stones are put inside and heated by an open fire. The food, wrapped in banana leaves, is cooked slowly on top of the hot stones.

Traditional Fijian Recipes
Here are some traditional Fijian recipes which are quite simple to prepare:

Palusami
12 *dalo* (taro) leaves
250g ground corned beef or smoked chicken, or pumpkin and/or sweet potato (for vegetarians)
one onion, diced
one tomato, diced
one tin of coconut cream
seasoning to taste

Mix the meat, onion and tomato with the seasoning. Divide the mixture into 12 portions and wrap each in a dalo leaf. Place in a baking dish and add the coconut cream. Cover with foil or a lid and bake in an oven for one hour at 200°C. Serve with cassava (tapioca) and sweet potato.

Kokoda
500g of very fresh, white fish (Fijians usually use *walu*, Spanish mackerel)
one cup of freshly squeezed lemon or lime juice
¼ cup of *lolo* (fresh coconut cream)
two tablespoons of white or spring onions, chopped very finely
two tablespoons of ripe tomatoes, chopped finely
chilli, freshly chopped (to your taste)
salt (to your taste)

Cut the fish into cubes. Marinate in lemon juice for at least two hours or overnight. Drain the juice and set aside. Add lolo, onions, tomatoes, chilli and salt, and some of the juice to taste (should be tangy). Serve chilled, garnished with spring onions, a wedge of lemon or lime and a chilli and ideally in a half coconut or clam shell. Kokoda is good as an entrée.

Nama
Nama, or grapeweed, is a seaweed which looks like miniature green grapes. During the summer it can be found floating on the surface above reefs and lagoons. Fresh nama must be served the same day that it is collected. You will see nama sold at the markets on a bed of green leaves to keep it cool and fresh, accompanied by a packet of *kora*, or fermented coconut, which Fijians like to eat with nama.

250g of nama
lolo
two small tomatoes, diced
chilli, freshly chopped (to your taste)
lemon or lime juice (to your taste)

Make a thick lolo (coconut cream) by scraping out the meat of a few coconuts and squeezing it. Dice tomatoes, chillies and lemon or lime juice and add this to the lolo. Pour this mixture on top of the nama and serve as a wet and juicy salad. ■

Vegetarian Food

The Hare Krishna restaurants in Lautoka and Suva are the best places for vegetarian fare. Most Indian and pizza restaurants have some vegetarian dishes and McDonald's has vegetarian burgers.

Self-Catering

Every large town in Fiji has a fresh fruit-and-vegetable market and a supermarket where you can get basic groceries. Most villages have a small shop, but the range of food items is normally very limited as villagers grow their own fresh produce. Some backpacker places have cooking facilities and also sell basic groceries. If you are a guest in a village it is a good idea to buy some goods at the local shop for your host family.

Useful Fijian food words include:

bele – green leafy vegetable, served boiled
bu – green coconut
bulumakau – beef
luve ni toa – chicken
dalo – taro, the starchy root, usually boiled
ika – fish
ivi – nut of the *ivi* tree, similar to/type of chestnut
kokoda – raw fish marinated in lime juice, served with chilli and onions
lolo – coconut milk
lovo – food cooked in a underground oven on hot stones
nama – seaweed which looks like miniature green grapes
niu – brown coconut
palusami – corned beef, onions and lolo wrapped in dalo leaves and baked in a lovo
rourou – dalo leaves boiled (similar taste to spinach)
ura – freshwater prawns
uto – breadfruit, baked, boiled or cooked in lovo
tavioca – cassava
vakalolo – a pudding of mashed starchy roots like cassava and dalo, and fruit such as breadfruit. Vast quantities of this delicacy were made for traditional feasts. The pudding is made with a sweet sauce of caramelised sugar-cane juice mixed and boiled with lolo, kneaded and rolled into balls, coated with more sweet sauce and wrapped in leaves.

DRINKS
Nonalcoholic Drinks

Both local and imported mineral water is available in Fiji. Most milk available is long-life. Fresh local fruit juices are great, but be careful as 'juice' on a menu often means cordial. The water of green coconut is especially refreshing when chilled. Local soft drinks include a sickly sweet banana flavour.

Alcoholic Drinks

Most restaurants and bars stock a variety of local and imported beer and spirits. Locally brewed beers are Fiji Bitter and Fiji Gold. Most of the wines available are from Australia or New Zealand. Expect to pay about F$2 for a glass of beer although the upmarket resorts will charge more. A 750 ml bottle of Fiji Rum is about F$20.

Yaqona

Yaqona is the national drink, and is an integral part of Fijian life. It is mildly narcotic, looks like muddy water, and you won't escape trying it! Refer to the Society & Conduct section in Facts about the Country.

ENTERTAINMENT

In Nadi and especially in Suva you will find some night life. The larger mainland resort hotels have discos, live bands, mekes, lovo nights, and fire-walking performances. Some offshore resorts, such as Beachcomber in the Mamanucas, have a reputation as being fun for young travellers. Suva, with its cosmopolitan and student population, is the night-life capital. Here there are a variety of entertainment options including bars, an 'Irish pub', nightclubs (with recorded or live music), a country-music venue and a jazz club. Restaurants normally close early, so don't expect to find many places to eat after 10 pm.

Small towns and remote islands, however, can be pretty dead at night. A popular pastime is to join a kava-drinking session. They are often accompanied by guitar playing, singing and story telling till the wee hours. Such sessions can be fun to participate in and are a great way to meet locals.

Cinemas

Every major town has at least one cinema. Suva has the largest range, and a new cinema complex is being built in the centre. Screenings include fairly up-to-date mainstream English-language productions and Indian 'Bollywood' films. Admission costs only F$2 to F$3. Check the entertainment section in the *Fiji Times* for what's showing.

SPECTATOR SPORT

Rugby and soccer are Fiji's major competitive sports. Rugby, especially popular with indigenous Fijians, is the one sport which has continually put Fiji on the world sporting scene. Every village has a rugby field, and any (invited) visitor would be welcome to join an informal game. It's a fun idea to visit a local rugby match on Viti Levu. It is interesting watching the crowd, even if you don't like rugby. Soccer is especially strong with the Fiji Indians and Gujeratis have their own competition.

The British brought the golfing habit to Fiji. There are courses in Denarau, the Coral Coast, Pacific Harbour and the Fiji golf club in Suva. Other popular sports include cricket, basketball, netball, volleyball, squash, badminton, tennis, lawn bowls, surfing, chess, athletics and boxing.

Refer to the sports pages of the *Fiji Times* for venues and events.

THINGS TO BUY

There is no shortage of handicraft shops in the main tourist centres of Nadi, the Coral Coast and Suva. Lautoka is quieter and the salespeople less aggressive. Watch out for sword sellers on the streets who will try to sell you a piece of rubbish with your name carved on it (refer to Dangers & Annoyances). Shops in little towns on the outer islands such as Taveuni may have interesting items at a cheaper price.

The Government Handicraft Shop in Suva has better quality goods than most of the articles in the Suva Handicraft Centre, where many of the artefacts are not even genuinely Fijian. However, the centre is interesting for a stroll. There are lots of desperate stall holders who will try to entice you to buy their goods, which are usually the same as those in the next stall. Occasionally one has better quality items or a better deal. Beware: if there is a cruise ship in port, prices will usually skyrocket.

Fiji was once a duty-free mecca, but now there is nothing particularly special about the shopping. When buying duty-free electric equipment check that the voltage and cycle are compatible with those of your home country.

Popular mementos include traditional artefacts such as war clubs, spears and chiefly cannibal forks, yaqona bowls of various sizes (miniature ones for salt and pepper!), *tapa* cloth (bark cloth in the form of wall hangings, covered books, postcards), shell buttons, and sandalwood/coconut soap. Pottery is also popular and is a good buy – if you can get it home in one piece. Don't buy any products derived from endangered species such as turtle shell.

Shops such as Tiki Togs in Suva and Nadi have clothes by local fashion designers in colourful tropical prints. There are also T-shirts and sulus made by local artists and many shops selling colourful Indian saris and Indian jewellery. Fijian ceramic jewellery is sold in the Government Handicraft Shop in Suva.

The Fiji Museum Shop in Suva has some interesting books, posters and postcards for sale. Posters include the Fiji Natural Heritage series. *Children of the Sun* is a beautiful photography book and should be available at the Fiji Visitors Bureau.

Getting There & Away

Most visitors to Fiji arrive at Nadi International Airport, though a few flights from nearby Pacific countries also land at Nausori airport near Suva. Centrally situated in the South Pacific, Fiji is one of the main airline hubs of the Pacific region (Hawaii is the other). Many travellers visit Fiji on round-the-world tickets, or on a stopover between Australia, New Zealand and North America.

AIR
Airports & Airlines
Nadi International Airport Nine km north of central Nadi, this is the main airport in Fiji. A taxi ride to Nadi should cost about F$8. Frequent local buses cost 45 cents (the bus stop is just outside the Queens Rd entrance).

The arrivals and customs area has a board displaying the names and rates of hotels in the Nadi area that are members of the Fiji Hotels Association. The best source of information, however, is the Fiji Visitors Bureau (FVB) office (☎ 722 433; fax 720 141) located to your left as you exit the customs area. As you enter arrivals you will be greeted by a sea of smiling faces and guitar serenading, which can be a bit overwhelming. Normally, representatives of the FVB will be there to help you, and it's worth escaping the crowd and going to their office to get an update on available accommodation and activities. Most of the other people will be representatives of local accommodation and the many travel agencies on the ground floor and first floor concourse.

The airport has a 24-hour ANZ bank with currency exchange (F$2 commission fee per transaction) just next to the FVB office. There are also many travel agencies, airline offices and car-rental offices in the arrivals area. There is a post office diagonally across the car park from the arrivals area.

If you walk outside to the corner and other leg of the L-shaped building you will find the international long-departure lounge, restaurants (one is upstairs), duty-free shop,

newsagency, and luggage storage at the far end next to the snack bar and domestic departures and arrivals.

Airlines with direct services to Nadi include Fiji's Air Pacific, Qantas, Air New Zealand, Korean Air, Air Caledonie, Air Nauru, Royal Tongan Airlines, Solomon Airlines and Air Marshall Airlines.

Nausori International Airport Fiji's second airport is situated 23 km north-east of downtown Suva. Royal Tongan Airlines, Air Marshall Islands and Air Nauru have international flights which arrive at Nausori, but otherwise it is mostly used for domestic flights. The airport premises are small and low key, and include a newspaper stand with magazines and books, and a snack counter.

Taxi rides to/from Suva cost about F$20. There is no direct local bus service to/from Suva and the airport, but there is a bus service departing from the Travelodge Hotel in Suva. Another way to get from the airport to town is to take a taxi to the Nausori bus terminal by taxi (four km; about F$5) and then catch one of the frequent local buses to Suva for about 80 cents.

The following airlines have representatives in Fiji:

Air Calédonie
    Nadi (☎ 733 145; fax 720 236)
    Suva (☎ 302 133; fax 301 928)
Air Nauru
    Nadi (☎ 722 795)
    Suva (☎ 312 377; fax 302 861)
Air New Zealand
    Nadi (☎ 722 955, 722 472; fax 721 450)
    Suva (☎ 313 100; fax 302 294)
Air Pacific
    Nadi (☎ 304 388; fax 302 860)
    (General Sales agents for Air Canada, British Airways, Cathay Pacific, Malaysian Airlines, Polynesian Airlines)
Canadian Airlines International
    Nadi (☎ 722 400; fax 722 523)
    Suva (☎ 311 844; fax 305 800)

Qantas
    Nadi (☎ 722 880; fax 720 444)
    Suva (☎ 311 833; fax 304 795)
Royal Tongan Airlines
    Nadi (☎ 723 555, 723 539; fax 720 085)
    Suva (☎ 315 755)
Solomon Airlines
    Nadi (☎ 722 831; fax 722 140)
    Suva (☎ 315 755)
Air Marshall Airlines
    Nadi (☎ 722 192; fax 720 302)
    Suva (☎ 303 888; fax 303 890)

Buying Tickets

A plane ticket will probably be the single most expensive item in your budget, and buying it can be an intimidating business. There is likely to be a multitude of airlines and travel agents hoping to separate you from your money, and it is always worth putting aside a few hours to research the current state of the market. Start early: some of the cheapest tickets have to be bought months in advance, and some popular flights sell out early. Talk to other recent travellers – they may be able to stop you making some of the same old mistakes. Look at the ads in newspapers and magazines, consult reference books and watch for special offers.

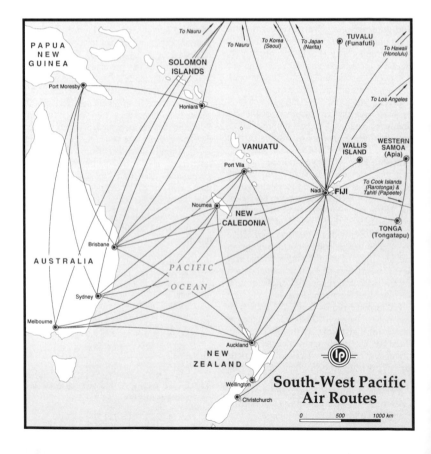

Then phone round travel agents for bargains. (Airlines can supply information on routes and timetables; however, except at times of interairline war they do not supply the cheapest tickets.) Find out the fare, the route, the duration of the journey and any restrictions on the ticket. (See restrictions in the Air Travel Glossary.) Then sit back and decide which is best for you.

You may discover that those impossibly cheap flights are 'fully booked, but we have another one that costs a bit more...' Or the flight is on an airline notorious for its poor safety standards and leaves you in the world's least favourite airport in mid-journey for 14 hours. Or they claim only to have the last two seats available for that country for the whole of July, which they will hold for you for a maximum of two hours. Don't panic – keep ringing around. Use the fares quoted in this book as a guide only. They are approximate and based on the rates advertised by travel agents at the time of going to press. Quoted airfares do not necessarily constitute a recommendation for the carrier. If you are travelling from the UK or the USA, you will probably find that the cheapest flights are being advertised by obscure bucket shops whose names haven't yet reached the telephone directory. Many such firms are honest and solvent, but there are a few rogues who will take your money and disappear, to reopen elsewhere a month or two later under a new name. If you feel suspicious about a firm, don't give them all the money at once – leave a deposit of 20% or so and pay the balance when you get the ticket. If they insist on cash in advance, go somewhere else. And once you have the ticket, ring the airline to confirm that you are actually booked onto the flight.

You may decide to pay more than the rock-bottom fare and opt for the safety of a better-known travel agent. Firms such as STA, who have offices worldwide, Council Travel in the USA or Travel CUTS in Canada are not going to disappear overnight, leaving you clutching a receipt for a nonexistent ticket, but they do offer good prices to most destinations.

Once you have your ticket, write its number down, together with the flight number and other details, and keep the information somewhere separate. If the ticket is lost or stolen, this will help you get a replacement. It's sensible to buy travel insurance as early as possible. If you buy it the week before you fly, you may find, for example, that you're not covered for delays to your flight caused by industrial action.

Round-the-World Tickets & Circle Pacific Fares

Round-the-World (RTW) tickets have become very popular in the last few years. Airline RTW tickets are often real bargains, and can work out to be no more expensive or even cheaper than an ordinary return ticket. Prices start at about UK£850, A$1800 or US$1300.

Official airline RTW tickets are usually put together by a combination of two airlines, and permit you to fly anywhere you want on their route systems so long as you do not backtrack. Other restrictions are that you (usually) must book the first sector in advance and cancellation penalties then apply. There may be restrictions on how many stops you are permitted and usually the tickets are valid from 90 days up to one year. An alternative type of RTW ticket is one put together by a travel agent using a combination of discounted tickets.

Fiji can be included in the following RTW tickets:

Air New Zealand/Ansett Australia/Northwest Airlines/KLM/South African Airways SSA/Emirates/Air UK/Air Calédonie
   World Navigator A$2499/3099 for low/high season
Qantas/British Airways/US Air
   Global Explorer A$2599/3199 for low/high season
Qantas/Air Pacific/American Airlines
   A$3199

Qantas/Air Pacific/Air New Zealand/ have a triangle fare for A$1093 between Australia (Melbourne, Sydney, Brisbane), Fiji (Nadi) and New Zealand (Auckland). Polynesian

Airlines/Air New Zealand/Air Pacific have a Pacific Triangle Fare between Tonga, Apia (American Samoa) and Nadi for US$469 with a one-year validity.

Polynesian Airlines also have a Polypass for A$1399. It entitles you to visit five different countries in 30 days: Australia (Sydney, Melbourne), New Zealand (Auckland, Wellington), Fiji, Western Samoa (Apia), American Samoa and Tonga. Flights are limited to one or two a week. Honolulu can be included for an additional A$199. North Americans should enquire about Air Pacific's Pacific Air Pass and Boomerang Pass.

Travellers with Special Needs

If you have special needs of any sort – you've broken a leg, are vegetarian, travelling in a wheelchair, taking the baby, terrified of flying – let the airline know as soon as possible so that they can make arrangements accordingly. You should remind them when you reconfirm your booking (at least 72 hours before departure) and again when you check in at the airport. It may also be worth ringing round the airlines before you make your booking to find out how they can handle your particular needs.

Airports and airlines can be surprisingly helpful, but they do need advance warning.

Air Travel Glossary

Apex Apex, or 'advance purchase excursion' is a discounted ticket which must be paid for in advance. There are penalties if you wish to change it.

Baggage Allowance This will be written on your ticket: usually one 20-kg item to go in the hold, plus one item of hand luggage.

Bucket Shop An unbonded travel agency specialising in discounted airline tickets.

Bumped Just because you have a confirmed seat doesn't mean you're going to get on the plane – see Overbooking.

Cancellation Penalties If you have to cancel or change an Apex ticket there are often heavy penalties involved; insurance can sometimes be taken out against these penalties. Some airlines impose penalties on regular tickets as well, particularly against 'no show' passengers.

Check In Airlines ask you to check in a certain time ahead of the flight departure (usually 1½ hours on international flights). If you fail to check in on time and the flight is overbooked, the airline can cancel your booking and give your seat to somebody else.

Confirmation Having a ticket written out with the flight and date you want doesn't mean you have a seat until the agent has checked with the airline that your status is 'OK' or confirmed. Meanwhile you could just be 'on request'.

Discounted Tickets There are two types of discounted fares – officially discounted (see Promotional Fares) and unofficially discounted. The lowest prices often impose drawbacks such as flying with unpopular airlines, inconvenient schedules, or unpleasant routes and connections. A discounted ticket can save you other things than money – you may be able to pay Apex prices without the associated Apex advance booking and other requirements. Discounted tickets only exist where there is fierce competition.

Full Fares Airlines traditionally offer first class (coded F), business class (coded J) and economy class (coded Y) tickets. These days there are so many promotional and discounted fares available from the regular economy class that few passengers pay full economy fare.

Lost Tickets If you lose your airline ticket an airline will usually treat it like a travellers' cheque and, after enquiries, issue you with another one. Legally, however, an airline is entitled to treat it like cash and if you lose it then it's gone forever. Take good care of your tickets.

No Shows No shows are passengers who fail to show up for their flight, sometimes due to unexpected delays or disasters, sometimes because they simply forget, sometimes because they made more than one booking and didn't bother to cancel the one they didn't want. Full-fare passengers who fail to turn up are sometimes entitled to travel on a later flight. The rest of us are penalised (see Cancellation Penalties).

On Request This is an unconfirmed booking for a flight, see Confirmation.

Open Jaws This is a return ticket which allows you fly out to one place but return from another. If available this can save you backtracking to your arrival point.

Most international airports will provide escorts from check-in desk to plane where needed, and there should be ramps, lifts, accessible toilets and phones. Aircraft toilets, on the other hand, are likely to present a problem; travellers should discuss this with the airline at an early stage and, if necessary, with their doctor.

Guide dogs for the blind will often have to travel in a specially pressurised baggage compartment with other animals, away from their owner. They are subject to the same quarantine laws (six months in isolation etc) as any other animal when entering or returning to countries currently free of rabies such as Britain or Australia. Deaf travellers can ask for airport and in-flight announcements to be written down for them.

Children under two travel for 10% of the standard fare (or free, on some airlines), as long as they don't occupy a seat. They don't get a baggage allowance either. 'Skycots' should be provided by the airline if requested in advance; these will take a child weighing up to about 10 kg. Children between two and 12 can usually occupy a seat for half to two-thirds of the full fare, and do get a baggage allowance. Push chairs can often be taken as hand luggage.

Bicycles can travel by plane. You *can* take

Overbooking Airlines hate to fly empty seats and since every flight has some passengers who fail to show up (see No Shows) airlines often book more passengers than they have seats. Usually the excess passengers balance those who fail to show up but occasionally somebody gets bumped. If this happens guess who it is most likely to be? The passengers who check in late.

Promotional Fares These are officially discounted fares like Apex fares which are available from travel agents or direct from the airline.

Reconfirmation At least 72 hours prior to departure time of an onward or return flight you must contact the airline and 'reconfirm' that you intend to be on the flight. If you don't do this the airline can delete your name from the passenger list and you could lose your seat. You don't have to reconfirm the first flight on your itinerary or if your stopover is less than 72 hours. It doesn't hurt to reconfirm more than once.

Restrictions Discounted tickets often have various restrictions on them – advance purchase is the most usual one (see Apex). Others are restrictions on the minimum and maximum period you must be away, such as a minimum of 14 days or a maximum of one year. See Cancellation Penalties.

Stand-by This is a discounted ticket where you only fly if there is a seat free at the last moment. Stand-by fares are usually only available on domestic routes.

Tickets Out An entry requirement for many countries is that you have an onward or return ticket – in other words, a ticket out of the country. If you're not sure what you intend to do next, the easiest solution is to buy the cheapest onward ticket to a neighbouring country, or a ticket from a reliable airline which can later be refunded if you do not use it.

Transferred Tickets Airline tickets cannot be transferred from one person to another. Travellers sometimes try to sell the return half of their ticket, but officials can ask you to prove that you are the person named on the ticket. This is unlikely to happen on domestic flights, but on an international flight tickets may be compared with passports.

Travel Agencies Travel agencies vary widely and you should ensure you use one that suits your needs. Some simply handle tours while full-service agencies handle everything from tours and tickets to car rental and hotel bookings. A good one will do all these things and can save you a lot of money but if all you want is a ticket at the lowest possible price, then you really need an agency specialising in discounted tickets. A discounted ticket agency, however, may not be useful for other things, like hotel bookings.

Travel Periods Some officially discounted fares, Apex fares in particular, vary with the time of year. There is often a low (off-peak) season and a high (peak) season. Sometimes there's an intermediate or shoulder season as well. At peak times, when everyone wants to fly, not only will the officially discounted fares be higher but so will unofficially discounted fares or there may simply be no discounted tickets available. Usually the fare depends on your outward flight – if you depart in the high season and return in the low season, you pay the high-season fare. ■

them to pieces and put them in a bike bag or box, but it's much easier simply to wheel your bike to the check-in desk, where it should be treated as a piece of baggage. You may have to remove the pedals and turn the handlebars sideways so that it takes up less space in the aircraft's hold; check all this with the airline well in advance, preferably before you pay for your ticket.

Australia
Air Pacific is the main carrier between Australia and Fiji and Qantas tickets to Fiji are usually seats on Air Pacific planes.

Excursion fares from Sydney or Brisbane are typically A$735/785/835 return for low/shoulder/high (school holidays) season for a minimum five days and a maximum 120 days. Apex fares are cheaper, but less flexible. You will need to pay 14 days in advance, no changes are permitted and cancellation penalties apply. These are about A$685/735/785 for low/shoulder/high season. Add A$50 to the above fares from Melbourne. The flight time is about 3¾ hours from Sydney and 4½ hours from Melbourne. Children pay 67% of the adult fare.

A return economy fare (low season with a six-month validity) from Sydney to west-coast USA with a stopover in Fiji costs around A$2270.

It is possible to get better deals so you should shop around. STA and Flight Centres International are major dealers in cheap air fares. Check the travel agents' ads in the *Yellow Pages* and ring around.

New Zealand
Air Pacific operates Nadi-Auckland, Nadi-Wellington and Nadi-Christchurch services. Air New Zealand also flies Nadi-Auckland and has shared services on the other routes. Prices on Air New Zealand from Auckland to Fiji are NZ$798/954 for low/high season (flight time about three hours). Flights from Wellington are about NZ$170 extra and from Christchurch NZ$222 extra. Air New Zealand flies Auckland/LA with a stopover in Fiji. Return fares are about NZ$2270 for a seven-day advance purchase, six-month

validity, low-season ticket. With Air New Zealand, Fiji can also be a stopover from Auckland on the way to Japan, Korea, Singapore and Canada.

As in Australia, STA and Flight Centres International are popular travel agents in New Zealand.

Other Pacific Countries
There are many airline connections between Fiji and other Pacific countries: Air Nauru flies Nadi-Nauru and Suva-Nauru; Air Marshall Islands flies Nadi-Funafuti (Tuvalu); Air Calédonie flies Nadi-Noumea (New Caledonia), Nadi-Wallis Island and Nadi-Papeete (Tahiti); Solomon Airlines flies Nadi-Honiara (Solomon Islands); Royal Tongan Airlines flies Nausori-Fua'amotu (Tongatapu, Tonga) and Nausori-Lupepau'u (Vava'u, Tonga), and Nadi-Honolulu; Air Pacific flies Nadi-Honiara, Nadi-Apia (Western Samoa), Nadi-Port Vila (Vanuatu), and Nadi-Fua'amoto; Air New Zealand flies Nadi-Port Vila, Nadi-Honiara, Nadi-Apia and Nadi-Fua'amoto.

The USA
Fiji is a major stopover between west-coast USA and Australia and New Zealand. Fiji is about six hours from Hawaii and 12 hours from west-coast USA. Fares from the USA range greatly in price depending on season and ticket restrictions. An LA/Nadi ticket with Air Pacific begins at about US$848 for a low season, maximum one-month stay, 21-day advance-purchase excursion fare. You can buy a 14-day advance purchase, maximum six-month validity ticket from between US$1123 and US$1273.

The *New York Times*, the *LA Times*, the *Chicago Tribune* and the *San Francisco Chronicle/Examiner* all produce weekly travel sections in which you'll find any number of travel agents' ads. Council Travel and STA Travel have offices in major cities nationwide. The magazine *Travel Unlimited* (PO Box 1058, Allston, MA 02134) publishes details on the cheapest air fares and courier possibilities for destinations all over the world from the USA.

Canada

Canadian Airlines International combined with Air New Zealand have an excursion fare (seven days minimum, 12 months maximum), for C$1739/1917/2116 in the low/shoulder/peak season, flying to Fiji from Vancouver via Honolulu. A three-month, seven-day advance-purchase ticket from Toronto will cost about C$2119/2297/2496 for low/shoulder/peak season. Fiji is also a popular stopover between Canada and Australia and New Zealand, and for travellers on RTW tickets. Air Pacific has also introduced flights from Nadi to Vancouver.

Travel CUTS has offices in all major cities. The *Toronto Globe & Mail* and the *Vancouver Sun* carry travel agents' ads. The magazine *Great Expeditions* (PO Box 8000-411, Abbotsford BC V2S 6H1) is also useful.

Europe

Most people travelling to Fiji from Europe will be using an RTW ticket or making a stopover between North America and Australia or New Zealand.

Trailfinders in west London produces a lavishly illustrated brochure, which includes air-fare details. STA also has branches in the UK. Look in listings magazines such as *Time Out*, plus the Sunday papers and *Exchange & Mart* for ads. Also look out for free magazines widely available in London – they can usually be found outside main train stations. Most British travel agents are registered with the Association of British Travel Agents (ABTA). If you have bought a ticket from an ABTA-registered agent who then goes out of business, ABTA will provide a refund or a replacement ticket. Unregistered bucket shops are riskier but also sometimes cheaper.

The Globetrotters Club, BCM Roving, London WC1N 3XX, publishes a newsletter called *Globe*, which covers obscure destinations and can help in finding travelling companions. In Amsterdam, NBBS is a popular travel agent.

Asia

There are direct flights from South Korea and Japan to Fiji, but most flights to/from South-East Asia go via Australia or New Zealand to connect to Fiji.

Air New Zealand also flies Nadi-Tokyo and Nadi-Nagoya, and Air Pacific flies Nadi-Tokyo and Nadi-Osaka. Air Pacific tickets (sold only in Japan) for flights from Tokyo cost ¥160,000/342,400 for instant purchase/special economy. This ticket is for a four-day minimum, three-month maximum stay, and other conditions apply.

Both Air New Zealand and Korean Air fly Nadi-Seoul. A three-month excursion fare with Korean Air costs A$1956/2136 (W1,254,400/1,311,700) for low/high season.

Hong Kong is the discount plane-ticket capital of the region. Its bucket shops are at least as unreliable as those of other cities. Ask the advice of other travellers before buying a ticket. STA, which is reliable, has branches in Hong Kong, Tokyo, Singapore, Bangkok and Kuala Lumpur.

Africa

Both the *World Navigator* (including South African Airways and KLM) and the *Global Explorer* (including British Airways and Qantas) RTW tickets include Africa in their itinerary options, the major hub being Johannesburg. Refer to the RTW ticket section. Otherwise a Johannesburg-Nadi ticket via Melbourne, joining Qantas/Air Pacific, will cost from A$1981 (conditions apply), or for full economy $A4457!

South America

From Santiago you can fly to Nadi by Air New Zealand and Lan Chile, via Papeete and Rarotonga. A 180-day ticket costs about A$2240/2520 for low/high season. Santiago-Nadi return costs around A$1626. The World Navigator RTW ticket (including Air New Zealand, KLM and South African Airways) includes South America, the major hubs being Santiago, Buenos Aires, Sao Paulo and Rio de Janeiro. Refer to the RTW ticket section.

SEA

Travelling to Fiji by sea is now difficult unless you're on a cruise ship or yacht. Few of the shipping companies will take passengers on cargo ships and those that do will usually charge hefty rates. However, you could try asking your local shipping agents, or go to the docks and personally approach the captains. It is virtually impossible to leave Fiji by cargo ship unless passage has been prearranged.

Shipping companies include Burns Philp (☎ 304 282; fax 301 127) and Carpenters Shipping (☎ 312 244; fax 301 572), both in Suva.

Cruise Ship

Some cruise ships have Fiji on their itinerary, but usually only stop over for one or two nights in Suva. From Australia, P&O's *Fair Princess* (replacing the *Fair Star*) has a 14-night cruise starting in Sydney and stopping at six ports for between A$2800 (no porthole) to A$4060 per person for a twin cabin.

Yacht

Fiji's islands are a popular destination or stopover for yachts cruising the Pacific. It is often possible to catch a ride with a yacht looking for extra people to crew their boat or share day-to-day costs . If you are interested, approach marinas, ask around and look on noticeboards. Yachts should enter Fiji through the designated ports of entry at Suva, Lautoka or Levuka. Other marinas include Vuda Point Marina (between Nadi and Lautoka), Savusavu Yacht Club on Vanua Levu and Musket Cove Marina on Plantation Island in the Mamanucas. Refer to the Getting Around chapter & Activities in the Facts for the Visitor chapter.

Entry & Departure Procedures On reaching Fijian waters, yachts must first call at a designated port of entry to be cleared from by customs, immigration and quarantine officials. Documents required include: a certificate of clearance from the previous port of call; a crew list with accompanying personal details and passports. Yachties intending to visit outer islands within the Fiji group must have the approval of the Department of Fijian Affairs in Suva, or if in Lautoka or Levuka the approval can be obtained from the Commissioner's Department at the district offices. Before departing, you'll need to complete clearance formalities (within 24 hours), providing inbound clearance papers, your vessel's details and your next port of call. Customs must be cleared before immigration, and you must have paid all port dues and health fees.

Information Yacht Help (☎ 667 222) PO Box 4799, Lautoka, publishes the *Yacht Help Booklet, Fiji*, which has general information about services for yachties and up-to-date clearance formalities. Pacific Marine Yacht Consultants (☎ 668 214; fax 668 215) PO Box 4799, Lautoka, offers services to help sort out paperwork, cruising arrangements and obtaining parts not available in Fiji. The Royal Suva Yacht Club (☎ 312 021; fax 304

Isa Lei, a Fijian Farewell Song

Isa Lei is a traditional Fijian farewell song often played for travellers who are leaving a resort, a cruise, or the country.

Isa Isa Vulagi lasa dina
Isa Isa you are my only treasure
Nomu lako au na rarawa kina
Must you leave me so lonely and forsaken
Cava beka ko a mai cakava
As the roses will miss the sun at dawning
Nomu lako au na sega ni lasa
Every moment my heart for you is yearning

Isa lei, na noqu rarawa
Isa Lei the purple shadows fall
Ni ko sa na gole e na mataka
Sad the morrow will dawn upon my sorrow
Bau nanuma na nodatou lasa
Oh forget not when you are far away
Mai Viti nanuma tiko ga
Precious moments from Fiji

Vanua rogo na nomuni vanua
Isa Isa my heart was filled with pleasure
Kena ca ni levu tu na ua
From the moment I heard your tender greeting
Lomaqu voli me'u bau butuka
Mid the sunshine we spent the hours together
Tovolea ke balavu na bua
Now so swiftly those happy hours are fleeting ■

433) is also a good place to get the latest information and to meet local yachties.

Prevailing Winds The best time to sail is in the 'winter' from late April to early November when the south-easterly Trade Winds are blowing. During the summer months winds change direction more often and the chance of striking storms and hurricanes is greater.

Repairs The Neisau Marina Complex (☎ 664 858; fax 663 807) PO Box 3831, Lautoka, at the end of Bouwalu St, provides facilities for yachts in need of repair. The facilities include a working shed, tools and machinery for hire, a large stand area with cradles, a travel-lift marine hoist, and floating berths.

DEPARTURE TAXES

An international departure tax of F$20 applies to all visitors apart from children under 12.

ORGANISED TOURS

For those not interested in travelling independently, package tours may be the ideal option if you have limited time, prefer to pay an all-inclusive cost up front, wish to stay in a particular hotel or resort, or have special interests and activities such as diving. Many visitors from Australia, New Zealand and the USA visit Fiji on some type of package tour.

Most travel agents will be able to organise this type of trip and can often arrange cheap deals. There are many options available, and prices depend on the season, type of accommodation and length of time. Alternatively, some Pacific cruises (refer to the Cruise Ship section) include Fiji on their itinerary.

For tours within Fiji refer to the Getting Around chapter.

WARNING

The information in this chapter is particularly vulnerable to change: prices for international travel are volatile, routes are introduced and cancelled, schedules change, special deals come and go, and rules and visa requirements are amended. Airlines and governments seem to take a perverse pleasure in making price structures and regulations as complicated as possible. You should check directly with the airline or a travel agent to make sure you understand how a fare (and the ticket you may buy) works. In addition, the travel industry is highly competitive and there are many lurks and perks.

The upshot of this is that you should get opinions, quotes and advice from as many airlines and travel agents as possible before you part with your hard-earned cash. The details given in this chapter should be regarded as pointers and are not a substitute for your own careful, up-to-date research.

Getting Around

By using local buses, carriers and ferries you can get around Fiji's main islands relatively cheaply and easily. If you'd like more comfort or are short on time you can use air-conditioned express buses, rental vehicles, charter boats or the small interisland planes.

AIR
Domestic Services
Fiji is well serviced by internal airlines which have frequent and reliable flights. Some may find the light planes scary, especially if it's windy or turbulent, but the views of the islands, coral reefs and lagoons are fantastic.

The international airports of Nadi and Nausori near Suva, both on Viti Levu, also serve as the main domestic hubs. Other domestic airports include Savusavu and Labasa on Vanua Levu, Matei on Taveuni, Vunisea on Kadavu, Bureta on Ovalau and, in the Mamanucas, Malololailai and Mana islands. Many of the smaller islands also have airstrips. There are flights to outer islands where there is no accommodation for tourists, but an invitation is needed to visit – in some cases it is illegal to turn up uninvited. Rotuma, Gau, Koro, Moala and Vanuabalavu and Lakeba in Lau have airstrips but receive few visitors, while other islands such as Vatulele, Yasawa and Wakaya have their own airstrips to serve the up-market resorts.

The two main airlines are Air Fiji and Sunflower Airlines. Most of Air Fiji's services operate out of Nausori, while Sunflower's base and major hub is Nadi; their prices on shared routes are almost identical. Vanua Air Charters covers a smaller number of destinations, and charter services are available on Island Hoppers helicopters and Turtle Airways seaplanes.

The following companies operate interisland flights (refer also to the two Airfare charts):

Air Fiji
> Nadi (☎ 722 521; fax 720 555); Suva (☎ 313 666; fax 300 771); Labasa (☎ 811 188; fax 813 819); overseas reservations: Australia (☎ 1800 818 813; fax 02-9388 7829), New Zealand (☎ 09-379 4455), California (☎ 800 677 4277) and London (☎ 0171-253 2000).

> Previously named Fiji Air, the airline has a fleet of Bandits, Twin Otters, Harbins and Britten Norman Islanders. There are daily flights from Suva to Labasa, Levuka, Nadi, Savusavu and Taveuni, and five a week to Kadavu. There are also daily flights from Nadi to Suva, Savusavu, Malololailai, Labasa and Taveuni, and five a week to Kadavu via Suva.

> Air Fiji offers day trips in conjunction with Ovalau Tours to historic Levuka. The Suva/Levuka fare is F$149 and for Nadi/Levuka it's F$257 per person. It includes transfers, breakfast, guided walking tour, lunch and afternoon tea at a local resident's home. To include an overnight stay at Mavida Hotel is an extra F$25. There are also day trips to Musket Cove Resort (Malololailai) for F$75 per person, including

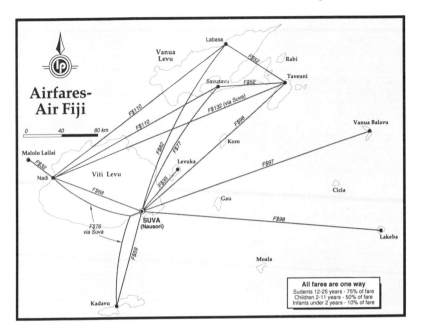

**Airfares-
Air Fiji**

All fares are one way
Students 12-25 years - 75% of fare
Children 2-11 years - 50% of fare
Infants under 2 years - 10% of fare

lunch at the resort and use of its facilities, for only F$11 more than the normal return fare.

Sunflower Airlines

Nadi Airport (☎ 723 016; fax 723 611); Suva (☎ 315 755; fax 305 027); Labasa (☎ 811 454; fax 281 9542); overseas offices: Australia (☎ 02-9211 6135; fax 9281 9542), New Zealand (☎ 09-413 9542; fax 413 9666), Hawaii (☎ 808 539 3627; fax 539 3630), California (☎ 800 224 0220; fax 909 659 5830) and Germany (☎ & fax 49 7476 2615).

Most Sunflower flights operate out of Nadi, with daily services to major tourist destinations (except Ovalau), including Suva, Labasa, Savusavu, Taveuni, Kadavu, Malololailai (Plantation and Musket coves) and Mana Island. The fleet of small planes includes Britten Norman Islanders, Twin Otters and Shorts 330 aircraft.

Seven-day excursion fares are available for the Nadi-Suva, Nadi-Labasa and Suva-Labasa routes for about 20% less than the normal return fare.

Vanua Air Charters

Suva (☎ 313 726; fax 313 902), 58-60 Yatulau Building; Nausori Airport (☎ 477 711); Labasa (☎ 811 655; fax 813 900).

Vanua Air Charters serves a number of desti-

nations, including Vanua Levu and Taveuni. There are daily (except Sunday) Suva-Savusavu-Labasa flights for F$80, and Suva-Taveuni flights three times a week for F$88 – cheaper than Air Fiji. It also flies from Suva to islands of the Lau and Lomaiviti groups which don't have places for travellers to stay: Gau, Moala, Cicia, Vanua Balavu and Lakeba. Infants pay 10% of the fare, children pay 50% and students 75%.

Turtle Airways

Newtown Beach, Nadi (☎ 722 389; fax 720 346).

Turtle Airways has a fleet of Cessna seaplanes which can carry up to four passengers. As well as flight seeing, they provide transfer services to Mamanucas, the Fijian Resort, Pacific Harbour, Suva, Toberua Island and other islands as required.

A flight to Malololailai by seaplane costs F$190 return (compared with F$64 by Sunflower or Air Fiji). The charter service is F$700 per flying hour.

Island Hoppers

Nadi Airport (☎ 720 410; fax 720 172).

Island Hoppers operates helicopter flight-seeing tours departing from Denarau Island. It also transfers guests to island resorts such as Vomo and Tokoriki. A 20-minute flight is F$107 per person, 40 minutes F$184 per person.

Airfares-
Sunflower
Airlines

All Fares are one way
Children under 12 years - 50% of fare
Infants to 3 years - 10% of fare
* Charters can be arranged from
• Nadi to Yasawa Island
• Nadi to Vatulete

Air Passes

Air Fiji has a four-coupon Discover Fiji Pass which lasts for 30 days and costs A$250 (US$199). An unlimited number of additional flights are A$50 each. Some routes cost less than F$52 anyway, so consider which flights are worth including in the pass. Vanuabalavu and Lakeba are excluded routes.

The pass was formerly only available from within Fiji, but now it is only sold outside Fiji in conjunction with an international air fare. You have to pay seven working days prior to departure; there is a A$50 pre-departure cancellation fee, and reimbursement is minimal once in Fiji. There is no discount for children except for infants at 10% of the pass fare. If you change your mind it will cost A$50 per change to reroute. It's best to book your seats, as the small planes often fill up quickly.

If you are eligible for the 25% student discount that may be more economical. Alternatively think about excursion fares (minimum one day, maximum seven), which usually work out to be about 20% less than the normal return fare. Enquire with both Sunflower and Air Fiji.

BUS

Fiji's larger islands have an extensive and inexpensive bus network. Catching the local buses is a cheap and fun way to get around, assuming you have the time. While fairly noisy and smoky, they are perfect for the tropics with open unglazed windows and a rolled-up tarpaulin, which everyone helps pull down when it rains. There are bus stops but you can often just hail the buses down, especially in rural areas.

Viti Levu's main bus stations are at Lautoka, Nadi and Suva. Express buses operate along the Queens Road and Kings Road. There are also many different bus companies operating on a local level. Even remote inland villages, such as Nadarivatu in Viti Levu's highlands, have regular (though less frequent) services. These trips might take a while, stopping in many villages along the way, but it is an opportunity to mix with the locals. Before heading to an isolated area, check if there is a return bus so you don't get stranded without any accommodation. Refer to the island chapters for information on local bus services.

Bus companies on Viti Levu include:

Pacific Transport Limited
Nadi (☎ 700 044); Lautoka (☎ 660 499); Sigatoka (☎ 500 088); Suva (☎ 304 366); Taveuni (☎ 880278).
Pacific Transport has regular buses (open-air type) serving Lautoka to Suva via the Coral Coast, on the Queens Road. There are five staged buses (F$7.60) which take about six hours and at least five express buses daily for a 20-cent sur-charge. Express buses take about five hours from the Lautoka bus terminal to the Suva terminal and about half an hour less from Nadi. If you are not in a hurry it's good to have a break along the way and catch another bus an hour or two later. The first bus leaves Lautoka at 6.30 am, the last at 5.30 pm, or 6 pm on Friday. It is generally OK to turn up at the bus station, but you can book in advance for an extra 50 cents. Pacific Transport Limited also runs the local buses in Taveuni.
Sunbeam Transport Limited
Lautoka (☎ 662 822).
Sunbeam has a Kings Road as well as a Queens Road service. Lautoka-Suva via the Kings Road costs F$8.80 and takes about six hours. The trip along the partially unsealed Kings Road is scenic, especially near Rakiraki.
UTC (United Touring Fiji)
Nadi Airport (☎ 722 811; fax 720 389); Suva (☎ 312 287).
UTC has an express air-con coach service from Suva to Nadi along Queens Road, stopping at the larger hotels along the way. It departs daily at 1.30 pm from Nadi and arrives in Suva at 6 pm, then departs Suva at 8 am and arrives in Nadi at 12.30 pm. From Nadi Airport to Korolevu costs F$19, to Suva F$27.
Fiji Holiday Connections
Nadi Airport (☎ 720 977, 701 823 ext 22), Suite 8, Arrival Concourse.
This company operates a minibus shuttle between Nadi and Suva along the Queens Road that will pick up and drop off at hotels along the Coral Coast. It departs Nadi at 9 am, arriving in Suva at 12.30 pm, returning from Suva at 2 pm and arriving in Nadi at 5 pm. The express service leaves Nadi at 8 am, arriving in Suva at 11 am, departing Suva at 1 pm and arriving back in Nadi at 4 pm. Book a day in advance. It also has minibuses for hire within Viti Levu.

Reservations

Reservation are not necessary for the regular local buses; you just need to ask around the bus terminals for departure times or get an up-to-date timetable. However, if you are on a tight schedule or have an appointment, it may be a good idea to buy your ticket in advance. For coach trips and tours over longer distances (ie Suva to Nadi), book with the respective company.

CARRIERS & MINIBUSES

Many locals drive small trucks, with a tar-paulin-covered frame on the back. These often have passenger seating and some run trips between Nadi and Suva. You can pick up a ride in main street Nadi. They leave when full and are quicker than taking the bus. Similarly, Viti Minibuses also shuttle along the Queens Road between Lautoka (pick up near the bus station) and Suva (pick up near the market), and charge F$10. However, the drivers are notorious for speeding.

TRAIN

The only passenger train is on Viti Levu's Coral Coast between the Fijian Resort and Natadola Beach. It is a scenic jaunt for tour-ists. Sugar trains use the railways in the cane-growing areas of Viti Levu and Vanua Levu.

CAR & MOTORCYCLE

Ninety percent of Fiji's 5100 km of roads are on Viti Levu and Vanua Levu, of which about one-fifth are sealed.

Road Rules

Driving is on the left-hand side of the road as in Australia and New Zealand. The speed limit is 50 km/h in town areas and 80 km/h outside town on the highway. Most of the villages have speed humps to force drivers to respect the village pace. Seat belts are compulsory for front-seat passengers. Should you pick up a parking fine in Suva, it's likely to be only F$2.

As a rule, local drivers are maniacs, often speeding, stopping suddenly and overtaking on blind corners, so take care, especially on gravel roads. Buses also stop where and when they please. There are lots of pot-holes, and sometimes the roads are too narrow for two vehicles to pass, so be aware of oncoming traffic. Pedestrians often stroll along the road, and animals (including dogs, cattle, horses and goats) are free to wander onto the roads in both towns and country. Driving at night can therefore be risky, especially along the south-east coast of Viti Levu. In cane-cutting season watch for sugar trains which have right of way. Ask the Fiji Visitors Bureau (FVB) for further information.

Rental

Rental cars are relatively expensive in Fiji; however, it is a good way to explore the larger islands, especially if you can split the cost with a group. Motorcycles are not very common in Fiji and we did not come across any for hire. Viti Levu is easy to get to know by car, with Queens Road and most of Kings Road being sealed. Most other roads are unsealed and are better for 4WD vehicles. Some agencies, such as Central, will not allow their cars to be driven on unpaved roads, which would mean that, unless you wanted to risk invalidating your insurance, the Queens Road/Kings Road loop would not be able to be completed. It would also mean that exploration off these main roads would be restricted.

It is possible to take vehicles on roll-on roll-off ferries to Vanua Levu or Taveuni, but again, some companies do not allow this. If you intend to take a hire car on a ferry to Vanua Levu it's best to hire a 4WD.

The shorter the hire period, the higher the rate. Delivery and collection charges apply. Avis rates for four to seven days unlimited travel are F$110/132 per day for a small, air-conditioned car/4WD. Alternatively, for the same vehicles, you could pay F$66 per day plus 44 cents per km. Khans has small air-con cars for F$82 per day with unlimited travel, or F$28 per day plus 30 cents per km, and it also hires minibuses. Khans hires at an hourly rate or per half-day, while some firms have a minimum hire of three days. Some companies offer discounts for advance bookings. It's usual to pay a deposit by credit card, although some companies such as Central require a minimum F$350 cash per day as well as a passport-size photograph. You will be required to present a valid overseas or international drivers licence. Third party insurance is compulsory and personal accident insurance is highly recommended if you are not already covered by travel insurance. The minimum-age requirement is 21, or in some cases 25.

Ask the FVB about the respective companies. The cheaper companies are notorious for providing faulty cars which conk out during your trip. Often, when you add up the hidden costs, the price may not be that cheap anyway. Consider what's appropriate for you, including how inconvenienced you might be if the car breaks down, what support services is provided, the likely travel distance, insurance, if VAT is included, and the excess/excess waiver amount (Thrifty's excess is F$700, whereas Central's is F$1500). Common exclusions include tyre damage, underbody and overhead damage, and theft of the vehicle. Check brakes, water, tyre pressure and condition before heading off.

The main towns have service stations, but fill up the tank before heading inland. If you do run out of fuel, it might be available in village shops Fuel costs between 90 cents and F$1 per litre.

The easiest place to rent vehicles is Viti Levu, and some of the many agencies are listed below. Most have offices at Nadi International Airport. The established companies also have offices in other towns and rental desks at larger hotels.

Rental Agencies – Viti Levu Car-rental agencies on Viti Levu include:

Avis
  Nadi Airport (☎ 722 233; fax 720 482)
  Nausori Airport (☎ 478 963)
Budget Rent a Car
  Nadi Airport (☎ 722 735; fax 722 053)
  Nausori Airport (☎ 479 299)
Central
  Nadi Airport (☎ 722 771, 722 450)
  Suva (☎ 311 866; fax 305 072)
Dove Rent a Car
  Nadi (☎ 721 606)
  Suva (☎ 311 755; fax 311 755)
Hertz
  Nadi (☎ 723 466; fax 723 650)
  Suva (☎ 302 186)
Khans
  Nadi Airport (☎ 723 506; fax 702 159)
  Suva (☎ 385 033)
Rental Cars (Fiji) Ltd
  Nadi Airport (☎ 723 922; fax 700 040)
Satellite
  Nadi Airport (☎ 721 957)
  Nadi (☎ /fax 701911)
Sharmas
  Nadi Airport (☎ 721 908)
  Nadi (☎ 701 055; fax 702 038)
  Suva (☎ 314 365)
Tanoa Rent-a-Car
  Nadi Airport (☎ 722 544; fax 720 667)
Thrifty Car Rental
  Nadi Airport (☎ 722 935; fax 722 607)
  Suva (☎ 314 436)

Rental Agencies – Vanua Levu Car-rental agencies here provide only 4WD vehicles due to Vanua Levu's rough roads. Budget Rent a Car has offices in Savusavu (☎ 850 799) and Labasa (☎ 811 999).

Rental Agencies – Taveuni Taveuni's agency has rental cars and 4WD vehicles for drivers aged over 25 years. The agency (☎ 880 058; fax 880 202) is at Kaba's Supermarket in Somosomo.

BICYCLE
Fiji's larger islands have good potential for cycling, although some areas are too hilly and rugged. If you are thinking about bringing a bicycle, mountain bikes would be best for exploring the interior. Viti Levu has long, flat stretches of sealed road along the scenic Coral Coast and it is possible to cycle around the island by Kings Road and Queens Road. You could also cycle on Vanua Levu's

unsealed roads from Savusavu along Natewa Bay (no accommodation here), and along the Hibiscus Highway from Buca Bay, where you can take the ferry to Taveuni. Ovalau has a scenic unsealed (mainly flat) road along the coast.

The biggest hazard is the unpredictable traffic. Avoid riding in the evening, as traffic can be dangerous when visibility is low. Travel light but carry plenty of water. You can usually buy coconuts and bananas from villages along the way. Storage at Nadi Airport is relatively expensive; the cheapest place to store bikes is at backpacker hostels. There are a few places to rent bicycles (Coral Coast, Taveuni and Ovalau) while Independent Tours near Sigatoka runs mountain-bike tours. Refer also to Cycling under Activities in the Facts for the Visitor chapter.

HITCHING
Hitching is never entirely safe in any country in the world, and we don't recommend it. Travellers who decide to hitch should understand that they are taking a small but potentially serious risk.

Hitching is still relatively safe in Fiji, especially in country areas. Locals do it all the time, especially hopping in the back of carriers. It is customary to pay the equivalent of the bus fare to the driver. People who do choose to hitch will be safer if they travel in pairs and let someone know where they are planning to go. Crime is more prevalent around Suva, although cases of tourists being mugged are occurring in Nadi.

WALKING
Fiji has many interesting places to go walking. The most accessible and probably the most interesting treks are in the Viti Levu highlands and in Taveuni. Other islands with good areas for walking or trekking include Kadavu, Ovalau and Vanua Levu. Almost everywhere you go, even in the most remote areas, the land is owned by *matagali* or villages, and if you intend to go trekking or walking you will usually need guides and permission. See Trekking under Activities in

the Facts for the Visitor chapter and the individual islands chapters.

BOAT

With the exception of the up-market resort islands, often the only means of transport to and between the islands is by small local boats. Lifejackets are rarely provided and usually the boats have no radio-phones. If the weather looks ominous or the boat is over-crowded, you may prefer not to go!

In most areas it is difficult to explore and hop from island to island unless you have a charter boat or yacht. In Kadavu for example, transport is mostly by small village boats or those owned by the various resorts. Apart from the Suva/Kadavu ferry there is no organised transport and resorts do not share services. Similarly, in the Yasawas it is expensive to hop around the islands unless you're on an organised cruise. The back-packer resorts on Waya, Waya Sewa and Tavewa use small boats from Lautoka to transport their guests. If you're dubious about the small boats, Westside Watersports (☎ & fax 661 462) is now running weekly transfers from Lautoka to Tavewa Island. It also picks up and drops off at Waya Sewa (Dive Trek) for four or more passengers.

Interisland hopping for sightseeing and transfers is available in the Mamanucas, but is relatively expensive. South Sea Cruises (☎ 722 988, 750 445; fax 720 346) operates various cruises and boat charters to the Mamanucas, as well as the regular *Island Express* service. The air-con catamaran does twice-daily transfers between Denarau, Malololailai, Malolo, Castaway and Mana islands. Mana Island costs F$78 return.

Ferry

Regular ferry services operate between Viti Levu, Vanua Levu and Taveuni (Patterson Brothers, Beachcomber Cruises and Consort Shipping); between Viti Levu and Ovalau (Patterson Brothers and Emoisi's Shipping); and between Viti Levu and Kadavu (Whippy's). The Patterson Brothers, Beach-comber Cruises and Consort Shipping boats are large roll-on roll-off ferries, carrying pas-sengers, vehicles and cargo. They have can-teens where you can buy drinks, snacks and light meals. The times given should be taken as a guide only, as ferry timetables are noto-rious for changing frequently. There is often a long waiting period at stopovers.

Patterson Brothers Shipping
Suva (☎ 315 644; fax 301 652), Suite 1 & 2; Lautoka (☎ 661 173); and offices in Labasa, Levuka and Savusavu.
Ellington Wharf (Viti Levu) **to Nabouwalu** (south-west Vanua Levu) on the *Ashika* costs F$28.60 or F$31.90, including the 3½-hour bus trip from Lautoka. The ferry trip is 3¾ hours, and Labasa is a further four hours by bus through Bua and Macuata provinces.
Natovi Landing to Nabouwalu on the *Jubilee* costs F$28.60. The trip involves 1½ hours by bus from Suva to Natovi, four hours by ferry across the Bligh Waters, followed by four hours by bus to Labasa. (Note that Nabouwalu is an isolated town, with not much to interest the traveller.)
Natovi Landing to Savusavu, on the *Ovalau*, is F$20, plus F$5 for the bus fare from Suva to Natovi. The boat trip takes 6½ hours. Connec-tions to Taveuni are as noted below; to Labasa it's two hours by bus. Suva to Labasa via either Nabouwalu or Savusavu is F$37.40.
Vanua Levu to Taveuni from Savusavu is a 1½-hour bus trip along the Hibiscus Highway to Natuvu, Buca Bay and the ferry across the Somosomo Strait (1¾ hours) to Waiyevo, Taveuni. Connection is also available by bus from Labasa (2¾ to 3½ hours to Buca Bay).
Viti Levu to Ovalau (Natovi Landing to Buresala Landing) costs F$17.60, or F$19.80 from Suva to Ovalau. From Suva the trip involves a bus trip of 1½ hours to Natovi, followed by one hour on the ferry across the Northern Bau Waters and another hour by bus to Levuka.

Beachcomber Cruises
Suva (☎ 307 889, 300 863; fax 306 189), Taina's Travel Service, Suite 8, Epworth Arcade (agent).
Viti Levu to Vanua Levu is served by the *Adi SS (Dana Star)* departs Narajan's Jetty, Walu Bay in Suva, each Thursday at 4 pm for Savusavu on Vanua Levu, arriving about 12 hours later. Check in one hour beforehand. The ferry, originally from Sweden, takes 15 cars, 12 trucks, freight and up to 500 passengers. On Monday, Tuesday, Friday and Saturday passengers are transported by bus to Natovi Landing, where the ferry departs at 1.30 pm, arriving in Savusavu about seven hours later. The one-way trip costs F$30/38 per adult for economy/first class.
Vanua Levu to Taveuni is serviced on Wed-nesday, when the ferry continues on a five-hour trip from Savusavu to Taveuni, arriving at 6 am

and returning at 2 pm. The one-way trip from Natovi via Savusavu to Taveuni costs F$34/40 per adult. All boat fares are half-price for children between five and 16 years; younger children pay a quarter of the adult fare. Bus fares from Suva to Natovi are F$2/4 for children/adults.

Consort Shipping Line
Suva (☎ 302 877; fax 303 389), ground floor, Dominion House; Savusavu (☎ 850 279; fax 850 442).

Suva to Savusavu: the MV *SOFE (Spirit of Free Enterprise)* does a weekly voyage (departing Suva at midnight on Tuesday) via Koro return, as well as one Suva to Taveuni trip (departing Suva early Saturday morning) via

Koro and Savusavu return. Prices are F$28/52 for economy/cabin from Suva to Savusavu, and the trip takes between 11 and 14 hours.

Savusavu to Taveuni (about six hours) is F$15/33 for economy/cabin. The boat pauses at Koro for about one hour and the Suva/Taveuni trip involves an 11-hour stopover in Savusavu.

Whippy's Boatyard Limited
Suva (☎ 311 507, 340 015; fax 340 015), PO Box 9.

Viti Levu to Kadavu on the *Gurawa* departs twice weekly at 6 am from the Ports Authority Local Shipping Wharf, Rona St, Walu Bay. On Tuesday the boat passes Dravuni and sails down the eastern side of Ono Island, calling into Albert's Place (Lagalevu; F$40) and Nukubalavu

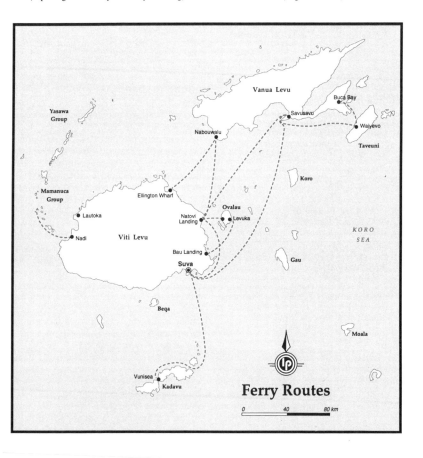

Ferry Routes

0   40   80 km

Resort (Waisilima), and then around the northern side of the main island to Vunisea (F$42).

On Friday the boat takes a different route, passing Dravuni, then heading down around the western side of Ono Island to Jona's Resort (Kenia; F$37). It then goes across the channel, calling at Nukubalavu Resort and Albert's Place, and around the south-eastern side of the main island as far as the Great Astrolabe Hideaway (Kadavu-Koro; F$42). Fares given are per adult from Suva one way.

Kadavu Shipping

Suva (☎ 311 766), ground floor, Procera House, Waimanu Road.

Suva to Nabukalevu-i-Ra, on the ferry MV *Bulou-ni-ceva* departing Suva for Vunisea, Kavala Bay and Nabukalevu-i-Ra. The fare is F$35 per person one way. This service is mostly for cargo and local use, and is less regular and not as reliable as the Whippy Service.

Emoisi's Shipping

Suva (☎ 313 366) 35 Gordon St; Levuka (440 057/440 013).

Viti Levu to Ovalau: a daily service by minibus from Suva to Bau Landing and small boat to Leleuvia Island for F$15/33 one way/return. On Monday, Wednesday, Friday and Saturday the boat continues to Levuka. This trip costs F$18/39.60 one way/return.

Kaunitoni Shipping Office

Suva (☎ 311 109; fax 305 529), ground floor, NATCO Building, Edinburgh Drive.

Viti Levu to Rotuma costs F$90/130 for deck/saloon. Permission to visit is required.

Cakauniika Shipping Office

Suva (☎ 312 962) Muaiwalu Jetty (Old Millers Wharf), Walu Bay.

Viti Levu to the Lau Group: Suva to Moala costs F$49.50 per person one way; Suva to Lakeba and Vanua Balavu costs F$60.50 per person with meals included. Permission is required for foreigners to visit Lakeba.

Yacht

Yachting is a great way to explore the Fiji archipelago. It is possible to charter boats or hitch a ride on cruising vessels. Refer to the Sea section of the Getting There & Away chapter and Boat Chartering & Fishing and Sailing in the Activities section of the Facts for the Visitor chapter.

LOCAL TRANSPORT
Taxi

You will find taxis on Viti Levu, Vanua Levu and Taveuni. The bus stations in the main towns usually have depots and there is often an oversupply of taxis, with drivers competing for business. There are some phone cabs, but most are rickety old dinosaurs bound for or retrieved from the wrecker. Most drivers are Fiji Indian, usually with relatives in Australia, New Zealand or Canada, and are keen to discuss life and local politics.

Unlike in Suva, taxi drivers in Nadi, Lautoka and most rural areas don't use their meters. Ask locals what the acceptable rate is for a trip. If there is no meter always confirm an approximate price with the driver beforehand. Cabs can be shared for long trips. For touring around areas with limited public transport such as Taveuni, forming a group and negotiating a taxi fee for a half-day or day may be an option.

Always ask if the taxi is a return cab. If the taxi picks you up on a return trip, you can expect to pay F$1 per person or less (confirm the going rate with locals), as long as the taxi doesn't have to go out of its way. To make up for the low fare, the driver will usually pick up extra passengers from bus stops. You can easily recognise a return cab, as most taxis have the name of their home depot on the bumper bar.

ORGANISED TOURS

Fiji has many companies providing tours within the country, including trekking, cycling, kayaking, diving, bus or 4WD tours.

Cruises to the outer islands such as the Mamanucas and Yasawas are also popular. The main concentration of organised tours is on Viti Levu, with some on Ovalau, Taveuni and Vanua Levu.

For an overview, refer to the Activities section in the Facts for the Visitor chapter, and the individual island chapters for specific information on tours and operators.

Viti Levu

Geography

Viti Levu (Great Fiji) is Fiji's largest island, with an area of approximately 10,400 sq km. It has about 75% of Fiji's total population and is the political and administrative centre of the whole archipelago. The principal industries are located here, and it has the most extensive transport and communication system.

The island is roughly oval in shape, and measures about 146 km from east to west and 106 km from north to south. The main geographical feature is the mountain range which runs north-south. The highest Fijian peak, Tomanivi (Mt Victoria) at 1323m, is near the northern end of the range. On either side of this backbone there are rugged ranges and hills sloping steeply towards the lowland coastal areas. Different areas of the highlands have their own drainage systems: the Colo East Plateau is drained by the Rewa River; the Navua Plateau, to the south, by the Navua River; the Colo West Plateau by the Sigatoka River; and the Navosa Plateau by the Ba River.

Climate

The central highlands lie in the path of the prevailing south-east Trade Winds, resulting in higher rainfall on the eastern side of the range. On this side of the island the slopes are predominantly covered with greener vegetation and rainforest. In contrast, the western slopes have mostly open grasslands, which turn light yellow to brown according to the season; see the Facts for the Visitor chapter for more information about climate.

Orientation

Viti Levu's mountains divide the island into two distinct regions: the wetter eastern side and the drier western side. The country's capital, largest city and main port is Suva on the eastern side of Viti Levu. The main international airport, however, is on the western side at Nadi, with Lautoka, Fiji's second

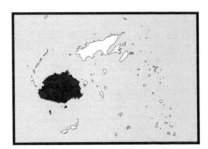

largest city and second port, nearby. Nadi and Suva are linked by the fully sealed Queens Road, along the southern perimeter of Viti Levu (221 km), and Kings Road (mostly sealed), around the northern side of the island (265 km). Expect to find lots of people and animals walking on the edge of the roads during day or night. There are regular buses along the Kings Road and Queens Road.

South of Nadi, the Queens Road winds through cane fields with a few interesting detours, including Momi Bay, Natadola Beach and the Kulukulu Sand Dunes near Sigatoka. The Sigatoka River is Fiji's second largest river and the Sigatoka Valley, which extends up into the highlands, is known as Fiji's 'salad bowl'. The Queens Road passes Korotogo and Korolevu along a beautiful stretch of coast known as the Coral Coast. Past Korolevu, Queens Road turns away from the shore and climbs up over the southern end of the main mountain range that divides east and west Viti Levu. Deuba and Pacific Harbour have the last OK beaches before Suva, and Beqa Lagoon is visible directly offshore.

The Kings Road is just as spectacular as the Queens Road, and is perhaps more interesting due to the variety of landscapes it passes through. Heading north from Suva, the Kings Road passes Nausori town on the

ROBYN JONES

HOLGER LEUE

ROBYN JONES

ROBYN JONES

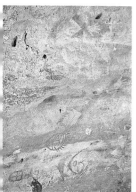
ROBYN JONES

HOLGER LEUE

A	B
C	D
E	F

Viti Levu

A: Naiserelagi Church
B: Sri Siva Subramaniya Temple, Nadi
C: Temple doors, Orchid Island

D: Navala Village, Nausori Highlands
E: Rock paintings, Vatulele
F: Sunset, Suva

ROBYN JONES

Viti Levu
Seashore, Vatulele Island

margin of the Rewa River and up to Korovou, where it heads inland. Another route follows the coast past Natovi Landing, rejoining the Kings Road further north near Viti Levu Bay, but as this road is unsealed, it's best suited to 4WD. The Kings Road is also unsealed from Korovou for about 50 km up to Dama, but is reasonably well maintained and suitable for any type of car. This stretch passes through more isolated Fijian villages. From Dama the newly sealed road heads down through the hills to Viti Levu Bay and along the coast to Rakiraki, with some spectacular views of the mountains, coast and offshore islands, including Nananu-i-Ra. Just before Tavua is the turn-off to Nadarivatu and Mt Victoria. Beyond Tavua the Kings Road becomes less scenic, passing through Ba and sugar-cane country and finishing at Lautoka.

There are many minor roads leading to isolated coastal areas or into the highland interior. Most are unsealed and often too rough for non-4WD vehicles. Sometimes, especially during the wetter season, these roads can become muddy and flooded.

Activities

Activities such as cycling, trekking, bird-watching, horse riding, surfing, windsurfing, boat chartering, fishing, rafting, sailing, canoeing, snorkelling and diving are all available on Viti Levu. It is also possible to visit villages and archaeological sites; see Activities in the Facts for the Visitor chapter.

Organised Tours

Trekking in the Interior Organised treks are a good way to have a look at the beautiful Fijian high country and interior villages. Rosie Tours (or Adventure Tours, ☎ 722 755; fax 722 607) is the largest tour operator in Fiji, and has an office at Nadi airport and tour desks at most major hotels. It has daily (except Sunday) full-day trekking to the Nausori Highlands from Nadi for F$58 including lunch. It also offers more expensive six-day, five-night tours to the Central Highlands for F$600, including meals and accommodation.

Peni Inland Adventures (☎ /fax 703 801) at 10 Westpoint Arcade in Nadi offers mountain tours and village stays at Bukuya in the highlands; see the Interior section. Peni also organises four-day treks from Mt Victoria to Bukuya, which cost F$240 per person, including meals, accommodation and guides.

German International Eco-Touring Fiji (☎ /fax 723 360) has an office almost next door to the RB supermarket, Main St, Nadi town. It offers four-day, three-night trekking to the Central Highlands for F$370 or to Mt Victoria for F$438. It also offers package tours in association with Sunflower Airlines to host villages on Moala Island in the southern Lau group. Prices start at F$388 for two nights.

The Tourist Information Centre (☎ 700 243; fax 702 746), which is actually a commercial travel agent, is run by Victory Travel and Tours Ltd and is also known as Island Adventures, Jungle Trek Safari, Inland Safari and Victory Inland Safaris. It has an office in Nadi town and in Martinar near the Dominion International Hotel. It offers a variety of budget tours: a day trip to the Nausori Highlands, for example, costs F$52.

Mountain Bike & 4WD Tours Independent Tours (☎ 520 697, 520 678; fax 520 678), based in Korotogo, near Sigatoka, started up in late 1995. It has guided bike tours for groups of two to six people, as well as bike hire and 4WD tours. A deposit of F$200 or credit card or other ID is required and there is a 15% discount for those who bring their own bicycle. It is advisable to book at least 10 days ahead. A German guide is available. Cyclists should be reasonably fit, especially for the trips into the mountains, although a service car can pick you up if you are lagging. Equipment, including 21-speed mountain bikes, helmets, gloves and water bottles, is provided, and supplies of water, fruit drinks and food are carried in an accompanying truck and are included in the price.

A half-day tour to the Nausori Highlands, departing from Nadi, costs F$39. You will be

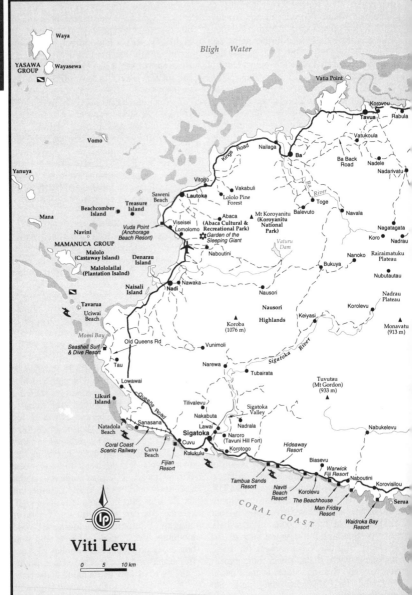

Viti Levu

0   5   10 km

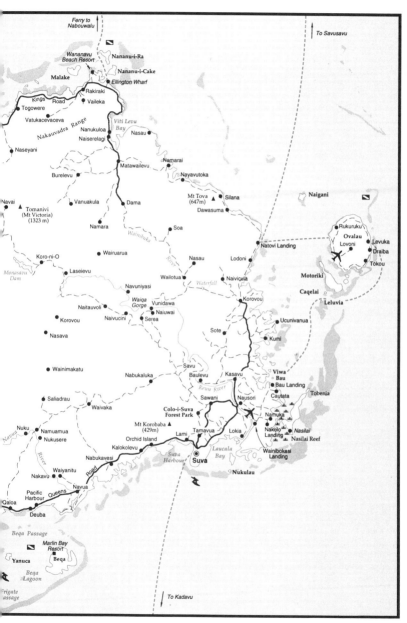

transported up into the hills, from where you ride back down.

Most of the tours depart from Korotogo and there is free pick-up from hotels along the Coral Coast. A half-day trip by 4WD up Sigatoka Valley and return ride down to the Coral Coast costs F$49. Day tours from Sigatoka (F$69) involve being transported to a hill overlooking the Coral Coast. You ride along the ridges, past cattle farms and settlements, downhill to and along the Sigatoka River, stopping for a swim and to visit Nawamagi village for *lovo* lunch and kava, and continuing on to Tavuni Hill Fort. It also has a day trip from Korotogo to Natadola Beach involving a one-hour bike ride past villages and farmland, and barbecue lunch, for F$49.

Another bike tour through the Sigatoka Valley, Nausori Highlands and down to Nadi Bay (160 km) takes three days and two nights and costs F$275. This route is also offered as a one-day trip by 4WD. An annual eight-day trip around Viti Levu is F$385. It is scheduled for August, but ring/fax to confirm departure dates. Cyclists travel about 50 km a day so they have to be reasonably fit.

Road Tours If you are short on time or prefer not to travel around independently, then organised road tours may be an option. Road tours from Nadi with Rosie Tours include trips to Suva for F$46, which is a long way for a day trip. A half-day tour to the sights between Nadi and Lautoka, including Vuda Lookout-Viseisei village-Garden of the Sleeping Giant, is F$45. Better value is a full-day tour to Sigatoka Valley-Tavuni Hill Fort-Kula Bird Park for F$55. Entrance fees are normally included in the price, but not lunches.

UTC Fiji (☎ 722 811), at the airport, offers day tours by bus from Nadi to Suva via the Orchid Island Cultural Centre for F$56 per person. Half-day tours to the Garden of the Sleeping Giant and Viseisei village are F$37 per person.

River Trips If you are looking for a bit of adventure you might try river rafting. Eco

Touring Fiji (☎ 703 844; fax 703 360) offers white-water rubber rafting on the Ba River. It is a scenic drive to the starting point upriver, through cane fields with views of the coast. The volume of water in the river influences how fast your ride will be. If it has been raining before you go you might get a thrilling ride. When it is calm the raft will drift along over crystal waters through the scenic bush surroundings. The tour includes swimming, a picnic lunch, guide, helmet and life vest, and pick-up and transport to/from Nadi and Lautoka hotels.

Trips up the Sigatoka River to pottery villages are offered by Bounty Cruises; see Sigatoka and Around later in this chapter. From Suva and Pacific Harbour hotels you can take canoe, raft or motorboat tours of the Navua River; see the Queens Road section of this chapter. Short jet-boat tours of the mangroves near Denarau Island, Nadi, are offered by Shotover Jet Fiji; see the Nadi section.

Cruises to the Mamanucas & Yasawas
Cruises to the stunning Mamanuca and Yasawa islands are very popular; refer to these two island chapters for more information. Most leave from Nadi's Denarau Marina or Lautoka's Queens Wharf. Half-and full-day cruises are available to the Mamanucas; operators include Beachcomber, South Seas Cruises, Captain Cook Cruises and the Whale's Tale. Longer cruises to the Yasawas are offered by Westside Watersports, Blue Lagoon Cruises and Captain Cook Cruises.

Scenic Flights
Most domestic flights are scenic, especially on a clear day. The islands, coral reefs and depths of blues and greens are gorgeous from above– snorkellers and divers will drool at the sight. Flights over the Nausori Highlands and the Sigatoka Valley are also spectacular.

Turtle Airways (☎ 722 389; fax 720 346), based at Newtown Beach, Nadi, has a fleet of Cessna seaplanes, which can carry up to four passengers. As well as transfers they have scenic flights. The charter service is

F$700 per flying hour. Island Hoppers (☎ 720 410; fax 720 172) has an office at Nadi airport and offers helicopter flights departing from Denarau Island. A 20-minute flight over the Sabeto mountain range and the gorges of Mt Evans east of Lautoka is F$107 per person. The 'Islands & Highlands' trip is F$184 per person for 40 minutes. A 'Tag-a-Long Tour' joins transfer guests to one of the offshore islands for F$107 and takes 40 to 60 minutes.

Day trips can also be taken from Nadi to Malololailai and Mana Island in the Mamanucas and to historical Levuka in Ovalau; see the Getting Around chapter. UTC Fiji organises a full-day 'cruise and flightsee' tour to Mana Island, including barbecue lunch and return via seaplane for F$180 per person.

Accommodation

On arrival at Nadi airport you will be bombarded with a huge range of accommodation options, especially in the Nadi/Lautoka and Coral Coast areas. If you haven't already decided where to go we recommend a night or two in Nadi to assess your options and hear other traveller's tales. In Nadi you can either stay downtown, at the 'beach' or close to the airport for convenience while awaiting connections. The town has good restaurants and infrastructure for travellers.

If Nadi is too hectic, Lautoka is quieter and easier to get around. There is also accommodation between the two towns at Vuda Point. There are many places to stay along the Queens Road, and Fiji's capital, Suva, has a range of options. Along the Kings Road accommodation is relatively sparse. Korovou (eastern Viti Levu), Rakiraki, Tavua and Ba have one basic hotel each. Rakiraki also has one up-market resort, as does offshore Nananu-i-Ra Island, along with four budget options. With the exception of beautiful Natadola Beach and the OK beaches of the Coral Coast, to find idyllic beaches, peace and quiet, you must pay extra for boat transportation or domestic flights to the offshore and outer islands.

Getting There & Away

Most travellers arrive in Fiji at Nadi International Airport or a lesser number at Nausori airport near Suva. Refer to the Getting There & Away chapter for details on the airports and airline offices. These airports also have domestic flights to most other islands. Refer to the Getting Around chapter and individual island chapters for interisland flights and ferry services.

Getting Around

There are regular domestic light plane flights between Nadi and Suva, and the airstrip at Deuba near Pacific Harbour has recently reopened, with two services per week from Nadi. To get to/from Nadi airport and to/from Nausori airport, see the Getting There & Away chapter. Local buses are a cheap and interesting way to get around, and Viti Levu has a good bus network with many different bus companies operating on a local level. Express buses link the main centres along the Queens Road and Kings Road. The main bus stations are at Lautoka, Nadi and Suva. There are also minibuses and carriers shuttling along the Queens Road. Taxis are plentiful but don't always use meters, so confirm the price in advance. Viti Levu is easy to explore by car; see the Getting Around chapter for details and a list of car-rental companies.

Nadi, Lautoka & Around

Nadi town and Lautoka are 33 km apart, on the western coast of Viti Levu and set against a mountain backdrop. The Nadi airport is nine km from Nadi town and 24 km from Lautoka, and there are a few places of interest in between. Sugar cane, well suited to the hot and relatively dry climate of western Viti Levu, is grown extensively. There is a high proportion of Fiji Indians in the area, who are mostly fourth-generation descendants of indentured labourers brought to Fiji to work in the cane fields.

NADI

Nadi is Fiji's third-largest city, with a population of 15,220 within the urban area. This rapidly expanding town relies almost totally on tourism, and while not a particularly appealing place, it is a convenient base to organise your trip around Viti Levu, to the interior or to offshore islands. Nadi has an abundance of places to stay, from budget dorms to luxury resort hotels such as the Sheraton and Regent. Its main street is cluttered with restaurants and duty-free, clothes and souvenir shops. The Swami Temple at the southern end of the main street is worth a visit, as is the produce market. To the east lie the beautiful Nausori Highlands and to the north the Sabeto Range.

Orientation

It is not difficult to get to Nadi from the airport (nine km). The Queens Road heads south from Lautoka into Nadi, passing Nadi airport and crossing the Nadi River, to enter town as its main street, which then terminates in a T-intersection (at the Hindu temple). The Queens Road continues towards Suva, while the Nadi Back Road bypasses the busy centre and rejoins the Queens Road towards the airport. The Nausori Highlands Road leads off into the mountains from the Nadi Back Road; see the Inland section at the end of this chapter. The market, bus terminal, post office and telephone exchange are to the east of the main street.

Just north of the Nadi River bridge and to the west (on the right if coming from the airport) is the road to Denarau Island, four km away and about 20 minutes from the airport. The 255-hectare island is reclaimed mangrove swamp and has dark-sand beaches, which may be disappointing for some. It has Nadi's two most up-market resorts and the Denarau Golf & Racquet Club; see Activities below. The Denarau Marina opened in mid-1994 and it is from here that most tours and boat services to the Mamanuca islands depart.

Wailoaloa Rd turns west off the Queens Road near the Dominion Hotel (to the right

if you are coming from the airport). Wailoaloa Beach is about 1¾ km from the highway. To get to Newtown Beach turn off Wailoaloa Rd to the right after 1¼ km and continue for another 1¼ km. Here there are several budget places to stay, a golf course and the Turtle Airways seaplane base. You can also get to Wailoaloa Beach along Enamanu Rd.

Information

Tourist Office The Fiji Visitors Bureau (FVB; ☎ 722 433; fax 720 141), PO Box 9217, Nadi airport, is a very good source of current information about what is happening in the tourism scene in Fiji. The office is just on the left of the ANZ bank as you come out of arrivals, and it has an extensive stock of brochures for you to browse through, and probably get lost in. If you brief the staff about what you are after you are more likely to obtain useful information. Places other than the FVB purporting to be 'tourist information centres ' are actually travel agents; see Travel Agencies below.

Money The ANZ bank at the airport is open 24 hours every day, and is therefore a convenient place to change money. They charge F$2 per transaction. There are ANZ, Westpac and National Bank of Fiji (NBF) banks on the Main St in Nadi that will change foreign currency and travellers' cheques without transaction fees. There is also a Thomas Cook money exchange in the main street and another next to the Morris Hedstrom supermarket. Many hotels will change money but normally they pay a bit less than the banks.

Post & Telecommunications Both the post office and the telephone exchange are in downtown Nadi near the market. There is also a post office at Nadi airport, across the car park from the arrivals area near the cargo sheds. Public cardphones are not usually too hard to find; see the Facts for the Visitor chapter.

Travel Agencies Nadi has a plethora of travel agencies, most of which have offices

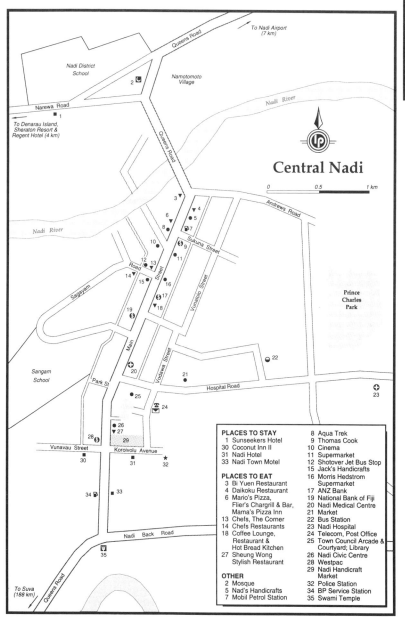

Central Nadi

0   0.5   1 km

PLACES TO STAY
1 Sunseekers Hotel
30 Coconut Inn II
31 Nadi Hotel
33 Nadi Town Motel

PLACES TO EAT
3 Bi Yuen Restaurant
4 Daikoku Restaurant
6 Mario's Pizza,
   Flier's Chargrill & Bar,
   Mama's Pizza Inn
13 Chefs, The Corner
14 Chefs Restaurants
18 Coffee Lounge,
   Restaurant &
   Hot Bread Kitchen
27 Sheung Wong
   Stylish Restaurant

OTHER
2 Mosque
5 Nad's Handicrafts
7 Mobil Petrol Station

8 Aqua Trek
9 Thomas Cook
10 Cinema
11 Supermarket
12 Shotover Jet Bus Stop
15 Jack's Handicrafts
16 Morris Hedstrom
   Supermarket
17 ANZ Bank
19 National Bank of Fiji
20 Nadi Medical Centre
21 Market
22 Bus Station
23 Nadi Hospital
24 Telecom, Post Office
25 Town Council Arcade &
   Courtyard; Library
26 Nadi Civic Centre
28 Westpac
29 Nadi Handicraft
   Market
32 Police Station
34 BP Service Station
35 Swami Temple

at the Nadi International Airport arrivals area on the ground and 1st floors. It is a good idea to have a look at the FVB before booking anything with the agents, who all receive commissions from different places and therefore may not give an unbiased opinion. Some specialise in budget accommodation and offer good deals for the budget traveller, but be careful with the arrangements and forms of payment for your trip or tour. Avoid paying too much money up front. Often they ask for full payment in advance, and then you may have difficulty with refunds if required. Ideally you should try to get more information on details such as: the safety of the transport you are going to be using, especially if it includes boat trips; the cleanliness and facilities of the accommodation; the type and price of food available; and any hidden costs. If possible, quiz other travellers who have recently been to the place, as that's a good way to get the current picture and avoid unwanted trips.

Agents include:

Rosie, The Travel Service
    Nadi airport concourse (☎ 722 755; fax 722 607)
    Australia: East Towers, 9 Bronte Rd, Bondi Junction, Sydney, NSW 2022 (☎ 02-9389 3666; fax 02-9369 1129; toll-free 008-659 867)
    USA: 1620 Redesdale Ave, Los Angeles, CA 90026 (☎ 213-660 1023; fax 213-660 0415)
Margaret Travel Service
    Nadi airport concourse (☎ 721 988; fax 721 992)
    Fiji Bayrisches Tourist Information Centre, Grace Bros Building, Main St 1, Nadi Town (☎ 703 922; fax 721 022)
Tourist Information Centre
    cnr Market Rd & Main St, Nadi Town (☎ 700 243; fax 702 746)

Bookshops Nadi doesn't have many good bookshops. Desai on Main St near the Civic Centre (☎ 703 444) and Paper Power in the Town Council Arcade (Civic Centre) have a limited selection. You might be able to find some interesting books at hotel and handicraft shops.

Medical Services For medical treatment, contact:

Nadi Hospital
    Market Rd, Nadi (☎ 701 128)
Namaka Medical Centre
    Namaka Lane (off Queens Road), Namaka (☎ 722 288)

Emergency Emergency phone numbers include:

Emergency (☎ 000), free
FVB emergency hotline (☎ 0800 721 721), free
Police (☎ 700 222)
Ambulance (☎ 701 128)

Dangers & Annoyances Refer to the Facts for the Visitor chapter. The main annoyance in Nadi is pestering by souvenir and duty-free vendors downtown. You may also come across sword sellers. While Fiji is a relatively safe place to travel, muggings and theft are unfortunately becoming increasingly common in the Nadi area, even during daylight, and the danger is not limited to lone travellers. Avoid walking along quiet roads such as Wailoaloa Rd or even the road to Denarau Island, as well as the stretch along the Queens Road from downtown Nadi to Kennedy Ave. Leave valuables at your hotel and if you are carrying a pack it may be best to take a bus or taxi.

Sri Siva Subramaniya Swami Temple

At the southern end of Nadi's main street, set against a beautiful mountain backdrop, is this large, elaborate and colourful Hindu temple (☎ 700 016; fax 703 777). Devotees originally worshipped here in a small *bure*. Following traditional south-Indian Hindu temple architecture, its reinforced concrete shell is covered by ornate sculpture and paintings depicting lotus leaves and deities. *Silpi* (craftsmen) were imported from India for the construction. For the opening ceremony in July 1994 a chief priest was brought from India and a helicopter hovered overhead to shower heavenly blessings in the form of flowers.

The Hindu Lord Shiva takes on various forms, all incarnations being manifestations of the One Supreme Lord. This is a Murugan temple and worship of Lord Murugan is

PLACES TO STAY
1   Tokatoka Resort Hotel
2   Raffles Gateway Hotel
4   Tanoa International
    Hotel
5   Fiji Mocambo
6   Tanoa Apartments &
    International Hotel
7   Melanesian Hotel
9   Skylodge Hotel
11 Travellers Beach
    Resort
12 Horizon Beach
    Resort
14 New Town Beach
    Motel
15 Club Fiji Resort

17 Rosie Serviced
    Apartments
20 Dominion International
    Hotel
21 Westin Plaza Hotel
22 Sandalwood Inn
23 Capricorn
    International Hotel
24 Nadi Bay Motel
26 Sunny Holiday Motel
28 Nadi International
    Youth Hostel
29 White House
30 Hotel Kennedy

PLACES TO EAT
8   Maharaj Restaurant

16 Colonial Plaza
    (Mama's Pizza Inn,
    Tandoori Haven)
18 Cafe Blewzz
25 Hamancho Restaurant
27 MacDonald's

OTHER
3   Nadi International
    Airport
10 Turtle Airways
13 Inner Space
    Adventures
19 Shell Service Station
31 BP Service Station

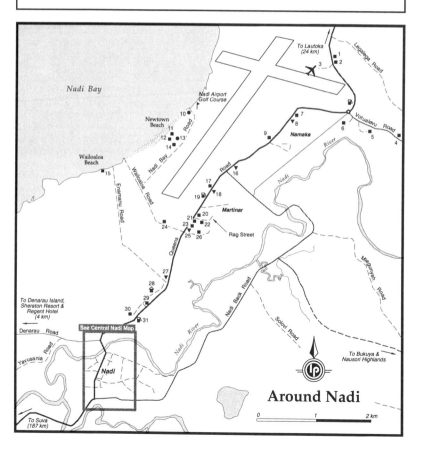

Around Nadi

equivalent to the worship of nature. He is the guardian deity of seasonal rains. Paintings on the ceiling show Lord Murugan in various encounters. Other deities enshrined in the temple include Ganesa, Muruga, Siva and Laxmi.

Visitors are welcome but are requested to wear neat and modest dress, and to have consumed no alcohol or nonvegetarian food that day. The temple is open daily from 5 am to 8 pm and closed Monday to Friday from 1 to 3.30 pm. There is a devotees' lunch on Sunday. Annual festivals such as Karthingai Puja (23 March), Panguni Uthiram Thirunaal (1 to 3 April) and Thai Pusam attract devotees from around the world. The temple has four full-time priests who perform eight pujas daily and for a fee are available for home and vehicle blessings.

Activities
There are many organised tours which leave the Nadi area, including scenic flights, road tours, treks to the interior, cycling, island cruises and river trips; see Organised Tours earlier in this chapter.

Diving Aqua Trek (☎ 702 413; fax 702 4120) has a shop at 465 Main St, Nadi town. It is the largest dive operation in the area and one of the best equipped in Fiji, and as a result you will have to pay a little bit more. It has a dive shop on Mana Island and also offers day trips from Nadi. Dives include the popular shark-feeding dive. A boat dive including tank and weights is F$60 or with all gear F$80. Night or dawn dives are F$70 and packages are also available (F$330 for six tanks plus F$10 gear hire per dive). A scuba-diving course is F$130 and a PADI open-water course (minimum four days) is F$520. It is advisable to book in advance.

Inner Space Adventures (☎ 723 883) at Wailoaloa Beach near the Travellers Beach Resort offers cheaper dive trips to the Mamanuca sites, but don't expect the standards you would get from Aqua Trek. It charges F$60/77/99 for a one/two/three-tank dive trip, which includes all gear, lunch and a transfer from hotels in the Nadi area. Open-

water courses cost F$320 and advanced-diver courses are F$240. Snorkelling trips cost F$25, including equipment.

Horse Riding Nadi Bay Pony Club (☎ 720 136), Newtown Beach, Nadi, offers beach and cross-country rides and day treks into the mountains. A one-hour ride along the beach costs F$15, and half-day/full-day treks go for F$50/90, including lunch.

Jet-Boat Trip Also on Denarau Island is the New Zealand company Shotover Jet Fiji (☎ 750 400; fax 750 666), which opened in Fiji in 1994. The jet boats depart Denarau Marina for a hair-raising half-hour trip to the Nadi River mangroves. The thrilling adrenalin rush is probably out of the price range of most budget travellers: F$55 for adults and F$24 for children under 15 years old. The jet boats carry 12 passengers and are powered by eight-litre V8 engines and are designed for speed on as little as 10 cm of water. While the drivers are trained to perform 360-degree spins and frighteningly close shaves, Shotover has carried over a million passengers without incident. A similar trip operates in Queenstown, New Zealand. There's a courtesy minibus for transfers from hotels in the area and from the Nadi town pick-up point opposite Chefs Restaurant.

Golf & Tennis The Denarau Golf & Racquet Club (☎ 750 477; fax 750 484) caters mainly for guests of the Regent and Sheraton hotels. They have an 18-hole golf course with bunkers in the shape of sea creatures. The club house has a restaurant and bar, pro-golf shop, meeting and change rooms. Green fees are F$81 for 18 holes and F$49 for nine holes. There are also all-weather and grass tennis courts. Fees are F$17.60 per hour and racket hire F$5 per person.

A much cheaper alternative for less discerning golfers is the Nadi Airport Golf Club (☎ 722 148), which is open seven days a week from 7 am to 7 pm (daylight hours) and is located opposite Turtle Airways, Newtown Beach. Green fees here are F$15 for 18 holes. It is F$20 to rent a full set of clubs and F$5 for a pull cart. They have a bar and pool table. Discounts can be arranged.

Places to Stay – bottom end
Consider whether you want the convenience of staying close to downtown (where there are lots of options for places to eat), at the black-sand Wailoaloa Beach (fairly isolated but away from the chaotic centre) or along the Queens Road between the airport and downtown Nadi. Obviously, proximity to the airport will affect the level of aircraft noise. The only place which allows camping is the Sunny Holiday Motel. Some places get a commission for selling travellers certain tours.

Along the Highway There are two budget places to stay on Kennedy Ave, which runs parallel to the Queens Road. Both of these hotels are within a 15-minute walk from downtown; however, there have been a spate of muggings along this stretch so avoid walking in the dark by yourself, especially if carrying packs. Consider catching the bus or a taxi for F$2.

The *White House Visitor's Inn* (☎ 700 022; fax 702 822), 40 Kennedy Ave, is recommended. This small hotel is reasonably clean and has a friendly atmosphere. Rooms with private facilities and air-con are F$27.50/33 for singles/doubles. A twin room with shared toilet and bathroom is F$22 and a four-bed dorm is F$8.80 per person. There are communal tea and coffee-making facilities and a simple breakfast is included in the price.

A short walk from the White House is *Nadi International Youth Hostel* (☎ /fax 703 200), a new three-storey building at 115 Kennedy Ave. It has dorm beds for F$5.50 and private double rooms inside the dormitory area for F$16.50. A breakfast of tea, bread and jam is included. HI card holders get a 10% discount. You can cook in the kitchen on the top floor and wash your clothes at troughs on the back balconies, or they will do your washing for F$5.

The *Sandalwood Inn* (☎ 722 044; fax 720 103) is a small, clean, well-run hotel on Ragg St, just off Queens Road near the Dominion International Hotel. All rooms have tea/coffee-making facilities. It has fan-cooled rooms with shared toilet and shower for F$26/33 for singles/doubles, or F$33/40 for rooms with private facilities and fridge. Air-con rooms cost F$50/57 for singles/doubles.

The *Sandalwood Lodge*, which is 200m from the Sandalwood Inn, has self-contained units with a small kitchen and private balcony for F$64/70/77 for singles/doubles/triples.

The *Sunny Holiday Motel* (☎ 722 158; fax 701 541), Northern Press Rd, near the Hamacho Restaurant, is a bit of a dump and best avoided unless you are camping, in which case you can use their front lawn for F$2. Dorm beds are F$5; the downstairs dorm is stuffy with no external window, but the upstairs room is a bit better. Although it describes itself as a youth hostel it is not affiliated with the IYHF. Rooms with share facilities are F$11/16.60 or with private facilities F$19.80/22. A self-contained apartment is F$27.50/33; air-conditioning costs an extra F$5.50.

The *Nadi Bay Motel* (☎ 723 599; fax 720 092) on Beach Rd (Wailoaloa Rd) is a few hundred metres off Queens Road. It's in a bit of a no-man's-land, neither close to downtown nor the beach, which is a long, dusty walk away. The downstairs dorm is crowded and can be noisy with 12 bunk beds for F$8.80 per head. The upstairs dorm is better. Breakfast is extra. Rooms with shared facilities are F$23/31, and those with private bathroom are F$31/38. Air-con rooms with private facilities cost F$38/46/54 and apartments with cooking facilities are F$46/54/62 with F$8 surcharge for an extra person. The hotel has a pool, bar and restaurant with meals for about F$6, and credit cards are accepted. The hotel seems a bit run-down, and feedback from travellers about cleanliness, food and service has been mixed.

If you want to stay close to the airport, the *Melanesian Hotel* (☎ 722 438; fax 720 425) on Queens Road is an option. It is about three minutes (F$3 taxi) drive from the airport. It

VITI LEVU

has a couple of reasonably good five-bed dormitories for F$12 per bed. Standard rooms with fan are F$33/40, or with air-con for F$43/50/60. There is a swimming pool and a small restaurant with breakfast for under F$4.50 and meals under F$8.50.

The *Rosie Serviced Apartments* (☎ 722 755; fax 722 607), on Queens Road, look fairly unattractive from the outside but can be a cheap way to stay in Nadi if you are in a small group or family. Reasonably comfortable self-contained apartments with cooking facilities are F$50 and sleep four to five people. Weekly rates are F$40 per night.

At the Beach There are four budget options at Wailoaloa Beach on Nadi Bay, three of which are grouped together about five km from Nadi town and three km (a long dusty walk) from the Queens Road. The beach is fairly unattractive but is an alternative to the bustling town. The disadvantage of staying here is that food and transport are limited. Ring in advance to check availability of accommodation. To get to town you can either catch a local bus (50 cents) or taxi for about F$3 (although they will try to charge F$5). A taxi to the airport costs F$7. Buses depart Wailoaloa Beach every hour till 11.30 am and less frequently in the afternoon until the last one at 5.30 pm. Boats leave from here to Mana Island backpacker 'resorts'.

The *Horizon Beach Resort* (☎ 722 832; fax 720 662) has good-value, clean rooms and friendly staff. Dorm beds are F$5.50 per person. The dorm rooms can get crowded, but are usually clean and have hot showers. Fan-cooled rooms are F$19.80/28.60, F$27.50/33 with a sea view. Air-con rooms with a sea view are F$31.90/37.40. There are no cooking facilities but meals are good and reasonably priced at between F$5.50 and F$8. They have a washing machine but F$10 for one load is too expensive.

New Town Beach Motel (☎ 723 339; fax 720 087), at 5 Wasawasa Rd, has fan-cooled rooms for F$11 per person in the small, five-bed dorm with a bathroom. Twin/double rooms are F$33 and family rooms are

F$41.80. The dining room has lunches for F$6 and dinner for under F$8.

Travellers Beach Resort (☎ 723 322; fax 720 026) has 20 rooms in a two-storey block. Dorm rooms cost F$8.80 per person. Double rooms with fans are F$33 or F$38.50 with air-con, but it may be possible to bargain. The hotel has a small pool on the beach, and it accepts Visa and MasterCard. There have been mixed reports from travellers, and complaints of being pushed into arranged trips, being disturbed during the night by very friendly female staff, and of being difficult to deal with over payments.

Club Fiji Resort (☎ 702 189; fax 720 350) is further south than the other three places and has more of a resort feel. It seems a bit misplaced on this black-sand beach. Staying here can get expensive because of the isolation, which limits you to the resort bar and restaurant. It has 24 rooms and a large dining/bar bure. Beach-front rooms are F$70.40, ocean-view rooms are F$59.40 and back garden-court rooms are F$42.90. Two rooms are used as dormitories and are F$9.90/12.90 per person without/with breakfast. There are 12 beds crammed in each and despite the limited space, solar hot water and lack of security, management allows people who have checked out from other bures to use the dorm showers. There is a daily shuttle bus to downtown Nadi at 10 am, returning at 1 pm, or a taxi ride costs F$5.

Downtown Nadi The *Sunseekers Hotel* (☎ 700 400) is conveniently located near the north end of town on the Naceura Rd to Denarau. Although not in the centre, it is only a few minutes walk away over the bridge. The hotel houses up to 100 guests, is reasonably clean and organised, and is a good option for budget accommodation. Dorm beds cost F$6.60 a night. Prices for fan-cooled rooms are in the range of F$27 to F$38. Some rooms have private toilet and shower. They also have a small shop, tourist information, a bar, outdoor deck with tables, a swimming pool and a small restaurant serving snacks all day.

The *Nadi Town Motel* (☎ 700 600) is a

rock-bottom dive located on the main street towards the seedier end of town, near Nadi's nightclubs. Up the dodgy stairs, rooms are smelly and not very clean. Dorm beds cost F$6 and shabby double rooms F$25. They are pushy in the promotion of transfers to Nananu-i-Ra Island. The *Coconut Inn II* in Vunavau St charges F$11 per person in the dorm, F$22/33 for standard singles/doubles with no window and F$25/45 for better rooms.

The *Nadi Hotel* (☎ 700 000; fax 700 280), on Koroivolu Ave, is centrally located downtown near the post office, market and bus terminal. It has 33 relatively clean rooms in a two-storey building with a garden and swimming pool. Dorm beds are F$10, but it can be noisy due to the disco next door. Standard fan-cooled rooms cost F$22/27.50, and air-con rooms cost F$33/38.50. There can be a problem with water supply to the upstairs rooms. The restaurant, also open for outsiders, has a simple menu with sandwiches for F$4.50 and grill of the day for F$6.50.

Places to Stay – middle

Most of the middle-range hotels are located on the Queens Road near the airport, an important consideration given the very early morning departure times of many international flights. The disadvantage is their distance from most restaurants and entertainment. Club Fiji Resort at Wailoaloa Beach may also be an option; see Places to Stay–bottom end, earlier in this chapter.

The *Raffles Gateway Hotel* (☎ 722 444; fax 720 620), conveniently located directly opposite Nadi airport, has 100 air-con rooms at F$100 for singles/doubles and F$110 for triples. Day rooms are F$50 for a maximum of six hours between 6 am and 6 pm. Up to two children under 16 years can share with parents for free. There are no cooking facilities and restaurant meals cost F$14 to F$17.

Tokatoka Resort Hotel (☎ 720 222; fax 720 400) is popular among ex-pats when staying in Nadi. It is located almost opposite the airport a km towards Lautoka. The hotel has 74 villa-style units ranging from studios

for F$130 (doubles), villa studios for F$140 (up to three people), villa apartments for F$180 (up to four people) and full villas (maximum seven people) for F$286. All units have cooking facilities. The atmosphere and facilities are good for families and it has an interestingly designed swimming pool, a water slide and restaurant, and child-minding for F$3.50 per hour.

The *Skylodge Hotel* (☎ 722 200; fax 790 212), which was built as a consequence of Nadi airport's expansion, is now part of the Tanoa group of hotels. It has 53 rooms on 4.4 hectares and amenities include pitch and putt golf, mini tennis and a swimming pool. Rooms in the building near reception start at F$100 for singles or doubles with air-con. Cottages are spaced around the garden. The four self-contained units appear to be run-down and are F$125 each. They are also available for long-term rental. Security may be a problem as there is no check at the gate.

The *Dominion (International Hotel)* (☎ 722 255; fax 720 187) is on the Queens Road about 4.5 km from Nadi airport. Prices are F$102/109/116 for deluxe rooms, F$119/126/133 for superior rooms. An extra bed in the same room is F$6 and children under 12 years are half-price. Staff are friendly and helpful, and amenities include a reasonably good swimming pool and gardens, tennis courts and night entertainment including a meke. The restaurant serves all-day snacks for F$5.50 to F$6.50 and has an overpriced mixed-style dinner menu, including seafood, for F$15 to F$23.50. If they don't appear busy, ask for their reduced 'walk in rates'.

The *Westin Plaza Hotel* (☎ 720 044; fax 720 071), also on Queens Road, now has the same owners as Tokatoka. It used to be known as the New Westgate Hotel and is being refurbished. Standard rooms with air-con and ceiling fan, tea and coffee-making facilities and a fridge cost F$66. The front upstairs rooms are better. The standard rooms, however, are being phased out and replaced with deluxe versions with air-con and ceiling fan for F$99. Try asking for local rates. The hotel has a nice swimming pool, bar and restaurant (mains cost F$8 to F$12) but otherwise there is little to do at night. Budget rooms with shared facilities are F$29/36.30 for singles/doubles.

The *Capricorn International Hotel* (☎ 720 088; fax 720 522), just south of the Westin Plaza Hotel on Queens Road, used to be called the Metro Inn. The new owners are renovating some of the rooms, and there is a shop, dining room and bar. Rooms with fridge, telephone, sink and air-con are F$72 for singles or doubles. Deluxe rooms, with a door opening onto the pool, are a bit bigger and are F$82. A family suite is F$115.

The *Hotel Kennedy* (☎ 702 360; fax 702 218), on Kennedy Ave, is a 10-minute walk from downtown. It is clean and reasonably maintained but in need of some redecoration. Fan-cooled standard rooms are F$35/40 for singles/doubles and deluxe air-con rooms with a huge bathroom are F$50/55. An apartment with two bedrooms and cooking facilities is F$99. They also have a not-so-clean dorm in the old section for 16 people for F$10 each. Facilities include a good gym and swimming pool. The food at their restaurant is reasonably priced.

Places to Stay – top end

The *Fiji Mocambo* (☎ 722 000; fax 720 324) is on a 17-hectare property in the Namaka Hills, a few minutes drive south of the airport. It is managed by Shangri-la Hotels, but don't expect the same standards here, even the superior rooms are plain and getting a little shabby. Most rooms have a restful view out over farmland to the hills beyond. The hotel has 128 rooms with mountain views, air-con, TV and refrigerator. Standard rooms cost F$137. There are also corporate rates. On Monday, Wednesday and Friday it has meke and lovo nights and there are live bands on Saturday night.

A step down from the Mocambo is the *Tanoa International Hotel* (☎ 720 277; fax 720 191), which used to be the Travelodge but is now locally owned. It has 114 air-con studio rooms (fairly tight) with TV (including a Japanese channel), 24-hour room service, one double bed and one single bed.

Prices are F$160 for a studio and F$190 for a suite. Interconnecting rooms are also available. The restaurant has dinner for F$11 to F$32 and lunches F$10 to F$18.50. Amenities include a fitness centre.

Tanoa Apartments (☎ 723 685; fax 721 193) has 23 self-contained and serviced apartments in a new building on a hill with great mountain views and a swimming pool. Rates are F$140 for a deluxe bedroom or F$210 for a three-bedroom apartment. Some units accommodate up to six people. Weekly and long-term rates are negotiable.

Denarau Island The *Regent Fiji* (☎ 750 000; fax 750 259) was the first luxury hotel to be built in Fiji and has been operating continuously for the last 20 years. It has a rather interesting ambience, with the buildings blending in with the well-established gardens. Despite having 285 rooms, its spacious grounds and garden design avoid a crowded feeling. The lofty foyer, which has survived various hurricanes, has a deep, richly coloured decor and houses temporary art exhibitions. Rooms are decorated with bark cloth and rattan. Prices start at F$291.50 for garden-view rooms and F$398.20 for beach-front rooms.

For the food lover it has various restaurants with different food styles: there's fine dining in the Garden View, a mixed international menu on the Ocean Terrace, fish and grills in the Steak House, light lunches on the Terrace and Japanese food in the new Hamacho Japanese Restaurant. It's not the cheapest option around Nadi, but normally you can get a good-quality meal from these places. Amenities include tennis courts, a pitch and putt green, archery and lawn bowling facilities. The resort also offers guests scuba diving, game fishing, windsurfing and sailing.

While the Regent has more of a traditional Fijian style, its rival next door, the *Sheraton Fiji Resort* (☎ 750 777; fax 750 818), has a more modern Mediterranean feel. It has 300 deluxe rooms, all of which have ocean views, with prices starting at F$412.50 for singles or doubles. The Beachside Terrace

Restaurant is pleasant in the evening and the Ports of Call Restaurant is of a high standard, and therefore not cheap. A room-service American breakfast costs F$38.50. The resort caters well for young families and there is a daily entertainment programme for children, including a kid's barbecue around the pool for F$10. The baby-sitting service is F$2.75 per hour. Amenities and activities include a fitness centre with nine work-out stations, water aerobics, beach masseur, snorkelling and fishing trips, and scuba diving. Nonmotorised water activities are included in the rate.

Places to Eat

Nadi has the largest variety of restaurants and eating places in Fiji. Most places serve a mixture of Fijian, Indian, Chinese and Western dishes, and there are lots of cheap lunch-time eateries downtown. The tiny *Indian cafe*, in the courtyard next to the Nadi Civic Centre, while not particularly clean, has good, cheap food and is popular with locals. The *Coffee Lounge Restaurant* in the main street has good food for F$4 for a main. *Chefs, the Corner*, on the corner of Sagayam and the Queens Road, is an air-con cafe and takeaway. It's a bit more expensive but has excellent food, including meals, cakes, coconut pies, coffee and ice cream. It is open until 6 pm, and closed on Sunday. A fast-food alternative is *McDonald's* on the corner of Queens Road, which made its Fiji debut in mid-1996. It is extremely popular with locals and has vegetarian burgers.

Fijian For authentic Fijian dishes and a clean, homely atmosphere, the best place is *Cafe Blewzz* (☎ 721 022). It is a bit out of the way, in the suburb of Martinar on the Queens Road towards the airport, opposite the Rosie Apartments. It has breakfast, lunch and dinner at very reasonable prices.

International Chefs have three different places to eat: Chefs, the Corner (see above), Chefs, the Edge and Chefs, the Restaurant, all on Sagayam Rd, just off the main street. All have air-con. The medium-priced restau-

rant, *Chefs, the Edge*, is open from 9 am until 10 pm Monday to Saturday and serves excellent food at justifiable prices. *Chefs, the Restaurant* (☎ 703 131) is one of the most expensive restaurants in Nadi, offering international cuisine and candle-lit dinners. It is open for lunch from 10 am to 2 pm and dinner from 6 to 10 pm, but is closed on Sunday.

Fliers Chargrill & Bar (☎ 703 629), downtown on the main street opposite the Mobil service station, is open for dinner only. The restaurant/bar is frequented by airline crews and locals. It has music and steaks for F$10 to F$15.

The *Aeroview* restaurant and bar, upstairs at Nadi airport, has air-con and accepts credit cards– a good place if you have spent the last of your cash before flying out. The seafood bisque is recommended. The up-market resort hotels on Denarau Island have fine dining restaurants, which are open for visitors; see Places to Stay.

Italian For pizza and pasta and a comfortable atmosphere, *Mama's Pizza Inn* downtown is the best. The large pizza is huge and vegetarian bolognaise spaghetti is yummy. *Mario's Pizza* (☎ 703 903) a few doors up is OK and has medium pizza or pasta for around F$10. There is another Mama's at the Colonial Plaza, a new development halfway between Namaka and Nadi on the Queens Road.

Indian *Tandoori Haven* (☎ 720 811), which opened late 1995 at the Colonial Plaza, Namaka, has good food and atmosphere. It serves giant portions as starters and most main courses are between F$6.50 and F$15. It is closed on Monday and Sunday lunch. A banquet for lunch or dinner is F$20/30 for vegetarian/nonvegetarian. *Maharaj* (☎ 722 962), on the Queens Road near the airport, is good but not very conveniently located. Prices range from F$6 to F$15 per main dish. One reader has recommended the red-hot-chilli curried goat. Other Indian places include the *Curry Restaurant* (☎ 700 960), a run-down place downtown, opposite the

Mobil service station. The food is OK at F$7 to F$10 per dish.

Chinese *Bi Yuen Restaurant* (☎ 703 771), just next to the bridge in Nadi town, has quick, friendly service and reasonably cheap F$5 to F$8 meals that include unlimited rice, a pickled appetiser and ice cream. The *Sheung Wong Stylish Restaurant* (☎ 703 245) opened mid-1996 near the Civic Centre in the main street. Chow mein and chop suey dishes range from F$3.50 to F$8. They also have Indian curries from F$5 to F$18. Sichuan dishes (more spicy) and sea food ranges from F$6 to F$18.

Japanese Nadi has two good Japanese res-taurants. *Daikoku Restaurant* (☎ 703 622), downtown near the bridge, has à la carte for F$18 to F$25, teppan-yaki for F$22 to F$38 and sushi for F$5 to F$7: best avoided if on a budget. The spacious restaurant has air-con and is open for lunch from 11.30 am to 2 pm and dinner from 6 to 10 pm.

Hamacho (☎ 720 252), on the Queens Road near the Capricorn Hotel, has a com-fortable bar and table seating. A la carte is from F$4 to F$8 and yaki-tori (skewers) goes for F$3 to F$4, but the serves are small.

Self-Catering Nadi has a large produce market, which sells lots of fresh fruit and vegetables. Good-quality meat, however, is fairly difficult to come by. There are also several large supermarkets as well as baker-ies downtown.

Entertainment

Nadi has nowhere near the variety of nightlife as the capital, Suva. The up-market hotels usually have something happening at weekends. The *Fiji Mocambo Hotel* is the place to go for fine dining and live bands on Saturday night. There is a cover charge, a dress code and cars often wait in line to get into the grounds.

The *Regent* and *Sheraton* hotels on Denarau Island also have bars and night-time entertainment including mekes and fire walking. *Fliers*, opposite the Mobil service station, is a good place for a drink down-town.

Alternatively, there are a few cinemas downtown, which show a mix of Hollywood and Indian movies for under F$3 admission. The *West End Cinema* on Ashram Rd has four screenings daily except Sunday. Check the *Fiji Times* for information on what's showing.

Things to Buy

There are no shortage of souvenir and duty-free shops in Nadi's Main St. Jack's Handicrafts, in a large two-storey complex, sells handicrafts, clothing and jewellery, and has a small art gallery. Nad's Handicrafts sells similar items. Nadi also has an outdoor handicraft centre where you can bargain. Check if the items are hand or machine made. There are also many stores selling Indian clothing.

Popular items are *masi* (bark cloth), kava bowls (*tanoa*) from huge to miniature, war clubs, Fijian combs, *sulus*, woven baskets and mats, and local pottery. Some shops also sell handicrafts from other Pacific islands, such as face masks from Papua New Guinea and canoe prows from the Solomon Islands. Tania Whiteside at 381 Main St has a selec-tion of clothing by local designers; see the Things to Buy section in the Facts for the Visitor chapter.

Getting There & Away

See the Getting There & Away chapter for information on Nadi International Airport and the Getting Around chapter for inter-island air and boat services, and car rental. Many tours leave Nadi for the Mamanucas, mostly from Denarau Island.

Getting Around

There are regular local and express buses that travel along the Queens Road. There are local buses to Newtown Beach but not to Denarau. Taxis are plentiful in Nadi but do not use meters, so prices should be con-firmed in advance; see Taxi in the Getting Around chapter.

LAUTOKA

Lautoka, the administrative centre of the Western Division, is Fiji's second port and largest city after Suva, with a population of about 40,000. As a backdrop it has the beautiful Mt Evans Range. While not an especially interesting city, if you want to avoid the tourist hype of Nadi, it is a much simpler place to get around on foot and a good base for taking trips to the Mamanucas and the Yasawas. The town has a large produce and handicraft market and a reasonably organised bus station, where buses leave for the Kings Road to the north and the Queens Road to the south. The main street is lined with royal palms.

The local economy revolves around cane growing and the large Lautoka Sugar Mill has been operating since 1903. Cutting and crushing season is in the latter half of the year, when you will see lots of little sugar trains transporting the cane to the mill. There is a high proportion of Fiji Indians, mostly descendants of indentured labourers now working in business or farming leased land. Wood-chip export is another major industry. About nine km north of Lautoka on the Kings Road is a turn-off to the right along Vakabuli Rd to the Lololo Pine Plantation and the Drasa Timber Mill, about eight km inland.

Information

There are several banks downtown, including ANZ, Westpac and NBF, where you can change money and travellers' cheques. The Cathay Hotel will also change money at bank rates. The post office is on the corner of Vitogo Pde and Tavewa Ave, where there are a few public telephones.

Travel Agencies The following travel agencies are in Lautoka:

Air Pacific
    159 Vitogo Pde (☎ 664 022)
Sunflower Airlines
    Vidilo St (☎ 664 753)
Blue Lagoon Cruises
    Vitogo Pde (☎ 661 662; fax 664 098)

Beachcomber Cruises/Ferries/Resort
    1 Walu St (☎ 661 500; fax 664 496)
Westside Watersports
    Shop 1, Wharf Rd (☎ 661 462; fax 661 462)
Patterson Brothers Shipping
    15 Tukani St (☎ 866 1173)

Medical Services For medical treatment, contact:

Lautoka Hospital
    Thomson Cres, Lautoka (☎ 660 399)
Vakabale St Medical Centre
    Vakabale St, Lautoka (☎ 661 961)

Emergency In an emergency, contact:

Emergency (☎ 000), free
FVB emergency hotline (☎ 0800 721 721), free
Police (☎ 660 222)
Ambulance (☎ 660 399)

Neisau Marina

Neisau Marina (☎ 664 858; fax 663 807) at the end of Bouwalu St has berths for yacht repairs, swing moorings, a marine hoist, a workshop with tool and machinery hire and a boat refit service. Travellers should look on the notice board and ask around if they are interested in crewing on a yacht bound for the offshore islands. There are bathroom facilities, lockers, washing machines that sometimes work and a bar and nice sun-deck area.

Places to Stay

Lautoka has two rock-bottom hotels. The *Diamond Hotel* (☎ 661 920) at 8 Nacula St has fairly clean, simple rooms in a small building with a bar downstairs for F$18.60/24.80 for singles/doubles and dorm rooms for F$7.60.

The *Mon Repo Hotel* (☎ 661 595), on the corner of Vitogo Pde and Yasawa St, has fan-cooled rooms with shared bathroom for F$16.50/24 singles/ doubles and a three-bed dorm for F$11 per person. The rooms are mostly used for short-term business by prostitutes. Better options for low-budget accommodation within Lautoka are the dorms or double rooms at the Lautoka or

VITI LEVU

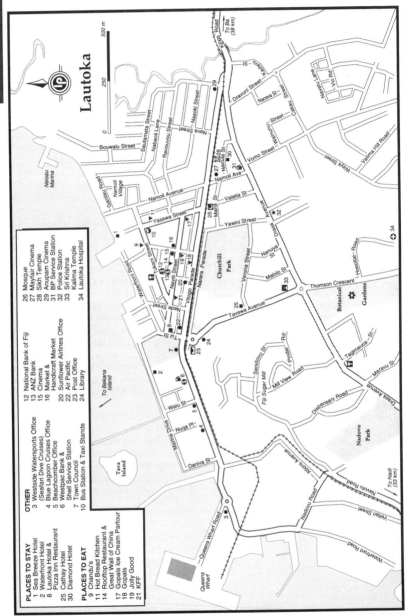

Lautoka

PLACES TO STAY
1 Sea Breeze Hotel
2 Waterfront Hotel
8 Lautoka Hotel &
  Pizza Inn Restaurant
25 Cathay Hotel
30 Diamond Hotel

PLACES TO EAT
9 Chandu's
11 Hot Bread Kitchen
14 Rooftop Restaurant &
  Great Wall of China
17 Gopals
18 Gopals Ice Cream Parlour
19 Jolly Good
21 KFF

OTHER
3 Westside Watersports Office
  (Seafari Dive Cruises)
4 Blue Lagoon Cruises Office
5 Beachcomber Office
6 Westpac Bank &
  Shell Service Station
7 Town Council
10 Bus Station & Taxi Stands
12 National Bank of Fiji
13 ANZ Bank
15 Cinema
16 Market &
  Handicraft Market
20 Sunflower Airlines Office
22 Air Pacific
23 Post Office
24 Library
26 Mosque
27 Mayfair Cinema
28 Sikh Temple
29 Anupam Cinema
31 BP Service Station
32 Police Station
33 Sri Krishna
  Kalima Temple
34 Lautoka Hospital

Cathay hotels and there is also camping and dorms at Saweni Beach.

The *Lautoka Hotel* (☎ 660 388; fax 660 201) is conveniently located at 2-12 Naviti St at the opposite end to the market. It is popular among locals and travellers. In the old wing they have good-value rooms which are fairly grungy but spacious with fans and sink, and clean, shared-bathroom facilities, for F$16.80/22 for singles/doubles. Dormitory rooms are F$8.80/11 per person with fan/air-con. There are also rooms with air-con and private bathroom for F$44 for singles or doubles. The new wing has good air-con motel rooms with private bathroom, fridge and telephone for F$65 singles or doubles. There is a swimming pool, a reasonably good restaurant, bar and TV lounge with a friendly, easy-going atmosphere. At the front desk you can book several trips to outer islands and tours.

The *Cathay Hotel* (☎ 660 566; fax 660 136), at Tavewa Ave up from the post office roundabout, is another good option for budget accommodation. They have a swimming pool and bar, a TV lounge and a restaurant, which serves mediocre meals for F$4 to F$7, but has good fruit juice. Here fan-cooled rooms with private bathrooms cost F$27.50/36.50 for singles/doubles, and air-con rooms with private facilities cost F$36/44. A bed in one of their various dorms (up to four people in each) costs F$8.80. Trips to the Yasawas can be arranged at reception.

The *Sea Breeze Hotel* (☎ 667 711) is at the end of Bekana Lane on the waterfront. In a convenient location in a quiet cul-de-sac close to the market and bus terminal, it is a three-storey building with an internal garden courtyard. All rooms have ensuites. Air-con rooms cost F$35, or F$40 with a sea view. Rooms with ceiling fan are F$25/30 for singles/doubles but these are often booked out. An extra person is F$5.50. Despite being a bit expensive for the budget traveller it is a good option for getting rid of jet lag before deciding where to go, especially if you intend to visit the Yasawas. They have a breakfast room upstairs, a quiet bar and TV lounge downstairs, and a cloudy swimming pool.

The *Waterfront Hotel* (☎ 664 777; fax 665 870) is the only up-market hotel in Lautoka, catering to local business travellers and conferences as well as tourists. Its 43 rooms are in a modern two-storey building on Waterfront Rd. The lobby is linked to a bar, spacious lounge and outdoor deck from which you can gaze at the passing ships and Bekana Island. It also has a nice swimming pool and its Old Mill Restaurant is quite good (see the following Places to Eat section). Prices are F$110/121 for standard rooms/ suites for singles or doubles.

A five-minute boat ride (about one km offshore) from Lautoka wharf on Bekana Island, is *Paradise Island Resort* (☎ /fax 665 222). The island is far from idyllic by Fijian standards, but it has a nice harbour view, mangroves and a small beach. Although the place has obviously been allowed to become run-down over the last few years, it may be an option for a brief stay or day visit for the Sunday barbecue. Bring friends, otherwise you might be a bit lonely! It has 10 fan-cooled bures with private bathroom for F$135 each (maximum four people). The basic eight-bed dorm is F$15 per person or F$45 including meals; ask for low-season specials. Meal prices begin at F$5.50, and there is a barbecue plate if you wish to cook your own food.

There is a swimming pool, bar and restaurant, and activities include windsurfing, snorkelling, use of a Hobie Cat, nature walks and kayaking around the island (about 1½ hours of hard work). Equipment hire is F$7.50 per day. The generator is turned off by 10 pm and water has to be barged in from the mainland. Transfers from Lautoka are F$15 return.

Places to Eat

Lautoka has nowhere near the variety of restaurants that Nadi or Suva have. There are, however, various cheap restaurants near the bus station which serve Indian, Chinese and Fijian fare for lunch. *Chandu's* at 15 Tukani St opposite the terminal, above

Shiu's hardware shop, has quite good quality meals for around F$6 for both lunch and dinner. *Jolly Good* at the corner of Naviti and Vakabale Sts is a popular outdoor venue for snacks and New Zealand ice cream. It looks like a converted car sales yard with outdoor tables behind a fenced area. Inexpensive Indian, Chinese and Fijian fast food is under F$4, while burgers and hot dogs are under F$2.50. The *Morris Hedstrom Hypermart Cafe* at the rear of the supermarket opposite the NBF bank has a variety of good value fast-food lunches including soup, sandwiches, curries, chicken and chips, and Indian, Chinese and Fijian meals for under F$3. New Zealand ice cream is 80 cents. The cafe is open Monday to Thursday 8 am to 7 pm, Friday until 8 pm and Saturday from 8 am until 6 pm.

For the best vegetarian meals in town try the Hare Krishna restaurants. *Gopals*, at 117 Vitogo Pde, open from 11 am to 2 pm, has air-con. *Gopals Ice Cream Parlour and Quick Service Bar* is on the corner of Naviti and Yasawa Sts near the bus station and market, and is open from 9 am to 6 pm. Both are closed on Sunday. Prices range from F$1.50 for simple dishes and soups to F$6.50 for a fruit juice and a food platter with assorted curry, relish and rice or naan. They also have lots of interesting-looking bright-coloured sweets.

The *Rooftop* (☎ 668 988), at 21 Naviti St on top of Coco's Night Club and the Great Wall of China, is open seven days a week for lunch and dinner. It is a pleasant place with a licensed bar and live music on Thursday, Friday and Saturday nights, and a happy hour from 5 to 7.30 pm every day. The restaurant serves good steak dishes for reasonable prices. The *Great Wall of China Restaurant* (☎ 664 763) serves large portions and average-quality Chinese dishes, and the *Empress of China*, 143 Vitogo Pde, has a Chinese, Indian and European menu. *KFF* serves Indian and Chinese food in a clean, air-con restaurant. The Korean owners are about to open a fine-dining Korean restaurant on the same premises.

The *Bula Restaurant* at the Lautoka Hotel offers three-course meals daily for around F$10, and next door the *Pizza Inn Restaurant* serves reasonable pizzas. The *Old Mill Restaurant* at the Waterfront Hotel serves light meals (all day) for F$7 to F$11.50 and main meals for F$13.50 to F$19.50. The hotel also has a bar and nice views out to the harbour. You can also get lunch at *Spencer's Bar* at the Neisau Marina for F$3 to F$8; it has a bar and a pleasant outdoor deck.

Entertainment

Lautoka has a couple of cinemas and on Thursday, Friday and Saturday nights there are a couple of nightspots. The *Rooftop Restaurant* on Naviti St has live music; see Places to Eat above. For more of a nightclub scene try *Coco's*, on the floor below the Rooftop, and *Hunter's Inn*, around the corner from the Lautoka Hotel on Tui St.

Getting There & Away

Lautoka is 33 km north of Nadi town and 24 km from Nadi airport. Local buses shuttle between the two towns every 15 minutes during the day and less frequently during the evening. There are also regular express buses along Kings Road and Queens Road (see the Getting Around chapter), as well as carriers and Viti buses to Suva. Both Sunbeam and Pacific Transport have offices in Yasawa St opposite the market.

Getting Around

It is easy to get around Lautoka on foot. Taxis are plentiful and short rides are cheap.

AROUND LAUTOKA
Abaca Cultural & Recreational Park

Abaca Cultural & Recreational Park (☎ 661 511 or 664 047; fax 661 784), part of Koroyanitu National Park, is in the mountains about 10 km east of Lautoka. Abaca village, pronounced 'Ambatha', is at the base of Mt Koroyanitu (Mt Evans). The park is being developed by the Native Lands Trust Board (NLTB) and South Pacific Regional Environment Programme (SPREP) to provide income for the locals through ecotourism. The area has beautiful nature walks, hikes through native rainforest, archaeological sites and swimming.

Visitors can stay in a 12-bed dormitory with cooking and bathroom facilities. Beds are F$15 per person. Camping is not allowed. Take some groceries as there is only a small village shop. There are also barbecue facilities and a lovo and entertainment on Thursday night. Meals can also be provided for F$5 each. Alternatively, you can ·stay with a host family and work as a volunteer. This costs F$20 per person per night for a minimum stay of three nights.

Admission to the park is F$5, plus F$1 to F$3 for guided treks. Treks include a full-day hike to Mt Koroyanitu and to the remains of a fortified village. There is also a two-hour hike to the terraced gardens at Tunutunu and to the Navuratu village site. Those who make the one-hour climb to the summit of Castle Rock will be rewarded with panoramic views of the Mamanucas and Yasawas.

Getting There & Away A carrier departs Lautoka (daily except Sunday) from the Cathay Hotel at 9 am, returning at 4 pm. The return trip costs F$8 per person. Alternatively, hire a carrier on Yasawa Street next to the bus station for about F$10 one way. The Tavakubu bus only goes as far as the Abaca junction. From Nadi, at the first roundabout before entering Lautoka, turn right and drive for about 1.4 km, turn into Tavakubu Rd and drive for a further five km, then turn right into the signposted Abaca Rd. The 10-km Abaca Rd up to the village is gravel and requires a vehicle with high ground clearance.

Saweni Beach
While littered and not particularly attractive, this is one of the few beaches between Nadi and Lautoka. It is popular with locals for weekend picnics. Saweni Beach Apartment Hotel has camping and budget accommodation; see below. On the road into Saweni Beach is **South Sea Orchids** (☎ 662 206; fax 666 283). The property is owned by Donald and Aileen Burness, whose great-grandfather was the interpreter on the

signing of the deed of cession of Fiji to Great Britain (the man with the long white beard on the F$50 note). They have an interesting collection of old Fijian artefacts, landscaped gardens, a private collection of orchids and a commercial nursery.

Place to Stay Saweni Beach Apartment Hotel (☎ 661 777; fax 660 136), six km south of Lautoka, has campsites for F$5 per person and a dorm for F$12 per person (maximum of four people). They also have 12 one-bedroom apartments, which are self-contained and fan cooled. Apartment doubles are F$40/46 for ocean view/beach front, with a F$9 surcharge for each extra person. This place is an option if all you want is a peaceful time without much action since they don't organise activities. They have a small swimming pool and a bar, but no restaurant, which leaves no option but to cook your own meals. At the time of writing there was a grocery shop under construction nearby.

Getting There & Away To get to Saweni Beach, turn off the Queens Road about six km south of Lautoka, from where it is about two km to the beach. Local buses leave from Lautoka bus station to Saweni Beach six times a day, with the first at 6.45 am and the last at 5.15 pm, otherwise catch any local bus to Nadi and walk in from the turn-off. Taxis from Lautoka are about F$6, and to the airport F$18. South Sea Orchids offer 1½-hour tours, which are normally prebooked with Fiji Tours Tourist Transport (☎ 723 311), or you can arrange your own visit by contacting them in advance. Expect to pay F$30 for a return taxi ride from Lautoka if you want the cab to wait.

Vuda Point
Vuda Point is a peninsula between Nadi and Lautoka, which juts out towards the Mamanucas. Historically this site is believed to be where the first Melanesians arrived to populate Fiji. The area is mostly farmland with a couple of resorts and a new marina, which aims to attract big yachts and more

business to the area. The First Landing Restaurant and bar next to the marina is a good place to eat, especially at sunset. It's a pity that Shell, Mobil and BP oil terminals also occupy this beautiful point.

Places to Stay Vuda Point has a couple of places to stay. On the left as you turn off the Queens Road along Vuda Point Rd is the *Mediterranean Villas Hotel* (☎ 664 011; fax 661 773). It looks uninviting from outside, but its position high on the Vuda Hill offers a panoramic view of Nadi Bay. Prices for the ocean-view Italian-style villas begin at F$90. The Italian and seafood restaurant offers main meals from F$8.50 to F$18.50. About two km further along the road on the left is *Anchorage Beach Resort* (☎ 662 099; fax 665 571). It is also sited on a hill with good views of the Vuda Point area. The beaches here are a bit better than the ones around Nadi, but don't expect bright white sand and crystal water – you will probably spend more time in the swimming pool. The resort has a pleasant atmosphere and personalised treatment. There are 10 rooms for F$70/75 singles/doubles, a cottage unit with three beds (maximum six people) for F$85 per double and F$10 per extra adult, and a dorm with cooking facilities for F$15 per person. It is possible to get discounts during the low season. They have a restaurant and bar with panoramic views and breakfast for F$9.50, lunches for F$6.50 to F$8.50 and European-style dinners for F$12.50 to F$16. For the location of places to stay around Lautoka, see the Mamanuca Group map.

Place to Eat Next to the Vuda Point Marina is the appropriately named restaurant and bar First Landing (%y666 171; fax 668 882). They have a wooden deck and outdoor tables overlooking a white-sand beach and the Mamanuca islands. It is an interesting place to have a meal at sunset, with a wood-fired oven for slow-baked seafood and pizza. Main meals cost F$9.50 to F$15 for good seafood, steak, curry and pasta dishes. It is an isolated spot, so you will need to take a taxi or your own transport to get there.

Getting There & Away The turn-off to Vuda Point is about 10 km south of Lautoka and about 13 km from Nadi airport, at the top of a steep hill. The marina is about 3.5 km off the Queens Road.

Viseisei Village
Viseisei is 11 km south of Lautoka and 12 km north of Nadi airport on the Queens Road. This village is not a typical Fijian village and receives many tourists on organised visits (except Sunday). It has a couple of handicraft bures, one of which together with a new house was burnt down in 1996 due to interfamily rivalries. The villagers are relatively wealthy, as the *mataqali* own and lease several of the Mamanuca islands to resorts. Viseisei was the home of the late Dr Timoci Bavadra, whose government was deposed by the coup in 1987. Local buses between Nadi and Lautoka stop at the village.

Garden of the Sleeping Giant
These landscaped gardens have the Sabeto Mountains (or Sleeping Giant Ridge) as a backdrop, and are a peaceful place to have a picnic or spend a couple of hours relaxing amongst the orchids (Fiji's largest collection), lily ponds and tracks up into the forested foothills. Founded by American actor Raymond Burr in 1977 to house his personal orchid collection, it is now owned by a Hawaiian corporation. Admission is a bit steep at F$9.35/17.60/22 for singles/doubles/families. Children up to 15 years get in for F$4.40, and it's free for those under five. A complimentary fruit drink is included. The gardens are open daily from 9 am to 5 pm or Sunday by appointment (☎ 722 701).

Getting There & Away The gardens are about six km north of Nadi airport. The turn-off is at Wailoko Rd. Head inland from the Queens Road for about two km along the gravel. A taxi will cost about F$12 from Nadi or alternatively take a local bus (Nadi-Lautoka) then walk/hitch from the turn-off. There are also organised tours.

Lomolomo Guns

Also at the foot of the Sabeto Mountains is an abandoned WWII battery, built to protect Nadi Bay. If you feel like a walk and a great view, ask to be let off the bus at the dirt road (about 8.5 km from the airport), which leads to a school about 400m up the road. Be sure to ask the locals if it's OK to visit, and also ask for directions. The easiest track is to the left of the school.

Queens Road & the Coral Coast

The Queens Road follows the southern perimeter of Viti Levu, from Lautoka to Suva. It is a sealed road and a scenic drive/bus ride, hugging the coast most of the way. Most of the roads heading inland off the highway are unsealed. The stretch of coastline along south-western Viti Levu is known as the Coral Coast because of the wide fringing reef offshore, which is broken only by passages adjacent to rivers and streams. There are many resorts spread along the Coral Coast, as well as a few budget places suitable for backpackers. Highlights are Natadola Beach, the Sigatoka Sand Dunes and the Tavuni Hill Fortification, which is of archaeological interest and has great views of the Sigatoka Valley.

NAISALI ISLAND

Naisali is a 42-hectare privately owned island, about 12 km south of Nadi. It is a long, flat island, just off the mainland, with a dark-sand beach. *Sonaisali Island Resort* (☎ 720 411; fax 720 392) opened in 1991. There are 32 hotel suites in a double-storey building. All have sea views to the Mamanucas, bar fridge, air-con, fan and a choice of one king-size bed or twin queen-size beds. There are also nine thatched bures, three with two bedrooms, and folding beds can be added at no extra charge. Rates for beach-front suites are F$220 and F$319 for one or two-bedroom beach-front bures. Res-

taurants include the *Poolside Pergola, Kula Koffee Korner* and the *Terrace*. A full American-style breakfast is F$16.50, European F$6 to F$9 and tropical buffet F$11. There is an all-day mixed menu with meals from F$5 to F$11, and dinner main courses are F$15 to F$25. A daily meal package is F$44/22 for adults/children, including a meke, lovo and theme nights. Child-minding is F$2.50 per hour.

The resort has a good swimming pool, a sunken bar and tennis courts. Windsurfing lessons and diving lessons in the pool are free. Other activities include Hobie Cat sailing, canoeing, water skiing, snorkelling and scuba diving.

Dive Sonaisali takes trips to the Mamanuca group. Dive locations about 20 minutes away by boat include: Kingfisher Reef, the Pinnacles, Namoto Passage, Salamanda and Jackie's Point. Prices including full equipment rental are F$89 for a two-tank dive day trip, to F$360 for 10 tanks over five days.

Getting There & Away

The Sonaisali Island Resort is a 25-minute drive from Nadi airport. Turn off the Queens Road at Nacobi Rd (unsealed) and drive for a couple of km across a swampy area to a landing. At the landing you will find a taxi stand. It is only about three minutes on a free boat shuttle from the mainland to Naisali Island. Most guests are on pre-arranged packages.

MOMI BAY

South of Nadi the Queens Road winds through cane fields, and the first interesting detour is towards Momi Bay and along the coast, recommended if you are taking a leisurely drive. The turn-off is about 18 km from Nadi (27 km from the airport). Some local buses take this route, but if you jump off you may have to wait a while for the next one. The 29 km of unsealed road, the old route of the Queens Road, takes you through beautiful farmland, cane fields and pine plantations. There are lots of small temples and mosques in the area. The general stores, mostly run by Fiji Indians, are barricaded with protective screens.

Momi Guns, a WWII battery on a hilltop overlooking the strategic Navula Passage, is worth a visit. It is about six km from the Queens Road turn-off, coming from Nadi. The camouflaged bunkers have been restored and there is a display with historical photos. The British naval guns were thought to have been used in the Boer War in the defence of Mafeking. Here, though, they were only fired for practice and once when a New Zealand ship was too slow to identify itself. During WWII Fiji formed a strategic link between US and Australia, and New Zealand and Fijian soldiers were posted here. The site, open daily except Sunday, is run by the National Trust and there is a F$2 entry fee.

Place to Stay & Eat
Seashell Surf & Dive Resort (☎ 720 100; fax 720 294), about 30 km from Nadi, is the only accommodation in the Momi Bay area. A reader's description sums up this budget resort fairly well: 'a strange, tacky place, the resort looks like a bad-taste remnant of the 70s or 60s'. It does have a variety of options, however, and the staff are friendly. Camping is F$7.90 per tent and dorm beds are F$11. The six dorm rooms (maximum five people) are on top of the restaurant/bar area in a big shed-like space. There are no fans so rooms can get a bit stuffy. Front rooms, which get the sea breeze and view, are better. Partitions are not full height but valuables can be locked in a separate room. Lodge rooms, with ceiling fan and basin with double or twin beds and shared facilities, cost F$38.50. Extra adults are F$15 each and children under 12 are free. Duplex and family bures with cooking facilities, fridge and ceiling fans are F$84.70/148.50 for doubles/up to six people. The small store nearby sells basics only, and bringing supplies from the markets in Sigatoka or Nadi is recommended if you wish to self-cater. However, there are no cooking facilities for campers or for the dorm accommodation. Meals are quite good,

although meal packages at F$23 may be out of some backpackers' budgets.

As with much of the Coral Coast, the beach here is not great, with swimming, snorkelling and windsurfing only practical at high tide. The resort has a swimming pool and tennis court, and other activities include volleyball, diving and surfing trips. Scuba Bula offer two-tank dive trips for F$77, ten-tank dive packages for F$340 (gear included) and a five-day PADI open-water course for F$330 (two people minimum). Snorkelling trips are F$11. Day trips to Plantation Island in the Mamanucas can also be arranged.

Surfing is expensive as it requires van and local boat transfers for F$25 out to the reef breaks around Namoto Island or F$35 for Cloud Break. Breaks include Namoto (left-hand wave), Wilkes (right-hand wave), Desperation and Swimming Pool. Whether or not you will be able to access Cloud Break is another matter as there are politics involved. At the time of writing Tavarua Island Resort had negotiated priority to surf Cloud Break with the local villagers. Refer to the Mamanucas chapter.

Getting There & Away
To get to the resort from Nadi, travel about 11 km along the old Queens Road, then take a turn-off to the right and drive for another 1.5 km. Local buses (Dominion Company) from Nadi to the Seashell Cove area depart Nadi bus station four times daily between 7.45 am and 4 pm. There are also regular buses from Sigatoka. The 30-minute taxi ride from the airport costs F$33, while airport transfers using the resort minibus are F$7.50.

NATADOLA BEACH
In between Momi and Sigatoka is the gorgeous white-sand Natadola Beach, which is good for swimming. This rates as the best beach on mainland Viti Levu; most of the other beaches in this area and along the Coral Coast have wide, flat fringing reefs that only allow swimming at high tide. Take care when swimming, however, as there can be a strong undertow. Sometimes there is good body

surfing here. If you want to snorkel, surf or windsurf take your own gear. The setting is idyllic, but watch your valuables and don't leave your gear unattended as there have been reports of theft. Camping is not recommended. The small up-market resort opposite the beach is the only development. If you don't want to eat at the resort, bring your own picnic and drinks.

Local villagers offer horse riding along the beach (F$5 to F$10) and sell green coconuts for drinking, shells, and seed and shell necklaces (F$2 to F$4). Sometimes they can be a bit pushy and seem to think that all travellers have spent F$250 per night on accommodation at the resort. Make sure you have loose change as the resort gets snitchy. Locals are not allowed to enter the resort and travellers cannot have a drink without buying lunch. There is no public telephone, although in an emergency you could beg the resort.

Places to Stay & Eat

Natadola Beach Resort (☎ /fax 721 000) is a new, intimate scale, 'boutique' resort, run by a New Zealand couple. At the time of writing it had four of its planned 10 rooms completed. They have fans, fridge, tea and coffee-making facilities and private courtyards, and there is an attractive landscaped swimming pool and garden area. Prices are F$250/325 for a room/two-bedroom suite. Packages including all meals, activities and airport transfers are F$495/605 per night for a room/two-bedroom suite (up to four people). Drinks are extra. The resort does not cater for children under 16 years old. Snorkelling gear and boogie boards are available for use by guests.

The restaurant/bar, with Spanish-style rendered walls and open-plan courtyard, is open to the public. House guests can also have their meals by the private pool or on the beach. The interesting menu changes daily, with lunches from F$6.75, dinner F$18 to F$28 and fresh fruit juices for F$3.50.

Local villagers are becoming interested in a share of the tourism dollar and it may be possible to arrange to stay in the nearby

village at the south end of Natadola Beach. A reader said they had been informed by Ilami Nabiau, a local from nearby Sanasana village, of accommodation for F$25 including meals in a two-bed bure with a toilet and bathroom. If you are interested contact Save (☎ 500 800) or Baravi (☎ 508 222), who are friends of Ilami, at Sanasana village c/o PO Box 551, Sigatoka. Let us know how you go.

Backpackers could consider *Robinson Crusoe Island* (Likuri Island), near the passage into Likuri Harbour, which is being set up by the same family who run the youth hostels in Nadi and Suva. Fresh water comes from a well and a generator runs for a few hours at night. There are two swimming pools and snorkelling off the beach. Bures are F$20/35 for singles/doubles or F$30/50 with three meals, and dorm accommodation for up to 20 people is F$10 per person or F$20 with meals. We will be interested to hear reports from travellers. Initial feedback has not been entirely complimentary. It is not recommended for lone female travellers. From Nadi, the boat landing is at the first bridge on the road to Natadola Beach off the Queens Road, and it takes about 15 minutes by boat to reach the island.

Getting There & Away

Natadola Beach is fairly isolated and makes a good day trip escape from Nadi. The Maro Rd turn-off to Natadola is 36 km from Nadi (45 km from the airport) along the Queens Road, where there is a temple on the corner with a life-size goddess. Turn right and continue along the gravel road for a further 9½ km, past a school, a mosque and two bridges, and turn left at a T-intersection. You will pass another mosque before reaching the beach. There are no direct buses from Nadi. There are Paradise buses from Sigatoka bus station to Vusama/Natadola, which take about one hour and cost about F$1.50. There are six buses daily (less during weekends), the first at 6.30 am and the last at 5.45 pm. The Coral Coast Railway, on the highway near the Fijian Resort, runs scenic tours to this beach; see below. Alternatively, it is a pleasant 3½-hour walk along the track to the beach from where you can catch the train or bus back. It is also possible to hire bikes or take an organised tour from Sigatoka and ride to the beach.

YANUCA ISLAND & AROUND

Past the turn-off to Natadola the Queens Road continues south-east, winding through hills and down to the coast at Cuvu Bay near the Fijian Resort on Yanuca Island (not to be confused with another Yanuca Island in Beqa Lagoon). This privately owned 43-hectare island linked to the mainland by a causeway is covered by the large *Shangri-La's Fijian Resort* (☎ 520 155; fax 500 402). The resort, built in the late 1960s, has recently undergone a F$7 million refurbishment with new restaurants and bars. The resort has 436 rooms in five different wings, all with private balconies, sea or lagoon views, air-con, 24-hour room service, tea and coffee-making facilities, minibar and fridge. Rates for singles or doubles are F$275 to F$341 for standard rooms, F$401.50 to F$528 for studios and suites, and F$632.50 to F$742.50 for self-contained beach bungalows. Up to two children can share with parents at no extra charge. It is considered good value for money among ex-pats (who get local rates!). Children can be entertained in the 'little chief club' – a special children's play area with trained staff supervising activities. Children under 12 can eat for free at buffet-style meals when accompanied by their parents. There are five restaurants serving good food, including the *Golden Cowrie* with main meals between F$18 and F$39. There are also convention facilities, TV and games rooms, beautiful gardens and plenty of space– although it can be a bit of a hike from some of the accommodation wings. There are over 500 staff employed at the resort.

The Fijian has an extensive range of activities and nonmotorised sports are included in the price. Facilities include a nine-hole golf course, a gym, two swimming pools (boasting the largest free-form swimming pool in the South Pacific), tennis courts, croquet and lawn bowls. Other activities include water skiing, para-sailing, fishing and sailing. Scuba diving is conducted by Sea Sports and there are free diving lessons in the pool.

Near the causeway entry to the Fijian Resort is the **Coral Coast Scenic Railway** (☎ 500 646; fax 520 688). It offers scenic rides along the coast on an old diesel sugar train, past villages, forests and sugar plantations to Natadola Beach. The railway was once used for transporting cane and passengers to the Lautoka Mill. Developed in the mid-1980s by New Zealander Peter Jones, it is now Fijian owned and run by an Australian consortium. The 14-km trip takes about 1¼ hours to get to the beach and 1½ hours to return, departing at 10 am and returning at 4 pm. The trip costs F$22/45 one way/return from the terminus, or F$59 including barbecue lunch at the Natadola Resort or F$69/79 from Coral Coast/Nadi hotels. Children under 12 are half-price or free if under six. It is a popular trip with guests of the Fijian Resort suffering hangovers or sunburn, but for backpackers and those on a tight budget it is probably a waste of money.

On the highway opposite the entrance to the Fijian Resort is the derelict Ka Levu Cultural Centre, which was closed in 1992 after cyclone damage. Behind this, *Tomlu's Restaurant* (☎ 520 729) is open for lunch and dinner, offering European, Chinese and Indian dishes for F$4 to F$13.50 and special seafood dishes for F$12 to F$32.

Getting There & Away

The Fijian Resort is about 50 km from Nadi (about a 45-minute drive) and 11 km from Sigatoka. There are regular express buses, minibuses and carriers travelling along the Queens Road; see the Getting Around chapter. There is an Avis desk at the Fijian Resort if you require a hire car.

SIGATOKA

Sigatoka is a small town 61 km south of Nadi, and 127 km west of Suva, on the banks and near the mouth of the Sigatoka River, Fiji's second-largest river. It is predominantly a farming community as well as a service town for tourists drawn to the Coral

Coast resorts. There is a produce market and bus station in the heart of town, duty-free shops and a large mosque. The most bizarre sight in Sigatoka is the fantasy-style mansion on the hill behind the town. Sigatoka has a few places to eat and a couple of budget places to stay, including a surf resort near the Sigatoka Sand Dunes.

Activities
Horse Riding Ratuva's Horse Riding (☎ 500 860) have horses for hire for riding along the beach. They charge F$20 per hour and F$15 per hour for groups of five or more. Their house is on a hill, about 5½ km from Sigatoka on the left heading towards Nadi.

Surfing Sigatoka has Fiji's only beach-break. Most other areas have fringing reefs but here the fresh water has prevented their formation. The break is a sandy bottom on top of a large submerged rock platform. Surfing is at the point-break at the mouth of the Sigatoka River and beach-breaks pound the shore.

River Cruise Bounty Cruises & Tours (☎ 500 963; fax 520 657) has two-hour cruises (F$15) three times daily, except Sunday, to a nearby village for mat weaving and pottery demonstrations. These boats were originally used to shuttle people across the Sigatoka River while the bridge was inoperational after cyclone damage. (You can also visit these villages independently; just hop on a local bus.) They also offer a five-hour cultural cruise three times a week to the sand dunes and then upriver to the Tavuni Hill Fort and Naroro village for a kava ceremony, meke and lunch. Their office is in Laselase village on the eastern side of the Sigatoka River.

Places to Stay
Sigatoka town is not the most interesting place to spend a night, but it may be a convenient stopover and base for exploring the local attractions. What's left of the *Sigatoka Hotel* (no phone), after most of it burnt down, can be found opposite the Shell petrol station on the right as you enter the town coming from Nadi. It still has five very basic rooms for F$20/25 for singles/doubles, and an eight-person dorm room for F$10 per head a night. The *Sigatoka Club* (☎ 500 026) by the river is a far better option. Its bar is the local watering hole, and has pool tables and a restaurant with F$4 meals. The spacious simple rooms upstairs are F$24/36 singles/doubles and a five-person dorm is F$10 each.

On the eastern (Korotogo) side of the river, about 500m past the bridge and 50m inland off Queens Road, is *Sigatoka Camping & Traveller's Rest* (no phone). It is a small block of land surrounded by cane fields. The site is not attractive and there is no beach, but there is a small toilet block with showers, and cooking facilities are also available. The fee is F$5 per person a night. Korotogo, seven km to the east, has more accommodation and places to eat.

Places to Eat
The market and the *Morris Hedstrom supermarket* are a good place for self-caterers to stock up in Sigatoka town. There are two bakeries near the market and bus station, and many cheap eateries. The *Fijian Kitchen* at the market serves simple, cheap Fijian dishes. The *Paradise Restaurant* (☎ 520 871) above a bakery is open for lunch and dinner except Sunday. It has Chinese, Indian, Fijian and Japanese-style meals for F$5 to F$9. The *Oriental Pacific Restaurant* (☎ 520 275), a busy spot near the bus station, is a bit grotty but cheap. As well as takeaway it has Chinese and European dishes for F$3 to F$8.

There are a few good eateries within a short walk from the market area. *Le Cafe* (☎ 520 668) on Valley Rd, a good place for refreshments, is only open for breakfast and lunch.

The Furage Cafe on the main street near the new bridge is owned by the same people who run the Chefs restaurants in Nadi. It is another good option, offering pastries, salads, sandwiches, burgers and a yummy Thai chicken dish with rice for under F$6. It also has cappuccinos, cakes, ice cream and, importantly, air-con.

Upstairs from the Furage Cafe is the *Sea Palace Restaurant* (☎ 500 648), which offers a mixed menu with Indian and Chinese dishes for F$6 to F$8, and European dishes for up to F$20. This place is open from 10 am to 10 pm.

Getting There & Away

The cheapest and most fun way to travel along the Coral Coast from either Suva or Lautoka is by open-air bus. Both Sunbeam Transport Limited (☎ 500 168, Sigatoka) and Pacific Transport Limited (☎ 500 088, Sigatoka) have regular buses along the Queens Road. Express buses running from Suva to Sigatoka take about 2¾ hours, while Sigatoka to Lautoka takes about 2¼ hours. Add about an hour for nonexpress buses.

Alternatively, UTC has express air-con coaches (going from Nadi International Airport to Korolevu costs F$19) and Fiji Holiday Connections has a minibus shuttle.

There are also carriers and Viti minibuses as well as taxis; see the Getting Around chapter.

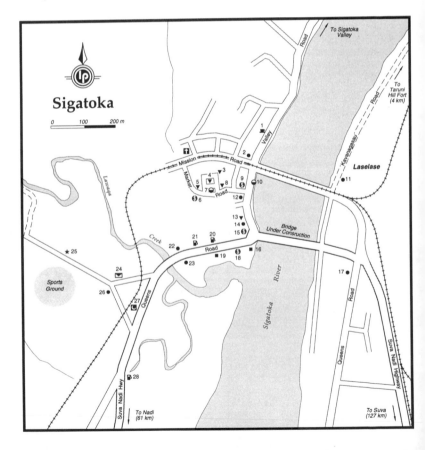

AROUND SIGATOKA
Sigatoka Valley

The Sigatoka River's tributaries originate as far away as Mt Victoria (Tomanivi) and the Monasavu Dam. It has long provided a line of communication between the mountain peoples and the coast dwellers, and the fertile river flats serve as productive agricultural land. Almost 200 archaeological, cultural or historically significant sites have been found in and around the valley, many of which are being taken over by farmland or housing.

This fertile river valley is known as Fiji's 'salad bowl'. Cereals, vegetables, fruits and peanuts as well as sugar cane are grown here, mostly on small-scale farms. The Sigatoka Valley Rural Development Project (SVRDP) coordinates cropping programmes and provides training for farmers on up-to-date techniques and irrigation systems. Much of the produce ends up at the municipal markets, and vegetables such as eggplant, chillies, okra, taro leaves and root crops like dalo, cassava and yams are also exported to Canada, Australia, New Zealand and the USA.

There are two **pottery villages** just north of Sigatoka, further up the valley. Nakabuta village is home to one of Fiji's best potters, Diana Tugea. Visitors are welcome here, as well as to Lawai village. If turning up unannounced, always ask the first person you meet if you can see the pottery. They will take you to a pottery bure with various potters' work on display. The traditional pottery style of this area is large, smooth cooking pots, but small items such as pigs and bures are also sold to tourists. The patchwork valley between the mountains is a fantastic sight to fly over, with the muddy brown waters of the Sigatoka River flowing into the blue ocean and Coral Coast fringing reefs disappearing into the distance.

Getting There & Away The Paradise Valley bus travels up the Sigatoka Valley on the western side, as far as Keiyasi village about 55 km upriver. It is a scenic ride, which takes about four hours return and costs about F$4. There are also regular Paradise buses to Naduri, which pass Nakabuta, every one to two hours from 6.30 am to 7.30 pm. On Sunday the service is less frequent. A taxi to Nakabuta (a 10 minute drive) will cost F$3 to F$5, or it's about 50 cents on the bus. It is about a four-km walk to Lawai village from Sigatoka. Some people may enjoy going upriver by boat; see organised tours below. The boat trips offer the same beautiful scenery that you'd see if you headed inland by local bus.

Sigatoka Sand Dunes

This large formation of wind-blown dunes is along a windswept beach near the mouth of the Sigatoka River. The dunes are about five km long, up to one km wide and on average about 20m high, rising to about 60m at the western end. The view is quite spectacular and it is a great place for a walk. However, don't expect golden Sahara-like dunes, as the

---

PLACES TO STAY
16 Sigatoka Club
19 Sigatoka Hotel

PLACES TO EAT
1   Le Cafe
3   Bakery & Paradise Restaurant
4   Market & Fijian Kitchen
5   Oriental Pacific Restaurant
8   Hot Bread & Cake Shop
13 Sea Palace Restaurant & Furage Cafe

OTHER
2   Tappo Duty Free
6   ANZ Bank
7   Bus Station
9   Westpac Bank
10 Taxi Stand & Wishing Well
11 Bounty Cruises Booking Office
12 Morris Hedstrom & Prouds Duty-Free
14 Jack's Handicrafts
15 National Bank of Fiji
17 School
18 Fiji Development Bank
20 Shell Petrol Station
21 BP Petrol Station
22 Angel Theatre
23 Town Council
24 Post Office
25 Police Station
26 Provincial Council
27 Mosque
28 Mobil Petrol Station

VITI LEVU

fine sand is a grey-brown colour and covered with vines and shrubs. The dunes have been forming over millions of years from the alluvial sediment washed downriver and out to sea, from where it is brought ashore by waves and then blown inland by the southeast Trade Winds.

Archaeological investigations have been carried out by the Fiji Museum, and human skeletal remains and pottery shards have been discovered, suggesting that there was a village near the eastern end of the dunes in prehistoric times. The state-owned part of the area was declared a national park in 1988

in an attempt to help preserve the site, and a visitor centre is being built on the Queens Road.

Place to Stay *Club Masa Resort* (no phone locally, 800 468 5643 or 213 473 451 in the USA), PO Box 710, Sigatoka, is a bit of a surfie hang-out near the beach at the edge of the Sigatoka Sand Dunes near Kulukulu village. Camping is F$11.50 and dorm beds (maximum 10 people) are F$16.50. Double cabins are F$21.50 for singles or doubles and F$43 in a self-contained unit. Prices include breakfast and dinner, which is good value,

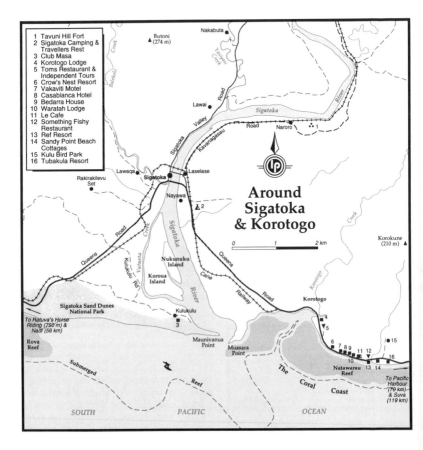

1 Tavuni Hill Fort
2 Sigatoka Camping & Travellers Rest
3 Club Masa
4 Korotogo Lodge
5 Toms Restaurant & Independent Tours
6 Crow's Nest Resort
7 Vakaviti Motel
8 Casablanca Hotel
9 Bedarra House
10 Waratah Lodge
11 Le Cafe
12 Something Fishy Restaurant
13 Ref Resort
14 Sandy Point Beach Cottages
15 Kulu Bird Park
16 Tubakula Resort

Around Sigatoka & Korotogo

and lunch can be ordered. There is generator power, a kitchen/bar, sitting room and dining on a verandah. The people who run it are fun and it is a great place to relax. The resort has ocean and river access for water sports including swimming, surfing, windsurfing, boogie boarding and canoeing, but you need to bring your own gear; see Activities for information on surfing.

Getting There & Away The dunes are southwest of Sigatoka near the mouth of the river. The turn-off from the Queens Road is Kulukulu Rd, about two km south-west of Sigatoka. It is a further two km along the dusty road and an extra km hike across the paddock to the dunes. It's a long way to walk from Sigatoka, especially in the heat, so take drinks. A better idea is to catch one of the Sunbeam buses that depart from Sigatoka bus station for Kulukulu village six times daily, from 6.30 am to 5 pm. Services are reduced on Sunday. A taxi will cost about F$4 one way from Sigatoka. The dunes are about a 50-minute drive from Nadi airport.

To get to Kulukulu village and Club Masa by car, turn left at the T-intersection facing the dunes at the end of Kulukulu Rd and continue for about one km. Club Masa is about a 200m walk across the paddock from the village towards the beach.

Tavuni Hill Fort

The Tavuni Hill Fort is one of the most interesting sights in the area. Defensive sites such as this were used in times of war, and while there are many such sites scattered all over Fiji, this is the most accessible one for visitors. The site has been restored and an information centre built in a combined effort between the Ministry of Tourism and the people of Naroro, whose ancestors lived in the fort. It has been funded by the Pacific Regional Tourism Development Scheme, a programme funded by the European Union (EU), and now provides income to the local villagers.

The defensive fort was established by a clan of Tongans led by Chief Maile Latemai. The mid to late 18th century was an era of political and social upheaval in Tonga and the chief left his country to avoid a family dispute. He and his entourage of servants sailed all the way in a great double-hulled canoe and arrived in the Sigatoka area in about 1788. They originally set up in Korotogo but were kept on the move by constant tribal warfare. Eventually the newcomers were accepted by the local tribes, and the chief was given some land and a local wife.

The steep limestone ridge, about 90m high at the edge of a bend in the Sigatoka River, was an obvious strategic location to set up a

---

The Kai Colo Uprising

The last significant tribal conflict in Fiji was the Kai Colo Uprising of 1875-6. The Kai Colo (mountain people of inland Viti Levu) had not agreed to the ceding of Fiji to Great Britain in 1874 and were understandably put out by the new colonial regime imposing its new politics and religion.

The measles epidemic of 1875 destroyed about a third of Fiji's population, totally wiping out some villages. The Kai Colo interpreted this both as a deliberate effort by the European invaders to destroy them, and as a punishment from their traditional gods for discarding them. Any faith in the new church dissolved and they returned to the old religion and tribal warfare, descending into the Sigatoka Valley and attacking and burning villages. The hill people and the coastal tribes had long been traditional enemies.

This was seen by the colonial government as a direct threat to the viability of their fledgling administration. To quash this 'rebellion' and set an example to others, Sir Arthur Gordon formed a constabulary of over 1000 Fijian men under the Nadroga Chief Ratu Luki. This force ascended the valley, destroying hill forts and either hanging, imprisoning or dispersing the chiefs involved. Sir Gordon's strategy was to pit Fijian against Fijian, on the one hand reinforcing the link with the new laws and, on the other, distancing the colonial government from the bloodshed. ∎

fortification. From this position the surrounding area could be easily surveyed both upstream and downstream. Substantial earthworks were carried out to form *yavus* (bases for houses) and terraces for barricade fencing. There are also a number of grave sites, a *rara* (ceremonial ground) and a *vatu ni bokola* (head-chopping stone). There are some beautiful curtain figs and an *ivi* tree on the site. The guide will probably joke about his cannibal past and pinch you to see how tasty you might be!

Later the site was again settled during the Kai Colo wars and the fort is thought to have been burnt down by the Native Constabulary in 1876. The reigning Noitoga Chief Kunatuni died as a result of wounds incurred in the preceding battle.

Admission is F$6 for adults, F$3 for children or F$15 for a family; locals get cheaper rates. The reception bure has display material and toilets, and sells souvenirs, posters and drinks. It is open daily, except Sunday.

Getting There & Away Tavuni is about four km north of Sigatoka on the eastern side of the river, above Naroro village. Regular local buses pass Tavuni Hill and cost about 50 cents. They leave Sigatoka bus station along Kavanagasau Rd heading for Mavua, seven times daily from 7.45 am to 5.30 pm. Taxis to the fort are about F$8 return.

KOROTOGO & AROUND

Past Sigatoka and across the river, the Queens Road heads back towards the shore at Korotogo. The next section of the Coral Coast past Korotogo to the Korolevu area is one of the most beautiful along Queens Road. The road winds along the shore, with scenic views of bays, beaches, coral reefs and mountains, and travelling at sunset or by early morning light it can be quite spectacular. The area known as Korotogo is about five to eight km east of Sigatoka. It has a range of dormitory, self-catering and resort accommodation options on or across the road from the beach. Except for nearby Sovi Bay, most parts of the beach here are suitable for swimming and snorkelling at high tide only.

Korotogo Souvenir Centre (☎ 504 432 after hours), across the road from the Reef Resort, sells wood carvings, kava bowls and dishes, coffee tables, tapa cloth, sea shells and shell jewellery.

Kula Bird Park

The Kula Bird Park (☎/fax 500 505) is located next door to the golf course, just past the Reef Resort on the left if heading towards Suva. It used to be privately owned but has now been taken over by the government after a cyclone and floods damaged the park and the business. While it used to have a large number of birds, there are now only 60 birds. There are 20 different species from Australia, Africa, South America and New Zealand, and also a few native Fijian birds including the Taveuni parrot. It also has a crested iguana and a few turtles in fish tanks. The bushwalk through some of the 45 hectares of forest takes about 15 minutes and passes through native species of trees, shrubs and flowers as well as introduced species. It is open from 9 am to 4 pm daily and admission costs F$5.50 for adults and F$7 for families with children under 15 years old.

Activities

Mountain Bike Hire & Tours Independent Tours (☎ 520 697, 520 678; fax 520 678), based in the same building as Tom's Restaurant, about 5 km east of Sigatoka, started up in late 1995. It offers bike hire and various bike or 4WD tours. Bike hire is F$8 per half-day and F$15 per day. A deposit of F$200 or credit card or other ID is required. Special 21-speed mountain bikes are reserved for tours. It has half-day, full-day and three day tours, and an annual eight-day guided tour for a minimum of two and a maximum of six people. Prebooking is recommended; see the Tours section at the beginning of this chapter for details on trips around the Sigatoka area, Nausori Highlands and Natadola Beach.

Diving *Sea Sports* (☎ 530 149; fax 530 279) has daily dive trips and picks up from Coral Coast hotels and resorts. It offers free pool

ROBYN JONES

T RESORT

ROBYN JONES

ROBYN JONES

A	
B	C
D	

Mamanuca Islands
A: Mana Island
B: Island home

C: Telecom man
D: View from lookout, Malolo Island

A	B
	C
	D

Suva
A: Ratu Sukuna, Government Buildings
B: Thurston Gardens
C: Suva cemetery
D: Hindu festival

sessions and dives at Coral Coast sites such as Naviti's Treasure and Morgan's Wall.

Places to Stay – bottom end

The *Vakaviti Motel* (☎/fax 520 424) is located on the steep hillside just across the road from the beach in a tropical garden, about 500m west of the Reef Resort. It has a block of four rooms opening onto a swimming pool and overlooking the ocean. There's one dorm with bunks for six people, costing F$12 per person; rooms cost F$45/55 for singles/doubles. All rooms have ceiling fans, cooking facilities and private bathrooms. There is a cabin for up to six people at the bottom end of the garden for F$65. Discounts for long stays are available. The friendly owners, Salote and AJ, took over the resort at the end of 1995. AJ, an ex-Rugby Union player who was the first Fijian to play for the New Zealand All Black team, will be happy to help you organise activities or tours around the area, and he takes guests for free Sunday drives.

Another good place is *Tubakula Beach Bungalows* (☎ 500 097; fax 660 136), on the beach front east of the Reef Hotel. It is run by the same people who have the Cathay Hotel in Lautoka, Saweni Beach Apartments, and Travel Inn and South Seas Hotel in Suva. It has 27 A-framed self-contained bungalows with fans. Prices for singles, doubles or triples vary according to their position: with garden it's F$49; with poolside position it's F$51; an ocean view costs F$55; and a beach-front position costs F$61. It costs F$10 per extra person. Dormitory accommodation is F$12 per night (maximum three beds) in eight small rooms. Rooms in beach-front bungalows sharing facilities are F$27.50/33/38.50. They have a swimming pool, minimarket for basic groceries and are building a restaurant.

The Mediterranean-style *Casablanca Hotel* (☎520 600; fax 520 616) next door to Vakaviti looks a bit incongruous for the South Pacific, but the price is fair and the staff are friendly and helpful. It is managed by an Egyptian/Australian and his Fijian wife. The eight clean, self-contained rooms

with cooking facilities and fridge are F$45/55 for singles/doubles and F$8 for an extra person. Rooms have balconies with ocean views and there is a pleasant garden and salt-water swimming pool; see Places to Eat for information on their restaurant.

The *Crow's Nest Resort* also has a 10-bed dorm room with no cooking facilities for F$11; see Places to Stay – middle.

The *Waratah Lodge* (☎500 278; fax 520 219), situated between Bedarra House and Le Cafe, has five A-framed cottages in a garden with a swimming pool. The cottages have fridges and cooking facilities and are F$33/44 for singles/doubles, and F$5 for each extra person up to a maximum of eight. The cottages weren't in top condition but it could be a way for a group to stay cheaply while exploring the surrounding area.

Korotogo Lodge (☎500 755; fax 520 182) is five km east of the Sigatoka bridge on the inland side of the road. The place is run-down and the rooms are pretty dingy but the Fiji-Indian couple is friendly and will give you free fruit from the garden. The dorm room has six beds and costs F$10 per night including breakfast with toast and jam. There are also four units with double beds and minimal cooking facilities. Tom's Restaurant is nearby.

Places to Stay – middle

Sandy Point Beach Cottages (☎500 125; fax 520 147) is a family-oriented resort with four self-contained cottages in spacious grounds on a nice stretch of beach next door to the Reef Resort. Prices for accommodation here per night are F$55/72 for singles/doubles or triples and F$121 for a family cottage, which sleeps five people. There are 10% discounts if you stay over 28 days and you should book ahead for the busy months of July, August or September. There is a fresh-water swimming pool but no restaurant. Resort owner Bob Kennedy uses his parabolic bowl to receive the latest weather maps via satellite and keep an eye on cyclones.

The *Crow's Nest Resort* (☎500 513; fax 520 354) is seven km east of Sigatoka town in Korotogo. Set in a garden area on the hillside across the road from the beach, the 18 self-contained split-level villas have balconies and sea views. Each are of identical design with one double bed on the upper level and two single beds below, ceiling fans, cooking facilities and refrigerator. The maximum number of people per unit is five and accommodation rates are F$75/99 single/double to quad, with each extra person costing F$9.90. It has a swimming pool and a sun-deck platform next to the restaurant.

Places to Stay – top end

The *Reef Resort* (☎ 500 044; fax 520 074) has 70 rooms with air-con, minibar, tea/coffee-making facilities and sea views. It's rated as the most popular moderately priced resort in the area, and has good food and friendly staff. Rooms, while not deluxe, are comfortable and clean. Prices for the standard double rooms are F$160, family suite rooms cost F$180 and luxury two-room suites are F$230. The resort has a kids club, and a creche service is provided for children under three years old from 9 am to 4 pm and from 7 to 9 pm daily. Meal packages are available; see Places to Eat below for information on the restaurant and bars. The daily activities programme includes complimentary snorkelling, hand-line fishing, kayaking and use of coral-viewing boards, and there is a nine-hole golf course across the road. Village visits are F$2 per adult and F$12 to see fire-walking performances.

Bedarra House (☎ 500 476; fax 520 116) just east of Casablanca Hotel opened in late 1994 and specialises in personal service. The building, more like a mansion than a hotel, has only four rooms (two family, two double), catering for a maximum of 12 guests. They have a good swimming pool, nice gardens and a lofty restaurant/bar and reception area. The daily tariffs including breakfast and three-course dinner is F$165 per double, and an extra adult/child is charged F$30/20.

Alternatively, you can hire the whole place for F$600 per night, which can work out to be very good value for a group; see below for details on the restaurant.

Places to Eat

The restaurant at the *Crow's Nest Resort* has an interesting nautical theme and has European and local dishes. Main meals cost F$5 to F$13.50. The *Sinbad Restaurant* at the front of the Casablanca Hotel serves Chinese, curries and European dishes for F$4 to F$10 and special Middle Eastern dishes are made to order. They intend to open a supermarket and bottle shop adjacent to the restaurant. The *Reef Resort* has casual all-day dining with a choice of burgers, salads, curries and Fijian dishes for F$5 to F$11. International-style dinners including steaks and seafood are F$16 to F$20. The Friday Fijian-feast buffet serves a good variety of Fijian food. The two bars have a happy hour from 6 to 7 pm. The *Bedarra House Restaurant* is open for visitors, and meals cost around F$8 for lunches and F$28 for a three-course dinner.

Outside the resort restaurants you can eat for nearly half the price. *Tom's Restaurant* (☎ 520 238), about five km east of Sigatoka town, has good-value Chinese, Indian and European dishes for F$4 to F$12. It has good seafood and very good Chinese meals. It is open weekdays from noon to 3 pm and 6 to 10 pm, and also on Sunday night. They provide free transport for customers within the Korotogo area after 9 pm. Also in Korotogo just opposite the Reef Resort is *Le Cafe* (☎ 520 668), open from 4 pm until 10 pm and a good place for dinner. The Swiss chef Jean Pierre offers a European-style menu with sandwiches, salads, pizzas, omelettes and burgers under F$5, and steak dishes under F$10. The small group of shops next door includes a general store and two more places to eat: the *Something Fishy Restaurant* (☎ 520 619) offers average seafood and mixed-menu dishes for around F$10, and *Fasta Food Pizza* has eat-in or takeaway pizzas.

KOROLEVU & AROUND

Korolevu village is 31 km east of Sigatoka

(24 km from Korotogo) and 71 km west of Pacific Harbour. There are many resorts spread along this stretch of the coast, from backpacker to top-end places. Nearby is **Biausevu Waterfall**, where you can swim. The turn-off to Biausevu village is about a 15-minute drive east of the Hideaway Resort. Continue along the track for 2.5 km till you reach the village, from where the waterfall is an easy 15 to 30-minute walk. Villagers will guide you to the falls for a small fee. Waterfall Tours (☎520 833) has five-hour trips that include a village visit (kava etc), lunch at a restaurant and visit to a handicraft store.

There is a souvenir shop east of Korolevu, 13 km from Sigatoka: Baravi Handicrafts (☎/fax 520 364) sells local handicrafts, clothes and jewellery and is open Monday to Saturday from 7.30 am to 6 pm.

East of Korolevu the Queens Road turns away from the shore and climbs up over the southern end of Viti Levu's dividing mountain range. To the east of this range the road improves, with wider sections, and the area is scenically different, with more rainforest. From here the road winds its way past wider bays.

Activities
The larger hotels have tour desks offering various trips along the Coral Coast including the sights at Sigatoka, horse riding and trips to waterfalls. They also have car-rental desks. Sea Sports offer dive trips for guests of most of the hotels and resorts along the Coral Coast. Waidroka Bay Resort has their own dive set up; see below. Surfing is possible at Hideaway Resort as well as Waidroka Bay Resort.

Places to Stay – bottom end
The Beachhouse is seven km east of Korolevu, 127.5 km from Suva, just off the Queens Road on a bend near the beach. This new accommodation was completed in early 1996 and is recommended for budget travellers for its good atmosphere and nice beach setting. It is run by friendly couple, Andrew and Jessica, who also run the Coconut Cafe in the restored cottage on the site; see Places to Eat. They have a couple of two-storey timber buildings (designed by Jessica) with double rooms upstairs, and dorm rooms downstairs (maximum of four in each). Prices are F$15 per person. Bathrooms and toilets are in an adjacent building. No

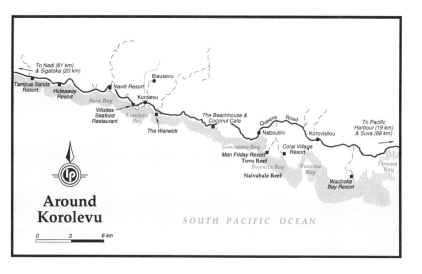

Around Korolevu

cooking facilities were available at the time of writing but they were planning to set some up in the near future. They have canoes and snorkelling equipment for hire. There are plenty of buses shuttling along the Queens Road (Suva or Nadi cost approximately F$5) and drivers will pick up and drop off at the gate from both directions.

Another new resort, which began construction in late 1995, is at Waidroka Bay in a beautifully secluded section of the Viti Levu coast. Waidroka is the Fijian word for fresh water, referring to the spring creek that flows through the forest to the bay. *Waidroka Bay Resort* (☎ 944 944; fax 303 160), run by two American couples, caters mainly for adventurous divers or surfers, but also for families and other visitors. It is 20 km west of Pacific Harbour, 69 km from Suva and four km off the Queens Road through steep hills and forest. At the time of writing it still looked a bit like a muddy building site. They were building five simple traditional-style bures near the beach on the edge of the forest. Accommodation rates for the ocean-front bure will be F$75/110 for a double/triple per night. The lodge (maximum of four people in a room with shared facilities) is F$48 per person per night. The big dormitory bure for 20 people will be F$12 per night. A restaurant was also under construction. They offer a three-meal package for F$25 per day, and otherwise lunch snacks are F$2.50 to F$5.75. The resort is remote and there are no self-catering facilities.

Scuba diving in the bay and off the outer reef is F$55/90 for one-tank/two-tank dives. Snorkel trips are F$10 per person but you can also snorkel along the shore. If conditions are right, it is possible to surf a couple of breaks a half-hour paddle from the beach. Alternatively, take the half-hour boat trip to surf at Frigate Passage for F$30 per person or F$135 per boat trip for a group. The resort can hire surfboards but ideally bring your own. Other activities include fishing and island trips, water skiing, paddle boating, trekking, village visits and trips to Pacific Harbour. The road into the resort is a bit rough but you shouldn't need a 4WD. Trans-

fers from Nadi airport or from the Queens Road can be organised if you call ahead.

Vilisite's Restaurant (☎ 530 054), on the Queens Road between the Naviti and Warwick resorts, have a building next to their restaurant with three fan-cooled rooms with ensuite, fridge and a double and single bed for F$75. The rooms are OK but they have a small window facing the back of the building and are not designed to make the most of the sea views.

Coral Village (☎/fax 500 807) is in a coastal valley next to Namaqaqa village and near Man Friday Resort. The turn-off is 50 km from Sigatoka and 77 km from Suva. It is a small-scale resort in an isolated spot with a good beach lagoon and offshore reef for swimming and snorkelling. Under new management since late 1995, the resort has double or twin fan-cooled bures for F$50/300 daily/weekly, family bures for F$75/450 and dorm beds for F$12/75. Camping is also available for F$6/38 daily/weekly per person. There is hot water but the toilets are a bit far from the campsite. There are no cooking facilities but the dining room/bar offers good food with breakfast for F$3 to F$5, lunch for F$2.50 to F$3.75 and dinner F$6 to F$9.50, including salad and rice or vegetables. There are two small stores selling basic groceries in the nearby village. Diving can be arranged through Man Friday Resort, and other activities include volleyball and nature walks. They also have a boat for fishing trips. There is a local dance, as well as kava drinking, on Tuesday night for F$5 per person. The road into the resort is about five km off the Queens Road, so call ahead to be picked up at the turn-off. There are regular buses to/from Nadi and Suva.

Places to Stay – middle

The *Hideaway Resort* (☎ 500 177; fax 520 025) is one of the most popular resorts in the area in its price range. It has a nice beach and good swimming, but be aware of the channel as the current can be dangerous under certain conditions (the channel area is marked by poles). The accommodation is smart, in a nice, well-maintained garden setting. Standard bungalows (maximum four people) have fans, tea and coffee-making facilities and a refrigerator, and cost F$121. Family bungalows (maximum six people) cost F$181.50. There were dorms for F$38 including meals, but these are going to be transformed into standard bungalows. Main meals in the open-plan restaurant/bar are between F$10 to F$17. They have lovo nights on Sunday, and there is a stage for performances, where a house band plays most nights; a meke is held twice weekly and a kava ceremony once a week.

Activities included in the tariff are shore snorkelling, minigolf, tennis, volleyball, archery and use of the gym. Scuba diving, windsurfing, deep-sea fishing and night tennis are also available. There is a small swimming pool but a new one is under construction. There is a right-hand reef-break about 100m from the shore – one of the few sites in Fiji where you don't need a boat to go surfing. It is possible to surf all year round here but your chances of good surf are better between May and September. The resort also has boutiques with local and Australian fashion, a Thrifty car-rental desk and a foreign-currency exchange. Child-minding and baby-sitting can be arranged.

Tambua Sands Beach Resort (☎ 500 399; fax 520 265), located approximately halfway between Nadi and Suva, west of the Hideaway resort, has a good beach for Coral Coast standards. The bures spread along the beach in a pleasant garden setting are an option for those after a quiet, relaxing time and a friendly atmosphere. The resort, under Korean management since 1996, has 25 bures and six garden rooms with private bathrooms, tea and coffee-making facilities, but no cooking facilities.

Rates are F$114 per bure. The restaurant has breakfast from F$6.50 to F$9.50, lunch for F$9, dinner buffet F$20.50 or à la carte for F$16 to F$19. They have weekly lovo, Chinese and Indian nights. Most activities, including village tours, horse riding, bike, snorkelling and kayak hire, and deep-sea fishing, are extra. Baby-sitting is available upon request.

Places to Stay – top end
There are two resorts, which are members of the Warwick International Hotel chain, within a few km of each other and guests can use either resort's facilities. The *Naviti* (☎ 530 444; fax 530 343) is on an interesting site on a protected beach, with a hilly backdrop and a small private island in the lagoon. The 140 rooms (maximum four people), decorated in pastel colours with cane furniture, have air-con, tea and coffee-making facilities, minibar, music and telephone. Prices are F$181.50 for mountain-view rooms, F$192.50 for ocean view and F$385 for suites. The three restaurants have main meals for F$15 to F$24. The resort has five tennis courts, a nine-hole golf course, a good swimming pool, a games room, a couple of shops and a currency exchange. They have an extensive list of activities and nonmotorised sports are included in the price. Baby-sitting is available 24 hours for F$1.50 per hour and there is a baby pool, children's playground and children's menu. There is reasonably good access for disabled people. The resort is 90 km from Nadi airport. Taxis are about F$55 for the 1½ -hour ride. A return taxi to Sigatoka (28 km, a 20-minute drive) is F$30.

There is a free shuttle bus (five minutes) to its sister hotel, *The Warwick* (☎ 530 555; fax 530 010). This is one of the largest resorts in Fiji, with 250 rooms in a recently refurbished building. It has a spacious lobby, shops, tour desk, laundrette, gym and convention facilities. All rooms are air-con and have marble bathrooms. Mountain-view rooms cost F$210 for singles/doubles or F$250 for triple with a maximum of two kids. Ocean-view rooms are F$25 extra. The Warwick Club has rooms on the third level for F$352 and suites for F$400, including breakfast, afternoon tea and cocktails in the club lounge, slippers and gowns. The resort has a good pool and bar areas, and four restaurants including the Wicked Walu; see Places to Eat below. Entertainment includes a meke and fire walking. Activities include golf, tennis, squash, horse riding, diving, windsurfing and fishing. The resort is about two km east of Korolevu.

Man Friday Resort (☎ 500 185; fax 520 666) is located in a beautiful, hilly beachfront setting well off the beaten track. Under new management since late 1995, the resort is now promoted as 'very gay friendly', but straight people and families are also accepted as long they are gay friendly. There is a special 'lesbian in grass skirts' fortnight every year. The resort's name comes from the Daniel Defoe character 'Friday', who saved Robinson Crusoe from cannibals on a tropical island. There are 27 spacious, fan-cooled bures with mosquito nets, tea and coffee-making facilities, but no cooking facilities. Some of the units are on the hill and others are close to the beach, each with two queen-size beds and double showers. Room rates are F$232/258/309/360 per night for single/twin share/triple/quad, including transfers to and from Nadi airport, breakfast and various activities for a two-night stay. The longer you stay the cheaper the rate, and over six days is F$176/196/234/272.

Dinner is served buffet style with different themes (lovo, barbecue, pasta or Chinese) and costs F$16, or F$20 to F$22 for the seafood night. Visitors can come to the restaurant/bar but not use the resort facilities. There is a tennis court and a saltwater, foot-shaped swimming pool. Use of sailboards, catamarans, glass-bottom boat, banana boats and snorkelling equipment is included in the daily rate. Entertainment includes amateur nights, frog races, horse races and chocolate-mousse-eating competitions. Diving is extra, and can be arranged with Sea Sports. Man Friday is 90 km from Nadi, 80 km from Suva, and five km from the Queens Road. If you ring ahead they can pick you up from the turn-off.

Places to Eat

The *Coconut Cafe* and restaurant in a colonial cottage at the beach front has been recommended as a pleasant place to stop along the Coral Coast for a break. It offers a varied menu with Devonshire tea, cakes, coffee and fresh-fruit smoothies, and European-style light meals for around F$8. See Places to Stay for the new Beachhouse dormitory accommodation behind the cafe.

Vilisite's Seafood Restaurant (☎ 530 054) is located on the Queens Road between the Naviti and Warwick hotels. It has a verandah with tables overlooking the beach, and Vilisite is a good cook. There are five different three-course set menus for lunch or dinner; one including octopus, fish fillets and fruits is F$18, while whole lobsters or 16 king prawns, fried rice plus a fruit platter is F$32.

Many of the resorts also have restaurants where visitors are welcome. At the Warwick Resort the *Papagallo Restaurant* serves good pizza and pasta dishes for F$10 to F$18 and main meals for F$16.50 to F$26.50. They also have an interesting seafood restaurant (dinner only), the *Wicked Walu*, which is on a tiny island linked to the resort by a causeway. Meals here cost F$18 to F$34. The *Cafe Korolevu*, also at the Warwick, has a mixed-style lunch menu with main dishes for F$7.50 to F$19.

The restaurant at the gay-friendly Man Friday Resort (☎ 500 185) has good food and is open for visitors. House guests usually eat at a single, large dinner table and you may be asked to join them.

PACIFIC HARBOUR

Past Korolevu heading towards Suva the scenery along the Queens Road begins to change. The vegetation becomes greener and denser as you approach the wetter eastern side of Viti Levu. In the Deuba and Pacific Harbour area the Queens Road runs near the shore, with Beqa Island in sight.

Pacific Harbour is 78 km east of Sigatoka (139 km from Nadi) and 49 km west of Suva. It is an unusual town for Fiji, planned as an up-market housing and tourism development with meandering drives, canals and a golf course (one of the best in Fiji) in the middle. The town itself is fairly boring for visitors, but the Beqa Lagoon offshore has world-class diving and a surf-break, and the beach at Deuba, about one km west of the Pacific Harbour Hotel, is the closest reasonable beach to Suva. Just 45 minutes by car from Suva, Pacific Harbour is a convenient weekend beach escape from the capital, and some residents even commute daily to work there. Pacific Harbour has two large hotels, villa units and apartments for rent and a couple of budget places to stay in nearby Deuba. It also has a few restaurants and a large cultural centre and tourist marketplace. East of Pacific Harbour is a 50-km-long section of the Queens Road with only the Orchid Island Cultural Centre perhaps worth a stop before Suva.

Things to See
The Fijian Cultural Centre & Marketplace (☎ 450 177; fax 450 083) is about one km east of the Pacific Harbour Hotel. The complex, with gift shops, boutiques, restaurants and a cultural centre, is unashamedly geared towards tourists and specifically tour groups by the busload. It is OK for a quick glimpse of Fijian culture and for purchasing souvenirs. There is a **Lake Tour** around an artificial village in a drua (old-style canoe) with a 'warrior' as skipper and guide. The small islands have a reconstructed temple, chief's bure, cooking area with utensils and a weaving hut. Fijian actors dressed in traditional costumes carry out a mock battle. The boat stops along the way to show traditional techniques for canoe making, weaving, tapa and pottery. Visitors are not allowed to disembark at the 'sacred islands'. The hour-long tour costs F$18/9 per adult/child.

The **Dance Theatre of Fiji** performs *Spirit of the Land* shows on Monday, Wednesday, Thursday and Friday, and villagers of Beqa Island have fire-walking rituals on Tuesday and Saturday. Shows cost F$18/9 per adult/child or F$33/16.50 for a double attraction programme.

Activities
The Pacific Harbour Hotel allows visitors to join their organised tours and use the resort's facilities. Hourly rates for guests/nonguests are as follows: dinghy sailing, windsurfing or coral viewing costs F$12/18; and horse riding costs F$7/14 (half-price for children). Nonguests can also use the tennis courts for F$6.60 to F$13.20 per hour (equipment rental is extra) and canoes for F$6 per hour. Water skiing is F$36 per 20 minutes. Cruises to Yanuca Island are F$60.50/30.50 for adult/child.

Diving There are several operators that dive the Beqa lagoon, two of which are based at Pacific Harbour. Dive Connections (☎ 450 541; fax 450 539), next to the canal at 16 River Drive opposite the Pacific Harbour Hotel, is run by Leyh and Edward Harness. They take dive trips on either the 12m *Scuba Queen* or seven-metre aluminium *Dive Master*. A two-tank dive, including all equipment, picnic lunch and soft drinks, costs F$105, or F$90 for just tanks and weights. For snorkellers, trips are F$45 including lunch. Dive courses cost F$120 for introductory dives, F$365 for PADI open-water certification and F$300 for PADI advanced-diver certification. They also have a comfortable, self-contained one-bedroom unit to accommodate their divers.

Beqa Divers Fiji (☎ 361 088; fax 361 047) has a dive shop at the Pacific Harbour Hotel marina and are part of Scubahire in Lami, near Suva. They are one of the oldest diving operations in Fiji and have a five-star PADI training facility. A two-tank dive trip, including all equipment and lunch, costs F$126.50. An introductory dive is F$137.50 and open-water PADI courses are F$450. Snorkellers are included on trips for F$60.

Diving is also available at Beqa Island Resort; see below.

Fishing Dive Connections also charters its dive boats for fishing trips for F$440/660 for half-day/full day, including lunch and all fishing gear. Baywater Charters (☎ 450 235; fax 450 606) also has charter boats for fishing as well as for picnic and snorkelling trips to Yanuca Island. Charters through the Pacific Harbour Hotel are F$60.50/72.60 for guests/nonguests and F$550/880 for half-day/full-day game-fishing tours.

Surfing There is first-class surfing at Frigate Passage; see Yanuca Island later in this chapter. Trips to the break can be organised with Penaia of Frigates Surfriders (☎ 450 472; fax 724 059). You can also enquire at the newsagency at the Pacific Harbour marketplace; it runs a camp at Yanuca Island. You could also try Michael Fairfax (☎ 970 011; fax 303 160), who organises surf trips to the passage.

Golf The Pacific Harbour Golf & Country Club (☎ 450 048) has an 18-hole, par-72 championship course, considered one of the best in Fiji. Designed around lakes and canals, it has a club house and restaurant, and is about two km off the Queens Road. Green fees are F$11/22 18/9 holes for Pacific Harbour Hotel guests and F$22/44 for 18/9 holes for other visitors. Hire of clubs and carts is extra and golf lessons are also available.

Organised Tours
Wilderness Ethnic Adventure Fiji (☎ 387 594; fax 300 584) offers tours to the Navua River, picking up passengers from Pacific Harbour as well as from Suva hotels, and Discover Fiji Tours (☎ 450 180; fax 450 549), based at Pacific Harbour, also have several tours in the area; see Navua below. Discover Fiji Tours also offers one to four-day guided treks across Namosi Province, camping overnight in villages, and an all-day Suva city tour and shopping expedition from Pacific Harbour.

Places to Stay – bottom end
Deuba is on the Queens Road about one km west of the Pacific Harbour Hotel and a few minutes walk from the local beach. It is a good place for budget travellers to stay while organising trips to Beqa Lagoon. The *Coral Coast Christian Centre* (☎ 450 178), run by Jo and Heather, has a spacious garden area and good value accommodation. Tent sites cost F$5.50. 'Cozy corner' cabins (maximum of five people in each) with shared bathroom and kitchen facilities are F$13/22 for singles/doubles, with each extra adult/child costing F$9/5. They also have six self-contained units, each with private bathroom, hot water, refrigerator and cooking

facilities, for F$22/40 singles/doubles, and F$18/6 per extra adult/child. Discount rates are given for stays of over one week. Alcohol isn't permitted here.

The *Deuba Inn* (☎ 450 544; fax 361 337) next door used to be an old homestead and pineapple-canning factory. It is now accommodation, with a pleasant garden and restaurant area. It has beds in simple prefab buildings with shared bathroom facilities but no cooking for F$16.50/26.40 for singles/doubles, or for F$35 in a dorm that can fit five people. There are also four self-contained units of varying size with cooking facilities for F$40 to F$60 for three people and F$5 per extra person (maximum five people at a squeeze); see Places to Eat for information on the restaurant and cafe.

Places to Stay – middle
Pacific Harbour Villas (☎/fax 450 959) can be a good option for families or groups. They are spacious houses in a quiet location around the golf course, in the back streets across the Queens Road from the Pacific Harbour Hotel. The villas have twin or double bedrooms, open-plan lounge, dining and kitchen areas, and gardens, some with private swimming pools. They are mostly owned by people who live abroad and are normally rented for long terms. The set-up won't provide the ultimate Fijian experience but might be convenient to use as a base to go diving or visit the surrounding area. Prices for villas are F$75 per night for standard two-bedroom units for a minimum stay of three days. Long-term discounts are available. Ideally, if you stay at one of the rear units you should have your own transport.

Fiji Palms Beach Club (☎ 450 050; fax 450 025) is right next to the Pacific Harbour Hotel. It has spacious self-contained two-bedroom apartments (with cooking facilities, air-con and fans) that can sleep six people. Prices are F$180 for one night, F$135 per night if you stay for two to six nights or F$900 per week. Club facilities include a bar, swimming pool and spa pool, barbecue and shop, and guests can also use the facilities of the hotel next door.

The *Korean Village* (☎ 450 100; fax 450 153), previously known as the Atholl Hotel, is now Korean owned, and caters mainly for Korean tour groups. The modern building has 22 rooms and is now painted lolly pink. Prices have dropped considerably since the changeover. Tariffs for singles or doubles are F$90 for standard rooms, F$95 for deluxe rooms, F$100 for huge suites and F$1100 for the penthouse. The bar and restaurant has an international-style menu with lunch and dinner main courses for F$13 to F$18.50 and a Korean menu for F$12 to F$20, which includes a broiled-eel dish for F$40. To get there, turn down Great Harbour Drive just west of the Pacific Harbour Cultural Centre. It is located near the golf course, on Fairway Place, just north of the canal.

To get more of an insight into local lifestyle try *Vunimaqo Lomery* (☎ 450 095), an English-style B&B. Ita Wilson, a Fijian, and her Scottish husband, Des, have a colonial-style home in a private garden on the water's edge. They have two rooms, which are F$30/60 for singles/doubles per night including breakfast, and share their bathroom, kitchen and company. They give preference to couples passing by looking for a quiet place to stay for a night or two. It is located past Lomery Church and school, seven km east of Pacific Harbour on Queens Road towards Suva.

Places to Stay – top end

The *Pacific Harbour Hotel* (☎ 450 022; fax 450 262) was built in the early 1970s. The resort has a reasonably good beach for swimming, a couple of shops and money exchange. Rooms with air-con, fridge, TV, telephone, tea and coffee-making facilities are F$156/176 for singles/doubles, including breakfast. Up to two children under 16 years old can share with parents free of charge. The hotel has two restaurants and two bars; see Places to Eat. There are special meke and theme nights. Included in the room rate is canoeing and day-time tennis. Most other activities and organised tours cost extra, including golf at the 18-hole Country Club Golf Course and scuba diving with Beqa

Divers. Bicycle rental is F$6 per hour; see Activities above.

Places to Eat

Kumaran's Restaurant and Milk Bar (☎ 450 294), located just across the road from the Pacific Harbour Hotel entrance, offers simple but good Indian, Chinese and European eat-in or takeaway main dishes for F$5 to F$10.

The Deuba Inn, in Deuba one km west of Pacific Harbour, has a restaurant, cafe and bar: *Loraini's Restaurant* specialises in seafood dishes; the *Banana Leaf Cafe* has snacks and cheaper meal options for breakfast, lunch and dinner for F$4.50 to F$7; and the *Planters Bar* has happy hours from 5 to 7 pm.

The Pacific Harbour Hotel has two restaurants, the *Kana Snack Bar* and the *Nautilus Restaurant*, with lunches under F$11.50 and dinner for F$16.50 to F$26.40. *Sakura House* (☎ 450 300) is a Japanese restaurant, just across the road from the hotel entrance. Its menu has tempura, sashimi and sukiyaki, with main dishes for F$20 to F$30 and European-style steak dishes for F$10 to F$15. It is open daily from 6 pm to midnight.

The Pub Restaurant (☎ 450 509), on the western side of the marina opposite the Pacific Harbour Hotel, has a blackboard menu including steaks and seafood mains for F$13 to F$17. Daily opening hours are 5.30 to 11 pm for dinner (happy hour 5.30 to 6.30 pm), and 11.30 am to 4 pm for Sunday lunch. The Fijian Cultural Centre & Marketplace, about one km east of the Pacific Harbour Hotel, also has a couple of places to eat: the *Oasis Restaurant* (☎ 450 617) has light meals and snacks for F$3.50 to F$7 and main meals for around F$10; and the *Cultural Centre Tree Top Restaurant* (☎ 450 095) has traditional Fijian cooking.

Getting There & Away

Pacific Harbour is 139 km from Nadi and 49 km from Suva. It is about an hour's express bus ride from Suva and around three hours from Nadi. There are frequent Pacific Transport and Sunbeam Transport Lautoka-Suva buses travelling the Queens Road as well as Viti minibuses and carriers. The first bus to Lautoka is at 7.50 am and the last at 7 pm; the first to Suva is at 8.45 am and the last at 9.40 pm.

The Deuba airstrip reopened in 1996. Air Fiji has two services per week from Nadi on Thursday and Sunday.

NAVUA

This agricultural region is 39 km west of Suva and 143 km from Nadi. Early this century sugar cane was planted in the area and a sugar mill was built, but this activity ceased with the shift of cane plantations to the more productive, drier western region. Since then the delta region turned to other farming activities such as dairy farming, cattle grazing, rice and other crops. Farmhouses are scattered around the district. The small town of Navua, about a 20-minute drive from Suva on the banks of the large Navua River, serves the local farming community and has a produce market. Many of the old buildings in the town date from the turn of the century.

Upriver there are beautiful gorges, waterfalls, forest and spectacular mountain backdrops. The best way to explore the relatively inaccessible area is by river.

Organised Tours

Discover Fiji Tours (☎ 450 180; fax 450 549), based at Pacific Harbour, have several tours to the Navua River area. The Magic Waterfall trip costs F$54 per person and includes lunch and *bilibili* (bamboo rafting) down the Navua River to Nakavu village. They pick up and drop off from Pacific Harbour and Suva hotels. A five-hour trip with a cruise up the Navua River in a 25-horsepower punt (1½ hours upriver, one hour return) to Namuamua village for lunch costs F$45. They also offer one to four-day guided treks across Namosi Province, camping overnight in villages, and a three day, two-night camp on the Navua River.

Wilderness Ethnic Adventure Fiji (☎ 387 594; fax 300 584) offers several tours, which pick up from Suva and Pacific Harbour

hotels. An all-day trip with canoeing/rubber rafting on the Navua River including barbecue lunch costs F$65 per person. Expect to get wet. The minimum age is 15 and if any older than 45 years you have to sign a liability disclaimer! Lifejackets are provided but you must be able to swim. A trip up the Navua River by motorboat with a village visit costs F$33/54 per child/adult.

There are also market boats and local buses to/from Namuamua and Nukusere villages about 20 km upriver. The trip can take up to two hours depending on the river's water level.

Getting There & Away

The regular express buses along the Queens Road stop at Navua. They take about 50 minutes from Suva and about 3¼ hours from Nadi.

ORCHID ISLAND

The **Orchid Island Cultural Centre** (☎ 361 128; fax 361 064) is seven km west of Suva and 42 km from Pacific Harbour. While it used to offer good demonstrations of traditional Fijian customs, at the time of writing it appeared to have gone downhill. It still has an interesting replica of the *bure kalou*, a large ancient temple, as well as a tour through the chief's house, demonstrations of bark-cloth making, basket weaving and

---

Bure Kalou

In the days of the old religion, every village had a temple, or *bure kalou*. These had a characteristically high pitched roof and usually stood on terraced foundations. The *bete*, or priest, an intermediary between the villagers and the spirits, lived in the temple and performed various rituals, including feasting on slain enemies and burying important people. A strip of white bark cloth, usually hung from the ceiling, served as a connection to the spirits. These bures were also used as meeting houses for the men. The construction of such a temple required that a strong man be buried alive in each of the corner post holes. ■

pottery. A historical display with a section about cannibalism is mildly interesting. It also has the remains of a small zoo containing a banded iguana, snakes and Fijian flora. Admission at F$10 per person (free for children under 15 years) is a bit steep for what's offered. The centre is open Monday to Saturday from 8 am to 4.30 pm. You can get there on nonexpress Queens Road buses.

Islands off Southern Viti Levu

BEQA LAGOON

Beqa and Yanuca islands are enclosed in the 360-sq-km **Beqa Lagoon** with its 64-km barrier reef. The lagoon is famous for its dive sites, which include: Side Streets, with soft corals, coral heads and gorgonian fans; Frigates Pass, a 48m wall dive with large pelagic fish including white-tip reef sharks; and Caesar's Rocks, with coral heads and swim throughs. Surfing is first class at **Frigate Passage** south-west of Yanuca Island. It has left-hand waves, which can get really big. The break has three sections, which join up under the right conditions: the outside take off; a long, walled speed section with a possibility of stand-up tubes; and an inside section breaking over the shallower section of reef and finishing in deep water.

Beqa Island

Beqa is a volcanic island about 7½ km south of Viti Levu's Navua Delta, and is visible from the Queens Road near Pacific Harbour and even from Suva. It is 35 minutes by boat from Pacific Harbour. The island is about seven km in diameter with an area of 36 sq km and a deeply indented coastline. The rugged interior is dominated by ridges averaging 250m high and sloping steeply down to the coast. The island is surrounded by a coral reef famous for its dive sites. Beqa has eight villages, and the villagers of Rukua, Naceva and Dakuibeqa are famous for their

fire-walking tradition. Apart from one up-market resort there are no other places for visitors to stay on the island.

The *Marlin Bay Resort* (☎ 304 042; fax 304 028) is on a nice coconut-tree fringed beach on the western side of Beqa Island. This resort caters mostly for a dive-oriented clientele. It has 12 luxury bures near the beach and a large central bure with a restaurant, lounge area and office. Singles/doubles cost F$302/495 per night for a minimum of three nights, plus boat transfers for F$50 per person. Children under 10 years old are half-price. Rates include all meals and activities including a two-tank dive-boat trip and unlimited shore diving. Other activities include snorkelling, kayaking, hikes to waterfalls and village visits. Game fishing can be arranged for an additional price.

Yanuca Island

Not to be confused with Yanuca Island (Fijian Resort) near Sigatoka, this small island with beautiful beaches is located within the Beqa Lagoon, nine km west of Beqa Island. It is visited mainly by people on day excursions, divers and overnight campers. It has one small village and a surf camp.

Frigate Surfriders (☎ 450 472; fax 724 059) has a camp on a small white-sand beach. It is run by Penaia Drekeni and you can usually find him at the newsagency/video shop at the Pacific Harbour Cultural Centre. He charges F$65 per person per night or F$30 for nonsurfers, and F$20 for the island shuttle. The rate includes accommodation in tents, three meals in a beach hut, surfing, windsurfing or fishing trips. They have recently set up piped water for the camp and are planning to build some simple hut accommodation. Other activities can be arranged, including snorkelling, diving, canoeing and trekking.

VATULELE ISLAND

Vatulele is 32 km south of Korolevu off the Viti Levu coast, to the west of Beqa Lagoon. The island is 13 km long with a total area of about 31 sq km. It is mostly flat, the highest point being just 33m above sea level, and has scrub and palm vegetation. The western coast is a long escarpment broken by vertical cliffs formed by fracturing and uplifts. The northern and eastern ends are protected by a barrier reef up to three km out from the shoreline, forming a lagoon. There are two navigable passages at the northern end of the barrier reef.

The island has four villages with a total population of around 950, and one exclusive resort on land leased from the mataqali. Vatulele is one of Fiji's two main producers of bark cloth and the population lives mostly off subsistence farming and fishing. Vatulele is known for its **archaeological sites**, including ancient rock paintings of faces and stencilled hands, geological formations, limestone caves and pools inhabited by sacred red prawns.

The exclusive *Vatulele Island Resort* (☎ 720 300; fax 720 062; ☎ 02 326 1055 in Australia; 800 828 9146 in the USA) ranks as one of the best island resorts in the world. It was developed by Australian TV producer Henry Crawford together with Martin Livingston from Fiji. Martin also manages the resort and ensures there is never a dull moment. Architecturally it is the most interesting of Fiji's resorts, with a stunning mix of Santa Fe style with thick rendered walls, together with lofty thatched roofs in tradi-

tional Fijian bure style. The materials, including huge, sculptural, strangled fig trunks, were imported from the main island, and the site was selectively cleared using 100 men with cane knives in order to minimise impact on the natural surroundings. Everything was placed by manpower only, and motorised sports are not available at the resort. After 2½ years of construction the resort was opened in 1990. The 16 bures are well spaced, each fronting onto its own stretch of white-sand beach facing an idyllic turquoise lagoon. While each site has an individual character, the bures have identical layouts with an open-plan, split-level sleeping and sitting area, and bathroom opening onto an outdoor terrace. The space, facilities, view and use of natural materials promote a feeling of complete relaxation and privacy. Every element is thoughtfully designed, right down to the shower outlet!

Gourmet-quality meals, beverages and alcohol are included in the rate and can be served anywhere you wish, although everyone usually dines at the same table in the main bure. The minimum stay is four nights at a nightly price of F$858/1276 for singles/doubles at high season, and F$748/1056 for low season. Children are only accepted during family weeks (early July and late September) and cost F$44 if under 12 years or F$66 up to 15 years. Low season

---

Sacred Red Prawns

Near the north end of Vatulele the limestone is honeycombed with caves and pools which, despite being inland from the shore, are affected by tidal movements. These pools are the habitat of the famous red prawns, or *ura buta*, meaning cooked prawns. The red prawns are regarded with great respect by the islanders, who won't eat or harm them. They believe that anyone who takes the prawns will be shipwrecked when they sail away from the island. The prawns are known to respond when called by traditional magic chants and there is a local legend to explain their origin.

There was once a beautiful but cold-hearted young woman called Yalewa, who treated her many suitors with disdain, preferring to play with her friends. She told her chiefly father that she would only accept a man who was brave and creative with godly powers and would never marry anyone who came to the island by mere canoe. One day an ingenious and hopeful young chief arrived from across the sea on a string of stepping stones, bringing with him a basket of cooked prawns as a present. Yalewa angrily and ungraciously struck him with the basket, scattering its contents. The prawns came alive and can be found in the pools of Vatulele to this day. The frightened suitor fled home across the stepping stones and never returned. ■

is during June, from November to 20 December and from 11 January to 27 March.

Activities such as snorkelling, windsurfing, tennis and hiking are included. Dive trips to nearby sites cost F$99 for a single dive and F$825/1320 for singles/doubles for a certification course. Packages are available for two-tank dive trips (one to four days) for F$132 per day, or 10 tanks over five days for F$550. Sport game fishing is F$440 for four hours. The island has an airstrip, and return transfers by charter plane cost F$341 per person (half-price for under 12 years).

Suva

While Nadi in the west is the tourism centre, Suva is the political and administrative capital, the major port and the centre of educational, commercial and industrial life in Fiji. The city ranks as the largest and most sophisticated in the South Pacific and is an important regional centre, with the University of the South Pacific, the Forum Secretariat and overseas embassies.

Suva and its surrounding urban area has a population of over 141,000 people, about half of Fiji's total urban population. It is a multiracial and multicultural centre with many churches, mosques and temples. There are a large number of public servants, ex-pats and students from throughout the Pacific region. About 60% of Suva's inhabitants are squatters living in settlements on land with no formal title. Urbanisation, poverty and crime are becoming increasingly problematic.

The landscape is quite beautiful, with scenic views to the mountains across the bay, and there are some interesting old buildings, gardens and remnants of the colonial past, as well as some nondescript high-rise blocks. The climate is notorious for being hot, wet and humid, although the tropical rain (about three metres annually) often comes as refreshing change at the end of afternoon.

History

The Fijians who lived on the Suva Peninsula were traditional rivals with the Rewans to the east, as was chief Cakobau of Bau. In the 1850s, with help from King George of Tonga, Cakobau defeated the Rewans in the battle of the Kaba Peninsula.

Until the 1870s there were few Europeans in the area. The majority of Suva's original settlers and fortune hunters came from Melbourne, Australia, where there was an economic downturn after the gold rushes. In 1868 the newly formed Polynesia Company had agreed to clear Cakobau's inflated debts (owed to American settlers) in return for land, including over 9000 hectares in the Suva area, and the right to trade in Fiji. While not his land to sell, the powerful chief Cakobau had the Fijian village relocated from the present site of Government House. Cakobau, claiming to be *Tui Viti* or King of Fiji, had already attempted to cede Fiji to Britain for payment of these debts in 1862.

In 1870 a group of forty Australians from Melbourne arrived in what is now downtown Suva. The dense reeds were cleared for farming and they tried growing cotton and then sugar cane. Their attempts at farming on the thin topsoil and soapstone base of the Suva Peninsula failed, and most of the settlers' efforts ended in bankruptcy. Two Melbourne merchants, WK Thomson and S Renwick, turned this financial ruin to their advantage by encouraging the government to relocate the capital from Levuka to Suva so as to increase land values. Levuka had insufficient room for expansion, being squeezed between the beach front and tall hills immediately behind, and the government was looking for a fresh start for White settlement. Nadi and Galoa, in Kadavu, were also considered as sites for the new capital, but the merchants gave incentives in the form of land grants. Colonel WT Smyth, who recommended the move, had not visited Suva during the hottest and rainiest season, and opinion has it that he might have decided otherwise if he had.

The government officially moved to Suva from Levuka in 1882. In the 1880s Suva was

VITI LEVU

a township of about a dozen buildings. Later, sections of the seashore were reclaimed and trading houses constructed, and by the 1920s it was a flourishing colonial centre with many prominent public and private buildings. Large-scale land reclamation was carried out in the 1950s for the Walu Bay industrial zone.

The contorted layout of downtown Suva is blamed on Colonel FE Pratt, who was Surveyor General of the Royal Engineers in 1875. Although many were not happy with the layout, the original plans were not modified due to a lack of funds, and in some areas

the town grew haphazardly anyway. The area south of the Nubukalou Creek was developed first and the mud and soapstone roads were often impassable. Later the town extended east to the Domain and north-east to Toorak. This residential suburb on the hill overlooking the bay was once one of the premium areas, and though it has now fallen from grandeur it is thought to have been named after Melbourne's exclusive suburb.

Orientation

Suva is on a peninsula, with Laucala Bay to the east and the downtown area facing the

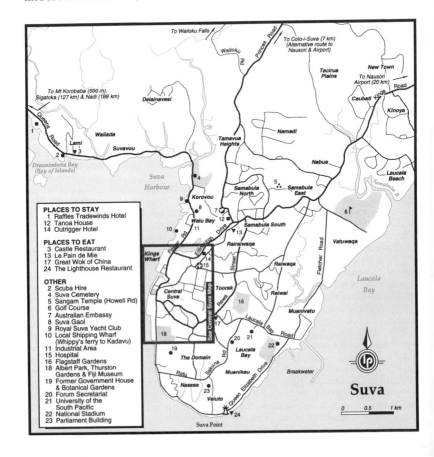

PLACES TO STAY
1 Raffles Tradewinds Hotel
12 Tanoa House
14 Outrigger Hotel

PLACES TO EAT
3 Castle Restaurant
13 Le Pain de Mie
17 Great Wok of China
24 The Lighthouse Restaurant

OTHER
2 Scuba Hire
4 Suva Cemetery
5 Sangam Temple (Howell Rd)
6 Golf Course
7 Australian Embassy
8 Suva Gaol
9 Royal Suva Yacht Club
10 Local Shipping Wharf (Whippy's ferry to Kadavu)
11 Industrial Area
15 Hospital
16 Flagstaff Gardens
18 Albert Park, Thurston Gardens & Fiji Museum
19 Former Government House & Botanical Gardens
20 Forum Secretariat
21 University of the South Pacific
22 National Stadium
23 Parliament Building

Suva

0   0.5   1 km

protected Suva Harbour to the west. Apart from the relatively flat downtown area near the wharf and market, the rest of the peninsula is hilly. There are three major roads in and out of the city: the Queens Road via Lami to the west, Princes Rd along the Tamavua ridge to the north and the Kings Road to the north-east via Nausori. Suva's town layout is maddeningly complicated, especially for drivers. Many of the meandering streets are one way, intersecting at varying angles and forming contorted loops. If you can't find your bearings go to a rooftop hotel restaurant to get a bite or a drink and a better idea of the city layout.

If you are arriving via the Queens Road from Nadi you will enter Suva heading south, with Suva Harbour on your right. Pass the prison and industrial area and cross the bridge over the Walu Bay inlet, where you will find a roundabout. At this roundabout, Edinburgh Drive heads uphill to the left to Samabula, and from there you can follow the Kings Road through to Nausori International Airport. Princes Rd heads north from Samabula through Tamavua Heights and is also a scenic route to Nausori. Alternatively, at the roundabout at Walu Bay follow Rodwell Rd past the bus station and market, across the Nubukalou creek to the central Suva area.

The area on the hill overlooking the market is the suburb of Toorak, which has many no-through streets. Waimanu Rd, an extension of Victoria Pde and Renwick Rd, takes you up to Suva Hospital.

Suva's downtown area has the GPO and business section along Victoria Pde, and the main drag, which runs parallel to the waterfront. If you keep heading south you will pass the Government Buildings, Albert Park and Thurston Gardens, where Victoria Pde becomes Queen Elizabeth Drive. This then passes Government House and winds all the way around the tip of the peninsula (Suva Point). Queen Elizabeth Drive finishes on the eastern side of the peninsula at Laucala Bay, near the University of South Pacific and the National Stadium. From Laucala Bay you can head north to meet the Kings Road

or head west back to central Suva via Laucala Bay Road.

Maps The best source of maps in Fiji is the Lands & Surveys Department, Room 10 in the Records & Reprographic Subsection, Government Buildings, Suva. Here you can buy a *Suva, Lami & Environs* map as well as maps of other towns and areas of Fiji. Opening hours are 9 am to 3.30 pm (3 pm on Friday), but it's closed from 1 to 2 pm for lunch. Bookshops downtown, including Desai at 12 Pier St opposite the FVB, stock this map. The FVB also has brochures and maps.

Information
Tourist Offices The main source of tourist information is the FVB (☎ 302 433; fax: 300 970; PO Box 92; Internet: http://www. fijifvb.gov.fj; email: infodesk@fijifvb. gov.fj), which has its head office in Suva on the corner of Thomson and Scott Sts. This office is bigger and better organised than the one at Nadi airport, and can consequently provide more useful information about what is available for travellers. Like the Nadi office, it has an extensive stock of brochures for you to browse through, and it now has a 24-hour, toll-free visitors' help line (☎ 0800 721 721) to handle complaints and emergencies.

The Tourism Council of the South Pacific (☎ 304 177; fax 301 995; email: spice @is.com.fj) has an office on the corner of Loftus St and Victoria Pde on the 3rd floor above Dolphins Food Court. It promotes cooperation among the South Pacific island nations for the development of tourism in the region. Funding by the EU will cease in 1988, and the plan is for the council to become self-sufficient by commercialising services. It has an interesting service on the Internet (http://www.infocentre.com/spt), in the format of a travel directory including Fiji, Cook Islands, Kiribati, New Caledonia, Niue, Papua New Guinea, Solomon Islands, Tahiti, Tonga, Tuvalu, Vanuatu and Western Samoa.

VITI LEVU

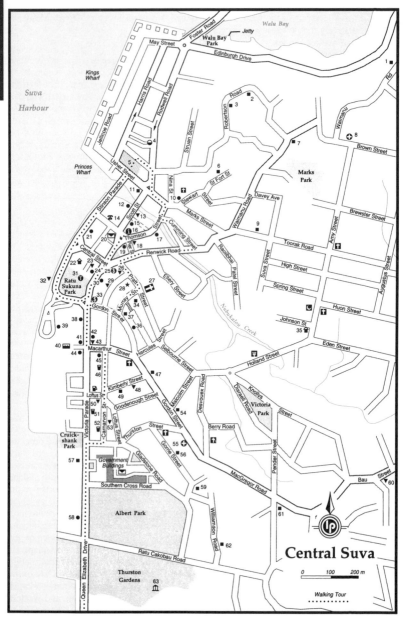

Central Suva

0   100   200 m

Walking Tour
. . . .

PLACES TO STAY	23	Cardo's Chargrill	21	Curio & Handicraft
1 Outrigger Hotel	26	Lantern Palace, Hare		Centre
2 Saf's Apartment Hotel		Krishna Restaurant	24	Regal Cinema
3 Tropic Towers	29	Palm Court Bistro	25	ANZ Bank
Apartment Hotel	32	Tiko's Floating	27	Roman Catholic
6 Capricorn		Restaurant		Cathedral
Apartment Hotel	43	Bad Dog Cafe &	28	Central Police Station
7 Ocean View		Lucky Eddie's	30	Air New Zealand
Private Hotel		Urban Jungle	31	Public Toilets
9 Bouganvillia Motel		Nightclubs	33	National Bank of Fiji
11 Metropole Hotel	48	Swiss Tavern	36	Emoisi's Ferry Service
22 YWCA Hostel	50	Dolphin Food Court &	38	FINTEL
34 Townhouse Hotel		Tourism Council of	39	Town Hall & City
35 Suva International		the South Pacific		Council
Youth Hostel	53	Old Mill Cottage	40	Suva Olympic Pool
37 Sunset	60	Noble House	41	Old Town Hall
Apartment Hotel			42	Air Fiji
47 Southern Cross Hotel	**OTHER**		44	Suva City Library
49 Coconut Inn	4	Bus Station &	45	Government Crafts
54 Berjaya Hotel		Taxi Stands		Centre & Ratu
56 Travel Inn	5	Suva Municipal Market		Sakuna House
57 Suva Travelodge	8	Hospital	46	Birdland Blues Bar
59 Suva Motor Inn	10	Beachcomber &	51	Golden Dragon
61 Suva Peninsula Hotel		Patterson Brothers		Nightclub
62 South Seas	12	Cinema Complex	52	The Barn
Private Hotel	14	Telephone Exchange	55	Medical Centre,
	15	Consort Shipping Line		Pharmacy &
PLACES TO EAT	16	Fiji Visitors Bureau		Fiji Recompression
13 Pizza King, The Wish-	17	Morris Hedstrom		Chamber
bone & The Wedge	19	Desai Bookshop,	58	Grand Pacific Hotel
18 Sichuan Pavillion		Sunflower Airlines	63	Fiji Museum
Restaurant	20	GPO		

In addition to those publications already mentioned in the Books section of the Facts for the Visitor chapter, some useful sources of information available in Suva are:

Fiji Magic (☎ 313 944; fax 302 852; Internet: http://www.fijimagic.com) a free monthly magazine listing current happenings on the Fiji tourism scene, including accommodation, restaurants, tours and activities.

Spotlight on Suva is a local advertising newspaper (free) that also has information on restaurants, shops, tours and activities.

Suva – A History and Guide by Albert J Schutz, Pacific Publications, Sydney, 1978.

The Fiji Hotel Association (☎ 302 975; fax 300 331), 42 Gorrie St, Suva. Most of the country's middle and top-range hotels and resorts are members of this organisation. They have a pamphlet with a table summarising the facilities of each member hotel.

The Ministry of Information, Government Buildings, Suva (☎ 211 218) has a few brochures including *Fiji Today* and *Fiji Facts and Figures*.

Foreign Embassies & Consulates The following foreign embassies and consulates are in Suva:

Australia
37 Princes Rd, Tamavua, PO Box 214 (☎ 382 211; fax 382 065)
China
147 Queen Elizabeth Drive, Suva (☎ 301 833; fax 300 950)
European Union
4th Floor, Fiji Development Bank Building, Victoria Pde, Suva (☎ 313 633; fax 300 370)
France
1st Floor, Dominion House, Thomson St, Suva (☎ 312 233; fax 301 894)
Israel
5th Floor, Parade Building, 69 Joske St, Suva (☎ 303 420; fax 300 415)
Japan
2nd Floor, Dominion House, Thomson St, Suva (☎ 302 122; fax 301 452)
Korea
8th Floor, Vanua House, Victoria Pde, Suva (☎ 300 977; fax 303 410)

Malaysia
5th Floor, Air Pacific House, Butt St, Suva, PO Box 356 (☎ 312 166; fax 303 350)
Marshall Islands
41 Borron Rd, Samabula, PO Box 2038 (☎ 387 899; fax 387 115)
Micronesia
37 Loftus St, Suva (☎ 304 566; fax 304 081)
Nauru
7th Floor, Ratu Sukuna House, Suva, PO Box 2420 (☎ 313 566; fax 302 861)
New Zealand
10th Floor, Reserve Bank Building, Pratt St, Suva, PO Box 1378 (☎ 311 422; fax 300 842)
Papua New Guinea
16 Lovoni Rd, Tamavua (☎ 381 612)
Tuvalu
16 Gorrie St, Suva, PO Box 14449 (☎ 301 355; fax 301 023)
UK
Victoria House, 47 Gladstone Rd, Suva, PO Box 1355 (☎ 311 033; fax 301 046)
USA
31 Loftus St, Suva, PO Box 218 (☎ 314 466; fax 300 081)

Money The Westpac Bank (☎ 300 666; fax 300 275), at 1 Thomson St, and the ANZ Bank (☎ 301 755; fax 300 267), at 25 Victoria Pde, are the best places to change money in Suva. Bank hours are Monday to Thursday from 9.30 am to 3 pm (Friday to 4 pm). Thomas Cook (☎ 301 603), at 21 Thomson St next to the Post Office, also changes travellers' cheques and foreign currency and is open during weekdays from 8.30 am to 5 pm, and Saturday from 8.30 to noon. Many of the hotels, including the budget South Seas Hotel and Travel Inn, will also change travellers' cheques for guests at the going bank rate. The Travelodge Hotel will exchange foreign currency on Sunday, but at lower rates than banks.

Post & Communications There are many cardphones scattered around the city, including the arcade next to the GPO, but this can be noisy. A quiet place to make calls is the foyer of the Travelodge. FINTEL or Fiji International Telecommunications (☎ 312 933; fax 301 025), 158 Victoria Pde, provides international services only, including phone calls, faxes and telegrams. It is open

from 8 am to 8 pm, Monday to Saturday. If you are carrying a computer and have problems with it, Alpha Computer Centre (☎ 300 211; fax 302 089) at 175 Victoria Pde is one of several shops that sell PCs in Suva. If they can't repair your PC themselves they should be able to put you in touch with others that can; see the Facts for the Visitor chapter for more information.

Travel Agencies Travel agencies in Suva include:

Hunts Travel
Dominion Building Arcade (☎ 315 288; fax 302 212). Hunts is a general agent for International air tickets.
Qantas Airways
CML Building, Victoria Pde (☎ 311 833; fax 304 795)
Air New Zealand
Queensland Insurance Building, Victoria Pde (☎ 313 100; fax 302 294)
Air Pacific
CML Building, Victoria Pde (☎ 304 388; fax 302 860)
Air Fiji
185 Victoria Pde (☎ 314 666; fax 303 326)
Sunflower Airlines
30 Thomson St (☎ 315 755; fax 305 027)

See the Getting There & Away section later in this chapter for interisland-ferry agencies.

Bookshops The University of the South Pacific (USP) has two good bookshops: the USP Book Centre at the Services Centre stocks textbooks as well as books about the South Pacific; the Institute of Pacific Studies (☎ 313 900; fax 301 594) is a publisher with an interesting catalogue, including over 250 titles by local authors. Its small bookshop, also at the USP, accepts cash and mail orders. The Fiji Museum has interesting books for sale, and there are Desai bookshops (☎ 314 088; fax 302 321) at the GB Hari Building, 12 Pier St opposite the FVB and at the Dominion House Arcade in downtown Suva, also near the FVB.

Libraries The Suva City Library, Victoria Pde next to the old town hall, has a small library on the ground floor. The Fiji Museum has a good reference library. You need to request to visit in advance and pay a small fee/donation.

The best Pacific collection is at the University of South Pacific Library, a large, new resource centre for the whole of the South Pacific region. Visitors can pay a F$30 deposit to borrow books from the general library. Books from the Pacific collection, however, cannot be borrowed and visitors can only use this part of the library for one day. Opening hours are 8 am to 10 pm from Monday to Thursday (to 6 pm on Friday and Saturday), and 1.30 to 6 pm on Sunday. Reduced hours apply during vacation breaks.

The South Pacific Action Committee for Human Ecology & Environment has a small reference library at the USP. The organisation aims to create awareness of issues that affect environment, sustainability and growth in the South Pacific region. It is next to the 2nd Hall, Student Quarters. Refer to the Facts about the Country chapter.

Cultural Centres The Fiji Museum, in the grounds of Thurston Gardens, is the major centre for the promotion of indigenous Fijian culture; see Fiji Museum later in this section. Other cultural centres include:

Indian Cultural Centre
    271 Toorak Rd, Suva (☎ 676 800). This cultural centre was established to promote Indian culture with lectures, language classes, theatre, music and dance classes.
Alliance Française
    77 Cakobau Rd, Suva (☎ 313 802; fax 313 803)

Laundry Most resorts and hotels will do your laundry for about F$5 a load. Same-day laundry and dry-cleaning services are also available in Suva.

Medical Services The Gordon Street Medical Clinic has a good reputation and is conveniently located in downtown Suva. It also has a pharmacy and the Fiji Recompression Chamber Facility. If you have an International Student Card you should be able to attend the university medical clinic free of charge.

Gordon Street Medical Clinic (and pharmacy)
    96-100 Gordon St (☎ 313 355, 313 155), Recompression Chamber (☎ 305 154).
Colonial War Memorial Hospital
    Waimanu Rd, Suva (☎ 313 444)
Central Pharmacy
    corner of Cumming St and Waimanu Rd (☎ 301 877).
AJ Swann & Co
    in the arcade next to the GPO, Thomson St (☎ 302 743). Opening hours are Monday to Friday from 8 am to 6 pm, Saturday 8 am to 1.30 pm and Sunday and Public Holidays from 9 am to noon.
Flagstaff Pharmacy
    7 Rewa St in Flagstaff (☎ 304 001), a 10-minute drive from downtown Suva towards the University of South Pacific. It's open on Sunday and Public Holidays, but ring to confirm opening hours.

Emergency Some useful emergency numbers follow:

Emergency (☎ 000), free
FVB emergency hotline (☎ 0800 721 721), free
Police (☎ 311 222)
Ambulance (☎ 301 439)

Walking Tour
Central Suva is easy to get to know on foot and most of the remaining colonial buildings and places of interest are concentrated here. Allow a few hours, and avoid the midday heat, which can be oppressive. Ideally, start in the early morning and take breaks along the way. Most places close on Sunday, and Saturday mornings are the busiest, especially at the market; see the Central Suva map.

Begin at the **FVB** building (1912). Opposite is the **Garrick Hotel** (1914), which now houses the Sichuan Pavilion Restaurant upstairs. Pause at the tiny park with an *ivi* tree on the corner known as the **Triangle**, in front of Proud's duty-free shop, to have a look at the historical marker, which commemorates the arrival of the first missionaries in 1835, the annexation of Fiji by Britain in 1874, public land sales in 1880 and the proclamation of Suva as the capital in 1882. Head down **Victoria Pde**, Suva's main street, which is lined with shops, banks, airline offices, nightclubs and many important colonial buildings. Cross Ratu Sukuna Park to the waterfront. The mountain ranges across Suva Harbour include the distinctive Joske's Thumb. Turn back to the **Curio & Handicraft Centre** for a browse through the souvenir stalls (8 am to 5 pm from Monday to Saturday). Walk along the foreshore towards the **Suva Municipal Market**. This produce market is another must-see for its exotic fruit and vegetables, *nama* (seaweed), kava, fish, crabs and spices as well as for the fascinating multiracial and multicultural mix. Vendors sell brightly coloured Indian sweets and savouries, and fruit drinks are sold from glass tanks. The top floor has the dry produce, mostly tobacco and kava as presentation bundles or pounded root. You will probably be offered to try a bowl.

Head back to busy Cumming St, which in the 1920s was known for its *yaqona* saloons and 'dens of iniquity'. Across the Nubukalou Creek is the **Morris Hedstrom building** (1918) with its Venice-like canal and arcaded seating area. At the end of Cumming St turn right into Renwick Rd and left at Pratt St, which was originally a creek. On the left past the Reserve Bank Building is the **Roman Catholic Cathedral** (1902), one of the capital's most prominent landmarks. Head

down Murray St, turn right at Gordon St and then left back on to Victoria Pde and continue along past the **Fiji International Telecommunications building** (1926) and the **former town hall** (1904). The old town hall building now houses a Chinese restaurant but once the main hall was used for dances, bazaars and performances. The municipal offices and council chambers were on the ground floor with a museum above. Shoppers may be interested in the craft shop at the front. The **Suva Olympic Pool** is set back between this building and the **Suva City Library** (1909), which houses the library downstairs and an engineering department upstairs. Victoria Pde runs parallel with the water. Most of the land on the sea side is actually reclaimed and, unfortunately, views are being built out by high-rise developments, which turn their backs on the foreshore, ignoring the great potential of the waterfront with its beautiful views to the mountains.

Turn left at Macarthur St (consider the Bad Dog for refreshments) and have a browse in the Government Crafts Centre. Turn right along Carnavon St, where you can stop for food at the Dolphin or better still the Old Mill Cottage Restaurant. Opposite the Old Mill Cottage is a rusting cog wheel uncovered during excavations for the NLTB building behind. It is believed to be part of the machinery of the sugar mill previously

---

Ratu Sukuna & the Native Lands Trust Board

The plaque on Sukuna's statue outside the Government Buildings reads: 'Ratu Sir Lala Sukuna, Tui Lau, Statesman Soldier, Paramount Chief and Leader of Men, 1888-1958'. Ratu Sukuna was the first Fijian to be educated overseas and the first to receive a university degree (a law degree from Oxford). He also served with the French Foreign Legion during WWI and was decorated for bravery in the Fiji Labour Detachment. One of this influential and respected character's main contributions to Fiji was the setting up of the Native Lands Trust Board (NLTB). He spent years studying the boundaries of land owned by the many *mataqali* and *yavusa*, Fijian land-owning groups. By 1905, 17% of the land had been sold to non-Fijian landowners (about half of this before cession to Britain in 1874), when a decree was imposed to prevent the sale of any more native land. Sukuna negotiated with every mataqali in Fiji and the Great Council of Chiefs to avoid disputes over land ownership. The NLTB aimed to prevent Fijians from leasing their land for long periods for quick profits at the expense of the needs of future generations, and to make surplus land available for lease and use by others. The anniversary of his death is commemorated with a national holiday. ■

on this site. Built in 1873 and owned by Brewer & Joske, the mill was the first in Fiji, but growing sugar cane in this area turned out to be a failure. The mouldy but impressive looking **Government Buildings** (1939 and 1967) are at the end of the street. The buildings required heavy foundations as they are built on reclaimed land over a creek bed. Of interest is the Department of Lands & Survey, as it was the scene of the 1987 coup. Parliament has now moved to new premises, but government departments and the courts remain. The statues of two influential Fijians (Ratu Cakobau and Ratu Sukuna) are in the front gardens on Victoria Pde.

Further along Victoria Pde you will find the Grand Pacific Hotel building and **Albert Park**, which was named after Queen Victoria's husband. This land was given to the government by the Polynesia Company as an incentive for moving the capital to Suva. It has a cricket ground and tennis courts up on the hill. Kingsford Smith Pavilion is named after the famous aviator who landed here. Opposite the park is the **Grand Pacific Hotel** building (1914), built by the Union Steamship Company on a fantastic site on the foreshore looking over to the mountains across the bay. Its ship-style architecture is reminiscent of the first-class ship accommodation of the era, with rooms opening onto a deck-like verandah and an internal balcony over an entertainment area. Elegant in its heyday, the hotel has unfortunately not yet undergone its promised renovations and stands boarded up and

neglected. It is owned by the people of Nauru, whose country is now bankrupt.

Before visiting **Thurston Gardens** (1913) continue along Victoria Pde, which becomes Queen Elizabeth Drive, to the **former government house** (1928). Now that there is no governor it is the president's residence. The precinct is not open to the public and the entrance is guarded by a soldier in a red shirt and white handkerchief sulu. The original Government House (1882), built on this site for Governor Des Voeux, was struck by lightning and burnt down in 1921. Return to the Thurston Gardens next door. These botanical gardens are named after Sir John Bates Thurston, an amateur botanist who introduced many ornamental plant species to Fiji. Gates are open from 6 am to 6.30 pm. The **Botanic Gardens Clock Tower** was built in 1918. Finish the walking tour at the Fiji Museum, and if you still have the time and energy, visit the parliament buildings (it's probably worth taking a taxi).

Fiji Museum

The Fiji Museum is one of Suva's highlights and is definitely worth a visit. Located in the grounds of Thurston Gardens, its fascinating collection of artefacts includes drua, weapons, ceremonial *tabua* and kava bowls, necklaces, breastplates, tools, cooking utensils and the Reverend Baker's old boot, which was reportedly cooked along with his body parts. There is a thermally stable room upstairs that houses beautiful examples of

Kingsford Smith

Charles Kingsford Smith, in his Fokker trimotor *The Southern Cross*, was the first aviator to cross the Pacific, flying from California to Australia. The longest leg of the flight was the 34-hour trip from Hawaii to Fiji. Suva's Albert Park, with its hill at one end and the Grand Pacific Hotel at the other, was made into a makeshift landing strip. Trees were still being cleared after he had already left Hawaii. Kingsford Smith and his crew arrived on 6 June 1928, welcomed by a crowd of thousands, including colonial dignitaries who had gathered at the Grand Pacific Hotel to witness and celebrate the major social event of the era. The pilot had to spin the plane around at the end of the park in order to stop in time. Because the park was too short to takeoff with a heavy load of fuel, they had to unload, fly to Nasilai Beach and reload for take off to Brisbane and Sydney. Kingsford Smith and his crew were presented with a ceremonial *tabua* as a token of great respect. ■

bark cloth. Exhibits explain other aspects of Fiji's history including the Tongan influence, early traders and settlers, blackbirding and Indian indenture.

The museum also undertakes archaeological research, the collection and preservation of oral traditions, and publishes such works as *Domodomo*, a quarterly journal on history, language, culture, art and natural history. It also organises exhibitions and craft demonstrations. Fiji's best known potters, Taravini Wati and Diana Tugea, give joint demonstrations at the museum on the first Thursday of each month, and Wati can also be seen each Thursday and Friday.

Lack of space and funding are perennial problems. A design competition for new premises was held recently, but it remains to be seen if anything will eventuate. Admission is F$3.30, and children are free. Opening hours are Monday to Friday from 8 am to 4 pm, and 9 am to 4.30 pm on Saturday. The Friends of the Fiji Museum Society publishes a quarterly newsletter called *Time Connections*. Annual subscriptions cost F$15/30 for students/individuals living abroad. For more information call☎ 315 944, fax 305 143, or write to PO Box 2023, Government Buildings, Suva. Volunteers are needed in the Collections, Archaeology and Education departments to organise archives and artefacts, and to organise children's projects and archaeology field programmes; see Organised Tours later in the Suva section for trips on the Fiji Museum's replica of a traditional Fijian drua.

Parliament of Fiji

The new parliament complex (☎ 305 811) was opened in June 1992. It consists of the *vale ni bose lawa* (parliament house) and separate buildings for parliament, government and opposition offices, and committee facilities. Both the house of representatives and the senate meet in the same chamber at different times.

The parliament is very interesting architecturally. Designed by Viti Architects, the concept was to integrate traditional Fijian building forms and crafts with a contemporary feel and modern technology, addressing shade, natural light and ventilation. It also reinforces the new direction in government towards maintaining traditional indigenous-Fijian values.

The site of the parliament house is elevated, and the building, with its stone base and dominant roof form, is based on the traditional vale. The overall site planning is in keeping with that of a traditional village. The site and landscaping form a symbolic link between the land and the sea. The complex is planned around courtyards and uses landscaping and covered walkways to link the different buildings. This, together with the use of natural materials, suggests an Asian influence in the design. Internally, Fijian elements include bark-cloth banners, *lalawa-magimagi* weaving of the ceiling structure, round columns (concrete), extensive use of timber, and furniture designed to give a crafted appearance.

The buildings are visible from Queen Elizabeth Drive but the visitor's entry is off Battery Rd, with ceremonial access from Ratu Sukuna Rd. The complex is five km from the city centre and the easiest way to get there is by taxi; otherwise take a bus along Queen Elizabeth Drive and walk along Ratu Sukuna Rd for about one km. Visiting hours are 8 am to 1 pm and 2 to 4.30 pm weekdays.

University of the South Pacific

The Laucala campus (☎ 313 900; fax 301 305) is the main campus of the regional university for 1½ million people of 12 South Pacific countries. It has about 2000 full-time students and many more taking distance education courses in the Schools of Humanities, Pure & Applied Sciences and Social & Economic Development. There are also six institutes: Applied Science; Education; Marine Studies; Pacific Studies; Research Extension; and Training in Agriculture, Social & Administrative Studies. The Law Department and Pacific Languages Unit are in Vanuatu, while the Agriculture Department is at the Western Samoa campus.

USP is a fee-paying institution and most

students rely on scholarships to help them continue their studies. Scholarships are highly competitive and the government's policy of 'positive discrimination' is controversial. Scholarships are awarded by the Government Public Service: 50% are allocated to indigenous Fijians, while Indian, Chinese, European and other races compete for the remaining 50%. The Native Lands Trust Board (NLTB) also has scholarships specifically for indigenous Fijians. There are problems with overcrowding, student-housing shortages and occasional outbursts of racism.

The campus, on the site of a former New Zealand seaplane base, is a pleasant place to visit. Many of the buildings have been financed by the Australian or New Zealand governments. The main entrance is off Laucala Bay Rd and is a 10 to 15-minute drive from downtown Suva. Inside the entrance on the right is a small botanical garden and herbarium, with Pacific plants, which is open from 8 am to 4 pm.

There are frequent buses to the USP; the Vatuwaqa bus departs from in front of the Morris Hedstrom building in Thomas St. The taxi fare from the city is about F$2.

Activities

Not much happens in Suva on Sunday so it's a good idea to organise activities in advance or attend a Fijian church service to hear some great singing. For canoeing and rafting, see Organised Tours later in the Suva section of this chapter.

Swimming Since Suva has no beautiful sandy beaches, locals escape on weekends to the nearest decent beach at Deuba, Pacific Harbour, a 50-minute drive from Suva, although by local bus it can take much longer. Alternatively, there are the freshwater pools at **Colo-i-Suva Forest Park** and **Wailoku Falls**; see Around Suva later in this chapter. There are regular Wailoku buses from the Suva bus station: get off at the end of the line, walk down the gravel road to the creek and then upstream for about five minutes.

In Suva itself the Suva Olympic Swimming Pool, at 224 Victoria Pde next to the City Library, is a welcome retreat on a hot day. It's an interesting place, cheap, seldom crowded and reasonably clean. The pool is open weekdays from 10 am to 6 pm from April to September and through October to March on weekdays from 6 am to 7 pm and Saturday from 8 am to 6 pm. Admission for adults is F$1.10, 55 cents for children under 14 years old. Cubicles (change rooms) are an extra 22 cents, with a F$2 deposit for keys. Another option if you are keen to swim laps is the University's 25m pool. Entry is F$2 for adults and it is open between 7 am and 6 pm.

Diving Scuba Hire (☎ 361 088; fax 361 047), 75 Marine Drive, Lami, has dive trips to Beqa Lagoon and runs PADI courses. The *Nai'a*, a 33m live-aboard yacht (☎ 361 382; fax 362 511), is based at Lami. It has a 12-person crew, camera room with E6 processing, and takes up to 18 passengers.

Surfing There is a surf-break near Suva lighthouse, but you need a boat to get there. Ed Lovell at the Fiji Surf Association (☎ 361 358) may be able to give some advice on local conditions; see the Pacific Harbour section.

Sailing Honorary membership of the Royal Suva Yacht Club (☎ 312 921; fax 304 433) is given to visiting yachties. Fees to use the new marina, which opened in 1996, are F$15 per week for solo yachts and F$30 per yacht with two or more people. Bathrooms with toilets and hot water are open 24 hours. Even without a yacht, overseas visitors are welcomed and can be signed in for weekend social activities. The clubhouse has great views of the Bay of Islands and the mountains, including Joske's Thumb, and is a pleasant place to spend a few hours. One reader suggested that it's easy to get a free trip across the bay on weekends with one of the practising crews. The office is open weekdays from 8 am to 5 pm and 8 am to noon on Saturday. On Tuesday evening there is a barbecue with half-price beer from 6 to

7.30 pm; see Organised Tours later in this section for information on the Fiji Museum's drua.

Bushwalking Colo-i-Suva Forest Park is an easy place for bushwalking close to Suva; see Around Suva later in this chapter. You can also hike to Mt Korobaba, about one to two-hours walk from the cement factory near Lami. **Joske's Thumb** is an enticing spectacle from Suva. A climb to this peak was featured in the Juniper film *Journey to the Dawning of the Day*.

Keen walkers should contact the Rucksack Club. The president and membership regularly changes, as most of the 80 to 100 members are ex-pats on contract in Fiji. Try John Furbank (☎ 302 039) or ask the FVB for the latest contact. The club is dedicated to appreciating Fiji's natural beauty and culture through outdoor-walking adventures. It has fortnightly meetings, with guest speakers and performers, on Wednesday night at St Andrew's Church (a small, simple weatherboard structure that dates back to 1895) on the corner of Gordon and Goodenough Sts.

Weekly activities include bushwalks and trips inland or to other islands. Visitor membership for two months is only F$2. For further information, write to PO Box 2394, Government Buildings, Suva.

Organised Tours

You can experience sailing in a replica of a traditional drua or double-hulled canoe in the Fiji Museum's *Tabu Tabu Soro*. It runs one-hour tours of the Bay of Islands, two-hour tours of Suva Harbour and day trips to Nukulau Island. The canoe is moored at the Tradewinds Hotel; you can book through the Fiji Museum (☎ 315 944, 315 043; fax 305 143).

Wilderness Ethnic Adventure Fiji (☎ 387 594; fax 300 584) offers several tours, which pick up from Suva hotels. An all-day trip with canoeing/rafting on the beautiful Navua River (see the Navua section earlier in this chapter) includes a barbecue lunch and costs F$65 per person. A trip up the Navua River

---

Drua

The drua (double-hulled canoe) *Ra Marama* was given by Ratu Cakobau to King George of Tonga for help in his war against the people of Rewa. Built in the early 1850s, it was over 30m long, with an 18m-high mast, 90 sq metres of deck space and could carry more than 150 people. It could sail faster than the European sailing ships of the era. Some drua could carry up to 300 people and building could take as long as seven years. Work began with the felling of two large trees, which were spliced together to form the keel. The hulls were made from split logs, and mulberry bark was used as a caulking material. Construction involved ceremonial human sacrifices, and the completed vessel was launched over the bodies of slaves serving as rollers under the hulls. ■

---

by motorboat with a village visit costs F$33/54 for child/adult. A half-day/full-day Rewa Delta and Nasilai village tour is F$35/49 for adults and F$20/25 for children. The tour includes a visit to a Hindu temple and St Joseph Catholic Church (1901), as well as entertainment and demonstrations of pottery or mat weaving.

Wilderness Ethnic Adventure Fiji also has a five-hour trip to Colo-i-Suva Forest Park and a visit to a 75m waterfall (with a picnic lunch) for F$39. If you are very short of time, it also has a two-hour whirlwind tour of Suva costing F$15 for children under 12 and $25 for adults.

Discover Fiji Tours (☎ 450 180; fax 450 549), based in Pacific Harbour, has a Magic Waterfall trip to the Navua River, which will pick up and drop off at Suva. It costs F$54 per person, including lunch and rafting on bamboo raft from about 15 km upriver down to Nakavu village.

Air Fiji, in conjunction with Ovalau Tours, offers day trips to the historic town of Levuka on the island of Ovalau for F$149 per person. This includes transfers, air fares, breakfast, guided walking tour, lunch and afternoon tea at a local resident's home. An overnight stay at Mavida Hotel is an extra F$25.

Special Events

Check with the FVB to see if there are any special events coinciding with your stay. Suva has a week-long festival in August, known as the **Hibiscus Festival**, which has lots of floats, processions and Fijian fire-walking demonstrations.

There are several Hindu religious festivals observed in Suva as well as around the country. In March or April each year the birth of Lord Rama is celebrated with a party on the shores of Laucala Bay, with offerings, flowers and swimming. In August fire walking is held at the Mariamma Temple, Howell Rd, Samabula, and Durga Gram Puja, involving body piercing and other ordeals, is held at Wailekutu, near Suva.

Places to Stay

The capital has a variety of places to stay. There are several good budget options, as well as many medium-range hotel rooms and long-term apartments, and several top-range hotels. The closest island resort is Toberua Island to the east; see Nausori & the Rewa Delta in the Kings Road section later in this chapter. It is possible to camp at Colo-i-Suva Forest Park, which is 11 km out of the city.

Places to Stay – bottom end

Hostels *Suva International Youth Hostel* (☎ /fax 314 670), 11 Amy St, is a colonial style weatherboard house, formerly a girls hostel, up in the Toorak area. It has old but clean rooms that accommodate a maximum of 35 people. There is one toilet inside the house and two toilets and a cold shower outside, and there are cooking facilities and a dining table in a covered area at the back. Rates are the cheapest in Suva. Including simple breakfast (bread, butter, jam, tea or coffee), the dormitory bunks are F$5.50 per person, or singles/doubles with shared facilities are F$16.50/22. A bag of clothes is washed for F$5. There is a 10% discount for HI card holders; doors close at 11 pm. The hostel is about 10 minutes walk from downtown. There is a mosque, a Methodist Church and a Hindu temple nearby and you can hear prayers and singing, sometimes at the same time.

The Cathay chain runs two budget accommodation in Suva, both with clean and spartan rooms. They are affiliated with the HI New Zealand and Backpacker Resorts International. The *Travel Inn* (☎ 304 254; fax 340 236) is the smaller of the two. It is conveniently located at 19 Gorrie St, a quiet street near the Government Buildings, within an easy walk to the city centre. The old building, a bit reminiscent of a prison with rooms in a U-shape around a central stair, has good-value singles, doubles or twin fan-cooled rooms. Rooms are paired to share one bathroom as well as a small area with a table, sink, refrigerator and a common door to the outside. Singles/doubles cost F$16.50 /22. It also has four self-contained apartments for F$40/51 for three/four people. There is a good communal kitchen and dining area, which is open from 7 am to 7.30 pm. Local potter Taraivini Wati has a studio next door at the back of the Wilson Addison Advertising office.

Cathay also runs the *South Seas Private Hotel* (☎ 312 296; fax 340 236). This is another classic, old, double-storey weatherboard building at 6 Williamson Rd, near the Thurston Gardens. Dormitories (maximum of five people) cost F$8.80 per person, single rooms F$13, double or twin rooms F$20.50. Triple rooms and single or double rooms with private bath and toilet are F$27.50. Rooms have fans and the bathrooms are clean and have solar hot water. Downstairs there is a communal kitchen and dining area (that can be tight if the place is busy) and a reading room/lounge area; there's book exchange available and a range of travel guides is sold at the reception area. You can store gear in a storage room, and staff are generally friendly. As with many budget places you may find the occasional cockroach. At both Cathay hotels travellers' cheques are accepted, but not credit cards. Discounts are available for long stays and for those with Nomads Dreamtime cards, YHA or VIP cards.

The *Coconut Inn* (no phone), 8 Kimberley

St, is a small rock-bottom hotel that was popular with backpackers in the past but now appears to be poorly managed. It has tight dormitories with four to six beds in each for F$8 per person; single/double rooms are F$16.50/22. There is a small sitting area at reception, a kitchen where you can cook, cold showers, a washing machine costing F$5 per load, and storage for 50 cents per day. Rooms are very stuffy and there are no mosquito nets on the windows. Security could be a problem as there are broken locks on the rooms. One reader complained of unfriendly staff and of being refused a refund when trying to leave early.

The *YWCA* (☎ 304 829), PO Box 534, Suva, is conveniently located on the 4th floor of a tall building adjacent to Ratu Sukuna Park, but it only has accommodation for four female travellers. Beds are F$10 per night, and you will probably need to book in advance to get a room here. Showers have cold water and rooms have fans. There is a cafeteria downstairs.

Hotels & Motels *Tropic Towers Apartment Hotel* (☎ 304 470; fax 304 169), 86 Robertson Rd, is a short walk up the hill from the bus terminal and the Suva Municipal Market. The budget rooms in this old building cost F$33/44 with fan/air-con for singles or doubles with shared bathroom and kitchen. The rooms upstairs are better. There is a sitting room with TV and guests can use the hotel's pool facilities and have a load of washing done for F$5. They also have middle-range rooms; see Places to Stay – middle, later in this section. A bit further up the hill is *Saf's Apartment Hotel* (☎ 301 849), 100 Robertson Rd. Rooms with a double bed on the ground floor go for F$25, and two-bedroom apartments upstairs are F$35. Rooms are fairly small but new. They were building a third floor at the time of writing that will house apartments with cooking facilities for F$45. The dining room serves curry meals for F$4 and breakfast with toast, tea and coffee for F$1.20.

Bougainvillia Motel (☎ 303 690; fax 305 443), above a furniture shop at 55 Toorak Rd,

looks dodgy from the outside but is surprisingly clean inside and has friendly staff. It has 13 rooms, which are good value. The dormitory (maximum of six) is F$12. Large double rooms with fan, private bathroom, fridge and phone are F$35 for singles or doubles, and deluxe rooms with air-con and TV are F$45 for singles or doubles.

Metropole Hotel (☎ 304 124, 304 112), Scott St near the market, is very conveniently located and well looked after by helpful staff. There are four clean rooms upstairs, which have small washbasins and fans, but bathrooms and toilets are shared. The rooms cost F$16.50/24.75 for singles/doubles. There is a rowdy bar downstairs and it can be noisy in the mornings due to the fish market outside. If the main entrance is closed try the side entrance through the bar. There is another bar upstairs as well as a Chinese restaurant.

Sunset Apartment Motel (☎ 301 799; fax 303 446), on the corner of Gordon and Murray Sts, is also very close to the city centre. The four-storey building (no lifts) has 15 self-contained apartments, nine of which are two-bedroom units with TV, phone, kitchen, sitting area and verandah. They cost F$66/77/88 for doubles/triples/quads. Double rooms downstairs without cooking facilities cost F$41.60/46 singles/doubles. It also has a clean 12-bed dormitory with one bathroom, two toilets, refrigerator and small sitting area, but no cooking facilities for F$8.60.

Tanoa House (☎ 381 575), 5 Princes Rd, is a run-down old guesthouse in Samabula on a hill with a small garden. It is about a 10-minute ride on the Samabula bus from downtown, and is located just across from the Fiji Institute of Technology. Tariffs for rooms are F$15/25 for singles/doubles. Rooms have share facilities and some are a bit cramped or open directly onto the living area, which has a TV and an OK atmosphere. It also has a bar and dining area and offers breakfast for F$5, lunch for F$6.50 and diner for F$8.

Outrigger Hotel (☎ 314 944; fax 302 944), 349 Waimanu Rd near the hospital, looks run down and several readers have complained that it is too expensive for what is offered, that rooms are smelly, dirty, dark and full of cockroaches, the hot water is erratic and the staff are unpleasant. It has dormitory accommodation for F$12, and 20 air-con rooms with private bathrooms for F$44/49 singles/doubles and F$66 for a family of four. Some rooms have a good view of the Suva Harbour and the mountains. See Places to Eat later in this section for information on the roof-garden restaurant.

The *Kings Hotel* (☎ 304 411), at the city end of Waimanu Rd near Marks St, isn't the most salubrious place to stay. There are a few bars downstairs and if you wake up here on a Sunday morning you may find the most repulsive toilets in all of Suva's hotels. Nevertheless, it offers rooms with shared facilities for F$17/20 singles/doubles, and rooms with private toilet and bath for F$25/35.

There are also a few places frequented by prostitutes and their clients, which you may prefer to avoid. The *Oceanview Private Hotel* (☎ 312 129), 270 Waimanu Rd, has three accommodation buildings on a large sloping site, and a covered communal area with pool table, booth seating, TV and bar. Its 48 rooms, old and a bit neglected, have share facilities and cost F$14/20 for singles/doubles. The *New Haven Motel* (☎ 315 220), 587 Waimanu Rd, has grotty rooms for F$17 singles or doubles. *Motel Capital* (☎ 313 246), at 91 Robertson Rd near the Tropic Towers, offers rooms for F$18 single or doubles with shared facilities and F$20 for rooms with a bathroom. *Amy Apartment Hotel* (☎ 315 113), 98 Amy St, has ground-floor rooms for F$20/25, or F$30/33 upstairs.

Places to Stay – middle
Hotels & Motels *Tropic Towers Apartment Hotel* (☎ 304 470; fax 304 169), 86 Robertson Rd, is a four-storey apartment block on the hill up from the bus terminal and the Suva Municipal Market. It offers standard apartments with air-con, phone, TV and cooking facilities for F$60.50/71.50/82.50 for singles/doubles/triples. It has a swimming pool, bar, a small shop and a secure parking area.

The *Southern Cross Hotel* (☎ 314 233; fax 302 901), 63 Gordon St, now has Korean owners. It has 34 rooms with air-con, minibar and TV for F$86 singles or doubles. There is a nightclub downstairs with a bar and music for dancing during the evenings (some rooms can therefore be noisy) and a kidney-shaped pool at the back. See Places to Eat for information on the Korean restaurant on the top floor and Entertainment for information on the disco.

The *Suva Peninsula Hotel* (☎ 313 711; fax 300 804), on the corner of Macgregor Rd and Pender St, has 40 units with air-con, phone, tea and coffee-making facilities, kitchenette and refrigerator in the suite units. Accommodation here starts at F$49.50/60.50 for singles/doubles and from F$70 for suites.

The *Town House Hotel* (☎ 300 055; fax 303 446), 3 Foster St, is a five-storey building with very simple if a bit shabby, self-contained units with air-con, TV, cooking facilities and refrigerator. A bed sitting room goes for F$46/57 singles/doubles and one bedroom apartments for F$57/68. It is F$12 per extra adult, F$7.70 per extra child. You can get to the rooftop restaurant via a rickety external lift with perspex sides, which provides good views of the cathedral, city and bay; see Places to Eat later in this section.

Apartments Suva has a good number of middle-range apartments with self-catering facilities, ranging from small blocks to hotel-style amenities such as the *Suva Motor Inn* (☎ 313 973; fax 300 381), on the corner of Mitchell and Gorrie Sts. This is a new and well-organised establishment conveniently located near the Government Buildings and parks. The building is designed around a central courtyard with a swimming pool and water slide. It has 37 modern units with air-con, a double bed and one convertible sofa, TV, wardrobe, alarm clock/radio and kitchenette, costing F$88 single or double per night and F$20 per extra person. There are also eight good two-bedroom apartments with one double bed and two single beds, kitchenette and table for F$154 a single or double and F$10 for each extra person, up to maximum of six people.

Capricorn Apartment Hotel (☎ 303 732; fax 303 069), 7-11 Fort St, is a four-storey building also arranged around a swimming pool and garden area. It has 25 studio rooms and nine deluxe apartments, which are reasonably well maintained with private facilities including a kitchenette and refrigerator, TV and air-con, and some have balconies overlooking Suva Harbour. Prices for standard rooms are F$93.50/104.50 upstairs/downstairs for singles or doubles, and F$115.50/126.50 for deluxe one bedroom/two bedroom (maximum of five people).

Opposite the Berjaya Hotel, on the corner of Malcolm and Gordon Sts, are the *Elixir Motel Apartments* (☎ 303 288; fax 303 383); Gordon St can be busy and noisy at times. The entrance has a security door and camera. The 15 two-bedroom apartments (maximum of three people) with cooking facilities are good value for F$55/66 with/without air-con. There is a 10% discount for stays of more than one week.

The accommodation wing at *Noble House* (☎ 304 322; fax 300 504), 16 Bau St, was about to change management at the time of writing. It has 10 spacious older-style rooms and is set in a pleasant garden among tall palms. Rooms here are normally for long-term rent, but rooms with cooking facilities can be rented for F$95 per night.

Other self-contained apartments include: the *Pender Court Apartments* (☎ 314 992), 30 Pender St, F$35/35 for singles/doubles; the *Suva Apartments* (☎ 304 280), 17 Bau St, F$30/35 for singles/doubles and F$12 per extra person; the *Duncan Apartments* (☎ 313 973), 9 Duncan Rd; and the *Annandale Apartments* (☎ 311 054; fax 302 171), 265 Waimanu Rd.

Places to Stay – top end

The *Suva Travelodge* (☎ 301 600; fax 300 251) is on Victoria Pde on the waterfront opposite the Government Buildings. It is popular with business travellers for its proximity to the central business area. There are 131 standard rooms that are nothing special, with air-con, TV, phone, tea and coffee-making facilities. Rooms are F$181.50/198 for singles or doubles/triples and suites are up to F$395. There is a newsagency/gift shop in the lobby area as well as a cafe, restaurant and entertainment area and fairly small swimming pool; see Places to Eat below, for information on the cafe and restaurant.

Also in central Suva, the Best Western chain of hotels operates the *Berjaya Hotel* (☎ 312 300; fax 301 300) on the corner of Malcolm and Gordon Sts. The nine storey building, previously the Suva Courtesy Inn, has 50 air-con rooms and suites. Rooms are all of similar layout with one double bed, a couch, tiled floor, dark timber furniture, TV, minibar, coffee and tea-making facilities. Rooms on the lower floors cost F$134 for singles/doubles, while upper-floor rooms with views of the mountains and harbour are F$146 for singles/doubles. Amenities include a swimming pool, coffee shop and a Malaysian restaurant.

The 110-room *Raffles Tradewinds Hotel* (☎ 362 450; fax 361 464) is about a 10-minute drive west of Suva at Lami. Located on the water's edge, it has great views over the Bay of Islands. Rooms here cost F$132/148.50/170.50. The hotel has a swimming pool, tour desk, shops and an interesting floating restaurant; see Places to Eat below.

Places to Eat

Restaurants Suva doesn't have as much variety as Nadi, but does have some good restaurants. The *Old Mill Cottage* (☎ 312 134) at 49 Carnavon St, just around the corner from the Dolphin Food Court, is absolutely the best bet for lunch, or for a fruit-salad break. The old weatherboard home with verandah has been converted into a cute cafe\restaurant, which is popular with government workers on their lunch break. The Fijian, Indian and Chinese food is well prepared and very good value with dishes for around F$5. Try the *palusami* (corned beef wrapped in taro leaves cooked in coconut milk), which is a traditional Fijian dish. Unfortunately, the restaurant is not open for dinner. Hours are 7 am to 6 pm weekdays and to 5 pm on Saturday.

Cardo's Chargrill (☎ 314 330), Regal Lane, behind the Regal Cinema, specialises in beefsteak dishes, but also has chargrilled chicken and seafood. The meals are cooked in different styles, from Japanese to Cajun. Prices are F$14.50 for a 250g steak, or if you are really craving beef badly, F$23 for 400g. The steaks are great by Fijian standards and the air-con restaurant also has a bar. The owner claims to be the fourth-generation descendant of an Argentinian stockman, Espero Cardo. A shipment of Argentinian cattle bound for Australia was pirated while passing through Fiji's Koro Sea during the 19th century and Cardo's life was spared to look after the animals.

Noble House (☎ 304 322; fax 300 504), at 16 Bau St towards Flagstaff, is a small entertainment complex owned by the amiable Jackson Yee. The grandiose building was built to replace the original house, which burnt down. It has two fine-dining restaurants on the premises. The *Aberdeen Grill* serves steak and seafood dishes for F$15.50 to F$16.50. It is open during the week from noon to 2.30 pm and 6.30 to 10.30 pm, and on Saturday from 6.30 to 10.30 pm. In a large ballroom setting, the *Taipan Restaurant* offers mostly Cantonese dishes for F$5 to F$28. The Taipan has fine food but is not up to the standard of the Great Wok; see below. It is open on Sunday from 6.30 to 10.30 pm, but closed on Monday. There is also a disco on the premises; see the Entertainment section.

Suva has two floating restaurants. *Tiko's Floating Restaurant* (☎ 313 626) is an old Blue Lagoon Cruiser converted into a restaurant and anchored at the sea wall near Ratu Sukuna Park. Seafood is its specialty, but there are also steak and chicken dishes on the menu. Seafood dishes go for between F$10 and F$27.50 (for lobster). Steak dishes are F$14 to F$18 and specials F$16.50 to F$19.

The restaurant is open for dinner only and there is a disco below deck. When there is a bit of a swell the rocking and the fresh sea breeze can be interesting even if the food isn't the best value. Raffles Tradewinds' *Floating Restaurant* (☎ 362 450) in Lami, a 10-minute drive west of Suva, is a pleasant spot to enjoy a beer, a meal and the views of the yachts and Bay of Islands, especially on a warm, breezy day. Lunches cost F$7.50 to F$17 and dinner F$11 to F$26.

Another spot on the water's edge to dine, snack or just have a drink and watch the sunset is the *Lighthouse* (☎ 314 467), a small, informal restaurant at 1 Queen Elizabeth Drive, Veiuto. Unfortunately the high windowsills block the view of the water and fishing activity, but they are also building an outdoor deck. While the food can be variable, it is worth a try for the location. The place is popular with locals. The mixed menu has cakes and pastries and main dishes for F$3.50 to F$15. It is open Monday to Saturday from 7 am to 10 pm. To get there from town take a taxi (F$1.50) or catch the Laucala Bay bus from the terminal. The restaurant is opposite a school ground. If you are keen for a walk it's about three km around Suva Point from Thurston Gardens towards Laucala Bay.

Other restaurants include the *Suva Travelodge Restaurant*, where dinner from the international-style menu costs F$17.50 to F$29.50. The *Roof Top Restaurant* at the Town House Hotel, while a bit grotty, has good views of the cathedral, city and bay, and may be an option for escaping the busy city streets for a beer. It is also a good place to find your bearings. Meals here cost F$7.50 to F$10 for salads and steaks.

Indian The *Hare Krishna* (☎ 314 154), on the corner of Pratt and Joske Sts, offers one of the best deals for vegetarian meals in town. The downstairs cafe (open Monday to Thursday from 9 am to 8 pm, Friday to 9 pm and Saturday to 3.30 pm) has good-quality ice cream, including exotic flavours and gaudy coloured sweets. The air-con restaurant upstairs is open daily for lunch from 11 to 2.30 pm, and dinner on Friday from 6 to 9 pm. Another good place for curry is the *Curry House Restaurant* (☎ 313 756), 87 Cumming St, near the Nubukalou Creek.

Chinese Suva has lots of Chinese Restaurants. Perhaps the best is the *Great Wok of China* (☎ 301 285), on the corner of Bau St and Laucala Bay Rd, Flagstaff. Though not cheap and fairly up-market, the food is excellent and definitely worth a try. The menu specialises in Sichuan cuisine and even includes bêche-de-mer. It is open Monday to Friday from noon to 2 pm and 6.15 to 10.45 pm, as well as Saturday night. The *Castle Restaurant* (☎ 361 223), 6 Fenton St, Lami, also has good-value Chinese meals for F$4.50 to F$10.50 (seafood up to F$25.30) and also serves European meals. It is open Monday to Saturday from noon to 3 pm and 5 to 10 pm. The only drawback is its distance from Suva.

More conveniently located downtown is the *Sichuan Pavilion* (☎ 315 194), opposite the FVB in Thomson St, which also serves good meals. Upstairs in the old Garrick Hotel building, it has a balcony with a glimpse of the bay and mountains. Meals cost around F$8, with seafood dishes for F$12 to F$18. One reader maintained the food was delicious, as good as the Great Wok, but the wine list is limited. The *Lantern Palace* (☎ 314 633) at 10 Pratt St is another convenient option. The atmosphere is simple and pleasant, with friendly staff and good-value, reliable dishes for F$5.50 to F$8. It also serves sizzling Mongolian dishes, steaks, salads and fish & chips for F$4 to F$9. This restaurant is open every day for lunch from 11.30 am to 2.30 pm, and for dinner from 5 to 10 pm.

Other Chinese restaurants include the *Ming Palace* (☎ 315 111) inside the old town hall building. While the atmosphere is grandiose, catering for up to 250 people, there are usually only a few people dining and the bland food doesn't justify the price. Chinese and European dishes average F$8 to F$10. It is open Monday to Friday from noon to 2 pm and 6 to 10 pm. The *New Peking* (☎ 312 939), 195 Victoria Pde, just opposite the new Suva City Council building, offers Chinese meals for F$4 to F$5, European dishes including steaks and fish & chips for F$3.50 to F$7.50, and seafood F$4 to F$16.50. *Foon's Seafood* in the GPO arcade has dalo nest and spicy fish on their inexpensive menu. The *Ocean Restaurant* upstairs at the Metropole Hotel is popular with wharfies and the Asian fishing crowd, and has karaoke sessions.

Malaysian The Berjaya Hotel has a reasonably good Chinese-Malaysian restaurant, the *Kampong Ku*, with an extensive and interesting menu. The steam boat is recommended. Main dishes are F$8 to F$15 and they have a swimming-pool buffet, which is pretty good for F$12.

Korean The Southern Cross Hotel now has a Korean restaurant, the *Seoul House*, which mostly caters for groups of Korean tourists. Korean main dishes are F$9 to F$16, European dishes go for F$11 to F$15, and they have sashimi on Sunday afternoon.

Swiss The *Swiss Tavern* (☎ 303 233), 16 Kimberly St, specialises in Swiss cuisine. It offers a variety of main-course dishes, including veal schnitzel, lamb, beef, fish or prawns for F$18 to F$21. Snack dishes such as pasta, goulash, French-onion soup and home-made bratwurst cost F$8 to F$12. Special dishes such as fondue and seafood bouillabaisse cost F$28. It also offers a good wine list and has a bar downstairs. The food is good, though on the expensive side, and service is slow.

Pizzerias *Pizza King* (☎ 315 762) at the Harbour Centre has fairly ordinary pizza. Small pizzas are around F$5. It is open every day, including Sunday, from noon to 2 pm and 7 to 10 pm. *Pizza Hut* (☎ 311 825) on Victoria Pde near the Bad Dog Cafe has reasonable pizzas. The *Outrigger Motel* is pretty run-down but the roof-garden bar and *Papa La Pizza* (☎ 314 944) has great views and is worth a try as the pizza is OK. Large pizzas are F$13 to F$20. You can get up there from downtown by taxi for F$1.50, or by the frequent hospital bus from the terminal for 30 cents, or it's around half-an-hour away on foot.

Cafes The best cafes are the *Old Mill Cottage* (see restaurants below) and *Palm Court Bistro* (☎ 304 662) at shop 17, Queensland Insurance Arcade on Victoria Pde. The latter is recommended for quick lunches and good cakes. Sandwiches and salads are F$1.50 to F$4, burgers F$3.50, and pizzas, quiches and pastries are under F$2. It is open weekdays from 7 am to 5.30 pm, Saturday from 7 am to 2.30 pm. The *Bad Dog Cafe* on the corner of Macarthur St and Victoria Pde is also recommended. It serves breakfast, lunch, dinner, coffee and cakes, and is open Monday to Wednesday from 7 am to 11 pm, Thursday to Saturday to 1 am, and Sunday to 10 pm. It is trendy but good value for quality food and huge coffees. Snacks are well presented and tasty, and they have an extensive list of foreign beers as well as wines available by the glass. It is a good place to escape the midday heat and receive a blast of air-con or for watching nightclubbers go by on Friday and Saturday nights.

The *Curry House Cafeteria* (☎ 313 000), in the old town hall building, offers curry dishes including dhal soup, chutney and two rotis or rice for F$3 to F$6, and roti parcels for F$1.10 to F$2.75. Since quality here varies, have a good look at what's on display before deciding what to eat. *Time Out Foods* (☎ 313 723), a cafeteria on the ground floor of the YWCA building at Ratu Sukuna Park, has good views of the mountains across the bay. Open Monday to Saturday from 7.30 am to 10 pm, it offers sandwiches, burgers and pasta lunches for F$3.50 to F$6, and a variety of European-style dinner meals for F$8 to F$13.50.

Several hotels have cafes that are open to the public. *Penny's Coffee Shop* at the Suva Travelodge has interesting paintings in a changing exhibition on the wall, but overpriced lunches. The Berjaya Hotel also has a coffee shop with light meals for F$7 to F$11.

The Suva Motor Inn's *Waterfall Cafe* (by the swimming pool) is open to visitors and offers curries, burgers, salads and sandwiches for F$7 to F$9.50 and main dinner dishes including seafood and steaks for F$9.50 to F$11.50.

The *Fiji Museum Cafe*, on the verandah overlooking Thurston Gardens next to the Fiji Museum entrance, is run by an Indian lady who serves curries and roti for F$3.50. It opens at 7.30 am and closes with the museum at 4.30 pm.

If you are near the University a cheap place to eat is the *USP Canteen*; it's F$3.50 for visitors, but the food is predictably pretty ordinary. The food is much better and still cheap at *Mango Tree Kona*, which has quite a good spot to sit on the verandah and watch the students go by.

Fast Food The *Dolphin Plaza Food Court* on the corner of Loftus St and Victoria Pde can be a good option for a quick meal. There are a variety of takeaway-food shops and tables, including pizza, pasta, Chinese, curries and Fijian dishes for around F$5. It is popular with locals for Sunday lunches.

The Wishbone & the Wedge, in the arcade near Nubukalou Creek, has takeaway food as well as a restaurant/bar with air-con. Spicy chicken and chips or burgers cost F$3, curry or pasta goes for F$7. *Jo's Takeaway* (☎ 313 997), 67 Amy St, Toorak, is open 24 hours a day. On Friday and Saturday night there are barbecue stands along Victoria Pde to cater for nightclubbers. The market has cheap meals for lunch, but is not recommended for dinner.

Self-Catering The *Morris Hedstrom Supermarket* downtown has a large selection of grocery items and fresh food. A trip to the Suva Municipal Market for fish, fruit and vegetables is obligatory. *Le Pain de Mie* at 492 Waimanu Rd in Samabula South is a French bakery open 24-hours every day; it's great for French sticks, croissants and quiches. There are also a couple of bakeries downtown, including a *Hot Bread Kitchen* in the Harbour Centre opposite Morris Hedstrom.

Entertainment

Suva, with its cosmopolitan population and high numbers of students, has the most diverse nightlife in Fiji. Nightclubs and bars are popular and Victoria Pde swarms on Friday and Saturday night. Most of the nightclubs and pubs have a happy hour/hours with cheaper drinks. All are closed on Sunday. Fights sometimes break out and recently a student was killed by a bouncer. The bar at the *Metropole Hotel* and the *Bali Hai Nightclub* have the reputation of being the roughest nightspots. The *Fiji Times* has an entertainment section with information on upcoming events and what's on at nightclubs.

Cinemas The *Regal Theatre* (☎ 311 376), 54 Victoria Pde near Sukuna Park, and the *Phoenix* (☎ 300 094), 192 Rodwell Rd near the bus terminal, both screen international movies. Indian movies are screened at the Lilac, Regal and Eros theatres. A new Village Cinema complex (☎ 311 109) is to be opened on Scott St near the Nubukalou Creek. Cinema tickets are cheap, only F$2.50 to F$3; see the cinema section in the *Fiji Times* for what's screening.

Discos *Lucky Eddies* & *Urban Jungle* (☎ 312 884), on Victoria Pde opposite the old town hall, are the most lively and relaxed of the main nightclubs. They are both on the same premises and their music competes across the dividing stairwell. Lucky Eddies, open Monday to Saturday from 7 pm to 1 am, has strobe lights, mirror balls and white light, while Urban Jungle, open Thursday to Saturday from 9 pm to 1 am, has more hard surfaces and a grungy graffiti feel. Entry to both is F$4.

Also on Victoria Pde are the *Golden Dragon* (☎ 311 018) and *Signals* (☎ 313 590). The Golden Dragon, opposite the Fiji Development Bank, has disco and reggae dance music every night except Sunday from 7.30 pm to 1 am. Admission is F$2 Monday

to Wednesday, and F$4 Thursday to Saturday. It has booths, tables and a dance floor. Signals, opposite the Suva Library, has a lounge bar with disco, reggae and rap music. It is open from 6 pm to 1 am Monday to Saturday. Admission is generally F$3, but is free before 9 pm.

If you prefer a smaller-scale bar and less threatening atmosphere, try *Tingles* (☎ 313 626), below deck on Tiko's Floating Restaurant moored off Ratu Sukuna Park. They play disco and reggae music. It is an interesting setting in a small space with a low ceiling, and the boat rocks with the waves. It is open every night until midnight except Sunday, with a F$3 entry charge on Thursday, Friday and Saturday unless you have dined at the restaurant, in which case it is free.

Other discos include *Chequers* at Waimanu Rd between Cunningham and Marks Sts, which has a house band nightly except Sunday and lucky draws for stubbies and spirits, and *Scandals* at Noble House on Friday and Saturday (frequented mainly by under-25-year-olds, but often empty). The *Southern Cross Hotel* has a disco and live house band every night playing Fiji rock 'n' roll. Happy hours are from 4 to 7 pm. Admission is F$2, and it is open till 1 am Monday to Saturday. *Bali Hai* at the Walu Bay end of Rodwell Rd has a reputation for being rough.

Jazz *Birdland Jazz Club* (☎ 303 833), 6 Carnavon St, is an underground venue offering live jazz and rhythm & blues on Thursday and Saturday night. Admission is free and happy hours are from 6 to 9 pm. The *Suva Travelodge* also has jazz on Thursday night from 5.30 to 8 pm as well as a 'Friday fever' night. It has a friendly atmosphere, with free wine for ladies from 9.30 to 11 pm on Thursday, and happy hours from 6 to 9 pm Monday to Saturday. *Traps Bar* also has live jazz on Wednesday; see Pubs & Bars below.

Country Music *The Barn* (☎ 307 845) on Carnavon St is a popular venue for older crowds. It has live bands playing mainly

HOLGER LEUE

HOLGER LEUE

ROBYN JONES

LEONARDO PINHEIRO

A	
C	B
D	

Yasawa Group
A: Turtle Island
B: Cruising the Yasawas
C: Coconut leaf fishing, Yaroma Island
D: Volcanic formations, Yasawa Island

ROBYN JONES

ROBYN JONES

ROBYN JONES

Yasawa Group
Top: Volleyball competition, Wayasewa
Middle: Village House, Wayasewa
Bottom: Meke performance, Wayasewa

country music, and a spacious bar with lots of tables and seats. Admission is F$5. The bouncers wear cowboy hats and make you tuck in your shirt to enter. It is open Monday to Saturday from 5.30 pm to 1 am, with happy hour from 5.30 to 9.30 pm. There is a barn dance at 10.30 pm.

Folk & Traditional Music Suva Travelodge has meke and traditional Fijian dances on Wednesday night, along with a *lolo* and seafood buffet.

Pubs & Bars *O'Reilly's* (☎ 312 968) is a very popular Irish bar on the busy corner of Macarthur St and Victoria Pde. It is great for an evening beer, with a friendly atmosphere, pool table and music. Evidently the back right-hand side of the bar the place to be if you are gay. On the opposite corner, *The Office* (☎ 313 927) has outdoor seating and happy hours from 5 to 8 pm. It usually screens rugby on the TV. Further down Victoria Pde before the Shell service station, *Traps Bar* (☎ 312 922) also has happy hour (half-price drinks) from 5 to 8 pm and live jazz on Wednesday. The Fiji Writers Association's Niu Wave Writers have monthly performances here with music and comedy. The bar has lots of small rooms with Spanish-style white rendered walls and dark timber; it also plays videos. *Jackson's Bar* at Noble House is open on Thursday, Friday and Saturday. Most bars open from 5 or 6 pm until 1 am on weekdays, midnight on Saturday, and are closed on Sunday.

Spectator Sport
Fijians are fanatical about their rugby and even if you don't like the game it's worth going to a match to watch the crowd. Ask at the FVB if there will be a match during your stay.

Things to Buy
See the Facts for the Visitor chapter. The Government Handicraft Centre (☎ 211 222; fax 302 617), on Macarthur St, assists rural artisans and has good-quality reproductions, but is generally more expensive than else-

where. It's a good idea to look around and compare quality and price. Opening hours are Monday to Thursday from 8 am to 4.30 pm (Friday to 4 pm) and Saturday from 8 am to 12.30 pm. The Craft Gallery (☎ 304 445), Studio 10 on Victoria Pde next to the Ming Palace Restaurant (open Monday to Friday from 9 am to 5 pm and Saturday from 10 am to 2 pm), has a few items that you may not see elsewhere. The Suva Travelodge often has exhibitions of work by local artists and items for sale (not cheap). The Suva Curio & Handicraft Centre is interesting for a stroll and occasionally one stall has better quality or a better deal. Some of the artefacts are not even genuinely Fijian and if there is a cruise ship in port prices will skyrocket. Watch out for annoying sword sellers who will pretend to be your friend and then demand that you buy a souvenir with your name on it – just walk away, you are under no obligation to buy.

Try South Pacific Recordings (☎ 313 405; fax 304 883), in Usher St near the Suva Municipal Market, for tapes or CDs of local musicians. Tiki Togs (☎ 312 664), at 38 Thomson St and on 199 Victoria Pde, have some clothing by local designers. The Fiji Museum Shop has good postcards, posters and books. The Fiji Philatelic Bureau (☎ 312 928; fax 306 088) at the GPO building, PO Box 100, Suva, has stamps and first covers from Fiji and other Pacific Islands. The Suva Municipal Market is a good place to buy kava for village visits (the unpounded roots are better) and to sample local foods.

Getting There & Away
Suva is well connected to the rest of the country by air, interisland ferry and to western Viti Levu by buses and carriers; see the Getting There & Away chapter for international flights to Nausori airport.

Air Nausori airport is 23 km north-east of central Suva. Air Fiji is Sunflower Airlines' main domestic carrier. Vanua Air Charters also has some passenger flights; see the Getting Around chapter for air routes and prices.

Air Fiji
185 Victoria Pde (☎ 313 666; fax 300 771; Nausori airport ☎ 478 077), the major domestic operator out of Nausori.

Sunflower Airlines
Thomson St (opposite the GPO) (☎ 315 755; fax 305 027; Nausori airport ☎ 477 310)

Vanua Air Charters
58-60 Yatulau Building (☎ 313 726; fax 313 902; Nausori airport ☎ 477 711)

Bus & Carriers Many locals drive small trucks or carriers with a tarpaulin-covered frame on the back. These often have passenger seating and some run trips between Nadi and Suva. They leave when full and are quicker than taking the bus: they usually speed! Similarly, Viti Minibuses also shuttle along the Queens Road to Lautoka. In Suva they pick up passengers in Robertson Rd near the market, charging F$10 per person.

There are frequent express buses operating along the Queens Road and Kings Road. Pacific and Sunbeam express buses leave from the bus terminal. If you can put up with busy bus stations and sometimes crowded buses, they are more fun and better value than the 20-seater tourist buses, which stop at all hotels along the Coral Coast.

Pacific Transport Limited
(☎ 304 366, Suva) has regular buses (open-air type) from Lautoka to Suva via the Coral Coast, on the Queens Road.

Sunbeam Transport Limited
(☎ 662 822, Lautoka) has a Kings Road as well as a Queens Road service to Lautoka.

UTC (United Touring Fiji)
(☎ 312 287, Suva) has an express air-conditioned coach service from Suva to Nadi along Queens Road, stopping at the larger hotels along the way.

Fiji Holiday Connections
Operates a minibus shuttle between Nadi and Suva along the Queens Road that will pick up and drop off at hotels along the Coral Coast.

Boat From Suva there are regular ferry services to Vanua Levu and Taveuni (Patterson Brothers, Beachcomber Cruises and Consort Shipping); to Ovalau (Patterson Brothers and Emoisi's Shipping); and to Kadavu (Whippy's Boatyard and the less reliable Kadavu Shipping). It is also possible to get to Lau and Rotuma by boat; see the Getting Around chapter for details on ferry services.

Patterson Brothers Shipping
Suite 1 & 2, Epworth House, Nina St, Suva (☎ 315 644; fax 301 652). Suva to Taveuni, Vanua Levu and Ovalau. The trip to Ovalau from Suva involves a bus to Natovi Landing to catch the ferry and then another bus to Levuka. Trips to Vanua Levu involve a bus trip to Natovi and a ferry to either Nabouwalu or Savusavu. From Nabouwalu there is a bus on to Labasa. From Savusavu there is a bus connection to Buca Bay and another ferry to Taveuni.

Beachcomber Cruises
c/o Taina's Travel Service, Suite 8, Epworth Arcade, Nina St, Suva (☎ 307 889, 300 863; fax 306 189). The *Adi SS (Dana Star)* departs Narajan's Jetty, Walu Bay, once a week for Savusavu. Four other days per week there is a bus service to Natovi Landing to meet the ferry to Savusavu, and once a week the ferry continues to Taveuni.

Consort Shipping Line
Dominion House Arcade, Thomson St, behind the FVB (☎ 302 877, 313 344; fax 303 389). The office is open Monday to Friday from 8 am to 4 pm (closed noon to 1 pm for lunch), and Saturday from 9 am to noon. The *MV SOFE (Spirit of Free Enterprise)* does a weekly voyage between Suva and Savusavu via Koro return, as well as one between Suva and Taveuni, via Koro.

Emoisi's Shipping
35 Gordon St, Suva (☎ 313 366). Emoisi has a daily Viti Levu to Ovalau service by minibus from Suva to Bau Landing, and a small boat to Leluvia Island.

Whippy's Boatyard Limited
PO Box 9, Suva (☎ 311 507, 340 015; fax 340 015). The *Gurawa* departs twice weekly for Kadavu.

Kadavu Shipping
Ground floor, Procera House, Waimanu Rd, Suva (☎ 311 766). The ferry MV*Bulou-ni-ceva* is mostly for cargo and local use and is less regular and not as reliable as the Whippy Service.

Cakauniika Shipping Office
Muaiwalu Jetty (Old Millers Wharf), Walu Bay, Suva (☎ 312 962). Runs a service from Viti Levu to the Lau group.

Getting Around

The best way to get around central Suva is on foot. The local buses are cheap and plentiful. The terminal is next to the market and is busy and crowded. The best thing to do is to ask bus drivers or locals where buses leave from and where they go to. There are relatively few buses in the evening and a reduced service on Sunday. Taxis are cheap and plentiful, and in Suva they actually use the meter! The drivers are usually friendly, chatting and telling stories. Suva's one-way streets and contorted loops may make you think the taxi driver is taking you in the wrong direction. The traffic in downtown Suva can be confusing even for local drivers, and invariably the unsuspecting driver, attempting to browse along Victoria Pde, will get caught on a long run around the market and wharf area; see the Getting Around chapter for information on car rentals and the Nausori section for how to get to/from Nausori airport, which is about 23 km from Suva.

COLO-I-SUVA FOREST PARK

The Colo-i-Suva Forest Park (pronounced Tholo-ee-Suva) is about 245 hectares of forest in the hills north of Suva. Great for escaping the capital on a hot day, it has three pools (with rope swings) that are good for swimming, about 6.5 km of walking track and a half-km-long nature trail. The park is fairly well developed, with toilets, shelters, barbecue pits and picnic tables.

The Waisila Creek flows down to Waimanu River and is the water catchment for the Nausori/Nasinu areas. The forest here was logged in the late 1940s and early 1950s, and while the surrounding area has been extensively cleared, the park area was replanted with introduced mahogany.

The park is now managed by the Department of Forestry and they have a Visitor Information Centre (☎ 320 211). The entry fee is F$5 per person for foreigners and F$2 for locals.

It is about two km along the gravel Kalabu Rd from the forest station to the Upper Pools car park and about a 250m walk to the pool. If on foot, hike in along the Falls Trail; from Princes Rd to the Waisila Falls it's about 800m, and then it's a further 570m to the Upper Pool. There is a security booth at the car park, manned from 9 am to 4 pm daily, but watch your belongings anyway. Leave anything valuable at the Visitor Information Centre, not in cars or tents.

The park is popular with bird-watchers. There are about 14 bird species, among which you may see or hear barking pigeons, sulphur-breasted musk parrots, Fiji warblers and golden doves. It is theoretically a nature

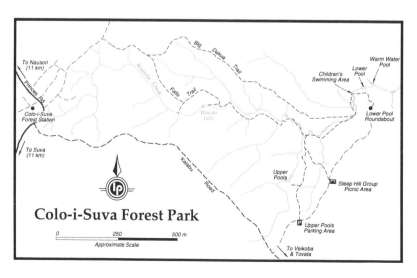

Colo-i-Suva Forest Park

sanctuary, but fish, prawns and eel are poached by locals.

Good hiking boots are recommended as it can be slippery in the wet. High-speed films are best, especially if the weather is overcast, due to the low light levels under the dense vegetation.

Camping is allowed in designated areas as long as you inform the forestry station. However, it is not recommended that you camp alone as the area is remote and there has been some trouble in the past.

Getting There & Away The park is about 11 km north of Suva. The Sawani bus leaves Suva bus station every half-hour, and it takes about 20 minutes to reach the forest station on the left on top of the hill. The fare is 61 cents. If driving, take Princes Rd out of Suva, past Tamavua and Tacirua villages.

Kings Road (Suva to Lautoka)

The Kings Road around northern Viti Levu has some beautiful scenery and is recommended for travel either by bus or car. The road is in good condition and mostly sealed, except for the section between Korovou and Dama (about 65 km). There are relatively few places to stay along this route. Korovou, Tavua and Ba each have a simple hotel, as does the Rakiraki area, and there is an up-market resort and several other resorts on Nananu-i-Ra Island. It is 265 km from Suva to Lautoka on the Kings Road, compared to 221 km along the Queens Road.

NAUSORI & THE REWA DELTA

Nausori, 20 km north-east of downtown Suva on the eastern bank of the Rewa River, is an important agricultural, market, transport and service centre, with the country's second-largest airport. It is also the headquarters for district offices of the Central Division. Nausori has a population of 14,000, mostly farm labourers and industry workers. The town grew up around the CSR sugar mill that operated here between 1882 and 1959. The bridge across the Rewa River opened in 1938. Sugar growing was more successful on the drier western side of Viti Levu, and alternative industries including light manufacturing, stock food, timber milling and rice milling were developed. The sugar mill became the Rewa Rice Mill, which still operates today. Irrigation developments during the 1970s turned the Rewa Delta, together with the Navua Delta and the Bua River flats in south-western Vanua Levu, into major rice-producing areas.

The town itself isn't very interesting for travellers. There are a couple of banks, some inexpensive eateries near the market and bus station, and if you are desperate the *Kings Hotel* (☎ 478 833) in the main street has a couple of very ordinary rooms around the back of the pub/nightclub for F$16.50/21.45 for singles/doubles. They have their own bathrooms and are usually rented to customers by the hour.

There are three important boat landings near Nausori: Bau Landing (see Bau Island), Wainibokasi Landing (see Nasilai village) and Nakelo Landing (see Toberua Island). There are regular buses to all three landings from Nausori. From Nakelo Landing there are local village boats, which you may be able to join or hire to explore the area. Chat with locals and you may be invited to visit their villages.

Getting There & Away

Air Nausori International Airport is about three km south-east of Nausori, 23 km from Suva. Royal Tongan Airlines, Air Marshall Islands and Air Nauru have international flights that arrive here, but otherwise it is mostly used for domestic flights. The airport premises are small and low key, and have a newspaper stand, with a few magazines and books, and a snack counter.

Bus The stretch of Kings Road from Suva to Nausori is the country's busiest and most congested highway. Taxi rides from the airport to/from Suva cost about F$20. There

Ring-Ditch Fortifications

Defensive fortifications in lowland areas took the form of ring-ditches (*korowaiwai*). There are many of these eroded circular mounds remaining in the Rewa Delta and you may be able to spot some if you fly over the area. In times of war these were necessary for the survival of a village as protection against surprise attack. Typically, each mataqali occupied such a settlement surrounded by their food gardens. The habitation area was encircled by a war ditch, usually about 10m wide with steep battered sides and a palisade, or strong fence, on top of the inner bank. Entry was through narrow causeways or drawbridges and gates. The ditch was sometimes implanted with dangerous bamboo spikes hidden in the muddy water. Important villages could be surrounded by up to four concentric ditches with offset causeways to divide and expose attackers. Fences were made of coconut posts and bamboo or bundles of reeds. According to AJ Webb, writing in 1885, 'Before the introduction of firearms, these places were simply impregnable to assault, and could only be taken through treachery or by starving the beleaguered'. ■

are no direct local buses to/from Suva and the airport, but Nausori Taxi & Bus Service (☎ 312 185, 304 178) has a bus service to/from the Travelodge Hotel. Alternatively, cover the four km to the Nausori town bus terminal by taxi (about F$5), and catch one of the frequent local buses to Suva bus terminal for about 80 cents. Allow plenty of time, as some buses crawl while others speed. The Nausori bus terminal is in the main street. Sunbeam Transport (☎ 479 353) has regular buses to Lautoka via the Kings Road and there are four express services on weekdays (the first at 7.15 am and the last at 5.45 pm; ring to confirm weekend timetables).

Naisilai Village & Naililili Catholic Mission

Naisilai village is home to the well-known potter Taraivini Wati; see the Arts section in the Facts about the Country chapter. Pottery is a major source of income for the village, and when large orders are placed for hotels and embassies everyone participates in the process, helping to collect and prepare the clay and make the pots. When a baby girl is born in the village, a lump of clay is placed on her forehead. They believe that she will then automatically know how to carry on the pottery-making tradition.

The Naililili Catholic Mission was built at the turn of the century by Catholic missionaries from France. Inside, the church is decorated with stained-glass windows imported from Europe, which interestingly contain writing in Fijian. The delta area is on a flood plane and the resident priests have now moved away.

Getting There & Away Wilderness Ethnic Adventure Fiji runs tours of the Rewa Delta and Nasilai village, departing from Suva hotels; see Organised Tours, Suva. There are regular buses to Wainibokasi Landing from Nausori bus terminal. If driving, from Nausori head south-east for about six km on the road running parallel with the Rewa River, pass the airport entrance and turn right at the T-intersection. The landing is a further one km before the bridge across the Wainibokasi River. There you can catch a boat to the Naililili Catholic Mission almost opposite or take a short trip downriver to Naisilai village. Ask for permission to visit the village and take some kava.

Bau Island

If you fly over Bau today it is bizarre to think that such a tiny speck of an island was the power base of Cakobau and his father, Tanoa, in the 19th century and is still a seat of traditional power; see the History section in the Facts about the Country chapter. In the 1780s there were 30 bure kalou (temples) on the small chiefly island, including the famous Na Vata ni Tawake, which stood on a huge *yavu* (house mound) faced with large panels of flat rock.

Also of interest is a chiefly cemetery, an old church and a sacrificial killing stone on which enemies were slaughtered prior to being cooked and consumed.

To visit the island you must be invited by someone who lives there or have permission from the Ministry of Fijian Affairs. If you do manage a visit, dress conservatively, take a large *waka* of kava root for presentation to the *turaga-ni-koro* (chief), and don't wear hats or walk around unescorted; see the Dos & Don'ts section in the Facts for the Visitor chapter.

Getting There & Away There are regular buses from Nausori bus terminal to Bau Landing, which is north-east of Nausori airport. If you are driving, from Nausori turn left before the airport and after about four km turn left at the intersection and follow the road to its end. Local boats cross to Bau Island opposite. Boats also leave for Viwa Island from here.

Toberua Island

Toberua Island is a small island just off Kaba Point, the easternmost point of Viti Levu, about 30 km from Suva. Despite being close to Suva, Toberua has its own weather patterns, receiving about a third of Suva's annual rainfall. *Toberua Island Resort* (☎ 302 356; fax 302 214) was originally built in 1968 as an American millionaire's hideaway and was one of the earliest luxury resorts established in Fiji. It can accommodate a maximum of 28 people and accepts children of any age. Baby-sitting costs F\$9/15 per evening/daytime. Its 14 bures have polished hardwood interiors with one king-size bed and one single bed, ceiling fan, indoor/outdoor bathrooms, small bar, and tea and coffee-making facilities. Prices are F\$325/352 single/twin, and F\$42 extra for a third adult per day. Up to two children under 16 years old can share with parents free of charge. Meals for adults are F\$68/82 for two/three meals per day and for children F\$19/36 up to 12 years/up to 16 years.

The island's total area is just under two hectares at high tide, but when the tide is out it extends to 12 hectares and the exposed beach is used for golf. The golf course is par 27 with nine holes between 90m to 180m long. Clubs and balls are provided free, and the Toberua Open Men's Championship is played annually between Christmas and New Year. Other free activities include snorkelling, windsurfing, Hobie-Cat sailing, paddle boating and tours to the nearby island bird sanctuary and mangrove forest. Diving trips to sites at Toberua Passage are F\$60 per dive, or F\$330/500 for six/10 dives. Open-water certification courses are F\$420, including all equipment.

Getting There & Away There are regular local buses from Nausori bus terminal to Nakelo Landing, which is on the banks of the Wainibokasi River, south-east of the airport. If driving from Nausori, turn left before the airport and then take the first right. Follow the road for about five km and turn right before Namuka. The Toberua Island Resort boat transfers guests from Nakelo Landing.

KOROVOU & AROUND

The Kings Road is sealed from Suva to Korovou, then gravel until Dama on the way to Rakiraki. Korovou (one of many towns known literally as 'new village') isn't a must-see. It is a transport intersection about 50 km from Suva and 31 km from Nausori airport. There are a few shops near the bus stop, where you can buy a snack, and there's a post office across the river near the roundabout. At the roundabout, Kings Road continues to the north-west through prime dairy-farming country and into the hills, while the unsealed road to Natovi Landing, about a 20-minute drive away, follows the coast. It is possible to meet the Kings Road again further on, but only if you have a 4WD, as the road deteriorates as you approach Mt Tova.

If you have to stay in Korovou for some reason, the only accommodation is the *Tailevu Hotel* (☎ 430 028; fax 430 244), on top of the hill above the roundabout. Dorm accommodation is F$8 or F$18 with three meals. Rooms with ensuite, small bar and TV are F$28/45 singles/doubles, including breakfast. There is a family room that sleeps five for F$50, as well as self-contained cottages (maximum four people) for the same price. You can also camp; sites cost F$8 per night. Meals in the restaurant are from F$4 to F$7.50 for a main or up to F$10.50 for seafood; half a cray goes for F$15.50. A nightclub operates here on Thursday, Friday and Saturday night.

The Tailevu Hotel can arrange trips and activities, including a visit to **Wailotua Snake God Cave** about 23 km west of Korovou on the Kings Road. Alternatively, enquire about the cave at Wailotua village and for a small fee they will arrange a guide. The cave is about 1½ to two hours walk from the village. It is an interesting trip along the Kings Road from Korovou to Rakiraki; the road winds through hills and along the Wainibuka River past many small villages. You may see the occasional bilibili on the river. About 14 km from Korovou the Kings Road crosses the beautiful **Uru's Waterfall**.

Natovi Landing
Beachcomber Cruises' bus/ferry service departs from Natovi Landing for Savusavu (daily except Wednesday) and weekly to Taveuni. Patterson Brothers has a Natovi-Savusavu service and a weekly Natovi-Taveuni ferry, as well as one to Nabouwalu, Vanua Levu (daily except Sunday). Patterson Brothers also have a Natovi-Ovalau ferry (daily except Sunday) to Buresala then bus on to Levuka. There is a general store at Natovi Landing but not much else. Ferries also depart for Vanua Levu from Ellington Wharf, where you can cross to Nananu-i-Ra Island and catch ferries to Vanua Levu; see the Getting Around chapter.

Getting There & Away
Sunbeam Transport has regular buses to Suva on weekdays between 10.55 am and 9.20 pm, and to Lautoka between 8 am and 6.30 pm.

RAKIRAKI & AROUND
The trip from Korovou across the mountains, past Viti Levu Bay and down to Ra province and Rakiraki, has some stunning scenery. The climate on the northern side of the mountains is similar to that of western Viti Levu, and it is sugar-cane-growing country. The turn-off to Ellington Wharf is about five km east of Rakiraki off the Kings Road (at the 112.4 km post from Lautoka), and it is then a further 1.5 km to the wharf. From there you can cross to Nananu-i-Ra Island, which has several budget and one up-market place to stay. Ferries also leave here for Vanua Levu. Rakiraki is the northernmost town in Viti Levu. Inland from Rakiraki, about two km off the Kings Road past the sugar mill, is the township of Vaileka, where you will find the bus station and taxi stands, banks, market and shopping area. According to local legend, the imposing mountains of the **Nakauvadra Range** to the south are the home of the great Snake-God Degei, creator of all the islands. The opening and closing of his eyes is the cause of night and day, and thunder is said to be Degei turning in his sleep.

Heading out of Rakiraki towards Nadi, look out for **Udreudre's Tomb**, the resting place of Fiji's most notorious cannibal. It is on the left by the roadside about 100m to the west past the turn-off to Vaileka.

About 10 km west of Rakiraki near Vitawa is a large outcrop known as **Navatu Rock**. There was once a fortified village on top and it was believed that from here spirits would depart for the afterlife.

Naiserelagi Catholic Mission
About 25 km east of Rakiraki overlooking Viti Levu Bay is an old mission built in 1917, which is famous for its mural depicting a black Christ. The painting is the work of French artist Jean Charlot, carried out in 1962. The three panels incorporate biblical scenes with Christ on the cross in a barkcloth sulu, and Fijians are depicted offering mats and tabua and Indians offering flowers and oxen. There is also a tanoa at Christ's

---

Ratu Udreudre

In 1849, some time after Ratu Udreudre's death, the Reverend Richard Lyth, who was staying in Cokova in north-eastern Viti Levu, saw a long line of stones placed together in a row. Each stone represented one of the chief's victims and amounted to a personal tally of at least 872 corpses, in addition to any eaten in his youth. The Reverend recounted a conversation with Udreudre's son:

Ravatu assured me that his father eat all this number of human beings – he was wont to add a stone to the row for each one he received – they were victims killed in war he eat them all himself – he gave to none, however much he had on hand – it was cooked and recooked (by which it was preserved) until it was all consumed – he would keep it in a box so that he might lose none... he eat but little else very little vegetable – and being an enormous eater he was able to get through a great deal. ∎

---

feet. Visitors are welcome and a small donation is appreciated.

From Vaileka take the Flying Prince local bus for F$1.20, ideally before 9 am when buses are more regular. Naiserelagi is just south of Nanukuloa village on the right past the school. The mission is half a km up a winding track on the hill. Alternatively, the Rakiraki Hotel has half-day tours departing at 8 am.

Places to Stay

There are two places to stay on the mainland in the Rakiraki area. The *Rakiraki Hotel* (☎ 694 101; fax 694 545) on the Kings Road is well maintained with simple, reasonably good-value rooms with fans for F$33/38.50 for singles/doubles, and air-con rooms for F$66/77. You can get about a 30% discount for air-con rooms between November and early April. They have a swimming pool, half-size tennis court, lawn bowling and nine-hole golf course nearby. It also has a bar and restaurant; see Places to Eat below.

A good middle-range option for those wanting more of a resort feel is *Wananavu Beach Resort* (☎ 694 433; fax 694 499). The resort, opened in mid-1994, is located at the northernmost point of Viti Levu, about four km off the Kings Road east of Rakiraki. From its hillside position there are beautiful views of Nananu-i-Ra Island and Viti Levu's coastline. Each of the 12 deluxe bures have ceiling fan, refrigerator, tea and coffee-making facilities and good views from the

balcony and at a pinch can accommodate up to four people.

Rates per person are about F$365 for three nights and F$87 per additional night, including breakfast and airport transfers. They have a restaurant/bar where you can have your meal on a deck and gaze at the sunset, and an à la carte dining restaurant with international and Fijian dishes. There is a sandy beach nearby, a marina, swimming pool in the garden, tennis and volleyball courts and snorkelling. Scuba diving is available with Ra Divers; see below.

Places to Eat

The Rakiraki Hotel Restaurant and bar is open to visitors. Main courses here are F$9.50 to F$14.50, including curries, roasts, fried fish, grilled steak and vegetables. Vaileka has a few places to eat near the bus station, including *Gafoor & Sons*, *Rakiraki Lodge* and *Va's Cake Shop* at the Community Centre building. Ellington Wharf has a kiosk called *Taste of Paradise* (☎/fax 694 474), which sells sandwiches, hot dogs, pies, cakes, burgers, fresh juices and home-made ice cream at reasonable prices.

Getting There & Away

Rakiraki is 157 km north-west of Suva, along a partially sealed road, and 141 km north-east of Nadi, along a fully sealed road. Sunbeam Transport has regular express buses along the Kings Road from Suva and Nadi, which stop at Vaileka and the turn-off to Ellington Wharf; see the Getting Around chapter. There are taxis at the bus terminal at Vaileka, which charge about F$7 to get to Ellington Wharf. The island is a 15-minute boat ride from Ellington Wharf. Each of the resorts on Nananu-i-Ra have their own boat service to the island; call in advance (before reaching Ellington) to arrange for a pick-up. Ellington Wharf has a kiosk (see above) and cover, which can be used while waiting for boats to Nananu-i-Ra or for the Patterson Brothers' ferry three times a week to Nabouwalu, south-west Vanua Levu; see the Getting Around chapter.

Alternatively, PVV Tours (☎ 720 959; fax 701 541) have daily transfers by minibus between Nadi and Ellington Wharf for F$20 (2½ hours) and a boat to Nananu-i-Ra (F$8.25 one way per person). It is more expensive than the ordinary bus; however, they do pick up from hotels and stop along the way for picking up supplies. Sharing a taxi is another option (about F$65).

NANANU-I-RA ISLAND

Nananu-i-Ra is a 350-hectare island roughly triangular in shape with steep hills, many scalloped bays, white-sand beaches and mangroves. To the north is Bligh Water and reefs in the surrounding area are good for diving. Nananu-i-Ra is popular among travellers for its relative ease of access, good beaches, relatively dry climate and good snorkelling. It is a quick and inexpensive option for getting away from the Nadi area. Most of the residents are of European descent, so don't come here expecting much contact with indigenous Fijian culture.

The island has no roads and much of the land is privately owned, so stick to the beach unless you have permission. One reader said it took them about seven hours walking time and two hours waiting for the boat back: 'this waiting time we spent on a lovely stretch of uninhabited beach on the north-western end of the island, the sea was as warm as I have ever felt– like a warm bath'. While snorkelling, expect to see OK coral, abundant fish and, on the north side of the island, many sea snakes.

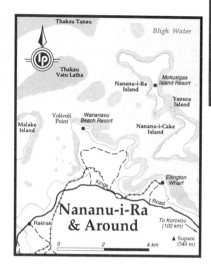

Ra Divers, PO Box 417, Rakiraki (☎ 694 511), will pick up from each of the budget resorts. Scuba diving costs F$83 for a two-tank dive. They will also take snorkellers for F$7.70 if they have space on the boat. PADI or NAUI open-water certificate courses are F$363. Ra Divers also take people fishing, including day trips to Turtle Bay (a turtle-breeding ground in October/November). Mokusigas Resort also has diving and fishing for its guests and may allow others to join trips if the resort is not full.

Places to Stay & Eat

There are four inexpensive places to stay on the island and one more up-market resort. Three of the budget places are close together on the same beach, so if you do not like one for some reason there is the option of moving next door. Take cash as none of the budget places accept credit cards. It is a good idea to pick up some supplementary food supplies (especially fruit and vegetables), although each of the places to stay will also provide food, and there is a small store at both Betham's and Kon Tiki. All of the budget places provide linen and cutlery. It's a good idea to book accommodation in advance,

VITI LEVU

Nananu-i-Ra

0   0.5   1 km

1 Kon Tiki Lodge
2 Mokusiga's Resort
3 Ancient Fijian Lookout
4 Nananu Beach Cottages (MacDonald's)
5 Betham's Beach Cottages
6 Charlie's Place

are F$16.50 return. They have a small shop, with reasonable prices, which sells a good range of food items including bread, milk and frozen meat. Snorkelling gear can be hired for F$8 per day and kayaks for F$2 per hour.

Nananu Beach Cottages (☎ 694 633), also known as McDonald's, has dorm accommodation (maximum of six people) for F$16.50, and twin rooms with shared bathrooms for F$38.50 for singles or doubles. Self-contained cottages are F$55 for doubles plus F$6 per extra person. They have an outdoor cafe, which serves toasted sandwiches for F$2.50 and large pizzas for F$8 to F$12. Meal packages for three meals are F$24.20 and return boat transfers from the wharf are F$15 per person. Snorkelling gear can be hired for F$5 per day and kayaks for F$2 per hour.

Kon Tiki Lodge (☎ 694 290) is located on a lovely beach with good snorkelling, about 1½ hours walk from the other budget places, near the north-west point of the island. It has beach-front self-contained bungalows for F$38.50 for a double. Double or twin bures with shared facilities are F$33. The dorms (up to seven beds) cost F$16.50. There are good cooking facilities for the dorms and there is also a small shop that has a few basics like water, eggs, juices, soft drinks, biscuits, cheese, pasta, canned food and snack bars. Meal packages are F$11 and include breakfast, lunch and dinner. Staff are friendly and it is a good place to sit up at night exchanging stories with fellow travellers and drinking kava. Activities include volleyball, fishing, snorkelling (F$3 equipment hire) and diving through Ra Divers. Transfers from Ellington Wharf are F$17.60 per person return.

The more up-market *Mokusigas Resort* (☎ 694 444; fax 694 404) was opened in 1991. It is on an interesting site on a narrow, steep ridge with beautiful views to the water on either side. The name translates loosely as 'lazy bones', but if you don't like steep paths you'd better avoid this resort. It has 20 suites, each with ceiling fans, fridge and balcony, which are F$220/270 for lagoon/ocean view for a maximum of three people. Main meals

especially if you want a cottage, as the island can get crowded. The water supply is sometimes a problem. Outsiders may be allowed to use Mokusiga Resort's bar and restaurant if they are not busy, but it is essential to book first.

Charlie's Place (☎ 694 676) is popular among travellers as it's good value for money. It has a dorm for F$17.60 (maximum of nine people). The spacious cottage has a bedroom, sitting room, verandah, a well-equipped kitchen and laundry facilities for F$50 a double, plus F$8 for each extra person (up to a maximum of eight). It has a view of the beach from the hill. Dinner costs F$7. They will give guests mangoes when in season.

Betham's Beach Cottages (☎ 694 132), in the middle between Charlie's and McDonald's, has two dormitories with cooking facilities, one sleeping six and the other eight to 10 people, for F$16.50 each. Beach-front cottages cost F$55. Transfers in Bligh's Restaurant are in the F$18 to F$19 range. Activities include snorkelling, windsurfing, canoeing, fishing, tennis and working out in the gym. Dives cost F$55 per single trip or ten dives go for F$510, and an open-water certificate course costs F$440. One-way boat transfers to/from Ellington Wharf are F$11 per person.

Getting There & Away

For getting to/from Ellington Wharf and the island, see Rakiraki & Around – Getting There & Away, above.

TAVUA & AROUND

Midway between Rakiraki and Tavua is **Yaqara**, the largest cattle station in Fiji (7000 hectares), with land extending from the Kings Road all the way up to the mountain ridge. It is run by the government for commercial and research purposes and has 4000 head of cattle as well as orchards.

Tavua is a small, quiet agricultural town

67 km from Lautoka and 100 km from Nadi. It has a market, so if going inland do your shopping here. Buses leave here at 3 pm daily for the hill town of Nadarivatu. Further along is Monasavu Dam and the road continues through to Suva, but don't attempt this trip unless you have a 4WD; see the Interior section later in this chapter.

From Tavua, the road past the hospital leads inland about nine km to the gold-mining town of **Vatukoula**, which has about 5000 residents. The Emperor Gold Mining Company began mining here in the 1930s. The ore is mined from a narrow vein on the edge of an extinct volcano. Most mining is underground, but there are also open cuts. Gold is Fiji's third-largest earner of foreign exchange and about 1500 people are employed by the company. In the early 1990s there were bitter strikes by workers over wages and conditions.

There are many buses which travel daily to Vatukoula. If you have time to kill it may be worth taking a ride to see the difference between the housing for workers and their bosses.

From Vatukoula, drivers may take the scenic back road to Ba, which passes cane farms and Indian settlements. Rosie Tours has excursions which include Vatukoula on their itinerary, and the Tavua Hotel can also organise trips.

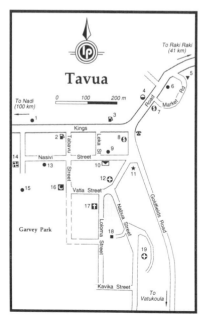

Tavua

To Raki Raki (41 km)

To Nadi (100 km)

0   100   200 m

Kings Street

Nasivi Street

Vatia Street

Garvey Park

Kavika Street

To Vatukoula

1	Farmer's Club
2	Mobil Service Station
3	Shell Service Station
4	Bus Stop
5	Hot Bread Shop
6	Market
7	ANZ Bank
8	Westpac Bank
9	Theatre
10	Post Office & Court House
11	Police Station
12	Medical Clinic
13	Tavua Club
14	Temple
15	School
16	Mosque
17	Church
18	Tavua Hotel
19	Hospital

VITI LEVU

Places to Stay & Eat

The only place to stay in the area is the *Tavua Hotel* (☎ 680 522; fax 680 390). It is a classic old hotel with a colonial character and rather sleepy service. It has 11 rooms with private bathrooms, which are reasonably good value at F$33/44 for singles/doubles. There is a spacious semicircular lounge upstairs with good views and a bar and large dining room downstairs.

The restaurant serves unexciting meals (mixed menu) for between F$10 and F$16, but tables near the window are quite pleasant. There is a swimming pool at the back, which is presumable sometimes clean. This is a possible place to spend a night if you intend to go inland to Nadarivatu (Mt Victoria/Tomanivi).

Unfortunately, our experience of the Tavua Hotel was tainted by the sound of an altercation in the room next door and the refusal of the security man to do anything about it!

BA

Ba is a fairly unattractive agricultural town, 38 km north-east of Lautoka and 71 km from Nadi. The Ba district is the largest in Fiji, with a predominantly Fiji-Indian population of 12,500. It's an expanding commercial centre, dependent on cane growing and the Rarawai Sugar Mill. There's also a sawmill that harvests pine and local hardwood. Other industries include clothing, building materials, steel, confectionery, poultry and chalk.

A new bridge is being built over the Ba River, financed by the EU, and the Kings Road will be diverted to bypass the town. The old bridge was wiped out by Cyclone Kina in 1993 and the town was cut off for about eight months until a temporary bridge was installed on loan. There is a large mosque downtown near the Elevuka Creek.

Soccer is popular in the region and the local team often wins national tournaments. Ba also boasts the best race course in Fiji. The town's horse-racing and bougainvillea

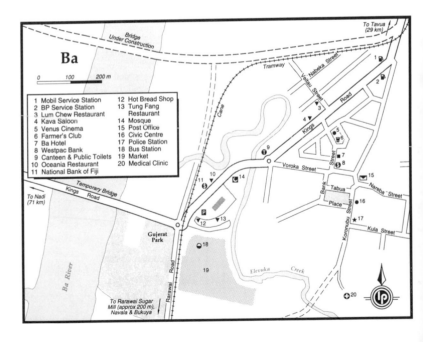

Ba

0   100   200 m

1 Mobil Service Station
2 BP Service Station
3 Lum Chew Restaurant
4 Kava Saloon
5 Venus Cinema
6 Farmer's Club
7 Ba Hotel
8 Westpac Bank
9 Canteen & Public Toilets
10 Oceania Restaurant
11 National Bank of Fiji
12 Hot Bread Shop
13 Tung Fang Restaurant
14 Mosque
15 Post Office
16 Civic Centre
17 Police Station
18 Bus Station
19 Market
20 Medical Clinic

festivals are in September; see River Trips under Organised Tours earlier in this chapter for Ba River rafting.

Places to Stay & Eat

There is not much reason for the traveller to stay in Ba. The *Ba Hotel* (☎ 674 000) on Bank St is the only place to stay, catering mainly for business people. It has 14 rooms with air-con, private bathrooms, tea and coffee-making facilities, fridge and phone. A night in one of their gaudy but clean rooms is F$40/52 single/double. It also has a restaurant with main meals for around F$7, a bar and reasonable swimming pool. The *Farmer's Club* next door is not a bad place for a drink. There are lots of very cheap but fairly grotty places to eat in Ba. *Lum Chew Restaurant* is upstairs and around the corner from the *Kava Saloon* (a Fiji-Indian haunt with fast food and a pool table).

On the western side of the river, *Tung Fang Restaurant* has Chinese lunch dishes for F$2 to F$3, but a very smelly toilet. Another Chinese restaurant is the *Oceania* next to the NBF bank, which has air-con and dishes for F$2.50 to F$4.

The Interior

The Interior of Viti Levu is one of the best places to experience traditional Fijian culture. There are small villages and settlements scattered through the hills, which are largely self-sufficient.

NADARIVATU, NAVAI & KORO-NI-O

About three km east of Tavua, a gravel road heads inland off the Kings Road to Nadarivatu and cross-country to Suva. The gravel road winds up gently at first, then climbs sharply to Fiji's highest mountain range. Views become more and more spectacular with vistas of the coast and offshore islands.

Nadarivatu, 30 km south-east of Tavua, is a forestry settlement, located in one of the most beautiful highland areas of Fiji. A good

part of this area is covered with pine plantations, which are harvested and replanted. The cool and fresh mountain air will give you the opportunity to make use of that forgotten jumper or jacket. Almost opposite the now dilapidated and disused Forestry Rest House is a fragment of the legendary **stone bowl** after which the town is named. Locals believe the spring, which originated from the bowl, to be the source of the mighty Sigatoka River. From Nadarivatu there is a walking trail up to the old fire tower on Mt Lomalagi (sky or heaven in Fijian). The hike is about 1½ hours each way and the view from the top is great on a clear day.

It is possible to camp at Nadarivatu but seek permission from the Forestry Office (☎ 689 001) first. They can also arrange for you to stay with one of the forest worker's families, which can be fun, or in the forest worker's dormitory, which has access to showers. Bring provisions from Tavua. Either give some money, groceries or clothing to cover your costs – it will certainly be appreciated. Nadarivatu used to be a summer-vacation destination for Vatukoula mine bosses and there is a gold-mine rest house, which is spacious and has an open fire. It is for mine workers but, on the off chance that space is available, seek permission to stay there from the manager at Vatukoula (Colin Patterson). You may have to pay in advance at Vatukoula. Buli Tamani and family are the caretakers (☎ 689 005).

Navai is about eight km south of Nadarivatu at the foot of Fiji's highest peak (1323m), **Tomanivi** (Adam and Eve's place) or Mt Victoria. The Wainibuka and Wainimala rivers (eventually merging to form the Rewa) originate in this area, as well as the Sigatoka River. Fiji's staple root crop, cassava, doesn't grow well here (believed to be Adam's punishment), but many other vegetables thrive at this altitude. Villagers only grow food for their own use nowadays, after a farm scheme failed because it could not compete with imported produce.

The trail to Tomanivi begins from Navai village. Guides can be hired for F$10. Allow at least three hours for the climb and two hours to return. The last half of the climb is practically rock climbing and can be extremely slippery after rain.

Past Navai the road deteriorates, and is recommended for 4WD vehicles only. The **Monasavu Dam** and **Koro-ni-O** (village of the clouds) are about 25 km to the south-east. The Wailoa/Monasavu Hydroelectric Scheme provides about 93% of Viti Levu's power needs (about 89% of Fiji's needs), with a generating capacity of 80 MW. It was completed in 1983 at a cost of F$233 million, and has greatly reduced Fiji's reliance on diesel imports. The road improves again at Serea and continues on to Suva.

Getting There & Away

Local buses depart from Tavua (opposite the market) at 3 pm daily (except Sunday) to Nadrau, a village near the Monasavu Dam. The bus returns to Tavua the following morning at about 7 am. The winding bus trip up into the mountains takes about 1½ hours. If going up by car, ideally you should be in a 4WD. Cutting across from Vatukoula, the road is barely passable; avoid it unless you have a 4WD or are hitching with a carrier.

NAUSORI HIGHLANDS

The Nausori Highlands have some fantastic landscapes and remote villages, which retain many interesting traditional beliefs and culture. Sunday is a day of rest, church and spending time with the family, so visits may be disruptive and unappreciated.

Navala

Navala is Fiji's most picturesque village, set in a superb landscape. It is high up in the hills on a sloping site on the banks of the Ba River. While most Fijian villages now have a preference for concrete block and corrugated-iron construction, Navala retains traditional bures; only the school and radio shed are concrete blocks and these are out of sight. Obviously the chief enforces strict town-planning rules! Navala is a relatively large village and the houses are laid out in avenues with a central promenade down to the river. The buildings are rectangular with sloping stone plinths, hipped thatched roofs of timber-pole structure and woven walls. Kitchens are in separate bures. The stunning, timeless beauty is a photographer's paradise but you need to get permission to take shots, theoretically even from across the bridge. The turaga-ni-koro, Karoalo Vaisewa, allows tourists to visit and take photos but they must present a *sevusevu* and donation of F$5 or F$10. If you arrive independently, ask the first person you meet to escort you to the chief. The people of Navala follow Catholicism. The village has a radio telephone for emergencies.

Places to Stay & Eat One reader wrote of a new backpacker hostel, Boulou's Lodge & Backpacker Hostel (no phone) near Navala village. He said it's run by a retired Fijian couple, Seresio and Bulou N Talili, and their son Tui. You can usually stay in their house and be part of the family; they have no electricity and a cold-water improvised shower. All meals and kava drinking are included in the F$35 per person per night fee. Take some food as a present and leave a donation for the village community centre project.

Tui will take you tramping up to their farm, which is a two-hour walk uphill. The place is well worth seeing, no 20th-century influence up here at all. There is also a good view from up there, you can see the sea in the distance. They also offer horse riding and rafting on the river. All these activities cost extra.
Ulrich Guenther

Coming from Ba, the lodge is one km past Navala and on the right about 50m before a river crossing. It may not have a sign so ask. We will be interested to hear reports from travellers.

Getting There & Away There is a local bus from Ba to Navala (1½ hours) at midday. Carriers are much more expensive, about F$18. The road is rough and gravel, with a few patches of bitumen on the really steep bits. While only a distance of about 26 km, Navala is about an hour's drive from Ba, past the Rarawai Mill, through beautiful rugged

---

Traditional Vales & Bures

Traditionally, Fijians lived in two types of houses. A family house was called a *vale*, while men's houses (where circumcised males of the clan met, ate and slept) were known as bures. These buildings were dark and smoky inside with no windows and usually only one low door. Vales had hearth pits where the women cooked, and the packed earth floor was covered with grass or fern leaves and then pandanus leaf or coarse coconut-leaf mats. Sleeping compartments were at one end, behind a bark-cloth curtain. Finely woven mats and wooden headrests were used for sleeping. Storage was in baskets hanging from walls, on overhead racks and suspended multipronged wooden hooks with broad-rimmed rat guards. Coconut-fibre string (from the pounded husk of a ripe nut) was used for lashing and decorating the roof structure. Houses were mostly rectangular, but in Western Viti Levu some were round or, later, square with conical roofs supported on a central post (thought to be a New Caledonian influence). In eastern Fiji, rounded gables were a Tongan influence. ∎

---

scenery. Sometimes the Ba River floods and the concrete bridge just before the village becomes impassable. There are tours from Nadi that visit Navala, as well as white-water rafting trips to the Ba River; see Organised Tours earlier in this chapter.

Bukuya

The village of Bukuya is at the intersection of the roads from Sigatoka, Nadi and Ba. The drive from Sigatoka up the Sigatoka Valley is about 1½ hours. From Nadi along the Nausori Highlands Road, it takes about 1½ to two hours, and from Ba via Navala about 1½ hours. Bukuya has a population of about 700 people. The chief is an ex-boxing champion.

Places to Stay & Eat Located on a hill on the edge of the village is *Peni's* (☎ /fax 703 801, Nadi). The thatched bures for travellers are about the only traditional bures in the village. Rates for accommodation, including meals, transport and activities, are F$130/ 200 for singles/doubles for three days and two nights. Five days and four nights cost F$165 per person and F$10 per extra night thereafter. Campsites are F$10 per person per night for a minimum of three nights, plus F$40 for return transport to Nadi. Bures are small and very simple with lino over compacted earth floors and various living things making their home in the roof. There are shared flush toilets and cold showers.

Food is good and plentiful, and based around home-grown fruit and vegetables. Meals provided include palusami, taro leaves, roots, pineapple, pawpaw, potatoes and noodles mixed with green beans and canned meat. They also have lovo nights. Villagers here are more or less self-sufficient in food, except for salt and meat. The small shop opposite Peni's sells confectionery, soap, dried biscuits, tinned fish and cigarettes. Another shop in the village has refrigerated meats.

Activities include waterfall tours, horse riding, visits to the chief's bure and local school, Sunday church services (Methodist), river fishing, jungle treks and visits to neighbouring villages. Peni's tours are a bit of an adventure and their success depends on the traveller's expectations. Do not expect anything to be strictly organised or coordinated: 'Fiji time' operates here. You are likely to be offered one activity per day and some activities are not feasible in wet conditions, or if their carrier is otherwise engaged. A polite push to keep things moving may sometimes be appropriate; otherwise just appreciate the good food and get into the slow-paced village lifestyle. It is one of the best places to get an insight into traditional Fijian village life. One reader with a three-year-old son wrote:

We spent two weeks at Peni's place in Bukuya... accommodation is basic and activities sometimes haphazard but after all, this is Fiji time. We loved it, and if you go there expecting a taste of village life and are prepared to take things as they come, you'll have a better time than at any of the beach resorts! If you're travelling with kids it's nothing short of perfect – the villagers love children.

Adrienne Robinson

Getting There & Away All roads to Bukuya are rough and unsealed, and best suited to a 4WD. Peni's son George hurtles up and down the hills in his carrier with his load of travellers bouncing in the back. Don't expect comfort – it's a bone-crunching ride and if you are lucky there may be a few bits of sponge to sit on. There are several operators that take trips into the highlands; see Organised Tours at the beginning of the chapter.

The Reverend Baker

The Wesleyan Methodist missionary Thomas Baker was killed on 21 July 1867 by the Vatusila people at Nabutautau village in the isolated headwaters of the Sigatoka River in the Nausori Highlands. A few years earlier he had been given the task of converting the people of the interior of Viti Levu to the new religion. Out of impatience, martyrdom, foolhardiness, or the urge for success, he ignored advice to keep to areas under the influence of already converted groups. Many believe that it was almost inevitable that he would offend the highlanders in some way.

One theory maintains that the Reverend's death was political. The highlanders associated conversion to Christianity with subservience to Bau and were opposed to any kind of extended authority. Another story is that the local chief borrowed Baker's comb while the missionary was out. Baker later snatched the comb from the chief's hair. Villagers, observing the missionary touching their chief's sacred head, were furious and killed and ate him in disgust, sharing the flesh among neighbouring villages. One local laughingly recounted the story of his ancestors: 'We ate everything, even tried to eat his shoes'. Baker's shoe is exhibited in the Fiji Museum.

Twenty years after his death a mission teacher, guided by a repentant eater, recovered the Reverend's humerus from within the overgrown fork of a large shaddock tree. The bone had been placed there as a trophy. ■

Mamanuca Group

The Mamanucas is a group of about 20 small islands of various shapes and sizes and of varied geological formations: volcanic, limestone or coral-sand islets. The group is located just off the western coast of Viti Levu in a lagoon formed between the Great Sea Reef and the mainland.

Like the Yasawa group to the north, the Mamanucas are very scenic with beautiful white-sand and reef-fringed beaches. Only a few of the smaller islands such as Monu and Monuriki still retain significant areas of forest with native birds and reptiles. Most of the islands have grassland vegetation and some have dry forest areas. Coconut palms are found on the small sandy islands. Fire, goats and other introduced animals have degraded the original vegetation.

Normally the Mamanuca islands are sunnier and drier than Viti Levu. You often see heavy rain clouds hanging over Nadi and Lautoka while these offshore islands remain unaffected. Most of the habitable islands support a Fijian village community and/or a tourist resort. The resorts usually barge their water in from the mainland and rely on generator power. The majority are on leased land owned by nearby villages. Due to their proximity to Nadi and Lautoka, the Mamanucas are popular for day trips and most of Fiji's tourists visit or stay at one of the Mamanuca resorts.

Activities

Most resorts have their own activities, including snorkelling, windsurfing, fishing and other water sports.

Diving Mamanuca dive sites have an abundance of fish and corals. Gotham City is three pinnacles in a passage in the outer barrier reef which has soft coral and is named after the batfish. You are likely to see big fish at the Big Ws which is outside the Barrier Reef on the edge of an abyss.

Inside the Malolo Barrier Reef is the

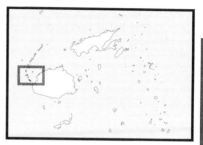

famous Supermarket, at a depth of between five and 30m, where several currents converge. Here brave divers feed grey, white and black-tip reef sharks and the occasional bronze whaler.

North Reef, also known as the Circus, has lots of clown fish, schools of pelagics, plate corals, nudibranches, feather stars and a series of pinnacles. Other sites include the Fish Store, Driwas Dream, Yadua Island, Barrel Head, Camel Humps, a cruise-ship wreck and the remains of a WWII B26 bomber. See Activities in the Facts for the Visitor chapter for a further description of diving in the Mamanucas. The decompression chamber in Suva is 45 minutes away by helicopter.

Many resorts have their own dive operations for guests. Mamanutha Diving has a dive shop on Malololailai Island (Plantation Island). See the Viti Levu chapter for information on Aqua-Trek and Inner Space which take trips to the Mamanucas from Nadi.

Surfing There are excellent surf-breaks at Malolo and Namotu passages. Surfers will have to weigh up the cost and convenience of staying at resorts close to the breaks with the option of cheaper accommodation on the mainland, but with additional transport costs for each surf trip. Seashell Cove Resort, near Momi Bay, arranges trips to the Mamanuca

MAMANUCA GROUP

breaks (see the Viti Levu chapter and Surfing in the Facts for the Visitor chapter).

Dangers & Annoyances

Travelling by small boat in rough weather can be a problem. This mostly applies to backpackers travelling from Nadi to Mana and Malolo islands. You and your gear are likely to get wet. If the weather conditions look suspect, the boat is overcrowded or there are no lifejackets on board, consider alternative means of transport. Flying is not much more expensive. See the Facts for the Visitor chapter.

Accommodation

There are only a few budget places to stay in the Mamanucas: the backpacker hostels on Mana Island, a camp on Malolo Island and a dorm at Beachcomber Resort. Unless your time is very limited, other places such as the Yasawas, Nananu-i-Ra and Taveuni have better options for budget travellers.

Most of the resorts cater for those willing to pay middle to top-range prices, and most guests are package-deal customers who have pre-arranged their trip from overseas. Some resorts have excellent facilities and services for families, while others don't accept young

children. In the southern Mamanucas, the resorts on Tavarua and Namotu specialise in surfing for budget travellers.

Getting Around

It is relatively difficult and costly to explore the Mamanucas, unless of course you have your own yacht. Yachts can be hired at Musket Cove Marina on Malololailai Island. Most resorts have island-hopping trips for their guests but, as they don't like to promote their competition, they stop only briefly.

The South Seas catamaran shuttles between Malololailai, Malolo, Qalito and Mana islands. It has coach pick ups from hotels and resorts in Nadi (free) and Coral Coast (F$10 one way). It also has a water-taxi service which is expensive unless you are in a large group.

If you are travelling to Mana Island (Sun-flower Airlines) or Malololailai Island (Sunflower Airlines, Air Fiji and Island Air) the price of a light plane ticket is comparable with the price by catamaran, but the trip by air is much quicker and more scenic. Turtle Airways offers seaplane flights from Newtown Beach, Nadi, to all of the Mamanuca resorts, as does Island Hoppers by helicopter. Note that weight limits apply to all flights.

Local boats are used for transporting backpackers to/from Mana and Malolo islands.

Organised Tours Several operators offer cruises of the Mamanucas.

Captain Cook Cruises This company (☎ 701 823; fax 702 045) offers a chicken 'n' champagne cruise on board the *Ra Marama* a 33m sailing ship for F$59, which includes lunch; snorkelling gear costs F$2. The trip stops at Malololailai Island for about an hour, where you can hire the resort's facilities. They also have a three-day, two-night cruise/camping trip to the Mamanucas and the southern Yasawas; see the Yasawas chapter for this and for longer trips on board the *Reef Escape*.

South Sea Cruises South Sea Cruises (☎ 722 988; fax 720 346) offers catamaran transfers and water taxis from Denarau, as well as combination and full-day cruises on board the *Seaspray* to Qalito/Malololailai for F$60/50, including lunch. A half-day/full-day cruise to Aqualand is F$33/45, including pick up from Nadi hotels and lunch. Aqualand is a small coral island which is mostly sand with a few trees and huts. There are water sports such as snorkelling, water skiing, windsurfing, para-sailing and banana rides, and use of viewing boards and water scooters is extra. There is also a F$65 pass for all activities except diving. South Seas also offers scuba-diving trips to the Mamanucas and boat charters. A full-day sightseeing trip of eight islands in a small boat is F$660.

Oceanic Schooner Co This company (☎ 722 455; fax 720 134) offers a five-island champagne cruise aboard the 30m schooner *Whale's Tale*, including champagne, continental breakfast, buffet lunch, an open bar

1	Sheraton Vomo Resort
2	Tokoriki Island Resort
3	Matamanoa Island Resort
4	Mana Island Resort
5	Ratu Kini's Hostel & Mereani Backpackers Inn
6	Beachcomber Island Resort
7	Treasure Island Resort
8	Mediterranean Island Resort
9	Paradise Island Resort
10	Saweni Beach Apartments
11	Mediterranean Villas
12	Anchorage Beach Resort
13	Vuda Marina & First Landing Restaurant
14	Navini Island Resort
15	Castaway Island Resort
16	Club Naitasi Resort
17	Musket Cove Resort
18	Plantation Island Resort
19	Airport
20	Sheraton Fiji, The Regent, Denaru Marine
21	Sonaisali Island Resort
22	Namoto Island Resort
23	Tavarua Island Resort
24	Seashell Surf & Dive Resort

MAMANUCA GROUP

and snorkelling gear. What else do you need? Well, F$150.

Fun Cruises Fiji Fun Cruises (☎ 722 455, 723 590) offers full-day trips to uninhabited Malamala (Daydream Island), which cost F$69 on weekdays or F$79 on weekends. Children under 16 years are half-price. Included is BBQ lunch, drinks including wine and beer, snorkelling and coral viewing. The cruise to the island takes one hour.

Blue Lagoon Cruises This company has a combined Mamanuca and Yasawa islands cruise; see the Yasawas chapter.

TAI ISLAND

Tai (Beachcomber) Island and nearby Levuka (Treasure) Island lie about 20 km offshore from Nadi airport. *Beachcomber Island Resort* (☎ 661 500, 662 600; fax 664 496) has been operating for more than 25 years. The island measures only two hectares at low tide but has a great garden and is circled by a beautiful beach. It only takes 10 minutes to walk around the island which is completely covered by the resort. The resort receives lots of day trippers and caters to a maximum of 160 house guests. While it is not a secluded oasis, it has the reputation for having the best party atmosphere in the Mamanucas and attracts a young singles crowd. Entertainment includes live music and grooving on the sand dance floor.

The huge dorm bure sleeps 40 in two-level bunks. Lockers are provided. It costs F$69 each with meals included. Alternatively, private lodges – with fan-cooled rooms with fridge, vanity basin and shared facilities – are F$150/200/269 for singles/doubles/triples. There are 18 bures on the beach front for F$216/266/335. Each has an ensuite, fan, fridge and tea/coffee-making facilities. Children under six are free. Prices include buffet-style meals.

Most activities cost extra, but snorkelling equipment is free for house guests. On offer are water skiing, para-sailing, giant tobogganing, windsurfing, jet skiing, canoe-

ing (F$4 per hour) and fishing trips. Island hopping is F$48 for a half-day and there are also whole-day cruises to uninhabited Monuriki and a visit to a village on Yanuya Island.

The diving operator Subsurface Fiji (☎ 666 738; fax 669 955) operates from Tai Island and has Japanese as well as English-speaking instructors. Mixed gas diving (nitrox) is also available. A single-tank dive costs F$70 and a four-tank package is F$240. An introductory dive is F$95 and open-water courses are F$450. Specialty courses are also available. Diving is half-price at Beachcomber during February and March for those staying at least five nights.

Getting There & Away

Beachcomber Island Resort arranges for a courtesy bus pick up from the airport and Nadi and Lautoka hotels. The trip aboard the *Tui Tai* takes 70 minutes and leaves Lautoka's Queen's Wharf twice daily at 10 am and 2 pm. Transfers cost F$60/30 return for adults/children under 16; children under two are free. There are also boat transfers for Regent and Sheraton guests which leave Denarau Marina at 9 am. Beachcomber also offers speedboat transfers for late flight arrivals. Flights by Turtle Airways seaplane are F$95/190 one way/return or F$110/220 by Island Hopper helicopter. Discounts apply for children.

LEVUKA ISLAND

Levuka Island is a short distance from Beachcomber. The six-hectare coral island is covered by *Treasure Island Resort* (☎ 661 599, 666 999; fax 663 577), which used to be owned by Beachcomber, and caters mostly to a family clientele. There are 67 units close to the beach, each with private bathrooms, fridge and tea/coffee-making facilities. The units cost F$280 for up to three adults or up to two children under 16 in the same room as their parents. A meal package for adults/children under 12 is F$47/24 daily for breakfast and dinner, or F$55/28 for three meals. Meals for infants under two are free.

There is nightly entertainment in the large

open dining room/bar, a games room with pool, table tennis and darts, a boutique, and a fresh-water pool. The resort caters well for kids, with a children's pool, playground and baby-sitting provided. Activities included in the price are windsurfing, canoeing, snorkelling, volleyball, golf and use of catamaran, paddle boats and sail boats. Water skiing, tobogganing, para-sailing, jet skiing, fishing and diving are also available. Diving with Tropex Divers (☎ 661599; fax 663577) starts at F$45 for a one-tank beach dive, F$70 for a one-tank boat dive, and a five-tank dive package is F$290. Scuba diving in the pool is free and introductory dives are F$110. Open-water certification is $475. Tropex also offers specialty courses and underwater photography.

Getting There & Away
Levuka Island is 17 km from Lautoka Wharf. The *Tui Tai* departs the wharf twice daily at 10 am and 2 pm. Transfers for Treasure Island Resort guests cost F$54/27 for adults/children under 16. South Seas Cruises has a twice-daily service, at 9.45 am and 2 pm, from Denarau Marina for F$33/56 per person one way/return. The trip takes 1 hours; children under 16 are half-price and infants under two are free.

TIVOA ISLAND
This tiny coral island has the *Mediterranean Island Resort* (☎ 664 011, 663 700; fax 661 773) which caters for a maximum of six people at a time. There's an open-air restaurant and two beach cottages on opposite sides of the island. Prices are F$173 per person including three meals. The whole island can be chartered for a three-day, two-night package for Tuesdays and Wednesdays only. Blue Lagoon Cruises stop at the island for lunch on other days. Activities include swimming and snorkelling, and sunbathing on the white-sand beach.

Getting There & Away
The island is a 20-minute trip by resort boat from Lautoka wharf. Day cruises are offered

for F$60, including lunch and snorkelling gear. Children under 12 are half-price.

NAVINI ISLAND
Navini, a tiny island centrally located in the Mamanucas, is surrounded by a white-sand beach and offshore reef. The intimate *Navini Island Resort* (☎ 662 188; fax 665 566) caters for a maximum of 20 guests. It is a good place for families or couples who want a friendly atmosphere away from crowds of tourists. The 27 friendly staff outnumber the guests, one of the reasons why there are lots of return guests. The resort shop has souvenirs, toiletries, books and book lending.

The eight bures are all within 10m of the beach. The four one-bedroom bures (maximum three people) are F$265. The honeymoon bure costs F$385, and has two rooms, a verandah and a private courtyard with spa. A duplex bure with sitting room (maximum five people) is F$330. A 10% discount applies for stays of over one week. There is a bar and small dining area and all guests eat at the same table. A meal plan is F$57 per adult, F$30 for children five to 12 years old or F$20 if under five. The food is good, especially the fresh fish.

Activities include kayaking, windsurfing, volleyball, use of viewing boards and snorkelling, in particular along the edge of the reef that surrounds the island. All water sports and morning trips, including fishing and visiting other resorts or villages, are included in the price. Diving can be arranged with Subsurface at Beachcomber. Guests staying on other islands cannot visit Navini, however. Live-aboard cruises on *Sereki Mai* around the Mamanucas and Yasawas can also be arranged. A three-day, two-night cruise for four people is F$835 per person including meals and transfers.

Getting There & Away
Most guests are picked up from Nadi or Lautoka hotels and taken by car to Vuda Point Marina, from where the resort is a half-hour ride away by speed boat. Return transfers cost F$96 per adult or F$48 per child between five and 12 years old; children

under five are free. By Turtle Airways seaplane the flight is F$95/190 one way/return. A South Seas water taxi (maximum 10 people) costs F$260 from Denarau.

MALOLOLAILAI ISLAND

Malololailai (Plantation) Island lies 20 km west of Denarau. The island is fairly large for the Mamanucas, 240 hectares, and has a good white-sand beach. Apart from the two resorts, there is a time share, a marina, a dive shop, a grocery store and a restaurant near the airstrip, and a gift shop on the hill above Musket Cove resort.

Musket Cove Marina

The Musket Cove Yacht Club hosts Fiji regatta week and the Musket Cove to Port Vila yacht race. Yachts can anchor at the marina and stock up on fuel, water and provisions from the general store nearby. The Moorings (☎/fax 666 710) operates out of the marina. It has yachts for hire for sailing to the Mamanucas and Yasawas. Boats have showers, toilets, fridges, linen and towels and a BBQ on deck. Snorkel gear, dinghy and outboard are also provided. Boats are 12-15m and take up to six people. Prices range from F$605 in the low season (January to March), up to F$880 for peak season per day. A local guide is included, but add F$27.50 per day for insurance, F$100 per day if you need a skipper and F$80 for a cook. A full crew can also be provided.

Diving

Mamanutha Diving (☎ 622 215; fax 662 633) has a dive shop at the marina. A one-tank dive costs F$65 and a six-tank package is F$250. Introductory dives are F$89 and open-water courses are $400/500 for a group/private lesson. There are also specialty courses and accommodation packages with Musket Cove Resort. Mamanutha Diving also service Club Naitasi and Namotu Island Resort. The Plantation Island Resort has its own concern, Plantation Divers. One dive is F$65 and a six-dive package is F$250. Open-water courses are F$390 for a group or F$500 for private

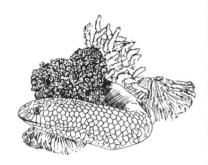

Sea Snake

lessons. Day trippers are welcome and can hire the resort's equipment. South Seas Cruises offers trips on a semisubmersible reef viewer.

Places to Stay & Eat

Self-caterers will be glad to know there is a general store near the airstrip. *Ananda's Restaurant* next door has meals for around F$15.

Plantation Island Resort (☎ 669 333; fax 669 200), established in the late 1970s and one of Fiji's first resorts, used to be considered one of the finest offshore resorts in the region. However, some of its buildings are now looking a bit tired, and the garden is relatively sparse, but this may change with plans for a new management. The 18 two-bedroom bures cost F$385/302.50 for garden/beachfront for singles or doubles, or F$412.50/495 for six adults. The 53 one-room studio bures set in the garden are F$247.50. There are also 40 spacious, air-con hotel rooms in a double-storey building for F$187 or F$159. Some of these rooms can be noisy and have no views. All have private bathrooms, fans, tea/coffee-making facilities and fridges. Up to two children under 16 can stay in the same room as their parents free of charge. A discount of 20% applies from November to mid-December and late January to the end of March.

Food is not included in the price and no cooking facilities are provided. Breakfast ranges from F$6 to F$15.50 for full American style. Lunch is F$7.50 to F$9.50 for a main, F$15.50 to F$19 for dinner or F$25 for a Fijian night. A disco is held every night. The resort has a creche and baby-sitting service, a children's menu, a swimming pool and games room that make it popular with families. Activities included in the room rate are snorkelling, volleyball, putt putt golf, canoeing and windsurfing. Other activities such as water skiing, diving, para-gliding, game fishing, island hopping and jet skiing are additional.

Adjacent to the Musket Cove Yacht Club & Marina is *Musket Cove Resort* (☎ 662 215; fax 662 633). The beach is not as nice as Malololailai Island's and at low tide the water is distant, but it does have a swimming pool. The present owners, Dick and Carol Smith, built and run both Castaway and Plantation Island resorts. The double-storey villas, which have a spa, two bathrooms and cooking facilities, sleep up to six people and cost F$330 for singles or doubles. Beach-front bures sleep three people and are F$260 for singles or doubles. Seaview Bures have cooking facilities and sleep four people, and cost F$220 for singles or doubles. In each of the bures each additional adult is charged F$15 and there is no additional charge for children under 16. All units have ceiling fans. Ask about the special 'lomaloma' seven-night package deal. *Dick's Place*, the resort's bistro and bar, serves international cuisine with some Indian and Fijian dishes, weekly barbecues and pig on the spit. Activities such as water skiing, windsurfing, canoeing, hand line fishing and snorkelling trips are included in the room price. Game fishing, diving and use of Hobie Cats are additional.

Lagoon Resort Time Share (☎ 662 215 or New Zealand: 09 357 0503; fax 09 358 4269), adjacent to the marina, has five two-bedroom and 15 single-bedroom thatched-roof bures. The units are spacious, clean and have kitchen facilities. Although a time share, you may be able to arrange to stay here if you ring the New Zealand number. Guests can also use the Musket Cove Resort's facilities. Building began in 1992 and there is a

tennis court, but the swimming pool is still under construction and the garden is not yet well established.

Getting There & Away
Malololailai has a landing strip with shuttle services by Sunflower, Air Fiji and Island Air. Air Fiji also has day trips to Musket Cove Resort, Malololailai Island, for F$75 per person, including lunch at the resort and use of its facilities, for only F$11 more than the normal return fare. A flight to Malololailai Island by Turtle Airways sea-plane will cost F$190 return (compared with F$64 by Sunflower or Air Fiji).

The South Sea Cruises Island Express cat-amaran departs twice daily from Denarau and costs F$33/62 one way/return. The after-noon trip takes a little over one hour, while the morning trip stops at Mana, Qalito and Malolo islands, arriving at Malololailai Island about three hours later. Both South Seas Cruises and Captain Cook Cruises have sailing trips which visit Malololailai Island.

MALOLO ISLAND
Malolo Island is the largest of the Mamanuca islands and has two villages, a resort, a back-packer camp and a time share (Lako Mai). It has a variety of vegetation, including man-groves and coastal forest. The island's highest point is Uluisolo (218m), which was used by locals as a hill fortification and by the US Forces in 1942 as an observation point. There are panoramic views of the Mamanuca islands and the southern Yasawas.

Club Naitasi (☎ 669 999; fax 669 197) has 28 bures which cost F$295 for up to three adults, or two adults and two children. The 10 villas have two separate bedrooms and cost F$425 for up to six people. The accom-modation has cooking facilities and basic food items can be purchased at the resort shop. Self-caterers should consider bringing groceries from the mainland. Meal packages are also available for dining at the Terrace Restaurant up on the hill or at the deck bar down near the water. Naitasi has a good information leaflet on flora and fauna, nature

Americans on Malolo

In 1840 there was a conflict between a US expedition led by Commandant Charles Wilkes and the people of Malolo. When Wilkes and his sailors tried to take a local as a hostage, the Fijians retaliated and killed some Americans, including Wilkes' nephew. In response the Americans set two villages alight and killed more than 50 people. American troops again 'invaded' Malolo in 1942, while training for combat with the Japanese. They set up an observation and signals station on Mt Uluisolo. ■

and cultural walks around the island and archaeological sites. There's an activities programme for kids and baby-sitting at F$3.50 per hour. The daily rate includes all nonmotorised water sports. Diving is arranged with Mamanuca Divers from Malololailai Island.

The backpacker option is *Malolo Camp*. Camping is F$8.80 and dorm accommodation costs F$13.20. A meal package for breakfast, lunch and dinner is F$8.80 but big eaters may find the food insufficient. Activities include fishing trips for F$6.60 per person, four-island hopping for F$22, snorkelling at Sandy Island for F$5.50 plus F$5.50 gear hire, and a village visit by boat for F$11 per person. Malolo Island is very quiet but you can walk to both Club Naitasi or Malololailai Island for more action. Advance bookings are essential. Enquire with Fiji Island Adventures (☎ 700 243; fax 702 746), also known as the Tourist Information Centre, in Nadi. It may not give independent information, however, and could try to encourage you to go to Malolo Island.

Getting There & Away

The Island Express leaves Denarau Marina twice daily, at 9 am and 1.30 pm, and passes Malolo Island; it costs F$40/70 one way/return. Children under 16 are half-price. The 10-minute flight by Turtle Airways seaplane is F$95/190 one way/return. Children under 16 are half-price and under two 10%.

Transfers to Malolo Camp are made by village boat for F$27.50 per person.

QALITO ISLAND

Reef-fringed Qalito (Castaway) Island covers an area of 70 hectares and is 27 km west of Denarau. *Castaway Island Resort* (☎ 661 233; fax 665 753) covers about one-eighth of the island and the remainder has tropical vegetation. The 66 fan-cooled bures are quite spacious, sleeping four adults or a family of five, and have a fridge and inter-esting tapa-lined ceilings. Beach-front bures cost F$390, ocean view F$370 and garden F$330. A new pool was being built at the time of writing. There is a great dining terrace perched on the point overlooking the water. Buffet breakfast is included in the price. The all-day casual dining menu has meals for F$5 to F$14 and the à la carte dinner is F$16 to F$27 for mains or F$60 for the seafood platter.

There is a creche and a club to keep the children very busy. It is complimentary during the day for those over three years old. The resort has a clinic with a registered nurse. Catamaran sailing, snorkelling, surf-ski paddling around the island, windsurfing, volleyball and tennis are all included in the price. Other activities such as diving, jet skiing, para-sailing, water skiing, fishing and island hopping are extra.

Castaway Dive School has one-tank dives for F$90 and six-tank packages for F$325. There is a discount if you have your own equipment. PADI open-water courses are F$450 per person or F$600 for individual lessons. Underwater photography courses are also offered.

Getting There & Away

The Island Express leaves Denarau Marina twice daily, at 9 am and 1.30 pm, and costs F$40/70 one way/return. Children under 16 are half-price. The 10-minute flight by Turtle Airways seaplane is F$95/190 one way/return. Children under 16 are half-price and under two pay 10%. By Island Hopper heli-copter the flight is F$143/286. Alternatively, the resort's speedboat can be chartered for

F$350 for eight people. Castaway Island Resort is about half an hour by speedboat from Mana Island. South Sea Cruises has a full-day cruise aboard a 21m ketch with lunch and use of facilities at Castaway.

MANA ISLAND

Beautiful Mana Island is located about 30 km west of Denarau. With its grassy hills, lovely beaches and wide coral reef, the island is spectacular to fly over. Accommodation includes a large luxury resort and two backpacker hostels. Mana Resort stretches between the north and south beaches, over 80 hectares of leased land. The Sunset beach at the far western end of the island is where the resort holds weddings. The snorkelling is quite good with lots of tiny colourful fish. Also check out the south beach pier at night where the fish go into a frenzy under the lights. It is worth hiking up to the tallest hill for the view of water, beach and other islands.

Diving

Aqua-Trek (☎ 702 413; fax 702 412) has a dive shop at Mana to cater for resort divers as well as an office in downtown Nadi. A one-tank boat dive is F$60 or F$80 including equipment, and a six-tank package is F$330. Courses include discover scuba for F$130 and open water for F$519.

Places to stay – bottom end

There are two backpacker hostels on the south-eastern edge of the Mana Resort near the south beach. The resort has erected a huge fence to make it clear that its facilities are for its own guests only. Some brochures carry photos of beach shelters and deckchairs but they are for the exclusive use of resort patrons.

While the hostels appear to be part of the same complex, they are run by b others who are very competitive. Even thou 1 everyone is crammed together in the s me restaurant/bar area, you cannot sit at the tables belonging to the other hostel. Politics aside, the staff of both are usually friendly and the party atmosphere can be fun, but it's not the place to go if you want a quiet escape. The place is often overcrowded and there have been mixed reports about both hostels. Avoid paying too much up front so that you have an option to change if you are not happy. The drawbacks are lots of rubbish and the sight of mountains of empty beer bottles. Only cash is accepted and beware of theft on the beaches and in the dorms. The power supply can be a problem, as can water, and you may need to resort to a natural shower in the rain or bathing in the ocean. BYO soap, towel, snacks, torch, kava and mosquito repellent. Meals are an important issue here as there is nowhere to buy ingredients and backpackers are not allowed to use the resort's restaurants. Activities include bushwalking, swimming and snorkelling, kava parties and volleyball.

Ratu Kini Boko's Village Hostel (☎ 667 520, 669 143) has five dorms of various types, from a concrete house to traditional bures. The largest takes a maximum of 16 people. Prices are F$27.50 per person including meals. There are also two double rooms available for F$66 or F$77 with own bathroom, and including meals. Beer is sold by the half-dozen only. Food is usually OK and served buffet style, including fried rice, curries, fried cassava, homemade cakes and bread, porridge and fruit. Activities include a BBQ at a 'honeymoon island' and snorkelling trips for F$5 per person for the boat plus F$5 to hire gear.

One reader described her trip to Mana Island as follows:

Mana Island was gorgeous but it left much to be desired: rats in the kitchen, food very average...but it was still good. I stayed at Ratukini's, which was right in the middle of the village, so I met a lot of Fijians... Most backpackers are less finicky than me so they will love Mana. If anyone goes to Mana they should fly rather than take a boat. I got the boat out there, and got horribly sunburnt after two hours under the sun, all my stuff got soaking wet and then I flew back in 15 minutes for only F$15 more. Also the flight was quite fun and scary; it was an eight-seater aircraft including the pilot and it was a really stormy day, so I got to spend 15 minutes with five terrified Japanese tourists, all lurching round in a lawn mower.
Sara Anderson

Mereani Vata Backpacker's Inn (☎ 703 466, 663 099) has up to 24 people squeezed into one dorm for F$27.50 per person, including three meals. There are also four rooms which are F$33/66 for singles/ doubles including meals. The weekly *lovo* night is F$5.50 and the barbecue night F$25. It seems that food quality and quantity vary. Activities available include reef-fishing trips for F$5.50, four-island sightseeing for F$22, snorkelling (including equipment) for F$5.50 and a weekly kava ceremony.

Places to stay – top end
The Japanese-owned *Mana Island Resort* (☎ 661 210; fax 662 713) is one of the largest resorts in Fiji. It was established in the early 1970s when the original Australian owner built 60 of the garden bures. Presently it has 170 rooms and the government has given permission to expand this up to 600! The 90 garden bures cost F$235 or F$370 for a duplex for a maximum of six people. Up to two children under 16 can share a room with parents free of charge. The six executive bures are F$385 for singles or doubles. The ten deluxe duplex bures are F$585 for a maximum of six people, and the 12 deluxe bures are F$350 for singles or doubles. The deluxe bures are very spacious, elevated with a porch, and have both a fan and air-con, fridge, and solar panels on the corrugated-iron roofs. There are also 32 deluxe hotel rooms on the northern beach front for F$320. The hotel and deluxe bures were built in 1994.

The Mamanuca restaurant and bar are in the main entertainment bure. Meal plans are available and children are about half-price. There is a weekly lovo and a *meke* or floor show three times a week. The Coffee Shop and Bulumakau Steak House on the north beach is for Mana guests only (bad luck backpackers, you'll be asked to give your room number). It has great steak and seafood, and mains are F$15 to F$26.50. Resort facilities include a circular pool, two lit tennis courts, volleyball and a games room. Nonmotorised water sports are included in the price. South Seas Cruises

offers trips on a semisubmersible reef viewer.

Getting There & Away
The quickest and most scenic way to get to Mana is to fly. Sunflower Airlines has a 15-minute shuttle from Nadi airport to the Mana island airstrip seven times daily which costs F$40 each way. Island Hoppers heli-copters are much more expensive. Turtle Airways seaplanes cost F$95/190 one way/return.

The Island Express catamaran departs twice daily from Denarau Marina and is F$43/78 one way/return. The morning trip is direct to Mana and takes 1¾ hours, while the afternoon trip first passes by Malololailai, Malolo and Qalito islands and takes 2½ hours. The first child is 50% of the fare and it's 25% per additional child.

The backpacker resorts charge F$25 per person each way for transfers in an open boat. Boats depart from Wailoaloa Beach daily and the trip takes 45 minutes to 1½ hours. The boat to Ratukini's departs from Horizon Beach Resort weekdays at 12 noon and weekends at 9.30 am. This can vary, however, due to tide and weather conditions. As each resort has its own transport, you are forced to decide in advance where you will be staying.

MATAMANOA ISLAND
Matamanoa is a small, high island north of Mana. *Matamanoa Island Resort* (☎ 660 511; fax 661 069) is on a point and a hill overlooking a beautiful beach. It boasted the second best occupancy rate of Mamanuca resorts, after Castaway, for 1995. There are concrete paths through the garden setting to the 20 thatched-roof bures. The layout is fairly tight but buildings are staggered to increase privacy. Each bure has a verandah and views to the beach (half facing sunrise, half sunset), ceilings decorated with tapa, and tea/coffee-making facilities. Prices are F$320 per bure for a maximum of four people. There are also eight air-con units without beach views for F$160 for doubles. Matamanoa does not cater for children under

10 and is best suited to couples who want a relaxing holiday.

The resort has a swimming pool and tennis courts which are shaded during the day and lit at night, and guests can trek up the hill behind the resort. Activities offered include a 'honeymoon island' picnic for F$70 a couple, island hopping for F$50 per person for a minimum of four people and trips to the nearby village of Tavua, which is famous for its pottery. Nonmotorised water sports are included in the price.

The dive operation based at the resort is Fiji Deep (☎ 662 266; fax 661 069). One dive costs F$65 or F$80 including equipment. A six-dive package is F$350 or F$295 if you have your own gear. Courses include F$65 for discover scuba and F$495 for open-water certification.

Getting There & Away

It is a 2½-hour boat trip by Island Express from Denarau Marina to Mana, followed by a shuttle to Matamanoa or Tokoriki for F$67/116 per person one way/return for adults.

Sunflower Airlines has a 15-minute flight from Nadi airport to Mana which connects with the 11 am boat shuttle to Matamanoa/Tokoriki for an extra F$47/94 per person one way/return. Alternatively, a 20-minute trip by Turtle Airways seaplane is F$116/232 per person one way/return. It flies to Matamanoa/Tokoriki direct but the return trip involves a boat to Mana and seaplane to the mainland. The helicopter trip takes the same time and costs F$143/286 per person one way/return from Nadi airport or Denarau.

TOKORIKI ISLAND

The small, hilly island of Tokoriki has a beautiful, long white-sand beach facing west. Its position near the northern end of the Mamanucas gives a special feeling of remoteness. The *Tokoriki Island Resort* (☎ 661 999; fax 665 295) opened in 1989 and used to have the same owner as Matamanoa. New owners took over in late 1995; their clientele is mostly families and couples, much of it repeat business. The 19 beach front bures, similar in design to those of Matamanoa, are F$320 and sleep up to four people. Three of the bures are slightly bigger and sleep up to five. On top of the hill is a cross in memory of the initial owner and developer, Australian Gordon Morris, who died in an accident while building the resort.

Tokoriki has a pleasant dining terrace area where lunch is served for F$9.50 to F$12.50 and dinner F$16.50 to F$22. There is a smorgasbord three nights a week, a lovo and meke once a week, and a special children's menu. A visit to the resort's 'honeymoon island' costs F$70 per couple including lunch. Activities include tennis, canoeing, sailing, reef fishing, snorkelling, a visit to Yanuya village (F$9/4.50 for adults/children) and island hopping (four people for F$50 each). All nonmotorised water sports are included in the rate. Diving is with Fiji Deep based at Matamanoa resort.

Getting There & Away

See Getting There & Away for Matamanoa. The Island Express catamaran and shuttle via Mana and Matamanoa is F$67/116 per person for one way/return. Tokoriki also accepts day trippers.

VOMO ISLAND

This wedge-shaped 90-hectare island rises to a magnificent high ridge and has lovely beaches, good snorkelling and diving. Its interesting shape is recognisable from a distance from boats on the way to the Yasawas from Nadi or Lautoka.

The exclusive *Sheraton Vomo Island* (☎ 667 955; fax 667 997 or Australia ☎ 1800 07 3535; New Zealand ☎ 0800 443535; UK ☎ 0800 353535; USA/Canada ☎ 800 325 3535) is an alternative to Denarau's black-sand beach. Maintaining mainland luxury standards and service on a remote island does have its difficulties, however. It has 30 very comfortable air-con villas, each with a spacious bathroom and spa, a mosquito-net-enclosed deck and a partitioned-off lounge. Prices vary with the time of year, but are in the range of F$1078/1250 for standard/

deluxe villas for singles or doubles, including breakfast and helicopter transfers. A maximum of three people can stay in each villa and there is a minimum stay of three nights.

Facilities include a pool, a nine-hole golf course and three venues for dining, depending on the weather. One couple is allowed to picnic on the beautiful 'honeymoon island' Vomolailai. Activities include day trips to other islands and diving through Dive Connections.

Getting There & Away
Most guests arrive by helicopter (F$585 return) and the resort does not accept day trippers.

TAVARUA ISLAND
This 12-hectare island is at the southern edge of the reef which encloses the Mamanucas. It is surrounded by beautiful white-sand beaches and has great surf nearby at Cloud Break and Restaurants. Waves are for experienced surfers only, as they're overhead to well overhead on good days. Cloudbreak, about 2.5 km offshore, has waves averaging two to three metres and the waves at Restaurants, about 400m paddling distance from the resort, average around two metres.

Tavarua Island Resort (☎ 723 513; fax 720 395) or Tavarua Island Tours, California, USA (☎ 805 686 4551; fax 805 683 6696), is run by Americans John Roseman and Rick Isbell. This resort has 12 double/twin bures and a restaurant/bar area overlooking the Restaurants break. The daily rate is F$200/331 for singles/twin, which includes meals, drinks and transfers. The simple but comfortable bures are elevated and spaced along the beach. They have an open-air shower behind a screen with a solar bag (plastic sack). There is one toilet block near the restaurant, which is a bit of a walk in the night from the more distant bures, and the resort runs on generator and solar power. The minimum stay is four days and bookings need to be made in advance. Groups can charter the whole island for around F$4045 per day.

Serious surfers are advised to bring three boards since they can easily be snapped by the powerful waves. A boat with a radio stays with surfers out at Cloud Break and, if necessary, any accident victims can be transferred quickly to the mainland by helicopter. Game fishing, windsurfing and diving can also be arranged. Depending on the group of guests, nonsurfers may feel a bit left out.

Getting There & Away
Tavarua organises pick ups from the Nadi area. Guests are driven to Uciwai landing and there's a half-hour boat ride to the island.

NAMOTU ISLAND
The gorgeous 1.5-hectare island of Namotu (Magic) Island looks more like a white sand bar. The *Namotu Island Resort* (☎/fax 720 439; email: fiji@maui.net) and a few trees compete for the higher land. Windsurfing champ Mike Waltze and his wife, Dannette, are part-owners/managers of this very intimate resort, which caters for a maximum of 18 people. The resort relies on wind and solar power. While ideally suited to surfers and windsurfers, it is also popular with divers, fishermen and honeymooners.

There are two dorm rooms with shared bathroom facilities, which take a maximum of four people in each, for F$111 per day per person. A deluxe bure is F$207/173/138 per person for doubles/triples/quads. It has a verandah with a great view of the ocean, and has its own toilet and bathing facilities which are covered, but outside. The showers are solar-bag type.

The 'Love shack' bure, F$173 for a double, is about half the size of the deluxe bures and has its own bathroom facilities. Additional bures were under construction at the time of writing. The hexagonal restaurant and bar building is circled by a verandah. Accommodation prices include three meals a day (varied cuisine) and unlimited surfing. Drinks from the bar are extra.

Surf breaks include Swimming Pool, which is good for beginners, Wilkes and Namotu. Use of kayaks and snorkelling gear is included in the price and surfboards can be hired for F$10 per hour. Windsurfers have to bring their own equipment. Trips across to nearby Tavarua are free and an island hop is F$10 return to Malololailai's Plantation and Musket Cove resorts. Diving is with Mamanuca Divers, which is based at Musket Cove Marina, Malololailai Island. There are seven dive sites in the area, including the Outer Reef, Supermarket and night diving at the Fish Store. Snorkelling trips can also be arranged.

Getting There & Away

Generally guests book and pay in advance, but Namotu does take 'walk ins'. They will arrange for a driver to pick up from Nadi airport or Nadi hotels. The cost of transport is included if you stay longer than three days, otherwise it costs F$30 for a taxi from the airport to Uciwai landing and F$20 per boat each way.

Yasawa Group

The Yasawa group is a chain of 20 ancient volcanic islands extending almost in a straight line for 90 km within the Great Sea Reef. The southern islands begin 40 km north-west of Viti Levu. Of the 17 islands in the group there are six main ones, four of which are large and elevated, with summits up to nearly 600m above sea level. The land is mostly hilly and rugged and the climate is relatively dry. The Yasawas' sun-drenched white-sand beaches, spectacular crystal-clear lagoons and rugged landscapes make them one of Fiji's main tourist destinations. Most people visit the islands on cruises as there are not many places to stay.

After the famous mutiny on the *Bounty* in 1789, Captain Bligh passed through the island group on his way to Timor. His longboat was chased by Fijian canoes.

The people of the Yasawa islands have their own dialect, known as Vuda. The traveller may notice that *cola* (pronounced 'thola') is sometimes used instead of *bula* ('cheers'), or *vina du riki* instead of *vinaka vakalevu* for 'thank you very much'.

The Yasawas are sparsely populated, with only about 5000 villagers. There are no banks, postal services or medical services. The up-market resorts have phones and some of the smaller resorts have radio phones for emergencies.

Activities

Hiking Bring hiking boots, as islands such as Wayasewa and Waya are great for trekking.

Kayaking Southern Sea Ventures (☎ 03 9670 72 52 Outdoor Travel, Australia) runs 10-day kayaking trips to the Yasawas. The trips, between July and October, last 10 days with eight days paddling for about three to four hours daily. The maximum is 10 people per group. Other activities include swimming, snorkelling, village visits and camping overnight. Prices are A$1395 (about

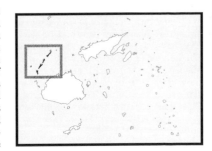

F$1520) including meals, two-person fibreglass kayaks, camping and safety equipment.

Diving The Yasawas have lots of spectacular reefs with brilliant corals, walls, underwater caves and many unexplored areas. Westside Watersports has a dive shop on Tavewa Island which caters for cruise passengers as well as the backpacker resorts. Diving costs F$66/88 for a one-tank/two-tank dive, F$110 for an introductory dive and F$55 for repeat introductory dives. There is also a diving operation run by locals at Dive Trek, on Wayasewa Island. The up-market resorts of Yasawa Island Lodge and Turtle Island offer diving for their guests, as do the cruise boats.

Dangers & Annoyances

By small boat the trip to the Yasawas is quite long and passes across a fairly exposed stretch of water, and weather conditions can quickly change. In the past passengers have been stranded adrift due to engine failure, and only rescued hours later. See below for trips in small boats.

Accommodation

Camping is possible at Dive Trek Wayasewa, Yalobi on Waya, and at Coralview and David's Place on Tavewa. In addition, other

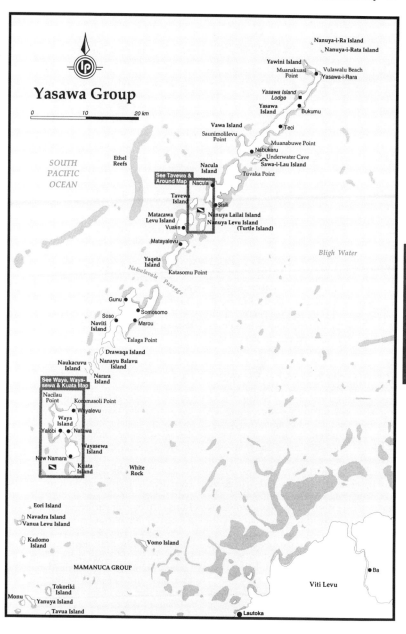

budget places are Octopus Club on Waya and Otto & Fanny's on Tavewa. Most places have a minimum stay and ask for payment up front. It is difficult to swap between islands as transport is limited. Self-catering is possible at Otto & Fanny's. On Waya and Wayasewa you will probably have more contact with village culture than on Tavewa. The Yasawas also have two luxury resorts: Turtle Island and Yasawa Island Lodge.

Getting There & Away
The up-market resorts have charter plane services for guests, while most visitors to the budget resorts travel by small boat. Unfortunately there is no really cheap and easy way to hop from island to island in the Yasawas unless you have your own yacht or sea kayak!

Small Boat Check if boats have marine radios for communication at sea and if there are sufficient lifejackets on board. Depending on the weather and your state of mind, the trip can be a fun adventure or uncomfortable, frightening and vomit-inducing! Exposure to rain or too much sun may be a problem if the boat doesn't have a roof.

Cruise/Transfers As well as cruises (see below), Westside Watersports offers transfers between Lautoka and the budget Yasawa resorts. It has a trip to Tavewa departing at 9 am on Tuesday and returning on Wednesday, for F$44 per person one way – a good idea if the weather looks rough and you don't want to brave the small boat transfers. For resorts in the Waya/Wayasewa area it will pick up and drop off at Dive Trek, if there are four or more passengers, for F$33 per person one way. The Westside Watersports office is at Shop No 1, Wharf Rd, Lautoka.

Cruises Cruising is a good way to see the beautiful Yasawas if you can afford it. There are a number of options:

Westside Watersports This company (☎/fax 661 462) has a three-day, two-night Seafari Dive Cruise which is a good alterna-

tive to the up-market cruises. This isn't a luxury cruise, as the MV *Tausala* is a cargo boat converted into a cruiser, but it's comfortable enough with a friendly and busy crew. The two nights are spent camping beside the beach in tents at Kuata and Tavewa islands. You will attend a *yaqona* ceremony and *meke* performance at Waya Island, a traditional *lovo* dinner, a barbecue, visit the Blue Lagoon and stop at Drawaqa Island. At all beach stops you can swim and enjoy free snorkelling.

Prices are F$395 (F$197.50 per night) per person for twin-share tent, F$198 for children 12 to 16 years old, and if you want the luxury of one tent for yourself it costs F$593. Prices include tents, bedding, morning teas and all meals. Drinks are extra, but prices are reasonable. The cruise is accompanied by the dive boat *Absolute* and Westside Watersports now has a dive shop on Tavewa Island. Cruises depart from Lautoka wharf.

Captain Cook Cruises This company (☎ 701 823; fax 702 045) has an office at 15 Narewa Rd, Nadi, and also one Australia (☎ 1800 804 843) and in New Zealand (☎ 0800 446 389). It offers several cruises on board the MV *Reef Escape*: a three-night Mamanuca and southern Yasawa cruise, a four-night Yasawa cruise and seven-night combination cruise. The huge 68m-long boat has a swimming pool, bars, lounges, a conference room and accommodation on three decks, including cabins with bunk beds, staterooms and deluxe staterooms. All rooms have air-con.

Cabin accommodation prices begin at F$385/257/205 per night for singles/twin/triples for the seven-night trip or F$428/570/684 for the three-night trip. Add about 17% for singles or doubles in staterooms and 23% for the deluxe staterooms. Children sharing with adults cost 10% if under three or F$70 per night if under 15. Cruises depart from Denarau Marina and also pick up Mamanuca resort guests at Likuliku Harbour, Malolo Island.

Captain Cook Cruises also has three-day, two-night cruises of the Mamanucas and

ROBIN JONES

ROBYN JONES

ROBYN JONES

ROBYN JONES

| A | B |
| C | D |

Kadavu
A: Making pandanus mats
B: Fisherman

C: Village church
D: Kadavu beach

ROBYN JONES

ROBYN JONES

JENNIFER BROOKS

LEONARDO PINHEIRO

A	
C	B
	D

Ovalau

A: Tuna cannery, Levuka
B: Marist Convent School, Levuka

C: Sacred Heart Church, Levuka
D: Provincial Bure, Nasora

southern Yasawas on board the *Ra Marama* tall sailing ship. You stop over at Beachcomber for use of the resort's water-sport facilities, visit villages and camp overnight. Prices are F$450 per person, including meals. It might be possible to arrange a discount.

Blue Lagoon Cruises This company (☎ 661 662; fax 664 098), with its six motor yachts company dominates the luxury cruise market. It has four-day, three-night cruises to the Yasawas (a club cruise, popular cruise and luxury cruise) and a seven-day, six-night Mamanuca and Yasawa cruise. Prices begin at F$469/235/196 per person per night for singles/twin/triples for cabin accommodation on the three-night popular cruise on a 39m, 20-cabin yacht. Children under two pay 11% and those under 16 years sharing with an adult are charged F$568 per night. Club cruises on the 50m, 33-cabin yachts are about 25% more expensive, and luxury cruises aboard the 56m *Mystique Princess* are at least 50% more. Accommodation has air-con and ensuites, and the boats have saloon and sundeck areas. Transfers, cruise activities and food are included but drinks, snorkel and other equipment hire is extra.

KUATA ISLAND

Kuata Island is a small island which has interesting caves and volcanic rock formations. There are coral cliffs on the southern end and great snorkelling. Seafari Dive Cruises camps here overnight. Dive Trek, Wayasewa, is just to the north.

WAYASEWA ISLAND

Also known as Wayalailai (little Waya), Wayasewa is in the Southern Yasawas, about 40 km north-west of Lautoka. It has good beaches and coral reefs offshore. After a rock slide from the cliff damaged some of the buildings, the Fijian Government declared Namara village unsafe and had it moved to its present location in 1975. Some of the villagers remained in old Namara village, and this beautiful overhanging cliff is the backdrop for the budget resort at its base.

The **New Namara** (Naboro village) site is also spectacular, with a large flat area between two beaches and high grassy hills to the south which look theatrical in the afternoon light. Villagers welcome tourist groups and present mekes and host *kava* ceremonies. Many of the photos in Glen Craig's photography book *Children of the Sun* were taken on Wayasewa and Waya islands.

Dive Trek Wayasewa (☎ 669 715), PO Box 6353, Lautoka, is owned and operated by the villagers of Wayasewa. The dorm accommodation is very basic and is crammed into the old schoolhouse which is

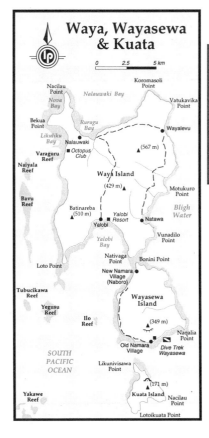

YASAWA GROUP

partitioned into 13 rooms. A twin dorm is F$35 per person including meals. These rooms share separate men's and women's cold-water showers and flush toilets. The water supply can be restricted.

There are six simple bures overlooking the beach, each with its own toilet and shower facilities. At F$90 per couple they are relatively expensive for what they are. One is used as a two-room dorm (four people per room) for F$50 per person including meals. Mosquito nets are provided. Drinks and snacks can be bought at reasonable prices and the evenings can be fun. A generator powers the refrigerator and lighting and there is a radio telephone for emergencies.

Swimming at low tide is a problem. Snorkelling is OK off the beach but gear (F$3 hire) is limited. Trips to Kuata beach/reef are F$4 to F$8. Diving is very good but equipment is basic. It costs F$75/110 for a one/two-tank dive including equipment. A resort course is F$100 and an open-water course is F$400. Guided hikes are taken around the island. The trek to the top of the cliff passes through high grass and trees, and over sharp rocks. From the hilltop you have excellent views of the reefs, neighbouring islands and all over the Yasawa group.

Other activities include fishing (F$4), volleyball, village visits and the inescapable kava ceremony. There are no boat trips or guided treks on Sunday, to respect the Fijian day of rest.

Getting There & Away

Transport to the island is by small boat (about 1½ to two hours), departing from Lautoka's Neisau Marina daily except Sunday. It costs F$40 per person each way. The boat picks up and drops off at Lautoka and Nadi hotels. The minimum stay is three days.

WAYA ISLAND

Waya has rugged hills and beautiful beaches and lagoons. There are four villages, a nursing station and a boarding school on the island. It is easy to walk around Waya and

hike to the top of Yalobi Hills, from where you can see the entire chain of the Yasawa islands.

Places to Stay & Eat

Octopus Resort (☎ 666 337 or 700 600; fax 666 210) is a tiny budget resort with a lovely beach, a good reef for snorkelling and a secluded atmosphere. It is a good alternative to the busier budget places. There is no electricity and facilities are simple but comfortable. It has only three bures, each with their own shower and toilet. Rates, including breakfast and dinner, are F$57/77 for singles/doubles or F$49 for twin share. Sharing a bure with a maximum of four people costs F$29 per person. Children under three are free.

Activities include island hopping, picnic or fishing trips for F$15 per person, a hiking tour for F$10, volleyball or simply hammock lounging. Diving can be arranged through Dive Trek. The use of snorkelling gear, canoes and windsurfers are all included in the price.

Yalobi (☎ 660 566 at the Cathay Hotel, Lautoka, or 703 922, Nadi), PO Box 1163, Lautoka, is located on a nice white-sand beach in a protected bay which looks across to Namara. Adi Sayaba offers simple accommodation for F$25 per person in a dorm, or F$30 per person in a double room. Camping is F$6 per tent. Three meals are provided for F$10 per person per day. Activities include snorkelling, volleyball and hiking to Eagle Peak. A trip to a nearby island is F$80 for five or six people; while island hopping (maximum of six people), including a visit to Sawa-i-Lau caves at the northern end of the Yasawas, costs F$400 for the boat.

Adi's cousin, Semi also runs a backpacker's resort, *Lovoni Beach Resort* (☎ 701 454 after hours), on another small beach on Waya. The price of dorm accommodation is F$16.50/27.50 per person without/with meals. There is one double bure for F$35/75 for singles/double including three meals. Activities available include snorkelling (F$6.60 per day), reef fishing trips (F$5.50), deep-sea fishing (F$22 per hour) and four-island sightseeing (F$22 including lunch).

Getting There & Away

Each resort has its own boat transport to the island; the trip takes about two hours. Octopus picks up its guests from Neisau Marina, Lautoka, and the boat trip costs F$66 return. Yalobi's boat transfers depart from Fisheries Wharf, Lautoka, and are F$35/70 per person one way/return. Transfers to Lovoni Beach Resort are also F$35/70 including pick up from Nadi/Lautoka hotels.

TAVEWA ISLAND

Tavewa, a small low island with nice beaches, is easy to walk around. The island is freehold land and there is no village and no chief, just three budget resorts and a dive operation. It can sometimes get overcrowded at the backpacker resorts. It's only a short walk between them, so if you are unhappy, check out the competition. Ideally, pay up front for only your one-way transfer. Although swimming and snorkelling here are excellent, there can sometimes be stingers, but they are more annoying than painful.

Places to Stay & Eat

Coralview Resort (☎ 662 648 or ☎ 660 566 at the Cathay Hotel, Lautoka), PO Box 3764, Lautoka, has spacious grounds, a coral and sand beach and a good atmosphere. There is very good coral about 30m from the beach. Previously known as Uncle Robert's Place, it is now run by Don & Alumita Bruce. The flat grounds are good for up to 50 campers with own tents, at F$16 per person including three meals. The four double bures and five dorm bures sleep from three to eight people. Rats and mice may visit your bure. The thatched bure accommodation is tight and each has concrete floors and mosquito nets. A dorm bed is F$25 or a double is F$55, including meals. For stays of over three weeks a discount can be negotiated. There is a shared facilities block with flush toilets. Shower water is from the well and rainwater is used for drinking. Near the beach there is a kitchen and dining hut with soft drinks for

F$1 and beer for F$2. There is also a small shop which stocks things such as tinned and frozen foods and toilet paper. A generator powers the restaurant and freezers.

Prices include one free activity per day, including snorkelling (F$2.50 equipment hire per day), fishing ($5 equipment hire per day), volleyball, a lovo night, kava and nightly music.

A trip to Malakati village on Nacula Island is F$12 per person, and trips to Sawa-i-Lau caves are F$20 per person. There are also beach trips across to Blue Lagoon Island about 10 minutes away. It is a 20-minute

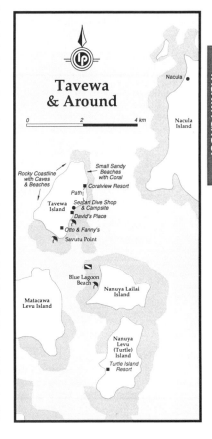

Tavewa & Around

0   2   4 km

Nacula

Nacula Island

Rocky Coastline with Caves & Beaches

Small Sandy Beaches with Coral

Coralview Resort

Path

Tavewa Island

Sealani Dive Shop & Campsite

David's Place

Otto & Fanny's

Savutu Point

Blue Lagoon Beach

Nanuya Lailai Island

Matacawa Levu Island

Nanuya Levu (Turtle) Island

Turtle Island Resort

YASAWA GROUP

walk along the beach to the lovely Savutu Point.

David's Place (☎/fax 721 820 or ☎ 663 939 island), run by David Doughty, has a friendly atmosphere. Rates are F$19.80 for campers, F$30.25 for a dorm bed and F$66 for a double bure. The traditional-style bures have mosquito nets and concrete floors which are occasionally visited by a few crabs and the odd mouse.

You will probably have to queue for the two showers and two WCs. There is no shop and no cooking; all prices include three meals a day with lovo and barbecue nights. There is usually plenty of food provided, with a mixture of fish, meat and vegetables. People gather in the dining room for music and dancing every night, along with a grog session.

Free activities include snorkelling at nearby islands, volleyball, hiking and fishing. Canoes and snorkelling gear can be hired. Trips to Sawa-i-Lau caves and a Naisisili village visit cost F$14 per person for a group of eight to 10 people.

Just inland from Savutu Point is *Otto & Fanny Doughty's* (☎ 668 714, son Harry in Lautoka). There are three self-contained units which are well positioned in the large grounds. The large bure is F$30 per person or F$20 each if used as a dorm for up to six people. It is private and very spacious, with solar lighting, and is close to the beach. The double unit costs F$45. All units have a kitchen, dining table and lounge chairs. Fanny can also provide meals for F$30 per day.

There is no shop on the island so bring your own food and drinks. The generator provides electricity from 6 to 10 pm. While the beautiful beach at Savutu Point is seemingly remote, avoid the temptation to skinny dip as Fanny does not appreciate the local kids being corrupted! For reservations write to PO Box 1349, Lautoka.

Fanny's afternoon tea, from 3 pm to about 4.30 pm, is very popular with backpackers from the other resorts. Three pieces of cake (chocolate or banana) with coffee, tea or juice is just F$2.

Getting There & Away
Tavewa is a 2½ to three-hour trip by small speedboat from Lautoka. Each resort has its own boat transport to the island and will charge more if you are going to another resort. The return trip to Coralview Resort costs F$80, departing from the Cathay Hotel, Lautoka, at 8 am on Tuesday and Saturday, and 2 pm on Wednesday, and returning from the island on Monday, Wednesday and Friday mornings. David's Place boats leave Lautoka for the island on Tuesday, Thursday and Saturday at 8.30 am and return on Monday, Wednesday and Friday at 11.30 am. Fares for guests are F$40/80 one way/return. Otto and Fanny charge F$80 for the return boat ride from Lautoka; with the other resort boats, it's F$50 one way.

SAWA-I-LAU ISLAND
Sawa-i-Lau is the odd limestone island in the group of high volcanic islands. As limestone forms only underwater, the island is thought to have been uplifted a few hundred metres. It has a great dome-shaped cave which extends to a height of about 15m above the water surface. You can swim through the pool and other caves lead off it. The colourful limestone walls have carvings, paintings and inscriptions of unknown meaning. Similar inscriptions also occur on Vanua Levu in the hills near Vuinadi village, Natewa Bay and near Dakuniba village on the Cakaudrove Peninsula, as well as at Naqilai on north-west Taveuni.

Getting There & Away
Many of the Yasawa backpacker resorts offer trips to the caves and many of the cruise ships call here.

NANUYA LEVU ISLAND
Nanuya Levu (Turtle) Island is a 200 hectare, privately owned island about 2.25 km long and about 900m wide. It has protected sandy beaches on the blue lagoon side and rugged volcanic cliffs and surf on the exposed

YASAWA GROUP

eastern side. The 1980 film *The Blue Lagoon*, starring Brooke Shields, was filmed entirely on Turtle Island, as was the original 1949 version starring Jean Simmons. A UK TV series *Swiss Family Robinson* is also to be shot on adjacent **Nanuya Lailai**, where Blue Lagoon Cruises stop overnight for use of the beach and for snorkelling.

Turtle Island Resort (☎ 722 921, 663 889; fax 720 007) claims to be the 'South Pacific's most beautiful and exclusive paradise'. The owner is American Richard Evanson, who after making his fortune in cable television bought the island in 1972 as his own personal hideaway. The resort is especially popular with Americans. No singles, kids or gays are allowed – guests are limited to English-speaking, straight couples only, 'who can communicate and enjoy each other's company and humour'! There are only 14 bures, each with two rooms, spaced along the western beach. There is a six-night minimum stay and prices are around F$640 per night for doubles. All food, drinks and activities are included in the price, so that guests can forget about the need for money. Guests can partake in deep-sea fishing, sailing, windsurfing, canoeing, snorkelling, diving, horse riding and village trips. The island has 14 private beaches for use by guests.

Getting There & Away
Guests are transferred to Turtle Island Resort by a chartered Turtle Airways seaplane, a 30-minute flight from Nadi.

YASAWA ISLAND
Yasawa is the northernmost of the Yasawa islands. It has four small villages and an up-market resort. *Yasawa Island Lodge* (☎ 663 364; fax 665 044) is a 16-bure luxury resort on a gorgeous beach. New management took over in early 1996. The spacious bures are split level with sundecks, separate living and bedroom areas, king-size beds, double showers, separate dressing rooms, ceiling fans and air-con. The rate is F$465/660 for singles/doubles, including all à la carte meals (drinks extra) and activities, except for diving and game fishing. Lobster omelettes are offered for breakfast. The resort has its own dive shop and pastimes include 4WD trips, picnics on deserted beaches, snorkelling, tennis, croquet, bushwalking, safari drives and use of dinghies, sailboards and mountain bikes. The bar/dining area is in a large octagonal bure which opens onto verandahs. There is no minimum stay.

Getting There & Away
Transfers to the resort's airstrip are by Sunflower Airlines charter. The flight from Nadi takes 30 minutes and costs F$150 per person each way.

Ovalau & the Lomaiviti Group

To the east of Viti Levu is the Lomaiviti group, also known as the central group. It has seven principal islands and many smaller ones. Ovalau, one of the closest to the east coast of Viti Levu, is also one of the most important – its main town, Levuka, was Fiji's earliest European settlement and the first capital. To the south of Ovalau are the islands of Motoriki, Caqelai and Leluvia. The tiny coral islands of Leluvia and Caqelai both have budget accommodation, good snorkelling and lovely beaches. Hawksbill turtles lay their eggs on these beaches.

Gau is the southernmost and the largest island of the group. Wedge-shaped Koro rises abruptly from deep water. Ferries stop here between Viti Levu, Vanua Levu and Taveuni. Both Koro and Gau have airstrips. Lying to the east are Nairai and Batiki, which are lower than their neighbouring islands and are surrounded by large coral reefs. Makogai is north-east of Levuka; formerly a leper colony for the south-west Pacific, it now has a Department of Agriculture research station. Wakaya is also to the north-east of Levuka and used to be a private plantation. It now has an exclusive resort and property development.

The climate of these islands is sunnier and drier than that of the east coast of Viti Levu.

Ovalau

Ovalau's volcanic landscape is beautiful and the island is definitely worth a visit for the historic town of Levuka. You can also hike to the extinct caldera at Ovalau's centre, the site of Lovoni village. This large volcanic crater has vents on the north and eastern sides, and is broken to the south-west by a river valley. The land surface of the whole island is rugged, with sharp peaks. The Bureta airstrip and Buresala ferry landing are on the western side of Ovalau, while Levuka

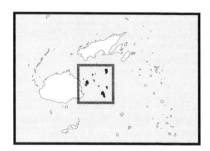

is on the eastern coast. A gravel road winds around the perimeter of the island and is quite steep in the northern section. Another road follows the Bureta River inland to Lovoni village.

There is plenty of budget accommodation in Levuka, and camping at Rukuruku and Ovalau Holiday Resort. For most people a couple of days is plenty of time to explore Levuka. Add another day for hiking to Lovoni. If you want beaches, consider the offshore islands.

LEVUKA

Levuka is the administrative, educational and agricultural centre for the Lomaiviti group and other parts of the Eastern Division. About 3000 people live in or near the town. Levuka is one of Fiji's official entry ports. Its harbour is protected by the offshore Lekaleka Reef.

As early as 1806 sandalwood traders stopped at Levuka for supplies of water and food. Traders began settling in Levuka in the 1830s, some marrying Fijians. With the protection of the chief of Levuka they built schooners and traded throughout Fiji for *bêche-de-mer*, turtle shell and coconut oil. Lovoni villagers from the centre of Ovalau sometimes raided the settlement. The town had its heyday in the mid to late 19th century.

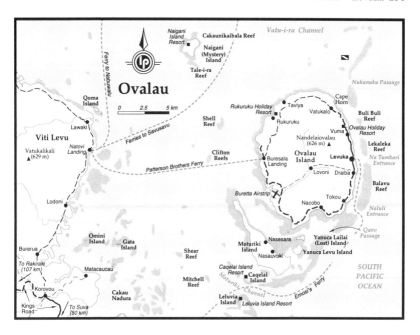

By the 1850s it had become increasingly rowdy, with a reputation for wild drunkenness and violence.

In the 1870s a flood of planters and other settlers came to Fiji, and the booming town had a population of about 3000 Europeans. Incredibly, tiny Levuka once had 52 hotels on Beach St and was the wild, lawless centre of the blackbirding trade and a popular port for sailors, whalers and traders. In 1888 and 1905, hurricanes swept away the buildings at the north end of the town.

Until 1825 the coastal villagers were allied to the chiefs of Verata (a village of Viti Levu's Rewa Delta), after which they changed allegiance to the chief of Bau (an island off the south-east coast of Viti Levu). The powerful Ratu Cakobau of Bau attempted unsuccessfully to form a national government in 1871, and in 1874 ceded Fiji to Great Britain. Fiji thus became a British colony and Levuka was proclaimed its capital. For more information, see the History section in the Facts about the Country chapter.

Due to limited space, Levuka could not develop as a capital and the government was officially moved to Suva in 1882. Business continued for some years but, at the turn of the century, trade shifted to Suva and, with copra markets plummeting, the town hit a serious decline in the 1930s. These days the local economy depends largely on fish packing at the Pacific Fishing Company (PAFCO) with some input from tourism.

Many surprisingly intact, colourful old buildings date back to Levuka's boom period. The PAFCO facility at the southern end contrasts with the rest of the town, which seems to have been frozen in time. It is now a slow-paced, picturesque place with buildings reminiscent of a Wild West tumbleweed town. The Department of Town & Country Planning designated Levuka a historic town in 1989 and the government subsidises paint if owners use heritage colours.

The population is mainly of mixed Fijian and European descent. Many descendants of traders – including those of American David Whippy, a beachcomber who was later appointed US vice-consul by Commodore Wilkes – live in the town.

Orientation & Information

Levuka is squeezed between the mountains and the water's edge. The Beach St oceanfront promenade is lined on its western side with historic shopfronts. This main street continues as a ring road around the island.

Useful sources of information are the Community Centre at the Morris Hedstrom building, the Whale's Tale Restaurant and Cafe Levuka.

Westpac and the National Bank of Fiji, both at the southern end of Beach St, will change travellers' cheques. The post office is open from 8 am to 1 pm and 2 to 4 pm Monday to Friday, and from 8 am to 10.30 am on Saturday. It is near Queens Wharf at the southern end of Beach St. There is a cardphone outside.

Cafe Levuka has a laundry service.

Travel Agencies Air Fiji Travel Centre (☎ 811 188; fax 813 819) is at Beach St, opposite the Community Centre. Patterson Brothers Shipping (☎ 440 125) is near the market on Beach St; see Getting There & Away for information on the Viti Levu-Ovalau bus and ferry service.

Ovalau Tours & Transport Limited (☎ 440 611; fax 440 405) Beach St, Levuka, near the Whale's Tale, is run by an American couple, Jennifer and Michael Brook. They offer day trips and overnight packages in Levuka; see Getting There & Away. Through their community tourism scheme, the Brooks are trying to involve the locals in tourism, and some of the money raised helps fund restoration of historic homes. The 'tea and *talanoa*' (have a chat) series takes you inside the homes of local residents such as Rosie Morris, Bubu Kara and Aunty Ella Bryson. It's a great way to get a local perspective. Most of their business is prearranged.

Niumaia's Tourist Information Centre (☎ 440 356) is a travel agency aimed at budget travellers and has a variety of organised tours around Ovalau; see Activities.

Medical & Emergency Services Levuka Hospital (☎ 440 105) is in Beach St. For an Ambulance, call ☎ 440 105; for police, call ☎ 440 222

Walking Tour

Start at the area known as Nasova, the location of the signing of the Deed of Cession in 1874. The **Cession Site**, surrounded by a picket fence, has three large stones with plaques commemorating the signing of the deed. Prince Charles once stayed in the **Provincial Bure** (1970), and **Nasova House** (1869) is thought to be part of the original colonial governors' complex. The weatherboard structure, with its top-hinged windows propped open, is typical of the domestic colonial style.

PAFCO, the Pacific Fishing Company, employs about 1000 people, roughly 30% of Ovalau's working population. It processes and cans about 15,000 metric tonnes of tuna (skipjack, yellow fin and albacore) per year from Fiji and other Pacific waters, including the Solomon Islands and Kiribati. Tuna is packed under about 30 different brandnames.

The factory was established in 1964 to boost Levuka's dying economy, and set up as a joint venture between two Japanese companies and the Fijian government. Originally it was a transhipment depot to service Taiwanese, Japanese and Korean long-line fishing vessels operating around the western Pacific. In 1987 the Fijian government bought out its partners, increasing its share holding to 98%, with 2% owned by Ovalau citizens. In 1989 Pacific Packaging Limited, a joint-venture can-making plant, was built next to the cannery. Further expansions took place in 1992, including a wharf development, a new office complex and freezer storage. The F$17 million extension was

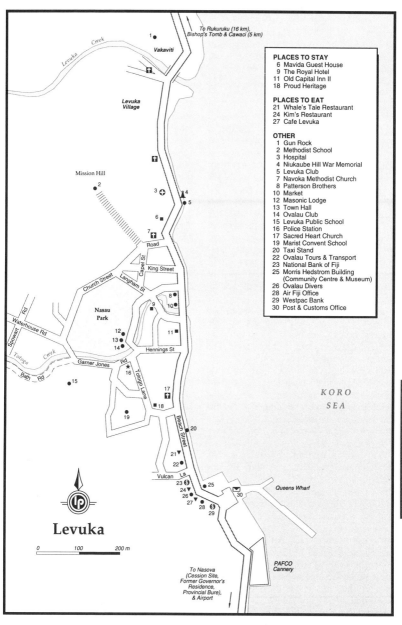

PLACES TO STAY
6 Mavida Guest House
9 The Royal Hotel
11 Old Capital Inn II
18 Proud Heritage

PLACES TO EAT
21 Whale's Tale Restaurant
24 Kim's Restaurant
27 Cafe Levuka

OTHER
1 Gun Rock
2 Methodist School
3 Hospital
4 Niukaube Hill War Memorial
5 Levuka Club
7 Navoka Methodist Church
8 Patterson Brothers
10 Market
12 Masonic Lodge
13 Town Hall
14 Ovalau Club
15 Levuka Public School
16 Police Station
17 Sacred Heart Church
19 Marist Convent School
20 Taxi Stand
22 Ovalau Tours & Transport
23 National Bank of Fiji
25 Morris Hedstrom Building
   (Community Centre & Museum)
26 Ovalau Divers
28 Air Fiji Office
29 Westpac Bank
30 Post & Customs Office

Levuka

LOMAIVITI GROUP

built with Australian financial and technical support. Canned fish exports are Fiji's largest earner after sugar, tourism and gold. Levuka's economy has always been insecure and rumours circulate about the plant being moved to Suva.

Walk north along **Beach St**. Levuka's shop architecture is typified by high facade parapets and verandahs linked together to form walkways. The streetscape dates from the late 19th and early 20th centuries. Most of the buildings are of simple timber construction. The former **Morris Hedstrom** trading store (1868) has retained its facade with massive graphics, but now houses the Levuka Community Centre, library, museum, YWCA and a school for the handicapped. The **museum** and **library** have a collection of old artefacts, clubs and adornments as well as traders' and settlers' carpentry tools, demijohns and other bottles, guns, photos, a sitar and a WWI gas mask. It also has a shell collection. The opening hours are from 9 am to 5 pm.

Levuka has retained many of its original religious and community buildings. Visit the **Sacred Heart Church** (1858) on the main street and then explore the backstreets. The **Marist Convent School** (1891) was established by the Marists (Congregation of Mary) who arrived from France and Australia. The large symmetrical form of the coral stone and timber building is set against the backdrop of mountains. Today it is a primary school for students from all over Fiji.

The **police station** (1920) is a little weatherboard building, still used for this purpose today. Across the creek you'll find the timber, colonial-style **Ovalau Club** (1904) Fiji's first private club. The bartender will show you a letter written by Count Felix von Luckner in 1917 during WWI, on Katafaga, northern Lau. Before his capture on nearby Wakaya, the German cruised the waters sinking Allied ships. During the war most of the German traders were forced to give up their businesses. Next door is the **town hall** (1898), also known as the Queen Victoria Memorial Hall. The building is typical of the British colonial style of the time. The **Masonic Lodge** (1924) is built in a classic revival style, Roman with Doric columns. It was the South Pacific's first masonic lodge.

Return across the creek and follow Garner Jones Rd and the Totoga Creek up to the **Levuka Public School** (1881). The building has been stripped of its once ornate trimmings. Many of Fiji's prominent citizens were educated here. It was Fiji's first formal school, with European-style education. If you continue up the steps you will come to a popular resting spot where you can pause and watch the passers-by. Walk along Church St past the Nasau Park. Many old colonial houses were built on the hillsides. If you are reasonably fit, the **199 Steps of Mission Hill** are worth climbing for the fantastic view.

The simple Gothic-style **Navoka Methodist Church** (1860s) is one of the oldest churches in Fiji. It is constructed of coral and stone. **The Royal Hotel** (1860s) is the lone survivor of the numerous pubs of the era. The timber-framed structure was rebuilt in 1903.

Niukaube Hill, on a point near the water, was the former location of Ratu Seru Cakobau's supreme court and parliament house. It now has a war memorial to local European descendants who fought and died in WWI and WWII.

Continue north to **Levuka village**. With the present chief's permission you can climb **Gun Rock**. In 1849 Commodore Wilkes, of the US exploring expedition, pounded this with his ship's canons to impress the Tui Levuka. From here you have a great view of the township of Levuka.

Walk or take a taxi the 5 km to Cawaci. The **Bishop's Tomb** (1922) is on a point, looking out to sea. The tiny domed structure has Gothic and Italianate influences. Fiji's first and second Roman Catholic bishops are entombed here. Another interesting building, **St John's College** (1894), is in view across the road. It was here that Fijian chiefs' sons were educated in English. The style is Gothic revival, and it is built of limestone and coral.

Activities

Cycling Cycling is a good way to get around Levuka. The road to the south is fairly flat and north is OK until about Vatukalo, after which it gets very hilly. Mountain bikes are available for hire at F\$3/6/10 per hour/half day/full day. Enquire at the Whale's Tale or with Greg at the YWCA near the Museum from 9 am to 4 pm.

Diving & Snorkelling Diving here is on the reefs to the north-east of Ovalau, where there are many unexplored sites. At Trevally Reef you are likely to see groupers and sea turtles. Ovalau Divers (☎ 440 028; fax 440 066) started in 1995 and has an office above Cafe Levuka opposite the Community Centre. Prices are F\$55/75 for one/two-tank dives including gear and boat transportation. Discover Scuba courses are F\$75 and PADI Open Water certification is \$F300 (five days). Reef snorkelling trips are F\$15 to F\$25.

Organised Tours

One of the highlights of Ovalau is hiking to Lovoni village, uphill through rainforest and into the crater of the extinct volcano in the centre of the island. There you can visit the village, have a Fijian lunch and swim in the river pools. Guides will tell you about local customs, the history of the Lovoni people and about the cultural, medicinal and traditional uses of plants. There are treks every day except Sunday, which is a day of rest for the village. Hikes are run by two competitors, Epi and Niumaia, both from Lovoni village.

Epi's tours are popular and recommended. They cost F\$15 including lunch and transport. Contact Epi at the Whale's Tale (☎ 440 235) or Cafe Levuka (☎ 440 028).

Niumaia has a variety of trips: two to four-hour treks to Lovoni from either Levuka, Draiba or Visoto, or from Lovoni to Rukuruku, are F\$15.50 per person, for a minimum of two people; a two-hour trek to Gun Rock costs F\$6.50. Prices include transport to and from Levuka, a guide and lunch. A hike to Lovoni's Korolevu Hill Fort involves a four-hour trek and costs F\$20.50 per person.

Niumaia can also arrange bamboo-rafting tours. Four-hour van tours around the island, for a minimum of four people, cost F\$20 per person. Levuka to Lovoni (a 45-minute drive) costs F\$15 per person return, and a two-hour tour of Levuka and Cawaci historic sites costs F\$6.50 per person. His travel agency is Niumaia's Tourist Information Centre (☎ 440 356) at the back of the museum and library within the Morris Hedstrom Building/Levuka Community Centre, or write to PO Box 82, Levuka.

Michael and Jennifer Brook at Ovalau Tours & Transport Limited also offer day trips from Suva and Nadi, overnight packages and local tours; see the Getting There & Away section.

Places to Stay

Fiji's oldest hotel, *The Royal Hotel* (☎ 440 024; fax 440 174) is near the market, by the Totoga Creek. It oozes colonial atmosphere, even if it is getting a bit worn at the edges. It is run by the elderly Mrs Dorothy Ashley and has been in the family for generations. The old weatherboard building once had an open verandah with lace balustrading, but this has since been built in to increase the size of the rooms.

There is a licensed bar, a billiard room, a dining room with views of the garden, a guest lounge and video room. Only house guests are allowed in the bar. The video nights are very popular with TV-starved travellers. The staff can be a bit grumpy, but this perhaps adds to the character.

The hotel has 15 fan-cooled comfortable rooms upstairs, each with a small ensuite with shower and toilet. Singles/doubles/triples cost F\$15.40/25.30/27.50, or F\$20.90 for twin share. The dormitory downstairs sleeps 11 people for F\$6.60 per person. There are also three weatherboard cottages of two, three and five rooms, each sharing a kitchen and bathroom. Singles/doubles/triples cost F\$15.40/20.90/27.50.

The *Mavida Gust House* (☎ 440 477), PO Box 91, Levuka, is at the northern end of

LOMAIVITI GROUP

Beach St near Niukaube Hill. Parts of the guesthouse date from the late 1860s. It is a pleasant place with lots of sitting areas and is actually two buildings joined by a covered space for parties and kava drinking. There is a dorm for four people which costs F$8 per person. Fan-cooled singles/doubles are F$10/20 or F$12/25 in the old house. The shared bathrooms have hot water. All prices include breakfast. Lunch and dinner can be ordered for F$5 per meal. Mavida is owned by Rosie Patterson and run by her niece Pasepa.

The *Proud Heritage* (☎ 440 035) on Convent Road was previously called the Old Capital Inn I. Run by Saroj and Annie since late 1995, it is a double storey building at the back of the Sacred Heart church. It has a sitting room and rooms upstairs with shared facilities. Prices are F$11/18 for singles/ doubles. The dorm (maximum three people) costs F$7. Breakfast of toast, bacon, sausage and juice is included. There is a restaurant downstairs; see Places to Eat.

The *Old Capital Inn II* (☎ 440 013, 440 057) charges F$8.80/18.80 for singles/ doubles without breakfast, or F$9.90/19.90 with breakfast. Dorm accommodation (maximum four people) costs F$6.60/ F$7.70 without/with breakfast. You have to walk through the breakfast room to get to the showers and toilets. It also has two self-contained cottages. One costs F$15 and the other, which sleeps three people, costs F$25. The rooms have mosquito nets and fans.

Ovalau Holiday Resort (☎ 440 329) PO Box 113, Levuka, is across the road from a small bay at **Lawaki Toki** past Vuma village, north of Levuka. It's about 3 km from Levuka (about a 50-minutes walk, around F$5 by taxi). The sandy beach is not very nice but the snorkelling is OK (bring your own equipment). It might be an option if you want an extra quiet place to stay. Munim Praan, who also owns the supermarket opposite Cafe Levuka, took over the place in 1996. Camping costs F$5. The price for a dorm bed is F$7.50. The dorm unit has six fan-cooled bedrooms with 19 beds; it also has two toilets and a shower, a central kitchen and a sitting area for a few people. There are no mosquito nets but coils are provided. There are five self-contained weatherboard units with two bedrooms and a sitting area. Singles/doubles/triples cost F$22/35/45, and for a maximum of six people, F$75. There is a small swimming pool and pool table and the Bula Beach restaurant/bar has meals for F$4.50 to F$6.50 for lunch or dinner.

Places to Eat

The best food in town can be had at the *Whale's Tale* (☎ 440 235), a small restaurant run by Australians Liza and Julia Ditrich. The fresh fruit juices are a must, and they also make thick shakes and iced chocolate with rich chocolate ice cream. The cooking is home style with fresh ingredients, with dishes such as vegetable/chicken/beef pies, vegetable stir fry and good desserts. The average cost of a main meal is $5.50, or $2.50 for dessert. The *Proud Heritage* restaurant serves lunch and dinner. Soups are F$2 to F$4, and mains from the mixed style menu are F$4 to F$8.

Cafe Levuka (☎ 440 028) opposite the Morris Hedstrom building has main meals from a mixed menu for F$4 to F$6. It also serves alcoholic drinks. *Kim's Restaurant* (☎ 440 059) has huge soups for F$2 to F$3.50 and large main dishes of chicken, beef or fish for F$4 to F$5. Across the road from Kim's, the *Patterson Gardens Take-away Stand* next to the Community Centre, has cheap snacks. It has outdoor seating near the water and a good view of Levuka, but you have to put up with the noise of the town's generator.

Self-Catering There is a *produce market* near the Totoga Creek and a *supermarket* near the Community Centre.

Entertainment

Levuka's wild days are long gone and the sleepy town doesn't offer much night-time entertainment. For a drink try the *Ovalau Club*, *Levuka Club* and *Cafe Levuka*.

Getting There & Away

Air Air Fiji has twice-daily Levuka/Suva flights from Nausori airport to Bureta airstrip on Ovalau (12 minutes) for F$35/70 one way/return or F$50 as an excursion fare. The Buresala airport is on south-western Ovalau, about one hour's drive by minibus (F$3 per person) or taxi (F$17) to/from Levuka.

Air Fiji, in conjunction with Ovalau Tours & Transport Limited, offers a F$149 day-trip package from Suva to Levuka which includes return flights from Nausori airport, ground transfers on Ovalau, morning tea, a guided walking tour of the historic town and lunch and afternoon tea. Children from two to 12 years cost F$114, or F$25 if under two. For locals a package to Levuka is F$99. These trips may be a good idea if you have limited time. They are available daily, except Sunday. Connections from Nadi are an additional F$108 return. To include an overnight stay at Mavida Guest House is an extra F$25.

Boat Patterson Brothers Shipping (see the Getting Around chapter) has a bus and ferry service from Suva to Levuka. From Suva the trip involves a 1½-hour bus trip to Natovi, one hour on the ferry across the Northern Bau Waters to Buresala Landing (western Ovalau), followed by another hour by bus to Levuka. The trip from Natovi Landing to Levuka costs F$17.60, or F$19.80 from

Suva. Cars and bicycles can be taken on the roll-on, roll-off ferry for an additional charge.

From Natovi there are ferry services to Nabouwalu and Savusavu on Vanua Levu as well as to Taveuni; see the Getting Around chapter.

Emosi's Shipping (☎ 313 366 Suva, 440 057/440 013 Levuka) has four services weekly by minibus from Suva to Bau Landing (Ovalau), and a small boat to Levuka via Leluvia Island. This trip costs F$18/39.60 one-way/return and can take up to five hours. See the Leluvia section for more information.

Getting Around

Levuka is easy to get around on foot. There is a taxi stand near the Whale's Tale restaurant. Carriers can also be hired from here. Minibuses or taxis to the airport depart from outside the Air Fiji office. Regular trucks depart for Lovoni and Rukuruku. Mountain bikes can be hired; see Activities earlier.

LOVONI

Lovoni village is nestled within a spectacular extinct volcanic crater, in the centre of Ovalau. The village has no accommodation for travellers at present but there are guided walks to visit it from Levuka. Along the way the guide will point out the medicinal plants

The Enslavement of the People of Lovoni

During the Bauan war against the Lovoni highlanders of Ovalau in 1870-71, Ratu Cakobau tried four times to penetrate his enemies' fort but his warriors were repeatedly defeated. Instead he decided to send a Methodist missionary to subdue the people. Lovoni had a dwarf priest who could reputedly foresee the future and he was the first to see the missionary approaching. Noticing a kind of brightness emanating from the missionary, the priest believed himself to have been rendered powerless. The missionary held up a book and read from the Bible in Bauan. He referred to the people of Lovoni as the lost sheep of Fiji and invited them to a reconciliation feast being organised by Cakobau on 29 June 1871. The warriors came down to Levuka and in good faith put aside their weapons. Once they started their meal, however, they were caught off guard, surrounded and captured.

Ratu Cakobau offered the prisoners to anyone who wanted to buy slaves, and his takings helped him to form a government. Families were usually separated and other Lovoni villagers were dispersed to places such as Kavala in Kadavu, Yavusania near Nadi, Lovoni-Ono in Lau and Wailevu in Vanua Levu. The dwarf priest and two Lovoni warriors were sold to an American circus. Many people were returned to Lovoni in 1894. ■

of the rainforest. The trek can be steep and muddy so good boots are essential. Of interest is the **chief's burial site** opposite the church and **Korolevu hill fortification** high on the crater rim, where villagers took refuge in times of war.

The people of Lovoni are extremely proud and are known as the strongest Fijian tribe because they were never defeated in war by Cakobau, except through trickery. Lovoni men can therefore wear hats in other villages, even in the chiefly village of Bau, which would normally be disrespectful.

Every 7 July there is a big celebration in the village to commemorate the date of the enslavement of the people of Lovoni. All religions gather together in the same church and the history is read. A translation of the plaque at Lovoni church reads as follows:

This is a memorial stone commemorating the hundred years since Reverend Frederick Langham DDE walked up to Korolevu (old hill fort), Lovoni, Ovalau and ended the war of 1871. We should fear and worship God because our grandfathers never surrendered to any tribe, they only surrendered to God's word. We should worship him because there is no other god in this world that is greater than him.

Getting There & Away

You can hike or truck in from Levuka accompanied by a local guide; see Organised Tours in the Levuka section. There is a truck from Levuka to Lovoni at 7 and 11 am and 5 pm Monday to Friday, returning at 6, 7 and 8 am and 3 pm. Saturday is a busy market day, so the truck travels between Levuka and Lovoni several times. There are no services on Sunday.

RUKURUKU

The village of Rukuruku is on a black volcanic sand beach about 17 km from Levuka, on north-western Ovalau with a view of Naigani Island. Here you will find complete solitude, and perhaps boredom! There is a small **waterfall** about 20 minutes walk up the valley from Rukuruku Holiday Resort. Naigani Island Resort will pick up guests from **Taviya** village about 1 km north-east of Rukuruku.

Place to Stay & Eat

Rukuruku Holiday Resort (☎ c/o 440 235 Whale's Tale, Levuka or ☎ 385 838 in Suva) PO Box 112, Levuka, was run down and the staff seemed surprised to receive visitors when we came around. A camp site is F$5.50 per person with toilets, showers and cooking facilities. The dormitory accommodation has an ensuite bathroom and costs F$8.80 per person including breakfast. The rather musty bungalow sleeps seven at F$16.50 per person including breakfast. A portable gas stove is available. A 'deluxe' bure, for a maximum of four people, is F$66 per night. There is also a dining room. Breakfast is F$3.30 to F$4 and main meals are F$6 to F$8. The shop in Rukuruku sells canned food but not much else.

A Rukuruku sandbank snorkelling tour involves a 15-minute boat ride from Rukuruku. It costs F$10 for a minimum of four people, including lunch. From Levuka the trip costs F$5 per person for a minimum of six people – bring your own snorkelling equipment.

Getting There & Away

The Rukuruku carrier (a large, red-framed truck with a green canopy) departs from Beach St, Levuka at 7.30 am, noon and 5 pm and returns from Rukuruku at 6 and 9 am and 3 pm, Monday to Saturday. The trip costs F$1.50 and takes about one hour. Hiring a van, which will carry up to 12 people and pick up and return at your leisure, will cost F$15 each way. The resort will pick up (20 minutes by boat) from Buresala Landing for $10 or cross to Naigani for F$50.

Other Lomaiviti Islands

YANUCA LAILAI ISLAND

Yanuca Lailai Island (Lost Island) is an uninhabited island close to Levuka and adjacent to Motoriki Island. The island has rudimentary accommodation, but when we visited no one was there and it does not seem to be a regular operation. Apparently people sometimes get stranded here. It has a hill with a short, golden-sand beach about 200m long, and the rest is rocky. It is too shallow to swim at low tide – bring your own snorkelling gear.

There are four very simple shed-type *bures* for F$8.50 per person. Facilities are one flush toilet, one pit toilet, one shower (pump type out in the open), one covered sitting area and a tiny kitchen. You can camp here for F$6 per person. A day trip with lunch costs F$20, three meals are F$8.50 and fishing trips F$5. Arrange trips with Levi if you can track him down at Levuka – try the Community Centre.

MOTURIKI ISLAND

Moturiki lies to the south-west of Ovalau in the Lomaiviti Group. It has a hilly topography and 10 villages, but no places for travellers to stay. Both Leluvia and Caqelai resorts will take guests to Niubasaga on Moturiki for Sunday church services.

CAQELAI ISLAND

Just south of Motoriki lies Caqelai – a gorgeous, unspoilt coral island. It is only a 10-minute walk around its beautiful white-sand beaches, which are fringed with palms and other large trees. If you are lucky you may see dolphins and baby turtles.

The island is owned by the Methodist Church of Motoriki, which runs the small budget *Caqelai Resort*. In contrast with Leluvia the average number of guests is 10, with a maximum of 20. Those who are after a secluded, relaxing, friendly atmosphere and don't mind roughing it will love it here. The staff are very friendly. Facilities are very basic: a pump-up shower with a hand bucket, and a nonflush toilet.

Camping costs F$16 per person including meals. There is spartan dormitory accommodation for up to six people in a weatherboard shed with foam mattresses on slatted beds or on the vinyl-covered raised timber floor. Mosquito nets are provided. The dorm is F$17 per person including meals. There are six bures spaced about 15m apart along the beach as well as three at the back which are kept for emergencies. They are small Fijian-style bures with pandanus leaf lining, and are partitioned into a room and a small verandah. Some have sand floors, others concrete. One bure has rough-hewn coconut-board walls and a raised floor. Bures are F$20 per person including meals. The food is very good. Alternatively, guests can use the kitchen for preparing their own meals. There is an open shelter on the beach with a long table. You can't buy any alcohol, drinks or snacks, but are more than welcome to bring your own.

There is good snorkelling off the beach. At low tide it is possible to walk out to Snake Island. It is named after the many black-and-white banded sea snakes found there and is a good spot for snorkelling. You have to bring your own snorkelling gear and diving can be arranged with Nautilus Dive Fiji, which operates from Leluvia Island close by. Guests are taken for village trips to Niubasaga on Motoriki for the Sunday church service.

Getting There & Away

Contact Cafe Levuka or Royal Hotel in Levuka to arrange transport by small boat (30 minutes) to the island. Caqelai to Levuka costs F$10 per person. There's a daily morning shopping run to Levuka for F$2.50 one way. Return transport to/from Verata Landing, Viti Levu, is F$15 leaving at 6 am to meet the bus to Suva.

LELUVIA ISLAND

Leluvia is a seven-hectare coral cay with yellow-white sandy beaches. At low tide a vast area of sand and rock is exposed. You can easily walk around the island and explore the rockpools (lots of sea slugs and tiny octopuses). At low tide it's not so far to walk out to swim on the western side. There is a view of the local 'honeymoon island'.

Unfortunately, *Leluvia Island Resort* (☎ 301 584, 313 366 Suva office) PO Box 50, Levuka, seems to be taking over the beautiful island. Emosi has accommodation for up to 50 people, plus campers, and the island can get crowded. Camping is F$8/15 without/with meals. There is an assortment of bungalows in different building styles and materials: coconut log cabins with tapa design cloth internal lining; thatched roof bures with woven walls; and very basic weatherboard units with concrete floors and private bathroom. Beachfront bungalows for singles/doubles are F$36/52 with meals or F$29/38 without meals. Inland bungalows are F$26/50 including meals. Bures for singles/doubles are F$23/44 with meals, F$16/30 without meals. Two of the bures have cooking facilities. The two dormitories sleep eight people in each, and cost F$13/20 per person without/with meals. Food quality and quantity tends to vary and can be monotonous, especially when Emosi is off the island.

The place is a bit run down and pretty grotty. Shared facilities include four showers (pumped rainwater) and four toilets. There is a small shop and a communal cooking area. The resort has a phone but charges are expensive: F$3 for three minutes to Suva, F$4 to Nadi and F$3.50 to Levuka. Pastimes include volleyball, a massage (F$10), socialising with fellow backpackers and lazing on the beach. The dive operation Nautilus Dive Fiji offers one/two-tank dives for F$50/80. Courses cost F$50 for Discover Scuba and F$310 for Open Water. Dive sites include Snake Island, Challis Reef, Coral Garden, Smiley's and Shark Reef. A boat trip for snorkelling at Shark Reef or Snake Island is F$5 per person and hire of snorkelling gear is another F$5. One reader writes:

The snorkelling was astonishing; it is worth going out with the dive boat to see corals, sharks and dolphins, the diving was supposed to be top notch, too... I've never seen cockroaches as big as in the dorm here.
Stephen Rush

Getting There & Away
Emosi has an office at 35 Gordon St, Suva. The bus leaves Suva at noon daily except Sunday. It stops to shop for supplies on the way to Bau Landing from where transfers to the island take about 2½ hours by small open boat. The boat passes near Bau, a tiny island of great historical importance. Leluvia-Suva costs F$16.50 and the Suva-Leluvia-Levuka

trip (three times a week) is F$19.80/39.60 for one-way/return. If you have your own transport from Suva to Bau Landing, deduct about F$2.30 one way. Conditions can get very choppy. Several readers have complained about overloading, the lack of lifejackets, and passengers and gear arriving drenched. To get there from Levuka enquire at the Old Capital Inn II.

WAKAYA ISLAND
Wakaya is an 880-hectare island, privately owned by David and Jill Gilmour, about 20 km east of Ovalau and visible from Levuka. It has forests, cliffs, beautiful white sandy beaches, and archaeological sites including a stone fish trap. Feral horses, pigs and deer roam the island. There are millionaires' houses, roads and a marina.

On 80 hectares at the north-west end of the island is the *Wakaya Club* (☎ 440 128; fax 440 406 or ☎ Australia 1800 816 717, UK 01 284 700 444, North America 800 255 4347). This is one of Fiji's most exclusive resorts, ranking with Vatulele Island Resort and Turtle Island. It caters for a maximum of eight couples and no children under 16 years are allowed. Each of the eight units has a living room, a separate bedroom, four poster king-sized bed, bar, CD player, shower and separate bath. Some units have air-con. Rates for singles/doubles are F$1140/1480 per night, with a five-night minimum stay. There are high and low season incentives for extended stays. If you would like the exclusive use of the eight bures it's a mere F$13,510 per night with a seven-night minimum stay. The resort has a nine-hole golf course, tennis, croquet and masseurs. Rates include all meals (fine cuisine), drinks, and use of sporting facilities and equipment except for deep-sea fishing, scuba diving courses and boat charters. The daily rate includes two one-tank dives a day from the glass-bottomed boat. A PADI Open Water course (four days) costs F$1366/2125 for singles/doubles and Discover Scuba Diving (three hours) is F$228 per person. There are dive sites five minutes by boat from the Club.

Getting There & Away

Resort guests are transferred by Air Wakaya in the island's own twin-engine 1992 Britten Norman Islander plane. The flight from Nadi International Airport takes 45 minutes. Transfers are in addition to the rates quoted previously: F$1184 per couple, or F$592 for each single person in a group. The island is a 20-minute speedboat ride from Levuka.

NAIGANI ISLAND

Naigani, also known as Mystery Island, is a beautiful mountainous island midway between Ovalau and Viti Levu, about 10 km offshore. It has an area of 220 hectares, with white-sand beaches, lagoons and a fringing coral reef, Fijian villages, the remains of a precolonial hillside fortification and 'cannibal caves'.

Located on an old copra plantation is *Naigani Island Resort* (☎ 300 925; fax 300 539). The resort caters mainly for families with young children, couples and groups. After renovations in 1996 it has garden and beachfront fan-cooled villas. Two-bedroom villas with one or two bathrooms cost F$198, while interconnecting villas (three bedrooms, two bathrooms) are F$165. Double rooms cost F$165. A group of four or five can share a villa, and they sometimes have backpacker specials.

The bar and restaurant is in the restored plantation homestead. A two-meal package is F$30 per day and a three-meal package is F$45 per day. Alternatively, for a stay of seven nights, an all-meals package is F$199/99 per adult/child under 12. The resort has baby-sitting and organises kids' camp-outs. There's a nine-hole golf course, a free-form pool with swim-up bar and a 10m water slide. Nonmotorised water sports are included in the rates. Snorkelling is good and other activities include following nature trails, kayaking, windsurfing, fishing, and day excursions to Levuka on Ovalau.

Getting There & Away

Return road and launch transfers to/from Suva via Natovi Landing are F$60/30 per adult/child. Return launch transfers to/from Taviya village near Rukuruku on Ovalau are F$27.50. It is about 1½ hours drive from Suva to Natovi jetty. Naigani have an office upstairs at 22 Cumming St, Suva.

NAMENALALA ISLAND

The 44-hectare volcanic island of Namenalala is on the Namena Barrier Reef, 25 km off the south-eastern coast of Vanua Levu and about 40 km from Savusavu. It has lovely beaches and the island is a natural sailors' refuge. There is an old ring fortification on the island but no longer any villages – just one up-market resort. *Moody's Namena* (☎ 813 764; 812 366) accommodates up to 10 guests in five hexagonal timber and bamboo bures with verandahs. They are on a ridge forested with huge trees. Rates are US$181.30/182.60 (F$250/252) for singles/doubles and the minimum stay is five nights. Children under 16 years are not accepted. The compulsory meal package is US$68.70 (F$95) per person for three meals. Wine is complimentary with dinner and heart of palm is a speciality.

Divers must be certified and bring their certification card as proof. Dives are US$42 per tank. Weights, weight belt, tank, air, boats and dive guide are provided, but, if you don't have your own gear, equipment has to be rented from Savusavu. All other activities are included: windsurfing, fishing, snorkelling, excursions to the barrier reef (for snorkelling and diving), beach barbecues, beach volleyball, use of canoes and paddle boards. The island has a nature reserve for bird-watching and trekking. It has a giant clam farm and is home to seabirds and red-footed boobies. Hawksbill and green turtles lay their eggs on the beaches between November and March.

Getting There & Away

Guests arrive by charter yacht from Savusavu (F$330). Alternatively, the one-hour flight by seaplane from Nadi is F$975 per charter. The resort arranges share fares.

Vanua Levu

Vanua Levu ('big land') is the second largest island of the Fijian archipelago and has the second largest population. With an area of 5538 sq km it is just over half the size of Viti Levu. It has 18% of the country's total population. The main industries are sugar, copra and, more recently, gold mining at Mt Kasi in the island's south-west. The Fijian administration divides the island into the provinces of Cakaudrove (the south-east), Bua (the south-west) and Macuata (the north-west). Vanua Levu, together with Kioa, Rabi, a number of smaller offshore islands, as well as Taveuni, Qamea, Laucala, Matagi and the Ringgold Isles, is known as Fiji's 'North'.

Vanua Levu has an irregular and deeply indented coast. A large peninsula to the north-east forms the huge Natewa Bay and there is another large bay, Savusavu Bay, on the southern side of the island. As on Viti Levu, a mountain range runs along much of Vanua Levu's length dividing the island into a wetter eastern side and a drier western side.

The south-east coast has a predominantly indigenous Fijian population and is very scenic with many bays, rainforests and coconut plantations. Savusavu, the main tourist destination, is in the island's south-east.

The north-west has a higher population of Fijians of Indian decent and lots of sugarcane plantations and native forests, as well as pine plantations for commercial use. Much of the western coast is remote and only accessible by boat. Labasa, Vanua Levu's largest town and administrative and business centre, is situated in the north-west.

Vanua Levu is relatively undeveloped and, except for around Savusavu, has limited infrastructure and services for travellers. Due to its proximity to Viti Levu and easy access via frequent ferry and flight services, Vanua Levu is attracting an increasing number of visitors. As in Viti Levu's interior, the traveller is more likely to gain an insight into the traditional Fijian way of life here.

The island is volcanic in origin and has few sandy beaches. It does, however, offer excellent snorkelling and diving, kayaking and bird-watching. The island's remote, wild and rugged interior and indented coastline has good potential for hiking, but there is little in the way of organised treks. Villagers are less familiar with tourists than on Viti Levu and you cannot wander through the countryside without permission from the landowners. There are interesting archaeological sites at Nabouwalu near Savusavu and at Wasavula near Labasa.

Activities
Diving Vanua Levu's diving operations are concentrated in the Savusavu area. The famous Rainbow Reef lies off south-eastern Vanua Levu, but is generally accessed from Taveuni. The Great Sea Reef, the world's third largest barrier reef, runs along the island's northern coast. Only the up-market Nukubati Resort is presently diving in this largely unexplored area.

Kayaking Fiji by Kayak has a seasonal operation (September to November) to Natewa Bay. The protected reef-fringed bay is 65 km long and 16 km wide. It offers seven-day trips for groups of up to eight people. The trip costs US$1040 (F$1435) per person for a double occupancy tent. Add US$50 (F$69) if you require a tent to yourself. Participants stay overnight at Kontiki resort, are transported to Drekeniwai, and then paddle along the coast to the end of Tunuloa (Natewa) Peninsula from where they are transported back to the resort. The price includes transfers to and from Savusavu, food and equipment. Supplies are carried in support boats and you are accompanied by a staff of four. Expect up to three hours paddling each day, as well as hiking into the rainforest, snorkelling, fishing and village visits. No kayaking experience is required and anyone over 13 years old is accepted. The first and last night's resort meals are not included, nor is initial transport to Savusavu.

Its best to book in advance. Contact PO Box 43, Savusavu (☎ 850 372; fax 850 344) or 4462 17th St, San Francisco, CA 94114 (☎ /fax 415 861 3508) from December to July. Alternatively, book through Adventure Express, 650 5th Street, Suite 505, San Francisco, CA 94107 (☎ 800 443 0799; fax 800 442 0289).

Eco Divers-Tours in Savusavu has kayaks for hire all year round.

Getting There & Away
The cheapest way to get to Vanua Levu is by ferry. If you are short on time and prepared to spend more, it's well worth flying: see the fare chart in the Getting Around chapter. Both Savusavu and Labasa have airports.

There are three boat companies operating passenger services between Viti Levu, Vanua Levu and Taveuni (Patterson Brothers' Shipping, Beachcomber Cruises and Consort Shipping). Prices are competitive. All three have services between Natovi Landing, eastern Viti Levu and Savusavu. Patterson Brothers also has services between Nabouwalu, Vanua Levu and Natovi Landing, as well as Ellington Wharf, northern Viti Levu. See the entries under Savusavu and Nabouwalu and the Getting Around chapter for details.

The roll-on roll-off ferries will take cars or bicycles, but since both can be hired in Savusavu it is probably not worth the expense. The return charge from Suva via Natovi to Savusavu on the Patterson Brothers ferry is F$96.80/217 for bikes/cars; or to Nabouwalu F$96.80/150. Many rental companies, however, won't allow their vehicles to be taken on the ferries.

Getting Around
There is an extensive road system around the island's perimeter, but it is mostly unsealed and poorly maintained. The road from Labasa to Savusavu through central Vanua Levu over the top of the mountain range is sealed and in good condition. The island is quite well serviced by buses, and Budget Rent a Car (Labasa and Savusavu) has 4WD vehicles for hire. It's probably best to avoid driving at night as there are lots of animals and pedestrians crossing the roads and service stations are scarce. If you make the trip around the north from Labasa to Savusavu you will pass small villages but don't expect to be able to buy lunch or petrol.

SAVUSAVU & AROUND
Savusavu is Vanua Levu's second largest town with a population of about 2000. It is located on the peninsula which divides Savusavu Bay from the Koro Sea. The small town has one main street which runs parallel to the water's edge, a market centre and a port. Nawi Island lies about 100m offshore to the north and beyond is western Vanua Levu's picturesque mountainous range across Savusavu Bay. Sunsets can be spectacular. The whole of Savusavu Bay was once a caldera and the area still has lots of geothermal activity with hot springs near the wharf and vents of steam along the water's edge. Locals sometimes use the springs behind the playing field for cooking.

Copra was the area's main business during the second half of the 19th century, but profitability began declining early this century. Until the mid-1980s, most copra was sent to Suva for processing. Despite the building of a copra processing facility in Savusavu, considerably reducing freight costs, farmers are being forced to subdivide their land. Tourism is expanding and the town is now well serviced by air and ferries. Its slogan is 'the

VANUA LEVU

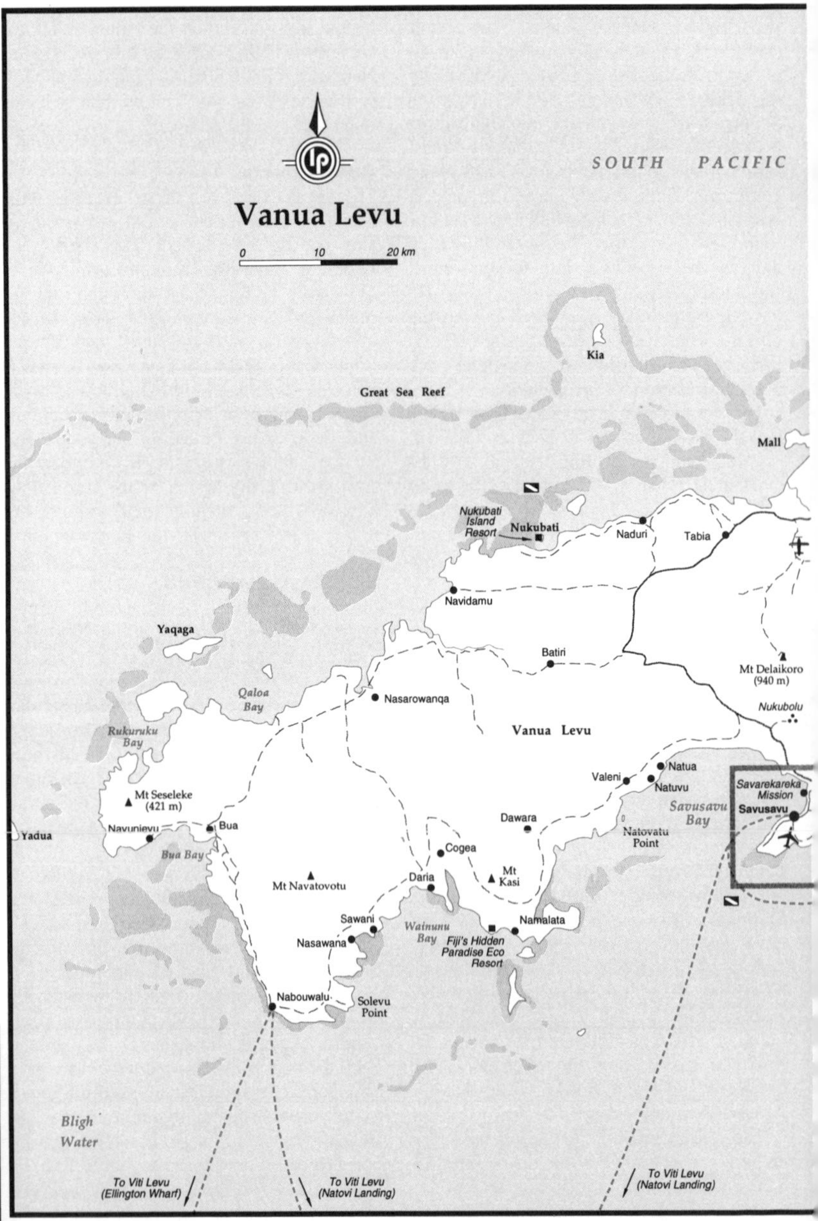

Vanua Levu

0   10   20 km

SOUTH   PACIFIC

Kia

Great Sea Reef

Mall

Nukubati Island Resort — Nukubati   Naduri   Tabia

Navidamu

Yaqaga

Batiri

Qaloa Bay

Mt Delaikoro (940 m)

Rukuruku Bay

Nasarowanqa

Vanua Levu

Nukubolu

Valeni   Natua
Natuvu

Mt Seseleke (421 m)

Navunievu   Bua

Dawara

Savarekareka Mission
Savusavu

Yadua

Bua Bay

Mt Navatovotu

Daria

Cogea

Mt Kasi

Natovatu Point

Savusavu Bay

Sawani

Wainunu Bay

Namalata

Nasawana

Fiji's Hidden Paradise Eco Resort

Nabouwalu   Solevu Point

Bligh Water

To Viti Levu (Ellington Wharf)   To Viti Levu (Natovi Landing)   To Viti Levu (Natovi Landing)

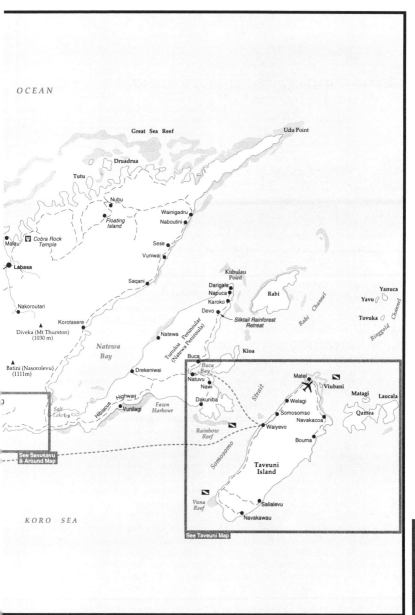

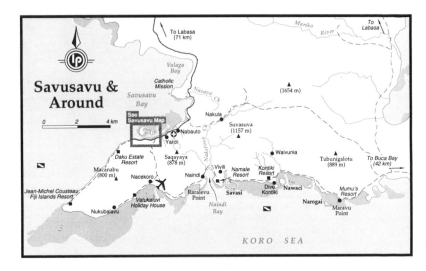

hidden paradise'. The port is a natural hurricane hole and is a popular stop for cruising yachties.

Information

The National Bank of Fiji, ANZ Bank and Westpac have branches in Savusavu. The post office is at the eastern end of the town near Buca Bay Rd. There are cardphones inside the post office and also at the Copra Shed Marina. Once a dilapidated old copra shed, the building has been renovated and turned into the service hub of the town. Here you can find Eco Divers-Tours, Beachcomber Cruises (☎ 850 266; fax 850 499), Patterson Brothers (☎ 850 161), Sunflower Airlines (☎ 850 141), the Savusavu Yacht Club and a bar, toilets, hot showers, two accommodation units, a boutique, a bookshop and a pizza restaurant on the water's edge. Hans at the Bula Bookshop Newsagency (☎ /fax 850 580) has a selection of books on Fiji, bus timetables, and gives advice on things to do in the area. The marina has a same day service laundry provided you put your washing in early in the morning. It costs F$1 per kg.

Moorings at the yacht club cost F$5 per

day, F$40 per week, or F$150 per month. At the time of writing yachts were required to get customs clearance in Suva, Levuka or Lautoka. Savusavu is endeavouring to obtain customs, immigration, health and quarantine services.

Medical & Emergency Services Call ☎ 850 444 for the hospital or an ambulance, or ☎ 850 222 for the police.

Nukubolu Archaeological Site

On the banks of a creek, near hot springs in a fertile volcanic crater north of Savusavu are the remains of an extensive village known as Nukobolu. There are carefully constructed thermal pools, stone building foundations and terraces which are well preserved. Locals dry kava on corrugated iron sheets laid over the pools and bathe in the hot springs when sick. They grow dalo, cassava, copra and kava (yaqona) in the area.

The Nukubolu people lived at the site until prior to the cession of Fiji to Britain. A war broke out after a disagreement between chiefs. Tui Cakau (chief of Cakaudrove) had sent a tabua along with a request for pigs to the Tui Koroalau, whose people were subjects of the Turaga Nukubolu. The request was rejected and the tabua sent back (a grave insult). The Nukubolu people retreated inland but could not escape and were defeated by the forces of Cakaudrove.

At the time of writing much of the site was overgrown while negotiations took place between villages over the pros and cons of introducing tourism. Ask if the site has been cleared otherwise you won't be able to see much amongst the tall grass. There is reportedly also a fortification in the surrounding mountains. The Nukubolu site is intended to become part of Vanua Levu's first national park (Waisali Rainforest Reserve) and an ecotourism project, with Eco Divers-Tours as park managers.

Eco Divers-Tours organises trips to the site. Alternatively, if you have your own 4WD, the turn-off up to Biaugunu village is about 20 km north-west of Savusavu, about eight km inland and over a couple of river crossings. If you turn up alone, make sure you have a *sevusevu* for the chief (Seru). You will have to pay F$5 for entry and a guide. Visiting the site involves walking for about 30 minutes along a muddy track through large stands of bamboo and across a shallow river.

Activities

Yachting is popular in Savusavu. The Yacht Club has sailboats for hire for F$5 to F$10 per hour. Fiji by Kayak has organised trips to Natewa Bay from September to November. Eco Divers-Tours takes trips to villages, copra plantations, mill tours, rainforest/waterfall walks.

There's also water-skiing (F$25 for 15 minutes), plus ocean kayaks (F$10 for a single, F$15 for a double per hour), windsurfers (F$10 per hour) and mountain bikes for hire (F$10 per day).

Diving & Snorkelling

The main attraction for most travellers to Savusavu is its reefs. There are good dive sites at the entrance to Savusavu Bay, the protected inner Savusavu Bay and along the coast towards Taveuni. Eco Divers-Tours, in conjunction with

L'Aventure Cousteau Dive Operation, has buoyed 21 dive sites including Big Blue, Shark Alley, The Grotto and Alice in Wonderland. L'Aventure Jean-Michel Cousteau Fiji offers snorkelling, diving and dive courses for their guests: see Places to Stay – top end.

Eco Divers-Tours (☎ 850 122; fax 850 344; e-mail: seafijidive@is.com.fij), run by Curly and Liz Caswell, has a dive shop with equipment sales and a travel agency at the Copra Shed Marina. Curly is national coordinator of the Fiji Recompression Chamber facility in Suva. A two-tank morning dive costs F$93.50 and a 10-tank special is F$400. PADI courses are available, including equipment hire. Discover Scuba costs F$75 and open water (with manuals) is F$380. Weekly accommodation/dive packages are available. Two-hour snorkelling trips are F$15 each for a group of four or F$25 each for two people. Combination diver/snorkelling groups can be accommodated.

Eco Divers has two six metre fast dive boats, and an 8.5m covered glass-bottom viewing/snorkelling/dive boat (for up to 20 people). It offers two-tank morning dives, one or two afternoon dives as well dusk and night dives. Pre-booking is suggested.

The dive shop Dive Kontiki (☎ 850 352), owned by German Andy Einberger, is located about 13 km east of Savusavu, adjacent to the marina opposite Kontiki Resort and about four km from Mumu's. A one-tank dive costs F$45 with tanks and weights only, or F$60 for full equipment supply.

For those who dive more than five days, the sixth day is free. A resort course costs F$75 and PADI open water is F$330. Snorkelling trips are available for F$5 including gear. There are dive sites close by. If you have your own snorkelling gear and would like to go for an exploratory snorkel, consider taking a bus along Natewa Bay and get off the bus about 40 km from Savusavu where the reef is close to the beach.

There are some white-sand beaches along this coast but it is largely rock, mud or coral. The bus from Labasa to Savusavu passes

VANUA LEVU

about 3 pm. Don't miss it – there is nowhere to stay in the area!

Places to Stay – bottom end

The Hidden Paradise Guest House (☎ 850 106; fax 850 344), run by Mrs Vidya Chand, is popular with locals and budget travellers who want somewhere quiet to stay. The six clean rooms are in a building at the back of her general store and restaurant. Security is obviously a priority judging by the bars on the windows and doors. There are shared toilets, cold showers, cooking facilities, and a covered clothes drying area. Prices are F$10.80/F$16.20/27 for singles/doubles/triples including breakfast of sweet porridge, eggs, toast and sausage. Locals play soccer in the afternoons at the sportsground at the back.

Near the hot springs behind the sportsground, *David's Holiday House* (☎ 850 216, 850 149) has a dormitory building that sleeps seven for F$9.30 per person. Tent sites cost F$6. The house has various rooms and a kitchen, dining area and shared bathroom. Singles/doubles are F$13.20/18.70 including breakfast (toast, eggs and fruit). The family room sleeps four for F$25.

PLACES TO STAY		OTHER	
3	Savusavu Bay Accomondation	1	Government Wharf
6	Hidden Paradise Guest House	2	Planters Club
7	Hot Springs Hotel	4	Consort Shipping
8	David's Holiday House	5	Shell Service Station
		9	Hot Springs
PLACES TO EAT		10	Morris Hedstrom
11	Captains Cafe (Copra Shed Marina)	11	Copra Shed Marina Complex & Savusavu Yacht Club
15	Kana Korna Coffee Shop	12	Eco Divers Tours
17	New Ping Ho	13	Taxi Stand & Bus Stop
		14	Market, Town Council & Police Post
19	Hot Bread Kitchen	16	Westpac Bank
20	Wing Yuen Restaurant	18	ANZ Bank
		21	National Bank of Fiji
		22	Air Fiji & Budget Rent-a-Car
		23	Post Office
		24	Shell Service Station

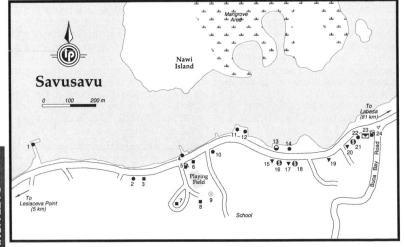

Savusavu

0   100   200 m

Nawi Island

Mangrove Area

To Labasa (81 km)

To Lesiaceva Point (5 km)

Playing Field

School

Buca Bay Road

VANUA LEVU

The place has a friendly atmosphere and, if you stay more than seven days, a 10% discount applies and laundry is free. Horse riding is free for guests and David has two bikes for hire at F$10 each per day.

Savusavu Bay Accommodation (☎ 850 100), upstairs in a double storey building on the main street, also calls itself 'hidden paradise' but has little atmosphere. Fan-cooled rooms, each with a small ensuite and porch, cost F$11/16.50 for singles/doubles or F$22 for singles or doubles with air-con. An air-con room with four beds costs F$33.

There is good accommodation at the *Copra Shed Marina*, but it is often booked out on long-term leases or rented by yachties. Studio 1, a one-bedroom apartment with a small deck on to the marina, can take up to three people and costs F$33 per night or F$450 per month. Studio 2 has two bedrooms and costs F$66 per night or F$660 per month. Both units have kitchens and mosquito nets.

The *Vatukaluvi Holiday House* (☎ 850 143, 850 561) is a 15-minute drive from the town on a rocky point. It overlooks the Koro Sea and a couple of cute islands with lone coconut trees. You can snorkel offshore and there are hot springs nearby. The house has a mezzanine and a deck and sleeps up to six people. It is ideal for a couple or a family interested in self-catering and costs F$45 per night. A taxi to Savusavu costs F$5. It is Geoff Taylor's mother's holiday house – he's a geologist who has an office at the Marina. Book in advance: PO Box 3, Savusavu.

An excellent place for budget travellers to stay is *Mumu's Resort* (☎ 850 416; fax 850 402), about 17 km east of Savusavu on a ruggedly beautiful site owned by Rosie and Gordon Edris (an American ex-colonel). They have a variety of accommodation sprouting up all over the site, products of Gordon's creative imagination. Concrete paths wind between the trees which cling to the volcanic rock. There is a sitting area and natural rock pool on the point where you can dip with the colourful fish.

The campsite is on top of the hill, under the pine, pandanus and coconut trees.

Camping costs F$5/7 for singles/doubles. The dormitory 'lagoon house' sleeps six for F$12 per person. It has cooking facilities, a shower and a toilet. Unfortunately, it is located adjacent to the noisy generator which runs from 4 to 9 pm.

The 'tank house' is a simple concrete block structure and costs F$35 for singles and doubles. A new Fijian bure is F$45 for a double.

The 'dream house' is fantastic, especially on a wild weather night. It is perched on a rocky, exposed cliff and has access down through a crevice to a rocky beach. The spacious front bedroom has a double and single bed, an adjoining room has two single beds, and behind is a simple kitchen and bathroom with cold water. It costs F$60 per night. Another new bure, small but with outdoor decks, was being built on the hill. Mosquito nets are provided in all bures. Rosie has lots of dogs guarding the property, but beware of leaving valuables in the bures near the road.

The main house has a comfortable meals/sitting area and pet parrots. Meal plans are available for F$20, otherwise breakfast is F$5, lunch F$7 and dinner F$10. The food is very good with nice curry chicken and fish, and octopus with coconut and home-made bread. There are also cooking facilities. It costs 80 cents for the gas.

While there is no sandy beach, there is excellent snorkelling offshore. At low tide you can walk out to the lagoon between the nearby islands. It has beautiful soft coral and lots of fish. There is another channel to the east of the resort where it is possible to swim through caves and see large parrot fish. Take care with the currents though. Diving can be arranged with Dive Kontiki which has a dive shop about four km down the road, towards Savusavu. Local buses (F$1 to Savusavu) pass five times a day (once only on Sunday) and a taxi to/from Savusavu costs F$12.

Eco Divers customers can take advantage of the Diver's Den rooms at the *Hot Springs Hotel* which are F$30 for singles, doubles or triples. See the following section for further information.

Places to Stay – middle

The *Hot Springs Hotel* (☎ 850 195; fax 850 430) is Savusavu's most prominent landmark. This four-level hotel, formerly part of the Travelodge chain, is built on the hill and has great views out to the Bay. When we visited, the hotel looked a bit tired and had a dull atmosphere but was undergoing renovations. New owners took over in mid-1996 and were giving a facelift to all 48 rooms and relocating the public bar down the hill away from the hotel building. It has a deck area with a freshwater swimming pool and great views.

Standard rooms have ensuites, a double and single bed, phone, fans or air-con, fridge, tea/coffee making facilities, and a verandah. Ground-level rooms cost F$50/65 for singles/doubles. Fan-cooled ocean view rooms on the third level are F$82/90 and air-con deluxe rooms on the fourth level are F$105/115. An extra person in any of the rooms costs F$11.

About 15-minutes walk south-west of Savusavu, is *Daku Estate Resort* (☎ 850 046; fax 850 334). This small, quiet resort, run by the Anglican Diocese of Polynesia, can cater for groups of up to 20 people. It has six fan-cooled bures with fridge, tea/coffee facilities and bathroom with hot water for F$60/100/140/160 per night for singles/doubles/triples/quads. Their very simple self-contained weatherboard cottage can sleep up to three people and costs F$62/82 for singles/doubles. The four fan-cooled villa units are clean, spacious and equipped with cooking facilities. They are ideal for families and can sleep up to five people. Villas cost F$72/120 for singles/doubles or F$210 for up to five adults. The unit on the hill has the best sea view. Children under 12 are half price. The restaurant menu changes daily. Breakfast is F$7.70, lunch F$11 and dinner F$19.80. Meal plans are available for F$38.50 per person. Package rates are also available and credit cards are accepted.

The resort has a pool, and activities and entertainment include volleyball, mekes, cultural programmes, guest speakers, visits to villages, schools and plantations, reef and snorkelling trips and island picnics. Diving can be arranged with Eco Divers. Free transport is provided for guests to/from the airport. A taxi to/from Savusavu costs F$1.50.

Kontiki Resort (☎ 850 262; fax 850 355) is on a nice sloping site with large trees 13 km east of Savusavu. The resort was quite run down at the time of writing and had very few customers. There are 16 bures of three different types. Up to four people can fit in the one-room units. Rates for singles/doubles/family are F$110/165/250 and children under six are free. The honeymoon bure, which costs F$180, is a bit more secluded than the rest and includes free champagne. A family unit with two rooms has the best views. It has a small fridge and a kitchen area but no cooking facilities. A meal plan including three meals and drinks is F$55 per day or F$185 for a seven night stay. Otherwise meals are F$8 to F$12 for lunch and F$13.50 to F$20 for dinner for seafood or steak, or F$23 to F$26 for lobster. The resort has a golf course and guests can dive with Dive Kontiki. Courtesy transport is provided for guests to/from the airport. A taxi to/from Savusavu costs F$10.

Places to Stay – top end

Jean-Michel Cousteau Fiji Islands Resort (☎ 850 188, 850 174; fax 850 340; USA toll free 800 246 3454 or ah 800 268 7832) has taken over Na Koro resort and refurbished and expanded the facilities. The seven-hectare property is about five km south-west of Savusavu at Lesiaceva Point, where Savusavu Bay joins the Koro Sea.

The resort offers luxury accommodation in 20 finely decorated, thatched-roof, fan-cooled bures with king size beds, mini-bar and tea/coffee making facilities. Rates for singles or doubles are F$374/510 for ocean-view/ocean-front bures. The ocean-view bures are set further back in the garden. A third person over 12 years old will cost F$70. The two-bedroom ocean-front family bures cost F$612. The open-air restaurant has a varied menu with Indian, Fijian and European dishes at F$17 to F$28 for a dinner, and lunches for F$6 to F$12. The resort also has a swimming pool, an interesting gift shop, a darkroom, and a well set up conference room with a video library.

According to the resort's philosophy, 'to completely experience nature we must become aware of the interactions between oceans, land and people'. Activities include underwater photography lessons, bird-watching, village visits, snorkelling, windsurfing, kayaking, volleyball, tennis, yoga, massage, rainforest hikes and learning about local customs and herbal medicine. The kids' programme has interesting theme days.

L'Aventure Jean-Michel Cousteau Fiji dive centre is unsurprisingly first class. A two-tank dive costs F$139, scuba certification is F$600 and advanced courses are F$431. There's a system whereby non divers can watch and talk to the people who are diving. Twice a year the resort holds a 'Project Ocean Search' programme. As well as diving, the two-week sessions involve marine science lectures, workshops and nature walks. For more information contact Jean-Michel Cousteau Productions on ☎ 805 899 8899; fax 805 899 8898 in the USA; see the Getting Around section later in this chapter.

Namale Resort (☎ 850 435; fax 850 400) is located on the Hibiscus Highway nine km east of Savusavu. The American owned resort is built on an interesting site with a multilevel landscaped garden. Rates for doubles are US$550 (F$759) for the honeymoon suite, US$522.50 (F$721) for an ocean-view bure and US$495 (F$683) for a garden-view bure. The price includes all meals, beverages, transfers from Savusavu airport and all activities apart from diving. The garden bures are very private, have outdoor decks and are a short walk from the beach. The honeymoon bures are near the beach and have bathtubs. The resort has an impressive entertainment/restaurant bure, but is for the exclusive use of guests.

Diving rates are US$77 (F$106) for two morning dives, and a PADI Discover Scuba Diving Course (two dives) is US$137.50

(F$190). Activities include tennis, village trips and waterfall and blowhole visits.

About 24 km offshore, south-west of Savusavu, is another up-market resort, Moody's Namena on Namenalala Island. See the Ovalau & the Lomaiviti Group chapter.

Places to Eat
Eatery options are pretty limited in Savusavu. The *Captain's Cafe* (☎ 850 511) at the Copra Shed Marina has OK pizza (F$8.50 to F$14 for a medium size). It's a great spot on the outdoor deck, with beautiful views of Viwa Island and of the volcanic mountains across the bay. The service is a bit slow. *Kana Korna Coffee Shop* opposite the bus station is a good daytime option for light meals.

The *New Ping Ho* has a Chinese menu with reasonable curry, chop suey, chow mein and rice dishes for F$2.80 to F$4.50. The restaurant at the front of the *Hidden Paradise Guest House* serves Indian curries and rice/roti/tavioka for F$1.70 to F$2.20. The *Sea Breeze* restaurant downstairs below Savusavu Bay Accommodation has curries and Chinese for F$3 to F$4 and the *Wing Yuen Restaurant* has fairly ordinary Chinese and European dishes for F$4 to F$7.

Meals at the *Hot Springs Hotel* are F$7 to F$8 for lunch and F$10 to F$15 for dinner. If you are after fine dining, consider the restaurant at *Jean-Michel Cousteau Fiji Islands Resort*. Ring to make a reservation.

Self-Catering Savusavu has a market, a small supermarket and a few grocery shops.

Entertainment
The *Savusavu Yacht Club* has a small bar upstairs at the Copra Shed Marina which has a good atmosphere. The *Hot Springs Hotel* has a happy hour from 5 to 7 pm and occasional dances. The 40 year old *Planters Club* is for the local copra farmers but will sign in and welcome visitors. The old colonial weatherboard building has a verandah with a view to the water. There are pool and table tennis tables. Bill and Mary McLaren have

been running the club for 20 years. Though copra farming is on the wane, they still organise dances once every three to four months where the oldies turn up in black tie, white jackets and evening frocks.

You might like to watch locals play rugby and soccer on the playing field behind the Shell service station.

Getting There & Away

Air Savusavu airstrip is three km south-east of the town. A trip from Nadi takes about an hour, and from Suva 45 minutes. The flight over the reefs and down to Savusavu through the coconut plantations is superb. The airport has toilets, and ladies sell roti, cake and fresh lemon juice at arrival and departure times. Sunflower Airlines has flights between Savusavu and Nadi twice daily, and Taveuni twice daily. Air Fiji has direct flights to Nadi once or twice daily, to Suva three times daily and to Taveuni three or four times daily. Refer to airfare charts in the Getting Around chapter for prices. Vanua Air Charters also has daily flights from Suva to Savusavu (F$80 one way).

Sunflower (☎ 850 141 Savusavu; 850 214 airport)
Air Fiji (☎ 850 538 Savusavu; 850 173 airport. The office in Savusavu is open from 8 am to 5 pm.

Bus The bus trip from Savusavu over the mountains to Labasa, on the mostly sealed highway, takes about three hours and costs F$4.30. Buses depart at 7.15 am, 9.30 am, 1 pm and 3.30 pm Monday to Saturday, and on Sunday at 9.30 am and 3.30 pm only. Buses from Savusavu to Labasa via Natewa Bay depart at 9 am daily. This trip takes about nine hours. At 1 pm a bus goes halfway to Wainigadru and, at 4.30 pm, to Yanuavou.

Savusavu to Napuca, at the tip of the Tunuloa Peninsula, takes about 3½ hours and costs about F$4.70. Buses depart at 10.30 am and 2.30 pm daily. The afternoon bus stays there overnight and returns at 7 am. A 4 pm bus goes to Drekeniwai and on to Buca Bay where it stays overnight. The trip costs F$3.20.

Buses also travel along the south-east coast towards Mt Kasi. The 11 am bus goes as far as Vaneni and the 2 pm travels to Mt Kasi goldmine (about two hours).

For confirmation of bus timetables ring Vishnu Holdings (☎ 850 276).

Boat Beachcomber Cruises has a weekly ferry (12 hours) direct from Suva to Savusavu and on to Taveuni (five hours). Four days a week the ferry does the trip between Natovi Landing and Savusavu (seven hours). There are bus connections from Suva to Natovi. See the Getting Around chapter for details.

Patterson Brothers also has ferries between Natovi Landing and Savusavu. There are bus connections (1½ hours) to Natuvu, Buca Bay and a ferry across the Somosomo Strait (1¾ hours) to Taveuni.

Consort Shipping Line (☎ 850 279; fax 850 442) has twice-weekly voyages between Suva and Savusavu (11 to 14 hours). Once a week the ferry continues to Taveuni after an 11-hour stopover in Savusavu.

There is also a ferry service between Taveuni and Vanua Levu on the *Grace* to Buca Bay and by bus to Savusavu. See the Taveuni chapter.

Getting Around

The Savusavu bus stop and taxi stands are downtown, near the market. There's no shortage of taxis. They can be hailed down, or if you need to ring for one try Hot Spring Taxis (☎ 850 226). Rates are about F$15 per hour. Local buses pass the airport but you will probably have to wait. A taxi to/from Savusavu costs F$2. There are buses from Savusavu to Lesiaceva Point (Jean-Michel Cousteau Resort) costs F$5. There are five buses daily, except Sunday. The trip takes 15 minutes and costs 50 cents. The bus departs at 6 am, 7 am, 12 noon, 3.30 pm and 5 pm.

Budget Rent a Car (☎ 850 799) in Savusavu has 4WD vehicles, which is a good way to explore the area if you can afford it. Eco Divers-Tours hires out mountain bikes.

TUNULOA PENINSULA

The Tunuloa Peninsula, also known as the

Natewa or Cakaudrove Peninsula, is the south-eastern section of Vanua Levu. It is a good area for bird-watching, hiking or for exploring by bus or 4WD. The gravel Hibiscus Highway runs from Savusavu to the road's end at Darigala. About 20 km east of Savusavu there is a turn-off to the north which follows the western side of Natewa Bay and is an alternative 4WD route to Labasa. About 35 km further along is the turn off into the village of Drekeniwai, where Prime Minister Rabuka was born.

Another road turns off to Buca Bay, which is about 65 km from Savusavu (1½ hours by bus). Most travellers pass through **Buca Bay** on the way to/from Taveuni. Ferries leave from Buca Bay and cross the Somosomo Strait to Taveuni. The beach here is black sand and there is not much reason to stay here but, if you get stranded, there is a shop and budget accommodation near the wharf. The ferry passes the island of **Kioa**, which is inhabited by Polynesians from Tuvalu (formerly Ellice Islands) who moved there after WWII.

South of Buca Bay, at the south-eastern end of Vanua Levu, is the village of **Dakuniba**, where petroglyphs on boulders can be found in a creek bed nearby. Similar alphabetic rock inscriptions are also found in the Sawa-i-Lau caves in the Yasawas. The inscriptions are thought to be of ceremonial or mystical significance but no-one knows who carved them and their meaning is a mystery. Dakuniba means 'behind the fence', and there is a theory that the rocks may have been part of a single structure. Offshore from Dakuniba is the Rainbow Reef, but there are no facilities for divers in the area. Dive boats from the Taveuni resorts travel across the Somosomo Strait to the reef.

The scenic road up to Napuca and **Darigala** follows the eastern coast and passes copra plantations, old homesteads, villages and forest areas. The island of **Rabi** east of the northern tip of the Tunuloa peninsula, is populated by Micronesians originally from Banaba (Ocean Island), in Kiribati. At the turn of the century the naive islanders sold phosphate mining rights in

return for an annual payment and their tiny island was eventually ruined. During WWII the Japanese invaded the island and many people perished. The British mining company purchased Rabi island for them and after the war the 2000 survivors were resettled there.

Places to Stay & Eat

Buca Bay Resort (☎ 880 370) PA Natuvu, Buca Bay, is within view of the ferry landing. The old residence has two rooms with separate bathroom for F$48.40 a double. In a separate building there is a six-bed dormitory with a bathroom. The dorm costs F$13.20 per person and camping is F$5. Restaurant meals can be provided if ordered in advance and there is a shop in town. There is no beach but the manager is friendly and takes guests to Kioa island for snorkelling on a beautiful reef.

Tunuloa Silktail Rainforest Retreat (radio ☎ 759RP6 or ☎/fax 09 232 0199 New Zealand) near Devo has been set up by a group of New Zealand bird-watchers, including Stuart Chambers, author of *Birds of New Zealand Locality Guide*, 1987. The two cottages have verandahs and are on a hill in a rainforest setting near a natural rock pool and small waterfall. The self-contained cottages have a gas stove and fridge and cost F$60 for up to three people. Another building has kitchen facilities and outdoor eating on the verandah. Dormitory accommodation is available in an older building for F$10 per person. There is a dining/sitting room and two rooms with two beds in each. Extra mattresses are available.

The area is the habitat of the silktail, a rare bird found only on this peninsula and on Taveuni. The silktail is on the world's endangered species list and logging on the peninsula has threatened the local population. The bird is about three inches high, black with a white patch on its tail. Apart from bird-watching, activities include bushwalking, cycling, snorkelling, swimming and trips to Rabi Island. It's about a 700m walk to the beach. The caretakers are Louisa Toronibau & family. Call the above

VANUA LEVU

number between 8 am and noon or 6 and 8 pm or write to Box 2686, Labasa, for more information.

Getting There & Away

The bus ride from Savusavu to Napuca takes about 3½ hours and costs F$4.40. It departs Savusavu at 10.30 am and 2.30 pm. The afternoon bus stays in Napuca overnight and returns at 7 am. The bus passes the Tunuloa Silktail Rainforest Retreat twice daily heading for Napuca and twice on the way back to Savusavu.

There is an afternoon (4 pm) bus to Drekenewai and on to Buca Bay where it stays overnight. The trip to Buca Bay costs F$3.20.

Timetables are liable to change so confirm in advance.

LABASA & AROUND

Labasa, with an urban population of 16,500, is the largest town on Vanua Levu. It is located on the north-western side of Vanua Levu's mountain range, on the banks of the meandering Labasa River about five km inland.

Labasa was a big centre for CSR in the colonial days. The Labasa sugar mill was opened in 1894 and the company established cane plantations in the fertile river valleys and on reclaimed mangrove swamps. The district is still predominantly a sugar cane growing area. Raw sugar and molasses, as well as timber, are exported from the port at Malau, north of the town. There are some lovely big colonial residences scattered around the district. Labasa has a predominantly Fiji Indian population, mostly descendants of indentured labourers brought to work on the plantations.

While Labasa is an important trade, service and administrative centre for western Vanua Levu, most travellers will find the town itself pretty dull.

There are a few interesting sites in the

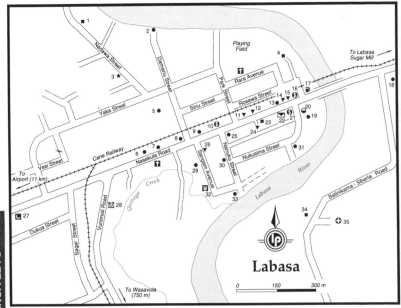

Labasa

district (see the following Things to See & Do section).

Information
Most shops and services can be found on the main street (Nasekula Rd), including the National Bank of Fiji, ANZ and Westpac banks, and the post office which has cardphones. The booking office for Air Fiji and Sunflower Airlines is on the corner of Nasekula Rd and Damanu St, and Patterson Brothers Shipping Office (☎ 812 444; fax 813 460) is a few doors away, also on Nasekula Rd.

The public library at the Civic Centre has

a small collection of books. It is open weekdays from 9 am to 1 pm and 2 to 5 pm, and Saturday from 9 am to noon.

East of the river is the hospital and the provincial council's multistorey office building. Note the stone monolith in front of the building. In the old Fijian religion, such stones were worshipped, as it was believed that they embodied the spirit of ancestor gods.

Medical & Emergency Services The police are in Nadawa St, Labasa; call ☎ 811 222. The hospital in Butinikama-Siberia Rd, Labasa, can be reached on ☎ 811 444 – the number is the same for an ambulance.

Things to See & Do
Just a couple of km south of town, on the river side of Vunimoli Rd, is **Wasavula Ceremonial Site**. It consists of two parallel linear platforms, each about two metres wide and 75m long, and spaced about four metres apart. The ceremonial platforms are lined with low stone walls, and transverse walls divide the site into segments. There are several tall stone monoliths and a head chopping stone. The site is behind some village houses so ask permission to have a look. You can get to Wasavula by bus or taxi.

The **Labasa Sugar Mill** (☎ 811 511) is about 1.5 km east of town. Tours are possible during the crushing season between June and December. **Waiqele hot springs** are three km beyond the airport. Take the Waiqele bus (75 cents).

Past the sugar mill and the Oawa River the main road turns left. After about five km there is a turn off to the left to the Malau Wharf. Another 4.5 km (about 11 km north of Labasa) on the right hand side of the road, is a Hindu temple built around the **Cobra Rock**.

The rock is about three metres high and its curved form resembles a poised cobra. Devotees bring offerings to the temple. They swear that the rock grows in size and that the roof has had to be raised several times over the years. Before entering you must remove your shoes and you should not have eaten

---

PLACES TO STAY
1 Labasa Riverview Private Hotel
4 Grand Eastern Hotel
23 Takia Hotel
30 Labasa Guest House
34 Friendly North Inn

PLACES TO EAT
11 Bhindi's Refreshment Bar
12 Joe's Restaurant
14 Wun Wah Cafe
15 Hot Bread Kitchen
23 Takia Hotel
24 Takia Sizzler
26 Isa Lei Restaurant

OTHER
2 Government Wharf
3 Police Station
5 Labasa College
6 Diamond Theatre
7 Patterson Brothers Shipping
8 Sunflower & Air Fiji Booking Office
9 Elite Cinema
10 Westpac Bank
13 Chemist
16 ANZ Bank
17 Mobil Service Station
18 Provincial Council Building
19 Market
20 Bus Station & Taxi Stand
21 National Bank of Fiji
22 Post Office
25 Morris Hedstrom
27 Mosque
28 Sikh Temple
29 School
31 Civic Centre
32 Hindu Temple
33 Labasa Club
35 Hospital

VANUA LEVU

Wasavula Ceremonial Site

Little is known about the origin of the Wasavula platforms, but they were thought to be related to similar sites of the *naga* cult found in Viti Levu's Sigatoka Valley. What is known about such sites is mostly based on hearsay and vague memories; the penalty for betraying ceremonial secrets was believed to be insanity followed by death.

Such sites were connected with spirit/ancestor worship. As well as being a venue for communicating with the founder gods, they formed a spiritual link between the people and the earth, time, crops and fertility. The sites were thought to have been used for performing ceremonies such as the installation of chiefs and priests, male initiation rites such as circumcision, or to tell the gods that the *bokola* (dead body of an enemy) had been prepared.

Stone monoliths, said to be actual gods or the shrines of the gods. They were also used as a refuge. Someone who had committed a crime could run to the village refuge stone. If they made it to the rock before being caught, their life would be spared. ■

---

meat that day. Several buses pass the temple including those to Natewa Bay, Vanikoro, Lakeba, Sangani and Lagalaga. A taxi costs F$10.

Further up the road on the left is a bus stand and a road which leads to the best **beach** in the area. It's about three km off the main road so it's difficult to get there unless you walk, have a car or are prepared to pay for a taxi. The road passes strange rock formations and runs through land which used to be a tidal swamp but now has rice and cane plantations. The beach is on private land owned by Durga Prasad & Sons and at the farm you'll have to pay F$5 per car to visit. Continue down through the coconut trees to the beach which is about 300m long, has a couple of huts, a toilet and a view to the port. It is popular with locals and can get crowded on holidays. It's a bit rocky and you can only swim at high tide.

About 50 km north-east of Labasa is **Floating Island**, in a small lake amongst the cane plantations. Pandanus palms grow on the small grassy platform which moves about. Locals say that no-one has ever reached the bottom of the lake.

You can get there by the 10.30 am Lagalaga Bisongo bus, but check return timetables to make sure you don't get stranded in the middle of nowhere. Ask the driver where to get off. Take the track about one km off the main road and ask to see the island at the farmhouse on the right. A return

trip by taxi will cost about F$45, which may be an option for a group.

Places to Stay

The *Labasa Riverview Private Hotel* (☎ 811 367; fax 814 337) in the suburb of Namara is a good option. It's about a five-minutes walk from town past the police station along Nadawa St and the river's edge. The double storey building has 10 fan-cooled rooms and a bar with snooker tables at the back facing the river. A deck extends out over the water and is a pleasant spot to have a beer as long as you have your mosquito repellent. Rooms with ensuite cost F$22/33 for singles/doubles. Rooms with shared bathroom are F$11/16.50. The upstairs rooms are more private and have a good view of the river. Half of the top floor is normally set aside as an apartment for long term lease. The friendly owner Pradeep is good for a chat and you can make tea or coffee in his office.

The *Grand Eastern Hotel* (☎ 811 022; fax 814 011) is also on the riverside, with Mobil storage tanks at the rear. The original double storey building has a bit of character, with its verandah covered in vines and the 'Sunset' bar outside the front entrance. There is a dining room downstairs and 10 fan-cooled rooms upstairs. It costs F$15/22 for a room with a basin but shared bathroom, or F$22/28 with an ensuite. An extra bed in the room costs F$6. Air-con rooms in the new wing, built in the mid-1980s, have ensuites,

ROBYN JONES

ROBYN JONES

ROBYN JONES

Vanua Levu

Top Left: Ganesa – Hindu god of prophecy
Top Right: Savusavu market
Bottom: Hindu women at the Savusavu market

LEONARDO PINHEIRO

ROBYN JONES

Vanua Levu
Top: Savusavu sunset
Bottom: Thermal springs, Nukubolu

TV, phone, tea/coffee-making facilities and cost F$52.80/59.60 for singles/doubles. A rooms in the old wing with similar facilities is F$33/39.60. Guests can hire videos for F$10 per night.

Labasa Guest House (☎ 812 155), Nanuku St, is conveniently located but has no atmosphere. However, it does have shared kitchen facilities. Singles/doubles cost F$11/16.50.

The Friendly North Inn (☎ 814 400, 814 094) is opposite the hospital, east of the river. The four blocks (10 rooms) were finished in 1996 and are a good deal for its price range. A room for singles or doubles costs F$27.50/44 with fan/air-con. A self-contained apartment costs F$33/49.50 with fan/air-con. Extra mattresses can be provided for F$5 each and a TV is F$10 per night. A restaurant/bar was under construction at the time of writing.

The three storey *Takia Hotel* (☎ 811 655; fax 813 527) is on the main street close to the bus station. With 38 rooms it is Labasa's largest hotel. It's a bit claustrophobic, with stuffy air-con and clashing 70s pub-style carpet. Fan-cooled rooms are F$35/45 for singles/doubles. Air-con rooms with clinical vinyl are F$55/65, or F$60/70 with gaudy carpet. Second floor air-con suites cost F$70/80. All rooms have their own ensuite, tea/coffee facilities and fridge. Credit cards are accepted but you will be charged about 5% to 10% extra. Children under 12 are free and an extra person in a room costs F$10.

Places to Eat

There is a Hot Bread Kitchen and supermarket near the bus station. *Bhindi's Refreshment Bar* further down the street is clean and has good homemade snacks including samosas and cakes. Mutton and vegetable pies cost F$1. It is open until 6.30 pm. Also recommended is the *Takia Sizzler*, the Takia Hotel's fast-food outlet. It is open 5 am to 6 pm, plays Indian music, and serves Chinese and Indian style meals such as chop suey or curries for F$2 to F$5, with rice, roti, cassava, dalo and chips.

Probably the best restaurant in town is *Joe's Restaurant* (☎ 811 766) for Chinese-style food. The *Wun Wah Cafe* has OK Chinese fare for F$2.50 to F$5. *Isa Lei Restaurant* (☎ 811 490) on Sangam Ave has Indian dishes for F$3-8. The *Tapa Restaurant* at the Takia Hotel has reasonable mixed style meals in the F$7.50 to F$12 price range for grilles and fish. It also has a lounge and salon bar. Lunch and dinner meals at the *Grand Eastern Hotel* average F$7 to F$8. Dishes include chop suey, curries and grilles, served with dalo, cassava, rice, roti or chips. The breakfast menu includes fruit and cereal, and a cooked breakfast is F$6.

Entertainment

Apart from the *Diamond Theatre* (☎ 811 471) and the *Elite Cinema* (☎ 811 260), both on Nasekula Rd, Labasa has little happening at night. Both the Grand Eastern Hotel and the Takia Hotel have bars.

Getting There & Away

Air Sunflower Airlines (☎ 812 121 airport), has four Nadi-Labasa flights daily, two Suva-Labasa flights daily, and three flights per week to Taveuni. Air Fiji (☎ 811 679 airport) has six Suva-Labasa flights daily and twice-daily Suva-Nadi flights. Vanua Air (☎ 811655; fax 813900) has Savusavu-Labasa flights, daily except Sunday, for F$80.

Bus There are regular buses between Labasa and Savusavu. Waiqele buses (☎ 817 680) depart Labasa four times daily (twice on Sunday) between 7.30 am and 4 pm and cost F$3. There are also buses which take the long route (about nine hours) to Savusavu around the north and down along Natewa Bay. Lagalaga Buses (☎ 811 062) have trips on this route (F$9) departing at 9 am. There are also regular buses between Labasa and Nabouwalu (see that section later in this chapter).

Getting Around

Taxis are plentiful and the main stand is near the bus station. There are several local bus companies. If you have time to kill, consider taking a bus ride around the district. There are no written timetables, so go to the bus station and ask around. You can hire 4WD vehicles from Budget Rent a Car (☎ 811 999).

The airport is about 11 km south-west of Labasa. It has a kiosk and a cardphone. The turn-off is about 4.25 km west of Labasa, just past the Wailevu River. During the day there are regular Waiqele buses from Labasa to the airport for 55 cents. A taxi from Labasa costs F$6.

NUKUBATI ISLAND

The privately owned island of Nukubati is just off the northern coast of Vanua Levu, about 40 km west of Labasa. It feels like it's in the middle of nowhere, certainly far from the usual tourist destinations. It is actually two small islands linked by mangroves. It takes about 30 minutes to walk around the island at low tide and 15 minutes to walk to its highest point. Once occupied by Fijian villagers, in the 19th century it was given by a local chief to a German gunsmith who settled here with his Fijian wife. In the colonial days it operated as a coconut plantation.

The secluded *Nukubati Island Resort* (☎ 813 901; fax 813 914), with its 21 staff, has four bungalows for a maximum of eight guests. Only adult couples are accepted, except for special weeks or if the whole resort is booked (F$2600 per night). The fan-cooled suites are spacious with a separate bedroom, bathroom and sitting areas. Each has a verandah facing the white sandy beach and a private courtyard off the bedroom. Prices, including meals and non-alcoholic drinks, are F$770 per night per couple. Discounts of 20 to 25% are available in low season (November to mid December and mid January to the end of March). They recommend a minimum stay of five nights. The restaurant has an extensive wine list and the menu specialises in seafood, fresh fruits and Fijian-style cooking including lovos and curries. The dining/bar/lounge pavilion has great views and plenty of room to find your own corner and read a book from the library. Wind generators and solar panels provide the electricity, and water is obtained by a desalination plant as well as from filtered rain water.

Activities include tennis, sailing, windsurfing, snorkelling off the beach or out on the reef, and fishing. The dive shop caters for experienced divers only and diving is included in the price. Nukubati is the only dive operation that dives the Great Sea Reef. Alternatively, you can just laze about and have a traditional Fijian massage for F$10. Game fishing and 4WD trips around Vanua Levu are extra.

Getting There & Away
Resort guests are transferred to the island by a one-hour boat ride along Vanua Levu's northern coast. Transfers are included in the price. The island can also be accessed by taxi – a drive along the coast past Naduri to the jetty, followed by a short boat ride.

NABOUWALU & AROUND

Nabouwalu is a small settlement on the south-western point of Vanua Levu. It has administrative offices, a post office, a small market and a store. Apart from taking the ferry service, there's not much reason to visit Nabouwalu itself. There is a new resort near Raviravi village about 55 km north-east of Nabouwalu on Wainunu Bay. The Mt Kasi goldmine is nearby.

Early in the 19th century, European traders flocked to the **Bua Bay** area north-west of Nabouwalu to exploit *yasi dina*, or sandalwood, which grew in the rugged hills. Offshore to the north-west, the island of Yaduatabu is home to the last sizeable population of rare and spectacular crested iguana. It became Fiji's first wildlife reserve in 1980.

Places to Stay & Eat
If you do wish to stay overnight in Nabouwalu, there is a *government guesthouse* (☎ 836 028; District Officer, Bua) which is generally used by government workers but may have vacancies. Prices are F$5.50 per person and there are cooking facilities. There is also a *YWCA* with beds for F$10.

Fiji's Hidden Paradise Eco Resort (☎ 63 82 4146, fax 63 82 7163 in Australia: e-mail: Mal@geko.com.au or Internet: www.

Precious Cargo

In 1800 the American schooner *Argo* was on her way to the penal colony on Norfolk Island when she was shipwrecked near Oneata, east of Lakeba in the Lau Group. Many of the sailors were killed and eaten by the locals, but Oliver Slater survived by befriending powerful chiefs and helping them in war with his knowledge of muskets and gunpowder.

The sailors brought with them a disease thought to be Asian cholera and a plague broke out in the Fijian islands. Known as *na lila balavu* (wasting sickness), it took a terrible toll, destroying whole communities. Sick people were walled up in caves, strangled, or even buried alive in an attempt to avoid the spread of the disease. Slater left Oneata and travelled with Fijians. He lived for a while in a village on Bua Bay until he was picked up by a passing Spanish vessel. He broke the news of the precious sandalwood to be found in the hills around Bua Bay and returned to Fiji to facilitate trade. Ships flocked to the area, which was also known as Sandalwood Bay. Cargoes of the fragrant timber, which fetched high prices in Asia, were traded for trinkets, muskets, alcohol and assistance in local wars. The chiefs of Bua gained prosperity and prestige.

The sandalwood trade was short lived as supply was soon exhausted. Slater's luck eventually ran out and the influential beachcomber was killed on Motoriki in the Lomaiviti Group. ■

allaustralian.com/fijishiddenparadise) is approximately 400m away from the village of Raviravi, and the village has a third ownership. It bills itself as an ecotourism resort. It has only three bures, each with their own flush toilet, shower and mosquito nets, accommodating a maximum of 14 guests. There is a common dining room. Rates including meals and activities are F$120 for singles or twin share. A family bure for three or more people is F$320. Meals are Fijian and Indian style, including fresh seafood, fruit, vegetables and rice. The resort uses gas lamps for lighting and solar power.

Activities include snorkelling/fishing tours, guided rainforest walks, bird-watching, massage and village visits. You can also learn about Fijian culture and bush medicine. Scuba diving can be arranged with Eco Divers in Savusavu for an extra cost: see Eco Divers rates under the Savusavu section. It usually involves staying in Savusavu. Rules are no bikinis and no sharing alcohol with the locals. BYO alcohol if you wish.

Getting There & Away

Patterson Brothers Shipping has a bus service from Lautoka, followed by a ferry service from Ellington Wharf, northern Viti Levu near Nananu-i-Ra, 60 km across Bligh Water to Nabouwalu. The ferry leaves Ellington Wharf early in the morning and you may be able to arrange to spend the night before on the boat. There are bus services to/from Lautoka and Ellington Wharf, and to/from Nabouwalu and Labasa (four hours). Alternatively, they have a daily (except Sunday) service from Natovi Landing, eastern Viti Levu, to Nabouwalu, with bus connections to/from Suva and Labasa. See the Getting Around chapter for details.

The long dusty road to Labasa through Bua and Macuata Provinces (136 km) also has regular buses (three times daily) which take five hours, while the express bus takes about four hours. The trip costs F$6.50. There are no direct buses from Nabouwalu to Savusavu, but you can travel through to Labasa and catch a bus from there to Savusavu. Alternatively, if you are not interested in visiting Labasa, ask the driver to drop you off at the junction with the road to Savusavu. You may have to wait at the intersection for about an hour for a bus coming from Labasa to Savusavu.

The road from Nabouwalu (127 km) around the southern coast to Savusavu is only passable by 4WD or carrier. Guests of Fiji Hidden Paradise Eco Resort are met at Savusavu airport and transported by 4WD vehicle to the resort. The trip around the southern coast to Raviravi takes 1½ to two hours and costs F$100 per vehicle for a maximum of four people.

VANUA LEVU

Taveuni

Taveuni is fairly sparsely populated, with 12,000 indigenous Fijians or people of mixed descent, together with many foreigners living on the island. Along with Eastern Vanua Levu, the islands of Qamea, Matagi and Laucala, Taveuni is included in the Vanua (or region) of Cakaudrove. Somosomo is the largest village and power base of the chiefly Fijian administration for the region. The island's main source of income is agriculture, specifically copra and to a lesser extent crops such as *dalo* and kava, but it is increasingly relying on tourism.

Taveuni's stunning natural beauty, both under and above water, is popular with divers, bushwalkers and nature lovers. Fortunately it is not too resortified (as yet anyway) and the island is relatively compact, easily accessible, and good for outdoor activities.

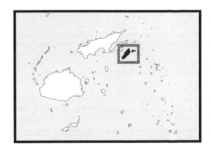

History

There are a few sites of archaeological interest on Taveuni, including the remains of the old Vuna village hill fortification in the south. Originally from Motoriki near Ovalau, the Paramount Chief Tui Vuna worked up a vast army which was long undefeated, partly due to the strategic location of his fort. The Tui Cakau of Somosomo eventually overcame his opponent by bribing relatives of Tui Vuna from Motoriki to abduct his son, rendering the chief helpless.

Before the Europeans arrived in Taveuni, the Fijian villagers had long been trading, and occasionally warring, with the seafaring Tongans. In the mid-19th century the Tongan warlord Ma'afu, already powerful in the Lau group and attempting to extend his influence, was defeated in a battle at Somosomo.

The first European traders and settlers arrived in southern Taveuni in the early 19th century. Land was bartered or purchased from the Tui Vuna and they established plantations and homesteads. Taveuni's deep fertile soil grew high quality cotton; how-

ever, when cotton prices collapsed, sugar cane was planted mainly in southern Taveuni in the Salialevu area, where the ruins of the 100-year-old Billyard sugar mill still stand. Sugar cane was a failure in Taveuni's wet climate. Farming of cattle and sheep among the palms had some success, as did coffee and tropical fruits, before copra plantations took over. Because of its agricultural importance, Taveuni developed good shipping services and roads for the time. Some of the descendants of the original settlers still own land in the area

Geography

The island of Taveuni, 42 km in length and about 10 km wide, is the third largest of the Fiji islands. It is located about 140 km northeast of Viti Levu and just nine km from the south-east end of Vanua Levu across the Somosomo Strait. One of main features in the island topography is the 1000m central ridge, which includes two of the highest peaks in Fiji: Des Voeux Peak at 1195m and Mt Uluigalau at 1241m, the second-highest summit in Fiji. The ridge lies perpendicular to the south-easterly prevailing winds, hence the high rainfall, especially on the south-eastern side. The summit is often hidden behind clouds. The abundant rainfall and volcanic soil covered with lush vegetation

PLACES TO STAY
1 Nai Kelekele
   Apartment
2 Lisi's Campsite
3 Beverly Beach
   Camping &
   Aquaventure
4 Maravu Plantation
   Resort
5 Dive Taveuni
7 Bibi's Hideaway
8 Margaret Peterson's
10 Lomalagi
   Beachfront Cottage
11 Sere-ni-ika
12 Niranjan's
   Accommodation &
   Airport Motel

14 Audrey's Sweet
   Somethings & By
   the Sea
17 Tovutovu Resort
18 Qamea Resort
19 Matagi Island Resort
20 Laucala Resort
22 Garden Island Resort
   & Rainbow Reef
   Divers
24 Kris Back Palace
25 Nomui Lala Resort &
   Vuna Reef Divers
26 Vatuwiri Farm

PLACES TO EAT
6 Karin's Garden &
   Restaurant

9 Coconut Grove Cafe &
   Beachfront Cottage
15 Little Dolphin
   Treehouse &
   Pizza Take Away

OTHER
13 Matei Airport
16 Bhula Bhai
   Supermarket
21 Government Wharf &
   Korean Wharf
23 Waikiri Missio

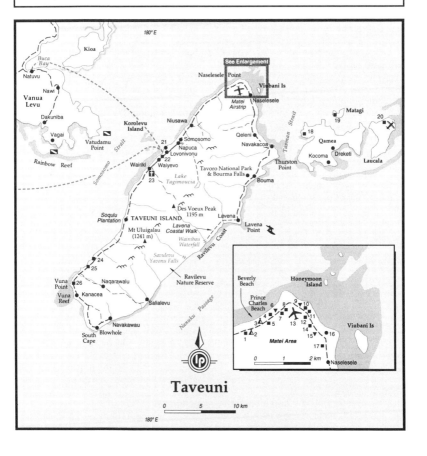

Taveuni

makes Taveuni one of Fiji's most fertile areas.

Taveuni is a typical example of a volcanic island. Its high volcanic ridge was formed by a series of volcanoes and its rich soils are derived from basaltic lava that was never submerged. In the south-east there are a number of lava flows reaching the coast. Being volcanic, Taveuni is not known for its beaches. Most of the coastline is rugged and there are some black-sand beaches such as Navakacoa. Lavena beach, and Prince Charles and Beverly beaches near Matei are exceptions with beautiful white sand. They are good for swimming and snorkelling. The smaller offshore islands of Qamea, Matagi and Laucala have stunning beaches, linking north-south along the protected western side.

Off Naselesele Point, Matei, on the northern point of the island, is a group of small rocky islets in a picturesque arrangement. For a further 10 km to the south-east the land is gently sloping until Thurston Point. Shallow water with reefs continue down to the village at Lavena Point. Hereon to Salialevu is a rugged, straight stretch of cliffs and open ocean, with no roads. About halfway along, the 20m high Savulevu Yavonu Waterfall flows directly into the sea. Salialevu has a small fringing reef and a channel, and at the south end of the island the volcanic coast is eroded by the sea, forming all sorts of caves and blowholes. At the southern cape the land turns flatter with a wide bay ending at Vuna Point where you again find village settlements. Along the coast around the south end and western side of the island all the way up to Wairiki there is deep water close to shore; the only reef is at Vuna Point where the inverted U-shaped coral formation extends for about three km out from the coast. Further north from Wairiki the currents through the Somosomo Strait form a submerged platform with abundant coral life.

Climate

In Taveuni expect lots of rain as it's a rainforest area. The island is especially hot and humid in January and February and the water

clarity is not as good due to plankton blooms and northerly winds from the equator; see the Facts about the Country chapter.

Flora & Fauna

Taveuni is known as the 'Garden Island of Fiji' for its dense and verdant rainforest and exotic flora and fauna above and below the sea. Its rugged geography hindered over-farming, leaving forests and wildlife relatively intact. Flora includes ferns, orchids, rare palms and native trees such as *evuevu*, *sinu*, *vutu*, *ivi* and *dilo*. A good place for viewing bats is Vatuwiri farm in the south. Fiji's national flower, the tagimoucia, or *Medinilla waterhousei,* only grows at high altitudes on Taveuni as well as on one mountain of Vanua Levu. Its petals are white and branches bright red. There are many copra plantations. Metal bands have been placed around the trees to stop rats and crabs climbing them and piercing the coconuts.

Bird-Watching Taveuni is one of the best locations in Fiji for bird-watching with over 100 species of birds. Its variety and number of birds is partly due to the mongoose never being introduced here. Try to make it to Des Voeux Peak at dawn and you may see the rare orange-breasted dove (male) and the silktail. Another good bird-watching site is near Qeleni, a village between Matei and Thurston Point. On the Matei side of the village, follow a 4WD track for 3.5 km up the mountain. Here you are likely to see the above-mentioned birds as well as parrots and fantails, especially between August and September when the birds are nesting. The forested Lavena coast is also a good spot to see orange or flame doves, Fiji goshawk, wattled honeyeater, and grey and white heron. Down south you are likely to see or hear magpies which were introduced to control insects in the copra plantations. The deep red feathers of the kula parrot were once an important trade item with the Tongans.

Language

One of the distinctions of the Cakaudrove dialect (which is common to Taveuni and its offshore islands and eastern Vanua Levu) is the dropped 'k'. The only difference that a traveller is likely to notice is 'vinaka', which is pronounced vina'a or even shortened to na'a or na'.

Activities

Hiking Taveuni's Lavena Coastal Walk and Bouma falls are a must-see for nature lovers. They have marked trails and don't require guides. Other places for keen trekkers to consider are from Somosomo to Lake Tagimoucia, or a walk to Des Voeux Peak.

Diving The Somosomo Strait (meaning 'good water' in Fijian) has strong tidal currents which provide a constant flow of nutrients, ideal for soft coral growth and diverse fish life. You are likely to see lots of fish, the occasional shark or turtle and fantastic coral. In November you may see pilot whales in the area. Taveuni is world renowned among divers for the spectacular, colourful soft corals at spots such as the Rainbow Reef, (a fringing reef almost 32 km long on the south-west corner of Vanua Levu but best accessed from Taveuni) and for drift dives along the Great White Wall. Other sites include Cabbage Patch, Blue Ribbon Eel Reef, The Ledge, The Pinnacle, Yellow Grotto, Annie's Bommie and The Zoo and Vuna Reef off southern Taveuni.

The patch reefs of the Somosomo Strait are fairly shallow (10 to 22m) but have strong tidal currents. The fringing reef has wall diving (15 to 30m) and larger fish, and is more exposed to weather and surge. The strongest current is actually in the shallow sections over the reefs, lessening with depth. Drift diving is done at some sites when the tides are right. Novice divers may find the currents in the Somosomo Strait challenging, but generally a descent line is placed. The area is not just for experienced divers as there are many different sites, and weather conditions vary.

The *Matagi Princess II*, a live-aboard 25m luxury yacht, based at Matagi Island Resort (☎ 880 260, 301 780; fax 880 274), is available for four to seven-day dive trips around northern Fiji. Catering for a maximum of 12 experienced divers, the yacht accesses the Somosomo Strait, as well as sites such as Noel's Wall, the Golden Dream, and exploratory dives on the Ringgolds and Exploring Isle. There are six 'staterooms' and film processing facilities on board. Two-day/three-night cruises are also offered for non-divers.

See the Diving sections throughout the chapter for more details. Dive Taveuni and Aquaventure are both based in Matei, Garden Island Resort in Waiyevo and Vuna Reef Divers in southern Taveuni. The upmarket resorts on the offshore islands of Matagi, Qamea and Laucala each have diving for their guests.

Kayaking From June to September each year Keni Madden and TC Donovan of Ringgold Reef Kayaking (☎ 880 083) take kayaking/camping tours around Taveuni. They also rent out kayaks during the year; enquire at Beverly Beach Garden Island Resort has ocean kayaks for hire and Little Dolphin in Matei has outrigger canoes. Some keen kayakers travel the Ravilevu coast.

Accommodation

Taveuni has a good variety of places to stay, ranging from very simple bottom end to more expensive offshore resorts. Waiyevo and around has several options for budget accommodation including one middle-range motel, Kaba's Motel, and the more upmarket Garden Island Resort which also has budget dorm rooms. While Napuca town, next to Somosomo, is not the most picturesque place to stay in Taveuni, it may be convenient for those who have just arrived by boat and want somewhere to crash. The accommodation in Southern Taveuni covers budget and middle range. Around the airport in Matei there are lots of budget and middle options as well as a couple of top end resorts. Eastern Taveuni is a beautiful area but, apart from camping, the only place to stay is backpacker style in the loft of Lavena's reception bure. Beverly, Lisi's and Tovutovu near

Matei have camping, as does Nomui Lala in the south. The up-market offshore resorts of Qamea, Matagi and Laucala cater mainly to pre-booked guests.

Power is by individual generators which usually run for limited time periods.

Entertainment

Taveuni has many outdoor activities but there is not much to do at night, except perhaps kava drinking. It is a place to go to bed early and pack in daytime activities instead. The **Meridian Cinema** in Wairiki shows movies on Friday, Saturday and Sunday at 7.30 pm.

Getting There & Away

Air The flights to/from Taveuni and either Suva or Nadi are stunning – you'll get especially excited if you are a diver! Sunflower (☎ 880 461) flies to/from Nadi twice daily, with an extra flight on Monday, Wednesday and Friday. The trip takes 1½ hours and costs F$132 one-way. Air Fiji (☎ 880 062) also flies this route for the same price (at least once daily). Both Air Fiji (three flights daily, F$98) and Vanua Air (twice on Tuesday, Thursday and Saturday; F$88) fly to/from Nausori near Suva. The flight takes about 55 minutes.

Flights to Savusavu or Labasa, Vanua Levu, cost F$50 on Sunflower and F$52 on Air Fiji. Sunflower flies twice daily to Savusavu and once daily to Labasa. Air Fiji flies three or four times daily to Savusavu. Refer also to the Getting Around chapter.

Matei airport is usually open from 8 am to 4 pm and has a cardphone, kiosk and a toilet block. There is a map of Taveuni painted on the wall showing locations of accommodation, although it's not necessarily up to date. Audrey Brown is sometimes there with her home baking and Margaret Peterson runs the kiosk selling roti parcels for F$1.40 as well as scones and other snacks.

Boat There are many services on the Taveuni-Vanua Levu-Viti Levu route so prices are competitive. Patterson Brothers Shipping (☎ 880 036, 880 382) has an office at the rear of the Lesuma supermarket, next to the National Bank of Fiji in Waiyevo. The trip to Savusavu, Vanua Levu involves a ferry across the Somosomo Strait for 1¾ hours to Natuvu, Buca Bay and then 1½ to two hours on a chartered bus to Savusavu. It can be a long, dusty bus trip, though quite scenic. There is a Patterson Brothers ferry from Savusavu on to Natovi Landing (6½ hours) and a bus service on to Suva. It leaves Korean wharf for Buca Bay every day except Sunday and twice on Wednesday and Friday, and costs F$5.50 per person or F$4.40 if you pay in advance at the office.

The *Grace* (☎ 880 134) also combines ferry and bus to Savusavu. It departs from Korean Wharf at 8.30 am daily (except Sunday), to Buca Bay for F$5, and has its own bus to Savusavu for an extra F$5. The boat returns at 1 pm. It also does transfers to Rabi Island on Thursday at 4 am (book by Wednesday afternoon). You have the choice of visiting for 1½ hours or staying one week until you can get the next ferry back to Taveuni. The only accommodation is a guesthouse or to camp and prior permission to visit is required.

The agent for Consort Shipping Line is at the Waiyevo market opposite Garden Island Resort. The MV *SOFE, Spirit of Free Enterprise* does a weekly Suva-Taveuni voyage via Koro and Savusavu. It takes five hours to get to Savusavu, usually stopping for a couple of hours and then taking 13 hours to get to Suva.

Beachcomber Cruises' *Adi Savusavu*, previously known as MV *Dana Star*, also does weekly trips to Savusavu and Suva and has better facilities than the SOFE. It departs from the Government Wharf. The Taveuni agent for Beachcomber is Raj's Tyre Repair (☎ 880 216; fax 880 202) in Napuca, which is open Monday to Friday from 8 am to 5 pm (noon on Saturday).

Timetables are always changing and the ferries are notorious for delays. The worst thing about the long trips is that the toilets can become disgusting. We recommend that you take your own toilet paper. See the Getting Around chapter for fares and other information, as well as the Vanua Levu chapter.

Getting Around

A gravel road hugs Taveuni's scenic coast from Lavena in the east to Navakawau in the south. There are also a couple of other inland 4WD tracks. Getting around Taveuni involves a bit of planning, the main disadvantage being the length of time between buses. To get around cheaply and quickly you need to combine buses with walking or hitching, or share taxis with a group.

Bus Getting around on the local buses is the best way to meet locals. Pacific Buses (☎ 880 278) has a depot centrally located at Naqara, Somosomo, opposite the Taveuni Central Indian School. Monday to Saturday buses depart for both the north (as far as Lavena) and the south (as far as Navakawau) at 8.30 am, noon and 5 pm. It costs about F$2.30 to travel to the end of the line. The southern bus goes up to Naqarawalu either on its way to or from Navakawau, depending on how full the bus is. If you wish to continue to Salialevu you will have to walk from Naqarawalu downhill about eight km – the only problem is getting back! It is better to hire a 4WD, taxi or take an organised trip. Beware of getting stranded at the end of the line as the last buses of the day return only the next morning. Lavena has simple accommodation but Naqarawalu and Navakawau do not. On Sunday buses go each way at 8 am, returning to the depot at 4 pm. Buses are sometimes full of schoolchildren and it can be frustrating if a bus passes you by and the next one is not for a few hours.

Car Kaba's Rentals, Kaba's Supermarket, Somosomo (☎ 880 058; fax 880 202) has rental cars for F$40 to F$50 per day plus 30c per km, and 4WD vehicles for F$55 per day plus 40c per km. Drivers must be over 25 years.

Taxi Taxis are readily available in the Matei and Waiyevo areas. It may be wise to book though if you need one on a Sunday. Hiring a taxi for a negotiated fee and touring most of the island's highlights in a day can be a good idea for a group of people and will probably work out cheaper than hiring a car. For destinations such as Lavena you can go one way by bus and arrange to be picked up at the end of the day at a designated time. From Matei airport expect to pay about F$12 to Waiyevo and F$25 to Vuna (Nomui Lala).

Organised Tours Tatadra Tours at Garden Island Resort (☎ 880 126) organises group excursions to the island's sights. Matei's Dive Taveuni and Maravu resorts also have organised trips including bird-watching and rainforest walks, village visits or to Bouma (about F$35), and the Lavena walk (F$55 for the whole day).

Around the Island

WAIYEVO, SOMOSOMO & AROUND

Waiyevo is the administrative centre of the island. While not a major population centre it has the island's hospital, police station, bank and representatives of the SOFE and Patterson Brothers' ferry services. It is a good base for trips to a number of nearby attractions.

The government wharf for large vessels and the **Korean Wharf** are both near **Lovonivonu**, one km north of Waiyevo (towards Matei). There is a small store on the bend in the road and a school. About 2.5 km north of Waiyevo is **Napuca**, Taveuni's main shopping centre, and to the north of the river is Somosomo, the island's chiefly village. The influential missionary William Cross is buried in this village. Napuca/Somosomo has schools, churches and the Great Council of Chiefs' meeting building, which was built in 1986 for the gathering of the important chiefs from all over Fiji. The hall is regularly used for general village meetings and three times a year for provincial council meetings.

The **180th meridian** passes through Taveuni about a 10-minutes walk south of

TAVEUNI

Tui Cakau

Ratu Glanville Wellington Lalabalavu became the new Tui Cakau (paramount chief of Somosomo and the whole Cakaudrove region) in May 1996. The former soldier, politician and administrator replaced the late Ratu Sir Penaia Ganilau. Dressed in *masi* cloth and a sash adorned with the sacred tagimoucia flower, he was installed by a traditional king maker, receiving *yaqona* as a symbol of acceptance of the title. Youths had climbed to Lake Tagimoucia to find the tagimoucia flowers. After the ceremony, Ratu Glanville had to remain at his home for four nights before bathing in the sea and removing the symbolic masi ceremonial attire. Ratu Glanville now has authority and power over land and fishing grounds in all the province, its people and all living things, and has to make decisions on land ownership and usage. ■

Waiyevo. There is a sign on the beach side of the road. It's not really very interesting, but the relief map of Taveuni is good for understanding the island's topography. For workability the International Dateline doglegs around Fiji so that everyone is operating on the same time. About two km south of Waiyevo is **Wairiki village**, which has a general store, cinema and a beautiful old Catholic Mission on the hill.

Information

The only bank on the island is the National Bank of Fiji at Waiyevo, just south of the Garden Island Resort. The Westpac Bank closed on Taveuni due to lack of business. The bank will cash travellers' cheques and you can get cash advances on MasterCard but not, at the time of writing, on Visa. The larger supermarkets and top end resorts accept credit cards, but you may be charged extra. Some resorts will also change travellers' cheques.

The post office, up on the hill in Waiyevo, opens Monday to Saturday from 8 am to 4 pm (closed for lunch 1 to 2 pm). There are card-phones located outside the supermarkets in Waiyevo and Somosomo. Club Coco handicrafts in Waiyevo has a fax service.

Wairiki Catholic Mission

Wairiki Mission, built in 1907, is about 20 minutes walk from Waiyevo, past the 180th Meridian sign. The Catholic Mission is on a hill overlooking a playing field to the Somosomo Strait and Vanua Levu in the distance. In the mid-17th century an important canoe battle took place off this beach between the Taveuni warriors and invading Tongans, who numbered in the thousands. At the time, Tongan chief Elene Ma'afu had gained control of much of the rest of Fiji. The locals managed to turn back the Tongan attack and reportedly the dead enemies were cooked in lovo and eaten with breadfruit! The building of the mission was a thank you to the French missionary priest who had advised the local warriors on a fighting strategy.

If you haven't been to a Fijian church, mass is worth attending for the fantastic singing (Sunday at 7 am and 9 am). A small donation is appreciated. The stained glass is thought to have been imported from France and there is a painting in the presbytery of the famous battle.

Waitavala Waterslide

This natural waterslide is about 25 minutes walk from Waiyevo supermarket. From the supermarket, with Garden Island Resort on the left, walk north towards Matei and take the first road to the right (about 500m past the resort). At the first fork in the road keep to the right. Continue up the hill, passing another turn off to the right, and then past a large shed. Take the next left turn downhill which leads to a creek and a bridge. The path to the waterslide, or rather waterslides, veers off before the creek following it upstream to the right. It is on the Waitavala estate, private land, so if you pass anyone on your way there ask, as a courtesy, if you can visit. It's probably best to watch a local before attempting a slide as the conditions vary with the water flow.

Des Voeux Peak

Des Voeux Peak is Taveuni's second highest mountain at 1195m, after Uluigalau at

TAVEUNI

1241m. On a clear day the views (between the vegetation) are great and it is possible to see Lake Tagimoucia. If you are a keen bird-watcher try to make it up there by dawn. Just before you reach Wairiki Catholic Mission (coming from Waiyevo), a turn-off heads inland and soon starts to climb steeply. Allow three to four hours to walk up (about six km) and at least two to return. It's an arduous climb in the heat so it's best to go up early. An alternative is to arrange for a trip up and then walk back at your leisure. On weekdays it is sometimes possible to hitch a ride with Telecom or PWD workers who go up to service their equipment. Driving requires a 4WD. Enquire at Kaba's supermarket for vehicle hire, or the travel desk at Garden Island Resort can organise trips for about F$60 to F$80 for the vehicle depending on the time spent. Alternatively, try the JP store near the Meridian Cinema at Wairiki.

Lake Tagimoucia
Lake Tagimoucia is in an old volcanic crater, 823m above sea level, in the mountains above Somosomo. Masses of vegetation float on the lake, and the national flower, the rare tagimoucia (*Medivilla waterhouse*, an

epiphytic plant) grows on the lake's shores. This red flower with a white centre blooms from late September to late December only at this altitude.

It is a difficult walk to the lake as it is often very muddy. Take lunch and allow eight hours for the round trip. The track starts from Napuca/Somosomo village. Hire a guide from the village yourself, or ask Garden Island Resort to arrange one for you which will cost F$40. Alternatively the lake can be viewed from a distance the lake from Des Voeux Peak.

Activities
At Garden Island Resort, Aquatrek, which took over from Rainbow Reef Divers in 1996, is a well-equipped dive shop with good boats. They dive the Rainbow Reef (about 20 minutes by boat) and the Vuna Lagoon down south. Two dives cost F$102, six dives (three days) F$290. They make two dives per morning, which is generally the calmest weather, returning for lunch. Prices include tanks and weight belts, but additional gear can be hired. Dive courses include PADI Discover Scuba Diving for F$102 and PADI open water for F$455.

Swimming at Waiyevo in front of the Garden Island Resort is possible two hours either side of high tide. Watch the current though and don't swim near Korean Wharf where fish may have been cleaned, attracting sharks. The small island of Korolevu, off the resort, has beaches with good snorkelling. Trips leave twice in the morning and return twice in the afternoon and cost F$8 per person. Snorkelling trips also go to Rainbow Reef; gear hire is F$5.50 per day. Ocean kayaks (which can carry lunch, snorkelling gear and scuba gear) are F$22/33 for half day/full day hire, and are a great way of exploring the coastline and Korolevu Island.

Places to Stay
Kool's Accommodation (☎ 880 395) is in Napuca. The friendly manager, Chitra Singh, has six very basic rooms in a long block for F$10/16 singles/doubles. There is electricity from 6 pm to 8.30 pm, but no fan. Shared

---

The Legend of the Tagimoucia Flower

One day a young girl disobeyed her mother by playing when she was supposed to be working. The mother lost her patience and, while beating her daughter with a bundle of coconut leaves, told her to go away so that she would never have to see her face again. The distraught girl ran away crying, as far as she could. Deep in the forest she came upon a large *ivi* tree with vines wrapped around it. She climbed the vines and became entangled. She cried and cried and the tears rolling down her face turned to blood, falling onto the vine and becoming beautiful flowers. Finally she did manage to escape and return home, relieved to find her mother had calmed down. The people of Taveuni believe that the exotic tagimoucia flower came from the young girl's tears. ■

facilities include a toilet, shower and a kitchen where you can cook for yourself, but there is no fridge. Security has reportedly been a problem in the past.

Kaba's Guest House & Motel (☎ 880 058) PO Box 4 Somosomo, in Napuca town, has two types of accommodation. The guesthouse consists of four spartan rooms which share a TV room, kitchen, two toilets, shower and laundry trough. Each room has a phone and costs F$20/28/30/40 for singles/doubles/twin/triples. Built in about 1990, the motel block has six deluxe rooms at F$33/40/44/56 for singles/doubles/twin/triples. They are very clean with tiled floors, ceiling fan, TV, telephone, hot water and kitchenettes. Kaba's supermarket is opposite.

Near the Korean wharf at Lovonivonu is the very basic *Sunset Accommodation* (☎ 880 406) run by Teresa and Baiya. The shack to the side of their small shop has a single and double room opening onto a small sitting area and kitchen for F$10/15 respectively. The generator provides electricity between 6 and 10 pm. Theresa will cook you a meal for F$3 or F$4. Another budget option is with Mere at the Waiyevo market. She accommodates people in her *home* nearby, for F$10 per person.

Garden Island Resort (☎ 880 286; fax 880 288) has good accommodation at middle-range prices. There is no beach but a pleasant pool and restaurant/bar area looks out to the Somosomo Strait and Vanua Levu beyond. There are some beautiful old flame trees on the site.

The double storey building used to be Travelodge in the 1970s. Typical rooms are clean with 70s furnishings, mosquito screens, ceiling fan, and sliding doors to the garden or upstairs verandah, with sea views. The resort quotes its prices in US$. Singles/doubles/triples cost US$50/66/75 and US$37.50/75/112.50 for meals. Interconnecting rooms are available. A family room is US$116 plus US$75 for meals. About half the rooms have air-conditioning which is an extra US$6 per night. There are seven-night package rates which are about

10% cheaper, as well as dive/meal/accommodation packages.

Two of the hotel rooms are used as dormitories (up to four people in each) for US$14 per person, great value when you consider what the rest are paying. There are also two double rooms (usually set aside for locals) for about US$30 per night. Located on the manager's side of the hotel, opening out onto the pool, the main difference here is that they have no fridge and the door doesn't lock. See the Activities section for information on Aquatrek, snorkelling and kayaking trips, and Places to Eat below for the resort restaurant.

Places to Eat

The Garden Island Resort *restaurant* has buffet-style breakfast for F$6.50, lunch is in the F$6.50 to 7.50 range and dinner is F$11 to 16. Outsiders are welcome in the restaurant and bar, but dinner needs to be ordered in the afternoon. The menu is a mixture of styles. Happy hour at the bar is between 6 and 7 pm.

If you find the Garden Island Resort restaurant a bit overpriced for what's on offer, try the *Wathi-po-ee Restaurant and Cannibal Cafe* next door. The menu is Chinese style and main dishes are in the F$4 to F$5 range; the kitchen is also a bakery. The restaurant is open from 8 am to 8 pm. On the water's edge is the outdoor cafe (enter through the restaurant's kitchen or the back of the Lesuma supermarket). It's a good spot to have a beer in the afternoon, overlooking the Somosomo Strait from the shade of a thatched roof. The cafe is open Monday to Friday from 7 am to 7 pm, and Saturday 7 am to 1 pm and 5 to 7 pm.

The Waiyevo market, directly opposite, has several takeaway stalls and sit-down eating, serving Fijian style food. *Mere's Takeaway* is quite good, open Monday to Friday from 8 am to 4 pm and Saturday from 9 am to 4.30 pm. Mere will also cook dinner if you order in advance. Stalls outside sell sweets and the market has a fresh fish section.

In Somosomo the *Island Restaurant*,

opposite Kaba's Motel, has very simple dishes of curry, chop suey or fried rice for F$2.30 to F$4. It is open 7.30 am to 8 pm.

Self-Catering Waiyevo has a good supermarket selling basics including bread and ice cream. There is also a small market but it can be difficult to buy fresh ingredients as Fijian villagers usually grow for their own use. Wairiki has a general store and Kaba's store/supermarket in Somosomo takes credit cards.

Things to Buy

Club Coco (☎ 880 017; fax 880 033) is next door to the supermarket and National Bank of Fiji in Waiyevo. The shop sells a variety of handicrafts including large pieces of stencilled tapa cloth (about F$48 for a piece measuring eight feet by two feet) and a small selection of books. Opening hours are Monday to Friday from 9 am to 5 pm, and to 1 pm on Saturday.

Most of the island's resorts have some sort of boutique. Garden Island Resort also has handicrafts by local craftspeople. Carpenters Agriculture, on the left about five minutes by taxi heading south from Waiyevo, sells local coffee beans that you'll need to roast yourself.

SOUTHERN TAVEUNI

The main villages on southern Taveuni are Naqarawalu in the hills and, on the southern coast near Vuna Reef, Kanacea, Vuna and Navakawau at the end of the road. The people of Kanacea are descendants of peoples whose island was sold by Chief Cakobau to Europeans. Their ancestors were displaced as punishment for siding with the Tongans in a war.

Things to See

The road south from Waiyevo to Vuna winds along the rugged coast through beautiful rainforest and coconut palms. About eight km (15 minutes drive) south of Waiyevo is a failed development project **Soqulu Plantation**, its grand scale and imported ideas obviously out of context. Some 1500 home sites were surveyed, but only about 25

people actually received a title and built homes. Bankruptcy left around 30 luxury condominiums stalled at only 85% completion. The nine-hole golf course, two tennis courts and a lawn bowls green are, however, open for public use (enquire about fees and equipment hire at Garden Island Resort). The rainforest in this area is an excellent place for bird-watching.

Also in the area is an ancient **Warrior Burial Cave**. This cave was once used as a hidden cemetery for warriors so that their death would be kept secret from enemies, for the same reason some chiefs were buried inside their own bures. The lava tube cave runs for about 360m down to the ocean. Guided tours can be arranged, but it is dark and muddy so take a torch.

At the end of the road past Naqarawalu is Salialevu, a large copra plantation and beef farm, of historical importance for the remains of **Billyard Sugar Mill** from last century.

Vatuwiri Farm, at Vuna Point, is another farm of interest. In its heyday it used to be one of the main copra estates in Taveuni. The 800 hectare farm is still one of the biggest on Taveuni (the largest has about 1600 ha). James Tarte established the estate in 1871 and introduced the magpie into Taveuni to control stick insects. There are some interesting old stone buildings, including tiny cottages and kitchens for the blackbirded and indentured labourers who worked here. Economic necessity has driven the Tarte family to diversify into cocoa, vanilla, sugar cane, cattle, Fijian asparagus, voy voy (tree for mats) and also to tourism. The remains of the old **Vuna village hill fortification** above the present village and partly on Vatuwiri Estate land, are worth a visit if you are interested in archaeology. The village was built on a strategic point and natural lookout, from where it was possible to survey the Vuna reef for intruding canoes. Large flat areas are linked by crossings over deep defensive ditches. Many stone foundations remain to tell their story: the tallest one would have been the chief's bure, linked to that of his wives; the one with a double base was the temple; and the largest was the meeting bure. Shells, pottery, axes and sea-washed rocks have been found at the site.

The **Blow Hole** past Vuna village performs best on a large south-westerly swell. However, don't come down to this end of the island just for this, unless you have never seen a blow hole before.

Activities

Nomui Lala offers activities including lava tube exploration with a local guide for F$5 per person plus an extra F$1 for torch hire, kayak rental, mountain trekking, volleyball, trips to Namoli Beach, the blow holes and 'mysterious hand prints'. A four hour horse ride through thick rainforest to a volcanic crater costs about F$25 per person. It also rents out mountain bikes for F$5/10/20 per hour/half-day/full-day.

Vatuwiri offers snorkelling, boat charters, reef and game fishing, horse riding, surfing transfers, fortified village visits, cattle mustering, bird-watching and trekking, but only to guests; see the Places to Stay & Eat section for full details.

Diving and snorkelling on the Vuna Reef is through Vuna Reef Divers at Nomui Lala Resort, or Noks Dive Centre at Kris Back Palace. You are likely to see lots of big fish, as well as beautiful coral and the occasional shark. Vuna Reef Divers has good dive equipment and dive boats, and lessons are available in English and German. It offers one-tank boat dives for F$50 and a six-tank special for F$250 with tanks, weights and dive guide included. Other equipment can be hired. The resort course is F$85 and PADI/NAUI open water courses are F$370, including all equipment. There is also a kayak diving course. A trip to the Great White Wall costs F$95 for a two-tank dive. Snorkellers are taken on the dive boat to Vuna Reef for F$25. With Noks Dive Centre a two-tank dive including equipment is F$77, a shore dive F$16.50, and PADI open water course is F$330.

Places to Stay & Eat

The Vuna area has a couple of small general stores including one near Vatuwiri Farm which is run by a Chinese couple. If the wife is by herself she will barricade the shop and only serve from a barred window at the back. Have patience as it can be difficult to communicate. The shop in Kanacea opens from 10.30 am to 1.30 pm and 4.30 to 8 pm daily, except Sunday. Families grow fruit and vegetables for their own use only, so it is almost impossible to buy fresh produce.

Kris Back Palace (☎ 880 246; fax 880 072), run by a friendly Fiji-Indian couple, Saviri and Bobby Shankaran, has budget (far from palatial) accommodation. It is fairly isolated, about seven km from Vuna, a bit less than two km north of Nomui Lala, on a rugged, scrubby section of rocky coastline. There is no beach, but snorkelling is good; it's possible to swim through underwater caves. The dorm, a simple thatched geometric bure, sleeps five people at F$11 per person. Mosquito nets and linen are provided. The double bure costs F$25. It is very basic, with a verandah and concrete floor, and is near the water's edge. The two toilets, two showers and laundry trough are a bit distant from the bures, so watch you don't sprain an ankle on the rough terrain at night! Camping is F$5 per person. Electricity is available from 6 to 9 pm. The very rustic kitchen hut, right on the water's edge, has a stove and sink but you can also cook at the owner's house across the road. Alternatively, Saviri will provide three meals (Indian and Fijian) for F$15 per day. Noks Diver Centre operates from here: see Activities above.

Nomui Lala Resort (☎ & fax 880 125; previously known as Susie's Plantation), was a copra plantation established in the 1850s. The name means 'group of friends' but it is still often referred to as Susie's. New owners Carolyn (American) and Eric (South African) took over in early 1996 and are endeavouring to revive the resort, which had been running down. There is no beach but the black lava rock contrasting with the turquoise water is quite beautiful. The large garden has fruit and coconut trees, and orchids. At the time of writing there was a problem with water supply and only rainwater could be used for drinking. Breakfast is F$5 for fruit and toast or F$9 for eggs, toast and cereal. Lunch is F$6 and three-course dinner is F$15. Kava drinking is the night-time entertainment. MasterCard and Visa are accepted but incur a 5% charge. See Activities above for information on Vuna Reef Divers.

Camping costs F$7 per person. The dormitory sleeps up to 12 people and costs F$12 per person. Sharing a double room is F$15 per person. Don't leave your valuables here, as the building is not far from the road and out of sight from reception. Basic kitchen facilities are provided and there is a toilet and shower, with cold water only.

The main house has a dining and sitting area and a few rooms of varying size and price. Rooms sharing a bathroom are F$25 for a single or double, or F$35 a double. The larger room with ensuite and ocean view is F$45. Across the garden the two private bures, each with self-catering facilities (no fridge, though), ensuites and mosquito nets are fairly rustic but comfortable. The corrugated iron roofs are used for catching rainwater and have palm lining internally. The 'Orchid bure', constructed from rough-hewn coconut timber, has a cute sitting room and is F$48 for a double. The 'Hibiscus bure' sleeps up to four or five people in two rooms divided by a partition for F$54 a double, F$10 per extra adult or F$5 per child. Gaps in the coconut tree floor boards add to the rustic effect. This bure has a verandah and the waves lap against the shore only a few metres away.

Vatuwiri Farm Resort (☎ 880 316) c/o PA Vuna, has a variety of accommodation for guests. Staying here will give you an insight into life on plantation from the viewpoint of a part-European family. The two small beachfront cottages are F$77 per night, each with a double bed and sitting area and a semi-detached ensuite. The one perched on the water's edge has a porch and a kitchen which can take a single bed. A room with ensuite in the homestead costs F$71.50 per night. A long weatherboard building with a verandah, which used to be the estate

workers' quarters and feels a bit like a stable, has been converted into six rooms for up to three people per room. Prices are F$22, or F$16.50 per night for stays of more than one week. There are no cooking facilities, but up at the homestead you can get three meals a day, afternoon tea, fruit and snacks for F$38.50. Solar electricity is available.

Snorkelling gear is free and diving can be arranged through Vuna Divers. Vatuwiri also offers reef fishing for F$16.50 per day for a minimum of two people, game fishing on its huge speed boat, horse riding for F$33 per day, surfing on Vuna reef (not reliable) for F$20 return transfer, trips to the fortified village remains in the hills, trips to a volcano crater, cattle mustering, fruit bat and bird watching, and trekking. The *Lady Vuna*, a 12m catamaran, can be chartered for F$1000 per night or F$750 for a day trip with food and drinks included.

Getting There & Away

It's about one hour by car or about two hours by local bus from Matei airport to Vuna along a winding gravel road which hugs the coast. It is a beautiful drive from Waiyevo to Vuna through dense verdant forest, past dalo and coconut plantations. See the Getting Around section earlier in this chapter.

MATEI & AROUND

Matei is a fast-growing residential area around the airport. The freehold land is popular with Americans and other foreigners searching for a piece of tropical paradise. One of the best beaches on the island is the white-sand Prince Charles Beach, good for sunbathing and snorkelling and swimming in crystal blue water. Beverly Beach nearby is also nice but snorkelling is not that great. Off Naselesele Point there are four small islands immediately offshore which have some good snorkelling (the third is known as the local 'Honeymoon Island'. Further to the east is the larger Viubani Island.

Activities

Scott and Lalita at Little Dolphin (see also Places to Stay) open between 8.30 am and

4.30 pm, and have sports equipment for hire, as well as being a source of useful information on Taveuni's sights. They have paddle boats (F$5 per hour or F$15 per day), outrigger canoes (F$30 per day), surfboards (F$15 per day) and snorkelling gear (F$5 per day). Snorkelling, surfing, fishing trips and tours can be arranged. To get to Honeymoon Island by small boat is about F$10 to F$11 per person.

The long established Dive Taveuni (see under Places to Stay) uses a 12m catamaran for dive trips. A two tank dive is F$120 per person per day. NAUI dive courses include: Resort Course F$150 for one or two people, or F$100 for a group; open water F$450 for one or two people, or F$395 for a group. Snorkelling trips are F$20 with lunch on the boat.

The resort is closed from mid-January to the end of February. The dive operation caters mainly to pre-booked guests. One reader raved about the operation's excellent planning and the food provided.

Aquaventure (☎ & fax 880 381) opened its dive operation at Beverly Beach in January 1996. Dive trips here cost F$65/100 for one/two-tank dives, less 10% if you have your own BCD regulator. Open water courses including full equipment hire (four to five days) are F$400, resort courses with one boat dive are F$100 and night dives are F$60. Multi-dive packages and other courses are also available. The owners, Tania and Alex, will also take snorkellers out to the reefs if space is available on their dive boat (maximum six).

Warwick and Dianne Bain, at Nai Kelekele Apartment Prince Charles Beach, (☎ & fax 880 141) offer a 13.5m charter yacht *Seax of Legra*, which departs Taveuni, Qamea, Buca Bay, and Vanua Levu. Charters are fully crewed, taking parties of one to four guests or a family of five. Rates include all meals, use of snorkelling gear and dinghies and a windsurf (on request). Diving can be arranged. Daily rates are US$650/690/725 for doubles/triples/four people. Weekly rates are US$4500/4750/5000 for doubles/triples/four people.

Places to Stay – bottom end

Margaret Peterson (☎ 880 171), the friendly lady at the airport kiosk, has two double *rooms* in her nearby house, which she rents for F$30/60 for singles/doubles including three meals. If you can't find her at the kiosk, try her house. It is about a five-minute walk from the airport towards Waiyevo through a beautiful stretch of forest. Hers is the third drive on the left before the bus stand and her house is up the hill. Margaret is also a good cook: see the upcoming Places to Eat section.

The best place for camping on Taveuni is *Beverly Beach Camping* about 15 minutes walk from the airport, southward past Dive Taveuni and Maravu resorts. The camp, managed by Bill Madden, is along the edge of a white-sand beach beneath fantastic, huge poison-fish trees. Set up for a maximum of 12 to 15 people, it's an excellent place to lay back and relax on the beach. Prince Charles Beach is a km further south. The facilities here are very basic, but the atmosphere can be fun especially if you strike a good group of people while you are there.

Tent sites cost F$5 per person or F$7 with tent provided. If you don't feel like staying in a tent there are also two very simple bures with sand floors, from where you literally step out on to the beach. The dormitory bure, with its floral cloth lining and mosquito nets, can fit a maximum of three people and is a good option at F$10 per person. The camp has flush toilet, shower, an open cooking bure with gas stove, utensils and a communal eating table. Bill brings around fresh fruit and vegetables in the morning. He also provides equipment for snorkelling and fishing. See the Activities section for information about Aquaventure, the new diving operation adjoining the camp.

Lisi's Campsite (☎ 880 194) Vacala Estate, PA Matei, is located across the road from the beautiful Prince Charles Beach, about two km or 20 minutes walk from the Matei airport towards Waiyevo. Camping costs F$5 and there are also two spartan bures with mosquito nets for F$10/20, singles/doubles. Out the back there is a shower, toilet, kitchen and communal laundry. There are also simple meals for guests: F$3.50 for breakfast and F$5 for dinner.

Tovutovu Resort (☎ & fax 880 560) began operating in 1996 and is located 20 minutes walk from Matei airport, past the Bhula Bhai Supermarket towards Naselesele village. It is run by Alan Petersen on the family's copra plantation. The front two bures are self-contained with small kitchenettes for F$60, sleeping a maximum of three in each. The two rear bures with private toilet and shower, but no cooking facilities, cost F$50 for singles or doubles. At the time of writing the newly constructed bures had mosquito screens and hot water, but no fans or fridges. A dorm for 12 people with a communal kitchen was being built on the higher ground at the back of the site and looks like it will be a good option for backpackers. The charge will be F$10 per head. Camping costs F$5. See Places to Eat for information on the restaurant. The property also has a family chapel on the hill, and further up past the end of the airport runway is an old village lookout site.

Niranjan's Budget Accommodation and Airport Motel (☎ 880 406) PA Matei, is three minutes walk east of the airport. It offers self-contained, rather shabby rooms with cooking facilities, for F$22/30 singles/doubles. Children under 10 cost F$8.80. The shop at the front has a limited selection of groceries, but there is a better supermarket only five minutes walk down the road. The family can also cook curry dinners for F$12. The *Airport Motel* next door looked as if it hadn't been used for a long time. Rooms with shared bathroom and basic cooking facilities (no fridge) are F$13.20/22 for singles/doubles.

Places to Stay – middle
It seems that just about everyone in Matei has a cottage or two for rent in their garden, some of which can be shared and are good value for groups or families.

Bibi's Hideaway (☎ 880 443, 880 365) PO Box 80, Waiyevo, is owned and run by the amiable James Biba. He has three good, self-contained cottages in his large garden in a quiet and convenient location. Walk for about seven minutes through the forest along the road from the airport towards Waiyevo. Another ten minutes walk will get you to the lovely Prince Charles Beach. Bibi is happy to give guests some of the produce from his garden: bananas, pawpaws, mangoes, pineapples, oranges, coconuts and guavas. The two simple cottages have spacious sitting rooms and kitchens, and there is a newer bure, built mostly with the rent money obtained when the film crew of 'Return to the Blue Lagoon' spent some time there. The oldest cottage costs F$27.50/38.50/77 for singles/doubles/family and can accommodate up to seven people. Each extra person over 13 years costs F$10. The other cottage has two rooms costing F$33 for singles or doubles, or F$55 to rent the entire unit. The self-contained bure, with its cane-lined interior, large window with a view to the garden and verandah, is F$44/55 a single/double. All units have fridges and mosquito nets.

Karin's Garden (☎ 880 511) PA Matei, is another new place to stay in the Matei area and is just across from Bibi's, on the ocean side of the road. The site is a long, narrow block of land ending in a steep cliff with a spectacular bird's eye view down on the reef. German couple Karin and Peter finished building their first accommodation unit in 1996. It is spacious, with plywood lining and timber floors. The two bedrooms open off a tall central kitchen/dining room, and onto a long verandah. Each double/twin room has its own ensuite, wardrobe, fan and generator power from 8 am to 10 pm. Price is F$55 per room.

Nai Kelekele Apartment (☎ & fax 880 141) is just next to Lisi's camping ground opposite Prince Charles Beach, five minutes drive from Matei airport. Warwick and Dianne Bain have a spacious, self-contained apartment on the ground floor of their two-storey house. It has a double bedroom, sitting room with two single beds, kitchen and bathroom and costs F$75 per night for up to four people. Refer to the Activities section for information on their charter yacht *Seax of Legra*.

Three minutes walk east of the airport is *Coconut Grove Beachfront Cottage* (☎ & fax 880 328). Ronna has a self-contained cottage with a double and a single bed, fan, fridge and cooking facilities, private outdoor shower and Fijian mats on timber floor at F$71.50 for singles or doubles and F$82.50 for a triple per night. Her restaurant is next door, but the cottage is still quite private. It has good views across the water to the small islets and access off the verandah down through the garden to a small private beach. If you wish to visit Honeymoon Island, Ronna will pack a picnic lunch. There is also a guestroom within the restaurant/house which has a double bed and ensuite with hot water at F$49.50/60.50 for singles/doubles, including breakfast. The generator runs for 18 hours a day (longer than most places). Refer to Places to Eat for details on the restaurant.

About three minutes walk further down the road from Coconut Grove is another self-contained apartment, *Lomalagi Beachfront Cottage* (☎ 880 299) c/o PA Matei. It can be rented for F$75 a night per couple, F$5 per extra person (maximum four) or for F$500 per week. Speak to Dolores Porter at the Sunflower desk at the airport or the caretaker that lives on the property (there is no sign on the gate). The unit has cooking facilities, fridge, solar power and can sleep four people. It is joined to the owner's unit by a common deck which overlooks the beach.

Sere-ni-ika (☎ 880 164) two doors down from Lomalagi, is a large house which belongs to Hawaiians who live there for about six months of the year. It has a spacious kitchen, living area and verandah which overlooks the sea, two doubles and a twin bedroom.

It costs F$40/80 singles/doubles per night and F$5 extra per additional guest, and you can arrange to rent the whole house. Caretakers Sili and Amelia Maikoro live on the property. The generator supplies power from 5.30 pm to 10.30 pm; F$2 per additional hour. Laundry service can be arranged for F$5 per load. Amelia will also cook for an additional charge.

American Audrey Brown, who is famous locally for her home-made biscuits, runs *Audrey's by the Sea* (☎ 880 039), a comfortable self-contained cottage in her garden costing F$65 for singles/doubles. Located on a small hill about 10 minutes walk down the road east of Matei airstrip, it is across the road from the sea and close to the local supermarket. The cottage has an open geometric plan like her house, with views to the water through the coconut trees. It has a tizzy plush interior, white and turquoise with lots of cushions and lacy curtains. No children are allowed.

Little Dolphin Treehouse (☎ 880 130) is in a beautiful spot between Audrey's and Bhula Bhai Supermarket, with a great view of the ocean and islands, and is good value at F$55 a day. The Treehouse is a cute double-storey building with polished timber floors, a double and a single bed upstairs, as well as a single bed, kitchen and bathroom with hot water downstairs. It has electricity from sunset to 10.30 pm. See the Activities section for information on sports equipment for hire.

Places to Stay – top end
New Zealanders Rick and Do Cammick have been running *Dive Taveuni* (☎ 880 441, 880 445; fax 880 466) since the mid-1970s. It's about ten minutes walk from the Matei airstrip towards Waiyevo, on a spectacular cliff site overlooking the Somosomo Strait and set in an immaculately maintained garden. You can walk down to a small beach which has white sand and large boulders. This resort is oriented primarily at divers and the majority of guests are on pre-booked packages. It is closed from mid-January to the end of February.

Accommodation here costs F$200 a night including meals and transfers; drinks are extra. Credit cards are accepted. The standard units have a double bedroom, tiled floor, fan, a fridge stocked with drinks, and an outdoor shower in a private courtyard. Meals include cooked breakfast with cereals, lunches on the dive trip or at the resort and dining on the restaurant deck. Another deck built out over the cliff is great for watching sunsets. See the Activities section for details on diving.

Located on the hill across the road from Dive Taveuni is *Maravu Plantation Resort* (☎ 880 555, 880 556; fax 880 600). The 22-hectare property is also a working copra plantation. 'Maravu' means calm and tranquil but this concept may change with the new ownership taking over in 1996. The 10 units all have an ensuite, ceiling fan, fridge, tea/coffee facilities and verandah with hammock. The seven deluxe bures have timber cladding, reed lining internally, parquetry flooring, and sleep up to four people. These cost F$165/198/227 for singles/doubles/triples. There are three honeymoon bures with private outdoor showers and sundeck for F$230 a double. Power is available all day except for three hours in the afternoon. The resort has a good pool and baby-sitting is available. See Places to Eat for information on the restaurant. Organised activities here include horse riding, volleyball and plantation tours as well as trips to the sites around the island. Diving is through Aquaventure.

Places to Eat

Restaurants & Cafes One of Taveuni's best places to eat is *Coconut Grove Cafe* (☎ 880 328), just east of the airport. It is the home of Ronna Goldstein and her well-mannered Doberman, Gracy. Dining is on her verandah, overlooking the water, islets and a cute beach. Try the best fresh fruit shakes on Taveuni for F$2.95. The restaurant offers breakfast from F$3 to F$6, including banana bread, and lunch for F$3.50 to F$10.50. Dinner, including a vegetable side dish and garlic bread, costs F$13.50 to F$16.50. The menu includes a backpackers' choice such as stir fry plus rice for F$7 to F$9.50 and there's a 20% discount for students. The menu changes daily and is displayed on the front door. Place your dinner order before 4 pm and if Ronna is not at home you can leave a note. In general, the menu includes fresh

vegetables, home-made pasta, salads, fish and sashimi, and delicious desserts such as home-made ice cream, passionfruit cream pie, chocolate cake, and real coffee. There is a Fijian lovo night and an Indian night once a week. Ronna also has a small gift shop with cards, jewellery and t-shirts. The restaurant may be closed during February.

Karin's Garden (☎ 880 511) also serves excellent European-style food. It is just across the road from Bibi's Hideaway. On offer are eggs, jam and toast for breakfast for F$6 to F$7; spaghetti and sandwiches for lunch at F$5 to F$12; and dinner from F$14 to F$18. Dinner dishes include pork, lamb, veal, chicken and fish. It is best to book for dinner before 5 pm and check what is on the day's menu. The bread and yogurt is homemade and the vegetables come from their garden. Future plans are to rebuild the restaurant further down the block on the cliff overlooking the water. The view from the cliff is spectacular at sunset, and on a clear day you can see large fish and dolphins swimming past.

Maravu Plantation Resort's *Wananavu Restaurant* just down the road serves good international and Fijian cuisine and is open for visitors. Another place to eat is the new *restaurant* at Tovutovu Resort, which has an outdoor deck overlooking Viubani Island. The food is reportedly good and the service is friendly, with main courses ranging from F$6 to F$10.

Audrey's Sweet Somethings is run by an American woman who serves local brewed coffee and scrumptious cakes on her verandah from 10 am to 6 pm. Audrey's home is about 10 minutes walk east of the airport. The selection of cakes includes: sponge torte with jam filling, almond meringue top, coconut and pineapple cake, chocolate chunk or chocolate centre cookies, lime tarts and fudge cake. Audrey sometimes takes her basket of goodies to the airport.

Fast Food The *airport kiosk* (☎ 880 171) which is open for plane arrivals and departures, sells roti parcels and scones. Margaret Peterson, who sells food at the airport kiosk, also prepares takeaway meals at her house (great food and lots of it) for F$15 per person. You need to let her know in advance. See Places to Stay above.

Five minutes east of the airport is *Little Dolphin Pizza Take Away* (☎ 880 130), next to Little Dolphin Treehouse. It is open from 4.30 to 6.30 pm and offers good pizzas (cheese, vegetarian and chicken) for F$12.50 to F$14.50 which are big enough for two. Put in your order before 3 pm if you want it for dinner. Another option for takeaway food is *Mahabir* (☎ 880 545), the taxi driver who lives just next to the Little Dolphin. He will deliver takeaway Indian curries, mutton or chicken with rice and dhal, in the Matei area for F$5 to F$7. Ring to order before 4 pm.

Mrs Harry's (☎ 880 404) takeaway curries are good value and popular among campers staying at Beverly. Bansraji (Harry's wife), prepares the meals at her house up on the hill almost opposite Beverly camp back towards Matei. It is best if you order before 4 pm for dinner, and she will also cook lunch if you order in advance. The food is Indian style. Curries and vegetarian dishes cost F$3 or F$5 for fish or meat with roti and dhal.

Self-Catering *Bhula Bhai Supermarket* in Matei (☎ 880 462; fax 880 050) is open from 7 am to 6 pm daily; closed on Sunday. It sells a good range of groceries, film, stationery, clothing and phonecards and accepts Visa and MasterCard (charge 10%, F$90 limit). The local cardphone and bus stop is also here. *Niranjan's shop*, five minutes walk closer towards Matei airport, also has a limited selection of groceries.

Getting There & Away
Matei is about 45 minutes by bus from Waiyevo; see the Getting Around section.

EASTERN TAVEUNI
Eastern Taveuni's beautiful, wild coast and lush rainforest is a magnet for nature lovers. Scenes for the 1991 Warner Brothers movie, *Return to the Blue Lagoon* were filmed at Bouma's Tavoro Falls and Lavena beach.

Rather than resort to activities such as logging, the Bouma Environmental Tourism Project is helping to preserve the land and sea resources of the Vanua Bouma while importantly bringing in income from visitors. The project is based on landowner initiative, with encouragement and assistance from the Native Lands Trust Board, the Forestry Department and Fiji Pine, and is funded by the New Zealand government. The people of Bouma invested, planned and built the extensive trails. The first stages of the project are the Bouma Forest Park, Tavoro National Park, and the Lavena Coastal Walk. Future stages plan to include the Waitabu Falls, which are similar to Bouma, and more cultural attractions such as the Navuga and Nasau fortified village sites.

Bouma Forest Park
Bouma Forest Park has seven km of bush walks, including three beautiful (modest size) waterfalls with natural swimming pools. The walking track begins directly opposite the reception bure, south of the river in Bouma. The first waterfall is about 24m high. It is only 10 minutes walk along a flat and easy path, which is well maintained and bordered by local flowers. There is a screened area for changing and a few picnic tables and barbecue plates.

The second waterfall, a bit smaller than the first, also has a good swimming pool. To reach it continue along the path for another 30 to 40 minutes. Initially the track is quite steep, but has formed steps, handrails and lookout spots with seats. The view through the coconut trees to the zigzagging reef and Qamea Island beyond is quite spectacular. Over the hill the track passes through rainforest and along the way a river crossing has a rope to help you jump from stone to stone. Reaching the third fall involves a hike along a less maintained, often muddy path through the forest for a further 30 minutes. Smaller than the other two (about 10m high), it has a great swimming pool and rocks for jumping off (always check for obstructions first!).

The park fee is F$5, or F$7 per person for a guided tour. Drinks and biscuits are available at the reception bure and there is an area where you can camp, with thatched shelters, toilets and baggage storage. Enquire on (☎ 880 390), or write c/o PA Bouma.

Getting There & Away It takes 45 minutes by local bus or about 20 minutes by car to reach Bouma village from Matei. A taxi (up to five people) will cost F$15 to F$20. See the Getting Around section for bus times.

If you are in the mood for a marathon it is possible to catch the early morning bus to Bouma, make a flying visit to all three waterfalls, and catch the early afternoon bus at about 1.45 pm on to Lavena. In a rush you can do the coastal walk before dark and either stay overnight at Lavena or be picked up by a pre-arranged taxi. The early afternoon bus returns to Matei and the late afternoon bus spends the night at Lavena.

Lavena Coastal Walk
Lavena village is the end of the road and, while it is not easy to get to as the bus service is limited, it's worth the trouble. The white-sand beach is good for swimming and snorkelling and there is even surf here, though not consistently. The currents can be strong here. The park entry fee of F$5 per person, payable at the reception bure, entitles you to use the beaches and the coastal walk.

The Lavena Coastal Walk is a beautiful hike along the forest edge, with the gorgeous **Wainibau Falls** as a reward at the end. The five km of well-marked path is mostly easy; allow at least three hours return. The first 1.5 km is parallel to a long, white-sand beach, changing to black volcanic sand beaches and becoming increasingly rocky. About halfway are strange pedestal formations caused by the coral base layer being eroded by the sea water, leaving bulbous rock shapes on fine bases. The track continues past a village, across a bridge at Wainisairi Creek (the only stream to flow out of Lake Tagimoucia) and up the valley of Wainibau Creek. This creek forms the boundary of the Bouma (Wainikeli) and Vuna lands and is also the boundary of the Ravilevu Nature Reserve to the south. To actually see and

reach the falls you have to walk over rocks and swim a short distance through two deep pools, so you'll need a waterproof camera to take shots. Two cascades fall at different angles into a deep pool with sheer walls. There are lots of fish in the creek.

Places to Stay & Eat The only accommodation at Lavena is at the *Reception bure* which has cooking, toilet and shower facilities and a place to crash on foam mattresses in the loft. It costs F$5 per person. It is also possible to camp if you have your own tent. The village *store* nearby has the usual tinned fish and meat, noodles and eggs, but you may need to buy fresh produce direct from the locals or bring your own.

Getting There & Away Lavena village is about 15 minutes drive past Bouma. From Matei it takes about one hour by local bus, or 35 minutes by car. If you have your own mountain bike allow about 3½ hours of hot, hard work one way. The bus trip from Waiyevo to Lavena takes less than two hours. The last bus does not return to Waiyevo until early the next morning so, if you need to return, arrange in advance for a taxi from Matei to pick you up. Expect to negotiate F$20 to F$25 for a taxi to/from Matei. See the Getting Around section for information on bus and taxi services.

Savulevu Yavonu Falls
The Ravilevu coast is the section from Lavena point down to Salialevu on the rough, exposed eastern side of Taveuni. It is a straight stretch of coast without any foreshore, but with cliffs and open ocean. About halfway along, the 20m high Savulevu Yavonu waterfall plunges off a cliff into the sea. During WWII, ships used the falls as a fresh water depot, going directly under the flow to refill their water reservoir. Access to the falls is by boat only, and is dependent on the weather as the ocean can get very rough on this side of the island. Trips cost about F$25 per person for groups of three to six. Enquire at Lavena's Reception bure.

Offshore Islands

Qamea, Laucala and Matagi are a group of islands just east of Thurston point across the Tasman Strait from north-eastern Taveuni. Qamea and Laucala islands are located inside a lagoon formed by a single barrier reef which wraps around the south-east side, broken only by a passage east of Laucala. The islands have beautiful white sand beaches. The original inhabitants of Qamea and Laucala were displaced in the mid-19th century by local chiefs for siding with Tongan chief Enele Ma'afu during a war. Laucala and Matagi are privately owned. Each island has an up-market resort, all catering mainly to diving and game fishing enthusiasts. Generally only resort visitors can go to these beautiful islands. Other travellers may be able to visit Qamea if invited by locals. If you are lucky enough to fly over, the view is superb.

MATAGI ISLAND
Horseshoe-shaped Matagi, formed by a submerged volcanic crater, is 10 km off Taveuni's coast. It is only about 100 hectares in area, with a steep elevation to 130m and a rainforest interior.

The bay faces north to open sea and there is a fringing reef on the south-west side of the island where the *Matagi Island Resort* (☎ 880 260, 301 780; fax 880 274) is situated along a white-sand beach. The Douglas family began the intimate scale resort in 1987, catering for a maximum of 24 guests at a time.

Children of any age are accepted and baby-sitting is available. There are eight spacious, circular plan bures with umbrella-like roofs, which sleep up to four people. A screen wall divides sitting areas and the rooms have an ensuite, ceiling fan, stocked fridge and tea/coffee beans. Rates are usually quoted in US dollars. Including all meals and transfers prices are F$297/525/725 for singles/doubles/triples, F$828

for two adults and two children between 12 and 16 or F$752 for two adults and two children under 12. Alternatively there is a tree house, perched about five metres above the ground, built around a beautiful old almond tree with a view to the beach, Qamea and Taveuni beyond. Kids would love it but it is reserved for honeymooners and couples only. The split level unit has an ensuite, separate lounge and outdoor decks and costs F$662 a double per night. The domed bure restaurant serves good food. The generator supplies power 24 hours a day and all bures have gas hot water.

Rates include a day trip to Taveuni, and non-motorised water sports (windsurfing, snorkelling, kayaking, sailing, paddle boarding). Diving, water skiing and saltwater fly fishing are also offered. Unlimited shore diving is included in the price, otherwise dive rates are F$124 for two tanks, or F$580 for a full certification course. Matagi boasts 30 dive spots within 10 to 30 minutes boat ride of the island. See the Diving section at the beginning of the chapter for information on the live-aboard *Matagi Princess II* based at the resort. For on-line information on the resort see the Internet web site at http://www.netilus.com/fijiisland-matagi. html; or e-mail: matagi@netilus.com.

Getting There & Away
The Matagi minibus meets guests at Matei airport. It is a 15-minute drive to Navakacoa village landing, a volcanic, black-sand beach, followed by a 20-minute boat ride to the island.

QAMEA ISLAND
Qamea is the closest of the three islands to Taveuni, only 2.5 km from Thurston Point. It is also the largest of the three, about 10 km in length and varying in width between 700m and five km. The island's coast has a number of bays with white-sand beaches and a narrow mangrove inlet on the west side. The interior, especially on the north side, is covered with steep green hills and sloping valleys, without much flat land. Qamea is rich in birdlife and is notable for the *lairo*,

the annual migration of land crabs. For a few days from late November to early December, at the start of their breeding season, masses of crabs move together from the mud flats towards the sea.

Qamea has six villages, but the up-market *Qamea Beach Club* (☎ 880 220; fax 880 092) is the only place for travellers to stay on the island. Opened in 1982, the resort is on 16 hectares, along a beautiful white sand beach. Each of the 11 rectangular bures has reed-lined interiors, cane-lined exteriors, ensuite, sitting area, fan, mini bar, tea/coffee facilities, hot showers and a hammock on the verandah. Bures can accommodate up to three people and cost F$385 per night. The meal package is an extra F$88 a day per person and airport transfers are F$88 per person. No children under 12 are allowed. The resort has a fresh spring water swimming pool and a large lofty entertainment/restaurant bure with a verandah. Just about everything is lacquered timber and cane, with huge backed cane chairs.

The resort has its own dive operation, Dive Qamea, which charges F$110 for a two-tank dive trip, and there is excellent snorkelling just offshore. Other activities include windsurfing, snorkelling, sailing, outrigger canoeing, nature walks, fish drives and village visits.

Trips can be organised to Bouma Waterfall, F$35 per person plus F$5 entry fee, and Lavena scenic walk and falls, F$45 per person plus F$5 entrance fee. A three-hour boat trip around Qamea is F$180 per boat including picnic lunch, and a trip to Nanuko Island (a beautiful atoll about 30 miles away) is F$250. Fishing costs F$10 to F$20 per hour.

Getting There & Away
Guests are picked up in the resort minibus from Matei Airport and driven about 10 km to Navakacoa village landing to pick up a speed boat to the island (about 15 minutes).

LAUCALA ISLAND
Laucala Island is about five km long and 3.5 km wide, just 500m east across the strait from Qamea, and is privately owned by the estate of the late US millionaire Malcolm Forbes. Most of the Fijians who live on the island work on the estate's copra plantations or at the up-market *Fiji Forbes Laucala Island Resort* (☎ 880 077; fax 880 099 or USA ☎ 719 379 3263; fax 719 379 3266). With only five bures, it caters for a maximum of 12 guests who tend to be mainly Americans and prices are quoted in US dollars. Rates are about F$3188 per person for seven nights, and F$455 per additional night. Children are half-price or free if under two. The resort offers scuba diving, deep-sea fishing and water skiing for its guests and all activities, meals and drinks are included in the rate. The bures each have a bedroom, lounge, dining area and kitchen, with air-con and a stocked bar. Groups of up to eight adults can book out the resort for a mere F$22,770 – plus F$2730 per extra person, and F$417 per person per additional night.

Getting There & Away
Laucala has its own airstrip and most visitors are flown to the island from Nadi.

Kadavu Group

KADAVU

The Kadavu Group is comprised of Kadavu (Fiji's fourth-largest island), Ono, Galoa and a numbers of smaller islands. The group is about 100 km south of Viti Levu. It is 411 sq km – comparable in size to Taveuni, but with a very irregular shape. The Kadavu coast is so deeply indented that it is almost cut into three by deep bays. Its highest peak is Mt Washington at 838m. There are few roads and most transportation is by boat.

The explorer Dumont d'Urville, who sailed past the island in 1834, named the Astrolabe Reef after his ship. When it was found that Levuka had no space for expansion, Kadavu's Galoa Harbour was considered, along with Suva, as a potential site for the new colonial capital. Kadavu, however, has remained removed from Fiji's major historical events and, due to its isolation, the villagers are very traditional. The local economy is small, based on subsistence agriculture and the export of local produce to the mainland. Tourism is also growing in the area, but it has been gradual due to the isolation and lack of infrastructure. Kadavu has a population of about 8000 people living in about 100 villages or settlements. Each village has its own fishing grounds, and resorts negotiate to use the areas for diving, surfing or fishing.

The prevailing south-easterly winds can batter the exposed south-eastern side of the island. Expect some rough weather from April to August.

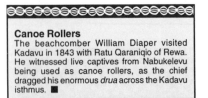

Canoe Rollers

The beachcomber William Diaper visited Kadavu in 1843 with Ratu Qaraniqio of Rewa. He witnessed live captives from Nabukelevu being used as canoe rollers, as the chief dragged his enormous *drua* across the Kadavu isthmus. ■

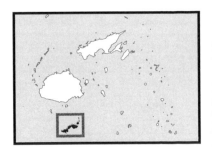

The rugged island has lush rainforests, especially on the eastern side, and boasts a wide variety of bird species. The Kadavu honeyeater, Kadavu fantail and the velvet fruit dove are indigenous. The beautiful Kadavu native musk parrot is red, blue and green.

Activities

Kadavu is a great place for nature lovers, hikers and bird-watchers. There are some nice beaches, but don't go with high expectations. The island is mountainous and quite rugged, especially on the eastern side, and has rainforest, numerous waterfalls and hiking trails (used mainly by school children). Ask locals if the track is clear before heading off. If visiting a village, ask to speak to the *turaga-ni-koro* first and don't wear a hat or carry things on your shoulders (see Dos & Don'ts in the Facts for the Visitor chapter). Most of the places to stay have equipment for snorkelling and other water sports. Stingers can sometimes be uncomfortable for swimmers and snorkellers.

Diving Most travellers are attracted to Kadavu by its reefs, which have some excellent diving. The famous Great Astrolabe Reef is about 50 km long, wrapping around the south-eastern side of Kadavu. It is one of the world's largest reefs and Fiji's longest

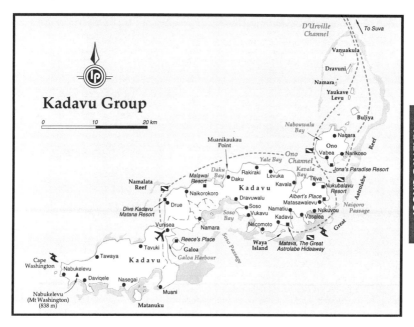

living organism. Expect brilliantly coloured soft and hard corals, vertical drop offs, and a wonderful array of marine life including lots of reef sharks. Diving on the Great Astrolabe Reef is variable, ranging from terrible to incredible. The weather quite often dictates which sites are suitable to dive. Visibility can range from 15m to 70m. Nukubalavu and Albert's Place resorts dive the Naiqoro Passage and, during rough weather, sites on the sheltered side of Ono Island. Matava dives from the SoSo Passage to Naiqoro Passage, offering cave dives, shark dives and unexplored sites.

The north-western side of the island (covered by Dive Kadavu and Malawai) is more sheltered from the prevailing winds than the Astrolabe Reef. Dive Kadavu sites include Yellow Wall, Evil Trench and Blue Tang on the Namalata reefs. Diving here is reportedly superb. Malawai dive sites include Rooper Reef, Semi's Cave, Purple Patch and Robert's Wreck. See the Facts for the Visitor chapter for more information on diving and dive operations.

Surfing Vesi Passage off Matava, The Great Astrolabe Hideaway, has powerful surf averaging 6ft (1.8m). It is only suitable on calm days. There is also surf at Cape Washington – the south-western point of Kadavu – but surfers have a poor reputation here as they have offended villagers in the past. One reader reports that a new resort will open on a small island just off the cape in 1997.

Sea & Dive Kayaking The season for organised kayaking trips is from May to September. Dive Kadavu Matana Resort has diving kayaks for hire with professional instruction available. Enquire about dive trips from Matana around Kadavu; these include a five-day trip around southern Kadavu or seven to 10 days around northern Kadavu. A boat follows the kayaks and sets up the base camp and tents. Jona's Paradise

---

The Battle of the Shark & Octopus Gods

Dakuwaqa the Shark God wished to take over Fijian waters and cruised the islands challenging other reef guardians. He heard that a monster who lived in Kadavu waters was reportedly stronger than himself, and sped down to the island to disprove the rumour. Dakuwaqa came across the giant octopus and adopted his usual battle strategy of charging with his mouth wide open and sharp teeth prepared to rip his opponent apart. The octopus, however, anchored itself to the coral reef and swiftly wrapped its free tentacles around the shark's body and jaws, clasping the shark in a death lock. Dakuwaqa was rendered helpless and had to beg for mercy. In return for lenience the octopus demanded that his subjects, the people of Kadavu, be forever protected from shark attack. In Kadavu the people now fish without fear and regard the shark as their protector. Most won't eat shark or octopus out of respect for their gods. ■

Resort on Ono Island also intends to run kayaking trips. Matava Resort has two-person kayaks for hire for F$10 for two hours.

Dangers & Annoyances

The ferry trip to Kadavu crosses an exposed stretch of water and the trip can be very rough. Transport around the island is by small boats, which often don't have life jackets or radios.

Places to Stay

Kadavu accommodation consists of several budget resorts (Albert's Place, Jona's Paradise, Galoa and Matava), middle-range resorts (Nukubalavu and Dive Kadavu) and one top-end resort (Malawai). Diving is the main reason for their existence. Consider transportation costs when choosing a place to stay. Albert's Place and Nukubulavu are within walking distance of each other so if you are not happy with one check out the other. Camping is allowed at Albert's Place as well as on Galoa Island and at Jona's Paradise on Ono Island.

Places to Stay – bottom end

Vunisea Travellers stranded in Vunisea should consider the *Vunisea Guesthouse* on the hill near the Namalata Bay wharf, about two km north of the airport. It has reasonable rooms for singles or doubles for F$30. Rooms open onto a common lounge room area. There is a grocery store nearby.

Alternatively, Thelma, who runs the airport kiosk, allows people to stay in her home for F$10 per person. She can arrange visits to a nearby waterfall.

Around Kadavu Island Most backpackers enjoy staying at *Albert's Place* (☎ 302 896), located on a bay beach on the north-eastern corner of Kadavu Island close to Naiqoro Passage. Camping here costs F$5.50 per person and dorm beds are F$6. There are 10 small very basic bures with mosquito nets and coral floors covered with woven mats which cost F$15/28 for singles/doubles. The two toilet blocks each have two flush toilets and one cold shower. There is no electricity. The entertainment bure was destroyed, leaving no place to gather at night on the beachfront, other than the dining room. The food provided is good and meals are F$22 per day or F$6/10/13 for breakfast/lunch/dinner. There is also a small shop with basic grocery items only. Self caterers can pay F$2 to use the kitchen and there is a wood stove outside.

Snorkelling is quite good in front of the resort at high tide. Diving is usually good but equipment and boats are very basic. The dive shop Naiqoro Divers offers Resort courses for F$75 and open water courses (five dives) for F$330 all inclusive. The Great Astrolabe Reef is a 10-minute boat ride from the resort. Other activities include volleyball, picnic trips to a waterfall for F$10 per person and reef trips for F$6 per person (minimum four). Day hikes to villages can also be arranged.

The ferry from Suva drops off at Albert's

Place twice weekly. Transfers from Vunisea airstrip to Albert's Place cost F$55 if there is one or two people or F$23 each for three or more. The trip takes about 1½ to two hours, depending on the weather, and they choose whichever side is the calmest.

Matava, The Great Astrolabe Hideaway is managed by four Australian guys and began operation early in 1996. 'Matava' (not to be confused with Matana Resort) is named after a battle that took place on this beach between the locals and warriors from Rewa (near Suva) back in the 17th century. The beach at the front of the resort isn't great; it's a bit muddy and the tide goes out a long way, meaning access to the boat can be a bit awkward with dive gear. However, a reef links it to a picturesque offshore island which makes a great snorkelling or kayaking trip. There is a beautiful view from the hill behind the resort. It can be windy and exposed on this side of the island, but the place has a rugged beauty and a sense of remoteness.

Accommodation consists of six bures set out on 11 hectares of land on the side of a hill near the water. The bures are rustic but comfortable, with timber floors and verandahs as well as solar-powered lighting, and cost F$15.50/30.80 for singles/doubles. There is spring water, 12V solar electricity and gas hot water for showers. The toilet block is a bit of a walk. There are plans to build additional self-contained bures. The food is good and costs F$20 for a meal package. A large restaurant/bar bure was being built at the time of writing.

It has good dive equipment and single dives cost F$38.50, while a six-dive package is F$220. A Resort course costs F$82.50, Open Water certification is F$308 and Advanced certification F$341. Other activities include reef ecology programmes, snorkelling, reef surfing, kayaking, organised bushwalking and horse riding treks, and village visits (for church services, meke and kava, and a waterfall visit). Sunday is a traditional day of rest so there is no diving or waterfall trip.

The resort only has a radio phone. You cannot call Matava directly, so contact Rosie

Tours in Nadi before you leave for Kadavu to arrange for pick-up at the airstrip or to tell them you are arriving by ferry. The boat trip from Vunisea airstrip up the south-eastern side of the main island to Matava takes 40 minutes to one hour and costs F$20 per person each way.

Nukubalavu and Matana also have dormitory accommodation: see the following section.

Places to Stay – middle

Nukubalavu Adventure Resort & Dive Centre (☎ 520 089 resort, 314 554 office; fax 302 212) is aimed primarily at divers. It has a range of accommodation options and a mixed clientele. Since upgrading, prices have doubled in one year and backpackers may now find the cost prohibitive, mainly due to the cost of meals and because there are no cooking facilities. Prices may be negotiable if you are on a tight budget. Tent sites are F$8.25 per person. The dormitory sleeps up to eight people and costs F$22 per person. Watch your valuables as the bure is far from the main area. There are hot showers. Beachfront bures with shared bathroom facilities are F$44/66/88 for singles/doubles/triples. Deluxe bures with ensuite are F$77/99 for singles/doubles.

The food is excellent in terms of variety and quantity, but is relatively expensive. A meal package is F$44 for three meals. Separately, breakfast/lunch/dinner costs F$13.20/17.60/24.20. The staff are friendly and at night all guests gather round a large table under an outdoor covered area, or sit inside and read books from the library or drink.

The long stretch of sandy beach is nothing special and you cannot swim at low tide. Divers have to lug their gear out to the boat at low tide and the dive boats are small and exposed. Rates are F$44/82.50 for one/two tank dives plus equipment rental of F$16.50 per day. A six-dive package (three days) costs F$247.50. Courses include Discover Scuba for F$82.50 and PADI Open Water for F$324.50. Additional activities include snorkelling, fishing, volleyball, trekking to a waterfall through rainforest and village visits.

Dive Kadavu, Matana Resort (☎ 311 780; fax 303 860) also caters mainly to divers. It is a relatively up-market resort and has excellent dorm rooms which are good value for divers, considering the resort's facilities. It is set in picturesque surroundings on the western side of Kadavu, sheltered from the prevailing south-easterly winds, and conveniently located for travellers arriving by plane. Airport transfers, about 15 minutes by boat from Vunisea, cost US$22 (F$30.50) per person return. The lovely beach is good for swimming and snorkelling. 'Matana' in the local dialect means 'all tide sandy beach'.

Prices are quoted in US$. Rooms with shared facilities in the Diver's Den are US$38.50/55/77 (F$53/74/106) for singles/doubles/triples with up to three people per room. As a dorm, rooms are US$26.40 (F$36.50) per person. The two fan-cooled, ocean-view rooms at US$82.50 (F$114) for a single or double, have their own bathroom, are well-ventilated and have fly screens, fridge and tea/coffee-making facilities. The two fan-cooled, deluxe, beach bures are US$110/132/154 (F$152/182/212.50) for singles or doubles/triples/quads. These have two rooms with a porch, and are ideal for a family or a maximum of four people. Laundry service is provided. The restaurant/bar on the hillside has gorgeous views of the water through the coconut palms and thatched bure rooftops to Nubukalevu (Mt Washington). The meal package costs US$44 (F$61) per day. There is a good swap library, with interesting books for divers and naturalists.

Dive Kadavu has an excellent set-up: four boats, two covered and specially designed for diving; good equipment; and a dive shop which has gear for sale. Up to four dives per day are offered. Three two-tank dive trips cost US$220 (F$303.50) including tanks and weights. Open Water certification costs US$280.50 (F$387). Snorkelling trips with the divers cost US$7/14 (F$9.50/19) for one afternoon trip/two sites in the morning. Underwater cameras are available for hire

and the resort has developing facilities. Using your own film it costs F$15 per film load for equipment hire and developing. Namalata Reef is about five km offshore and day trips to the sheltered Ono side of the Astrolabe are arranged with a stop for lunch at a village on Ono. Use of windsurfers and paddle boards are included in the rates. Other activities include use of dive and sea kayaks, forest walks in the hills, village visits and a weekly lovo.

Places to Stay – top end

Malawai (☎ 520 102; fax 361 536), 14.5 km north-east of Vunisea, is Kadavu's most up-market resort, catering for up to 10 guests only, and offering a quiet, relaxed atmosphere. It opened in early 1993 and is run by the McLauchlan family on their 140-hectare property. It consists of three colonial style cottages spaced along a white-sand beach. A minimum stay of three nights applies and children under 12 are only accepted as part of a group booking. The plantation cottages are US$253/330/440 (F$349/455/607) for singles/doubles/triples. The deluxe cottage costs US$286/363/473/583 for singles/doubles/triples/quad. Rates include all meals and return boat transfers. The fan-cooled cottages are spacious with private bathroom, coffee/tea-making facilities, a fruit bowl, biscuits and a fridge stocked with fruit juice, beer and soft drinks. The resort has good fresh water and a generator for power. The dining room in the Plantation house overlooks the water and a local band plays music for guests.

The resort is well-equipped with two 32 ft (9.6m) diving/fishing/transfer vessels and three 20 ft (six metre) boats which are used for water skiing, fishing and diving. Diving costs US$77 (F$106) for two tank dives per day. PADI dive courses include Discover Scuba for US$71.50 (F$99) and open water for US$220 (F$304). Accommodation/dive packages are available for those staying over seven nights. Boat charters for sports fishing are US$385/550 (F$531/759) for half/full day. Other activities include snorkelling, village visits, and hiking to other beaches and into the rainforest. Transfers by boat from the Vunisea airstrip take 40 minutes.

Places to Eat

Self-Catering Vunisea has a 'shopping centre', Albert's Place has a small store and there is a general store near Matava resort. Most of the resorts are remote, so even if all your meals are provided it may be an idea to take along some supplementary snacks just in case.

Getting There & Away

Air Air Fiji has five flights a week (Monday, Wednesday, Friday, Saturday and Sunday) to/from Kadavu and Nausori airport near Suva, with connections to/from Nadi. The flight time is 30 minutes. Sunflower Airlines has daily flights to Kadavu from Nadi airport. The flight time is 45 minutes; see the airfare chart in the Getting Around chapter.

It is a beautiful flight from either Nadi or Suva over stunning reefs. The approach to Vunisea airstrip (☎ Vunisea 42) over Namalata Bay has a spectacular view of Nabukelevu (Mt Washington), which rises steeply at the southern point of Kadavu. The flight can sometimes be turbulent. The airport has a small coffee shop. Ideally, have your accommodation and transfers booked in advance, otherwise you could be stranded in Vunisea: see the Places to Stay section.

Ferry See the Getting Around chapter for more detailed information. Whippy's Boatyard Ltd has a twice-weekly ferry service on the *MV Gurawa* to/from Suva and Kadavu. The ferry crosses open sea and can take from six to 11 hours depending on how much produce is being carried. On Tuesday it will drop guests off at Nukubalavu and Albert's Place on its way to Vunisea. On Friday it takes a different route, dropping off at Jona's Paradise and Matava as well as Nukubalavu and Albert's Place. Timetables can change so confirm in advance. Kadavu Shipping also has a Suva/Vunisea ferry, *MV Bulou-ni-ceva*. This service has no timetable and the stop-start trip can take anything from four hours to two days! It is mostly used for cargo.

The trip can be fine or terrible depending on the weather you strike. One reader described a trip to Kadavu as follows:

We took the Whippy's ferry to Nukubulavu. The crossing wasn't bad, but it was hard to get a seat downstairs as all the locals and their baggage were taking up every seat, lying prostrate across them with their eyes shut tightly. The return took ten hours and it seemed to stop off at every village on Kadavu to pick up locals and their supplies, including wood, goats and fish. The ferry was extremely top heavy and when we ran into a storm we nearly capsized. This, coupled with loads of people being sick everywhere, made the journey none too pleasant.

Dona Bray & Mark Tranter

Getting Around

Kadavu has only a few roads and these are restricted to the Vunisea area. There is one bus in Vunisea which only runs occasionally. However, it is fairly easy to hitch a ride around town. Small boats are the principal mode of transport to get around Kadavu. These trips are expensive due to fuel costs and mark-ups. Most of these boats don't have life jackets or radios. Make sure valuable gear is covered as things can get wet. There are no regular boats between the resorts. Each resort has its own boat transport and will arrange pick-ups from Vunisea airstrip. If you strike rough weather it can be a bone-crunching trip from Vunisea to Nukubalavu, Albert's Place and Matava. It is a pleasant walk between Nukubalavu and Albert's Place.

Vunisea

Orientation & Information Vunisea is Kadavu's administrative centre, with the island's only police station, post office, hospital and airstrip. The small town is situated on a narrow isthmus and is easy to get around on foot. To the west is Namalata Bay and to the east, North Bay. Vunisea itself doesn't have much to interest the traveller.

Money The National Bank of Fiji at the post office in Vunisea will not change travellers' cheques or handle credit card transactions. Most of the resorts are distant from Vunisea

KADAVU GROUP

anyway. Some do take credit cards but it may be best to bring cash.

Post & Communications The post office and telephone exchange is located at the top of the hill in Vunisea. There is also a small shop within the post office which sells clothes and stationery. Opening hours are Monday to Friday 8 am to 4 pm and Saturday 9 am to 1 pm.

Communication services in Kadavu are very basic. Calls need to be placed through the exchange. Some places have radio phones. If you need to make a call, approach the operator and make sure your number is in the queue, or you will wait forever. Opening hours are 7 am to 10 pm Monday to Saturday and 9 am to 1 pm on Sunday. Calls are quite expensive.

Medical Services Vunisea has a new hospital, completed in 1996, funded jointly by Australian aid and the Fiji government. The hospital building works were part of an overall F$7 million project to improve Kadavu's medical and health services. Divers suffering from the bends can be transferred to the Fiji Recompression Chamber in Suva by Medivac helicopter service, but this will be costly unless your travel insurance covers it!

Emergency In the event of an emergency, dial the following numbers:

Police (☎ 4)
Health Centre (☎ 8)

Getting There & Away Book by phone to arrange transport from Vunisea to nearby islands. Galoa is 10 to 20 minutes by small boat from North Bay and it costs F$6.60 per person each way.

GALOA ISLAND

The island of Galoa lies just to the east of Vunisea. A whaling station once operated here. On the northern point of the island is *Galoa Island Resort* (☎ 315 703), PO Box 6 Vunisea. Formerly known as Reece's Place

it is run by two Reece brothers and their wives. When we visited, the resort was semi-closed while they were upgrading the facilities which had been running down for some years. Bill loves to tell stories about the history of the island, medicinal plants and will show you the point where people went to die, so that their spirits could leave them for the afterlife. There is a large stone fish trap on the point and a beach graveyard where blackbirded labourers who died of smallpox were buried.

Camping costs F$4.40 per person and accommodation in bungalows with shared bathroom is F$11/17.60 for singles/doubles. Meals are F$3/5/7 for breakfast/lunch/dinner. Snorkelling trips are F$6.60 per person. Diving with Galoa Island Divers costs F$33/55 for a one/two tank dive. Shore dives are F$16.50. Equipment rental is extra.

A reader has also recommended *Bai's Place* (☎ 13), Bai Whippy PO Box 23, Vunisea, which is opening on Galoa. He said the accommodation was still a bit rough but it has plenty of water and a flush toilet. The two double bures (F$10 per night) are on a nice beach and there is a communal dining room. Fijian-style food is $10 per day. Campers pay $3.50 per person. Diving will be offered with PADI open water courses for F$275.

ONO ISLAND

Ono island is a roughly oval shaped island in the north-east of the Kadavu Group. *Jona's Paradise Resort* (☎ 315 889; fax 315 992) is at the southern end of the island. There are five bures spaced along the beachfront which cost F$40 per person or F$50 for the larger one, including three meals. The small huts are very simple with coral floors. Tent sites including meals cost F$25 per person. Facilities are rudimentary: one tin shed has a cold water shower and two pit toilets with buckets for flushing. The beach, however, is one of the best in Kadavu, with white sand and very good snorkelling directly in front of the resort, even at low tide. At the time of writing, diving was with either Nukubalavu or Albert's Place. The owners were planning to introduce diving and kayaking trips. Activities include fishing or scenic boat trips around Ono Island F$65/100 for a half/full day, shared between a maximum of six people. There's even a pet Kadavu parrot called Georgie.

Getting There & Away

Guests can arrive directly at the island by ferry or fly to Vunisea, from where transfers are F$25 per person each way by resort boat. Nukubalavu and Albert's Place are a short boat ride across the Ono channel.

KADAVU GROUP

Lau & Moala Groups

The Lau group of islands is located about halfway between the main islands of Fiji to the west and the Kingdom of Tonga to the east. The group is comprised of about 57 small islands spread over 400 km from north to south. The Moala group is to the west of southern Lau. Geographically Lau is subdivided into northern and southern Lau, but the whole of the Lau group, together with the Moala group, is under the administration of the Eastern Division. The climate in this region is drier than in most other parts of Fiji.

Most islands of the Lau group are made of composite materials; some are pure limestone and a few are volcanic. Interrupted periods of uplift permitted coral to grow over the limestone creating great masses of reefs. Relatively recent volcanic activity is evident by the lava domes on top of the limestone bases of some of the smaller islands.

The islanders of southern Lau are known for their crafts. Moce, Vatoa, Ono-i-Lau and Namuka produce tapa cloth and the artisans of Fulaga are excellent wood carvers.

History

Because of Lau's proximity to Tonga, the islanders have been greatly influenced by Polynesian people and culture. The southeast Trade Winds made it easy to sail from Tonga to Fiji, but more difficult to return. A revolution in canoe design facilitated traffic and trade between the island groups. Tongan and Samoan canoe-building craftsmen began settling in Fiji in the late 1700s, bringing with them their innovative canoe designs as well as other decorative skills and crafts. They intermarried with Fijians and the Tongan influence is expressed in names, language, food, decoration, architecture and facial features.

Both Captain Bligh and Captain Cook sighted the Lau group on their explorations in the late 18th century. The first real contact with Europeans was in 1800 when the American schooner *Argo* was wrecked on

Bukatatanoa reef east of Lakeba. The vessel was on its way to deliver supplies to the penal colony of Norfolk Island. Fijians of nearby Oneata looted the wreck obtaining muskets and gunpowder and the sailors lived with the islanders for a while until being either eaten or killed in disputes. Oliver Slater survived to become influential in Bua, Vanua Levu; see the aside in the Vanua Levu chapter.

The first Christian missionaries entered Fiji via Lau. Two Tahitians from the London Missionary Society tried unsuccessfully to set up in Lakeba, and then moved on to establish themselves in Oneata in 1830 where they managed to convert a small number of people. The Wesleyan missionaries, William Cross and David Cargill, settled in Lakeba in 1835. They arrived with an emissary of King George of Tonga, and out of respect for the king, the Tui Nayau (king or prominent chief of Lau) made them welcome. He and his people, however, were not interested in being converted. Cross and Cargill developed a system for written Fijian and produced the first book in Fijian. Eventually the Tui Nayau accepted Christianity in 1849.

Northern Lau was traditionally allied with Cakaudrove (Eastern Vanua Levu and Taveuni) but, by the mid-19th century, the region became dominated by Tongans. In 1847 the Tongan noble, Enele Ma'afu,

LEONARDO PINHEIRO

ROBYN JONES

ROBYN JONES

Taveuni
Top: Matei
Middle: Archaeological site, Vuna
Bottom: Labourer's cottages, Vuna

Taveuni

Top Left: Vuna Point
Top Right: Bouma Falls, Tavoro National Park
Bottom: Korean Wharf, Waiyevo

A Local Delicacy
One week after the full moon in November, the people of Vanuabalavu witness the annual rising of *balolo*, tiny green and brown sea worms. Worms by the thousands are collected at sunrise by Susui villagers. The catch is first soaked in fresh water, then packed into baskets and cooked overnight in a lovo (underground oven). The fishy-tasting baked worms are considered a delicacy. ■

cousin of King Taufa'ahau of Tonga, led an armada of war canoes to Vanuabalavu to investigate the killing of a preacher. Six years later the Tongan king appointed him governor of the Tongans in Fiji. After the murder of 17 Wesleyans, Ma'afu took Vanuabalavu by force and subjugated its inhabitants. He established Lomaloma (Sawana) as his base. The Tongans assisted in local Fijian wars in return for protection by Chief Cakobau of Bau. By 1855 Ma'afu had become a powerful force in the region and influential throughout much of Fiji. His aim was to conquer all Fiji and convert the people to Christianity.

Ma'afu was one of the signatories to the Deed of Cession to Britain and became officially recognised as Roko Tui Lau. After his death in 1881, Tongan power broke up, the title passed to the Tui Nayau, and many Tongans returned to their home country. Despite the distance from the rest of Fiji and their relatively small land area, the chiefs of the Lau group have always been surprisingly influential. Chiefs with the title Tui Nayau include the late Ratu Sukuna and the current president Ratu Mara.

Activities

Diving The Lau Group, due to its remote location as well as restrictions on tourism, is still relatively unexplored in terms of diving. The Lau waters are officially protected by the Fijian government, and commercial fishing is prohibited in the area. The up-market resorts of Vanuabalavu and Kaibu

have their own dive operations. Apart from introductory resort courses however, diving is limited to those with experience. A couple of live-aboard operators take trips to Lau. The *Matagi Princess II*, based at Matagi Island Resort, offers luxury diving and cruising the waters of the Exploring Isles of Vanuabalavu. Nai'a Cruises, operating out of Lami, near Suva, also offers special charters to Lau.

Accommodation
Tourism in the Lau Group is restricted and permission or an invitation to visit is required for foreigners. There are no banks and little infrastructure for tourism. However, budget accommodation is available on Moala, Lakeba and Vanuabalavu and there are up-market resorts on Kaibu and on Yanuyanu, just offshore from Vanuabalavu.

Getting There & Away
Moala, Vanuabalavu, Cicia, Lakeba and Kaibu have airstrips. Vanua Air Charters flies from Suva to Moala, Cicia, Vanua balavu and Lakeba. Sunflower Airlines flies from Nadi, via Suva to Moala. Air Fiji flies from Nadi, via Suva to Vanuabalavu and from Suva to Lakeba. Cakauniika Shipping has a Viti Levu/Lau Group boat service from Suva to Moala, Lakeba and Vanuabalavu. See the Getting Around chapter for details and airfare charts.

Northern Lau

Northern Lau's largest island is Vanua balavu. It has an airstrip and an up-market resort, as does Kaibu to the west. The islands of Naitauba, Kanacea, Mago, and Cicia are important for copra production.

VANUABALAVU ISLAND & AROUND
Vanuabalavu and the eight smaller islands within the same enclosing barrier reef were named the Exploring Isles by Commodore Wilkes of the US Exploring Expedition who charted the northern Lau group in 1840.

LAU & MOALA GROUP

Taveuni is visible in the distance, 115 km to the north-west. This beautiful island, roughly a reversed S-shape and averaging about two-km wide, has lots of sandy beaches and rugged limestone hills. The Bay of Islands at the north-western end of the island is used as a hurricane shelter by yachts. There is a road along the eastern coast which has occasional passing carriers.

The largest village on the island is Lomaloma on the south-eastern coast. In the mid-19th century Tongans conquered the island and built the village of Sawana next to Lomaloma. Lomaloma was Fiji's first port, regularly visited by sailing ships trading in the Pacific; in its heyday it had many hotels, shops and Fiji's first botanical gardens. Little remains of its past grandeur, however. Fifth-generation Tongan descendants still live in Sawana, the houses with rounded ends showing the influence of Tongan architecture. The Fijian inhabitants of Vanuabalavu trace their ancestry to Tailevu (south-east Viti Levu) and Cakaudrove (Taveuni and eastern Vanua Levu). Today the people of Vanuabalavu rely largely on copra and bêche-de-mer production for their income.

Places to Stay

You cannot just turn up on Vanuabalavu uninvited: permission is required for foreigners to visit; contact the Ministry of Foreign Affairs in Suva (☎ 304 200). There is a budget guest bure in Lomaloma village, and the tiny island of Yanuyanu, just offshore from Lomaloma, has the up-market *Lomaloma Resort* (☎ 880 446; fax 880 303). Yanuyanu is owned by Ratu Mara, the president of Fiji, who is also Tui Lau (paramount chief of the Lau group). The remote resort opened in 1994.

Lomaloma caters for a maximum of 22 guests in seven Tongan-style *bures*. Rates are US$210/335/460 (F$290/462/635) for singles/doubles/triples, including all meals, beer and soft drinks, and boat transfers from Vanuabalavu to the resort. The Great House has a bar, lounge and dining area. Seafood is the focus of the menu. Activities included in

the rates are snorkelling trips, nonmotorised water sports, treks, village tours, mekes, and trips to hot springs. Boats can be chartered for game fishing. Guests can snorkel off the beach and around the island but have to boat across to Vanuabalavu for sandy beaches.

Crystal Divers (☎ 880 446; e-mail Crystal Divers@netilus.com; Internet: http://www.netilus.com/Crystal Divers) offers one-tank dives for US$44 (F$61), plus US$14 (F$19.50) for equipment rental. An introductory dive (including equipment) costs US$100 (F$138). No other courses are offered at present. Dive/accommodation packages are available, as well as package rates for a non-diving partner. A four-night, three-day dive/accommodation package is US$845 or F$1166 per person.

The resort has a seven-metre open boat for a maximum of eight divers. As well as exploratory dives, sites include the Tonga Express (a fast current in the Tongan Passage) and Outer Limits, and Magic Kingdom on the protected side of Vanuabalavu. Some dive sites are an hour from the resort. Plankton can sometimes reduce visibility to 10 to 20m.

Getting There & Away

Vanuabalavu airstrip, centrally located on the island, is 355 km east of Nadi International Airport, about halfway to Tonga. Air

---

Fatal Attraction

There is a sacred freshwater lake near the village of Mavana on the north-east corner of Vanuabalavu. Annually, the people of Mavana gather here for a fun ceremony authorised by their traditional priest. Naked except for a leaf skirt, they jump around in the lake to stir up the muddy waters. This causes the large fish known as *yawa* (a type of mullet usually only found in the sea) to jump into the air. It is believed that the male fish are attracted to the female villagers and therefore easily trapped in the nets. Legend has it that the fish were dropped into the lake by a Tongan princess while flying over the island on her way to visit her lover in Taveuni. ∎

Fiji has twice-weekly flights from Nadi via Suva to Vanuabalavu. See the Getting Around chapter for fare charts. Vanua Air Charters flies (three times weekly) from Suva to Vanuabalavu for F$98 one-way. Guests of Lomaloma Resort are transferred from the airport to Yanuyanu by a 10-minute truck ride, then a five-minute boat ride. The boat trip from Suva to Vanuabalavu with Cakauniika Shipping costs F$60.50 per person with meals included.

KAIBU & YACATA ISLANDS
Kaibu is a 352-hectare, privately owned island in the northern Lau group, 55 km west of Vanuabalavu. It shares a fringing reef with the larger Yacata island. *Kaimbu Island Resort* (☎ 880 333; fax 880 334) is an exclusive resort with only three bures and a maximum of six guests. Each bure has its own beach and costs US$1094.50 (F$15110) per couple. The minimum stay is six nights. Generally only heterosexual adult couples are accepted, unless the whole island is reserved for US$2750 (F$3795), in which case children can be included. Rates include all meals, drinks, activities and return transfers from Suva.

Activities include diving on the barrier reef, snorkelling in the lagoon, sports fishing, sailing, water-skiing, wind surfing, catamaran sailing, trekking, visiting caves and picnics to an uninhabited island. Resort courses are available as an introduction to scuba diving.

Getting There & Away
The island has its own airstrip and guests reach the resort by charter plane.

Southern Lau

Lakeba, being the hereditary seat of the Tui Nayau (chief of Lau), is the most important island in Southern Lau. It is also Fiji's 10th largest island and the largest of the Lau Group. Southern Lau has 16 other islands which are mostly grouped within 100 km south-east of Lakeba. Vatoa and Ono-i-Lau are more isolated and further south.

LAKEBA ISLAND
Lakeba is a roughly circular-shaped volcanic island, approximately nine km in diameter, with a small peninsula at its southern end. A road circles the island and several roads cut across the interior. To the east is a wide lagoon enclosed in barrier reef. About 2000 people live in the island's eight villages. Yams, coconuts and *kumalas* (sweet potatoes) grow well on the fertile coastal lands and the interior is covered with grasslands, pandanus and pine plantations. The former prime minister and current president Ratu Sir Kamisese Mara (also the Tui Nayau), comes from Lakeba.

Lakeba was once a meeting place between Fijians and Tongans, and was also the place where Christian missionaries first entered Fiji via Tonga. It was also frequently visited by Europeans before the trading settlement was established in Levuka.

The island has several caves which are worth visiting, especially **Oso Nabukete**, which translates as 'too narrow for pregnant women'. Take some kava as a sevusevu to Nasaqalau village, where you can arrange a guide for about F$5. Ideally take your own torch. The island also has the remains of a fortification, where the people retreated in times of war.

The provincial headquarters for the Lau

Shark Calling
The villagers of Nasaqalau perform an annual shark-calling ritual in October or November. About a month prior to the ceremony the spot on the reef where the calling is to take place is marked by a post with a *tapa* (bark cloth) flag tied to it. A traditional priest ensures that no-one fishes in the area or goes near the post. On the designated day the caller stands up to his or her neck in the water and chants for up to an hour. A school of sharks, led by a white shark, will be drawn to the place. Traditionally all the sharks except the white shark are killed by the villagers and eaten. ■

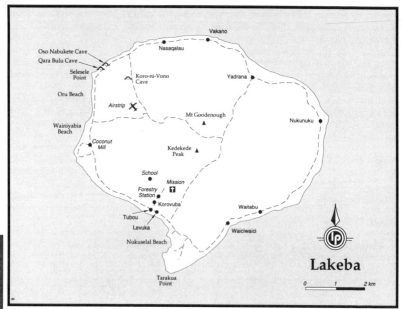

Vakano
Nasaqalau
Oso Nabukete Cave
Qara Bulu Cave
Selesele Point
Koro-ni-Vono Cave
Yadrana
Oru Beach
Airstrip
Mt Goodenough
Nukunuku
Wainiyabia Beach
Coconut Mill
Kedekede Peak
School
Mission
Forestry Station
Korovuba
Waitabu
Tubou
Levuka
Waiciwaici
Nukuselal Beach
Tarakua Point

Lakeba

0   1   2 km

group is in **Tubou** at the southern end of Lakeba. There is also a post office, telephone exchange, hospital, a government guesthouse and some good beaches nearby for snorkelling. The powerful Tongan chief Elene Ma'afu is buried here, as is influential Ratu Sir Lala Sukuna, Tui Lau (see the aside on him in the Suva section of the Viti Levu chapter).

Places to Stay

Restrictions on tourism seem to be softening in Lakeba. Call the provincial office (☎ 42 090) to check if you can visit the island and if you can book accommodation. The *government guest house* in Tubou has four rooms which cost F$10/15 for singles/doubles and good meals (lots of fish in *lolo*, *dalo*, *tavioka* and *rourou*) for F$5. There are plans for expansion. A *private guesthouse* with five thatched-roof bungalows, double beds and kitchenettes, was also being built in early 1996.

Getting There & Away

Both Air Fiji (twice weekly) and Vanua Air Charters (three flights weekly) have flights from Suva to Lakeba. Both charge F$98 one-way. See the Getting Around chapter for more information.

There is a bus from the airstrip to Tubou and carriers and buses circle the island. You can also reach the island by boat with Cakauniika Shipping. Suva to Lakeba costs F$60.50 per person with meals included. See the Getting Around chapter.

The Moala Group

The three islands of the Moala group, **Moala**, **Totoya** and **Matuku**, are geographically removed from Lau but administered as part of the Eastern Division. They are situated about halfway between Kadavu and the Southern Lau group, south-east of the Lomaviti Group. The islands, all of which have villages, are the eroded tops of previously submerged volcanic cones which have lifted more than three km up to the sea surface. Totoya's peculiar horseshoe shape is the result of a sunken volcano crater forming a land-locked lagoon. The volcano was active 4.9 million years ago. Its crescent shape shows the rim of a large crater still partially under the sea. Matuku has rich volcanic soil, steep wooded peaks and a submerged crater on the west side. This beautiful island is generally inaccessible to visitors.

MOALA ISLAND

Moala is the largest and most northerly of the three islands of the Moala Group. It lies about 160 km from Suva and 110 km from Lakeba. The 65-sq-km island is roughly triangular in shape with a deeply indented coast. The highest peak reaches 460m and there are two small crater lakes. The ances-tors of the inhabitants of Moala came from Viti Levu, and the island, with its extremely fertile soil, supports nine villages. The villagers produce copra and bananas which they send to Suva, a night's sail away.

Places to Stay

Do not turn up on Moala uninvited and without pre-arranged accommodation. Contact Eco Touring & German Tourist Information (☎ & fax 703 360) in Nadi for information on visiting the island. They can arrange stays with hosts Ota and Ravula Draunidalo and family. Package deals are available, including transfers by Sunflower Airlines and a room with private facilities. From Nadi the cost is F$388/478/548 for a two/four/seven night stay, or from Suva F$308/398/468. Longer stays are an extra F$30 per day.

Getting There & Away

Sunflower Airlines has three flights per week from Nadi, via Suva to Moala. See the Getting Around chapter for fare diagrams. Vanua Air Charters also flies from Suva to Moala three times weekly (F$83 one-way). Suva to Moala by boat with Cakauniika Shipping costs F$49.50 per person one-way with meals included. See the Getting Around chapter for details.

LAU & MOALA GROUP

Rotuma

Rotuma is an isolated, 30-sq-km volcanic island, located 470 km north of the Yasawa Group. It is shaped like a whale with the bigger body of land linked by the Motusa isthmus to the small tail end to the west. It is about 13 km long by five km at its widest. The landscape has extinct volcanic craters rising up to 250m. The smaller islands of Uea, Hatana and Hofliua lie to the west of Rotuma. Uea is a high, rocky island, and the spectacular Hofliua is also known as 'split island' because of its unusual rock formation. The offshore islands are important seabird rookeries. Endemic wildlife includes the Rotuman gecko and the red and black Rotuman honeyeater. Archaeological sites include the Graveyard of the Kings at Sisilo; Ki ne he'e; and the stone walls of Tafea Point.

Officially Rotuma is a province of Fiji but – unlike predominantly Melanesian Fiji – its indigenous population is Polynesian. Rotuma's distinct culture has developed over hundreds of years. Tongans invaded Rotuma in the 17th century and the Tongan influence is evident in the language and dances. In 1791 Europeans on the HMS *Pandora* stopped here to search for mutineers from the *Bounty*. Rotuma gained importance as a port, and the people were exposed to European traders, and runaway sailors and convicts. During the mid-19th century, Tongan Wesleyan and Marist Roman Catholic mis-

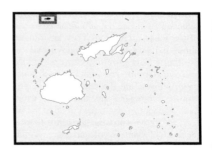

sionaries introduced their versions of Christianity. By the 1870s the religious groups were warring and, in response to the unrest, the Rotuman chiefs decided to cede their home to Britain. Rotuma was politically joined to the Fijian colony in 1881.

Rotuma has a population of about 3000. Most young people leave their remote island home to find work on other islands and about 6500 ethnic Rotumans live on other Fijian islands, mostly in Suva. The island has fertile soil: Villagers grow fruit (including oranges and bananas), root crops and coconuts. Fish is also an important food source. There is no shopping centre but a cooperative provides additional items. Rotuma produces copra which is processed at the mill near Savusavu. In 1988 Rotumans demonstrated their wish to become independent from Fiji, but the movement was quashed by the Fijian government. The island has recently hit the news over bad debts and bank loan scandals.

Accommodation

Do not turn up on Rotuma unannounced. For many years tourists have been decidedly unwelcome and cruise ships have been stopped from visiting the island. However, the Rotuman chiefs have decided to allow small numbers of visitors. Village stays cost F$33 per person, which includes meals. A self-contained apartment costs F$66 per

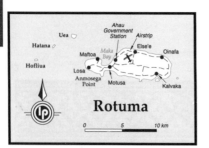

person without meals. Try to make arrangements with the island's District Officer (☎ 891 011) and enquire with Sunflower Airlines.

Getting There & Away

Air Sunflower Airlines has a twice-weekly flight (Tuesday and Saturday) from Nadi to Suva (Nausori) and on to Rotuma. The trip from Nadi takes 3¼ hours. See the airfare chart in the Getting Around chapter.

Boat There are no longer any regular passenger services to Rotuma. Yachts occasionally visit the island: obtain permission to anchor from the government station at Ahau, Maka Bay.

The Origin of Rotuma

A local legend Rotumans recount is that their ancestors came from Samoa. Where the island presently lies was once open sea until a Samoan chief, Raho, and his favourite grandchild arrived. The little girl was unhappy as her cousin was always annoying her and, to escape his torment, she convinced her grandfather to take her away to live on another island. For days and nights their entourage sailed westward in their outrigger canoe, but came across no land. Eventually the chief threw some Samoan soil overboard and it grew to form a beautiful, fertile island, which he named Rotuma. Some soil was scattered and formed the other small islands. Rotumans commemorate this legend with dance and song. ■

ROTUMA GROUP

Glossary

achar – Indian pickles
adi – female chief
arkatis – agents under commission collecting indentured labourers

baigan – eggplant
balabala – tree ferns
bêche-de-mer – a type of sea cucumber with an elongated body, leathery skin and a cluster of tentacles at the mouth; they were gathered by early traders and sold in China and South-East Asia as a delicacy and aphrodisiac
beka – flying fox
bele – leafy green vegetable
bete – priests of the old Fijian religion
bhaji – spinach, or any leafy green vegetable
bhindi – okra
bilibili – bamboo raft
bilo – drinking vessel made from half a coconut shell
breadfruit – a tree of the Pacific Islands, the trunk of which is used for lumber and canoe building; the fruit, which has a texture like bread, is cooked and eaten
bua – frangipani
bula – cheers (literally, 'life')
burau – ceremonial yaqona-drinking ritual
bure – thatched dwelling
bure kalau – ancient temple

choro – steal
cibi – death dance
copra – dried coconut kernel, used for making coconut oil

dadakulaci – banded sea krait, Fiji's most common snake
dakua – a tree of the kauri family
dalo – the taro plant, cultivated for its edible root stock
dele – (or *wate*), a dance in which women sexually humiliated enemy corpses and captives
dhaniya – coriander
drua – double-hulled canoe

girmitiya – indentured labourer

ibe – a mat
ibuburau – drinking vessels used in *yaqona* rites
ika – fish
ivi – Polynesian chestnut tree

jalebi – an Indian sweet
jira – cumin

kai colo – hill people
kaihidi – Fiji Indian
kaivalagi – 'people from far away', Europeans
kaiviti – indigenous Fijian
kanikani – scaly skin from excessive kava use
kasou – very drunk
kava – the Polynesian pepper shrub (*Piper methysticum*), or a drink prepared from its aromatic roots
kerekere – custom of shared property
kokoda – fish salad
koro – village headed by a hereditary chief
kumala – sweet potato

lagoon – a body of water that is bounded by an encircling reef
liku – the skirt of womanhood, made out of grasses or strips of pandanus leaves
lolo – coconut cream
lovo – feast in which food is cooked in a pit oven

malo – see *masi*
mangrove – a tropical tree that grows in tidal mud flats and extends looping prop roots along the shore
masala – curry powder
masi – (also known as *malo* or *tapa*), bark cloth with designs printed in black and rust; different styles are also made in other regions of the South Pacific
mataqali – extended family or landowning group

meke – a dance performance that enacts stories and legends

nama – an edible seaweed that looks like miniature green grapes
narak – hell

PADI – Professional Association of Dive Instructors, the world's largest diving association
paidar – on foot
paisa – money
pandanus – a plant common to the tropics whose sword-shaped leaves are used to make mats and baskets
piala – small metal enamel bowl
puri – deep-fried flat Indian bread

ratu – male chief
roti – flat Indian bread (like tortillas)
rourou – taro leaves

saqa – trevally fish
seo – an Indian savoury snack
sevusevu – a presentation of a gift such as *yaqona* or, more powerfully, a *tabua* as a request for certain favours
sulu – skirt worn to below the knees

tabu – forbidden or sacred, implying a religious sanction
tabua – the teeth of sperm whales, which have a special ceremonial value for Fijians; they are still used as negotiating tokens to symbolise esteem or atonement

taga yaqona – pounded *kava*
talanoa – to chat, to tell stories
tanoa – *yaqona* drinking bowl
tapa – see *masi*
tavioka – cassava, a type of root crop
tevoro – a god of the old Fijian religion
tikina – a group of Fijian villages linked together
trade winds – the near constant winds that dominate most of the tropics
tui – king
turaga – chief

vale – a family house
vale lailai – toilet
vanua – land, region, place
vasu – a system in which a chiefly woman's sons could claim support and ownership over the property of her brothers from other villages
veli – a group of little gods
vesi – ironwood, considered a sacred timber
vilavilairevo – fire walking (literally, 'jumping into the oven')
Viti – another name for Fiji

waka – kava roots
wakalou – climbing fern species
wate – see *dele*

yaqona – (also known as *kava*), a beverage drunk socially
yasana – a province formed by several *tikina*

Index

.

LONELY PLANET JOURNEYS

JOURNEYS is a unique collection of travel writing – published by the company that understands travel better than anyone else. It is a series for anyone who has ever experienced – or dreamed of – the magical moment when they encountered a strange culture or saw a place for the first time. They are tales to read while you're planning a trip, while you're on the road or while you're in an armchair, in front of a fire.

JOURNEYS books catch the spirit of a place, illuminate a culture, recount a crazy adventure, or introduce a fascinating way of life. They always entertain, and always enrich the experience of travel.

ISLANDS IN THE CLOUDS
Travels in the Highlands of New Guinea
Isabella Tree

Isabella Tree's remarkable journey takes us to the heart of the remote and beautiful Highlands of Papua New Guinea and Irian Jaya – one of the most extraordinary and dangerous regions on earth. Funny and tragic by turns, *Islands in the Clouds* is her moving story of the Highland people and the changes transforming their world.

Isabella Tree, who lives in England, has worked as a freelance journalist on a variety of newspapers and magazines, including a stint as senior travel correspondent for the *Evening Standard*. A fellow of the Royal Geographical Society, she has also written a biography of the Victorian ornithologist John Gould.

'One of the most accomplished travel writers to appear on the horizon for many years . . . the dialogue is brilliant' – Eric Newby

---

SEAN & DAVID'S LONG DRIVE
Sean Condon

Sean Condon is young, urban and a connoisseur of hair wax. He can't drive, and he doesn't really travel well. So when Sean and his friend David set out to explore Australia in a 1966 Ford Falcon, the result is a decidedly offbeat look at life on the road. Over 14,000 death-defying kilometres, our heroes check out the re-runs on tv, get fabulously drunk, listen to Neil Young cassettes and wonder why they ever left home.

Sean Condon lives in Melbourne. He played drums in several mediocre bands until he found his way into advertising and an above-average band called Boilersuit. *Sean & David's Long Drive* is his first book.

'Funny, pithy, kitsch and surreal . . . This book will do for Australia what Chernobyl did for Kiev, but hey you'll laugh as the stereotypes go boom'
– Time Out

LONELY PLANET PHRASEBOOKS

Building bridges,
Breaking barriers,
Beyond babble-on

Listen for the gems

Speak your own words

Ask your own
questions

Master of
your
own
image

- handy pocket-sized books
- easy to understand Pronunciation chapter
- clear and comprehensive Grammar chapter
- romanisation alongside script to allow ease of pronunciation
- script throughout so users can point to phrases
- extensive vocabulary sections, words and phrases for every situations
- full of cultural information and tips for the traveller

'...vital for a real DIY spirit and attitude in language learning' – Backpacker

'the phrasebooks have good cultural backgrounders and offer solid advice for challenging situations in remote locations' – San Francisco Examiner

'...they are unbeatable for their coverage of the world's more obscure languages' – The Geographical Magazine

---

Arabic (Egyptian)
Arabic (Moroccan)
Australia
 Australian English, Aboriginal and Torres Strait languages
Baltic States
 Estonian, Latvian, Lithuanian
Bengali
Burmese
Brazilian
Cantonese
Central Europe
 Czech, French, German, Hungarian, Italian and Slovak
Eastern Europe
 Bulgarian, Czech, Hungarian, Polish, Romanian and Slovak
Egyptian Arabic
Ethiopian (Amharic)
Fijian
French
German
Greek

Hindi/Urdu
Indonesian
Italian
Japanese
Korean
Lao
Latin American Spanish
Malay
Mandarin
Mediterranean Europe
 Albanian, Croatian, Greek, Italian, Macedonian, Maltese, Serbian, Slovene
Mongolian
Moroccan Arabic
Nepali
Papua New Guinea
Pilipino (Tagalog)
Quechua
Russian
Scandinavian Europe
 Danish, Finnish, Icelandic, Norwegian and Swedish

South-East Asia
 Burmese, Indonesian, Khmer, Lao, Malay, Tagalog (Pilipino), Thai and Vietnamese
Spanish
Sri Lanka
Swahili
Thai
Thai Hill Tribes
Tibetan
Turkish
Ukrainian
USA
 US English, Vernacular Talk, Native American languages and Hawaiian
Vietnamese
Western Europe
 Basque, Catalan, Dutch, French, German, Irish, Italian, Portuguese, Scottish Gaelic, Spanish (Castilian) and Welsh

---

LONELY PLANET TRAVEL ATLASES

Lonely Planet has long been famous for the number and quality of its guidebook maps. Now we've gone one step further and in conjunction with Steinhart Katzir Publishers produced a handy companion series: Lonely Planet travel atlases – maps of a country produced in book form.

Unlike other maps, which look good but lead travellers astray, our travel atlases have been researched on the road by Lonely Planet's experienced team of writers. All details are carefully checked to ensure the atlas corresponds with the equivalent Lonely Planet guidebook.

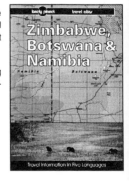

The handy atlas format means no holes, wrinkles, torn sections or constant folding and unfolding. These atlases can survive long periods on the road, unlike cumbersome fold-out maps. The comprehensive index ensures easy reference.

- full-colour throughout
- maps researched and checked by Lonely Planet authors
- place names correspond with Lonely Planet guidebooks
  – no confusing spelling differences
- legend and travelling information in English, French, German, Japanese and Spanish
- size: 230 x 160 mm

Available now:
Chile & Easter Island • Egypt • India & Bangladesh • Israel & the Palestinian Territories •Jordan, Syria & Lebanon • Kenya • Laos • Portugal • South Africa, Lesotho & Swaziland • Thailand • Turkey • Vietnam • Zimbabwe, Botswana & Namibia

---

LONELY PLANET TV SERIES & VIDEOS

Lonely Planet travel guides have been brought to life on television screens around the world. Like our guides, the programmes are based on the joy of independent travel, and look honestly at some of the most exciting, picturesque and frustrating places in the world. Each show is presented by one of three travellers from Australia, England or the USA and combines an innovative mixture of video, Super-8 film, atmospheric soundscapes and original music.

Videos of each episode – containing additional footage not shown on television – are available from good book and video shops, but the availability of individual videos varies with regional screening schedules.

Video destinations include: Alaska • American Rockies • Australia – The South-East • Baja California & the Copper Canyon • Brazil • Central Asia • Chile & Easter Island • Corsica, Sicily & Sardinia – The Mediterranean Islands • East Africa (Tanzania & Zanzibar) • Ecuador & the Galapagos Islands • Greenland & Iceland • Indonesia • Israel & the Sinai Desert • Jamaica • Japan • La Ruta Maya • Morocco • New York • North India • Pacific Islands (Fiji, Solomon Islands & Vanuatu) • South India • South West China • Turkey • Vietnam • West Africa • Zimbabwe, Botswana & Namibia

The Lonely Planet TV series is produced by:
Pilot Productions
The Old Studio
18 Middle Row
London W10 5AT UK

For video availability and ordering information contact your nearest Lonely Planet office.

Music from the TV series is available on CD & cassette.

PLANET TALK

Lonely Planet's FREE quarterly newsletter

We love hearing from you and think you'd like to hear from us.

When...is the right time to see reindeer in Finland?
Where...can you hear the best palm-wine music in Ghana?
How...do you get from Asunción to Areguá by steam train?
What...is the best way to see India?

For the answer to these and many other questions read PLANET TALK.

Every issue is packed with up-to-date travel news and advice including:

- a letter from Lonely Planet co-founders Tony and Maureen Wheeler
- go behind the scenes on the road with a Lonely Planet author
- feature article on an important and topical travel issue
- a selection of recent letters from travellers
- details on forthcoming Lonely Planet promotions
- complete list of Lonely Planet products

To join our mailing list contact any Lonely Planet office.

Also available: Lonely Planet T-shirts. 100% heavyweight cotton.

LONELY PLANET ONLINE

Get the latest travel information before you leave or while you're on the road

Whether you've just begun planning your next trip, or you're chasing down specific info on currency regulations or visa requirements, check out Lonely Planet Online for up-to-the-minute travel information.

As well as travel profiles of your favourite destinations (including maps and photos), you'll find current reports from our researchers and other travellers, updates on health and visas, travel advisories, and discussion of the ecological and political issues you need to be aware of as you travel.

There's also an online travellers' forum where you can share your experience of life on the road, meet travel companions and ask other travellers for their recommendations and advice. We also have plenty of links to other online sites useful to independent travellers.

And of course we have a complete and up-to-date list of all Lonely Planet travel products including guides, phrasebooks, atlases, Journeys and videos and a simple online ordering facility if you can't find the book you want elsewhere.

www.lonelyplanet.com
or
AOL keyword: lp

LONELY PLANET PRODUCTS

Lonely Planet is known worldwide for publishing practical, reliable and no-nonsense travel information in our guides and on our web site. The Lonely Planet list covers just about every accessible part of the world. Currently there are eight series: *travel guides*, *shoestring guides*, *walking guides*, *city guides*, *phrasebooks*, *audio packs*, *travel atlases* and *Journeys* – a unique collection of travel writing.

EUROPE

Amsterdam • Austria • Baltic States phrasebook • Britain • Central Europe on a shoestring • Central Europe phrasebook • Czech & Slovak Republics • Denmark • Dublin • Eastern Europe on a shoestring • Eastern Europe phrasebook • Estonia, Latvia & Lithuania • Finland • France • French phrasebook • German phrasebook • Greece • Greek phrasebook • Hungary • Iceland, Greenland & the Faroe Islands • Ireland • Italian phrasebook • Italy • Mediterranean Europe on a shoestring • Mediterranean Europe phrasebook • Paris • Poland • Portugal • Portugal travel atlas • Prague • Russia, Ukraine & Belarus • Russian phrasebook • Scandinavian & Baltic Europe on a shoestring • Scandinavian Europe phrasebook • Slovenia • Spain • Spanish phrasebook • St Petersburg • Switzerland • Trekking in Greece • Trekking in Spain • Ukrainian phrasebook • Vienna • Walking in Britain • Walking in Switzerland • Western Europe on a shoestring • Western Europe phrasebook

Travel Literature: The Olive Grove: Travels in Greece

NORTH AMERICA

Alaska • Backpacking in Alaska • Baja California • California & Nevada • Canada • Florida • Hawaii • Honolulu • Los Angeles • Mexico • Miami • New England • New Orleans • New York City • New York, New Jersey & Pennsylvania • Pacific Northwest USA • Rocky Mountain States • San Francisco • Southwest USA • USA phrasebook • Washington, DC & the Capital Region

CENTRAL AMERICA & THE CARIBBEAN

Bermuda • Central America on a shoestring • Costa Rica • Cuba • Eastern Caribbean • Guatemala, Belize & Yucatán: La Ruta Maya • Jamaica

SOUTH AMERICA

Argentina, Uruguay & Paraguay • Bolivia • Brazil • Brazilian phrasebook • Buenos Aires • Chile & Easter Island • Chile & Easter Island travel atlas • Colombia • Ecuador & the Galápagos Islands • Latin American Spanish phrasebook • Peru • Quechua phrasebook • Rio de Janeiro • South America on a shoestring • Trekking in the Patagonian Andes • Venezuela

Travel Literature: Full Circle: A South American Journey

ANTARCTICA

Antarctica

ISLANDS OF THE INDIAN OCEAN

Madagascar & Comoros • Maldives • Mauritius, Réunion & Seychelles

AFRICA

Africa - the South • Africa on a shoestring • Arabic (Moroccan) phrasebook • Cape Town • Central Africa • East Africa • Egypt • Egypt travel atlas • Ethiopian (Amharic) phrasebook • Kenya • Kenya travel atlas • Malawi, Mozambique & Zambia • Morocco • North Africa • South Africa, Lesotho & Swaziland • South Africa, Lesotho & Swaziland travel atlas • Swahili phrasebook • Trekking in East Africa • West Africa • Zimbabwe, Botswana & Namibia • Zimbabwe, Botswana & Namibia travel atlas

Travel Literature: The Rainbird: A Central African Journey • Songs to an African Sunset: A Zimbabwean Story

MAIL ORDER

Lonely Planet products are distributed worldwide. They are also available by mail order from Lonely Planet, so if you have difficulty finding a title please write to us. North American and South American residents should write to Embarcadero West, 155 Filbert St, Suite 251, Oakland CA 94607, USA; European and African residents should write to 10 Barley Mow Passage, Chiswick, London W4 4PH; and residents of other countries to PO Box 617, Hawthorn, Victoria 3122, Australia.

NORTH-EAST ASIA

Beijing • Cantonese phrasebook • China • Hong Kong • Hong Kong, Macau & Guangzhou • Japan • Japanese phrasebook • Japanese audio pack • Korea • Korean phrasebook • Mandarin phrasebook • Mongolia • Mongolian phrasebook • North-East Asia on a shoestring • Seoul • Taiwan • Tibet • Tibet phrasebook • Tokyo

Travel Literature: Lost Japan

MIDDLE EAST & CENTRAL ASIA

Arab Gulf States • Arabic (Egyptian) phrasebook • Central Asia • Iran • Israel & the Palestinian Territories • Israel & the Palestinian Territories travel atlas • Istanbul • Jerusalem • Jordan & Syria • Jordan, Syria & Lebanon travel atlas • Middle East • Turkey • Turkish phrasebook • Turkey travel atlas • Yemen

Travel Literature: The Gates of Damascus • Kingdom of the Film Stars: Journey into Jordan

ALSO AVAILABLE:

Travel with Children • Traveller's Tales

INDIAN SUBCONTINENT

Bangladesh • Bengali phrasebook • Delhi • Hindi/Urdu phrasebook • India • India & Bangladesh travel atlas • Indian Himalaya • Karakoram Highway • Nepal • Nepali phrasebook • Pakistan • Rajasthan • Sri Lanka • Sri Lanka phrasebook • Trekking in the Indian Himalaya • Trekking in the Karakoram & Hindukush • Trekking in the Nepal Himalaya

Travel Literature: In Rajasthan • Shopping for Buddhas

SOUTH-EAST ASIA

Bali & Lombok • Bangkok • Burmese phrasebook • Cambodia • Ho Chi Minh City • Indonesia • Indonesian phrasebook • Indonesian audio pack • Jakarta • Java • Laos • Lao phrasebook • Laos travel atlas • Malay phrasebook • Malaysia, Singapore & Brunei • Myanmar (Burma) • Philippines • Pilipino phrasebook • Singapore • South-East Asia on a shoestring • South-East Asia phrasebook • Thailand • Thailand travel atlas • Thai phrasebook • Thai audio pack • Thai Hill Tribes phrasebook • Vietnam • Vietnamese phrasebook • Vietnam travel atlas

AUSTRALIA & THE PACIFIC

Australia • Australian phrasebook • Bushwalking in Australia • Bushwalking in Papua New Guinea • Fiji • Fijian phrasebook • Islands of Australia's Great Barrier Reef • Melbourne • Micronesia • New Caledonia • New South Wales & the ACT • New Zealand • Northern Territory • Outback Australia • Papua New Guinea • Papua New Guinea phrasebook • Queensland • Rarotonga & the Cook Islands • Samoa • Solomon Islands • South Australia • Sydney • Tahiti & French Polynesia • Tasmania • Tonga • Tramping in New Zealand • Vanuatu • Victoria • Western Australia

Travel Literature: Islands in the Clouds • Sean & David's Long Drive

THE LONELY PLANET STORY

Lonely Planet published its first book in 1973 in response to the numerous 'How did you do it?' questions Maureen and Tony Wheeler were asked after driving, bussing, hitching, sailing and railing their way from England to Australia.

Written at a kitchen table and hand collated, trimmed and stapled, *Across Asia on the Cheap* became an instant local bestseller, inspiring thoughts of another book.

Eighteen months in South-East Asia resulted in their second guide, *South-East Asia on a shoestring*, which they put together in a backstreet Chinese hotel in Singapore in 1975. The 'yellow bible', as it quickly became known to backpackers around the world, soon became *the* guide to the region. It has sold well over half a million copies and is now in its 9th edition, still retaining its familiar yellow cover.

Today there are over 240 titles, including travel guides, walking guides, language kits & phrasebooks, travel atlases and travel literature. The company is the largest independent travel publisher in the world. Although Lonely Planet initially specialised in guides to Asia, today there are few corners of the globe that have not been covered.

The emphasis continues to be on travel for independent travellers. Tony and Maureen still travel for several months of each year and play an active part in the writing, updating and quality control of Lonely Planet's guides.

They have been joined by over 70 authors and 170 staff at our offices in Melbourne (Australia), Oakland (USA), London (UK) and Paris (France). Travellers themselves also make a valuable contribution to the guides through the feedback we receive in thousands of letters each year and on our web site.

The people at Lonely Planet strongly believe that travellers can make a positive contribution to the countries they visit, both through their appreciation of the countries' culture, wildlife and natural features, and through the money they spend. In addition, the company makes a direct contribution to the countries and regions it covers. Since 1986 a percentage of the income from each book has been donated to ventures such as famine relief in Africa; aid projects in India; agricultural projects in Central America; Greenpeace's efforts to halt French nuclear testing in the Pacific; and Amnesty International.

'I hope we send people out with the right attitude about travel. You realise when you travel that there are so many different perspectives about the world, so we hope these books will make people more interested in what they see. Guidebooks can't really guide people. All you can do is point them in the right direction.'

– Tony Wheeler

LONELY PLANET PUBLICATIONS

Australia
PO Box 617, Hawthorn 3122, Victoria
tel: (03) 9819 1877 fax: (03) 9819 6459
e-mail: talk2us@lonelyplanet.com.au

USA
Embarcadero West, 155 Filbert St, Suite 251,
Oakland, CA 94607
tel: (510) 893 8555 TOLL FREE: 800 275-8555
fax: (510) 893 8563
e-mail: info@lonelyplanet.com

UK
10 Barley Mow Passage, Chiswick,
London W4 4PH
tel: (0181) 742 3161 fax: (0181) 742 2772
e-mail: lonelyplanetuk@compuserve.com

France:
71 bis rue du Cardinal Lemoine, 75005 Paris
tel: 1 44 32 06 20 fax: 1 46 34 72 55
e-mail: 100560.415@compuserve.com

**World Wide Web: http://www.lonelyplanet.com
or *AOL keyword: lp***